Donald F. Brayton, MD

ANATOMY FOR SURGEONS: VOLUME 1

The Head
and Neck

ANATOMY FOR SURGEONS: VOLUME 1

The Head and Neck

BY

W. Henry Hollinshead, Ph.D.

PROFESSOR OF ANATOMY, MAYO FOUNDATION, UNIVERSITY OF MINNESOTA
HEAD OF THE SECTION OF ANATOMY, MAYO CLINIC
ROCHESTER, MINNESOTA

WITH 326 ILLUSTRATIONS

A HOEBER-HARPER BOOK

{ CONTENTS }

Surgical Consultants   vii

Preface   ix

1. THE CRANIUM   1

Scalp   1
Calvaria   5
Cranial Contents in
  General   8
Anterior Cranial Fossa   43
Middle Cranial Fossa   55
Posterior Cranial Fossa   67
References   87

2. THE ORBIT   94

Lids   94
Lacrimal Apparatus   105
Bony Orbit   109
Periorbita and Orbital
  Fascia   113
Eyeball   118
Muscles of the Orbit   128
Nerves   139
Blood Vessels   156
References   163

3. THE EAR   166

External Ear   166
Middle Ear   175

Internal Ear   200
References   223

4. THE NOSE AND PARANASAL SINUSES   229

External Nose   229
Internal Nose   234
Paranasal Sinuses   258
Anomalies   276
References   278

5. THE FASCIA AND FASCIAL SPACES OF THE HEAD AND NECK   282

Fascia and Spaces below
  the Hyoid Bone   284
Fascia and Spaces above
  the Hyoid Bone   292
References   305

6. THE FACE   306

Facial Muscles   307
Vessels   314
Parotid Gland   320
Nerves   325
Anomalies   336
References   337

CONTENTS

7. THE JAWS, PALATE, AND TONGUE — 340

Upper Jaw — 340
Palate — 346
Mandibular Region — 356
Suprahyoid and Lingual Regions — 372
References — 396

8. THE PHARYNX AND LARYNX — 401

The Pharynx — 401
The Larynx — 425
References — 452

9. THE NECK — 457

General Considerations — 457
Musculature — 460
Arteries — 467
Carotid Body and Carotid Sinus — 481
Veins — 484
Lymph Nodes and Lymphatics — 488
Nerves — 494
Visceral Structures of the Neck — 517
References — 543

Index to Volume 1 — 551

SURGICAL CONSULTANTS

The following men read and criticized for the author parts or all of the chapter or chapters indicated.

B. MARDEN BLACK, M.D.
Associate Professor of Surgery,*
Consultant in Surgery†

CHAPTER 9—THE NECK

•

W. McK. CRAIG, M.D.
Professor of Neurosurgery,*
Head of the Section of Neurosurgery†

CHAPTER 1—THE CRANIUM

•

JOHN B. ERICH, M.D., D.D.S.
Associate Professor of Plastic Surgery,*
Consultant in Plastic Surgery and Laryngology†

CHAPTER 5—THE FASCIA AND FASCIAL SPACES OF THE HEAD AND NECK
CHAPTER 7—THE JAWS, PALATE AND TONGUE

•

F. Z. HAVENS, M.D.
Associate Professor of Laryngology,*
Consultant in Plastic Surgery and Laryngology†

CHAPTER 6—THE FACE
CHAPTER 8—THE PHARYNX AND LARYNX

* Mayo Foundation, Graduate School, University of Minnesota
† Mayo Clinic, Rochester, Minnesota

SURGICAL CONSULTANTS

JOHN W. HENDERSON, M.D.

Assistant Professor of Ophthalmology,*
Consultant in Ophthalmology†

CHAPTER 2—THE ORBIT

•

JOSEPH M. JANES, M.D.

Assistant Professor of Orthopedic Surgery,*
Consultant in Orthopedic Surgery†

CHAPTER 9—THE NECK

•

S. A. LOVESTEDT, D.D.S.

Assistant Professor of Dental Surgery,*
Consultant in Dentistry†

CHAPTER 7—THE JAWS, PALATE AND TONGUE

•

C. S. MacCARTY, M.D.

Assistant Professor of Neurosurgery,*
Consultant in Neurosurgery†

CHAPTER 9—THE NECK

•

H. L. WILLIAMS, M.D.

Professor of Otolaryngology and Rhinology,*
Head of the Section of Otolaryngology and Rhinology†

CHAPTER 3—THE EAR
CHAPTER 4—THE NOSE AND PARANASAL SINUSES
CHAPTER 5—THE FASCIA AND FASCIAL SPACES OF THE HEAD AND NECK
CHAPTER 8—THE PHARYNX AND LARYNX

* Mayo Foundation, Graduate School, University of Minnesota
† Mayo Clinic, Rochester, Minnesota

PREFACE

In *Anatomy for Surgeons* I have attempted to present in readable form that regional anatomy which is of particular importance to the surgeon. It was thus not intended that this should be a complete descriptive anatomy; rather, my attempt has been to describe and interpret, with a minimal soporific effect, the anatomical facts and concepts which the surgeon has found useful.

It has been my good fortune to have taught anatomy to medical students and others, at Duke University School of Medicine, from 1930 to 1947, and since that time to have been engaged as consultant in anatomy to the more than 600 physicians of the Mayo Clinic and Mayo Foundation, and as a teacher of exclusively graduate courses to Fellows of the Mayo Foundation specializing in the various branches of surgery. This book is a direct outcome of that experience, for it represents an expansion of the material which I present in my several courses. In addition I have been exceedingly fortunate in receiving the aid of a number of specialists, my friends and colleagues of the Mayo Foundation and Mayo Clinic, in the preparation of this work. Every chapter has been read and criticized by one or more surgeons whose operating schedules keep them in constant touch with the particular anatomy described in that chapter. The modus operandi of this has been as follows: After I had completed and re-vised a chapter, a copy of the manuscript was given to a surgeon or surgeons particularly interested in all or a part of the chapter, with a request for criticism as to content and its applicability to the surgery of that area. Suggested changes, deletions, and additions were written directly upon the manuscript, which was returned to me. I incorporated them into the final text, often consulting again with the surgeon before so doing, and in some cases obtaining additional criticism after re-writing a part. It is a pleasure to acknowledge my debt to these men, who are listed on the two preceding pages as surgical consultants. It should be obvious, however, that they are in no way responsible for errors in facts, concepts, or phraseology, since I, as the author, solely bear the blame for these.

Our courses for Fellows involve not just discussions of the rationale of various operations in which these young surgeons are interested—that is just the dessert, so to speak—but also detailed expositions of the basic anatomy of the field in which they are interested. In my experience, it is very fundamental anatomy, especially that not so easily seen at the operating table, which must form the *pièce de résistance* of any graduate course in anatomy. With knowledge of or access to these fundamental details, the young surgeon has a firm foundation upon which to build his own clinical experience.

In preparing this text, I have, then, had two goals: first, to present to the younger surgeon not only a review of the broad basic anatomy with which the surgeon is necessarily concerned, but also a discussion of those details upon which the more mature surgeon, consciously or unconsciously, bases his daily work; second, to provide for the more mature surgeon both a refresher for those details which are, perhaps, slightly outside his own special field of interest, and a source of ready reference to the details which, although lying in his own field, he cannot expect to keep constantly in mind. To attain these goals, the text is so organized that any chapter can be read through as a whole, or that specific parts of a chapter can be consulted for discussions of particular points. To make the discussions of the various subjects complete in themselves, a certain amount of repetition is necessary; it is hoped that undue repetition has been avoided by the use of abundant cross references.

The book has been divided into three volumes: "The Head and Neck"; "The Thorax, Abdomen, and Pelvis"; and "The Back and Limbs." This subdivision is intended to serve two purposes: to prevent an individual volume from assuming such proportions that it cannot be readily packed or carried, or even read comfortably in bed if one has that habit; and to allow the surgeon interested in only one field, for instance the head and neck, to have the pertinent volume on his reference shelf if he so desires, without including a large mass of material on other parts of the body in which he has no interest.

No attempt has been made in the present work to describe the indications for or the detailed technic of specific operations, for these are matters that belong to surgery and not to anatomy. Nevertheless, certain anatomical facts and concepts are of importance only as they pertain to surgery, and most surgical procedures are based upon the anatomy, or the physiological anatomy, of the part concerned; an outstanding example of the latter, for instance, is the operation of fenestration, which is based upon an understanding of the functional importance of two mobile windows to the inner ear.

Throughout the book, reference is made to specific surgical procedures. Some of them will undoubtedly not stand the test of time, and will be superseded by others, based upon different concepts, refined technics, or newer knowledge, but—and this is worth emphasizing—the basic anatomy will remain the same, even though it may be regarded from an entirely new and different angle. In a similar fashion, if the text is to be both accurate and understandable, experimental work bearing upon various questions must be referred to, and at times the embryology underlying a certain condition must be understood. Every attempt has been made, therefore, to gather together pertinent material from all available sources.

Since no one can of his own knowledge possibly vouch for the numerous supposed facts presented in such a book as this, I have endeavored to supply appropriate references to the original literature. No pretense is made that the literature on any subject is exhaustively covered. Rather, I have selected references which have seemed to me to contribute something to the anatomy under discussion, and have proved useful to me in my teaching. When a number of articles upon the same subject have met these criteria, those actually cited have been chosen because they were relatively recent articles, because they presented new or opposing viewpoints or confirmed perhaps debatable concepts, or afforded a good review of the question as a whole. No question of priority, or even of superiority, is therefore implied in this selection. As will be noted, the references are almost without exception to literature written in English.

I would have real objections to the classification of this book as a "practical" or "surgical" anatomy, although it is intended to be directly useful to the surgeon. The terms are misleading: the former implies a sharp differentiation between that anatomy which is practical and that which is impractical from the standpoint of a clinician, while in reality any such attempted differentiation is necessarily ill-defined and subject to constant change, as exemplified by the fact that details and concepts of anatomy which were of no interest to the surgeon even ten years ago have become, through advances in technic, essential information; the latter term implies that there is some mysterious difference between plain or ordinary anatomy and surgical anatomy, whereas the difference really is only one of emphasis, and of point of view, concerning the same anatomical facts.

The illustrations are purely diagrammatic, and are planned to accompany the text in much the same manner that one draws diagrams upon the blackboard to illustrate points in a lecture. They are therefore intended to be simple and easily comprehended. For more complete depiction of various regions, and accurate representation of individual anatomical specimens, there are available a number of excellent atlases, of which the surgeon presumably owns at least one. Some of the illustrations in this text are original, so far as the author is aware; others are diagrams, or variations of them, that have been the common property of anatomists for years; still others are simplifications or modifications of more elaborate illustrations appearing in texts or the original literature; a few, which appeared as line drawings in other publications, have been directly borrowed in this form for the present work. The source of the original drawing, whether borrowed directly or modified, is acknowledged in the accompanying legend; I am indebted to the various authors and publishers for their permissions to use these drawings.

Except where a drawing has been directly copied, the general procedure has been that I sketched, as accurately as possible, the figure desired, whether it was original or an adaptation from another figure; this sketch was then turned over to Miss Jane Allen, of the Art Studio, and discussed with her; finally, after any necessary refinements and improvements, this sketch was converted by Miss Allen, with Mr. Russell Drake's supervision, into a finished pen and ink drawing which was reviewed and criticized by us together. The results, while still intentionally diagrammatic, much surpass my own skill, and I would be ungrateful indeed if I did not acknowledge my indebtedness to the patience, ability, and understanding of these medical illustrators.

It must be frankly admitted that anatomical terminology is at this time in a state of considerable confusion. The tendency among anatomists in the United States has been to use the B.N.A. terms in either their original Latin or, more frequently, their English translations. It is well recognized, however, that the B.N.A. is sometimes inadequate, and sometimes inappropriate, for certain structures have no official B.N.A. names, and the official terminology of others sounds strange unless one is thoroughly accustomed to it. Our British confreres, impatient of the long-overdue revision of international anatomical terminology, have adopted their own revision (the B.R. or Birmingham Revision), at least parts of which have found ready acceptance in the United States, especially among younger anatomists. Thus there is a growing tendency, for instance, to refer to the external maxillary artery by the more descriptive term "facial artery" and the submaxillary gland by the more accurate term "submandibular gland." Finally, it must be recognized, at least in a text for surgeons, that clinicians also often have their own patois, sometimes consisting of eponyms and sometimes of more or less descriptive terms; these may not coincide at all with the official anatomical terminology, and yet are handed down, by word of mouth and through the literature, from one intellectual generation to the next. Reconciliation of the varying terminology is often impossible, but in the present text an effort has been made to use at least the English translations of both the B.N.A. and the B.R., and supply in addition some of the more common synonyms.

In addition to the reading by estab-lished surgeons referred to previously, various chapters of the text have also been read by a number of Fellows of the Mayo Foundation. I am grateful to them for their suggestions. For the present volume these men include Drs. Joseph W. Begley, Jr., Paul M. Brickley, R. E. Casey, I. S. Cooper, A. B. Johnson, W. V. Kaplan, M. E. Kurth, C. B. Lamp, Jr., J. C. Lillie, H. B. Lockhart, and Lloyd M. Taylor.

Finally, I must also acknowledge my gratitude to the several people who have especially helped in the mechanics of the preparation of this book. These include, in addition to the medical illustrators, Dr. Carl Gambill, of the Section of Publications, who has carefully gone over the manuscript for me and given freely of his advice and experience; the publishers, who have been liberal with their enthusiasm for this, to me, formidable project, and who have given me every aid; and last, but by no means least, my secretary, Mrs. Lorraine Barnes, who has contributed to this book in all of the many ways that a good and careful secretary can.

W. HENRY HOLLINSHEAD

Rochester, Minnesota

ANATOMY FOR SURGEONS: VOLUME 1

The Head and Neck

CHAPTER 1

The Cranium

THE SCALP

THE three outer layers of the scalp—the skin, the subcutaneous tissue, and the aponeurotic layer (galea aponeurotica, epicranial aponeurosis) with its associated frontalis and occipitalis muscles—are intimately fused together and move as a unit with the contraction of the muscles. The dense subcutaneous tissue of the scalp contains the larger blood vessels and nerves, and its strong retinacula not only unite the skin and the galea, but afford support to the blood vessels. These outer layers are separated from the fifth or deepest layer of the scalp, the external periosteum or pericranium, by a loose fourth layer which allows easy movement of the outer layers and also ready spread of fluid or infections beneath the aponeurotic layer. Because of this latter fact, the subaponeurotic layer is sometimes referred to as the danger space of the scalp; fluids contained therein find exit with difficulty, typically into the periorbital connective tissue. The periosteum is fairly tightly attached to the bone, especially at the sutures; it is through the loose subapo-neurotic tissue that separation occurs most easily in tears or surgical reflections of the scalp.

NERVES AND VESSELS

The nerves and blood vessels of the scalp run up into it from below, the larger ones on the forehead and in the temporal and occipital regions; although the blood vessels anastomose so freely with each other that there is relatively little danger of reducing markedly the blood supply to an area of scalp unless a skin flap with an extremely narrow inferior pedicle is produced, the nerve supply must be taken into consideration when incisions for skin flaps are planned, or else an area of denervated or partially denervated scalp, with resulting numbness or paresthesia, will be produced.

Since the arteries of the scalp anastomose freely with each other and with those of the opposite side, they form a part of the potential collateral pathway available after ligation of the external or common carotid artery on one side. It is because of these abundant anastomoses, also, that wounds of the scalp involving the subcutaneous tissue typically show arterial bleeding from both cut surfaces. The profuseness of the bleeding is further contributed to by the fact that the blood vessels lie largely in the dense subcutaneous tissue, by which they are supported and to which they are attached,

pany the blood vessels of the scalp, which are derived largely from branches of the external carotid, but anteriorly are from the ophthalmic branch of the internal carotid.

As the nerves of the scalp approach it from all directions, and have of course a considerable overlap, it is usually impossible to produce adequate anesthesia of

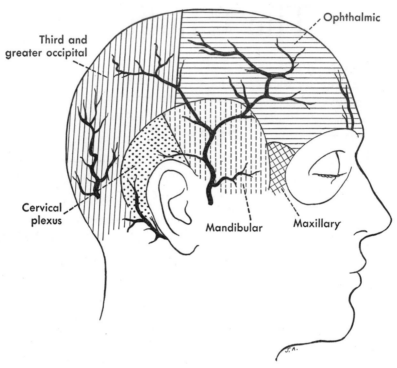

Fig. 1.   General areas of distribution of the chief nerves to the scalp, and the positions of the chief arteries.

and tend therefore to be held open by this tissue when they are cut. The arteries of the scalp supply not only the tissues of this, but also aid in supplying the underlying bones of the skull.

The nerves to the scalp are branches of cranial and spinal nerves (Fig. 1), the spinal nerves being derived both from the cervical plexus and from the posterior primary rami of the upper cervical nerves. Generally speaking, these nerves accom-

any large area of the scalp by a purely local injection; rather, the area in which anesthesia is desired must be ringed by a whole series of injections. Further, the nerves, like the vessels, run largely in the subcutaneous tissue, and the solution must therefore be placed in this layer rather than in the subaponeurotic layer where it could spread much more easily, but would be separated from the nerves by the tough galea aponeurotica.

SUPRA-ORBITAL NERVE AND ARTERY

The supra-orbital nerve (from the ophthalmic branch of the trigeminal) and the supra-orbital artery (from the ophthalmic artery) emerge through the supra-orbital notch or foramen to turn sharply around the upper margin of the orbit and be distributed to the scalp. At first they lie under the frontalis muscle but subsequently pierce this to run in the dense subcutaneous tissue of the scalp. The small supra-orbital artery forms anastomoses with the other vessels of the scalp, while the supra-orbital nerve supplies a very large area on the scalp, extending backward over the vault of the skull to approximately the interauricular line or slightly beyond it. Medial to the supra-orbital nerve and artery are the smaller supratrochlear nerve and frontal (supratrochlear) artery, also branches of the ophthalmic nerve and artery; they supply a limited medial region of the forehead.

Because of the extensive distribution of the supra-orbital nerve, frontal skin flaps or curved incisions over the front of the vault of the skull should be large if an area of denervated tissue is to be avoided. A longitudinal incision should therefore be close to the midline, while a transverse incision from the midline can be made safely only close to the level of the interauricular line; the flap must be left attached anteriorly and inferiorly, if the nerve and blood supply (much of the latter from the superficial temporal artery) are not to be interfered with.

AURICULOTEMPORAL NERVE

Laterally, in front of the ear, the auriculotemporal nerve (a branch of the mandibular division of the fifth nerve) extends upward with the superficial temporal vessels, to supply the chief portion of the temporal region of the side of the head as high as the superior temporal line on the skull—that is, especially over the area of origin of the temporalis muscle. More anteriorly, supplying skin behind the orbital process of the zygomatic bone, but not extending so far upward, is the zygomaticotemporal branch of the maxillary division of the fifth cranial nerve. To avoid interference with this nerve supply, and with the superficial temporal artery whose main branches, parietal and frontal, spread out in this same area, temporal skin flaps should be in the shape of wide open U's, or almost triangular, with the base widely attached below and anteriorly.

GREAT AURICULAR NERVE

While a small and probably variable area of skin behind the ear and over the mastoid process is innervated by the auricular branches of the seventh, ninth, and tenth cranial nerves (p. 170), the larger nerve distributed here, and extending upward to the scalp, is the great auricular from the cervical plexus (C-2 and C-3). The artery in this location is the posterior auricular branch of the external carotid, which roughly parallels the nerve. More posteriorly over the mastoid process is the mastoid branch of the occipital artery, which aids in supplying the scalp and also sends a branch into the bone to supply mastoid cells. Behind the area of distribution of the great auricular nerve is the lesser occipital nerve, also ascending from the cervical plexus (primarily second cervical). Small skin flaps over the mastoid region may be turned down by a U-shaped incision passing upward from the ear to the temporal line, and then curving backward and downward along this line, but if larger reflections of scalp are desired here the distribution of the auriculotemporal and occipital nerves should be taken into account.

GREATER OCCIPITAL NERVE

The greater occipital nerve is derived primarily from the posterior primary branch of the second cervical nerve; it typically appears in the suboccipital region at about the lateral border of the trapezius muscle, and becomes subcutaneous by piercing the fascia between the attachments of the trapezius and the sternocleidomastoid muscles to the skull; here it is joined by the occipital artery, and is distributed to the posterior part of the cranial vault to about the interauricular line. Its area of distribution here overlaps that from the supra-orbital branch of the ophthalmic, and laterally, at the level of the temporal line, overlaps the area of distribution of the posterior auricular and lesser occipital nerves. Medial to the greater occipital nerve the third occipital (representing the posterior ramus of C-3) extends also upward to the scalp, but rarely runs appreciably above the external occipital protuberance.

Obviously, if an area of anesthesia is to be avoided in turning occipital skin flaps, a transverse incision can be made safely only at about the level of the interauricular line; for a unilateral occipital approach a longitudinal incision may be extended safely backward from the interauricular line along the midline, and if desired another longitudinal but curved incision may be made along the temporal line; the important point is that the skin flap be turned downward, with its base left attached in the occipital region.

VEINS

The veins of the scalp parallel the arteries. They receive many of the emissary veins of the cranium, and through these communicate with the cranial venous sinuses. Arteriovenous aneurysms, more common in the head than elsewhere, occur most frequently in the scalp (Dandy, '46); they may be continuous through the skull with similar endocranial aneurysms, or formed by dural arteries which penetrate the skull —in either case, of course, being aneurysms of the external carotid system.

LYMPHATIC VESSELS

The lymphatic vessels from the frontal region of the scalp drain downward and backward into the parotid lymph nodes; those from the parietal and temporal regions pass downward both in front of and behind the ear to end in the parotid and the anterior and posterior auricular nodes; those from the occipital region drain for the most part into both the occipital and upper deep cervical nodes, but one large vessel from this region is said to follow the posterior border of the sternocleidomastoid muscle to reach lower deep cervical nodes.

SENSITIVITY OF THE SCALP

Ray and Wolff, in their study of the pain-sensitive structures in the head, found that while the skin of the scalp is sensitive to all the usual forms of stimulation to which skin is elsewhere, the *galea aponeurotica* is sensitive only to pain; where the extracranial blood vessels are in close contact with the galea the pain sensitivity was found to be greater than at other points. Like the galea, the fascia over the temporal and occipital muscles, and these muscles themselves, were reported as sensitive only to pain, this pain being appreciated near the point of stimulus.

The *periosteum* on the outside of the skull was found to be variable in regard to its sensitivity, that over the vertex being entirely insensitive; there was a general increase in sensitivity just over the eyebrows, low in the temporal regions, and low in the occipital region—that is, in the areas in which the nerves were approaching the scalp. Even here, however, the periosteum apparently is not particularly sensitive, since stripping of periosteum around the base of the skull produced only moderate pain in the neighborhood of the point of stimulation.

The *arteries* of the scalp were all found to be sensitive to pain, while the veins were either less sensitive or not at all so.

The *bony skull* itself, as also its veins, was found to be insensitive to all types of stimulation.

THE CALVARIA

THE bony vault of the cranium, the calvaria, consists, from before backward, of the unpaired frontal bone, the paired parietals, and the unpaired occipital bone. Laterally, the great wing of the sphenoid bone, and posterior to this the temporal bone, complete the sides of the brain case.

The calvaria is of course covered with periosteum on both its outer and inner surfaces; the inner periosteum is fused to the dura, forming its outer layer. The periosteum of the skull is, however, markedly deficient in osteogenic power, as compared with the periosteum of long bones, and relatively little regeneration of the bones of the skull may be expected following a craniotomy unless the bone flap is replaced. Areas of bone removed and replaced in the temporal region usually heal better than bone elsewhere, presumably because of the greater blood supply furnished them by the deep temporal arteries.

The bones of the vault of the cranium show three distinct layers: hard outer and inner tables (external and internal laminae) and a cancellous middle layer or diploë. The inner table is distinctly thinner than is the outer, and may be fractured by blows which leave the outer table intact, thus rendering more difficult the diagnosis of fractures of the skull.

Surgical approaches to the cerebral hemispheres, both diagnostic and operative, are usually made through the calvaria, as are also approaches to the other contents of the anterior and middle cranial fossae. A preliminary step is trephining the calvaria at a suitable and relatively safe spot; through the trephine opening a needle or other small instrument can be inserted or if a larger opening is desired several trephine openings can be made, and connected by sawing through the intervening bone.

In planning trephine operations on the calvaria, factors to be considered are not only the relations of the calvaria to the various subdivisions of the cerebral hemispheres (p. 29), but also the positions of the cranial venous sinuses—the superior sagittal and the lateral sinuses—related to the calvaria, and the position of the middle meningeal artery and its major branches. The relationships of the superior sagittal sinus are given on page 12, those of the lateral sinuses on page 29, and the middle meningeal artery is discussed on page 21.

THICKNESS OF SKULL

The bony vault of the skull is relatively thick, averaging perhaps about 5 mm., but average measurements of this are of little use to the surgeon. The thickness of the skull varies considerably with the individual, and in addition shows regional

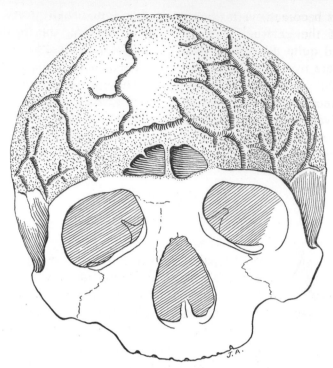

Fig. 2A.   The diploic veins from the anterior aspect. (Redrawn from Jefferson, G., and Stewart, D.: *Brit. J. Surg.*)

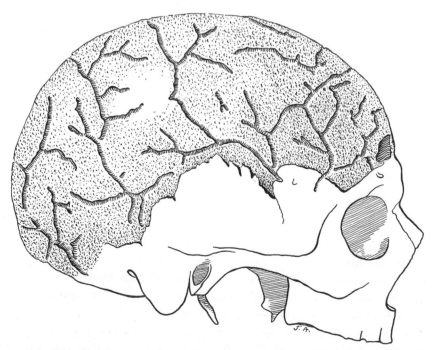

Fig. 2B.   The diploic veins from the lateral aspect. (Redrawn from Jefferson, G., and Stewart, D.: *Brit. J. Surg.*)

variations. It thus becomes much thicker in the region of the external occipital protuberance, and quite thin in the temporal region, where it is however in part protected by the overlying temporal muscle. The thinness of the temporal region is taken advantage of in "turning" frontal and temporal bone flaps, by sawing through the thicker bone and leaving

other, but usually form five chief veins on either side: the frontal, anterior temporal (typically two in number), posterior temporal, and occipital diploic veins.

The frontal diploic (Fig. 2A) veins communicate through the inner table with the superior sagittal sinus, but empty primarily downward into the supra-orbital branch of the ophthalmic vein, emerging

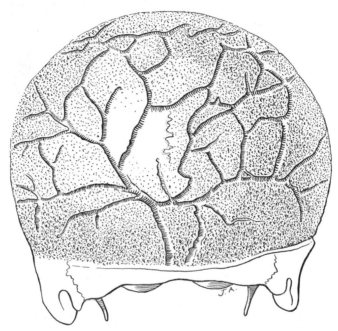

Fig. 2C. The diploic veins from the posterior aspect. (Redrawn from Jefferson, G., and Stewart, D.: *Brit. J. Surg.*)

the base of the flap in the temporal region, where it can be relatively easily fractured.

DIPLOIC VESSELS

The diploë contains the marrow, and is supplied by small but numerous diploic branches from the arteries both on the external and internal surfaces of the skull —that is, from the arteries of the scalp and from those of the dura mater. The diploic veins anastomose freely with each

from the skull through a small foramen located in the roof of the supra-orbital notch. The two *anterior temporal* veins (Fig. 2B) usually pass downward in front of and behind the coronal suture, respectively, to communicate both with the veins of the temporal muscle and with the sphenoparietal sinus. The *posterior temporal* diploic vein, in the parietal bone, drains downward to the mastoid region where it perforates the inner table to join the transverse sinus. The *occipital diploic vein* (Fig. 2C) empties either externally, into the occipital vein, or internally, into the transverse sinus. Thus the diploic veins may drain either into veins of the scalp or into the dural venous sinuses, or may form communications between the two. Through them an osteomyelitis originating, for instance, from the frontal sinus may involve not only the frontal bone but also the scalp and the dura.

Jefferson and Stewart, in their study of the diploic veins, found that generalized enlargement of these veins, as sometimes seen in roentgenograms, is no indication of increased intracranial pressure, but is rather usually perfectly normal, and it is sometimes stated that such enlargement is a usual concomitant of increasing age; they found enlargement of the grooves for the middle meningeal vessels to be much more often associated with increased intracranial pressure.

THE CRANIAL CONTENTS IN GENERAL

EXCEPT for the relations to the cranial vault, the relationships of many of the components of the cranial contents—for instance, those of nerves and vessels to each other—can be more usefully discussed in connection with the individual cranial fossae. The following account is therefore a general one; more specific details will in many instances be found in connection with the description of the cranial fossae.

DURA MATER

Where it is in contact with the bones of the skull the cranial dura mater, the general relations of which are shown in Figure 3, consists (except at the venous sinuses) of two layers closely fused together. The outer of these layers is the internal periosteum of the skull, and is continuous with the outer periosteal layer through the various foramina of the skull; the inner is the equivalent of the spinal dura, with which it is continuous at the foramen magnum.

CRANIAL EPIDURAL SPACE

While the spinal epidural (extradural) space is a large one, occupied by fat and venous plexuses, it ends above at the foramen magnum where the dura and the

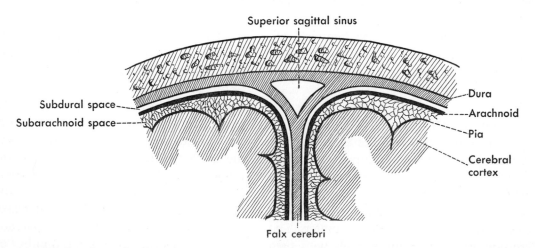

Fig. 3.   General relations of the three meninges to each other and to the cerebral hemispheres.

cranial periosteum fuse; the cranial epidural space is neither continuous with the spinal epidural space nor the homologue of it (Fig. 4). It is rather a potential space outside the inner periosteum, made possible by the loose attachment of this to the inner table of the skull. However, just as the major veins about the

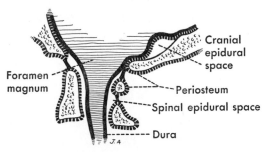

Fig. 4. Difference between the spinal and the cranial epidural spaces.

spinal cord (the internal vertebral venous plexuses) lie between the periosteum and the dura within the vertebral canal, so do the larger venous channels draining the brain lie between the periosteal and proper dural layers of the cranial dura (not, therefore, as about the cord, in the surgical epidural space). These channels are the dural venous sinuses, which receive support from the periosteal and proper dural layers between which they lie; because of this support, they have no walls of their own other than endothelium.

In addition to the venous sinuses, the dura also contains meningeal arteries and nerves, and some of the cranial nerves (notably those to the musculature of the eyeball) run for some distance in the dura.

STRENGTH OF ATTACHMENT

The strength of attachment of the periosteal layer of the dura to the skull varies considerably; according to Walker the strongest attachment to the vault of the cranium is in the midline, above the superior sagittal sinus; there is also some attachment to the sutures, and some along branches of the middle meningeal artery, but otherwise the attachment to the vault is quite loose, making removal of bone flaps relatively easy, and allowing the development of massive epidural hemorrhages.

In contrast to this, the attachments of the dura into the base of the skull are relatively strong; in the anterior fossa the dura is attached especially strongly to the crista galli and the cribriform plate, and about the optic foramen (Fig. 5). In the middle fossa the main attachments are about the edges of the numerous foramina through which nerves and vessels enter and leave this part of the cranium, especially the superior orbital fissure, the foramen rotundum and the foramen ovale, and the foramen lacerum. In the posterior cranial fossa the dura is attached especially to the basal portion of the sphenoid bone, to the margins of the foramen magnum and the jugular foramen, and to the internal acoustic meatus; it is less firmly attached about the venous sinuses.

SUBDURAL SPACE

The inner surface of the dura is lined not by epithelium but by fibroblastic tissue (Leary and Edwards), and this layer therefore forms the outer lining of the subdural space. The subdural space is usually described as being a potential space only, but Penfield ('24), by freezing the heads of dogs, apparently demonstrated that there is in this space an appreciable amount of clear, yellow fluid which probably normally prevents intimate contact between the arachnoid and dura. Penfield and Norcross suggested that it is displacement of this fluid locally, thus allowing close contact between

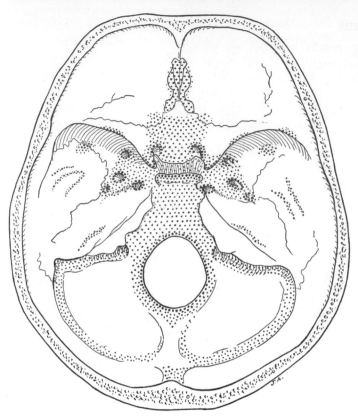

Fig. 5. Areas of stronger attachment of the dura to the base of the skull. (Redrawn from Walker, A. E.: *Anat. Rec. 55:*291, 1933.)

arachnoid and dura, that is responsible for posttraumatic headache. The origin of the subdural fluid is unknown, but apparently, as pointed out by Penfield, it does not arise in common with the cerebrospinal fluid, since it differs in color from the latter.

DURAL SEPTA

Not only is the inner layer of dura separated from the periosteal layer in certain locations by venous sinuses, but it also leaves this periosteal layer to form a reduplication of itself in the form of broad septa which project between certain parts of the brain, and therefore partially subdivide the cranial cavity.

FALX CEREBRI

The falx cerebri is a longitudinally directed septum of this nature, passing downward from the cranial vault in the sagittal plane, between the cerebral hemispheres; this large sickle-shaped fold is attached anteriorly to the crista galli, and posteriorly blends with the upper surface of the tentorium cerebelli. At its separation from the periosteal portion of the dura along the midline of the vault of the skull it helps to enclose the superior sagittal sinus; in its free margin it encloses the inferior sagittal sinus; and finally, at its attachment to the tentorium cerebelli it helps to form the walls of the straight sinus.

TENTORIUM CEREBELLI

The tentorium cerebelli is placed approximately transversely, its center being however much higher than its sides (Fig. 6) so that it fits fairly snugly between the posterior portions of the two cerebral hemispheres and over the somewhat convex upper surface of the cerebellum. The line of attachment of the tentorium cerebelli to the skull extends backward from the posterior clinoid processes along the superior borders of the petrous portions of the two temporal bones, and backward and medially along the occipital bone at the grooves for the transverse sinuses; thus the tentorium largely separates the middle from the posterior cranial fossa. The superior petrosal and transverse sinuses, from before backward, lie at its line of attachment to the periosteal dura, and, as already mentioned, the straight sinus lies at the junction of its raised center and the falx cerebri; anteriorly, the tentorium cerebelli is entered, close to the posterior clinoid processes, by the trochlear nerves.

The anterior edge of the tentorium cerebelli presents a deep concavity for accommodation of the brain stem as it passes into the posterior cranial fossa, this notch being known as the tentorial or trochlear notch, or the tentorial incisure; since the notch is little larger than is necessary to accommodate the brain stem, increased supratentorial pressure resulting in herniation of portions of the brain caudally through the notch may inflict severe damage on the brain (for instance, Reid).

In addition to the above-mentioned folds, there are others—the small falx cerebelli, the diaphragma sellae, and the arrangement of the dura about the semilunar ganglion of the trigeminal nerve—which are also of some importance and will be discussed in connection with the regions of the base of the skull in which they occur.

VENOUS SINUSES

The more constant dural venous sinuses are the superior and inferior sagittal, the lateral (transverse and sigmoid), the straight, the occipital, the superior and inferior petrosal, the cav-

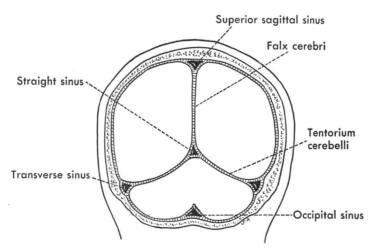

Fig. 6.   General relationships of the dura, and of the venous sinuses to it, illustrated in a frontal section through the posterior part of the skull.

ernous, and the sphenoparietal sinuses. Of these, the sagittal, straight, and occipital sinuses are unpaired, lying approximately in the midplane of the body, while the others are paired.

SUPERIOR SAGITTAL SINUS

The superior sagittal sinus lies on the inner surface of the vault of the skull, where it forms a slight groove in about the sagittal plane. It is approximately triangular in section, its upper wall being formed by the periosteum proper as it passes across the midline, its two inferolateral walls being formed by the two stems of origin of the falx cerebri. Occasional trabeculae (chords of Willis) cross the sinus, but are not numerous enough to affect its blood flow. At its anterior end, where the falx is attached to the crista galli, the superior sagittal sinus is quite small, but it enlarges rapidly as it runs posteriorly. At its front it receives communications from the frontal diploic veins, and may be connected to the veins of the nose by an emissary vein passing through the foramen caecum; this connection, which can allow nasal infections to be transmitted to the sinus, is said to be regularly present in the fetus and embryo, but apparently is only sometimes maintained during adult life. The sinus may also connect by emissary veins with the angular veins on the face, and farther back, through the parietal bone, is regularly connected by such veins to the superficial temporal and occipital veins of the scalp. At the internal occipital protuberance the superior sagittal sinus enters into the formation of the confluence of the sinuses (torcular Herophili), where it usually passes into the right transverse sinus (p. 17).

Laterally along the course of the superior sagittal sinus are irregular expansions which form the lateral lacunae, lying like the sinus itself largely within the dura but receiving the projecting arachnoid villi and Pacchionian granulations, and believed to serve as the chief drainage point for return of cerebrospinal fluid to the blood stream. According to O'Connell the lacunae develop after birth, and are reduced after middle age to a single pair, one on each side of the sinus.

The position of the superior sagittal sinus, its enlargement as it runs posteriorly, and the occurrence of the lacunae in connection with it must be taken into account in trephine operations upon the calvaria. The sinus lies in the midline except close to its termination, not far from the external occipital protuberance (torus), where it often deviates somewhat to one side, usually the right. However, the lacunae so increase its width that in trephining over the posterior half of the parietal region, where the lacunae are largest and most constant, the medial edge of the trephine should be not much closer than an inch (2 cm. or more) to the midline.

The superior cerebral veins, from the convexity of the cerebral hemispheres, empty into the superior sagittal sinus; they penetrate its walls quite obliquely, usually running forward so that they empty against the flow of blood within the sinus itself. Stopford ('30) has suggested that this direction of entrance is a mechanism for maintaining the circulation when the pressure of the cerebrospinal fluid is raised, assuring sufficient pressure in these thin-walled vessels to prevent their collapse, as they cross the subarachnoid space, by increases in the pressure of the cerebrospinal fluid.

Ligation and resection of the anterior portion of the superior sagittal sinus has been carried out a number of times, and more posterior portions have been resected after they have been slowly occluded by the growth of a tumor. Jaeger, who has reviewed the literature on this question, expressed the belief that the superior sagittal sinus can be safely ligated or resected anterior to the point at which the Rolandic veins (from the region of the precentral and postcentral gyri) enter the sinus; he found only 1 recorded case in which an unoccluded sinus had been resected so as to include the entrance of the Rolandic vein, and as this was followed by the death of the patient he was inclined to believe that resection of an unoccluded sinus posterior to the Rolandic vein may be incompatible with life. However, the adequacy of the normal anastomotic channels over the surface of the cerebral hemispheres is not known, and until there are reports of a number of cases of resection of the posterior part of an unoccluded sinus the question cannot be regarded as settled.

INFERIOR SAGITTAL SINUS

The inferior sagittal sinus runs in the free edge of the falx cerebri, where it receives small veins from the medial surfaces of the hemispheres and from the inferior part of the frontal region; it is quite small throughout its course, and at the junction of the falx and tentorium joins the much larger great cerebral vein (of Galen) to form the straight sinus. The straight sinus, in turn, runs posteriorly along the attachment of falx and tentorium to enter the torcular, the main stream of its blood typically going to the transverse sinus opposite to that which receives the blood from the superior sagittal sinus.

OCCIPITAL SINUS

The occipital sinus (Fig. 7) usually begins as right and left branches about the margins of the foramen magnum,

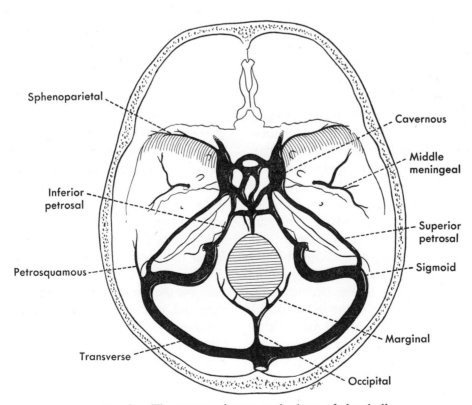

Fig. 7.   The venous sinuses at the base of the skull.

these branches being therefore known as the marginal sinuses and being continuous with the internal vertebral venous plexus of veins. After its formation at a variable distance above the margin of the foramen magnum the occipital sinus runs upward in the base of the falx cerebelli to join the torcular. Through plexuses accompanying the hypoglossal nerves the marginal sinuses, and therefore the occipital sinus, also communicate with the vertebral veins, which do not themselves enter the skull.

LATERAL SINUSES

The lateral or transverse sinuses extend from the torcular, at the internal occipital protuberance, to the paired jugular foramina; in the greater part of their courses they lie at the attachment of the tentorium cerebelli to the dura of the posterior occipital region, but after receiving the superior petrosal sinuses each curves downward into the posterior fossa, forming the S-shaped portion sometimes known as the sigmoid sinus. (Logically, the entire sinus should be known as the lateral sinus, and could then be described as composed of transverse and sigmoid portions, but there is no unanimity on this and "transverse" and "lateral" are often used synonymously.)

In its course each lateral sinus receives the internal auditory vein of its own side, veins from the pons, medulla, and superior surface of the cerebellum, and veins from the inferior surfaces of the occipital and temporal lobes of the brain. They communicate with the occipital and vertebral veins by way of the mastoid and condyloid emissary veins, and receive also the superior petrosal sinuses.

Both transverse sinuses are typically large, the right being usually somewhat larger than the left. The sigmoid portion of the lateral sinus ends by passing through the posterior part of the jugular foramen, outside of which it expands to form the superior bulb of the internal jugular vein. As the sinus passes through the jugular foramen it is usually separated from the inferior petrosal sinus by the emerging rootlets of the tenth and eleventh cranial nerves.

SUPERIOR PETROSAL SINUSES

The superior petrosal sinuses leave the cavernous sinuses, on either side of the sella turcica, to run along the attached margins of the tentorium cerebelli (therefore between middle and posterior cranial fossae) and empty into the lateral sinuses at the beginning of their sigmoid portions. Usually the superior petrosal sinus passes above the roots of the trigeminal nerve, but Coates found this to be true in only 30 of 55 cases; in 12 of the remainder the sinus passed beneath the trigeminal root, and in the other 13 it divided so that one portion passed above and one beneath the root.

INFERIOR PETROSAL SINUSES

The inferior petrosal sinuses, like the superior, originate from the cavernous sinuses, and therefore somewhat parallel these; they run backward along the petro-occipital sutures, in the posterior cranial fossa, to pass through the anterior compartment of the jugular foramen and empty into the superior bulb of the internal jugular vein. The inferior petrosal sinus receives veins from the lower surface of the cerebellum, from the brain stem and, usually, the vein of the cochlear canaliculus from the internal ear. As it leaves the cavernous sinus the inferior petrosal sinus passes beneath the petro-sphenoid ligament (of Gruber) in company with the abducens nerve; at its exit through the jugular foramen, it usually lies between the ninth and tenth nerves.

CAVERNOUS SINUSES

The cavernous sinuses (Fig. 7) are large venous spaces on the sides of the body of the sphenoid bone; they are connected to each other in front of and behind the hypophysis by small anterior and posterior intercavernous sinuses, the whole being therefore sometimes referred to as the circular sinus. Unlike the sinuses already described, which are typically open channels, the cavernous sinuses are much broken up by heavy trabeculae which cross them (their name is derived from the fact that they resemble cavernous or erectile tissue) and the flow of blood through them is therefore very much slowed; this, and the fact that the trabeculae markedly increase the endothelial surface, both contribute to the likelihood of thrombosis of the sinus as a result of its infection.

In the lateral wall of the cavernous sinus are the oculomotor and trochlear nerves, the ophthalmic division of the trigeminal, and sometimes the upper portion of the maxillary division of this nerve; medially, the carotid artery and the abducens nerve run through it. The cavernous sinuses receive the veins from the lower surfaces of the frontal lobes; into them also enter the ophthalmic veins, and therefore they may receive blood from the face, jaw, and pharynx by way of the communications between this vein on the one hand, and the angular vein and pterygoid plexus on the other. Small vessels passing through the foramen ovale, foramen rotundum, and foramen lacerum also form communications between the cavernous sinus and the pterygoid and pharyngeal plexuses. Laterally each cavernous sinus receives the sphenoparietal sinus, which communicates with the middle meningeal vein. Each sinus communicates with the internal jugular vein through the plexus about the internal carotid artery, and through the superior and inferior petrosal veins by which it is drained and with which it is continuous posteriorly; the two sinuses also communicate posteriorly with each other through an ill-defined plexus of small channels, the basilar plexus. Campbell expressed the belief that they are most frequently infected through their connections with the pharynx, as a sequel to tonsillectomy.

BASILAR PLEXUS

The basilar plexus lies in the dura mater of the posterior cranial fossa over the body of the sphenoid and the base of the occipital bones; anteriorly it communicates with the cavernous and inferior petrosal sinuses, posteriorly with the marginal sinuses and the internal vertebral venous plexus. It is, essentially, an upward continuation of the anterior internal vertebral venous plexus from the spinal column.

SPHENOPARIETAL SINUSES

The sphenoparietal sinuses arise from one of the meningeal veins, usually the middle meningeal, and run downward on the lesser wings of the sphenoid bone to empty each into the corresponding cavernous sinus, passing above the oculomotor nerve in the lateral wall of the sinus to do so. It is into these sinuses that the anterior temporal veins from the diploë usually end.

In addition to the venous channels already described in the dura, small sinuses likewise accompany the meningeal arteries, and are referred to as the meningeal veins. These vessels usually communicate with the diploic veins and with the various larger venous sinuses; the veins accompanying the middle meningeal artery are two in number, and in addition to their usual communications with the cavernous sinus (through the sphenoparietal) pass through the foramen spinosum with the artery to empty into the pterygoid plexus.

Of the other sinuses which may sometimes be present, the petrosquamous, though it is present only occasionally, is the most constant. It lies in the groove between the anterolateral surface of the petrous portion of the temporal bone and the squamous portion of this bone, and posteriorly opens into the superior petrosal sinus or the beginning of the sigmoid sinus; it may communicate anteriorly with a deep temporal vein outside the skull. Other venous sinuses which may be present as variations from the normal are discussed farther on in this chapter.

Major Variations

As a consequence of their development from a widespread venous network (Streeter) the cranial sinuses show numerous variations. Occasionally, as in the case described by Werden, multiple venous anomalies may be extreme and produce neurological symptoms, but besides such cases as these there are other variations which are much more common and yet are also of clinical importance. Probably the most frequent of these are variations at the torcular itself, often associated with variations in the lateral sinuses also. These have been analyzed by a number of workers.

In regard to the *sizes* of the vessels, Gibbs and Gibbs have measured the cross-sectional area of those emptying into the torcular and found them to be extremely variable, even relative to the cross-sectional area of other vessels at the same torcular. Their average values, however, were as follows: for the superior sagittal sinus, 20 sq. mm.; for the straight sinus, 15 sq. mm.; for the occipital sinus, 7 sq. mm.; for the right lateral sinus, 30 sq. mm.; and for the left, 24 sq. mm.

The varying disposition of the sinuses at the torcular, and the condition of the lateral sinuses, have been investigated both by dissection and from studies of roentgenograms or of dried bones; Hayner concluded that the cranial markings usually do not provide adequate data from which the formation of the torcular and the transverse sinuses may be accurately deduced, but Woodhall and Seeds, in a study of 100 good but routine roentgenograms of the occipital region, felt that they were able to interpret, sufficiently accurately for clinical purposes, the condition of the lateral sinuses from these; they found about the same percentage of types of variation as Woodhall found in a study of specimens by dissection.

In his analysis of variations at the torcular and in the transverse sinuses, Woodhall divided the types of confluence into five, of which the four chief types are shown in Figure 8. These were a common pool type (9 per cent) in which straight and superior sagittal sinuses meet and both lateral sinuses drain this junction; a plexiform type (56 per cent) which, although divisible into several subvarieties, was characterized by several channels that provided adequate communications between the two sides; an ipsilateral type (31 per cent) in which the sagittal sinus ran to one side and the straight sinus to the opposite side, though there was sometimes a foramen between the two; a unilateral type (4 per cent) in which both the sagittal and straight sinuses entered the same lateral sinus and there was absence of the opposite one; and a fifth type which he termed the occipital, overlapping with some of

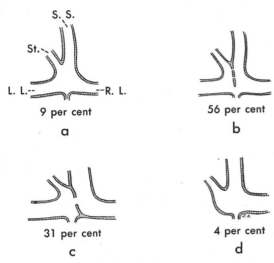

Fig. 8. Variation of the sinuses at the torcular. *a.* The common pool type. *b.* The plexiform type. *c.* The ipsilateral type. *d.* The unilateral type. *S.S.*, superior sagittal sinus; *St.*, straight sinus; *L.L.* and *R.L.*, left and right lateral sinuses, respectively. Percentages are those given by Woodhall.

the other types, but characterized by a persistence of a large single sinus or of paired occipital sinuses with large marginal sinuses.

Variations in the transverse portions of the lateral sinuses are only in part correlated with variations at the torcular. According to Woodhall, the lateral sinuses are usually of equal size when the torcular is of the common pool type; in the plexiform type the drainage varies, both sagittal and straight sinuses draining about equally into both sides, or one draining predominantly to one side, the other to the other side. In the majority of cases of unequal drainage the sagittal sinus drained to the right, the straight

sinus to the left. This tendency for the superior sagittal sinus to drain into the right lateral sinus and the straight sinus into the left one, when there is unequal drainage, is seen also in the ipsilateral type; among Woodhall's 31 cases this pattern occurred in 26, the reverse in only 5. This unequal drainage does not, however, necessarily affect the sizes of the lateral sinuses, for they were reported as being equal in size in 15, and the right as being only slightly larger in 6 more, while the left was the larger in only 3 cases. In the unilateral type the right lateral sinus was missing in 3 cases, the left in 1.

Of the variations in the region of the torcular, some of which were described by Knott as early as 1881, the most important one clinically is that in which one lateral sinus is much reduced or missing (Fig. 9). In this condition the Tobey-Ayer test may give misleading results, since occlusion of the internal jugular on the side of the normal sinus will give the expected rise in intracranial pressure, while occlusion on the side of the defective sinus will fail to produce a rise, and therefore may be interpreted as indicating a thrombosis of the lateral sinus on that side. Such a case has, for instance, been reported by Hilding.

According to Waltner variations of the transverse and sigmoid portions of the lateral sinus are independent of each other, since they are developed from separate anlagen, but the sigmoid portion shows greater constancy and fewer variations than does the transverse one. Some that have been described are shown in Figure 10. Hoople has stated that sometimes most of the blood from the transverse portion of the sinus may leave the skull through the mastoid foramen, the

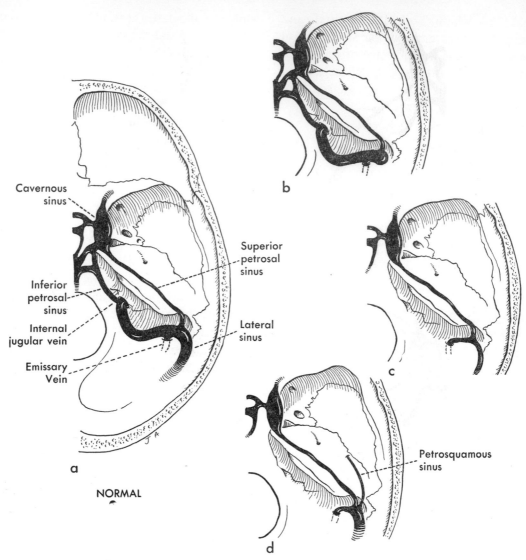

Cavernous
sinus

Superior
petrosal
sinus

Inferior
petrosal
sinus

Internal
jugular vein

Lateral
sinus

Emissary
Vein

a

NORMAL

b

c

Petrosquamous
sinus

d

Fig. 9.   Variations in the lateral sinus, with the normal arrangement, *a*, for comparison. In *b* the transverse portion of the lateral sinus is lacking. In *c* and *d* the sigmoid portion is lacking. (Adapted from Waltner, J. G.: *Arch. Otolaryng. 39*:307, 1944.)

jugular foramen then being markedly contracted, and the sigmoid portion of the sinus reduced or absent; he also reported a case in which the right transverse and sigmoid sinuses were small, and the sigmoid ended blindly at the jugular foramen, its drainage passing into sinuses of the middle cranial fossa.

Variations in the occipital and mar-

ginal sinuses, of importance in surgical approaches to the posterior fossa, are mentioned on page 73.

Doubling of one of the major sinuses is occasionally found; Woodhall found 2 cases of doubling of the superior sagittal sinus for a portion of its length, and both Knott and Hoople have noted that the transverse portion of the lateral

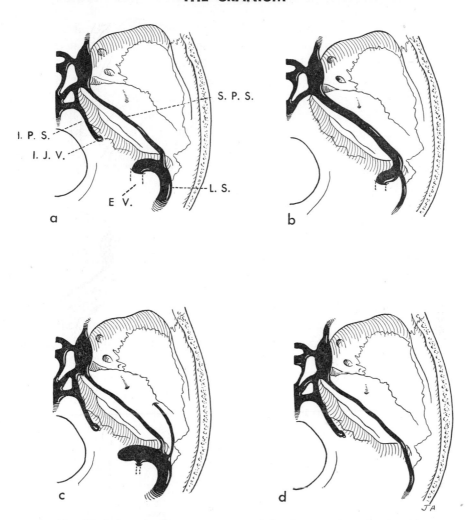

Fig. 10. Variations in the arrangement of the sinuses when the sigmoid portion is absent or fails to reach the jugular foramen. *I.P.S.* is the inferior petrosal sinus; *S.P.S.* the superior petrosal sinus; *L.S.* the lateral sinus; *I.J.V.* the internal jugular vein; and *E.V.* an emissary vein. (Adapted from Waltner, J. G.: *Arch. Otolaryng. 39:*307, 1944.)

sinus is sometimes similarly divided into separate channels.

FLOW OF BLOOD IN THE SINUSES

The usual anatomical disposition of the sinuses is such that one would expect practically all of the blood reaching the intracranial contents to make its exit by way of the large lateral sinuses into the internal jugular veins. In view of the fact that the straight sinus, formed by the great cerebral vein and the inferior sagittal sinus, receives blood bilaterally from the cerebral hemispheres and the more deeply placed structures of the brain, and that the large superior sagittal sinus also receives blood from both hemispheres, one would also expect rather thorough mixing of the blood entering by the paired carotid vessels supplying the two sides. Finally, in many cases one would also expect the blood from the superior sagittal sinus to be directed into one of the transverse sinuses, that from the straight sinus into the other. Only the latter expectation has been shown to be approximately true.

Gibbs and Gibbs, through perfusion experiments, have apparently substantiated the general belief that the torcular does usually direct the greater part of the flow from the superior sagittal sinus into the right lateral sinus, and that from the straight sinus into the left. In regard to the pathways of exit of blood from the cranium, however, Shenkin, Harmel, and Kety have found that a considerable proportion of internal carotid blood makes its way into the external jugular system; dye injections into the internal carotid indicated that approximately 22 per cent of the blood in the external jugular vein is derived from this vessel. Obviously, the rather insignificant emissary veins are of more importance than they would appear to be. As these authors found that only about 2.7 per cent of the blood of the internal jugular vein is derived from extracerebral sources, it is apparent that the flow of blood through the emissary veins is as a rule predominantly or entirely outward.

Shenkin, Harmel, and Kety have apparently shown also that there is a surprisingly incomplete mixing, on the venous side, of the blood derived from the two carotids; their experiments indicated that, of the carotid blood in the internal jugular, about 66 per cent is derived from the ipsilateral internal carotid, and only 34 per cent from the contralateral one.

Anomalous Accessory Sinuses

The most commonly occurring anomalous sinus is probably the *petrosquamous* (Fig. 9*d*); it usually begins anteriorly as a communication with the deep tem-
poral and middle meningeal veins, runs along the angle between the petrous and squamous portions of the temporal bone, and empties into either the lateral sinus or the posterior portion of the superior petrosal sinus. Knott found this vessel present in 7 of 44 cases on both sides, and in 19 additional cases on one side.

The *accessory sinus of Kelch* is described as passing backward from the superior orbital fissure, where it usually communicates with some of the vessels of the orbit, to cross the upper border of the petrous portion of the temporal bone and empty either into the superior petrosal or the lateral sinus.

The *ophthalmopetrous sinus of Hyrtle* is probably identical with the sinus of Kelch, as it is described as passing backward from the superior orbital fissure over the inner surface of the great wing of the sphenoid and the anterior surface of the temporal bone to terminate in the lateral sinus; it is said sometimes to leave the skull anteriorly through the foramen ovale, and sometimes to communicate with the middle meningeal veins. Knott found this vessel in 4 of 44 specimens examined.

The *accessory sinus of Verga* is a communication between the cavernous sinus or the ophthalmic vein, anteriorly, and the lateral sinus posteriorly, and may be another variation of those described above.

Occasionally, one of these accessory sinuses is of importance in the transmission of an infection. Thus Stewart has reported a case in which Kelch's accessory sinus became infected, apparently during the course of an operation on the middle ear, and noted that the petrosquamosal sinus has been said to be important in the passage of infection from the middle ear to the brain.

Stewart also described an additional accessory "sinus," which he termed the petro-occipital, though it probably should not be called a sinus since it lay for the most part outside the cranial cavity. According to Stewart it ran from the carotid venous plexus (at the point of communication of this with the cavernous sinus) to the jugular bulb, leaving the skull through an opening in the petro-occipital suture to run a largely extracranial course along the inferior surface of this suture.

MENINGEAL ARTERIES

While there are a number of arteries running in the dura and supplying it and the adjacent bone, most of these are small and are confined to the base of the skull. They include meningeal branches of the anterior and posterior ethmoidal arteries, themselves branches of the ophthalmic, to the floor of the anterior cranial fossa; twigs of the sphenopalatine artery (from the internal maxillary) to the same region; tiny unnamed branches from the internal carotid which are distributed largely in the neighborhood of the cavernous sinus and the semilunar ganglion; branches of the ascending pharyngeal artery to the floor of both middle and posterior cranial fossae; and branches from the vertebral and occipital arteries to the posterior cranial fossa. These are considered in the descriptions of the cranial fossae to which they are distributed. By far the largest of the meningeal arteries, and the most important one surgically, is the middle meningeal artery.

Gross and Savitsky have pointed out that, as would be expected from its size, the middle meningeal artery is the one most commonly involved in extradural hemorrhage, and therefore the subtemporal exposure of the middle cranial fossa is usually adequate to reveal such hemorrhages. They emphasized, however, that on rare occasions an extradural hemorrhage may be limited to the anterior cranial fossa, usually resulting here from hemorrhage from the meningeal branch of the anterior ethmoidal (or from this latter vessel itself?); they reported that extradural hemorrhages in the posterior cranial fossa are extremely rare. They also pointed out that extradural hemorrhages may occur without a fracture of the skull, and stated their belief that most extradural hemorrhages result from injury to the meningeal arteries and not from tears in the intracranial venous sinuses. Reichert and Morrissey agreed also that extradural venous hemorrhage is rare as compared with subdural venous hemorrhage or extradural arterial hemorrhage; they suggested, however, that a number of extradural hemorrhages which are supposed to arise from torn middle meningeal arteries actually arise from torn meningeal veins or sinuses. Kaump and Love, in discussing "subdural" hemorrhages, stated that most of them are really intradural, in the middle, vascular stratum of the dura.

MIDDLE MENINGEAL ARTERY

The middle meningeal artery, far the largest of the several meningeal arteries, supplies most of the supratentorial dura with the exception of the floor of the anterior cranial fossa, and even sends some branches into the posterior cranial fossa; it therefore spreads widely in the dura, and is of surgical importance both from the standpoint of its possible involvement in fractures of the skull (see the preceding paragraph) and because it is apt to be encountered in any lateral approach to the cranial contents. This artery, a branch of the internal maxillary (from the external carotid) enters the middle cranial fossa through the foramen spinosum, which lies just posterolateral to the foramen ovale.

Shortly after its entrance into the skull the middle meningeal artery divides into two major branches, anterior and posterior (Fig. 11); while some authors describe three branches, their so-called middle branch is derived from the posterior branch, from the main vessel between and the smaller branches are distributed more extensively to the bone than to the relatively avascular dura. The middle meningeal artery anastomoses with arteries of the opposite side, with the anterior and posterior meningeal arteries, and, through foramina in the bone, with the deep temporal arteries. It has usually also an orbital branch which anastomoses with the lacrimal branch of the ophthalmic artery; typically quite small, this

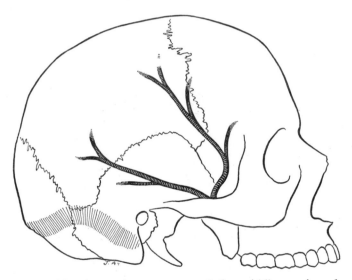

Fig. 11. Approximate course of the middle meningeal artery in relation to the cranial vault. The position of the lateral sinus is also indicated.

the anterior and posterior branches, or from the anterior branch. The anterior branch of the middle meningeal artery is distributed to the dura over the convexity of the brain in both anterior and middle cranial fossae, while the posterior is distributed to the remainder of the supratentorial portion of the dura, with a few twigs going also to the dura of the posterior fossa.

Although the larger branches of the middle meningeal artery lie in the dura, they form, with their accompanying veins, grooves on the interior of the cranium, vessel may be larger and form the stem of origin of the lacrimal artery, or even of the ophthalmic artery itself (p. 158); perhaps very rarely, as may have been true in the case described by Low, this anastomotic branch may form the origin of an anomalous middle meningeal artery.

COURSE

The *foramen spinosum* is located in approximately the deepest part of the concavity of the floor of the middle cranial fossa, about at the antero-posterior level of the posterior root of the zygoma. The middle meningeal artery may branch almost immediately after entering the cranium, or may run for some distance laterally and anteriorly before branching (Fig. 12). Chandler and Derezinski, in a study of 1200 half skulls, found no significant difference in the frequency of branching close to the foramen

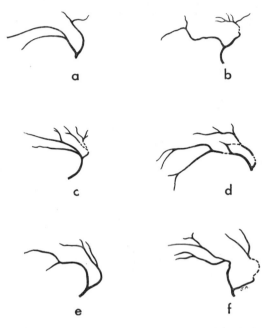

a   b

c   d

e   f

Fig. 12. Variations in the branching of the middle meningeal artery. The broken lines indicate that those parts of the vessels coursed in a canal in the bone. (Adapted from Chandler, S. B., and Derezinski, C. F.: *Anat. Rec. 62:* 309, 1935.)

spinosum, near the level of the great wing of the sphenoid, and between these two points. If the branching is far lateral, it is situated at about the level of the upper border of the zygomatic process, and at about the middle of the length of this process; in this case the posterior branch of the artery arches upward and backward almost parallel to the curved line formed by the zygomatic process, the supramastoid crest and the temporoparietal suture, but lying about a centimeter

above it. If the middle meningeal artery branches close to the foramen spinosum, the posterior branch does not come so far forward, and appears above the level of the zygomatic arch only toward the posterior end of this.

The *anterior branch* of the artery, whether it arises from close to the foramen spinosum or at the level of the middle of the zygomatic process, describes a broad curve with its concavity directed backward; the foremost part of this curve, and the point at which the artery can be fairly constantly located from externally on the skull, is the pterion, or region of junction of the frontal, sphenoid, parietal and temporal bones. This is covered by the temporal muscle, but can be located approximately by measuring about 2.5 cm. (a thumb's breadth) behind the zygomatic process of the frontal bone, and about 3.5 cm. (two fingerbreadths) above the zygomatic arch. Chandler and Derezinski found the anterior branch absent in only 9 of 1200 sides, and the posterior absent in only 7.

The anterior branch of the middle meningeal artery in more than 50 per cent of cases (677 of 1200, according to Chandler and Derezinski) runs in a canal in the bone, rather than simply in a groove, for part of its length, and is most apt to do so in the region of the pterion. For this reason, trephining over the pterion is to be avoided, and separation of the bone from the meninges at this particular level may lead to considerable bleeding unless the middle meningeal or its anterior branch is first secured below this point. The approach for ligature of this branch or the artery as a whole is over the middle of the zygomatic arch; if the artery sought is not found at this level, the dura lateral and inferior to the temporal lobe must be elevated; the an-

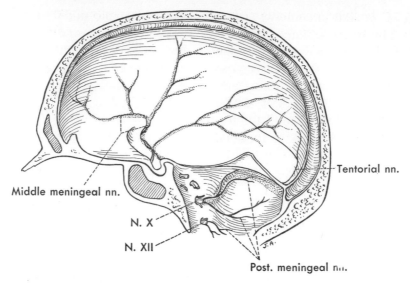

Fig. 13. Nerves of the cranial vault and the posterior cranial fossa. See also Fig. 34. (Redrawn from Penfield, W., and McNaughton, F.: *Arch. Neurol. & Psychiat. 44:*43, 1940.)

terior branch of the artery, in such a case, may be found by following the dura medially, but if the main stem of the vessel is to be located the dura must be followed not only medially but also posteriorly.

INNERVATION OF THE DURA OF THE CRANIAL VAULT

The vasomotor nerve supply of the dura mater is derived from plexuses accompanying the vessels, especially the middle meningeal artery, derived largely from the superior cervical ganglion. The sensory supply to the dura of the cranial vault is quite sparse, in contrast to that of most of the cranial floor, but like the latter is through recurrent branches of cranial nerves.

While the dura of the middle cranial fossa is supplied usually by branches from all three divisions of the trigeminal nerve, these branches are largely distributed at the base of the skull and to the tentorium or a limited area above this; the nerves to the dural vault run primarily with the middle meningeal artery, and are limited to its immediate neighborhood (Fig. 13, and see Fig. 34, p. 57). They consist of fibers arising from both the maxillary and mandibular divisions of the trigeminal, which largely accompany the middle meningeal artery and its branches. Tentorial branches from the ophthalmic nerve may reach the dura of the parietal region, however, according to Penfield and McNaughton; these workers found suggestive evidence that all the meningeal branches of the fifth nerve, regardless of their external origin, are derived actually from the ophthalmic. The nerves are described in more detail in connection with the middle cranial fossa (p. 56).

Anatomical investigations on the innervation of the dura of the cranial vault have been confirmed by clinical studies. Penfield and McNaughton, from stimulations of the dura at operation, concluded that all the supratentorial dura is innervated exclusively by the ipsilateral fifth cranial nerve. They were able to elicit only pain from the cranial dura, regardless of the type of stimulus used, and found that this pain was either local or referred; Figure 14 indicates their findings in regard to the latter. They noted that the convexity of the dura receives its nerve supply primarily from peripheral branches of the third division of the fifth nerve, with usually some also from the second, but believed that a contribution from the ophthalmic was less constant. Most important, they found that most of the dural convexity is insensitive, and that the sensitive points upon it coincide largely with the meningeal arteries, except for occasional points where nerves pass across the dura on their way to vascular channels.

Ray and Wolff, in their more extensive study of the sensitivity of cranial structures, agreed with Penfield and McNaughton that the dura between the branches of the middle meningeal artery is largely insensitive to pain; they reported that, except along the course of this artery and along the margins of the dural sinuses,

the supratentorial dura is sensitive to stimulation of any type only at the base of the skull.

LEPTOMENINGES AND SUBARACHNOID SPACE

The leptomeninges consist of the arachnoid and the pia, connected to each other by the arachnoid trabeculae but separated elsewhere by the subarachnoid space. The inner lining cells of the arachnoid, resembling mesothelial or endothelial cells, are continuous over the arachnoid trabeculae with the similar cells forming the outer surface of the pia; arachnoid and pia actually represent a splitting of a single layer, the leptomeninx, and the subarachnoid space is really then an intraleptomeningeal space, just as the peritoneal cavity is an intraperitoneal space.

CISTERNS

Since the pia is intimately attached to the surface of the brain, and therefore

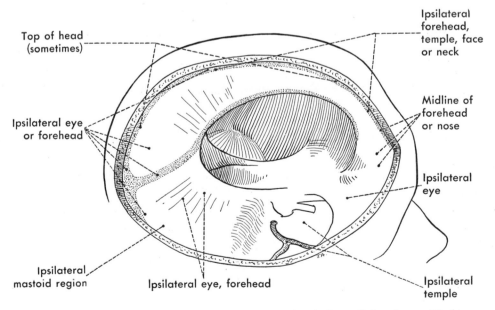

Fig. 14. Localization of referred pain from stimulation of the dura. (Redrawn from Penfield, W., and McNaughton, F.: *Arch. Neurol. & Psychiat.* 44:43, 1940.)

follows its form, while the arachnoid follows rather closely the conformation of the dura, the arachnoid space is much exaggerated in certain areas; these enlargements of the subarachnoid space are known as cisterns (Fig. 15). The largest and best known is the *cisterna magna* or *cisterna cerebellomedullaris,* lying between the postero-inferior surface of the cerebellum and the posterior surface of the medulla; this cistern receives the medulla, with its numerous vital centers and pathways.

The *cisterna basalis* (divided by the optic chiasma into a small anterior cisterna chiasmatis and a larger, posterior, cisterna interpeduncularis) lies at the base of the cerebrum, around the hypothalamus and the optic chiasma; the *cisterna pontis,* continuous anteriorly with the cisterna basalis, is sometimes referred to as Hilton's water bed, and

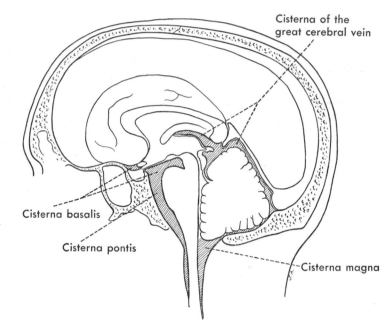

Cisterna of the great cerebral vein

Cisterna basalis

Cisterna pontis

Cisterna magna

Fig. 15. The chief subarachnoid cisterns about the brain.

the cerebrospinal fluid from the ventricular system of the brain, through paired lateral apertures (of Luschka) and the medial aperture (of Magendie) which open from the fourth ventricle.

Introduction of a needle into the cisterna magna, to record the pressure here in comparison with that at the lumbar level, or to secure cerebrospinal fluid from this area, has become a common practice; the tap is done through the foramen magnum but care must always be exercised not to thrust the needle against

lies especially about the basilar portion of the pons. The *cisterna of the great cerebral vein* lies deeply in the angle between the splenium of the corpus callosum, the superior surface of the cerebellum, and the colliculi of the midbrain.

Lesser cisterns are also sometimes described: for instance, one in each of the lateral fissures of the cerebrum (cisterns of the lateral sulci, lateral extensions of the interpeduncular cistern); since all of the cisterns are connected to each other, and represent only enlargements of the general subarachnoid space, it is obvious that it is sometimes difficult to draw a line between what should and should not be called a cistern.

The leptomeninges and the subarachnoid space are invaginated along blood vessels into the nervous system, where the arachnoid lies in contact with the outer wall of the blood vessel to form an inner lining to the perivascular space (the continuation of the subarachnoid space), and the pia forms the outer lining of this space (Fig. 16): Patek has emphasized

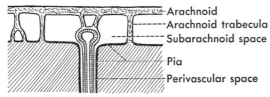

Fig. 16. Relation of the leptomeninges and the subarachnoid space to the perivascular spaces.

that the perivascular spaces are lined only in part by the pia and arachnoid, and in part by membranes composed of the glia itself; the arachnoid, according to Patek, extends along the blood vessels to the capillaries, while the pia extends about arteries for only a short distance, but about veins down to the smaller venules.

The subarachnoid space does not extend around the hypophysis (Wislocki; Sunderland, '45a), although it does encircle the infundibular stalk and is in contact with the upper surface of the hypophysis; below this point the dura is fused to the outer portion of the gland.

MENINGEAL RELATIONS OF NERVES

As the cranial nerves make their exits through the pia, the arachnoid, and the dura, each of these elements contributes

to the connective tissue of the nerve root; as the roots traverse the subarachnoid cavity they are covered by pia, and as they pierce the arachnoid they receive connective tissue from the outer layer of this (the cellular lining of the subarachnoid cavity being reflected of course at this point from arachnoid to pia). Similarly, as the nerves penetrate the dura the connective tissue of this element fuses with the connective tissue of the definitive nerve.

For the most part, the cranial nerves pierce the arachnoid and the dura in quick succession, and do not carry out with them portions of either the subarachnoid or the subdural spaces; the optic nerve, however, carries the meninges extracranially and is surrounded by a continuation of the subarachnoid space as far forward as the eyeball, while the facial and acoustic nerves are similarly surrounded by arachnoid and dura to the end of the internal auditory meatus; sometimes (Perlman and Lindsay) the subarachnoid space is prolonged about the facial nerve farther than this, extending even to the geniculate ganglion. Finally, there is an extension from the cisterna pontis around the root of the fifth nerve, as this latter passes across the petrous ridge, and enters a reduplication of the dura which in the middle cranial fossa forms Meckel's cave. This important relation of the fifth nerve is discussed on page 61.

NEUROGLIA IN NERVE ROOTS

While the pia covers the filaments of origin of the nerves throughout their courses through the subarachnoid space, the neuroglia can as a rule be traced for only a very short distance along the nerve roots as they leave the central nervous system. Tarlov ('37a, b) has shown that

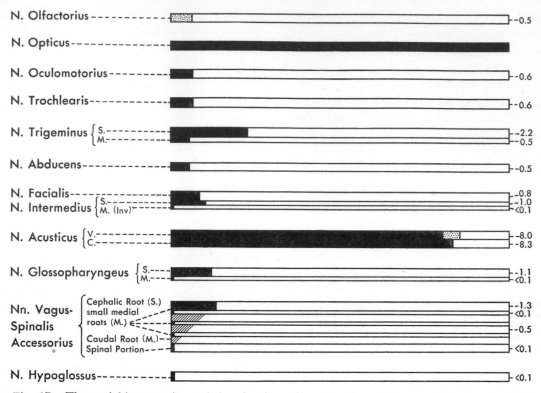

Fig. 17.   The variable extensions of the pia along the roots of cranial nerves. The lengths of the glial segments are given in millimeters, the sign < indicating that the measurement is usually less than that given. Stippling on the bars for the olfactory and vestibular nerves indicates common variations in the extent of the glia along these nerves; hatching on the vagus-accessory complex indicates a gradual decrease in the lengths of the glial segments of the successive rootlets from above downward. (From Tarlov, I. M.: *Arch. Neurol. & Psychiat. 37:*1338, 1937.)

for most cranial and spinal nerves the glia extends only a fraction of a millimeter beyond their external origins (Fig. 17). The optic nerve is an exception to this, but is really a tract of the brain rather than a typical nerve, and therefore contains neuroglia throughout its entire length.

The really outstanding exception to the distribution of glia along only a very short segment of a cranial nerve is the auditory nerve, which typically has glia extending for some 6 to 8 mm. along its course; this undoubtedly explains the far greater predilection of glial tumors to form on the auditory nerve than on other cranial nerves. Tarlov noted that occasional patches of glia may be found farther out in a nerve than they normally appear.

CRANIOCEREBRAL RELATIONS

The relations between various parts of the brain and certain markings or measured points on the skull are discussed in surgical texts, and this question will therefore be discussed here only in a very general way. It must be remembered, however, that not only do different skulls vary somewhat in the detail of their anatomy, but that there is also a very considerable variation in the morphology of the cerebral hemispheres themselves, and therefore no craniocerebral relations given here can be regarded as accurate and exact; rather they are only approximations which usually suffice for surgical purposes.

The cerebral hemispheres are entirely supratentorial, the frontal portion of the brain being lodged in the anterior cranial fossa, the temporal lobes fitting into the smooth lateral expansions of the middle cranial fossa, and the occipital lobes being located in the posterior part of the middle cranial fossa, resting upon the tentorium. The level of attachment of the tentorium, and therefore the lower surface of the occipital lobe, lies about an inch (2.5 cm.) above the plane through the upper borders of the external auditory meatuses and the superior margins of the orbits; the lower surface of the frontal lobe, since it rests upon the roof of the orbit, corresponds approximately to the level of the upper margin of the orbit; the temporal lobes, in the deeper anterior portion of the middle cranial fossa, descend to the level of about the upper border of the zygomatic arch. The midbrain lies at the tentorial notch, and the pons, the medulla, and the cerebellum lie in the posterior cranial fossa; most of the cranial nerves therefore arise within the posterior cranial fossa, and the majority of them enter the dura or make their exits from the skull through the walls or floor of this fossa. The third to the sixth, however, traverse also the middle cranial fossa.

The superior sagittal sinus has been discussed on page 12, and the middle meningeal artery on page 21. The course of the transverse portion of the lateral sinus may be approximated by a line, arching slightly upward, from the upper portion of the external occipital protuberance to the posterior aspect of the upper part of the root of the external ear (see also p. 73); the sigmoid sinus descends approximately along the posterior aspect of the root of the ear to the level of the lower border of the meatus and then curves forward to the level of the anterior border of the meatus, which approximates the anteroposterior position of the jugular foramen.

FISSURES, GYRI, AND LOBES

The pterion overlies approximately the stem of the *lateral (Sylvian) fissure,* the chief or posterior limb of which runs backward more or less parallel to but some 4 to 5 cm. above the zygomatic arch until it reaches the anteroposterior level of the mastoid process, after which it turns farther upward (Fig. 18).

Superiorly, the *central* or *Rolandic fissure or sulcus* begins slightly (about a centimeter) behind the midpoint of a sagittal line over the convexity of the skull extending from the nasofrontal suture (nasion) to the greater occipital protuberance (inion or torus); from this point in the midline the central sulcus extends downward and forward at an angle usually somewhat less than 70 degrees to end, of course, at the level of the lateral fissure. The lower end of the central sulcus is approximately vertically above the temporomandibular joint. Below the lateral fissure and slightly behind the level of the lower end of the central sulcus (therefore at approximately the anteroposterior level of the external meatus) is the transverse temporal gyrus, the area for hearing.

The *parieto-occipital sulcus* corresponds approximately to a short line drawn at right angles to the sagittal suture about a centimeter above or anterior to the lambda (the point of intersection between the sagittal and the occipitoparietal sutures, usually palpable as a

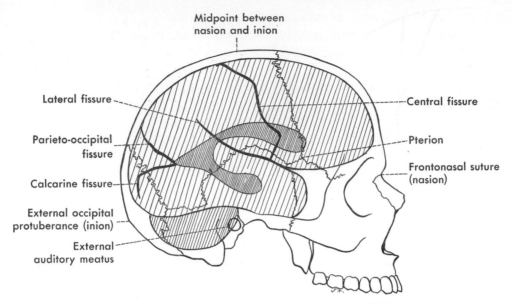

Midpoint between
nasion and inion

Lateral fissure

Parieto-occipital
fissure

Calcarine fissure

External occipital
protuberance (inion)

External
auditory meatus

Central fissure

Pterion

Frontonasal suture
(nasion)

Fig. 18. Some approximate relations of the brain to the skull. While these vary somewhat, this figure is fairly typical; the location of the fissures was recorded by roentgenograms after placing lead strips in the fissures. The lateral ventricle and the cerebellum are
more heavily shaded than the cerebral hemispheres.

depression). The calcarine area (center
for sight) lies in the occipital lobe just
above the level of the external occipital
protuberance.

These lines suffice to indicate the general positions of the lobes of the brain,
for the frontal lobe lies above the roof of
the orbit and the anterior part of the
lateral sulcus, and extends backward to
the central sulcus; the temporal lobe lies
below the lateral sulcus and extends
downward to about the level of the zygomatic process, and backward approximately to a line connecting the parieto-
occipital sulcus with the back of the root
of the external ear; the occipital lobe lies
behind the latter line, while the parietal
lobe lies between the upper part of this
line and the central sulcus.

It must be emphasized again that relationships between points on the skull and
the fissures and gyri of the cerebral hemispheres are really quite variable. For instance, a line directed vertically upward
from the external auditory meatus typ-

ically crosses the central sulcus, but sometimes crosses close to the base of this
sulcus and sometimes considerably higher,
depending upon the position and the inclination of the sulcus. Rowland and
Mettler, noting that the coronal suture
has been frequently used as a landmark
in lobotomy, investigated the relationships of this suture, and of the Freeman-Watts landmark, to the cerebral
hemisphere in a number of cadavers.
Even among only 6 skulls chosen at ran-
dom they found marked variations in
the inclination of this suture (Fig. 19),
as it formed an angle of anywhere from
69 to 86 degrees with the plane through
the external auditory meatus and the
lower rim of the orbit; investigating the
Freeman-Watts landmark—3 cm. behind
the lateral rim of the orbit and 6 cm.
above the zygoma—they found that this
point may overlie any one of the three
major subdivisions of the inferior frontal
gyrus. Observations such as these could
probably be repeated in regard to any

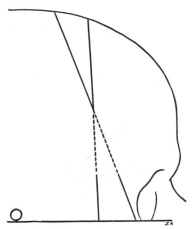

Fig. 19. Extremes in the inclination of the coronal suture among only 6 skulls. (Adapted from Rowland, L. P., and Mettler, F. A.: *J. Comp. Neurol. 89*:21, 1948.)

chosen landmark on the skull, and serve to emphasize the variability of cranio-cerebral relations.

DEEPER STRUCTURES OF BRAIN

As may be expected from what has already been said, the deeper structures of the brain also vary somewhat in their relations to the skull; Symington, among the early workers, has pointed out a few average levels for certain structures (Fig. 20). According to his findings, the genu of the corpus callosum usually extends forward to the level of the lower end of the coronal suture. The highest part of the body of the lateral ventricle is said to lie about 3 inches (7.5 cm.) above the roof of the external auditory meatus, therefore about 2 inches (5 cm.) from the top of the head; the anterior horn, like the callosum, reaches approximately as far forward as the coronal suture. The posterior horn is quite variable in its extent, although it is nearer the surface than any other part of the ventricle; Symington found it usually located about 2.5 cm. behind and 5 cm. above the external auditory meatus. It is customary to tap the lateral ventricle through its posterior horn, after a hole has been drilled in the upper posterior part of the parietal bone, anterior to the parieto-occipital suture; the horn lies at a depth

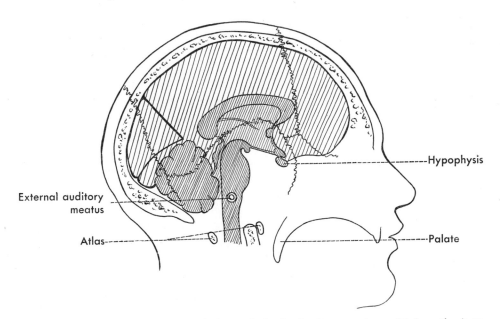

Fig. 20. Some approximate relations of the brain (as seen in sagittal section) to the skull. The brain stem, corpus callosum, and cerebellum are more heavily shaded; only the parieto-occipital and calcarine fissures of the cerebral cortex are shown.

of about 2½ inches (6 to 7 cm.) from the surface. The posterior horn may, however, be absent (Torkildsen).

The line of junction between midbrain and pons is said to be marked by a line about 1 inch (2.5 cm.) above the top of the external auditory meatus, and the junction of pons and medulla by a line about the level of the roof of the external auditory meatus, therefore at about the same level as the vault of the nasal part of the pharynx. The foramen magnum, and the junction of spinal cord and medulla, is at about the level of the hard palate. That useful landmark, the pterion, marks approximately the level of the anterior perforated substance and therefore of the optic chiasma and of the floor of the diencephalon.

BLOOD SUPPLY OF THE BRAIN

Arteries

The blood supply of the brain is derived from the vertebral and the internal carotid arteries (Fig. 21). The details of the relationships of these vessels and their branches to the base of the brain and to the cranial nerves are given in connection with the descriptions of the three cranial fossae; their general courses only are given here, therefore.

VERTEBRAL ARTERIES

The two vertebral arteries, after leaving the transverse foramina of the atlas, run posteriorly on the upper surface of the posterior arch of this bone to pierce the posterior atlanto-occipital membrane and the spinal dura and lie against the lateral side of the upper portion of the cord or lower end of the medulla, anterior to the spinal rootlets of the accessory nerve. They run upward through the foramen magnum on the ventral side of

the medulla, and unite at about the caudal end of the pons to form the basilar artery. Although, in the neck, each artery is accompanied by a vertebral venous plexus, this plexus does not enter the

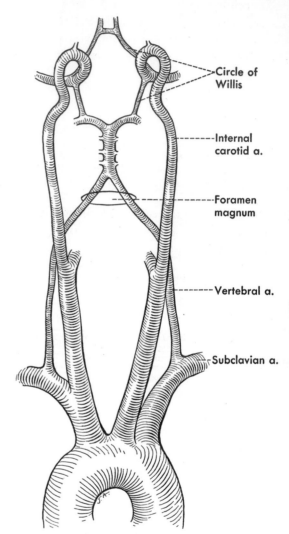

Fig. 21. Double origin of the blood supply to the brain.

cranial cavity with it but remains outside the dura, and normally receives, through emissary veins, only a very tiny proportion of the blood borne intracranially by the artery.

Before their union the two vertebral

arteries typically give off the anterior spinal arteries to the cord, and sometimes, though not usually (Stopford, '16a) the posterior spinal arteries. As they pass alongside the medulla they give off a variable number of small branches to this, and close to their terminations the large posterior inferior cerebellar arteries to the cerebellum and the posterolateral portions of the medulla (Fig. 22). The

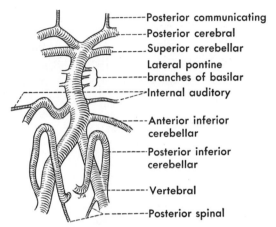

Posterior communicating
Posterior cerebral
Superior cerebellar
Lateral pontine branches of basilar
Internal auditory
Anterior inferior cerebellar
Posterior inferior cerebellar
Vertebral
Posterior spinal

Fig. 22. Schema of the vertebral arteries and their branches. The anterior spinal arteries are omitted; these and some variations of the vertebrals are shown in Figure 25. The more common origins of the posterior spinal and internal auditory arteries, from the posterior inferior and anterior inferior cerebellar arteries, respectively, are shown on the left side of the figure; the less common origins, from the vertebral and basilar, respectively, are shown on the right. Any of the vessels shown here may be asymmetrical in size, or more or less tortuous.

posterior inferior cerebellar artery normally runs upward along the dorso-lateral surface of the medulla and then loops dorsally and caudally to descend along the medulla and inferior surface of the cerebellum; before leaving the medulla and branching on the inferior surface of the cerebellum it usually gives rise to the posterior spinal artery.

BASILAR ARTERY

The basilar artery, formed by the junction of the two vertebrals at about the lower border of the pons, gives off in addition to a number of small pontine branches three or four main branches—the internal auditory artery, sometimes, and the anterior inferior cerebellar artery, the superior cerebellar, and the posterior cerebral; all of these vessels are of course paired, and the posterior cerebrals are the terminal branches formed by the bifurcation of the basilar artery at the upper border of the pons.

The *internal auditory artery* is a small vessel, passing on each side into the internal auditory meatus between the facial and auditory nerves; it is frequently described as a branch of the basilar artery, but Stopford ('16a) found it to arise from the anterior inferior cerebellar in 63 per cent of the cases in which he identified it, and Sunderland ('45b) reported a similar origin in 83 per cent of 264 sides which he examined, the artery arising from the basilar, therefore, in only 17 per cent. Watt and McKillop found the internal auditory artery to be double in 6 of 63 cases which they investigated.

The *anterior inferior cerebellar arteries* are paired branches which usually originate from the basilar soon after this vessel is formed, but may (Stopford, '16a) arise from the vertebral; each passes laterally and backward across the pons to the front part of the inferior surface of the cerebellum, often looping laterally in contact with the seventh and eighth nerves (page 81).

The *superior cerebellar arteries* are given off from the upper end of the basilar shortly before the ending of this vessel; they pass backward and downward around the cerebral peduncles or upper border of the pons to reach the superior surface of the cerebellum.

The *posterior cerebral arteries* are the terminal branches of the basilar, and pass laterally, where they lie at first parallel to the superior cerebellar arteries; close to their origins they are normally united to the internal carotids of their respective sides by the posterior communicating arteries. The posterior cerebral artery supplies most of the temporal lobe of the brain, except for the superior temporal gyrus, and most of the occipital lobe, thus including the important calcarine area.

The finer distribution of the vessels described briefly above, and the neurological symptoms resulting from their occlusion, cannot be entered into here. The former has been discussed in both its anatomical and clinical aspects by Stopford ('16b, '17); more recent discussions of some of the latter include that of Adams of a rare case of occlusion of the anterior inferior cerebellar artery, those of Merritt and Finland, and of Anderson, Lockhart, and Souter, on the more common occlusion of the posterior inferior cerebellar artery, of Kubik and Adams on occlusion of the basilar, and of Davison on occlusion of the anterior spinal artery.

Stopford ('17) has stated that occlusion of the vertebral artery is rare, but when it does occur it is more common on the left side. He also emphasized the variation in distribution of the posterior inferior cerebellar artery, with the resultant variation in symptoms resulting from its occlusion, and stated that it, of all the branches of the vertebral or basilar, is anatomically most prone to occlusion by emboli, a fact which is borne out by clinical experience. It may also be pointed out that the posterior cerebral artery supplies not only cortex, but also the medial and posterior portions of the thalamus, and gives off the posterior choroidal artery to the choroid plexus of the lateral ventricle and branches to the cerebellar peduncles and the corpora quadrigemina.

The vertebral ·arteries and their branches therefore supply an extensive area, including the upper portion of the spinal cord, the entire brain stem from the posterior portion of the thalamus downward, the entire cerebellum, and a large part of the postero-inferior portion of the cerebral cortex. It should be noted that while the cerebellar arteries anastomose freely with those of the opposite side on the cortex, the bulbar arteries are end arteries, like the deep vessels of the cerebrum.

INTERNAL CAROTID ARTERIES

The internal carotid arteries, the other great arterial trunks to the brain, are largely limited in their distribution to the cerebrum itself. The cranial course and chief branches of one of these vessels as seen in an arteriogram are shown in Figure 23. As the internal carotid artery passes upward through the carotid canal in the petrous portion of the temporal bone it lies in close relation to (anteromedial to) the middle ear cavity and the cochlea; it then turns sharply forward to run anteriorly and medially in the horizontal portion of the canal, at the end of which it enters the cranial cavity by turning upward upon the lateral surface of the body of the sphenoid bone, then turning again forward and proceeding along the lateral surface of the body through the cavernous sinus. Turning once again upward it leaves the cavernous sinus by piercing the dura medial to the anterior clinoid process. The two vessels converge somewhat in their course along the sphenoid; emerging from the dura, each vessel turns again caudally and divides, at the level of the anterior end of the lateral cerebral fissure, into its two terminal branches, anterior and middle cerebrals. The portion of the artery lateral to and above the sphenoid bone is frequently referred to as the carotid syphon.

In the cavernous sinus, the artery is in immediate contact with the abducens nerve, which crosses its lateral surface, but the oculomotor, the trochlear, and

Within the carotid canal the carotid artery gives off the small caroticotympanic branch to the middle ear cavity, but its first branch of importance after entering the cranium is the *ophthalmic artery*. This vessel arises from the internal carotid just as this latter perforates the dura at the medial surface of the anterior clinoid process, and therefore just posterior to the optic foramen. It enters the optic

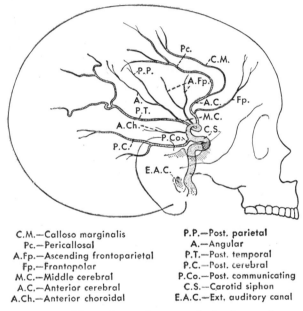

C.M.—Calloso marginalis	P.P.—Post. parietal
Pc.—Pericallosal	A.—Angular
A.Fp.—Ascending frontoparietal	P.T.—Post. temporal
Fp.—Frontopolar	P.C.—Post. cerebral
M.C.—Middle cerebral	P.Co.—Post. communicating
A.C.—Anterior cerebral	C.S.—Carotid siphon
A.Ch.—Anterior choroidal	E.A.C.—Ext. auditory canal

Fig. 23. Normal arteriogram of the internal carotid artery. Courtesy of Dr. Alfred Uihlein.

the ophthalmic branches of the fifth nerve lie more laterally, being in the lateral wall of the sinus. An internal carotid venous plexus accompanies the artery through a portion of its course, and forms a communication between the cavernous sinus and the internal jugular vein. The carotid artery is also accompanied by a nerve plexus, derived from the superior cervical ganglion; in addition to accompanying the branches of the artery, this plexus also gives rise to the deep petrosal nerve (to the sphenopalatine ganglion) and the sympathetic root of the ciliary ganglion.

foramen below the optic nerve, but within the dural sheath surrounding the nerve.

It is only shortly after giving off the ophthalmic artery that the carotid divides into its two terminal branches, the small anterior cerebral and the large middle cerebral arteries, this division taking place approximately lateral to the optic chiasma. Just before dividing, each carotid sends a posterior communicating artery to join the posterior cerebral artery of the same side and thus help to form the circle of Willis, and a choroidal artery into the inferior cornu of the lateral ventricle.

Small branches to the dura in the region of the cavernous sinus, and to the hypophysis, are also given off from the carotid in the cavernous sinus.

The *anterior cerebral arteries* pass forward and medially, above the optic nerves, chiasma, or tracts, to the intercerebral or longitudinal fissure, where they are connected by a short trunk, the anterior communicating artery. In the intercerebral fissure the two vessels lie close together and pass around the genu of the corpus callosum to be distributed to much of the medial side of the two cerebral hemispheres, anastomosing here with the posterior cerebral arteries at about the junction of parietal and occipital lobes.

The *middle cerebral artery*, anatomically the continuation of the internal carotid, passes laterally and upward in the lateral fissure, that is, between the temporal and frontal lobes of the brain; in the region of the insula it divides into cortical branches which are distributed to the lateral surfaces of the frontal and parietal lobes of the cerebral hemispheres, and to the superior portion of the temporal lobe. In its course the middle cerebral artery gives off a number of vessels to the basal ganglia and the cerebral peduncle, these sometimes being collectively known as the "artery" of internal hemorrhage. The distribution of these and other deep branches of the carotid system has been reviewed by Abbie, by Rubinstein, and by Finley; Beevor has described and beautifully illustrated the distribution of the three cerebral arteries.

Like the cerebellar arteries, the *cortical branches* of the three cerebral arteries have anastomoses with each other as they spread over the surface of the hemisphere. However, the deep group of vessels, to

structures of the brain stem, are similar to the bulbar vessels of the vertebral system, in that they are essentially end arteries, with no effective anastomoses.

CIRCLE OF WILLIS

The circle of Willis (circulus arteriosus) is normally formed by the origin of the two posterior cerebral arteries from the basilar, the junction of these to the internal carotid by the posterior communicating arteries, and by the anterior cerebrals and their anastomosis, the anterior communicating artery (Fig. 24). While it thus typically forms anastomotic channels by which blood can conceivably pass freely from any one vessel to all branches of the circle, Rogers has pointed out that actually there is very little evidence that any large amount of blood passes even from one internal carotid into the vessels of the opposite side or, normally, into the posterior cerebral arteries; injections of radiopaque materials into the carotid artery of one side usually outline that carotid system only, very little passing into other channels. He expressed the belief, therefore, that the circle of Willis probably does not permit mingling of the various blood streams from the main vessels, and should not be regarded as a distributor or equalizing station for the cerebral blood supply. Rather it provides a by-pass which is capable of opening up should one of the main channels become obstructed, and its value is largely potential only. Shenkin, Harmel, and Kety have also emphasized that the connections of the circle of Willis are potential rather than normally used ones. By use of dye injections they showed that there was little mixing of carotid blood on the arterial side, and even quite incomplete mixing on the venous side (see p. 20).

VARIATIONS

Variations of the vertebrals, the basilar, or their branches are the rule rather than the exception, and variations in the sizes of the vessels participating in the circle of Willis are quite common. It has often been stated that the brains of the insane

The *vertebral arteries* are usually (92 per cent—Stopford, '16a) unequal in size, the left being larger in somewhat more than half of these cases (Fig. 25, a ventral view). Stopford found an excessively small right vertebral artery in 5 of 150 brains examined, and 1 case in

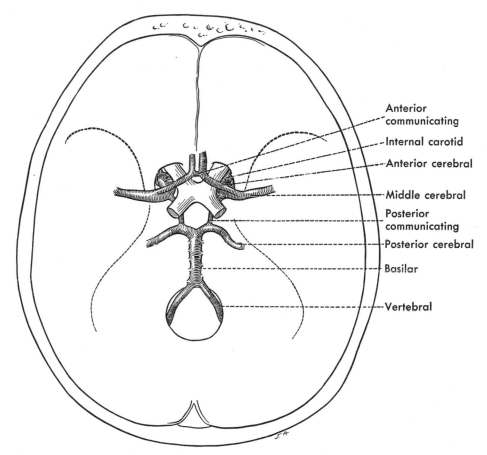

Anterior communicating

Internal carotid

Anterior cerebral

Middle cerebral

Posterior communicating

Posterior cerebral

Basilar

Vertebral

Fig. 24.   Relation of the circle of Willis to the base of the skull.

show arterial variations more frequently than do those of the sane, but apparently no causal relationship has been seriously suggested. In his own series, Stopford ('16a) found some discrepancy, such as absence, irregular origin, reduplication, or marked variation in size, of one or more arteries in 61 per cent of the brains from presumably sane individuals, and in 79 per cent of those from the insane.

which both vessels were minute. Batujeff has recorded an unusual case in which the left vertebral artery entirely failed to enter the skull, but was replaced by a branch of the internal carotid arising within the carotid canal and entering the skull through the condyloid foramen; this anomalous vessel represented all of the basilar artery except for the right posterior inferior cerebellar artery, which was formed as the terminal branch of the right vertebral artery.

Other variations in the formation, course, and branching of the basilar artery have been recorded in detail by Stopford ('16a). Among these were absence of the posterior inferior cerebellar artery bilaterally in 3 per cent, and absence on the right in 15 per cent and on the left in 6 per cent; doubling of the anterior in-

Fawcett and Blachford, Windle, Blackburn ('07, '10), and Stopford ('16a) have reported upon the *circle of Willis* and its branches in a total of approximately 1500 brains; they agree that the most common defect in the circle is absence of one or both posterior communicating arteries, the exact figure varying with the author (for instance, 7 per cent in Stopford's series of 150, 3.9 per cent in

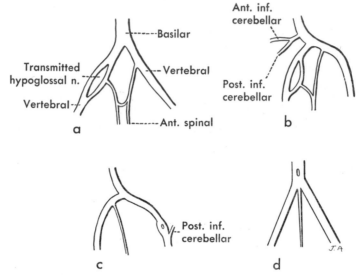

Fig. 25. Some variations in the vertebral arteries. In *b* a high and in *c* a low, origin of the posterior inferior cerebellar artery is indicated. Note also the variations in the origin of the anterior spinal artery. (Redrawn from Stopford, J. S. B.: *J. Anat. 50:* 131, 1916.)

ferior cerebellar artery once, and absence bilaterally once and on the left twice (among 150 cases); doubling of the superior cerebellar artery on both sides in 3 per cent, on the left only in 16 per cent, and on the right only in 12 per cent. Hochstetter, Flesch, and Smith have each reported an unusual variation, in which the internal carotid artery divided within the cavernous sinus, one of the two branches running downward to reinforce the basilar while the other proceeded as a normal internal carotid (see also p. 84).

Fawcett and Blachford's series of 700, 12.5 per cent in Windle's series of 200).

Another relatively common major variation is a major or entire origin of the posterior cerebral artery from the carotid, by way of an "enlarged" posterior communicating artery (Fig. 26). The occurrence of this origin averaged, in the series already cited, approximately 5 per cent on the right side, slightly less on the left, and about 2 per cent bilaterally, but Sunderland ('48) found a carotid origin of the posterior cerebral bilaterally in 6 per cent of 100 cases, and unilaterally in about 13 per cent each of right and left sides. Actually, this origin represents a retention of the embryonic condition, as the posterior cerebral is originally a branch of the internal carotid which subsequently transfers to the basilar. Apparently no major variations occur in the middle cerebral artery. The anterior cerebrals may be supplemented by a third, a so-called middle, anterior cerebral (Stopford found this in 6 per cent, Blackburn in about 10 per cent, Windle in about 4.5 per cent), or one may, rarely, be absent, or the two may be united for a part or much of their course (Windle). The anterior communicating artery is occasionally, but rarely, absent; more often it is double (7 to 9 per cent) or even triple (Fig. 27). It is of course absent as a

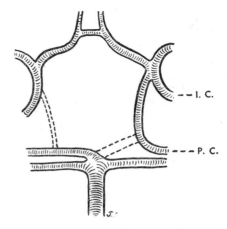

Fig. 26. The two origins of the posterior cerebral artery, the less common one being shown on the right. The parts of the circle of Willis that may be very small or entirely lacking are shown by the dotted lines. *I.C.*, the internal carotid artery; and *P.C.*, the posterior cerebral artery.

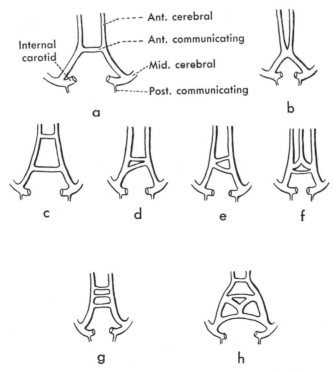

Fig. 27. Variations in the anterior communicating artery. (Redrawn from Stopford, J. S. B.: *J. Anat.* 50:131, 1916.)

vessel when there is fusion between the two anterior cerebrals.

ANEURYSMS

The circle of Willis and its branches are of importance from the standpoint of aneurysms. According to Dandy ('41) more than half of all intracranial aneurysms arise from the circle of Willis; he stated that about 80 per cent of these aneurysms are congenital, but Matas expressed the belief that only about 46 per cent are. The latter author found that aneurysmal defects, typically appearing at the forking of branches, are reported as being encountered in about 0.1 to 0.2 per cent of necropsies. Of 279 aneurysms reported in necropsy records as being of or adjacent to the circle, Matas found the middle cerebral to have 25.1 per cent, the basilar 16.1 per cent, the internal carotid 13.9 per cent, the anterior communicating 13.2 per cent, and the anterior cerebral 7.5 per cent.

Aneurysms of the circle of Willis are particularly apt to cause palsies of the third nerve, or may affect the visual pathway or other nerves to the eye muscles, in addition to pressure on the substance of the brain itself. Dandy ('39) has treated aneurysms of the internal carotid artery in the cavernous sinus by trapping them between two occlusions of the artery, one intracranially and the other in the neck.

INNERVATION

As they enter the skull, the arteries bring with them nerve plexuses which follow the smaller branches of the vessels into the pia and into the nervous system itself (Penfield, '32; Clark; Humphreys). The majority of the nerve fibers are probably vasoconstrictor or vasodilator, but Clark has described endings in the adventitia of vessels which appeared to be of sensory character, and Levine and Wolff expressed the belief that they have shown that the pial blood vessels possess an afferent as well as a motor supply, and that this afferent supply may be important in the regulation of the cerebral circulation. Apparently, however, there are no pain fibers among the afferent fibers on the smaller vessels, as Ray and Wolff were unable to obtain pain by stimulation of these vessels of the pia; only the larger blood vessels were found to contain pain fibers.

The causes of *headache* are not completely understood, but following especially the work of Wolff and his collaborators (for instance, Schumacher, Ray and Wolff; Schumacher and Wolff; Kunkle, Ray, and Wolff) it is generally granted that a major cause is distention of cerebral arteries, or of these and extracranial arteries of the head. While the distention of branches of the external carotid is stated by Ray and Wolff to be responsible chiefly for migraine headache and the headache associated with arterial hypertension, distention of intracranial arteries is said to be responsible for the headache produced by various chemical agents, such as histamine, and for that associated with septicemia and fever. Thus the larger arteries in the cranial cavity may play an important part in the production of symptoms. Kunkle, Lund, and Maher expressed the belief also that clinical headaches related to hunger, recent trauma of the head, or emotional tension are due to distention of intracranial or extracranial arteries, as they found that headaches of these types could be eliminated by exposure to a favorable increased gravity produced by the human centrifuge.

The *motor innervation* to the pial and

cerebral arterioles is believed to be a double one, from both sympathetic and parasympathetic systems. Pool, Forbes, and Nason, and Stavraky have stated that stimulation of the cervical sympathetic trunk produces constriction of the pial arteries which averages about a 10 per cent decrease in diameter. According to the former workers, the constriction is confined to the ipsilateral side, there being no change in the contralateral side. The parasympathetic supply to the pial vessels is said to be derived at least in part from the facial nerve, as stimulation of this at the geniculate ganglion produces vasodilation (Forbes, Nason, Cobb, and Wortman). The vasodilator fibers of the seventh nerve to the pial vessels are believed to reach their destination by way of the great superficial petrosal nerve and the internal carotid plexus, probably with a synapse upon cells located in this plexus (Chorobski and Penfield). Forbes, Nason, and Wortman, and Cobb and Finesinger have also described vasodilation of the pial vessels consequent to vagal stimulation, but suggested that this is a reflex involving the facial nerve on the efferent side. Fog ('39a) adduced evidence that the effect of the vasomotor nerves on the blood vessels is confined entirely to the larger arteries of the pia, and that there is none on the arterioles; he has stated ('39b) that while the pial arterioles respond to a fall in blood pressure by relaxing, and to a rise by contracting, these reactions occur after bilateral section of the cervical sympathetic trunk and bilateral section of various vasosensory nerves. Florey was likewise unable to obtain evidence of a nervous control over the vessels to the cerebral cortex.

In spite of the apparent demonstration of vasoconstrictors and vasodilators to the vessels within the cranium, the relative physiological importance of these is subject to some doubt. Forbes and Cobb stated that the regulation of the blood flow within the brain and the meninges is largely controlled by chemical agents, especially carbon dioxide; they reported that cerebral vasoconstrictor nerves are only about one tenth as effective on the vessels in the pia as are vasoconstrictor nerves in the skin, and that the vasoconstrictor nerves which are present are distributed unequally to different parts of the brain. Later Forbes ('40) stated that while the volume of blood flow through the brain is regulated largely by the arteriolar pressure, there are many other factors involved too; he also pointed out that although the blood vessels are particularly sensitive to slight variations in the tension of carbon dioxide, the resulting dilation of the arterioles may either increase the flow through the tissues of the brain, or, if it is general, may cause such a large fall in blood pressure that there is an actual decrease in cerebral blood flow.

Clinically, however, blocking the stellate ganglion is said to produce, frequently, marked improvements in patients suffering from disorders of the cerebral circulation, although there is no clear evidence that such block actually increases the total cerebral blood flow (Naffziger and Adams). Adson ('51), reporting that recurrent attacks of transitory hemiparesis in 2 individuals suffering from hypertension had apparently been halted by bilateral removal of the superior cervical ganglia, expressed his belief that the effect of this was probably extracranial, on the internal carotid artery, rather than on the middle cerebral itself.

VEINS

The venous drainage of the brain differs from that of most parts of the body in that the very thin-walled veins, containing no valves, do not at all correspond to the arteries, and do not accompany them. The veins resemble the arteries in only one essential respect, and that is that the cerebral vessels may be divided into two chief groups, a cortical group and a deep group (but see p. 43).

central gyri. Merwarth has described the syndrome resulting from occlusion of this vein, the symptoms being especially marked in the lower extremity since the vein drains especially the upper portions of the precentral and postcentral gyri. As already noted, the veins usually enter the sinus obliquely and in the direction oppo-

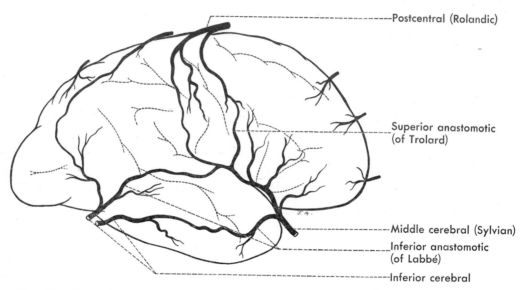

Fig. 28. General pattern of the cerebral veins. Details vary considerably, but in the schema here presented the general division into superior and inferior veins, and some of the larger anastomotic channels, are illustrated. It is a matter of opinion as to when a channel is large enough to be designated as an anastomotic vein.

CORTICAL VEINS

The veins of the cerebral cortex are usually divided into two groups, a superior and an inferior (Fig. 28). The *superior cerebral veins* communicate freely with each other, but do not form a constant pattern; they are usually described as forming some eight to a dozen trunks which empty into the superior sagittal sinus, but according to Merwarth usually unite into four principal trunks: a frontal, a precentral, a postcentral or Rolandic, and an occipital. Of these the postcentral or Rolandic is usually the largest and drains the precentral and post-

site to that in which the blood flows within the sinus.

The *inferior cerebral veins* drain into the cavernous sinus, and into the inferior sagittal, superior petrosal, and transverse sinuses; a vein from the occipital lobe usually also joins the termination of the great cerebral vein, and a vein from the inferior surface of the frontal lobe usually empties into the superior ophthalmic vein, but occasionally opens into the superior petrosal sinus. This small vessel is known as the ophthalmomeningeal vein.

One of the larger inferior cerebral veins runs in the lateral fissure to end in the cavernous sinus, and is therefore termed the middle cerebral or Sylvian vein. The middle cerebral vein is united posteriorly to the inferior cerebral veins in the posterior temporal and occipital regions, this connection being usually described as the inferior anastomotic vein of Labbé, but according to O'Connell being represented typically by two vessels. The middle cerebral vein usually has also a large anastomosis with one or more of the superior cerebral veins, this anastomotic channel being known as the superior anastomotic vein of Trolard. The superior anastomotic vein is, however, only one of several (according to O'Connell, usually at least three) vessels which unite the superior and inferior cerebral veins.

The veins on the superior surface of the cerebellum join the great cerebral vein, the straight sinus, and the transverse and superior petrosal sinuses; those on the inferior surface of the cerebellum join the inferior petrosal, transverse, and occipital sinuses.

DEEP CEREBRAL VEINS

The deep structures of the cerebrum, and of the brain stem above the region of the upper border of the pons, drain into paired internal cerebral veins which in turn unite to form the great cerebral vein (of Galen) that empties into the anterior end of the straight sinus. Since this venous drainage includes also the choroid plexuses, it has been suggested that obstruction of the great vein of Galen may be one cause of hydrocephalus; however, Bedford ('34a and b) has been unable to produce hydrocephalus or any obvious changes in the choroid plexus by operative occlusion of the great vein of Galen in either the dog or the monkey; he noted that there are considerable variations in the anatomy of this system, however, and that the disposition of the veins is somewhat different in these animals from that in man.

Schlesinger has found that in the monkey there are large intracerebral anastomotic venous channels in the white matter, which establish connections between the tributaries of the great vein of Galen and the veins on the surface of the hemispheres; apparently, therefore, the deep and superficial veins of the cerebrum are united by functional collateral channels (in sharp contrast to the arterial system) and drainage of the great cerebral vein and of the large veins on the surface of the brain overlaps to a very considerable extent. Schlesinger found, however, no anastomotic veins in the basal ganglia, which seemed to be drained primarily or exclusively by the great cerebral vein; occlusion of this vein, in his experiments, produced no hyperemia in the choroid plexus and no hydrocephalus, but did produce numerous hemorrhages into the head of the caudate nucleus.

The veins from the lower part of the brain stem—that is, from the pons and medulla—end in the inferior petrosal and transverse sinuses. According to Schlesinger, however, even the pontine vessels can be injected through the communications between the great vein of Galen and the veins on the surface of the cortex.

THE ANTERIOR CRANIAL FOSSA

THE anterior portions of the frontal lobes of the brain, and the associated olfactory nerves, bulbs, and tracts, lie in the anterior cranial fossa, while the optic chiasma and hypophysis, and the anterior ends of the temporal lobes, are immediately adjacent to it and may be approached through it.

The cranial vault of this fossa is largely formed by the frontal bone, hence the approach to it is usually through this bone. In order to avoid interrupting the supraorbital nerves and producing a denervated area of scalp in the parietal region, the skin can be incised in the sagittal plane beginning upon the forehead or at the hair line, carried back along this line and gradually curved downward toward the ear, or, alternatively, a transverse incision can be made close to the interauricular line. If after either of these incisions the skin flap is turned forward over the forehead and downward in the temporal region, major branches of neither the vessels nor the nerves of the scalp will be interrupted (see p. 1, ff.).

In "turning" a frontal bone flap, it is desirable to avoid the frontal sinus if possible, in order to prevent possible infection from this source; as the sinus varies quite considerably in regard to its upward extension into the frontal bone, its position should be ascertained by roentgenograms previous to operation. The bone flap is usually somewhat C shaped, with its base in the anterior temporal region at the thin squamous portion of the temporal bone, where it is most easily fractured. Nutrition of the bone flap may be maintained by leaving it attached to the temporal muscle, but this blood supply (through the deep temporal arteries) may be a source of troublesome bleeding, and has been found to be unnecessary for healing of the replaced bone. "Free" (that is, detached) bone flaps are preferred by many surgeons.

After the bone flap is reflected (a bilateral approach is sometimes preferred for access both to the region of the cribriform plate and to the optic chiasma and hypophysis), the dura may be incised directly, but if structures close to the floor of the anterior cranial fossa are sought the dura may be easily separated from the wall and most of the floor of the fossa. This approach has the advantage of allowing the dura to be retracted with the frontal lobe, thus lessening the possibility of damage to the latter. The firmer attachments of the dura are at the cribriform plate, toward the midline, and posteriorly along the sphenoid ridge (between anterior and middle cranial fossae); after it has been elevated from the inner surface of the cranium to these points, the dura must be incised.

FLOOR OF ANTERIOR CRANIAL FOSSA

The floor of the anterior cranial fossa consists largely of the orbital portion of the frontal bone; medially, the cribriform plate (lamina cribrosa) of the ethmoid, which has the olfactory bulb in contact with it, forms a small portion of the floor. A small, most posterior, portion of the anterior cranial fossa is formed by the anterior part of the body of the sphenoid bone and by its lesser wing, with the posteriorly projecting anterior clinoid process; the lateral portion of the lesser wing forms the sharp margin (sphenoid ridge) between anterior and middle cranial fossae.

Although it is correct anatomically to regard the sella turcica as being a portion of the middle cranial fossa, connecting the two larger paired portions across the midline, access to this region is most easily obtained through the frontal approach: the optic chiasma and the upper surface of the hypophysis lie at the level of the floor of the anterior fossa, but considerably above the lower surface of the temporal lobe, and therefore above the lateral part of the floor of the middle fossa. From the surgical standpoint the sella can be considered a part of the anterior fossa, the middle cranial fossa being therefore, from this standpoint, a paired structure.

FRACTURES

The floor of most of the anterior cranial fossa is particularly delicate, due both to its invasion by ethmoid and frontal sinuses and to its close relationship to the orbit and to the nose. Fractures of it may injure the olfactory bulb or tract, which lie in close contact with the cribriform plate; if they are accompanied by tearing of the meninges they may produce hemorrhage from the ethmoid branches of the ophthalmic artery, or their meningeal branches, which run along the lateral border of the cribriform plate; similarly, complete fractures of the floor of the anterior cranial fossa with tearing of the meninges may produce bleeding into the frontal sinus or directly into the nose, or, even in the absence of bleeding, an escape of cerebrospinal fluid into either of these (cerebrospinal rhinorrhea). According to Adson ('41a) from 2 to 5 per cent of fractures of the skull produce this latter result, but most of them heal spontaneously. Fractures across the floor of the anterior or middle cranial fossae extending to the region of the optic canals (optic foramina) may also produce lesions of the visual pathway, either through hemorrhage about the optic nerve in the canal, or by directly affecting this nerve.

DEFECTS

The floor of the anterior cranial fossa may present a congenital defect, through which a basal *encephalocele* or *meningocele* protrudes. According to Anderson basal encephaloceles or meningoceles typically pass either through the superior orbital (sphenoidal) fissure into the orbit (or on through the orbit into the pterygopalatine fossa) or protrude into the nose or nasopharynx through the ethmoid or sphenoid bones or through the suture between them. The latter he has termed the "sphenopharyngeal" type, though it might in some cases be more properly termed "ethmonasal." Mood, reviewing some 20 cases of anterior cerebral herniation, classified the majority as being nasofrontal ones, but found some, including the case he described, to be naso-ethmoidal, and 1 to be nasolacrimal. The distinctions here do not seem to be of particular importance. According to Anderson, however, basal meningoceles are more commonly "sphenopharyngeal," and it is the presence of these in the nasal cavity that has been shown to be sometimes responsible for the occurrence of "spontaneous" rhinorrhea, that is, not associated with fracture.

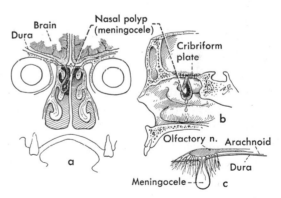

Fig. 29. Views of the cribriform region showing the meningeal sac in a case of cerebrospinal rhinorrhea. (From Adson, A. W., and Uihlein, A.: *Arch. Surg.* 58:623, 1949.)

SPONTANEOUS RHINORRHEA

Spontaneous rhinorrhea has been demonstrated in several cases to be due to protrusion of an arachnoid diverticulum into the nasal cavity through a defect in the ethmoid bone (Fig. 29); thus Adson

('41a) described a case in which at operation there was an opening 2 mm. in diameter in the cribriform plate, through which the meninges passed into the nasal cavity paralleling a filament of the olfactory nerve. Love and Gay have reported 2 similar cases, with small defects, in adults, and a large bilateral defect with herniation of a part of the frontal lobe in a child. Coleman and Trolard have attempted to distinguish between what they regard as truly spontaneous cerebrospinal rhinorrhea—that not due to a grossly demonstrable defect in the cribriform— and that in which a defect can be seen at operation, but it seems probable that the distinction is really one only of size. They inferred that in the former the fluid followed olfactory nerve filaments into the nose, although they suggested no reason for its escape. It seems reasonable to follow Adson in his belief that cerebrospinal rhinorrhea in the absence of fracture of the skull is due to defects in the cribriform plate with protrusion and thinning of the meninges, as it is difficult to believe that the lesion or multiple lesions could not sometimes be small enough to be overlooked at operation.

In the adult cases of Love and Gay, the rhinorrhea was precipitated by nasal infection—thus, although the condition is apparently congenital, symptoms may not occur, or may not be sufficiently marked, until some trauma precipitates them. It is generally recognized that meningitis is the most serious potential complication of this condition. The accepted method of repair is an intracranial approach (Adson; Love and Gay; Coleman and Troland; Wessels), a piece of muscle often being placed over the defect of the cribriform plate as a whole. Adson found the bilateral approach, with mobilization of the dura beneath both frontal lobes, most satisfactory.

ARTERIES AND NERVES

Laterally and superiorly, the dura of the anterior cranial fossa and its covering vault is supplied by the anterior branch of the middle meningeal artery. The floor of the anterior cranial fossa is supplied by the meningeal branches of the anterior and posterior ethmoidal arteries, themselves branches of the ophthalmic, which run in the dura on the lateral border of the cribriform plate. The branch from the anterior ethmoidal artery is usually the larger, and is sometimes referred to as *the* anterior meningeal artery. The meningeal branches of the ethmoidal arteries are reinforced by twigs of the sphenopalatine artery (from the internal maxillary), which ascend through the cribriform plate to anastomose with them.

Ray and Wolff found the dural floor of the anterior cranial fossa to be inconsistently sensitive to pressure, but uniformly sensitive to faradic stimulation; such stimulation produced pain which became localized in the general region of the homolateral eye (apparently, therefore, involving the ophthalmic division of the fifth nerve). The dura of the olfactory groove was found to be especially sensitive, as were portions of the arteries in the floor of the anterior cranial fossa; 2 cm. above the floor, however, the dura became insensitive. The innervation of the dura of the floor of the anterior cranial fossa is largely from the anterior ethmoidal (anterior nasal) nerve from the nasociliary branch of the ophthalmic, which like the artery enters the cranial cavity from the orbit and runs anteriorly along the lateral border of the cribriform plate to leave the cranial cavity and enter the nose; fine twigs also accompany the branches of the middle meningeal artery.

VENOUS SINUSES

The venous sinuses encountered in the anterior cranial fossa are small and easily avoided. The origin of the *superior sagittal sinus* lies in the attachment of the falx cerebri to the dura of the anterior wall and vault of the anterior fossa, while the small *inferior sagittal sinus* runs in the free edge of the falx. Toward its anterior end, where it attaches to the crista galli, the falx is often perforated; it can, if desired, be cut away from the crista without special precaution, since the inferior sagittal sinus at this level is practically nonexistent, and the superior sagittal sinus lies anterior to the crista.

At the posterior boundary of the anterior cranial fossa is the *sphenoparietal sinus*, running along the sphenoidal ridge; this is a slender connection between the middle meningeal vein and the cavernous sinus, and would be encountered only if an attempt were made to cut the dura away from its close attachment to the sphenoidal ridge.

The *cavernous sinuses* lie lateral to the sella turcica, and are therefore in the operative field in anterolateral approaches to the optic nerves and the hypophysis; their relations are of more importance in connection with the middle cranial fossa, however, and they are therefore described with this (p. 58). Anterior and posterior to the hypophyseal stalk the cavernous sinuses are connected by small anastomotic channels (anterior and posterior intercavernous sinuses, or the circular sinus) in the diaphragma sellae.

OLFACTORY BULB AND TRACT

By elevation of the frontal lobe, the olfactory bulb and tract may be examined throughout their length; the olfactory nerves themselves are fifteen or twenty delicate filaments on either side, which arise from bipolar cells situated in the mucous membrane, pass through the cribriform plate of the ethmoid and enter into the inferior surface of the olfactory bulb. The olfactory pathway is often interfered with in the frontal approach to the cranial contents, either accidentally or purposefully; although olfaction is not under ordinary circumstances a very important function in man, and the number of olfactory fibers present seems to decrease steadily after birth (p. 245), bilateral interruption of the olfactory tracts is to be avoided. There are no blood vessels of importance related to the olfactory nerves themselves, but aneurysms of the vessels at the base of the brain, such as the internal carotid, may damage an olfactory tract. Similarly, the olfactory system is of course subject to damage from tumors pressing upon it.

Associated with the olfactory nerve and tract is the *nervus terminalis* (rarely seen even by anatomists) from the nose; regarded either as sensory or autonomic, its functional significance is unknown. Intracranially, the nervus terminalis runs parallel to the olfactory bulb (Brookover). Between the two cerebral hemispheres are the anterior cerebral arteries; these, and the anterior communicating artery which usually connects them, are most closely related to the region of the optic chiasma and hypophysis and are therefore discussed in connection with this.

CHIASMAL AND HYPOPHYSEAL REGION

As the upper border of the sella turcica lies almost in the plane of the floor of the anterior cranial fossa, and considerably above that of the floor of the lateral portions of the middle cranial fossa, it is most easily approached by the frontal route; the importance of the structures concentrated in this immediate area, scarcely bigger than a nickel—the optic nerves, chiasma and tracts, the internal carotid arteries, the hypophysis and the hypothalamus—make the anatomical relations here exceedingly important.

Most anteriorly, and also most laterally, the optic nerves emerge from the optic foramina to be directed posteriorly and medially to join in the optic chiasma. Immediately posterior to the optic foramina, and under the backward projecting hook of the anterior clinoid processes, the internal carotid artery of each side emerges from the cavernous sinus on the side of the sella turcica, and occupies the lateral angle of the optic chiasma (between the optic nerve and the optic tract); here it proceeds to give off its branches.

Behind the optic chiasma and between the diverging optic tracts is the delicate *hypothalamus,* connected to the hypophysis by the slender hypophyseal stalk which passes downward in the midline behind the optic chiasma. The hypophysis occupies the sella turcica, its upper surface more or less covered by a reflection of dura (forming the diaphragma sellae). The depths of the sella are relatively inaccessible from the cranial cavity, for the anterior and posterior bony walls dip sharply beneath the general level of the cranial floor and its lateral walls are the two cavernous sinuses. These transmit the internal carotid artery, the third, fourth and sixth cranial nerves, and a portion of the fifth (p. 58). Posteriorly, the dorsum sellae with its more or less well developed anterolaterally projecting posterior clinoid processes, forms the

boundary of this region, and separates it from the posterior cranial fossa, the floor of which slopes sharply downward in contrast to the approximate horizontal disposition of the floor of the anterior cranial fossa.

As the frontal lobe is elevated, the *olfactory tract* may be seen just a little lateral to the midline; this is attached anteriorly, through the olfactory bulb and nerves, to the floor of the anterior cranial fossa, while posteriorly it attaches to the inferior surface of the frontal lobe of the brain just in front of the anterior perforated substance. Inferior to the attachment of the olfactory tract to the brain is the optic nerve, which may be traced from the optic foramen to the optic chiasma.

Lateral to the optic chiasma and posterolateral to the nerve, lying against the anterior perforated substance, is the *terminal portion of the internal carotid artery* and the first part of its major continuation, the middle cerebral artery; this latter runs laterally across the perforated substance, to which it is held by the numerous small branches (to the lenticular nucleus and internal capsule) which it gives off into this substance, and quickly disappears into the medial aspect of the lateral cerebral (Sylvian) fissure, between the frontal and temporal lobes of the brain.

The *anterior cerebral artery* arises from the anterior wall of the internal carotid, and passes medially and somewhat forward, lying inferior to the base of the olfactory tract, but crossing above the optic nerve or the optic chiasma; in the midline, between the bases of the olfactory tracts, the two anterior cerebral arteries come close together, are usually connected by the anterior communicating artery, and disappear as they turn upward between the two cerebral hemispheres.

The *posterior communicating artery* leaves the posterior surface of the internal carotid, proximal to the level of origin of the anterior cerebral, and passes posteriorly and somewhat medially about the hypothalamus, crossing below the optic tract, to form a posterolateral segment of the circle of Willis. Also from the posterior aspect of the internal carotid, lateral to the origin of the posterior communicating artery and sometimes under cover of the medial edge of the temporal lobe is the origin of the *choroidal* (anterior choroidal) *artery*; this vessel lies at first lateral to the posterior communicating artery, and then diverges farther laterally to disappear into the medial surface of the temporal lobe.

With the exception of the internal carotid artery (which curves upward and backward from its entrance through the dura—medial to the anterior clinoid processes and immediately posteromedial to the entrance of the optic nerves into the cranial cavity—to its attachment to the brain at the anterior perforated substance, just lateral to the optic chiasma), the cerebral vessels of this region lie entirely in close contact with the inferior surface of the brain, and are necessarily elevated with the frontal lobe. So also is the proximal end of the olfactory tract. However, the optic nerves and the internal carotid arteries necessarily extend across the subarachnoid space from the base of the skull to the base of the brain, and limit the space available for an anterolateral approach to the hypophysis. If, as sometimes occurs, the intracranial portions of the optic nerves are quite short and the optic chiasma lies well forward toward the chiasmal groove, an anterior approach, between the optic nerves

and below the chiasma, is impossible, and the approach must be a more lateral one, posterolateral to the optic nerve and either between this and the internal carotid, or behind this vessel. If, on the other hand, the optic nerves are long intracranially, the chiasma can be lifted with the base of the brain, and the upper surface of the hypophysis inspected through the gap enclosed by the anterior lip of the sella, the two optic nerves, and the chiasma. In such cases the hypophyseal stalk can be seen passing downward, or downward and forward, in the midline, as it runs from the tuber cinereum, just behind the optic chiasma, to the central aperture in the diaphragma sellae.

In the more lateral approach to the hypophysis, across the sphenoid ridge and therefore actually through an anteromedial corner of the middle cranial fossa, it should be remembered that the entire lateral dural wall of the sella is occupied by the cavernous sinus and the structures which traverse this sinus.

Optic Nerves and Optic Chiasma

As the optic nerves enter the cranial cavity at the optic foramen their dural and arachnoid sheaths, which extend about them to the eyeball, become continuous with these layers in the cranial cavity; the nerves then run through the basal cistern to the chiasma. The segments of the nerves within the cranial cavity may be relatively long or quite short, for the position of the optic chiasma varies. De Schweinitz, quoting observations of Schaeffer, has stated that in only 5 per cent of cases did the anterior portion of the chiasma rest directly in the chiasmal groove between the two optic foramina, so that much of it lay in front of the diaphragma sellae, and its posterior portion only was above this (Fig. 30); in 96 per cent of cases, including the 5 per cent already mentioned, the chiasma lay partly or wholly above the diaphragma, and in most of these the intracranial portions of the optic nerves were sufficiently long that the entire chiasma, or quite commonly its anterior part only, was intimately related to the diaphragma; in 4 per cent the chiasma lay entirely behind the diaphragm.

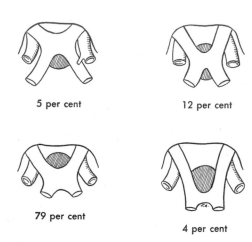

5 per cent   12 per cent

79 per cent

4 per cent

Fig. 30. Variations in the relation between the optic chiasma and the hypophysis. (From Hollinshead, W. H.: *S. Clin. North America* 32:1115, 1952, redrawn from de Schweinitz, G. E.: *Tr. Ophth. Soc. U. Kingdom* 43:12, 1923.)

Defects in the visual fields produced by enlargements of the hypophysis are dependent, therefore, not only upon the constant arrangement of the fibers within the optic nerve and chiasma, but also upon the variable relationship between the hypophysis and chiasma; enlargements of the hypophysis may, depending upon their positions and on the positions of the optic chiasma, affect different portions of the intracranial visual pathway.

LOCALIZATION OF FIBERS IN OPTIC NERVE

Within the optic nerve as it leaves the orbit the nerve fibers arising from the various quadrants of the retina are arranged almost exactly in the relative positions of these parts of the retina—that is, the fibers originating from the temporal half of each retina (representing the nasal portion of the visual field) occupy the lateral part of the nerve, while those from the nasal half of the retina (representing the temporal field) occupy the medial portion of the nerve. Similarly, fibers from the upper half of the retina (representing the lower visual field) lie uppermost in the nerve, while those from the lower half of the retina (representing the upper portion of the visual field) lie in the lower part of the nerve. Finally, the fibers representing macular vision lie in approximately the center of the nerve.

At the optic chiasma the fibers arising from the temporal half of each retina remain on the ipsilateral side, and thus occupy the lateral angle of the chiasma, while those originating in the nasal half of each retina cross to help form the contralateral optic tract; the fibers representing central vision apparently cross quite posteriorly in the chiasma. Thus pressure upon the anterior part of the chiasma will produce some bitemporal visual field disturbance, while pressure on the posterior part of the chiasma is especially apt to produce central visual defects; pressure upon the lateral part of the chiasma produces first a defect in the nasal portion of the visual field of the eye of the affected side.

VASCULAR RELATIONS OF OPTIC NERVE

The immediate vascular relations of the optic nerves, chiasma, and tracts in the region of the sella are to branches of the internal carotid artery. Since this vessel lies lateral to the chiasma in the angle formed by the converging optic nerves and the diverging optic tracts (Fig. 31), aneurysms of it may affect the optic nerves, the chiasma, or the tracts. The ophthalmic artery comes immediately into relationship with the inferior or latero-inferior surface of the optic nerve, and traverses the optic canal with this nerve; aneurysmal dilatations at the origin

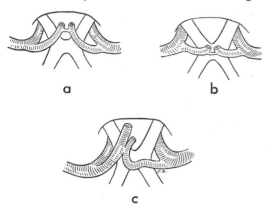

a   b

c

Fig. 31. Variations in the relation between the anterior cerebral arteries and the optic chiasma. (Redrawn from de Schweinitz, G. E.: *Tr. Ophth. Soc. U. Kingdom 43:*12, 1923.)

of this vessel may therefore early affect the optic nerve. The anterior cerebral arteries pass forward and medially just above the optic nerves, the chiasma, or the optic tracts, and pressure from one of these arteries may therefore produce various defects in the visual fields (de Schweinitz, Jefferson). Finally, the posterior communicating artery as it runs backward from the carotid crosses beneath the optic tract.

INTERNAL CAROTID ARTERY AND BRANCHES

The general course of the internal carotid and its branches has been described in connection with the blood supply of the brain (p. 34), and its important relations to the hypophyseal region and the optic system are described in the preceding paragraph and on page 48. To summarize, the internal carotid

artery leaves the dura and the cavernous sinus more or less under cover of the anterior clinoid process, and turns backward and upward to reach the lateral angle between the optic nerve and optic tract. Its exact relation to the optic nerve, chiasma, and tract obviously varies with the position of the chiasma.

The first branch of the carotid is the *ophthalmic,* which lies below the optic nerve and may or may not be visible lateral to it; this branch arises just as the carotid penetrates the dura. As the carotid crosses the basal cistern it has no branches, but as it reaches its definitive position against the base of the brain it gives rise to the *posterior communicating artery*. This passes posteromedially along the base of the brain, crossing inferior to the optic tract.

Shortly before it divides into its terminal branches, the anterior and middle cerebral arteries, the internal carotid gives off also the *anterior choroidal artery* which parallels but lies lateral to the posterior communicating artery.

The *middle cerebral artery* passes laterally into the medial edge of the lateral cerebral fissure, while the *anterior cerebral artery* swings medially and anteriorly, dorsal to the optic nerve, chiasma, or tract, and (above or anterior to the optic chiasma) is typically united to its fellow of the opposite side by the anterior communicating artery.

It is important to note that the anterior cerebral, the middle cerebral, and the posterior communicating arteries are all attached to the brain in this region by numerous delicate branches which enter the brain substance; those from the middle cerebral are particularly important, as some of them form the chief supply to the motor portion of the internal capsule (lenticulostriate arteries).

The fact that a large proportion of intracranial aneurysms occur in the carotid branches to the circle of Willis is mentioned on page 40.

HYPOTHALAMUS

Lying chiefly above and behind the optic chiasma, in the region bounded anteriorly and anterolaterally by the chiasma and the optic tracts, and laterally and posteriorly by the posterior communicating and posterior cerebral arteries, is the hypothalamus. The tuber cinereum, a downwardly directed projection of the floor of the hypothalamus, lies just behind the optic chiasma, and gives rise to the hypophyseal stalk connecting the hypothalamus to the posterior lobe of the hypophysis. The floor of the third ventricle is especially thin in the midline above the optic chiasma, and at the tuber cinereum. Numerous small vessels from all of the elements forming the circle of Willis converge toward the hypothalamus, to supply this and accompany the hypophyseal stalk to the hypophysis.

Because of the importance of the hypothalamus in the control of metabolic and endocrine functions, great care must be exercised in working in this region; in spite of such care it is not uncommon, for instance, for an alarming hyperthermia (due to a disturbance of the heat-regulating mechanism located in the hypothalamus) to develop following operations in this neighborhood.

HYPOPHYSIS

The hypophysis, or pituitary gland, normally lies entirely in the sella turcica (Fig. 32). Although it is connected to the hypothalamus by the hypophyseal stalk, it is largely separated from the other structures in this location by the diaphragma sellae, a fibrous layer largely derived from the inner layer of the dura. De Schweinitz has pointed out that the diaphragma varies markedly both in its strength and in the size of the central aperture which transmits the hypophyseal stalk, and this presumably influences in part the direction in which hypophyseal tumors expand. The varying relationship between the hypophysis and the optic chiasma has been mentioned on page 49. The subarachnoid cavity extends through the foramen in the diaphragma, and ex-

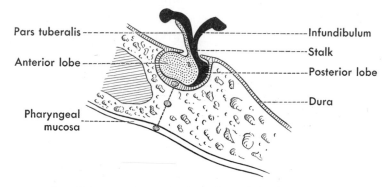

Fig. 32. Schema of a sagittal section of the hypophysis, and of the pathway of migration of the anterior lobe to the sella turcica. Various locations in which anterior lobe tissue might be left during this migration are indicated. (From Hollinshead, W. H.: *S. Clin. North America 32:*1115, 1952.)

pands over the upper surface of the hypophysis; except on its upper surface, however, the outer portion of the gland is fused to the dura, so that the gland is held in place both by the diaphragma and its attachments with the dura.

Within the sella turcica the hypophysis is related laterally to the cavernous sinuses, which are also connected to each other, anterior and posterior to the hypophysis, by small anterior and posterior

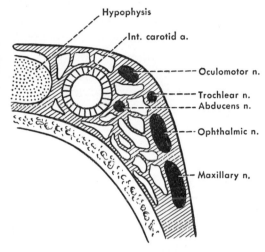

Fig. 33. Hypophysis and cavernous sinus in a frontal section. (From Hollinshead, W. H.: *S. Clin. North America* 32:1115, 1952.)

intercavernous sinuses. The cavernous sinuses and their contents are discussed in more detail in connection with the middle cranial fossa; it need only be mentioned here that since these sinuses form the lateral walls of the sella turcica, and since the anterior and posterior walls of the sella are bony, the intracranial approach to the hypophysis must be from above—a lateral approach through the dural wall of the sella is impossible because of the presence of the cavernous sinus and the structures which traverse it (the internal carotid artery and the third, fourth, sixth and part of the fifth cranial nerves—Fig. 33). The internal carotid

artery lies immediately adjacent to the hypophysis; tumors of the hypophysis expanding toward the cavernous sinus therefore tend to displace this portion of the carotid, which may therefore transmit its pulsations to the gland. Such tumors may also exert pressure upon the cranial nerves in the sinus; those most frequently affected are the third and fourth, the sixth sometimes being spared, apparently because it lies on the internal carotid and is therefore not subject to direct pressure from an hypophyseal tumor.

VASCULAR SUPPLY

The vascular supply of the anterior lobe of the hypophysis is by way of from fifteen to twenty small arteries which converge toward the stalk from all parts of the circle of Willis (Dandy and Goetsch). The pars intermedia is said to derive its blood supply from the vessels of the stalk, of the adjacent brain, and of the anterior lobe; the posterior lobe, according to these workers, receives its supply from a small artery formed by the union of two symmetrical branches, one from each internal carotid.

The *venous drainage* has been variously described as into the cavernous sinuses and also upward along the stalk to a venous circle immediately overlying the circle of Willis and draining into the great cerebral vein. Popa and Fielding described a system of veins of the hypophysis (hypophyseoportal system) as collecting blood from it and ascending as parallel vessels in the stalk to form a fine network beneath the infundibular recess of the third ventricle; a number of workers have offered evidence that this venous drainage is downward, however, from the infundibulum to the hypophysis; this has been most recently reiterated for the human being by Green, who has also actually observed this direction of blood flow in several animals, including the rat.

INNERVATION

Sympathetic nerve fibers reach the anterior lobe of the hypophysis from the carotid plexus by accompanying the arterial supply (Dandy, '13; Hair), but have not been shown to be of importance for the activity of the gland (for instance, Haterius; Markee, Sawyer, and Hollinshead). The numerous nerve fibers constituting the hypophyseal stalk end primarily in the posterior lobe. The importance of the nerve supply to the posterior lobe in the control of water balance has apparently been demonstrated by Fisher, Ingram, Hare, and Ranson and by Ingram and Fisher, and the relationship between damage to the stalk or the cells of origin of its fibers (the supraoptico-hypophyseal system) and the onset of diabetes insipidus is now generally recognized. Evidence has also been presented (Brooks) that this system of fibers may likewise be concerned with activation of the anterior lobe of the hypophysis, but there are other explanations of these findings and it seems more probable that the nervous control over the anterior lobe of the hypophysis is an indirect one (Leininger and Ranson; Dey; Sawyer, Markee, and Hollinshead).

ABERRANT TISSUE

Since the anterior lobe of the hypophysis (and the pars intermedia) develop from the diverticulum of the buccal epithelium known as Rathke's pouch, these portions of the gland are originally connected to the roof of the mouth. With increase in depth of the buccal pouch, this attachment becomes shifted poste-riorly until it lies at the caudal border of the nasal septum, and the stalk passes upward through the tissue that eventually forms the body of the sphenoid bone. As the hypophysis becomes detached from the pharyngeal wall, it leaves an apparently constant mass, the pharyngeal hypophysis, in this wall (Melchionna and Moore). Anterior lobe tissue has also been reported in the body of the sphenoid bone (for instance, by Suchannek), extending from the sella turcica to the pharynx (Fig. 32, p. 52). *Craniopharyngiomas,* thought to be developed from remnants of this stalk, are, however, according to Zeitlin and Oldberg, more commonly found above the sella turcica than below it—perhaps owing to the necessity for more room for these usually cystic tumors. One wonders, however, what proportion of tumors in this region are actually of Rathke's pouch origin, and especially how a tumor of such origin could possibly have arisen within the third ventricle, as Zeitlin and Oldberg thought to be true in a case they described. Tumors of the hypophyseal stalk proper—that is, of the stalk of the posterior lobe, connecting this to the brain—also occur; their symptomatology has been discussed by Beckmann and Kubie.

Remnants of the hypophysis within the body of the sphenoid bone are frequently described as lying in the course of the craniopharyngeal canal, a canalicular defect sometimes found in the bone (Sokolow); apparently this canal does not, however, represent the course of migration of the gland, but only roughly parallels that course (Arey). There is therefore no correlation between the presence of the canal and the presence of intrasphenoid remnants of the hypophysis.

THE MIDDLE CRANIAL FOSSA

IN ORDER to avoid the auriculotemporal nerve and superficial temporal artery, incisions of the scalp for an approach to the middle cranial fossa may begin above the ear and curve upward and forward along the superior temporal line, that is, at about the uppermost origin of the temporalis muscle from the side of the skull. If desired, the anterior end of the incision may curve downward somewhat behind the orbit. The origin of the temporal muscle from the parietal and temporal bones may be elevated as desired, and reflected downward. As in the case of frontal bone flaps, temporal bone flaps have been left attached to the muscle; detachment has the advantages of providing more room and, since a bone flap separated from its vascular connections does not bleed, lessening the hazard of a postoperative subdural hematoma.

In turning the bone flap for a temporal approach to the cranial contents, the position of the middle meningeal artery must be borne in mind. This is described on page 21 (and see Fig. 11). Briefly repeated, the anterior branch makes a broad curve upward, with its concavity directed backward; the most forward point of this curve, and the point at which the artery can be most easily located, is the pterion. If the middle meningeal artery branches late after entering the cranial cavity, this branching occurs at about the level of the upper border of the zygomatic process, and close to the middle of this process; the posterior branch of the middle meningeal artery then arches upward and backward, and almost parallels the zygomatic process, lying about a fingerbreadth above it.

FLOOR OF MIDDLE CRANIAL FOSSA

The bony floor of each of the large lateral expansions of the middle cranial fossa is formed anteriorly by the greater wing of the sphenoid bone, and posteriorly by the squama and upper surface of the petrous portion of the temporal bone; the two sides are connected toward their front by the sella turcica, in the body of the sphenoid bone. On each side of the sella, the middle cranial fossa is separated from the anterior cranial fossa by the sharp ridge of the lesser wing of the sphenoid, the sphenoid ridge; along this ridge runs the usually small sphenoparietal sinus. Posteromedially, the middle cranial fossa is separated from the posterior cranial fossa by the petrous ridges, or edge of the petrous pyramids, to which is attached the tentorium cerebelli; at the attachment of the tentorium to each petrous ridge lies the relatively large superior petrosal sinus. Posteromedial to the petrous ridge the posterior part of the temporal lobe, and the occipital lobe, rest upon the tentorium cerebelli, the two sides being separated from each other only by the falx cerebri.

The floor of the middle cranial fossa is distinctly thicker than that of the anterior fossa, but is nevertheless weakened by the numerous foramina which exist here. A large proportion of *fractures* of the base of the skull traverse the middle fossa. Fractures which extend across the body of the sphenoid bone may injure the internal carotid artery; or they may allow communication between the subarachnoid cavity and the sphenoid sinus, with discharge of cerebrospinal fluid through the nose, and ascending infection from the nose to the meninges. The middle meningeal artery is obviously particularly subject to damage in fractures of the middle fossa. If the fracture extends into or through the petrous portion of the temporal bone, facial paralysis and deafness are common sequelae. Fractures through the tegmen tympani (the thin portion of the floor of the middle cranial fossa, which is also the roof of the tympanic cavity and mastoid antrum) offer the same possibilities for the escape of blood or cerebrospinal fluid into the mastoid and middle ear cavities, and of infection of the meninges from these cavities, as exists in fractures involving the paranasal sinuses; if a fracture is so severe as to produce a tear of the tympanic membrane, or to extend into the roof of the external auditory meatus, blood and cerebrospinal fluid may also escape directly through this canal. Obviously, bleeding from the ear or nose, or both, in cranial injuries may be a sign of severe damage to the skull.

ATTACHMENT OF DURA

The dura of the middle cranial fossa is especially strongly attached about the numerous foramina of this fossa—the superior orbital fissure, the foramen rotundum and the foramen ovale, and the foramen lacerum in particular (see Fig. 5, p. 10). Anteriorly, it is attached to the sphenoidal ridge; medially, where it lies on the side of the sella turcica, it forms the walls of the cavernous sinus and must not be stripped from the bone; posteromedially, it is attached to the petrous ridge, which also receives the attachment of the tentorium cerebelli.

MENINGEAL VESSELS AND NERVES

MIDDLE MENINGEAL ARTERY

The middle meningeal artery enters the middle cranial fossa through the fo-ramen spinosum. From this position it runs forward and laterally in the dura; while it supplies twigs to the dura of the floor of the fossa, its distribution is largely to the calvaria, and it has already been discussed on page 21. While it lies in the dura of the floor of the middle fossa the middle meningeal artery supplies a superficial petrosal branch to the facial nerve and tympanum; this accompanies the great superficial petrosal nerve into the petrous bone, to anastomose with the stylomastoid branch of the posterior auricular artery. The middle meningeal also gives off a small superior tympanic artery to the tensor tympani muscle and the middle ear cavity.

Frequently there is an accessory middle meningeal artery, derived from the middle meningeal or directly from the internal maxillary, and reaching the dura through the foramen ovale; it is usually small and supplies the dura in the immediate vicinity of the semilunar ganglion, and the ganglion itself. In the absence of the accessory meningeal, small branches from the middle meningeal artery supply this same area; other branches to the dura of the middle cranial fossa include tiny unnamed branches from the internal carotid artery, distributed largely in the neighborhood of the cavernous sinus and the semilunar ganglion, and twigs of the ascending pharyngeal artery which pass through the foramen lacerum.

INNERVATION

The dura of the middle cranial fossa, including the upper surface of the tentorium, is supplied entirely by branches of the trigeminal nerve. All three divisions of the nerve may apparently participate in this, although Penfield and McNaughton suggested that the ophthalmic division of the ganglion may contain the cells of origin of all the trigeminal meningeal branches. In addition to variable twigs from the second and third divisions of the nerve to the dura close to the ganglion, both these divisions typically send branches to the middle meningeal artery to be distributed along it (Fig. 34). The branch from the mandibular, the nervus spinosus, typically arises outside the skull to join the middle meningeal artery here, and re-enter the

The tentorial nerve or nerves (of Arnold), derived from the ophthalmic, run a recurrent course across the trigeminal ganglion close to the trochlear nerve, and are distributed to the tentorium, the posterior third of the falx cerebri, and dura in the parieto-occipital region; Penfield and McNaughton, whose paper should be consulted for further details on the anatomy of the dural nerves,

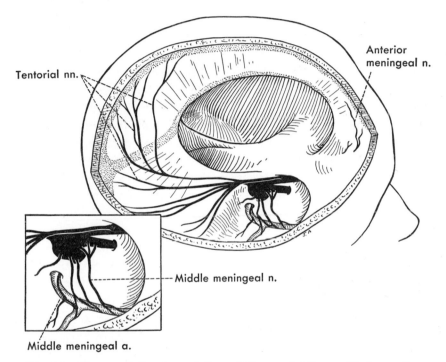

Fig. 34. Nerves of the dura of the middle cranial fossa. (Redrawn from Penfield, W., and McNaughton, F.: *Arch. Neurol. & Psychiat. 44:*43, 1940.)

skull along the artery through the foramen spinosum; a part or all of it may join the artery intracranially, however. The meningeal or recurrent branch (middle meningeal nerve) of the maxillary, sometimes double or triple (Grzybowski), joins the plexus on the anterior branch, or sometimes both branches, of the middle meningeal artery intracranially. The artery usually receives extracranially a twig from the otic ganglion, presumably vasomotor in function.

found the tentorial nerve to be constantly present.

Penfield and McNaughton, and Ray and Wolff, have agreed that most of the dural convexity is insensitive, except where the dura contains the meningeal arteries (p. 25). Similarly, the falx cerebri is said to be largely insensitive except along the margins of the superior sagittal sinus, but the floor of the middle cranial fossa and the upper surface of the tentorium are generally and uniformly sensitive to pain (although the lower surface of the tentorium is not, except close to the venous sinuses).

VENOUS SINUSES

The venous sinuses in or adjacent to the middle cranial fossa include the small sinuses (meningeal veins) accompanying the middle meningeal artery, and the sphenoparietal, cavernous, and superior petrosal sinuses. There are typically two venous channels with the middle meningeal artery; they communicate with the cavernous sinus through the sphenoparietal sinus, and also pass through the foramen spinosum with the artery to empty into the pterygoid plexus.

The *sphenoparietal sinus* forms a communication between the meningeal veins and the cavernous sinus, running downward and medially on the sphenoidal ridge to empty into the cavernous sinus above the oculomotor nerve as it lies in the lateral wall of the sinus. The sphenoparietal sinus usually also receives the anterior temporal diploic veins.

The *cavernous sinuses* lie on the sides of the body of the sphenoid bone, therefore on the sides of the hypophyseal fossa and just anterior to the semilunar ganglion of the trigeminal nerve. The oculomotor and trochlear nerves, the ophthalmic division of the trigeminal, and sometimes the upper portion of the maxillary division of this nerve run in the lateral wall of the sinus, and, more deeply, the carotid artery and the abducens nerve traverse it. Posteriorly, it lies against the anterosuperior edge of the semilunar ganglion, and gives off the superior petrosal sinus which runs backward along the petrous ridge close to the root of this ganglion. Its connections are described in more detail on page 15.

The *superior petrosal sinus* lies along the petrous ridge in the attached margin of the tentorium cerebelli; it forms a communication between the cavernous sinus and the lateral sinus, emptying into the latter at the beginning of its sigmoid portion. It is typically fairly small; in dividing the tentorium cerebelli from its attachment to the petrous ridge, in order to approach from above a laterally lying tumor in the posterior fossa, care need only be taken not to section the tentorium at its very attachment to the petrous ridge; section within a few millimeters of the ridge is usually safe, however (although the trochlear nerve on the lower surface of the tentorium should be avoided). An incision into the tentorium should not, of course, encroach upon the lateral sinus, and if extended posteriorly must be curved so as to parallel the anterior border of this sinus as it lies in the attachment of the tentorium to the occipital bone.

The roots of the trigeminal nerve also pass across the petrous ridge, and are therefore closely related to the superior petrosal sinus; the latter more commonly passes above the trigeminal roots, but may pass beneath them, or even divide so that one portion passes above and one beneath the roots (p. 14).

In addition to the sphenoparietal, cavernous, and superior petrosal sinuses, which essentially border the middle cranial fossa, other sinuses, usually small, may pass across the concavity of the fossa. These include the petrosquamous sinus, present on at least one side in approximately 50 per cent of individuals, the ophthalmopetrous sinus of Hyrtle, and the accessory sinuses of Kelch and of Verga. The latter three are relatively rare, and probably variations of the same fundamental pattern. All four of these sinuses are discussed on page 20.

The chiasmal and hypophyseal regions may be approached through the temporal or subtemporal route, but can be less well exposed than through the frontal approach, because of the marked concavity of the floor of the middle fossa. The cavernous sinuses cover the sides of the hypophyseal fossa, and the internal carotid arteries emerge from the cavernous sinuses to lie lateral to the optic chiasma; anterior and posterior to the chiasma the anterior cerebral and posterior communicating arteries pass respectively anteriorly and posteriorly, the former running above the optic nerves and the latter beneath the optic tracts; the middle cerebral artery, the continuation of the internal carotid, passes laterally and slightly upward into the medial side of the lateral cerebral fissure. These relationships have been described in more detail on pages 48 and 50, and the course of the internal carotid artery in the skull is described on page 34.

CRANIAL NERVES TRAVERSING THE MIDDLE FOSSA

Motor Nerves to the Orbit

All three of the motor nerves to the orbit pass through the cavernous sinus, and therefore through the middle cranial fossa; their relationships within the sinus to each other are described in detail in connection with the orbit, but are actually of relatively little clinical importance: the nerves are so closely grouped here that a lesion—for instance an aneurysm of the internal carotid, or an adenoma of the hypophysis—is very apt to affect all three nerves simultaneously, causing a complete ophthalmoplegia; the abducens

nerve is sometimes spared in hypophyseal enlargements, at least temporarily (p. 53). The distribution of these nerves is also described in connection with the orbit; in brief, they together supply all of the voluntary muscles of the eyeball, the levator palpebrae superioris, and two sets of involuntary muscle within the eyeball, the sphincter pupillae and the ciliary muscle.

The entrance of the abducens nerve into the cavernous sinus cannot be seen from the middle cranial fossa, since this nerve runs also intradurally in the floor of the posterior cranial fossa. The oculomotor nerve enters the dura mater just lateral and very close to the posterior clinoid process, passing between this process and the most anterior end of the free edge of the tentorium cerebelli. The trochlear nerve enters the dura just beneath the free border of the tentorium cerebelli (therefore technically in the posterior cranial fossa), only a little behind the posterior clinoid process. It would not be easily injured here in cutting the tentorium from the petrous pyramid unless the tentorium were cut very close to the bone (which should be avoided also for the sake of the superior petrosal sinus); however, in dividing the tentorium, it would probably be safer to identify the trochlear nerve and cut the free edge of the tentorium behind the entrance of this nerve. The tendency of the delicate trochlear nerve to cling to the lower surface of the tentorium may nevertheless lead to injury to the nerve in extending a tentorial incision posteriorly, unless the nerve is first separated.

The three nerves to the eye muscles are also discussed in connection with the posterior cranial fossa, in which they originate.

TRIGEMINAL NERVE

The trigeminal, or fifth cranial, nerve is not only the most important nerve of the middle cranial fossa, but also the largest of all cranial nerves except the optic. It is especially important clinically because of its involvement in major trigeminal neuralgia or tic douloureux, an accepted treatment of which is section of the sensory root of the fifth nerve, most commonly carried out through the middle cranial fossa.

The large sensory root (portio major) and the small motor and proprioceptive root (portio minor) of the fifth arise from the lateral pontine region, where the fibers pass through the brachium pontis. It is the sensory root that bears the large semilunar or Gasserian ganglion, the equivalent of the dorsal root ganglion of a spinal nerve, from which the three great branches of the nerve arise; the portio minor blends neither with the sensory root nor with the ganglion, but passes through the foramen ovale with the mandibular branch from the ganglion, and joins this branch just outside the foramen.

SEMILUNAR GANGLION

The cells of the semilunar ganglion give rise to fibers of general sensation which form the ophthalmic and maxillary branches of the nerve, and the major portion of the mixed mandibular nerve; these fibers are distributed peripherally to skin and mucous membrane of the head, while their central branches form the portio major. The portio minor supplies voluntary motor and proprioceptive (kinesthetic or muscle sense) fibers to the muscles of mastication and a few others derived from the mandibular arch; its distribution corresponds to that of the motor distribution of the mandibular nerve (p. 365).

It may be remembered that while the fifth nerve in its peripheral distribution is intimately connected with all four of the larger parasympathetic ganglia in the head, it does not contain any preganglionic fibers for these ganglia; similarly, although the lingual branch of the fifth nerve contains fibers for the taste buds of the anterior two thirds of the tongue, these fibers do not enter the brain stem with the fifth nerve, but are rather seventh nerve fibers (p. 383).

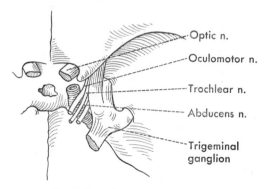

Fig. 35. Trigeminal ganglion in the middle cranial fossa.

Although the fifth nerve arises in the posterior cranial fossa, its roots extend anterolaterally and cross the petrous pyramid, so that the ganglion lies in the middle cranial fossa, on the sloping anterolateral surface of the petrous pyramid. Because of the slope of this surface of the petrous pyramid, the semilunar ganglion, closely applied to it, has somewhat complicated relations to the major planes of the body (Fig. 35). Thus its upper edge, almost horizontal, is also situated somewhat medially; moreover, since the petrous pyramids of each side converge toward each other, the upper edge of the semilunar ganglion, when traced forward, also inclines medially. Similarly, the posterior edge of the ganglion extends both laterally and downward from the root, and if it extends slightly forward at the same time it becomes an inferolateral rather than a strictly posterior border; the curved distal edge of the ganglion extends from a more posterior, inferior, and lateral position to a more anterior, superior and medial one.

PERIPHERAL BRANCHES OF TRIGEMINAL

From the ganglion the peripheral branches of the fifth nerve make their exits through three separate foramina of the skull. The *ophthalmic division* runs through the lateral wall of the cavernous sinus, in which position it gives off its recurrent meningeal branch, receives sympathetic fibers from the carotid plexus, and divides into three major branches which then enter the orbit through the superior orbital (sphenoid) fissure; the details of this are described in connection with the orbit (p. 148) and the face (p. 332).

The *maxillary division* of the fifth nerve runs along the lower portion of the lateral wall of the cavernous sinus, its relationship to the sinus varying with the size of the latter; it may be below the sinus, or the sinus may extend medial to and even below it. It leaves the skull by way of the foramen rotundum to enter the pterygopalatine (sphenomaxillary) fossa; its branches of distribution to the cheek, nose, palate, and upper jaw are described in connection with these structures.

The large sensory portion of the *mandibular nerve*, derived from the semilunar ganglion, passes through the foramen ovale with the portio minor, which lies deep (medial) to it; immediately outside the skull they join to form a mixed nerve.

TRIGEMINAL (MECKEL'S) CAVE

The relationship of the roots and ganglion of the fifth nerve to the arachnoid and dura is of importance in the surgical approach to the ganglion and its sensory root. Within the posterior cranial fossa the motor and sensory roots of the ganglion pass freely through the large subarachnoid space, but as they cross the petrous ridge they enter the dura, which at this point is evaginated to enclose a foramen through which the roots pass

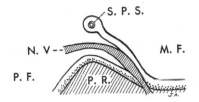

Fig. 36. Schema of the formation of Meckel's cave in a frontal section across the petrous ridge (*P.R.*). Other abbreviations: *N.V*, fifth cranial nerve; *S.P.S.*, superior petrosal sinus; *M.F.*, middle cranial fossa; and *P.F.*, posterior cranial fossa.

from the posterior to the middle cranial fossa (Fig. 36). This evagination of the dura is continued about the ganglion itself, and the space enclosed between the two dural layers is known as the trigeminal or Meckel's cave. A diverticulum of the pia-arachnoid also extends into Meckel's cave, so that the roots are surrounded, as they enter the middle cranial fossa, by a continuation of the subarachnoid space of the posterior cranial fossa (cisterna pontis); essentially, therefore, the three meninges of the posterior cranial fossa are evaginated out along the roots and ganglion of the fifth nerve in a fashion analogous to the evagination of the spinal meninges about the spinal nerves. The subarachnoid space surrounds the nerve roots as far as the ganglion; at the junction of root and ganglion it is obliterated on the anterolateral (outer) surface by fusion of the meninges to the ganglion, but on the posteromedial (deep) surface of the ganglion the subarachnoid space extends over about the proximal two thirds of the ganglion (Burr and Robinson). This relationship is of especial importance from the standpoint of attempted injections of the ganglion, as fluid delivered inadvertently into this space spreads readily backward toward the brain stem.

The oval mouth to Meckel's cave, transmitting the roots of the trigeminal nerve, usually lies below the superior petrosal sinus, for the latter normally runs in the free lip of the dura above the entrance to the cave. The sinus may, however (in more than 40 per cent?), pass below the mouth and therefore against the petrous ridge, or split to pass both above and below (Coates). Within the cave the semilunar ganglion is on the lateral surface of the anterior part of the petrous portion of the temporal bone, and is separated from the carotid artery only by dura and the thin structures of the foramen lacerum. The upper edge of the ganglion has a variable contact with the lateral wall of the cavernous sinus, and in the temporal approach to the sensory root this fact is taken into consideration; the dura along the upper and medial portion of the ganglion is avoided, and it is the dura along the posterior border that is incised to expose the sensory root. Above the ganglion, also in the lateral wall of the sinus, run the trochlear and oculomotor nerves.

Trigeminal Neuralgia

The cause or causes of major trigeminal neuralgia (tic douloureux) are not understood; it is widely believed that the precipitating cause may lie within the central nervous system (for example, Lewy and Grant), but it might be noted that Dandy ('34), in reporting upon his observations in 215 operations for this disease, stated that he found some type of gross anatomical involvement of the nerve root in 60 per cent of his cases; in the remaining 40 per cent no gross findings of any sort were noted, but he felt it possible that some might have escaped observation at operation. The concept that pressure upon the nerve root may be the cause of many cases of trigeminal neuralgia has been revived by Taarnhøj; he and others have reported considerable success in alleviating this condition by decompression of the ganglion, and of the nerve root as it crosses the petrous ridge (p. 66).

Regardless of the ultimate causative factor of trigeminal neuralgia, the paroxysmal attacks of this painful and disabling disease are ordinarily precipitated by stimulation of pain fibers from a so-called trigger zone, and the attacks may be alleviated or abolished by interruption of the pain fibers in this nerve. This has been attempted by injection of the ganglion with alcohol (Cushing, '20; Harris), extirpation of the ganglion (Cushing, '00), section of the sensory root, and section of the pain fibers as they course caudally in the medulla. Of these, section of the root has been more favored.

Trigeminal neuralgia involves apparently only the pain fibers of the fifth nerve, and most frequently arises in the zones of the mandibular or maxillary divisions of this nerve, being relatively rare in the first division; Grant reported that in a series of 100 cases of major trigeminal neuralgia the pain was primarily in the ophthalmic division in only 6. Because of these facts, the arrangement of the fibers in the sensory root has been in-

Trigeminal has
3 branches. One
can be cut?
? portio major

vestigated from the standpoint of the possibility of differential section of them, either close to the ganglion (by the temporal approach) or close to the brain stem (by a "cerebellar" or posterior fossa approach). Some workers have stated that there is no major rearrangement in disposition of the fibers in the sensory root close to the ganglion, and that the fibers are here arranged in the same order as the major branches of the nerve—that is, the fibers of the sensory root rep-

sensory loss; they therefore concluded that the arrangement of fibers in the sensory root of the trigeminal nerve varies and that the fibers may interlace or cross. The variation reported by these workers may be due to section of the sensory root at varying distances from the semilunar ganglion, as discussed in the following paragraph.

While a topographic arrangement of the sensory fibers in the root of the trigeminal nerve adjacent to the ganglion is

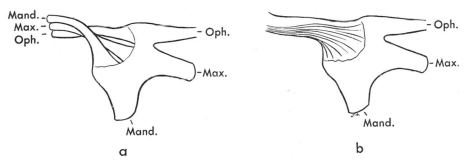

Fig. 37. Two concepts of the rearrangement of fibers said to occur in the sensory root of the trigeminal nerve between the ganglion and the brain stem. In *a* the three divisions are seen to be rotated upon each other, as in Fig. 38; in *b*, pain fibers from all three divisions are shown concentrated in the posterior part of the root at the pons.

resenting the mandibular division of the nerve lie laterally, posteriorly, and inferiorly, those representing the ophthalmic lie medially and superiorly, while those of the maxillary lie between the two. Thus Spiller and Frazier, and Taylor, have practiced and advocated differential section of the sensory root according to which peripheral division of the nerve is involved. Wilkins and Sachs stated that the fibers belonging to the ophthalmic division of the nerve are sometimes quite distinct from the other two divisions, but after attempting to spare the ophthalmic division, by cutting the outer and inferior two thirds of the sensory root (presumably close to the ganglion) they found marked variations in the area of

widely although not universally accepted, much less agreement exists as to their supposed arrangement between this point and the brain stem. Although, according to Grant, the sensory root of the fifth nerve is rarely more than 2 cm. long, it has been both claimed and denied that: (1) extensive intermingling of the fibers of the three major divisions of the trigeminal occurs proximal to the ganglion; (2) there is not a great deal of intermingling, but there is a definite rotation of the root between the ganglion and the pons (Fig. 37*a*); and (3) there is a grouping, at the pons, of the pain fibers from all three divisions (Fig. 37*b*).

From anatomical studies of the ganglion and sensory root Frazier and Whitehead stated that the nerve fibers derived from portions of the ganglion connected with the three major branches intermingle very little, while van Nouhuys reported much anastomosis and interlacing; Davis and Haven likewise have reported numerous anastomoses close to the ganglion, but expressed the belief that the various divisions nevertheless occupy definite positions in the root close to the pons. The latter workers have stated that there is a definite rotation of the sensory root between the ganglion and the pons: while

following partial section of the nerve close to the brain stem. Grant was certain that there is no sorting of pain fibers close to the ganglion, and found no evidence for it in his few cases of subtotal section close to the pons. Stibbe supported Dandy's concept, reporting that following section of the outer or posterior part of the fifth nerve root close to the pons in the monkey (1 case) the degenerated fibers could be traced exclusively into the spinal tract of the fifth nerve (known to be concerned with pain). Stibbe has also stated that

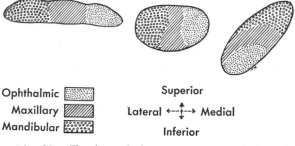

Ophthalmic ▧

Maxillary ▨

Mandibular ▨

Superior

Lateral ←--⤒--→ Medial

Inferior

Fig. 38.   Torsion of the sensory root of the trigeminal nerve between the ganglion and the pons, as seen in cross sections close to the ganglion, at the middle of the root, and close to the pons. (Redrawn from Davis, L., and Haven, H. A.: *Arch. Neurol. & Psychiat. 29:*1, 1933.)

at the ganglion the ophthalmic division is primarily medial, the mandibular lateral, they stated that at the pons the ophthalmic division is inferior and slightly medial, the mandibular division is superior and slightly dorsal (Fig. 38).

The third view, that there is a functional rather than an anatomical sorting of the fibers as they approach the pons, has been advocated by Dandy ('29, '32), who has stated that in his experience division of about the posterior (caudal or inferior?) half of the sensory root at the pons may completely abolish pain and yet produce only slight sensory changes, otherwise, over the face; he has not found an anatomical distribution of sensory loss

there are many ganglion cells on the sensory root of the fifth nerve in both the monkey and man, and suggested that regeneration of the peripheral fibers of these cells may bring about return of pain following successful section of the nerve root close to the ganglion.

Hyndman, comparing the effects of section of the sensory root close to the pons and close to the ganglion, has stated his belief that there is no rotation of the fibers between these two points; he has reported that section of the root from below upward, whether at the ganglion or at the pons, produces a loss of sensation which progresses from the lowermost distribution on the face upward, and from the midsagittal plane laterally. He concluded that there is extensive overlapping between the three divisions both in the ganglion and in the sensory root, yet at the same time appeared to agree somewhat with Dandy's concept, as he has stated that section of the inferior half of the root may eliminate the pain of tic, yet produce little loss of sensation.

The most that can be said concerning localization within the sensory root of the fifth nerve, therefore, is that it is a disputable question, and may perhaps vary from one individual to another. It appears that the careful surgeon, unless he is working with a patient under local anesthesia and tests the effect of partial root section at the operating table, may properly section the entire sensory root in order to relieve trigeminal neuralgia, regardless of which route of approach is used.

TEMPORAL APPROACH TO SENSORY ROOT

The temporal approach to the sensory root for section of it in trigeminal neuralgia is usually made largely extradurally, by elevation of the dura from the floor of the middle cranial fossa. In this approach the foramen spinosum and the middle meningeal artery are found by following the concavity of the middle cranial fossa to its deepest part; in order to retract the dura here the middle meningeal artery must be divided. After the dura is freed at the foramen spinosum by section of the artery, the foramen ovale and the mandibular branch of the fifth nerve may be found just anteromedial to the foramen spinosum (Fig. 39). The posterior border of the mandibular nerve and of the trigeminal ganglion leads medially and upward to the sensory root, and can be followed by carefully incising the enveloping dura about the posterior edge of

the mandibular nerve and ganglion (the so-called dura propria), and freeing it slightly from these structures. As the subarachnoid space of Meckel's cave is entered cerebrospinal fluid is released, and the sensory root of the nerve is exposed. The incision of the dura should not be carried upward to the edge of the petrous ridge itself, as the superior petrosal sinus here crosses the root of the fifth nerve—sometimes above it, sometimes below it, and sometimes on both sides of it (p. 14). The motor root is not visible here; although at the origin

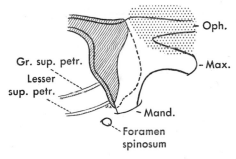

Fig. 39. Some approximate relations of the trigeminal ganglion. The heavily shaded area indicates the extension of the subarachnoid cavity of Meckel's cave on the outer surface of the roots and ganglion, the broken line on the ganglion its more distal extension deep to the ganglion; the stippled area indicates the cavernous sinus.

of the fifth nerve from the brain stem it lies somewhat anterior to the sensory root, it crosses obliquely beneath this root in order to reach the mandibular nerve, and as it enters Meckel's cave lies deep to (medial to and beneath) the sensory root. In sectioning the sensory root, great care should be taken to identify and spare the motor root, in order to avoid paralysis of the muscles of mastication on that side; sometimes, however, this is not possible, and the motor root also is sectioned. A rare anomaly is the presence of an artery of considerable size (an anomalous anastomotic branch between the internal carotid and the basilar) deep to the ganglion and the sensory root (Sunderland, '48).

Burr and Robinson stated that the trigeminal ganglion as it lies in Meckel's cave is closely fused to the dura on its anterolateral or outer surface, so that neither subarachnoid nor potential subdural space seems to exist here; Lockhart stated that the dura is, however, easily freed from the lateral surface of the ganglion and advocated an intradural approach, with incision of the dura over the lateral aspect of the ganglion. On its posteromedial or deep surface, and especially along its posterolateral or mandibular border, the ganglion is in contact with the subarachnoid space in at least its proximal two thirds, and fused with the dura only in its distal third; thus the extradural approach allows freer access to the subarachnoid cavity as it surrounds the roots of the nerve, without the potential damage to the ganglion as a whole that might easily result from dissecting the dura away from it, and especially with less danger of inadvertently opening the cavernous sinus.

If the dura along the posterior border of the semilunar ganglion is elevated from the base of the skull the great superficial petrosal nerve is necessarily elevated with this dura; this nerve runs in the dura, passing forward and somewhat medially to disappear beneath the deep surface of the trigeminal ganglion about halfway between the foramen ovale and the petrous ridge, and make its exit from the skull through the foramen lacerum.

A transient paralysis of the facial nerve sometimes occurs following section of the sensory root of the trigeminal nerve by the temporal route; this is usually thought to be due to damage to the facial nerve at its external genu through pulling upon the great superficial petrosal nerve; Grant expressed the belief that it might be due either to this or to rupture of the petrosal vein, a vein described by Dandy ('29) as leaving the lower surface of the cerebellum and crossing the subarachnoid space to join the petrosal sinus, usually anterior to the root of the fifth nerve, but sometimes upon it. It is difficult for the present writer to believe, from observations of the anatomy here, that tension upon the dura containing the great superficial petrosal nerve can usually be transmitted through the bony canal of this nerve to the main stem of the facial with sufficient force to injure the latter nerve. Dandy ('29) has stated that the geniculate ganglion itself may lack a bony covering and lie subdurally, and hence be subject to injury in elevation of the dura; perhaps in other cases the canal for the petrosal nerve is exceedingly short, and indirect trauma to the facial is therefore somewhat easier than under average conditions.

DECOMPRESSION

The anesthesia accompanying section of the sensory root of the fifth nerve is to some patients very annoying, and if it involves the first division of the nerve, care has to be taken to prevent ulceration of the cornea. Taarnhøj has reported a new operation for the relief of trigeminal neuralgia, which avoids sensory loss over the distribution of the nerve. This operation consists in removing the dura from over the posterior part of the trigeminal ganglion and sectioning the dural roof of Meckel's cave and the attached edge of the tentorium—thus decompressing this part of the ganglion, and the sensory root as it crosses the petrous ridge. Love has also reported success with the one operation of this type that he had tried and has since (personal communication) found it successful in a majority of more than two dozen cases.

The approach is a temporal one, as for root section, and has been made both transdurally and extradurally. Pertinent anatomical points to be considered are that the dura cannot be elevated from the anterior part of the ganglion without endangering the cavernous sinus, and that the edge of the dura over the nerve root at the entrance to Meckel's cave usually, but not always, contains the superior petrosal sinus, and hence may have to be divided between clips. Also, injury to the trochlear nerve, which may cling to the lower surface of the tentorium, is to be avoided.

CEREBELLAR APPROACH AND SECTION OF SPINAL TRACT

Hyndman has stated his belief that the cerebellar approach to the root of the fifth nerve is more dependable than the temporal, but is more difficult technically; this approach is discussed briefly on page 82. The pain of trigeminal neuralgia may also be abolished by section of the spinal tract of the fifth nerve in the medulla, as originally described by Sjöqvist, and more recently discussed by Grant, Groff, and Lewy; Grant and Weinberger; Weinberger and Grant; and Falconer. This operation is not so commonly attempted as section of the root, and is undoubtedly more difficult technically, but offers the advantage of differential section of the pain fibers of the fifth nerve without causing anesthesia. According to Brodal, trigeminal tractotomy may also produce analgesia over the areas of distribution of the seventh, ninth and tenth nerves, and may therefore prove useful in neuralgias of these nerves.

THE POSTERIOR CRANIAL FOSSA

THE posterior cranial fossa, roofed by the tentorium cerebelli, contains the midbrain, pontine region, medulla, and cerebellum, and therefore the attachments to the brain stem of all the cranial nerves except the first and the second. Of these nerves, the third is the only one which does not enter the dura while still within the posterior cranial fossa; it barely fails to do so, passing over the anterior attachment of the tentorium cerebelli to enter the dura just lateral to the posterior clinoid process, and therefore, strictly speaking, in the middle cranial fossa.

Although they arise in the posterior cranial fossa, the third, fourth and sixth nerves all traverse the cavernous sinus and actually leave the cranial cavity, to enter the orbit, through the superior orbital fissure. The fifth nerve likewise, although arising in the posterior cranial fossa, does not leave the cranium through this fossa; its roots pass anterolaterally, beneath the edge of the tentorium cerebelli and across the petrous ridge to enter the middle cranial fossa, in which the semilunar ganglion lies and through the walls of which the three major divisions of the fifth nerve leave the cranial cavity.

The posterior cranial fossa is usually approached posteriorly, through the occipital bone; this approach is referred to as the suboccipital or cerebellar approach. The upper surface of the cerebellum, and some of the higher cranial nerves in the fossa, may also be approached by the temporal route—after elevation of the temporal and occipital lobes from the upper surface of the tentorium cerebelli the tentorium may be cut close to its attachment to the petrous ridge, and reflected to uncover the structures. The structures in the attached edge of the tentorium are discussed on pages 58 and 59.

The skin of the occipital region is supplied primarily by the greater occipital nerve, supplemented by the third occipital nerve, and more laterally, toward the mastoid region, by the lesser occipital; the remainder of the skin over the mastoid region and behind the ear is supplied by the great auricular and the auricular branches of the seventh, ninth, and tenth nerves (p. 170). Since all of these nerves run upward onto the scalp, and since the chief blood supply to the scalp of this region is through the occipital artery which also runs upward, a transverse incision low in the occipital region is obviously to be avoided. Transverse incisions at about the interauricular line fall in the region of overlap between the distribution of the great occipital and the supraorbital nerves, and of the superficial temporal and occipital arteries, and therefore should produce no appreciable denervation of the scalp or interference with its vascularity; likewise, midline sagittal incisions do not affect the innervation or blood supply of the scalp significantly. A combination of these two incisions allows the turning down of a large flap of skin, with an extensive pedicle attached below, and can be done unilaterally or bilaterally; a midline incision alone, or a straight lateral incision some 3 cm. from and almost paralleling the mid-line (therefore somewhat between the distribution of the lesser occipital and the greater) has also been used (for instance, Adson, '41b).

OCCIPITAL MUSCULATURE

Since the occipital bone below the level of the transverse sinus is largely covered by the attachments of vertebral and other muscles, a brief statement of these relations is appropriate in discussing the posterior cranial fossa.

The occipitalis muscle arises from the occipital bone a little above the level of the external occipital protuberance and the superior nuchal line, and at this point, therefore, the galea aponeurotica is firmly attached to the skull.

Laterally, upon the superior nuchal line and the posterolateral aspect of the mastoid process, the *sternocleidomastoid* attaches (Fig. 40). Immediately beneath the sternocleidomastoid, and also on the superior nuchal line, is the attachment of the *splenius capitis*, which also extends onto the mastoid process. Beneath the lateral border of the splenius capitis, attaching not to the occipital bone but only to the mastoid process, is the *longissimus capitis* muscle.

Medially, on either side of the midline, the *trapezius* muscle typically arises from the skull along the superior nuchal line; the breadth of this attachment varies, and sometimes the trapezius fails to reach the skull. In any event, there is a gap, of variable size, between the lateral border of the upper portion of the trapezius and the medial or posterior border of the sternocleidomastoid. Through this gap (the upper part of the posterior triangle of the neck) the occipital artery usually becomes subcutaneous, and, passing superficial to the attachment of the trapezius, turns upward to perforate the galea. The great occipital nerve also becomes subcutaneous through the medial part of this gap if it is wide, or otherwise pierces the attachment of the trapezius muscle, and crosses superficial to the occipital artery, lateral to which it runs upward into the scalp.

Beneath the trapezius on either side of

the midline, and usually extending lateral to the line of attachment of this muscle, the heavy *semispinalis capitis* attaches to the skull, occupying much of the space between the superior and inferior nuchal but extends from the spine of the axis or epistropheus to the transverse process of the atlas).

In its course backward the occipital artery may pass either superficial or deep

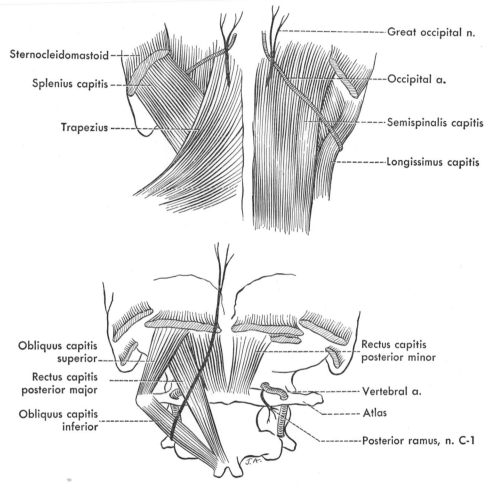

Great occipital n.

Sternocleidomastoid

Splenius capitis

Trapezius

Occipital a.

Semispinalis capitis

Longissimus capitis

Obliquus capitis superior

Rectus capitis posterior major

Obliquus capitis inferior

Rectus capitis posterior minor

Vertebral a.

Atlas

Posterior ramus, n. C-1

Fig. 40. The chief muscles, nerves, and vessels of the occipital region.

lines. The great occipital nerve emerges through it. In the midline, between the two semispinalis muscles, the ligamentum nuchae reaches the skull. Somewhat under cover of the lateral border of the semispinalis capitis, and attached largely to the lateral portion of the inferior nuchal line, is the *obliquus capitis superior* (the obliquus inferior does not reach the skull, to the longissimus capitis, but regularly lies superficial to the upper end of the obliquus superior, or entirely cranial to it, and passes around the lateral border of the semispinalis capitis. It runs almost transversely across the superficial surface of the semispinalis, just below the attachment of the muscle to the bone, until it makes its turn upward into the scalp.

Below the inferior nuchal line, and attaching therefore strictly to the base of the skull, are the attachments of the two other suboccipital muscles which reach the skull—the *rectus capitis posterior minor* and the *rectus capitis posterior major*. The rectus capitis posterior minor attaches on either side of the midline under cover of the semispinalis capitis and the medial edge of the rectus capitis posterior major. The rectus capitis posterior major attaches more laterally, extending to the attachment of the obliquus superior and with the two obliques forms the sides of the suboccipital triangle. In this triangle are the suboccipital (first cervical) nerve and a portion of the vertebral artery.

It is usually necessary to reflect most of these muscles from their attachments to the skull, in the suboccipital approach, and the more medial muscles must be reflected if an exposure through the posterior arch of the atlas is planned. If the scalp is not reflected from these muscles, and the latter are detached at their insertions on the bone, the base of the skull and the posterior arch of the atlas may be uncovered without sacrificing the nerve and blood supply to the scalp.

The posterior atlanto-occipital ligament or membrane stretches from the upper border of the posterior arch of the atlas to the posterior border of the foramen magnum, and is pierced by both the vertebral artery and the first cervical (suboccipital) nerve. The vertebral artery here at first runs medially and backward in the groove on the upper border of the posterior arch of the atlas, being covered by the oblique muscles, and then turns forward to enter the vertebral canal. The first cervical nerve typically emerges between the artery and the arch of the atlas, but may occasionally pierce the atlanto-occipital ligament above the artery.

CRANIAL FLOOR AND DURA

The floor of the posterior cranial fossa is formed largely by the occipital bone, but anterolaterally the temporal bone, especially the petrous portion, contributes to this, and anteriorly in the midline a small portion of the body of the sphenoid likewise contributes. The middle and posterior cranial fossae are separated from each other by the upward projection of the petrous portion of the temporal bone to form the petrous ridge, to which is attached the tentorium cerebelli.

This floor is frequently regarded as being especially sturdy, but is actually quite thin in places, and fractures of it are apt to be overlooked, although they may have very serious consequences. Even severe fractures of the posterior cranial fossa (unlike those of the middle and anterior cranial fossae, which are likely to lead to discharge through the nose and ear respectively) may not be easily recognized, both because of the mass of muscle covering this region and because blood and fluid in the posterior cranial fossa has no ready passageway into which it can escape. Fractures of the body of the sphenoid bone are a not uncommon cause of paralysis of the abducens nerve, which has a relatively long course in contact with this bone.

The dura of the posterior cranial fossa is firmly attached at the foramen magnum, at which level it splits into its definitive two layers—the periosteal layer which is reflected onto the outer surface of the skull and the dural layer proper which is continued downward as the dura about the spinal cord. It is also strongly attached to the basioccipital region, the basal portion of the sphenoid bone, and the jugular foramen. It is not, however, as firmly attached as one might suppose about the venous sinuses, and it is possible to dissect the occipital bone away from the posterior surface of the transverse sinus without injuring this vessel, just as in mastoidectomy the sigmoid portion of the sinus may be freed of bone.

The dura generally follows the conformation of the skull, but extending downward from the lower surface of the tentorium cerebelli at its posterior attachment to the midline is a usually small sickle-shaped fold, the falx cerebelli; this protrudes slightly forward between the two cerebellar hemispheres and contains the occipital sinus.

ARTERIES

The dura of the posterior cranial fossa, below the tentorium, receives some branches from the middle meningeal artery but is supplied largely by variable small branches from the ascending pharyngeal, the vertebral and the occipital arteries, none of which are of surgical importance. A fairly constant branch from the ascending pharyngeal enters the cranium through the jugular foramen, and is usually designated as the posterior meningeal artery; smaller twigs of this artery may pass along the canal for the hypoglossal nerve. The usually tiny meningeal branches from the occipital artery may variously enter the jugular foramen, the hypoglossal foramen, the condyloid canal, or the mastoid and parietal foramina, thus frequently accompanying emissary veins.

The artery from the mastoid branch of the occipital, traversing the skull with the mastoid emissary vein, is frequently the only one of these vessels to attain considerable size; it supplies the more lateral and posterior portion of the dura, and enters the dura at the posterior margin of the sigmoid sinus.

The posterior meningeal branch of the vertebral artery is said to arise usually from that vessel as it pierces the dura mater, to anastomose with other branches in the posterior fossa. The arteries to the dura of the posterior fossa vary considerably in size, and any one of the several vessels in this region may predominate.

INNERVATION OF THE DURA

Ray and Wolff found the dura on the lower surface of the tentorium to be insensitive to pain unless the venous sinuses were approached, but the dura of the floor of the posterior fossa, on the other hand, was found to be uniformly sensitive like the floor of the other fossae. In 1 patient of Ray and Wolff's, pain produced by stimulation of the more lateral portion of the dura of the floor of the posterior fossa, and referred to an area behind the ear, was abolished by section of the ninth and tenth cranial nerves. Pain from the more medial part of the dura usually was referred to a point low in the back of the head, and was abolished in 1 patient by section of the posterior roots of the first three cervical nerves.

The two nerves which are known to supply the dura of the posterior cranial fossa are the meningeal (recurrent) branches of the vagus and hypoglossal nerves (Fig. 41). The meningeal branch of the vagus, which ascends through the jugular foramen, is undoubtedly a branch of this nerve; on the other hand, the hypoglossal nerve contains neither sensory nor autonomic fibers in its roots, and the fibers of its meningeal branch must therefore be derived through its connections with other nerves. The meningeal branch of the hypoglossal is believed to contain fibers derived both from the superior cervical ganglion and from upper cervical nerves.

VENOUS SINUSES OF POSTERIOR CRANIAL FOSSA

The posterior cranial fossa is largely bounded by sinuses, which lie at the attachment of the tentorium cerebelli; the layers of the tentorium cerebelli where this attaches to the dura, while the sigmoid portion curves downward in a deep groove on the posteromedial aspect of the petrous ridge, to run forward and medially along the junction of the petrous ridge and the occipital bone and empty through the jugular foramen. As the sinus passes through the jugular foramen it is usually separated from the inferior pe-

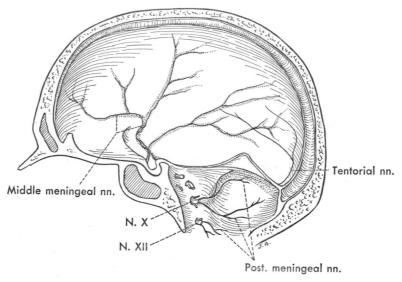

Fig. 41.   The nerves of the posterior cranial fossa and cranial vault. (Redrawn from Penfield, W., and McNaughton, F.: *Arch. Neurol. & Psychiat. 44*:43, 1940.)

sigmoid portions of the lateral sinuses, the inferior petrosal sinuses and the occipital sinus, and the basilar plexus, all lie within the posterior cranial fossa. Knowledge of the exact positions of the sinuses related to the posterior cranial fossa is obviously useful, but unfortunately the more important of these tend to vary somewhat, and real anomalies are sometimes encountered.

The *lateral or transverse sinuses* extend from the torcular, close to the internal occipital protuberance, to the paired jugular foramina; the transverse portion of each lateral sinus lies between the trosal sinus by the emerging rootlets of the tenth and eleventh cranial nerves.

The *superior petrosal sinus* has already been described as running along the edge of the petrous ridge, in the attachment of the tentorium cerebelli to this ridge; while it lies at the boundary between the posterior and middle cranial fossae, it is usually not of surgical importance except in the temporal approach to the sensory root of the trigeminal nerve; in the operation of decompression of the ganglion and sensory root (p. 66), it will frequently have to be divided, since it commonly lies above the entrance into Meckel's cave.

Each of the paired *inferior petrosal sinuses* leaves the posterior aspect of the cavernous sinus and runs along the groove between the petrous pyramid laterally and the basal portions of the sphenoid and occipital bones medially—that is, on the lateral aspect of the floor of the narrower upper portion of the posterior cranial fossa—and swings laterally to pass through the anterior compartment of the jugular foramen and empty into the superior bulb of the internal jugular vein. At its exit through the jugular foramen, the inferior petrosal sinus usually lies between the ninth and tenth cranial nerves. The two inferior petrosal sinuses communicate with each other across the floor of the posterior cranial fossa through the ill-defined basilar plexus.

The *occipital sinus* runs in the sagittal plane in the attachment of the falx cerebelli; it typically extends from the marginal sinuses at the foramen magnum to the torcular, and is also typically small. The occipital sinus varies markedly in its size, however, and may also have an aberrant course, and is always therefore a potential source of difficulty in posterior approaches to the fossa.

The usual relations of the lateral sinuses to external landmarks on the skull are described on page 29; however, it should be noted that there are variations in this regard. As the superior sagittal sinus reaches the torcular, it frequently does not remain in the midline but deviates to the right; the right transverse sinus is usually not only larger than the left transverse sinus, but its upper border may also lie almost a centimeter higher, while the left sinus may dip slightly downward in the posterior fossa, especially near the midline. Further, the internal occipital

protuberance, near which the torcular lies, does not correspond exactly in position to the external occipital protuberance, and the relation of the external occipital protuberance to the beginning of the transverse sinus varies. Thus while the transverse sinus is usually said to be marked on the external surface of the skull by a slightly curved line running from above the external occipital protuberance to the posterior border of the ear, the lower border of the sinus may actually lie 2 cm. or more below the level of the external occipital protuberance. Removal of bone from the posterior cranial fossa must therefore proceed carefully, for the upper limit at which the transverse sinus will be uncovered cannot be surely known beforehand.

The variations at the torcular have already been discussed (p. 16); for the most part, these do not markedly affect the actual carrying out of surgical procedures in the posterior fossa. An important source of variation in the posterior fossa, however, and one that may occasion considerable difficulty in the approach to this, is the occipital sinus (Fig. 42). While this sinus is usually so small that it may be ligated and divided with no difficulty in a bilateral or midline approach to the contents of the posterior cranial fossa, it is sometimes quite large, and may even replace one of the lateral sinuses. In such cases, the marginal sinuses are also large, since they serve as the point of exit for blood from the occipital sinus, and these sinuses then also offer difficulties in surgery. Even when the lateral sinuses are normal in their arrangement, the occipital sinus may be enlarged. Occasionally, instead of running in the midline, it deviates to one side to join the sigmoid sinus as this passes through the jugular foramen; if such a deviated occipital sinus is large (in one seen recently by the writer, it was a full 5 mm. in diameter) it may offer a definite hazard in approaches to the posterior fossa.

The cerebellar vermis marks the midline, while the lateral lobes largely fill the posterior and lateral, therefore the greater, portions of the posterior fossa, and must

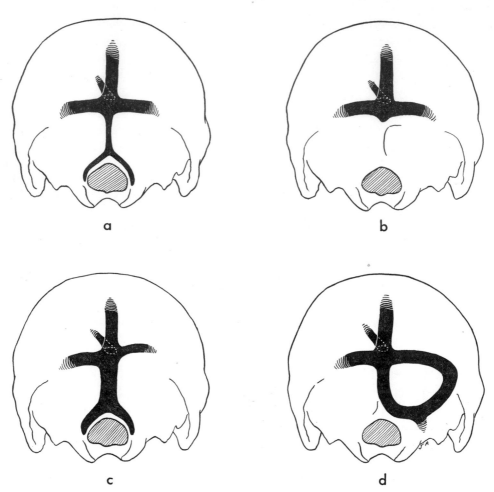

Fig. 42.   Variations in the occipital sinus.

CRANIAL NERVES AND ARTERIAL RELATIONS IN THE POSTERIOR FOSSA

Accessory, Vagus, and Glossopharyngeal Nerves

Reflection of the dura of the posterior fossa allows examination of the cerebellum and of the pontine and medullary portions of the brain stem with the roots of the cranial nerves arising from these.

be retracted in order to reveal the roots of the cranial nerves and the brain stem itself. Elevation of the cerebellum in the midline allows examination of the caudal portion of the roof of the fourth ventricle, with its contained choroid plexus, and, at the inferior end of this, the foramen of Magendie. The boundaries of the fourth ventricle as seen from this aspect are the nuclei of the posterior columns, and farther upward the restiform body. The posterior inferior cerebellar artery, descending along the lateral aspect of the medulla, curves onto the posterior surface of the medulla at about the level of the apex of the fourth ventricle (obex), and usually runs again upward between the cerebellum and the posterolateral aspect of the medulla before branching on the inferior surface of the cerebellum.

If the lateral lobe of the cerebellum is lifted, the roots of most of the more caudal cranial nerves may be examined

erally toward the jugular foramen, it receives from the side of the medulla additional rootlets, the bulbar rootlets of the spinal accessory nerve. Farther upward, arising from the side of the medulla in line with the bulbar rootlets of the accessory nerve, are the rootlets of origin of the vagus, and above this the one or more rootlets of the glossopharyngeal nerve.

All of these nerve roots arise along the same line on the posterolateral aspect of the medulla and largely just dorsal to the

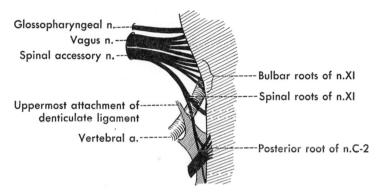

Fig. 43. Roots of origin of the ninth, tenth, and eleventh cranial nerves in a posterior view.

from their origin to their disappearance into the foramina by which they leave the cranial cavity. At the foramen magnum the uppermost denticulation of the *denticulate ligament* attaches to the dura and is crossed dorsally by the ascending spinal root of the spinal accessory nerve; ventral or anterior to both the denticulate ligament and the spinal root of the accessory nerve, and at first usually lateral to the nerve, the vertebral artery runs upward and somewhat medially, disappearing beneath the ventral surface of the medulla as it converges with its fellow of the opposite side (Fig. 43).

As the spinal root of the spinal accessory runs upward, diverging somewhat lat-

inferior olive; they form a series of rootlets which cannot be definitely assigned to any of the three cranial nerves to which they contribute until they are traced far enough laterally toward the jugular foramen to see the formation of the definitive nerves.

The roots of the ninth, tenth, and eleventh nerves are necessarily closely related to the *posterior inferior cerebellar artery*. This vessel typically ascends from its origin, and at first necessarily lies anterior or ventral to the roots of these nerves; the extent to which it is here related to the nerves varies, however, with the origin of the artery—the posterior inferior cerebellar may arise from the vertebral soon after this has entered the foramen magnum, or may not take origin from it until close to the formation of the basilar artery, therefore close to the caudal border of the pons. In this first, ascending, portion of its course the posterior inferior cerebellar artery may lie posterior to or upon the roots of the ninth, tenth, and eleventh nerves, but may also lie ventral or anterior to these nerves (Fig. 44); at the end of this ascending course the artery loops dorsally and caudally to descend along the side of the medulla and the inferior surface of the cerebellum, and this loop may lie above

ternal ramus (accessory branch to vagus) of the spinal accessory nerve (for instance, DuBois and Foley). The fibers of the bulbar rootlets arise from vagal nuclei and are distributed with the vagus, being associated with the spinal accessory for only a few millimeters—they join the spinal root of the accessory nerve within the cranial cavity, but as the accessory and vagus nerves pass through the jugular foramen the spinal and bulbar portions of the accessory nerves separate again (Fig. 45); the bulbar rootlets form the internal ramus of the spinal accessory and join the vagus, while the spinal roots

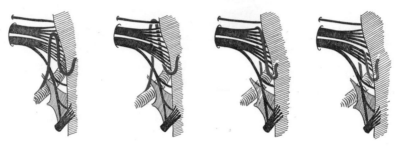

Fig. 44. Some variations in the relationship between the posterior inferior cerebellar artery and the roots of the ninth, tenth, and eleventh cranial nerves.

the origin of the ninth nerve, pass between the ninth and tenth or between the rootlets of the tenth and eleventh (Watt and McKillop). The most that can be said, therefore, concerning the relationship of the posterior inferior cerebellar to these nerve roots is that its loop, ascending and descending alongside the medulla, may lie largely ventral to the nerves, may lie largely dorsal to them, or may lie partly ventral and partly dorsal.

It has long been recognized that many of the voluntary *motor fibers* distributed in the vagus, that is, especially the fibers to the muscles of the pharynx and larynx, reach this nerve by way of the so-called bulbar rootlets (cranial root), and in-

form the external ramus of the accessory, which is distributed to the sternocleidomastoid and trapezius muscles. The bulbar rootlets of the accessory nerve are therefore more properly regarded as inferior vagal rootlets.

ACCESSORY NERVE

The spinal portion alone of the spinal accessory nerve thus corresponds to the extracranial spinal accessory nerve; although this nerve is joined outside the skull by sensory fibers from cervical nerves (for proprioception, but apparently not for pain, according to Windle and DeLozier), the spinal portion of the nerve is entirely voluntary motor and is distributed exclusively to the sternocleido-mastoid and trapezius muscles (Chase and Ranson). It can be sectioned intracranially, as for torticollis, below the level at which it is joined by the bulbar roots, to produce an isolated paralysis of these two muscles.

This part of the nerve arises by a series of rootlets from the lateral aspect of the spinal cord; among 40 cases investigated Holl found the lowermost rootlets to vary from the level of C-3 to that of C-7, but with the majority at C-5

anteroposterior relationship to this artery, and is joined here by the so-called bulbar rootlets of the nerve.

VAGUS NERVE

The vagus arises from the lateral surface of the medulla, between the restiform body and the inferior olive, as a series of rootlets in line with the more cranially placed roots of the glossopharyngeal nerve and the more caudally placed ones of the bulbar portion of the spinal accessory nerve. Foley and DuBois

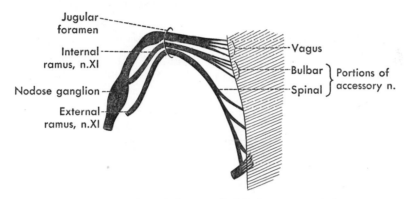

Fig. 45.   The grouping of the so-called bulbar roots of the accessory nerve as the internal ramus that joins the vagus, and the continuation of the spinal roots as the external ramus, or accessory nerve of gross anatomy.

and C-6. The fibers after their emergence turn and run upward between the anterior and posterior roots of the spinal nerves, being joined at successively higher levels by rootlets from these levels. Passing upward in this position in the subarachnoid cavity, and lying dorsal to the denticulate ligament, the spinal portion of the accessory nerve crosses dorsal (posterior) to the vertebral artery, to enter the cranial cavity through the foramen magnum. Alongside the medulla it usually lies lateral to the posterior inferior cerebellar artery, although varying in its

found that the sensory fibers in the vagus nerve (of the cat) constitute from 65 to 80 per cent of the total fibers, while the motor fibers number from 20 to 35 per cent of the total. Many of the voluntary motor fibers in the vagus, however, as already stated, leave the brain stem by way of the bulbar rootlets of the accessory rather than by way of the vagal rootlets themselves, and DuBois and Foley for the cat, and Tarlov ('40) for man, have described the main cephalic portion of the vagus-spinal accessory complex as primarily sensory. Delicate motor roots are said to lie ventromedial to the large cephalic sensory roots, while the caudal portion of the vagus-bulbar accessory complex is chiefly motor.

In a subsequent paper Tarlov ('42) has reported the results of section of the cephalic third of these rootlets in man: following such section no motor changes in the voluntary muscles could be demonstrated, and sensation of the posterior pharyngeal wall and soft palate appeared normal, but there was absence of sensitivity to pain over the right side of the epiglottis and diminished sensitivity to pain in the lower portion of the pharynx and in the larynx. Subsequent histological examination of the sectioned nerve rootlets again indicated that the uppermost roots were largely (about 95 per cent) sensory, although the more caudally sectioned ones contained greater numbers of motor fibers.

From their origins the rootlets of the vagus nerve run laterally and slightly anteriorly to converge to form the chief trunk of the vagus, and pass through the anterior portion of the jugular foramen, being usually separated from the ninth nerve by the inferior petrosal sinus, but closely paralleled by the accessory nerve; the sigmoid sinus passes through the posterior part of the jugular foramen, behind the accessory nerve, to form the superior bulb of the internal jugular vein, and the inferior petrosal sinus passes through the anterior portion of the jugular foramen, either anterior to the ninth nerve or between it and the tenth, to join the jugular bulb. As the vagus passes through the jugular foramen it bears its small, upper, jugular (superior) ganglion; from this arise both the auricular and meningeal or recurrent branches of the vagus, the latter passing upward again through the jugular foramen to be distributed primarily to the dura around the lateral sinus.

GLOSSOPHARYNGEAL NERVE

The glossopharyngeal nerve, like the vagal rootlets, arises from the lateral aspect of the medulla just caudal to the pons and in the groove between the inferior olive and the restiform body. According to Tarlov ('40) it usually presents two roots, a large sensory one and a small ventromedial motor root. These roots form the most superior or cephalic ones of the glossopharyngeal-vagus-accessory complex, represented by the entire series of rootlets in this position. From its origin the glossopharyngeal nerve runs laterally and slightly anteriorly in company with the vagus and spinal accessory nerves, where it usually comes in contact with the posterior inferior cerebellar artery (p. 75) and makes its exit through the most anterior part of the jugular foramen. In this position it is commonly separated from the vagus and spinal accessory nerves, which also make their exit through this foramen, by the inferior petrosal sinus as this latter passes through the jugular foramen to enter into the superior bulb of the internal jugular vein.

According to Partridge the nerve typically lies within a groove in the anterior part of the jugular foramen and is separated from the other structures in the foramen by a band of fibrous tissue which, in 25 per cent of the cases that he investigated, had been converted to osseous tissue. Thus in these cases the glossopharyngeal nerve passed through a bony canal of its own. Whether fibrous, osseous, or vascular, the separation between the ninth and tenth nerves as they pierce the dura at the jugular foramen facilitates intracranial section of the ninth nerve without damage to the tenth.

The glossopharyngeal nerve is largely a sensory one, though it contains some motor fibers; according to Foley and Sackett these number about 10 per cent of the total (in the cat). The motor fibers are of two types: voluntary ones to the only voluntary muscle, the stylopharyngeus, supplied by the ninth nerve, and preganglionic parasympathetic fibers to the otic ganglion, for the innervation of the parotid gland. The sensory fibers of the ninth nerve are distributed to the tympanic cavity and Eustachian tube, to almost the whole of the pharynx and the posterior third of the tongue, and to a limited region of skin of the external auditory meatus and ear.

The sensory distribution of the glossopharyngeal nerve accounts for the distribution of the pain of *glossopharyngeal neuralgia,* which is more commonly induced by swallowing and usually starts in the tonsillar region or the base of the tongue, but may extend to the ear, or may even begin in the ear. The pain is of the paroxysmal type, resembling trigeminal neuralgia, from which it can be distinguished by its distribution and the location of its trigger zone. The present accepted method of treatment is intracranial section of the root of the ninth nerve through a unilateral suboccipital craniotomy, as described by Adson ('24). In this operation advantage is usually taken of the fact that, as the ninth and tenth nerves pierce the dura, they do so distinctly separated from each other. I have, however, seen cases in which the dura at the jugular foramen and about the ninth and tenth nerves passed so deeply into the foramen that the actual points at which these nerves penetrated the dura could not be seen. In such a case it may be difficult to determine exactly which rootlets belong to the glossopharyngeal nerve; since, however, the upper vagal rootlets are largely sensory (p. 77), one or more of these may be divided without untoward damage.

The glossopharyngeal nerve has been sectioned extracranially for glossopharyngeal neuralgia, but the surgical approach here is difficult because of the close relations of the nerve to the carotid and internal jugular vessels; while it is possible to section it high enough to interrupt it before it has given off its pharyngeal branch—although this may come off quite high, only a little outside of the foramen—it is impossible to interrupt the branches to the ear by extracranial section, for these arise from the nerve as it traverses the jugular foramen. In such a case as that reported by Erickson, in which the pain was entirely limited to the tympanic branch of the ninth, extracranial section of the nerve would of course completely fail to alleviate the symptoms.

Section of the ninth nerve produces, as one would expect from the description of its distribution, loss of pain and touch over the fauces, the tonsils, and the pharyngeal wall from the larynx to the Eustachian tube; loss of the gag reflex; and loss of taste, pain, and touch over the posterior third of the tongue (Dandy, '27; Wycis; Erickson). While Wycis reported a case in which bilateral section of the ninth nerves was followed by a marked elevation of blood pressure, there is no evidence that the one was a cause of the other; the presence of depressor fibers in the vagus has long been known, and in experimental animals both these and the depressor fibers in the ninth (from the carotid sinus) must be destroyed in order to produce a sustained rise in blood pressure by section of nerves.

FACIAL AND ACOUSTIC NERVES

The seventh (facial) and eighth (acoustic or auditory) cranial nerves attach to the lateral surface of the brain stem close to the caudal border of the pons (Fig. 46a). These two nerves are closely related during their course through the subarachnoid space and into the in-

recess is a fold of choroid plexus, and at its end is the foramen of Luschka, one of the paired communications between the fourth ventricle and the subarachnoid space.

The acoustic nerve consists of two portions, which may or may not be grossly identifiable since they frequently

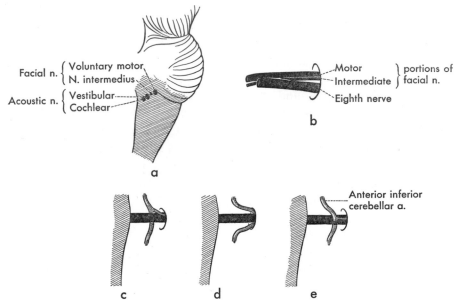

Fig. 46.   Some relations of the seventh and eighth cranial nerves. In *a* is shown, somewhat exaggerated spatially, the disposition of the four roots of these nerves at the brain stem and in *b*, also exaggeratedly spread apart, the relations of the three peripherally distinct components (cochlear and vestibular being ordinarily not separable here) as they might be seen from above. In *c, d,* and *e* are shown variable relations between these nerves and the anterior inferior cerebellar and internal auditory arteries as they might appear in a cerebellar approach, from which aspect the eighth nerve commonly hides the seventh.

ternal auditory (or acoustic) meatus. The eighth nerve lies dorsal and slightly caudal to the facial, which is therefore located somewhat more ventrally and slightly above or cranial to the eighth. From the cerebellar approach, therefore, the facial nerve may not be visible, being entirely hidden by the eighth. As the nerves leave the medulla they lie close against the cerebellum, and in contact with the lateral recess of the fourth ventricle; in this

form a single bundle; these are the cochlear (auditory) and vestibular divisions of the nerve. The cochlear division composes the more dorsal and caudal portion of the nerve, and passes dorsally over the restiform body, while the vestibular division forms the more superior and anterior portion of the nerve, and passes into the side of the medulla deep to the restiform body. The facial nerve also consists of two rootlets as it attaches to the brain stem; the voluntary motor rootlet is large and is situated anterior and cranial to the mixed sensory and parasympathetic root (nervus intermedius, nerve of Wrisberg or glossopalatine nerve), which is a rather small filament lying closely between the acoustic nerve and the voluntary portion of the facial nerve.

The acoustic and facial nerves pass laterally and slightly upward to enter the internal auditory meatus; as they pass across the subarachnoid space and enter the meatus the voluntary portion of the facial tends to lie most anteriorly, the auditory nerve most posteriorly with the nervus intermedius between these two. Within the auditory meatus the nervus intermedius typically joins the motor portion of the facial, and the common trunk crosses the anterior surface of the auditory nerve to lie above it at the distal end of the meatus.

As the seventh and eighth nerves pass laterally, they come in close but varying relationship to the *anterior inferior cerebellar artery,* which may lie either dorsal or ventral to them, loop around them or pass between any two of the three divisions (motor portion of the facial, nervus intermedius, or auditory nerve—Fig. 46c, d, e) as noted by Stopford ('16a); Watt and McKillop; and Sunderland ('45b, '48). Stopford found the artery lying more commonly ventral to the nerves, between them and the pons. Sunderland emphasized that the artery often loops laterally along these nerves, extending to their entrance into the meatus, or even out into the meatus; he found the artery to be related to the nerves at the meatus in 64 per cent of 264 sides. The varying relation of the anterior inferior cerebellar artery is of particular importance in operations at the cerebellopontine angle;

Atkinson has warned that occlusion of it may involve grave danger to the patient, especially if the posterior inferior cerebellar artery is small.

The seventh and eighth nerves are accompanied into the meatus by the *internal auditory artery,* which frequently insinuates itself between them; this artery is often described as a branch of the basilar artery, but Stopford ('16a) found it to arise from the anterior inferior cerebellar artery in 63 per cent of the cases in which he identified it, and Sunderland ('45b) reported a similar origin in 83 per cent of 264 sides which he examined—the artery then arising from the basilar in only 17 per cent. Watt and McKillop found the internal auditory artery to be double in 6 of 63 cases which they investigated.

DISTRIBUTION OF FACIAL NERVE

The voluntary motor fibers of the facial, constituting the bulk of the nerve, are distributed to all of the mimetic muscles of the face, including the buccinator, and to the platysma, the stylohyoid, the posterior belly of the digastric, and the tiny stapedius. The nervus intermedius root of the facial nerve contains preganglionic parasympathetic fibers which are destined for the sphenopalatine and submaxillary ganglia, and therefore especially for the glands and blood vessels of the nose and mouth.

This root of the nerve also contains sensory fibers which are derived from cells in the geniculate ganglion (located in the petrous portion of the temporal bone, at the external genu of the nerve); some of these fibers are for taste from the anterior two thirds of the tongue, while others are probably proprioceptive and still others may be concerned with cutaneous sensation and with pain. The further relations of this nerve in the skull are described in connection with the ear, with which it is closely associated in a part of its course, and its branching and distribution are discussed in connection with the face, nose, and tongue.

DISTRIBUTION OF ACOUSTIC NERVE

The fibers of both divisions of the acoustic nerve are of course distributed to the internal ear, but the two divisions have for the most part markedly different functions, for the auditory division is distributed to the cochlea, while the vestibular division is distributed primarily to the semicircular canals and to the maculae of the utriculus and sacculus. In addition to the afferent fibers, Rasmussen has stated that there are efferent fibers, of unknown function but derived from the superior olive, in the vestibular division of the nerve. Section of vestibular fibers close to the brain stem has been carried out for Ménière's disease; in such a case the more anterior and superior fibers of the eighth nerve have been cut, and this has been done with relatively little clinical evidence of damage to acoustic functions. Unless the two divisions are rather clearly delineated from each other, which rather commonly is not true, it is impossible to demonstrate anatomically how much of the nerve is composed of vestibular fibers, and differential section of the vestibular with sparing of the cochlear can be only approximate. Otolaryngologists currently favor other methods (p. 214) of dealing with Ménière's disease.

Trigeminal Nerve

The fifth (trigeminal) cranial nerve, like the seventh through the eleventh, attaches laterally to the brain stem, where its fibers penetrate the pons. It arises by two roots, a large sensory and a small motor one. The motor root lies above the sensory one, but in contact with it; as the roots run anterolaterally, the motor root is applied to the upper and anteromedial surface of the sensory root, and is therefore visible with difficulty or not at all from the cerebellar approach. Both roots, closely applied together, pass across the petrous ridge into the narrow mouth of Meckel's cave; the further relationships here, in the middle cranial fossa, have been described on page 61.

Section of the trigeminal root for neuralgia of this nerve has been carried out through an approach through the posterior fossa, as described by Dandy ('29), and some surgeons have preferred this approach; it presents certain obvious difficulties, especially that of avoiding injury to other cranial nerves in reaching the origin of the fifth. Dandy, whose paper should be consulted for details of technic, regarded this as much the superior approach, stating that it obviated the unpleasant sequelae—including facial paralysis—that sometimes occurred after section of the root by the temporal approach. The relationship of motor and sensory roots of this nerve at the brain stem is apparently constant and well known, though it may not be obvious to the surgeon working in this region; the arrangement of the sensory fibers of the various peripheral divisions of the nerve is, however, not absolutely known, may be variable, and is still subject to argument. This has been discussed on page 63. It might be added that Dandy stated that even complete section of the sensory root close to the pons does not abolish all sensation on the face, because of the presence of aberrant sensory rootlets (containing, however, apparently no pain fibers) which accompany the motor root.

Stopford ('16a) and Watt and Mc-Killop have called attention to an almost constant and particularly large pontine branch of the basilar artery that runs laterally across the pons to pass out along the ventral surface of the sensory root of the trigeminal nerve. This artery could stated that it commonly lay anterior to the nerve root, to which it could serve as a guide, but varied much in size and position (Fig. 47). He found no difficulty in occluding and dividing it when it lay against the nerve.

Dandy ('34) described a branch of

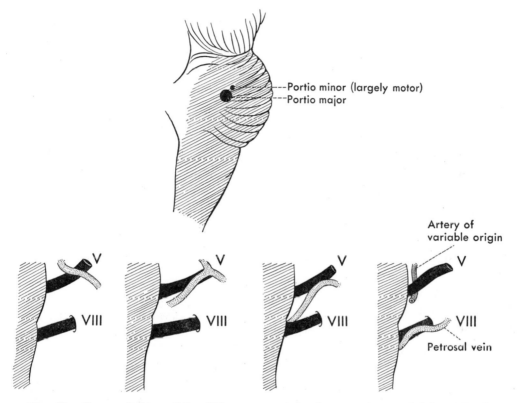

Fig. 47. Some relations of the fifth nerve roots in the posterior cranial fossa. In the lateral view of the brain stem the relation between the sensory and motor roots is shown; the remaining sketches, adapted from Dandy (*Arch. Surg. 18*:687, 1929), illustrate varying relationships between the fifth nerve root and the petrosal vein, with fifth and eighth nerves identified; in the last sketch an artery is shown related to the fifth nerve (see text).

apparently be a source of troublesome bleeding in section of the root through the posterior fossa. A venous connection to the superior petrosal sinus rather regularly passes along the lateral surface of the nerve, according to Sunderland ('48), and may also be a source of hemorrhage. Presumably this is the vein described by Dandy ('29) as the petrosal vein; he the superior cerebellar artery as lying either beneath the trigeminal root (that is, between it and the brain stem) or along its lateral surface; he stated that in 30.7 per cent of 215 cases of trigeminal neuralgia in which he had operated this artery had in some way affected the nerve, either lifting or bending the sensory root, or leaving a mark upon it. Larger arteries may also be related to the root in the posterior fossa: Sunderland ('48) has described the superior cerebellar, the posterior inferior cerebellar, and even the basilar artery, as being sometimes in contact with the trigeminal root, and in 3 cases found an anomalous anastomotic branch between the internal carotid and the basilar arteries accompanying this root.

TROCHLEAR NERVE

The trochlear nerve has the longest intracranial course, and the longest course through the subarachnoid cavity, of any of the cranial nerves. It is also the only one arising from the dorsal surface of the brain stem. From its external origin just caudal to the inferior colliculi the threadlike trochlear nerve passes laterally downward and somewhat forward, lying in the transverse fissure between cerebral and cerebellar hemispheres, and therefore in the cistern of the great cerebral vein. It is usually described as lying parallel to and between the superior cerebellar and the posterior cerebral arteries as it passes from its origin, but is actually, of course, separated from the latter by the tentorium cerebelli; it passes lateral to the cerebral peduncles, enters the basal cistern, and lying against the lower surface of the tentorium pierces the dura of this close to its free border, and only a little behind the posterior clinoid process. In its subarachnoid course this nerve is conceivably subject to compression against the tentorium by the superior cerebellar artery; in its further course through the cavernous sinus it is brought in close relation to the other nerves entering the orbit, and is here subject to damage from the same sources as these nerves. This nerve supplies only the superior oblique muscle.

HYPOGLOSSAL, ABDUCENS, AND OCULOMOTOR NERVES

The three nerves arising well ventrally from the brain stem, between this and the base of the skull in the posterior fossa, are the twelfth, sixth, and third (hypoglossal, abducens, and oculomotor).

HYPOGLOSSAL NERVE

The hypoglossal nerve arises from the ventrolateral surface of the medulla, between the inferior olive and the pyramid, its rootlets being in line with the anterior roots of the spinal nerves. From their origin the approximately dozen filaments of the hypoglossal nerve, which are entirely voluntary motor in function, unite to form two bundles that pass forward and laterad to traverse the hypoglossal (anterior condyloid) foramen. In or just external to the foramen these two trunks unite to form the main hypoglossal trunk; they usually pierce the dura separately, and may traverse separate bony canals. Lillie found no sign of subdivision of the bony hypoglossal canal in only about 50 per cent of the specimens which he examined, while in some 34 to 39 per cent there was a spur partially dividing the canal, and in 11 to 17 per cent there was complete division of the canal into two parts.

The two converging vertebral arteries usually lie medial and ventral to the hypoglossal nerves, and if they are tortuous and deviated laterally may produce pressure upon these nerves; occasionally, filaments of the nerve pass through an island in the vessel. The relationship of the posterior inferior cerebellar artery to the hypoglossal nerve varies considerably; as already noted in connection with the ninth, tenth, and eleventh nerves, this artery may lie largely dorsal to these nerves, or it may lie in part ventral to the nerves and therefore between them and the hypoglossal. The artery may arise from the vertebral either above or below the level of origin of the nerve from the brain stem, and in the former case especially has no intimate relation to the nerve. It might be recalled that there is normally a venous plexus accompanying the hypoglossal nerve through the hypoglossal foramen, and connecting the marginal sinuses with the vertebral vein; in

inferior cerebellar artery (Fig. 48); according to Stopford ('16a) the artery lies ventral to the nerve in more than four fifths of cases, but otherwise crosses dorsal to it or may even pass through the roots of the nerve. Both Stopford, and Watt and McKillop, have pointed out that when the artery lies dorsal to the nerve it may compress this against the basisphenoid bone. The internal auditory artery may have a similar relationship to the nerve

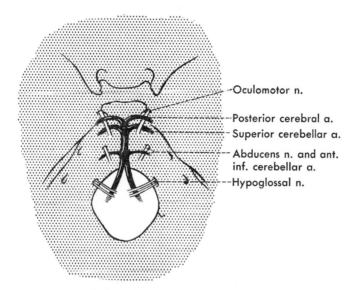

Oculomotor n.

Posterior cerebral a.

Superior cerebellar a.

Abducens n. and ant. inf. cerebellar a.

Hypoglossal n.

Fig. 48.   Relationships between the arteries and the nerves at the base of the brain. The more common relation between the abducens nerve and the anterior inferior cerebellar artery is shown on the left, a less common one on the right.

those cases in which the occipital sinus is much enlarged, the venous connection through the hypoglossal foramen may also be of considerable size.

ABDUCENS NERVE

The abducens nerve, like the trochlear supplying only one muscle in the orbit (the lateral rectus), emerges from the medulla at the posterior edge of the pons, just lateral to the pyramids and therefore not far from the ventral midline. Close to its origin it is crossed by the anterior

in that minority of instances in which it arises from the basilar. Cushing ('10), reporting compression of the sixth nerve by the anterior inferior cerebellar and internal auditory arteries, expressed his belief that constriction by an artery, due to displacement of the brain by a tumor or through edema, is one of the most common reasons for isolated paralysis of the sixth nerve. As is well known, such a paralysis of the sixth nerve is not uncommon in intracranial disturbances, and has little localizing value.

From its origin at the brain stem the abducens nerve passes forward and slightly laterally to enter the cranial dura on the side of the base of the sphenoid bone; it then continues upward and forward in the dura (that is, between the two layers of this) to pass over a groove in the petrous ridge just posterior to the base of the posterior clinoid process and enter the cavernous sinus. This groove is converted into a canal (Dorello's canal) by the petrosphenoid ligament (of Gruber), and contains also the inferior petrosal sinus, which usually lies medial to the nerve but may (Houser) lie above it. In this canal the abducens nerve is adjacent to the tip of the petrous pyramid, and therefore exposed to infection from petrous tip cells, and may be relatively close to the sphenoid sinus (less than 3 mm. in 15.7 per cent of cases studied by Houser). These relationships may also account for isolated paralysis of the sixth nerve. Further, any downward shift of the brain stem would necessarily quickly produce tension upon the sixth nerve, with possible injury to it.

These relationships, its fixed position in the dura of the cranial floor—where it may be involved by skull fractures—and perhaps other anatomical factors probably account for the frequency of involvement of this nerve; the often quoted statement that paralysis of the sixth nerve is due to its long intracranial course is illogical, for the sixth has a short subarachnoid course, and the trochlear nerve, very rarely paralyzed alone, has both a much longer subarachnoid and total intracranial course than has the sixth.

OCULOMOTOR NERVE

The oculomotor nerves arise at the upper border of the pons, emerging between or through the more medial fibers of the two cerebral peduncles. Unlike the other two motor nerves to the orbit the oculomotor nerve contains, in addition to its voluntary motor fibers (distributed to the levator palpebrae, superior, medial and inferior recti, and the inferior oblique), preganglionic parasympathetic fibers; these supply, through the ciliary ganglion, the ciliary muscle and the sphincter pupillae.

Close to its origin the oculomotor nerve typically passes between the posterior cerebral and the superior cerebellar arteries; in 50 per cent of cases, according to Stopford ('16a), the posterior cerebral artery lay in actual contact with the root of the nerve. Each nerve runs forward through the basal cistern, pierces the dura mater lateral and close to the posterior clinoid process, and thereafter traverses the cavernous sinus to enter the orbit through the superior orbital fissure.

Lying as it does usually between the posterior cerebral and the superior cerebellar arteries, the oculomotor nerve may be compressed by either, or by aneurysms of the anterior part of the basilar artery; as the nerve passes upward and forward it is also in close contact with the posterior communicating artery, and is therefore potentially subject to compression by aneurysms of that vessel.

ARTERIES

The general courses and connections of the arteries in the posterior cranial fossa have been described in connection with the blood supply of the brain (p. 32); their variable relations to the cranial nerves of the posterior fossa have been discussed in connection with these nerves.

Briefly summarized, the two *vertebral arteries* pass alongside the anteroventral aspect of the medulla, anterior or ventral to the roots of origin of the ninth, tenth and eleventh cranial nerves; as they converge toward their point of junction to form the basilar artery, they necessarily pass close to the hypoglossal nerves, which are more commonly affected by aneurysms of these vessels than are the more laterally lying nerves.

The *posterior inferior cerebellar artery* usually arises from the vertebral, but varies in the level of its origin and may even arise from the basilar; it typically runs cranially to loop dorsally and caudally, and in so doing is in close relation to the roots of the ninth, tenth, and eleventh nerves, but this relationship varies (p. 75). Finally, it usually turns upward, between the medulla and the cerebellum, before passing onto the latter.

The *basilar artery* is typically formed by the union of the two vertebrals at about the lower border of the pons, but may have a higher or a lower origin; although it should run in the midline, it is not unusual to find it deviated markedly to one side.

The *anterior inferior cerebellar artery* usually arises from the basilar, but may arise from the vertebral; it passes typically either above or below the sixth nerve, and in close relation to it, and as it passes toward the inferior surface of the cerebellum comes also into close relationship with the seventh and eighth nerves. It quite commonly loops laterally with these nerves, so that it lies adjacent to them at the internal auditory meatus. It may lie above or below the nerves, or between them.

The *internal auditory artery,* if it arises from the basilar, runs laterally with the seventh and eighth nerves; if it arises from the anterior inferior cerebellar artery, as it does more commonly, it usually arises from the loop on this vessel and may therefore leave it at or within the internal meatus.

The *superior cerebellar artery,* from the upper end of the basilar, passes laterally, backward, and downward around the pons; close to its origin it usually passes just below (caudal to) the oculomotor nerve, and farther laterally crosses the trochlear nerve. The *posterior cerebral artery* also passes laterally, paralleling the superior cerebellar; it usually lies above the oculomotor nerve, so that the roots of this nerve pass between the posterior cerebral and superior cerebellar vessels. From the posterior cerebrals the *posterior communicating arteries* pass forward on the sides of the hypothalamic region, to help complete the circle of Willis.

In addition to these larger branches, there are multiple small branches to the brain stem. Attention might be called again to the fact that an artery of appreciable size may be associated with the sensory root of the trigeminal nerve in the posterior fossa.

REFERENCES

ABBIE, A. A. The clinical significance of the anterior choroidal artery. *Brain 56:*233, 1933.

ADAMS, R. D. Occlusion of the anterior inferior cerebellar artery. *Arch. Neurol. & Psychiat. 49:*765, 1943.

ADSON, A. W. The surgical treatment of glossopharyngeal neuralgia. *Arch. Neurol. & Psychiat. 12:*487, 1924.

ADSON, A. W. Cerebrospinal rhinorrhea: Surgical repair of craniosinus fistula. *Ann. Surg. 114:*697, 1941a.

ADSON, A. W. A straight lateral incision for unilateral suboccipital craniotomy. *Surg., Gynec. & Obst.* 72:99, 1941b.

ADSON, A. W. Control of recurring hemiparesis by bilateral removal of the superior cervical sympathetic ganglia: Report of 2 cases. *Proc. Staff Meet., Mayo Clin.* 26:518, 1951.

ADSON, A. W., and UIHLEIN, A. Repair of defects in ethmoid and frontal sinuses resulting in cerebrospinal rhinorrhea. *Arch. Surg.* 58:623, 1949.

ANDERSON, A. G., LOCKHART, R. D., and SOUTER, W. C. Lateral syndrome of the medulla: Occlusion of the posterior inferior cerebellar artery; vascular lesions of the hind-brain. *Brain* 54:460, 1931.

ANDERSON, F. M. Intranasal (sphenopharyngeal) encephalocele: A report of a case with intracranial repair and a review of the subject. *Arch. Otolaryng.* 46:644, 1947.

AREY, L. B. The craniopharyngeal canal reviewed and reinterpreted. *Anat. Rec.* 106:1, 1950.

ATKINSON, W. J. The anterior inferior cerebellar artery: Its variations, pontine distribution, and significance in the surgery of cerebello-pontine angle tumours. *J. Neurol., Neurosurg. & Psychiat.* n.s. 12:137, 1949.

BATUJEFF, N. Eine seltene Arterienanomalie (Ursprung der A. basilaris aus der A. carotis interna). *Anat. Anz.* 4:282, 1889.

BECKMANN, J. W., and KUBIE, L. S. A clinical study of twenty-one cases of tumour of the hypophyseal stalk. *Brain* 52:127, 1929.

BEDFORD, T. H. B. The great vein of Galen and the syndrome of increased intracranial pressure. *Brain* 57:1, 1934a.

BEDFORD, T. H. B. The venous system of the velum interpositum of the Rhesus monkey and the effect of experimental occlusion of the great vein of Galen. *Brain* 57:255, 1934b.

BEEVOR, C. E. On the distribution of the different arteries supplying the human brain. *Philosoph. Tr. Roy. Soc.* s.B.200:1, 1909.

BLACKBURN, I. W. Anomalies of the encephalic arteries among the insane: A study of the arteries at the base of the encephalon in two hundred and twenty consecutive cases of mental disease, with special reference to anomalies of the circle of Willis. *J. Comp. Neurol.* 17:493, 1907.

BLACKBURN, I. W. On the median anterior cerebral artery as found among the insane. *J. Comp. Neurol.* 20:185, 1910.

BRODAL, A. Central course of afferent fibers for pain in facial glossopharyngeal and vagus nerves: Clinical observations. *Arch. Neurol. & Psychiat.* 57:292, 1947.

BROOKOVER, C. The nervus terminalis in adult man. *J. Comp. Neurol.* 24:131, 1914.

BROOKS, C. M. A study of the mechanism whereby coitus excites the ovulation-producing activity of the rabbit's pituitary. *Am. J. Physiol.* 121:157, 1938.

BURR, H. S., and ROBINSON, G. B. An anatomical study of the gasserian ganglion, with particular reference to the nature and extent of Meckel's cave. *Anat. Rec.* 29:269, 1925.

CAMPBELL, E. H. The cavernous sinus: Anatomical and clinical considerations. *Ann. Otol., Rhin. & Laryng.* 42:51, 1933.

CHANDLER, S. B., and DEREZINSKI, C. F. The variations of the middle meningeal artery within the middle cranial fossa. *Anat. Rec.* 62:309, 1935.

CHASE, M. R., and RANSON, S. W. The structure of the roots, trunk and branches of the vagus nerve. *J. Comp. Neurol.* 24:31, 1914.

CHOROBSKI, J., and PENFIELD, W. Cerebral vasodilator nerves and their pathway from the medulla oblongata: With observations on the pial and intracerebral vascular plexus. *Arch. Neurol. & Psychiat.* 28:1257, 1932.

CLARK, S. L. Innervation of the choroid plexuses and the blood vessels within the central nervous system. *J. Comp. Neurol.* 60:21, 1934.

COATES, A. E. A note on the superior petrosal sinus and its relation to the sensory root of the trigeminal nerve. *J. Anat.* 68:428, 1934.

COBB, S., and FINESINGER, J. E. Cerebral circulation: XIX. The vagal pathway of the vasodilator impulses. *Arch. Neurol. & Psychiat.* 28:1243, 1932.

COLEMAN, C. C., and TROLAND, C. E. The surgical treatment of spontaneous cerebrospinal rhinorrhea. *Ann. Surg.* 125:718, 1947.

CUSHING, H. A method of total extirpation of the gasserian ganglion for trigeminal neuralgia: By a route through the temporal fossa and beneath the middle meningeal artery. *J.A.M.A.* 34:1035, 1900.

CUSHING, H. Strangulation of the nervi abducentes by lateral branches of the basilar artery in cases of brain tumour. *Brain 33:* 204, 1910.

CUSHING, H. The rôle of deep alcohol injections in the treatment of trigeminal neuralgia. *J.A.M.A. 75:*441, 1920.

DANDY, W. E. The nerve supply to the pituitary body. *Am. J. Anat. 15:*333, 1913.

DANDY, W. E. Glossopharyngeal neuralgia (tic douloureux): Its diagnosis and treatment. *Arch. Surg. 15:*198, 1927.

DANDY, W. E. An operation for the cure of tic douloureux: Partial section of the sensory root at the pons. *Arch. Surg. 18:*687, 1929.

DANDY, W. E. Certain functions of the roots and ganglia of the cranial sensory nerves. *Arch. Neurol. & Psychiat. 27:*22, 1932.

DANDY, W. E. Concerning the cause of trigeminal neuralgia. *Am. J. Surg. 24:*447, 1934.

DANDY, W. E. The treatment of internal carotid aneurysms within the cavernous sinus and the cranial chamber: Report of three cases. *Ann. Surg. 109:*689, 1939.

DANDY, W. E. The surgical treatment of intracranial aneurysms of the internal carotid artery. *Ann. Surg. 114:*336, 1941.

DANDY, W. E. Arteriovenous aneurysms of the scalp and face. *Arch. Surg. 52:*1, 1946.

DANDY, W. E., and GOETSCH, E. The blood supply of the pituitary body. *Am. J. Anat. 11:*137, 1911.

DAVIS, L., and HAVEN, H. A. Surgical anatomy of the sensory root of the trigeminal nerve. *Arch. Neurol. & Psychiat. 29:*1, 1933.

DAVISON, C. Syndrome of the anterior spinal artery of the medulla oblongata. *Arch. Neurol. & Psychiat. 37:*91, 1937.

DEY, F. L. Evidence of hypothalamic control of hypophyseal gonadotrophic functions in the female guinea pig. *Endocrinology 33:* 75, 1943.

DuBois, F. S., and FOLEY, J. O. Experimental studies on the vagus and spinal accessory nerves in the cat. *Anat. Rec. 64:*285, 1936.

ERICKSON, T. C. Paroxysmal neuralgia of the tympanic branch of the glossopharyngeal nerve: Report of a case in which relief was obtained by intracranial section of the glossopharyngeal nerve. *Arch. Neurol. & Psychiat. 35:*1070, 1936.

FALCONER, M. A. Intramedullary trigeminal tractotomy and its place in the treatment of facial pain. *J. Neurol., Neurosurg. & Psychiat. n.s.12:*297, 1949.

FAWCETT, E., and BLACHFORD, J. V. The circle of Willis: An examination of 700 specimens. *J. Anat. & Physiol. 40:*63, 1905.

FINLEY, K. H. Angio-architecture of the substantia nigra and its pathogenic significance. *Arch. Neurol. & Psychiat. 36:*118, 1936.

FISHER, C., INGRAM, W. R., HARE, W. K., and RANSON, S. W. The degeneration of the supraoptico-hypophyseal system in diabetes insipidus. *Anat. Rec. 63:*29, 1935.

FLESCH, M. Ein weiterer Fall von Theilung der Arteria carotis interna in der Schädelhöhle. *Arch. f. Anat. u. Physiol. p.* 151, 1886.

FLOREY, H. Microscopical observations on the circulation of the blood in the cerebral cortex. *Brain 48:*43, 1925.

FOG, M. Cerebral circulation: I. Reaction of pial arteries to epinephrine by direct application and by intravenous injection. *Arch. Neurol. & Psychiat. 41:*109, 1939a.

FOG, M. Cerebral circulation: II. Reaction of pial arteries to increase in blood pressure. *Arch. Neurol. & Psychiat. 41:*260, 1939b.

FOLEY, J. O., and DuBois, F. S. Quantitative studies of the vagus nerve in the cat: I. The ratio of sensory to motor fibers. *J. Comp. Neurol. 67:*49, 1937.

FOLEY, J. O., and SACKETT, W. W. On the number of cells and fibers in the glossopharyngeal nerve of the cat (Abstr.). *Anat. Rec. 106:*303, 1950.

FORBES, H. S. Physiologic regulation of the cerebral circulation. *Arch. Neurol. & Psychiat. 43:*804, 1940.

FORBES, H. S., and COBB, S. Vasomotor control of cerebral vessels. *Brain 61:*221, 1938.

FORBES, H. S., NASON, GLADYS I., and WORTMAN, RUTH C. Cerebral circulation: XLIV. Vasodilation in the pia following stimulation of the vagus, aortic and carotid sinus nerves. *Arch. Neurol. & Psychiat. 37:*334, 1937.

FORBES, H. S., NASON, GLADYS I., COBB, S., and WORTMAN, RUTH C. Cerebral circulation: XLV. Vasodilation in the pia following stimulation of the geniculate ganglion. *Arch. Neurol. & Psychiat. 37:*776, 1937.

FRAZIER, C. H., and WHITEHEAD, E. The morphology of the gasserian ganglion. *Brain* 48:458, 1925.

GIBBS, ERNA L., and GIBBS, F. A. The cross section areas of the vessels that form the torcular and the manner in which flow is distributed to the right and to the left lateral sinus. *Anat. Rec. 59:*419, 1934.

GRANT, F. C. Major trigeminal neuralgia. *Am. J. Surg. 27:*430, 1935.

GRANT, F. C., and WEINBERGER, L. M. Experiences with intramedullary tractotomy: I. Relief of facial pain and summary of operative results. *Arch. Surg. 42:*681, 1941.

GRANT, F. C., GROFF, R. A., and LEWY, F. H. Section of the descending spinal root of the fifth cranial nerve. *Arch. Neurol. & Psychiat. 43:*498, 1940.

GREEN, J. D. The histology of the hypophysial stalk and median eminence in man with special reference to blood vessels, nerve fibers and a peculiar neurovascular zone in this region. *Anat. Rec. 100:*273, 1948.

GROSS, S. W., and SAVITSKY, N. Extradural hemorrhage in the anterior cranial fossa. *Ann. Surg. 116:*821, 1942.

GRZYBOWSKI, J. L'innervation de la dure-mère cranienne chez l'homme. *Arch. d'anat., d'histol. et d'embryol. 14:*387, 1931.

HAIR, G. W. The nerve supply of the hypophysis of the cat. *Anat. Rec. 71:*141, 1938.

HARRIS, W. An analysis of 1,433 cases of paroxysmal trigeminal neuralgia (trigeminaltic) and the end-results of gasserian alcohol injection. *Brain 63:*209, 1940.

HATERIUS, H. O. The genital-pituitary pathway: Non-effect of stimulation of superior cervical sympathetic ganglia. *Proc. Soc. Exper. Biol. & Med. 31:*1112, 1934.

HAYNER, J. C. Variations of the torcular Herophili and transverse sinuses. *Anat. Rec. 103:*542, 1949.

HILDING, A. False response to the jugular compression (Tobey-Ayer) test due to anomaly of the lateral sinus. *Arch. Otolaryng. 26:*143, 1937.

HOCHSTETTER, F. Ueber zwei Fälle einer seltenen Varietät der A. carotis interna. *Arch. f. Anat. u. Physiol.* p. 396, 1885.

HOLL, M. Ueber den Nervus accessorius Willisii. *Arch. f. Anat. u. Physiol.* p. 491, 1878.

HOLLINSHEAD, W. H. Anatomy of the endocrine glands. *S. Clin. North America* 32:1115, 1952.

HOOPLE, G. D. Anomaly of the lateral sinus: Report of a case. *Ann. Otol., Rhin. & Laryng. 45:*1019, 1936.

HOUSER, K. M. Anatomic relation of the sphenoid sinus to Dorello's canal: Abducens paralysis. *Arch. Otolaryng. 16:*488, 1932.

HUMPHREYS, S. P. Anatomic relations of cerebral vessels and perivascular nerves. *Arch. Neurol. & Psychiat. 41:*1207, 1939.

HYNDMAN, O. R. Tic douloureux: Partial section of the root of the fifth cranial nerve; a comparison of the subtemporal and cerebellar approaches from surgical and physiologic standpoints. *Arch. Surg. 37:*74, 1938.

INGRAM, W. R., and FISHER, C. The relation of the posterior pituitary to water exchange in the cat. *Anat. Rec. 66:*271, 1936.

JAEGER, J. R. Ligation and resection of the superior longitudinal sinus. *Arch. Neurol. & Psychiat. 48:*977, 1942.

JEFFERSON, G. Compression of the chiasma, optic nerves, and optic tracts by intracranial aneurysms. *Brain 60:*444, 1937.

JEFFERSON, G., and STEWART, D. On the veins of the diploë. *Brit. J. Surg. 16:*70, 1928.

KAUMP, D. H., and LOVE, J. G. "Subdural" hematoma. *Surg., Gynec. & Obst. 67:*87, 1938.

KNOTT, J. F. On the cerebral sinuses and their variations. *J. Anat. & Physiol. 16:*27, 1881.

KUBIK, C. S., and ADAMS, R. D. Occlusion of the basilar artery: A clinical and pathological study. *Brain 69:*73, 1946.

KUNKLE, E. C., LUND, D. W., and MAHER, P. J. Studies on headache: Analysis of vascular mechanisms in headache by use of the human centrifuge, with observations on pain perception under increased positive G. *Arch. Neurol. & Psychiat. 60:*253, 1948.

KUNKLE, E. C., RAY, B. S., and WOLFF, H. G. Experimental studies on headache: Analysis of the headache associated with changes in intracranial pressure. *Arch. Neurol. & Psychiat. 49:*323, 1943.

LEARY, T., and EDWARDS, E. A. The subdural space and its linings. *Arch. Neurol. & Psychiat. 29:*691, 1933.

LEININGER, C. R., and RANSON, S. W. The effect of hypophysial stalk transection upon gonadotrophic function in the guinea pig. *Anat. Rec. 87:*77, 1943.

LEVINE, M., and WOLFF, H. G. Cerebral circulation: Afferent impulses from the blood vessels of the pia. *Arch. Neurol. & Psychiat. 28:*140, 1932.

LEWY, F. H., and GRANT, F. C. Physiopathologic and pathoanatomic aspects of major trigeminal neuralgia. *Arch. Neurol. & Psychiat. 40:*1126, 1938.

LILLIE, R. D. Variations of the canalis hypoglossi. *Anat. Rec. 13:*131, 1917.

LOCKHART, R. D. The dural relations of the gasserian ganglion with reference to a new method of surgical approach. *J. Anat. 62:* 105, 1927.

LOVE, J. G. Decompression of the gasserian ganglion and its posterior root: A new treatment for trigeminal neuralgia (preliminary report). *Proc. Staff Meet., Mayo Clin. 27:* 257, 1952.

LOVE, J. G., and GAY, J. R. Spontaneous cerebrospinal rhinorrhea: Successful surgical treatment. *Arch. Otolaryng. 46:*40, 1947.

LOW, F. N. An anomalous middle meningeal artery. *Anat. Rec. 95:*347, 1946.

MARKEE, J. E., SAWYER, C. H., and HOLLINSHEAD, W. H. Activation of the anterior hypophysis by electrical stimulation in the rabbit. *Endocrinology 38:*345, 1946.

MATAS, R. Aneurysms of the circle of Willis. A discussion of Dr. Dandy's intracranial occlusion of the internal carotid for aneurysms of the circle of Willis, with supplementary remarks. *Ann. Surg. 107:*660, 1938.

MELCHIONNA, R. N., and MOORE, R. A. The pharyngeal pituitary gland. *Am. J. Path. 14:*763, 1938.

MERRITT, H., and FINLAND, M. Vascular lesions of the hind-brain: Lateral medullary syndrome. *Brain 53:*290, 1930.

MERWARTH, H. R. The syndrome of the rolandic vein: Hemiplegia of venous origin. *Am. J. Surg. 56:*526, 1942.

MOOD, G. F. Congenital anterior herniations of brain. *Ann. Otol., Rhin. & Laryng. 47:* 391, 1938.

NAFFZIGER, H. C., and ADAMS, J. E. Role of stellate block in various intracranial pathologic states. *Arch. Surg. 61:*286, 1950.

VAN NOUHUYS, F. The anatomy of the gasserian ganglion: Its relation to tic douloureux. *Arch. Surg. 24:*451, 1932.

O'CONNELL, J. E. A. Some observations on the cerebral veins. *Brain 57:*484, 1934.

PARTRIDGE, E. J. The relations of the glossopharyngeal nerve at its exit from the cranial cavity. *J. Anat. 52:*332, 1918.

PATEK, P. R. The perivascular spaces of the mammalian brain. *Anat. Rec. 88:*1, 1944.

PENFIELD, W. The cranial subdural space: A method of study. *Anat. Rec. 28:*173, 1924.

PENFIELD, W. Intracranial vascular nerves. *Arch. Neurol. & Psychiat. 27:*30, 1932.

PENFIELD, W., and McNAUGHTON, F. Dural headache and innervation of the dura mater. *Arch. Neurol. & Psychiat. 44:*43, 1940.

PENFIELD, W., and NORCROSS, N. C. Subdural traction and posttraumatic headache: Study of pathology and therapeusis. *Arch. Neurol. & Psychiat. 36:*75, 1936.

PERLMAN, H. B., and LINDSAY, J. R. Relation of the internal ear spaces to the meninges. *Arch. Otolaryng. 29:*12, 1939.

POOL, J. L., FORBES, H. S., and NASON, GLADYS I. Cerebral circulation: XXXII. Effect of stimulation of the sympathetic nerve on the pial vessels in the isolated head. *Arch. Neurol. & Psychiat. 32:*915, 1934.

POPA, G., and FIELDING, UNA. A portal circulation from the pituitary to the hypothalamic region. *J. Anat. 65:*88, 1930.

RASMUSSEN, G. L. The olivary peduncle and other fiber projections of the superior olivary complex. *J. Comp. Neurol. 84:*141, 1946.

RAY, B. S., and WOLFF, H. G. Experimental studies on headache: Pain-sensitive structures of the head and their significance in headache. *Arch. Surg. 41:*813, 1940.

REICHERT, F. L., and MORRISSEY, E. J. Extradural venous hemorrhage. *Ann. Surg. 113:* 204, 1941.

REID, W. L. Cerebral herniation through the incisura tentorii: A clinical, pathological, and experimental study. *Surgery 8:*756, 1940.

ROGERS, L. The function of the circulus arteriosus of Willis. *Brain 70:*171, 1947.

ROWLAND, L. P., and METTLER, F. A. Relation between the coronal suture and cerebrum. *J. Comp. Neurol. 89:*21, 1948.

RUBENSTEIN, H. S. Relation of circulus arteriosus to hypothalamus and internal capsule. *Arch. Neurol. & Psychiat. 52:*526, 1944.

SAWYER, C. H., MARKEE, J. E., and HOLLINSHEAD, W. H. Inhibition of ovulation in the rabbit by the adrenergic-blocking agent dibenamine. *Endocrinology 41:*395, 1947.

SCHLESINGER, B. The venous drainage of the brain, with special reference to the galenic system. *Brain 62:*274, 1939.

SCHUMACHER, G. A., and WOLFF, H. G. Experimental studies on headache: A. Contrast of histamine headache with the headache of migraine and that associated with hypertension; B. Contrast of vascular mechanisms in preheadache and in headache phenomena of migraine. *Arch. Neurol. & Psychiat. 45:* 199, 1941.

SCHUMACHER, G. A., RAY, B. S., and WOLFF, H. G. Experimental studies on headache: Further analysis of histamine headache and its pain pathways. *Arch. Neurol. & Psychiat. 44:*701, 1940.

DE SCHWEINITZ, G. E. The Bowman Lecture, 1923: Concerning certain ocular aspects of pituitary body disorders, mainly exclusive of the usual central and peripheral hemianopic field defects. *Tr. Ophth. Soc. U. Kingdom. 43:*12, 1923.

SHENKIN, H. A., HARMEL, M. H., and KETY, S. S. Dynamic anatomy of the cerebral circulation. *Arch. Neurol. & Psychiat. 60:* 240, 1948.

SJÖQVIST, O. Studies on pain conduction in the trigeminal nerve: A contribution to the surgical treatment of facial pain. *Acta psychiat. et neurol.* Suppl. *17,* 1938.

SMITH, G. E. Note on an anomalous anastomosis between the internal carotid and basilar arteries. *J. Anat. & Physiol. 43:* 310, 1909.

SOKOLOW, P. Der Canalis cranio-pharyngeus. *Arch. f. Anat. u. Physiol.* p. 71, 1904.

SPILLER, W. G., and FRAZIER, C. H. Tic douloureux: Anatomic and clinical basis for subtotal section of sensory root of trigeminal nerve. *Arch. Neurol. & Psychiat. 29:*50, 1933.

STAVRAKY, G. W. Response of cerebral blood vessels to electric stimulation of the thalamus and hypothalamic regions. *Arch. Neurol. & Psychiat. 35:*1002, 1936.

STEWART, J. P. The persistence of fetal blood sinuses and their relation to the middle ear spaces. *Arch. Otolaryng. 10:*266, 1929.

STIBBE, E. P. Some observations on the surgery of trigeminal neuralgia. *Brit. J. Surg. 24:*122, 1936.

STOPFORD, J. S. B. The arteries of the pons and medulla oblongata. *J. Anat. 50:*131, 1916a.

STOPFORD, J. S. B. The arteries of the pons and medulla oblongata: Part II. The precise distribution of the arteries supplying the medulla and pons. *J. Anat. 50:*255, 1916b.

STOPFORD, J. S. B. The arteries of the pons and medulla oblongata: Part III. The clinical application of Parts I and II. *J. Anat. 51:* 250, 1917.

STOPFORD, J. S. B. The functional significance of the arrangement of the cerebral and cerebellar veins. *J. Anat. 64:*257, 1930.

STREETER, G. L. The development of the venous sinuses of the dura mater in the human embryo. *Am. J. Anat. 18:*145, 1915.

SUCHANNEK. Ein Fall von Persistenz des Hypophysenganges. *Anat. Anz. 2:*520, 1887.

SUNDERLAND, S. The meningeal relations of the human hypophysis cerebri. *J. Anat. 79:*33, 1945a.

SUNDERLAND, S. The arterial relations of the internal auditory meatus. *Brain 68:*23, 1945b.

SUNDERLAND, S. Neurovascular relations and anomalies at the base of the brain. *J. Neurol., Neurosurg. & Psychiat.* n.s.*11:*243, 1948.

SYMINGTON, J. Observations on the relations of the deeper parts of the brain to the surface. *J. Anat. & Physiol. 37:*241, 1903.

TAARNHØJ, P. Decompression of the trigeminal root and the posterior part of the ganglion as treatment in trigeminal neuralgia: Preliminary communication. *J. Neurosurg. 9:*288, 1952.

TARLOV, I. M. Structure of the nerve root: I. Nature of the junction between the central and the peripheral nervous system. *Arch. Neurol. & Psychiat. 37:*555, 1937a.

TARLOV, I. M. Structure of the nerve root: II. Differentiation of sensory from motor roots; observations on identification of function in roots of mixed cranial nerves. *Arch. Neurol. & Psychiat. 37:*1338, 1937b.

TARLOV, I. M. Sensory and motor roots of the glossopharyngeal nerve and the vagus-spinal accessory complex. *Arch. Neurol & Psychiat. 44:*1018, 1940.

TARLOV, I. M. Section of the cephalic third of the vagus-spinal accessory complex: Clinical and histologic results. *Arch. Neurol. & Psychiat. 47:*141, 1942.

TAYLOR, A. S. Surgical treatment of trigeminal neuralgia. *Am. J. Surg. 20:*699, 1933.

TORKILDSEN, A. The gross anatomy of the lateral ventricles. *J. Anat. 68:*480, 1934.

WALKER, A. E. The attachments of the dura mater over the base of the skull. *Anat. Rec. 55:*291, 1933.

WALTNER, J. G. Anatomic variations of the lateral and sigmoid sinuses. *Arch. Otolaryng. 39:*307, 1944.

WATT, J. C., and MCKILLOP, A. N. Relation of arteries to roots of nerves in posterior cranial fossa in man. *Arch. Surg. 30:*336, 1935.

WEINBERGER, L. M., and GRANT, F. C. Experiences with intramedullary tractotomy: III. Studies in sensation. *Arch. Neurol. & Psychiat. 48:*355, 1942.

WERDEN, D. H. Intracranial venous anomaly. *Am. J. Surg. 29:*115, 1935.

WESSELS, A. Report of a case of spontaneous cerebrospinal rhinorrhea with operative cure. *Ann. Otol., Rhin. & Laryng. 48:*528, 1939.

WILKINS, H., and SACHS, E. Variations in skin anesthesia following subtotal resection of the posterior root: With a report of twenty-six cases illustrating a series of variations. *Arch. Neurol. & Psychiat. 29:*19, 1933.

WINDLE, B. C. A. On the arteries forming the circle of Willis. *J. Anat. & Physiol. 22:*289, 1888.

WINDLE, W. F., and DELOZIER, L. C. The absence of painful sensation in the cat during stimulation of the spinal accessory nerve. *J. Comp. Neurol. 54:*97, 1932.

WISLOCKI, G. B. The meningeal relations of the hypophysis cerebri. I. The relations in adult mammals. *Anat. Rec. 67:*273, 1937.

WOODHALL, B. Variations of the cranial venous sinuses in the region of the torcular Herophili. *Arch. Surg. 33:*297, 1936.

WOODHALL, B., and SEEDS, A. E. Cranial venous sinuses: Correlation between skull markings and roentgenograms of the occipital bone. *Arch. Surg. 33:*867, 1936.

WYCIS, H. Bilateral intracranial section of the glossopharyngeal nerve: Report of a case. *Arch. Neurol. & Psychiat. 54:*344, 1945.

ZEITLIN, H., and OLDBERG, E. Craniopharyngioma in the third ventricle of the brain: Partial surgical removal and pathologic study. *Arch. Neurol. & Psychiat. 43:*1195, 1940.

CHAPTER 2

The Orbit

THE external muscles, nerves, and vessels about the orbit are described in the chapter on the face; only those points of particular interest in connection with the orbit will be described here.

THE LIDS

THE structure of the upper and lower lids is similar, although the upper lid is more movable and presents certain features not found in the lower. The lids are essentially reduplicated folds of skin, the inner layer

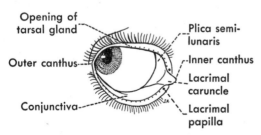

Opening of tarsal gland

Outer canthus

Conjunctiva

Plica semi-lunaris

Inner canthus

Lacrimal caruncle

Lacrimal papilla

Fig. 49.   Palpebral fissure with both eyelids everted.

of which is modified to form the conjunctiva. When the lids are open the interval between them is known as the palpebral fissure; this is limited medially and laterally by the inner and outer canthi, or angles, of the eye (Fig. 49). The medial (inner) canthus, unlike the lateral (outer) one, does not rest directly against the eyeball but is separated from it by a small space known as the lacrimal lake. The fleshy, yellowish projection within the lacrimal lake is the lacrimal caruncle, and the thin semilunar fold extending laterally from this is the *plica semilunaris*. The caruncle represents an area in which there are large modified sweat and sebaceous glands; the plica semilunaris is a vestige of the movable third lid, or nictitating membrane, of lower animals.

The eyelashes (cilia), or hairs on the free margins of the lids, are arranged in several rows which extend from the lateral canthus to about the level of the plica semilunaris. Associated with the hair follicles of the cilia are sebaceous glands (of Zeis) and rudimentary sweat glands (of Moll), the latter sometimes opening to the skin surface but frequently opening into the sebaceous glands or their ducts, or into a hair follicle. A stye is due to blockage of either type of gland.

At about the level of the lateral border

of the plica semilunaris, and always medial to the rows of cilia, each lid margin presents, when slightly everted, a posteriorly directed lacrimal papilla bearing a central opening or lacrimal punctum, these elevations and openings representing the origins of the lacrimal canaliculi which drain the tears from the lacrimal lake. Close to the posterior edge of the free margin of the lids may be seen

a plane along which the lid may be easily split into anterior and posterior portions.

Each eyelid consists, from without inward, of skin, subcutaneous tissue, voluntary muscle, orbital septum and tarsal plate, smooth muscle and conjunctiva (Fig. 50); in addition, the more freely movable upper lid receives the tendinous insertion of the levator palpebrae muscle. The skin of the eyelids is thin, and its

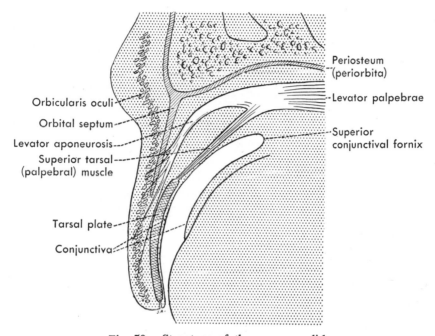

Fig. 50. Structure of the upper eyelid.

a row of minute apertures representing the opening of the tarsal glands (of Meibom), the glands themselves being visible as yellowish lines on the inner surface of the everted eyelid. A chalazion is due to blockage of this type of gland. A grayish line or a slight groove sometimes visible between the lashes and the openings of the tarsal glands represents the junction of the two fundamental portions of the lid, the skin and muscle on the one hand, and the tarsal glands and conjunctiva on the other, and indicates

texture is such that it is difficult to match it by skin grafts from other areas of the body. It is attached only by loose connective tissue to the underlying muscle; hence, in contrast to most areas of the face, relatively large quantities of fluid may accumulate subcutaneously in this loose connective tissue.

ORBICULARIS OCULI

The voluntary muscle in the lids is the *palpebral portion* of the orbicularis oculi, composed of rather thin bundles which are loosely held together by the subcutaneous connective tissue; between these bundles in the upper eyelid run expansions of the levator palpebrae to insert into the skin of the lid. This portion of the orbicularis arises largely from the medial palpebral ligament and inserts (Fig. 51), into the lateral palpebral raphe (not the lateral palpebral ligament), but a part of it closest to the margins of

pion) and results in improper drainage of tears with consequent spillage over the lower lid (epiphora). Induced paresis of the orbicularis oculi by injection of a local anesthetic into the fibers of the muscle at their insertion into the lateral raphe (technic of Van Lint) or by injection about the parotid plexus of the facial nerve (technic of O'Brien) has become a popular procedure in many intra-ocular

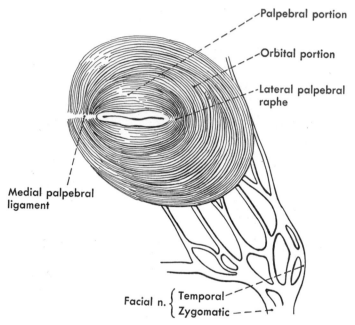

Fig. 51.   Orbicularis oculi from the front. For the relations of the pars lacrimalis see Fig. 58, page 107.

the lids arises from the posterior lacrimal crest (behind the lacrimal sac) and is known, at its origin only, as the pars lacrimalis, the tensor tarsi, or the muscle of Horner (see Fig. 58, p. 107). Some particularly delicate muscle fibers actually at the edge of the free lid have unfortunately been separately designated as the ciliary muscle of Riolan, a complication of no practical usefulness.

Paralysis of the orbicularis abolishes tight closure of the eye, allows the lower lid to drop away from the eyeball (ectro-

operations carried out under local anesthesia; this paresis forestalls the squeezing action of the eyelids upon the eyeball, with its tendency to produce loss of vitreous humor.

Behind the orbicularis oculi is another layer of loose connective tissue, in which run the chief blood vessels and nerves of the lid. It is through this layer that the lid may be most easily split. Behind this loose connective tissue is an area of dense connective tissue, formed in the lower lid by the tarsus (tarsal plate) and the orbital septum, in the upper lid by the orbital septum, the aponeurosis of the levator palpebrae and the tarsal plate.

ORBITAL SEPTUM

The orbital septum (palpebral fascia) extends into upper and lower lids from approximately the margins of the bony orbit, where it is continuous with the periosteum of the orbit (periorbita) and the periosteum of the outer surface of the skull. From this peripheral origin it extends as a membranous sheet into the eyelids. While it is not actually divided into upper and lower parts, for it is a continuous membrane, it is often convenient to speak of it in terms of its association with the lids; hence it is referred to, as a whole, as the orbital septum, or its upper and lower segments are referred to individually as the superior and inferior orbital septa.

Both superior and inferior orbital septa extend toward the free margins of the lids at least as far as the tarsal plates. The inferior septum is fused to the dense connective tissue on the front of the inferior tarsus, while the superior septum usually seems to overlap the front of the superior tarsus and to be separated from it by the aponeurosis of the levator palpebrae; however, according to some authors (for example, Wolff) it sends delicate septa through this aponeurosis to attach to the anterior surface of the tarsus. The superior orbital septum is stronger in appearance than is the inferior, but is perforated by a number of nerves and vessels which leave or enter the orbit to form communications between orbital and facial structures.

Medially, the orbital septum is fused with the medial palpebral ligament, while laterally it passes behind the lateral raphe (of the orbicularis oculi), which it rein-

forces; it lies, however, in front of the lateral palpebral ligament. It separates the connective tissue spaces of the lids from that of the orbit, and with expansions from the fascial sheaths of the ocular muscles restrains the orbital fat and forms a sort of fire screen which tends to prevent infections of the lid from passing backward into the orbit, and vice versa. Since the septum attaches medially to the posterior lacrimal crest, it thus excludes the lacrimal sac from the orbit proper.

TARSAL PLATES

The tarsal plates, or tarsi, consist of dense connective tissue in which are embedded enormous sebaceous glands, the

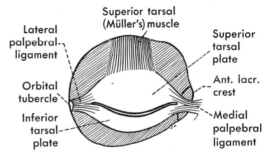

Fig. 52. Tarsal plates and their attachments.

tarsal or Meibomian glands; these plates give form to the upper and lower lids (Fig. 52). The edge of each plate adjacent to the free border of the lid parallels this, and is therefore straight, while the deeper border of each plate (that of the upper much more so than that of the lower) is curved so that the plates are somewhat semilunar in shape. The plates as a whole, in turn, are of course curved to conform to the outer surface of the eyeball. The superior tarsal plate is considerably larger than the inferior one, the greatest width of the superior being about 10 mm., that of the inferior about 5 mm. To forestall either inversion or eversion of the eyelid as the result of scar tissue formation in the tarsal plate, incisions into this are usually made in the frontal or vertical plane rather than a horizontal line.

MEDIAL PALPEBRAL LIGAMENT

The tarsi are anchored medially and laterally by the medial and lateral palpebral (tarsal) ligaments. The medial palpebral ligament, the stronger of the two, has an indefinite upper border but a lower border which is thick and prominent. This ligament is attached laterally to the medial angles of the two tarsal plates, and extends medially, adjacent to the lacrimal canaliculi, to pass in front of the lacrimal sac and attach to the frontal process of the maxilla in front of the fossa for the lacrimal sac. As a landmark for locating the lacrimal sac the medial palpebral ligament is quite important. This ligament can be demonstrated in the intact individual by drawing the lids laterally, so as to tense it, at which time the lower border is easily palpable. The ligament is frequently divided, or cut from its insertion into the periosteum of the anterior lacrimal crest, in order to gain access to the lacrimal sac in surgical procedures around this area.

In addition to its attachment to the anterior lacrimal crest the medial palpebral ligament is also said, by many authors, to send a weaker continuation lateral to and behind the lacrimal sac to attach to the posterior lacrimal crest, so that the nasal attachment is often described as being U shaped. Other investigators do not recognize the existence of a posterior part of the medial palpebral ligament, or describe it as being no more than delicate fascia on the anterior surface of the pars lacrimalis muscle. The majority of the fibers of the palpebral portion of the orbicularis oculi are attached firmly to the anterior surface of the medial palpebral ligament to form the medial raphe; the fibers of the pars lacrimalis are sometimes described as related to the posterior surface of the posterior lamina, and sometimes as arising from the anterior surface of this lamina, indicating again the indefiniteness of this supposed part of the ligament.

LATERAL PALPEBRAL LIGAMENT

The lateral palpebral ligament is frequently confused with the lateral palpebral raphe. This latter, however, represents merely an interlacing of muscle fibers at the lateral corner of the eye; it lies in front of the orbital septum, to which it is partly fused. Since it is not especially attached to the tarsal plates, it can hardly be regarded as a ligament of these. The true lateral palpebral ligament is completely separated from the raphe, for it lies behind both the orbital septum and the strong lateral horn of the levator aponeurosis. It consists of a band of connective tissue which attaches medially to the lateral angles of both tarsal plates, and laterally to the zygomatic bone at the orbital tubercle. At the tubercle the ligament is fused to the aponeurosis of the levator and to the check ligament from the lateral rectus muscle, but more medially it is separated from the check ligament by the lower edge of the palpebral portion of the lacrimal gland.

Probably because of its fusions with the other structures attaching to the orbital tubercle, and also because it is by no means as dense as the medial ligament, considerable variation exists in the manner in which this ligament has been described and illustrated. At and just lateral to its attachment to the tarsal plates it is usually distinct, but more laterally still it may blend completely with the lateral horn of the levator aponeurosis.

LEVATOR PALPEBRAE

In the upper lid, but not in the lower, the dense fibrous layer contains in addition to the tarsus and orbital septum a third element, the tendon of insertion, or aponeurosis, of the levator palpebrae (superioris). This muscle is usually described as dividing into two layers, an anterior and a posterior one, as it passes from the orbit into the lid.

The tendon or *aponeurosis* of the levator, the anterior layer, passes below the apparent free edge of the superior orbital septum, and above the tarsal plate, to lie in front of the plate (where it contributes to the connective tissue here) and to send connective tissue bands to the skin between the muscle bundles of the orbicularis. Through this attachment to the skin the levator produces the superior palpebral fold, and in paralysis of this muscle the fold disappears. The aponeurotic portion in the lid is much wider than the muscle from which it is derived, and its medial and lateral expansions are known as horns (or cornua). The lateral horn is prominent and deeply indents the anterior portion of the lacrimal gland to divide this gland into palpebral and orbicular portions; its attachment on the orbital wall is to the orbital tubercle, already mentioned as the point of attachment of the lateral palpebral ligament. The weaker medial horn of the levator aponeurosis blends with the medial palpebral ligament. From the upper surface of the levator as it passes into the lid a thin reflection from its fascia may usually be demonstrated passing upward behind the superior orbital septum to attach to the orbital rim.

The *superior tarsal or superior palpebral muscle* (of Müller), a thin sheet of smooth muscle, forms the so-called posterior or deep layer of the levator; it is firmly attached to the inferior surface of the levator, and passes downward behind the aponeurotic part. The insertion of this smooth muscle is into the upper border of the tarsal plate. Since it is attached to the levator, and has a function similar to this, it may be logical to describe it as a part of the levator, but it should not be forgotten that Müller's muscle (as it is generally called) is smooth muscle, and is innervated by the sympathetic nervous system. Many operations for ptosis involve manipulation of this muscle, with careful dissection of it from tarsal plate, conjunctiva, levator tendon, and orbital septum.

From histological observations a similar layer of smooth muscle has been described in the lower lid, as arising from a prolongation of the inferior rectus and inserting into the tarsal plate or (Whitnall, '21a) passing toward it but failing to reach it; it has been stated that this inferior tarsal or inferior palpebral muscle (also of Müller) can be seen in the living being through the conjunctiva, but the present writer has not been able to identify it with certainty in dissections.

CONJUNCTIVA

The conjunctiva forms the posterior layer of the eyelid. It begins at the free margin of the lid as a modification of the skin, is reflected upward or downward, as the case may be, to form the posterior surface of the lid, and from here is reflected onto the eyeball; that portion of the conjunctiva reflected from lid to bulb is sometimes termed the fornix, but the entire space between lid and eyeball is also referred to as the fornix. The superior fornix (in either sense) reaches to the orbital margin, and the inferior fornix almost does so; the outer or lateral fornix extends deeply, to just behind the equator of the globe, while the medial or internal fornix is largely nonexistent, due to the presence of the caruncle and the plica semilunaris.

The conjunctiva is intimately attached to the posterior surfaces of the tarsal plates, and is almost inseparable from them; above the tarsal plate in the upper lid, and below it in the lower lid, the conjunctiva lies relatively loosely on the smooth musculature of the lids, though it is so delicate that it is difficult to separate surgically. The superior fornix is described as having attached to it an expansion from the fascia of the levator palpebrae and superior rectus muscles, while the inferior fornix is said to receive an expansion from the fascia of the inferior rectus muscle; thus the fornices tend to move with movements of the lids and of the eyeball.

As the conjunctiva is reflected at the fornix onto the bulb it lies loosely on the anterior portion of the capsule of Tenon (fascia bulbi), and subconjunctival vessels lie in this position; at about 3 mm. from the cornea it becomes more closely applied to Tenon's capsule, and subsequently to the sclera and cornea, from both of which, however, it remains separable surgically until it fuses with the cornea. The line along which fusion of the conjunctiva to the cornea occurs is known as the conjunctival limbus. It is about 1 mm. anterior to the true limbus (the junction of cornea and sclera; see also p. 121 and Fig. 68). The limbus formed by the insertion of Tenon's capsule into the sclera lies about

1.5 mm. posterior to the true limbus; the area between the limbus of Tenon's capsule and the conjunctival limbus is of surgical importance as the site of various corneoscleral trephine procedures for glaucoma.

ANOMALIES

Notching or fissuring of the margin of a lid is referred to as a coloboma. When a part only of a lid is absent, it is usually the medial portion of the upper lid (Whitnall, '21a).

Cryptophthalmia is the condition in which the lids are entirely absent as such, the globe being covered with skin; associated with the absence of the lids and conjunctiva is absence of the latter's outgrowths, the lacrimal gland and its ducts.

The *muscles* of the lids may also fail to develop properly: absence of the levator produces a congenital ptosis; maldevelopment of the lateral raphe may produce an absence of the lateral canthus (Wheeler).

Hemi-absence of the external nose is accompanied by a deformation at the medial canthus; apparently the medial palpebral ligament is missing in such cases, and there is no normal drainage of tears (p. 276).

FASCIAL SPACES IN THE LIDS

Attention has already been called to the fact that the skin is only loosely attached to the underlying orbicularis oculi muscle, thus presenting here a fascial space in which fluid can readily accumulate. This space is largely limited to the orbit by the more dense connective tissue attaching the skin to the musculature over the remainder of the face and forehead. Behind the muscle, also, is an area of loose connective tissue, which is traversed by the chief blood vessels and nerves of the lid. In the lower lid this space is a closed one, and is known as the preseptal space.

In the *upper lid* (Fig. 53) this area of loose connective tissue is separated into two spaces by the aponeurosis of the

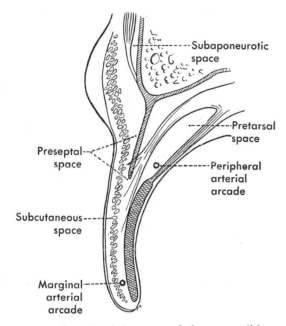

Preseptal space

Subaponeurotic space

Pretarsal space

Peripheral arterial arcade

Subcutaneous space

Marginal arterial arcade

Fig. 53.   Fascial spaces of the upper lid.

levator palpebrae muscle. The portion behind the levator tendon and the orbicularis, bounded posteriorly by the tarsal plate and Müller's muscle, is known as the *pretarsal space*; it contains the peripheral arterial arcade and laterally, extending beyond the edge of the tarsus, the palpebral portion of the lacrimal gland. It likewise is a closed space, as it is bounded above by the point of separation of the levator into its anterior and posterior laminae, and below by the attachment of the fibers of the levator to the front of the tarsal plate.

The second space in the upper lid is the *preseptal space*, bounded in front by

the orbicularis, behind by the septum, and behind and below by the fibers of the levator aponeurosis. It contains a certain amount of fat and, in its lower portion, the marginal arterial arcade. The preseptal space is often described as being continuous above, beneath the frontalis muscle, with the subaponeurotic or danger space of the scalp; Whitnall, following Charpy, states, however, that these two spaces are separated by the strong attachment of the galea to the orbital margin, and that injections into this space do not rise above the eyebrows, but rather pass back into the pretarsal space or pass outward between the fiber bundles of the orbicularis. This has been observed recently also by the present writer, in a case in which the preseptal space and the orbicularis muscle were thoroughly infiltrated and distended by injected latex, but none passed above the eyebrow into the subaponeurotic space. Clinically, according to Wolff, blood and pus may pass between the two spaces; this may occur, of course, along the branches of the ophthalmic artery and nerve which round the upper margin of the orbit to lie at first beneath the galea.

NERVES AND VESSELS OF THE LIDS

Nerves

The orbicularis oculi muscle is supplied by the facial nerve (temporal and zygomatic branches), branches of which enter the lateral portion of the muscle both above and below the lateral raphe, while some run deep to the lower border of the muscle to join the infra-orbital nerve and enter the muscle here. It might be noted, however, that the levator palpebrae, the other voluntary muscle of the lid, is an orbital muscle and is innervated by the oculomotor nerve. The smooth muscle in the lids is supplied through the superior cervical sympathetic ganglion.

Paralysis of the facial nerve results in an inability to close the lids tightly, and the lower lid tends to drop away from the eyeball and become everted. Paralysis of the oculomotor nerve produces a ptosis of the lid and inability to open the eye voluntarily; interruption of the sympathetic supply to the superior palpebral (Müller's) muscle, most frequently seen as a result of interruption of the cervical sympathetic chain (Horner's syndrome), interferes with the maintenance of a normal elevation of the upper lid, producing a constant ptosis of the lid.

In contrast to the ptosis produced by levator paralysis, however, paralysis of the superior palpebral muscle does not produce obliteration of the superior palpebral fold. Mahoney and Sheehan have shown on experimental animals that the superior tarsal muscle may completely overcome the ptosis of levator paralysis during moments of excitement.

The cutaneous nerves of the eyelids are branches of the ophthalmic and maxillary nerves which appear subcutaneously to supply skin of the face and of the lids themselves (Fig. 54). The cutaneous branches of the ophthalmic nerve traverse the orbit and therefore necessarily penetrate the orbital septum.

The supra-orbital nerve, the largest of these, leaves the orbit by the supra-orbital notch or foramen, and turns up to supply skin of the forehead; at the same time, however, it gives off minute branches which supply the larger portion of the upper lid. Medial to the supra-orbital the smaller supratrochlear nerve also rounds the orbital rim to supply the forehead, and similarly supplies the more

medial portion of the upper lid. Laterally, the upper lid near the lateral angle is supplied by twigs from the lacrimal nerve. The small infratrochlear nerve, another branch of the ophthalmic, supplies skin of both upper and lower lids at the inner canthus and along the side of the nose, while the major portion of the lower lid is supplied through upward running branches of the infra-orbital nerve (the terminal portion of the max-

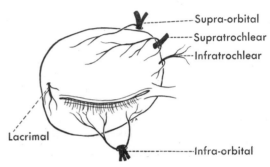

Fig. 54.   The cutaneous nerves related to the eyelids.

illary). Skin lateral to the outer canthus is likewise supplied by the maxillary nerve, through its zygomaticofacial and zygomaticotemporal branches.

VESSELS

ARTERIES

Passing upward between the medial corner of the eye and the side of the nose is the terminal (angular) branch of the facial or external maxillary artery, which anastomoses with branches of the ophthalmic in this position; accompanying this is the corresponding vein, the anterior facial or angular vein, which has here usually two or more large anastomoses with the ophthalmic veins (Fig. 55). The vein lies lateral to the artery, and is often visible through the skin, but in any case it is important to visualize the position of these vessels in an external approach to the lacrimal sac, since their cut ends tend to retract and make hemostasis difficult. It is preferable to avoid them, if at all possible, in incisions in this area. Inferior to the orbit are branches of the transverse facial artery, while lateral to and above it run branches of the superficial temporal artery. All of these vessels usually help to supply the skin of the lids, and anastomose with branches of the palpebral arterial ar-

upper eyelid. More medially, the frontal (supratrochlear) artery (one of the terminal branches of the ophthalmic) also pierces the orbital septum to turn upward on the forehead with the supratrochlear nerve. Close to the frontal artery, and immediately above the strong part of the medial palpebral ligament, the dorsal nasal artery (the other terminal branch of the ophthalmic) penetrates the orbital septum to supply skin at the base and side of the nose, give off

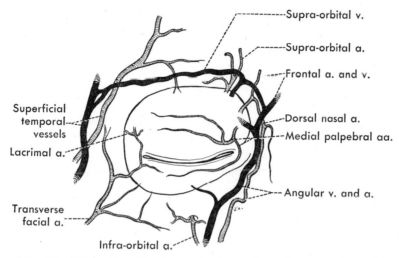

Fig. 55. The chief blood vessels about the orbital margin and in the lids; the veins of the lids are not shown.

cades, but the chief supply to the lids is from the ophthalmic artery itself.

The larger branches of the ophthalmic artery are concentrated in the upper nasal quadrant of the orbit and pierce this portion of the orbital septum; hence, in operations around the orbit, it is usually the vessels in this position that are the most difficult to ligate and section. The supra-orbital artery arises from the ophthalmic within the orbit, and accompanies the nerve of the same name through the supra-orbital notch or foramen; as it turns upward beneath the frontalis muscle it gives twigs to the

filaments to the lacrimal sac, and anastomose with the facial artery.

The large vessels of the upper and lower lids, however, are the superior and inferior medial palpebral branches of the ophthalmic, which arise either by a common stem or individually from the trunk of the ophthalmic (the frontonasal artery) or from one of the two terminal vessels. The *superior medial palpebral artery* passes above the medial palpebral ligament and usually divides to form two trunks which run laterally in the eyelid as the peripheral and marginal arterial arcades. The peripheral arcade runs behind the aponeurosis of the levator palpebrae, between this and Müller's muscle, while the marginal one lies on the front of the tarsal plate. The arcades of the upper lid may be completed laterally by small branches from the lacrimal artery, and give off in turn branches which supply the structures of the lid, and also most of the conjunctiva. These vessels usually anastomose also with the supra-orbital artery and with the orbital branch of the superficial temporal.

The *inferior medial palpebral artery* passes downward behind the medial palpebral ligament, perforates the inferior orbital septum, and then turns to run transversely between the orbicularis oculi and the inferior tarsal plate. The arch in the lower lid may also be completed laterally by a twig from the lacrimal artery, and usually communicates inferiorly with the transverse facial artery. As in the case of the upper lid, a secondary or peripheral arch may be present along the attached border of the tarsus, but this is inconstant in the lower lid.

The arterial supply of the conjunctiva of the upper lid is said to be largely from the peripheral arterial arcade, but to be supplemented toward the free margin of the lid by a supply from the marginal arcade. These branches supply not only the conjunctiva of the lid but also that of the fornix and most of the bulbar conjunctiva, and are said to show little anastomosis with each other. The ascending branches from the peripheral arcade penetrate the superior palpebral muscle and pass toward and around the edge of the fornix, to form posterior conjunctival vessels which descend behind the bulbar conjunctiva; it is these vessels which are prominent in acute conjunctivitis. About 4 mm. from the cornea they anastomose with the anterior conjunctival branches

of the anterior ciliary arteries, forming vessels which supply the pericorneal portion of the conjunctiva through a series of anastomosing branches. The branches to the conjunctiva of the inferior fornix are similarly distributed, but often are necessarily derived entirely from the marginal arcade.

VEINS

The veins of the eyelids are larger and more numerous than are the arteries, and drain into the ophthalmic and the angular veins medially, and into the superficial temporal laterally. One channel here (the supra-orbital vein), parallel to the superior rim of the orbit, is sometimes particularly well developed and may then form a broad anastomotic channel between the above-mentioned veins. The drainage of the posttarsal tissues, therefore especially of the conjunctiva, is into the ophthalmic vein, while that of the pretarsal tissues is into the angular vein medially and into the superficial temporal vein laterally. Accompanying the peripheral arterial arcade of the upper lid there is a small venous plexus which lies between the aponeurosis of the levator and the superior palpebral muscle, and connects with the veins of the levator and of the superior rectus, which are in turn tributaries of the ophthalmic vein.

LYMPHATICS

The lymphatics of the lids are, like the veins, divisible into pretarsal and posttarsal plexuses which are, however, connected to each other by anastomosing channels; the posttarsal vessels drain the conjunctiva and the Meibomian glands, while the pretarsal or superficial vessels drain the skin and adjacent layers. According to Burch the superficial lymphatics parallel the lid margins rather than run perpendicular to them as usually described. Both plexuses drain into the same nodes, those from most of the upper lid, from the lateral angle, and from a lateral portion of the lower lid (that is, the majority of the vessels) draining into anterior auricular and parotid lymph nodes, while those from the medial angle of the eye and the medial portion of the lower lid drain into submaxillary nodes (Most). In many severe types of conjunctivitis there is swelling of the preauricular nodes, evidencing spread of the infection via lymphatics, but enlargement of submaxillary nodes as the result of ocular disease is rarely seen.

THE LACRIMAL APPARATUS

THE lacrimal apparatus consists of a secretory portion, the lacrimal gland and its ducts; and of a drainage apparatus, the lacrimal lake, the lacrimal canaliculi and sac, and the nasolacrimal duct.

SECRETORY APPARATUS

The lacrimal gland is partially divided into two portions (Fig. 56) by the lateral horn of the aponeurosis of the levator palpebrae; that is, the gland is folded about the posterior border of the horn in such a fashion that a part lies above the aponeurosis, while another part ex-tends behind the aponeurosis into the lid. The larger orbital portion (superior lacrimal gland, B.N.A.) of the gland lies in the lacrimal fossa on the frontal bone and is in contact anteriorly with the orbital septum, which separates it from other structures of the lid. Behind the free posterior edge of the lateral horn of the levator aponeurosis it is continuous with the palpebral portion of the gland. The smaller and thinner palpebral portion (palpebral process, or inferior lacrimal gland, B.N.A.) Extends into the lateral part of the upper lid to lie against the conjunctiva, through which

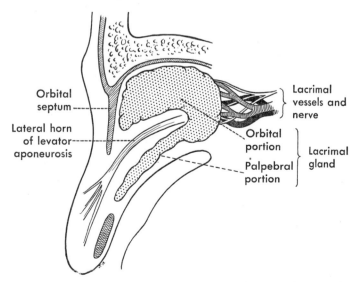

Fig. 56. Lacrimal gland in a parasagittal section of the front of the orbit.

it may be seen when the lid is everted; farther medially, it lies in front of the lateral portion of the superior orbital muscle. Its position should be kept in mind in surgical procedures upon the upper lid.

The lacrimal gland is supported and maintained in position by the aponeurosis of the levator and by the lateral rectus muscle, on the upper surfaces of which it rests. Some accounts of the fascia of the orbit describe the lacrimal gland as being surrounded by a capsule derived from a splitting of the periorbita, or as held in place by septa from the periorbita, but the gland has no very definite capsule and is normally only weakly attached to the periorbita. In malignant diseases of the gland it becomes firmly attached to the periorbita, and this in turn becomes more firmly attached to the adjacent bone. This invasion may account for the pain and tenderness evoked in this condition by palpation of the orbital rim.

The *nerves and vessels* to the lacrimal gland enter it at its undivided posterior border, and consist of numerous branches of the lacrimal artery and nerve. A branch of the infra-orbital artery may also sometimes supply the gland, extending upward from the inferior orbital fissure to reach its lower border. The branches of the lacrimal nerve proper to the gland are sensory, but this nerve is also joined by fibers from the sphenopalatine ganglion (see p. 149) which are secretory to the gland. The venous drainage of the gland is into the ophthalmic vein; the lymphatics are said to join the conjunctival lymphatics, and hence empty into the preauricular nodes.

The *ducts* (excretory ductules) of the lacrimal gland number approximately a dozen; those which come from the orbital part of the gland run through the palpebral portion and are largely joined by the ducts from this portion, though some of the palpebral ducts usually open independently. Removal of the palpebral portion might be expected to destroy the drainage of the entire gland, but apparently does not always do so; sometimes, however, the orbital portion must also be removed following excision of the palpebral portion. The ducts are delicate, and open for the most part into the outer part of the superior fornix, but one or more may also open into the inferior fornix. In addition to the lacrimal gland itself small accessory lacrimal glands (glands of Krause) lie adjacent to the conjunctiva, and are regarded as a continuation of the palpebral portion of the gland.

LACRIMAL DRAINAGE

Movements of the eyelid distribute the secreted tears over the surface of the eyeball, and any excess tends to accumulate in the lacrimal lake. The *lacrimal canaliculi* or lacrimal ducts drain the lacrimal lake. (Although the term "canaliculus" has been largely neglected in many texts for the B.N.A. term "duct," the former offers the obvious advantage of being not so easily confused with the excretory ducts of the lacrimal gland.) The lacrimal canaliculi begin at the puncta, which are so directed that their orifices face backward, therefore opening into the lacrimal lake. From the puncta the two canaliculi pass at first almost vertically away from the margins of the lids, but after about 2 mm. turn sharply medially, the upper canaliculus then running medially and downward, the lower one medially and upward so that they converge toward the lacrimal sac (Fig. 57). The canaliculi are largest at their bends, where each shows an ampulla; they are approximately 8 mm. long. After piercing the lacrimal fascia, the two canals enter the lacrimal sac either close together or by a common stem; when this common stem is somewhat dilated it is referred to as the sinus of Maier. In their courses the canaliculi lie for the most part behind the medial palpebral ligament and are surrounded by fibers of the pars lacrimalis (tensor tarsi) portion of the orbicularis. Those authors who describe two layers of the medial palpebral ligament describe the termination of the canaliculi as lying between the anterior and posterior lamellae.

The *lacrimal sac* lies in a fossa on the anteromedial wall of the bony orbit, but actually outside of the orbital cavity, since the orbital septum attaches behind

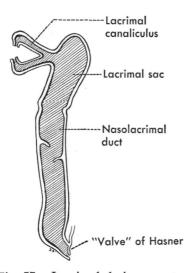

Fig. 57.   Lacrimal drainage system.

it. At the posterior lacrimal crest the periosteum splits into two layers which surround the sac and converge again at the anterior lacrimal crest, these portions of periosteum being referred to as

the lacrimal fascia (Fig. 58). Loose connective tissue in which is embedded a venous plexus lies between the lacrimal sac and the lacrimal fascia; because of this plexus, operations upon the sac may

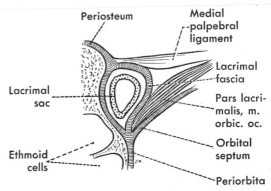

Fig. 58.   Relations of the lacrimal sac in a horizontal section; right side, from above.

be accompanied by considerable bleeding, even though the angular vein has been avoided. Anteriorly, the lacrimal fascia is in contact with the medial palpebral ligament while posteriorly it is in contact with Horner's muscle (and when the ligament is described as U shaped the fascia is then believed to be in contact also with the thin posteriorly reflected limb of the ligament).

The lacrimal sac is approximately 12 mm. long, and its upper end is covered by the medial palpebral ligament; in consequence, abscesses within the sac typically appear below the medial palpebral ligament, where incision should therefore be made for drainage. In approaches to the sac the presence of the angular vein must always be borne in mind. This vessel typically lies close to the side of the nose, although lateral to the corresponding artery (Fig. 55, p. 103), and therefore almost directly anterior to the lacrimal sac; hence the approach to the sac is usually made close to the medial canthus of the eye. The medial wall of the lacrimal sac roughly corresponds to the most anterior part of the middle nasal meatus and that portion of the nasal mucosa (a part of the atrium) lying just anterior and extending inferior to the middle concha of the nose, a fact worth remembering in attempting the intranasal approach to the sac or in searching for the opening of a dacryocystorhinostomy. Its usual relationship to ethmoidal air cells is stated on page 109.

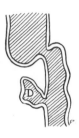

Fig. 59. Side-to-side junction of the lacrimal sac and nasolacrimal duct, making probing of the passage without tearing its mucous membrane impossible. *D* is a diverticulum of the duct. (Redrawn from Schaeffer, J. P.: *The Nose, Paranasal Passageways, and Olfactory Organ in Man.* Philadelphia, Blakiston, 1920.)

Since the lacrimal canaliculi open into the lacrimal sac approximately 2 to 3 mm. below its apex, the sac ends blindly above in a fundus or fornix; below, it narrows gradually or abruptly to be continued as the nasolacrimal duct.

The *nasolacrimal duct*, the connection between the lacrimal sac and the nasal cavity, lies within the bony nasolacrimal canal which is largely directed downward but slightly backward and laterally, lying in the thin bony wall between the maxillary sinus and the nasal cavity. It may be of the diameter of the sac itself, but the junction of sac and duct is typically narrowed; the two may even unite side-to-side rather than end-to-end (Fig. 59), thus making impossible probing of this system without injury to its walls. Within the nasolacrimal canal the duct is closely fused to the periosteum, in contrast to the separation between the lacrimal sac and its surrounding periosteum. The naso-

lacrimal duct terminates by passing through the nasal mucous membrane, usually in a fairly oblique fashion, to open into the inferior nasal meatus. This opening is usually about a fourth of the way back from the front border of the meatus, and according to Costen is more commonly placed quite high, just below the attached border of the lower turbinate. Schaeffer ('12a) has pointed out that the nasolacrimal duct develops by canalization of a solid epithelial cord, and this development undoubtedly explains the not unusual presence of valvelike folds of mucous membrane in this duct. The most constant of these folds, which apparently do not function as valves, is a flap of mucous membrane at the opening into the nasal cavity, known as the plica lacrimalis or "valve" of Hasner. Sometimes the ostium is completely occluded at birth by a membrane, but this usually perforates spontaneously by about the age of 6 months.

Schaeffer ('12b), and others since that time, have pointed out that there is no invariably typical form for the opening of the nasolacrimal duct, but that there are several normal types (see Fig. 134, p. 242). Thus the ostium may be rather indefinite and slitlike and guarded by a fold of mucous membrane, may pass almost directly through the mucous membrane of the nose, may empty into a deep groove, or even open on a raised projection; occasionally also there may be more than one opening. Geddes has reported a case in which the nasolacrimal duct opened into the middle instead of the inferior meatus.

Operations to establish a new communication between the lacrimal sac and the nasal cavity in cases of obstruction of the nasolacrimal duct (dacryostenosis) are designed to take advantage of the findings of Whitnall on the relations of the sac to the ethmoidal air cells. In 100 orbits which he examined, Whitnall ('21a) found some contact between one or more anterior ethmoid cells and the upper half of the fossa of the lacrimal sac in every case, and in more than half of these the whole medial wall of the upper part of the fossa was directly related to these cells; on the other hand, he found that approximately the lower half of the fossa was in every instance directly related to the middle meatus of the nose. Obviously, the formation of new communications should therefore take place in the lower part of the fossa, and preferably in the posterior part of this through the thin lacrimal bone. Rychener has discussed this operation.

The *blood supply* of the lacrimal sac and nasolacrimal duct is from the medial palpebral, dorsal nasal, angular, infraorbital, and sphenopalatine arteries; the veins, similarly, drain both toward the orbit and toward the nose. The *nerve supply* is largely from the infratrochlear branch of the ophthalmic, with twigs to the duct probably also coming from the anterior superior alveolar branch of the maxillary nerve.

THE BONY ORBIT

THE orbital cavities are, for convenience, usually described as being pyramidal in shape, though they obviously depart considerably from this. Under this analogy, the orbital rim represents the base of the pyramid, while the apex is at the optic foramen; the four sides of the pyramid are then the roof, the medial wall, the floor, and the lateral wall (Fig. 60). There are, however, several important deviations from this roughly pyramidal shape: The first is that the widest portion of the orbit is not at the base (the rim of the orbit) but lies about a centimeter and a half behind this, where the lacrimal gland and the greatest circumference of the eyeball are. The second deviation pertains to the medial wall, which, unlike the other walls, is not particularly triangular in shape, but rather quadrilateral. It is also important to note that the apex of the orbital pyramid does not lie di-

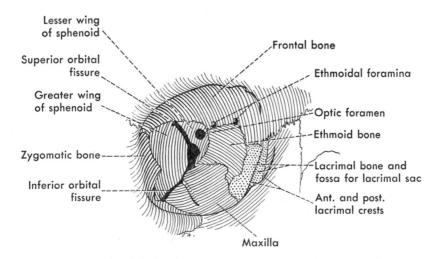

Fig. 60. The right bony orbit, somewhat from the lateral side.

rectly behind the middle of the base of the orbit, but decidedly to the medial side of this; the medial walls of the two orbital cavities are approximately parallel to each other, and therefore the apex (the optic foramen or canal) lies almost directly posteriorly along the medial wall of the orbit.

MEDIAL WALL OF ORBIT

The medial wall of the orbit is formed above by a part of the orbital process of the frontal bone, which also forms the major portion of the roof of the orbit; the remainder of the medial wall (the larger part) is formed by the lacrimal, ethmoid, and sphenoid bones, arranged anteroposteriorly in that order. Of these elements, the ethmoid forms the larger and more important component, this part of the bone being known as the lamina papyracea because of its extreme thinness. It is a common route through which sinus infections produce an orbital cellulitis, for it separates the orbit from the ethmoid air cells, and it is so thin that the outlines of these cells as their walls attach to the lamina may usually easily be seen in dried skulls. Ethmoid air cells typically invade also the lacrimal bone (p. 109), and may likewise invade the frontal, or the frontal sinus may extend backward in the upper portion of the medial wall and in the roof of the orbit. Behind the ethmoid is a portion of the body of the sphenoid bone, where this forms the medial portion of the optic canal; the sphenoid sinus may here be in close relation to the orbit. At the upper border of the ethmoid, on the fronto-ethmoidal suture, the anterior and posterior ethmoidal foramina may be seen. Anteriorly, the lacrimal bone and the frontal process of the maxilla lodge the fossa for the lacrimal sac; as already stated, the upper portion of this fossa is regularly in contact with anterior ethmoid cells, while the lower portion regularly shares a common wall with the middle meatus of the nose.

FLOOR OF ORBIT

The floor of the orbit slopes up on its medial side to join the medial wall, hence no sharp line can be drawn between these two walls; laterally and posteriorly the inferior orbital (sphenomaxillary) fissure may be considered as separating the floor from the lateral wall. The floor is formed primarily by the orbital process of the maxilla, supplemented anterolaterally, in front of the inferior orbital fissure, by the orbital process of the zygomatic, and posteriorly by a small portion of the palatine. Extending forward in the floor of the orbit from about the middle of the inferior orbital fissure is the infra-orbital groove, which transmits the infra-orbital nerve and vessels to their exit on the face.

LATERAL WALL OF ORBIT

The larger portion of the lateral wall of the orbit is the greater wing of the sphenoid bone; anterior to this, at and behind the orbital rim, is the frontal process of the zygomatic, and posteriorly, at the lateral rim of the optic foramen, is a portion of the lesser wing of the sphenoid bone, these bones together separating the orbital cavity from both the temporal and the middle cranial fossae (Fig. 61). A slight projection, the zygomatic tubercle or orbital tubercle of Whitnall, is usually present just behind the orbital margin and represents the area of attachment of the lateral horn of the levator aponeurosis, the lateral palpebral ligament, and the lateral check ligament, which attach in that order, from before backwards (although usually fused at their attachments here). This tubercle was identified by Whitnall in 95 per cent of 2000 skulls.

The greater and lesser wings of the sphenoid are separated by the superior orbital (sphenoidal) fissure, which is also prolonged anteriorly as a partial separation between the lateral wall and the roof of the orbit. The superior orbital fissure leads from the cranial cavity (middle cranial fossa) into the orbit; the inferior orbital fissure forms a communication in its posterior part from the pterygopalatine (sphenomaxillary) fossa to the orbit, while anteriorly it joins the orbit

thin, and lies between the orbit and the anterior cranial fossa above, and the orbit and the temporal lobe of the brain (middle cranial fossa) posterolaterally. The anterior portion of the roof is commonly occupied by a supra-orbital extension of the frontal sinus, the size of which varies considerably. The medial portion of the roof is a favorite route by which mucoceles invade the orbit; it is closely related to ethmoidal cells which may also spread laterally some distance in the roof. At the orbital rim the roof of the orbit presents medially a notch, the supra-orbital notch,

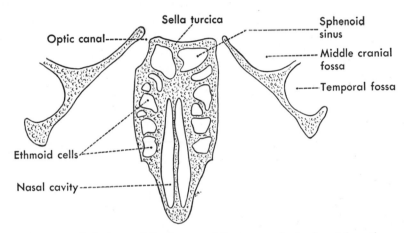

Fig. 61.   Relations of the bony orbits as seen in horizontal section.

and the infratemporal fossa. Anterior to the superior orbital fissure, where the lateral wall blends with the roof of the orbit, this wall is formed by a small portion of the frontal bone.

ROOF OF ORBIT

The roof of the orbit is formed largely by the orbital process of the frontal bone, with the lesser wing of the sphenoid contributing a minor portion posteriorly. Anteriorly, the roof presents in its lateral part a slight depression, the fossa for the lacrimal gland, and medially a more pronounced but much smaller depression, the trochlear fossa. The roof of the orbit is

which in about 25 per cent of individuals is converted into a foramen by ossification of the ligament crossing it. Multiple supra-orbital notches or foramina occur occasionally, and there may be a more medial notch or foramen for the supratrochlear nerve.

ORBITAL RELATIONS

The important relation of the floor of the orbit is to the maxillary sinus, or antrum of Highmore, which lies beneath almost the entire floor; the bone between the orbit and maxillary sinus may be as little as a half-millimeter or less in thickness, and therefore tumors of the antrum may easily invade the orbit. The relationship of much of the lateral wall of the orbit is to the temporal fossa, occupied by the powerful temporalis muscle; historically, this is the route through which optic nerve tumors were removed, and more recently, lateral decompressions of the orbit through this wall have been advocated for exophthalmos. Posteriorly, a rather thin portion of the lateral wall separates the orbital cavity from the middle cranial fossa and the temporal lobe of the brain.

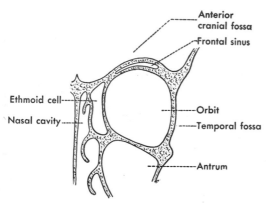

Fig. 62.   Relations of the bony orbit as seen in frontal section.

Since the orbit on three of its four sides comes in close relation to the paranasal sinuses (Fig. 62), it may be affected by infection or other pathological processes within these sinuses; Porter expressed the belief that a large majority of orbital infections, perhaps as many as 75 per cent, originate from infected sinuses. As would be judged by the thinness of the intervening wall, an ethmoiditis is one of the common causes of general infections of the orbital contents. Also, since the walls of the orbit are thin, sharp instruments may readily penetrate these walls and cause abnormal communications between the orbit and the various paranasal sinuses, or, more important still, enter the

anterior or middle cranial fossae and cause damage to the brain. The superior orbital fissure is sometimes the route of an encephalocele or meningocele, which may remain within the orbit or may leave it, by the inferior orbital fissure, to protrude into the pterygopalatine fossa.

OPTIC CANAL

The optic foramen—or better, since it is approximately 4–10 mm. long, the optic canal—is the rounded passageway at the apex of the orbit through which the optic nerve and the ophthalmic artery pass from an intracranial to an intraorbital position; it is formed medially by the body and laterally by the lesser wing of the sphenoid bone (Fig. 60). The walls of this canal thus have an important but varying relationship to the sphenoid sinus and to posterior ethmoid sinuses, depending upon the extent to which these sinuses may have invaded the lesser wing and the anterolateral aspect of the body of the sphenoid. The medial wall of the optic canal is rather regularly adjacent to the sphenoid sinus, unless this is particularly poorly developed, or partially replaced by an ethmoid cell; Van Alyea, in a study of 100 sphenoid sinuses, found the wall of the optic canal actually projecting into the sinus in 40, and Dixon found it projecting deeply, so as to be sometimes almost completely surrounded, in 7 per cent of 1600 skulls. Whitnall ('21a) quotes another worker as having found the sphenoid sinus projecting into the lesser wing of the sphenoid, above the optic canal, in about one third of skulls examined, and refers to the fact that the optic canal may be completely surrounded by the sphenoid sinus, so that it forms a very thin-walled tube passing through the sinus. A similar relationship to a posterior ethmoid cell has been described by

Goodyear, who stated that he has seen complete blindness follow surgical opening of the sphenoid sinus and of posterior ethmoid cells. Less extensive growth of a posterior ethmoid cell may bring it into relation with the optic canal only medially, or, through invasion of the bone between the canal and the superior orbital fissure, inferiorly and laterally; Van Alyea found the canal projecting into an ethmoid cell in 5 per cent of 100 cases. In any case, the bony wall between the cavities of the canal and sinus may be quite thin (0.5 mm. or less), or may even present dehiscences. Vail has pointed out that this wall may also vary in character, as it may be quite dense or may present large spongelike marrow spaces.

THE PERIORBITA AND THE ORBITAL FASCIA

PERIORBITA

THE periosteum of the orbit is usually referred to as the periorbita, but differs from periosteum on the outer surface of the skull only in the fact that it is for the of course continuous with the periosteum on the inner surface of the skull, and therefore with the dura (Fig. 63); in these places, also, the periosteum is rather tightly attached to the bone, as it is also

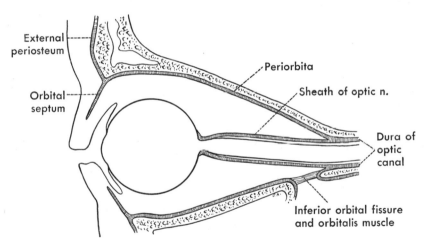

Fig. 63. Periorbita and dural sheath of the optic nerve in a sagittal section of the orbit.

most part rather loosely attached (as is much of the periosteal portion of the dura intracranially), so that it may be fairly easily lifted from the bone by accumulations of blood or pus. Where the orbit communicates with the cranial cavity— that is, at the optic foramen, the superior orbital fissure, and the anterior and posterior ethmoidal canals—the periorbita is at the sutures and deep to the lacrimal gland. At the margin of the orbit the periorbita thickens, and becomes continuous with the periosteum on the external surface of the skull; here also it gives rise to sheets of tissue which are reflected into the eyelids, like curtains, to form the orbital septa, already described in connection with the lids. At the posterior lacrimal crest the periorbita splits to surround the lacrimal sac and form the so-called lacrimal fascia, which at the nasolacrimal canal continues downward as the periosteum of this canal. It is sometimes stated that a thin sheet of periorbita passes on the lower surface of the lacrimal gland, and the gland is then described as being enclosed by the periorbita. This would appear to be a particularly strained description of the periorbita, since in fact the gland can be very easily separated from its bed against the orbital wall.

Posteriorly, about the optic foramen and a medial portion of the superior orbital fissure, the periosteum is thickened as it gives rise to the tendons of origin of the four rectus muscles, which are here fused to form a common tendon, the annulus or tendon of Zinn (Fig. 74, p. 131). The portion of the annulus arising from the rim of the optic canal represents a point of fusion between tendons of origin of the muscles, periorbita, and the dural sheath about the optic nerve. At the annulus, also, the periorbita is sometimes described as being continuous with the fascial sheaths on the muscles; since contiguous connective tissue layers generally are continuous with each other this seems entirely reasonable, but the fascial sheaths of the muscles are so thin posteriorly as to be practically non-demonstrable.

Over the inferior orbital fissure the gap in the periorbita is bridged by connective tissue which contains a quantity of smooth muscle, the inferior orbital or the *orbitalis muscle* (of Müller). It is this muscle that has been held to cause, by its contraction, the proptosis of exophthalmic goiter, though it is doubtful that this theory has any proponents today. Ruedemann, for instance, has pointed out that a very considerable increase in the orbital contents, amounting to approximately 1600 cu. mm., is necessary to move the eyeball forward 1 mm. It is impossible to imagine this muscle, slung as it is across the narrow infra-orbital fissure, causing any appreciable decrease in the orbital space by its contraction; nor is the alternative idea, that it can produce marked congestion of the veins, much more attractive, in view of the collateral circulation available to these veins. It is interesting that unilateral exophthalmos is not necessarily due to an orbital tumor, but may be associated with hyperthyroidism (for example, Hinton).

FASCIA OF THE ORBIT

Orbital fat fills the portions of the orbit not occupied by other structures, but in addition to the fibrous connective tissue permeating this fat there are certain rather definite layers of fascia within the orbit. Each of the muscles of the orbit has a fascial capsule or sleeve; as already noted, this is an histological rather than a gross anatomical feature posteriorly, but anteriorly a thick layer of fascia appears about each muscle as it approaches the eyeball. In the latter location the sheaths of the four rectus muscles gradually spread laterally so as to come in contact with each other, and it is frequently stated that a similar fusion of membranes between the muscles occurs posteriorly; the muscles and their connecting fascia (intermuscular membrane) are then said to separate the fat within the muscular cone from that between the muscular cone and the periosteum. While it is difficult to demonstrate an intermuscular fascial layer in the posterior part of the orbit, there seems to be clinical evidence that such a layer either exists or can be formed by compression of looser tissue, since Wolff states that infections within the cone of muscles do not necessarily spread outside the cone, and cites a case in which exploration of the orbital contents outside the muscle cone failed to reveal intraorbital pus, because this was entirely confined to the muscle cone.

FASCIA BULBI

The thickened sleevelike sheaths around the anterior portions of the mus-

limbus (the sclerocorneal junction). Between these two rings of attachment the inner surface of Tenon's capsule is attached to the sclera only by fine but numerous trabeculae which bridge the subcapsular space (interfascial space of Tenon). When these trabeculae are broken by dissection, the inner surface of Tenon's capsule presents a smooth, almost serous appearance. The outer surface is less distinct, as it receives the heavier

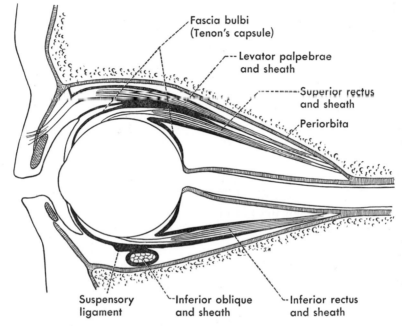

Fascia bulbi
(Tenon's capsule)

Levator palpebrae
and sheath

Superior rectus
and sheath

Periorbita

Suspensory
ligament

Inferior oblique
and sheath

Inferior rectus
and sheath

Fig. 64.   Fascia of the orbit in a sagittal section.

cles give rise to certain ligaments, which will be described later, and the sheaths of all four recti and of the two obliques contribute to the formation of the fascia bulbi, more commonly known as Tenon's capsule (Fig. 64).

Tenon's capsule is a definite fibrous layer intervening between the orbital fat and the eyeball itself; it is attached firmly to the sclera around the point of entrance of the optic nerve posteriorly, and likewise firmly attached anteriorly to the sclera about 1.5 mm. posterior to the

trabeculae from the surrounding orbital fat. While it was once held that the eyeball moved fairly freely within Tenon's capsule, it is now generally accepted that relatively little movement can take place between the bulb and the capsule, and that in most movements the two move together upon a bed of periorbital fat. When the eyeball is removed Tenon's capsule can serve as a socket for the prosthetic bulb used to replace it; it has the additional advantage, in such cases, of moving with the contractions of the orbital muscles, since, as described in the following paragraph, it is continuous with their sheaths.

As the six muscles of the eyeball reach Tenon's capsule their sheaths, well developed in the more anterior portion of the orbit, become continuous with the capsule; essentially, they expand and fuse together to form the capsule, and the tendons of insertion of the muscles then run between the capsule and the eyeball —or, put differently, Tenon's capsule is reflected onto the muscles of the eyeball to form the well-developed fibrous sheaths which surround these muscles as they approach the optic bulb. Thus when the eyeball has been removed from the capsule, the cut ends of the muscles can be seen protruding from individual sleeves of tissue which continue back around the muscles. The interfascial space of Tenon is therefore continuous with the individual spaces potentially present about each muscle, that is, between the muscle and its fascial sheath.

SUSPENSORY LIGAMENT

While the suspensory ligament (of Lockwood) is sometimes described and figured as if it were an entity apart from the fascia bulbi and the sheaths of the muscles which contribute to it, any sharp separation between these three elements seems to be artificial. The central portion of the ligament of Lockwood consists of fused thickenings of the fascia about the inferior oblique and inferior rectus muscles where they cross each other, at which point they are also contributing to Tenon's capsule; similarly, the lateral portion of the ligament represents a fusion between the central portion and the fascia about the lateral rectus muscle, and the medial represents a similar fusion with fascia about the medial rectus. The fasciae over

the medial and lateral recti, in turn, attach to the corresponding walls of the orbit to form the check ligaments.

These various fascial thickenings through their continuity with each other form the hammock-like layer of connective tissue stretching beneath the eyeball from the medial to the lateral wall of the orbit, and known as Lockwood's suspensory ligament. The ligament thus consists (Fig. 65) of fused fasciae of the medial,

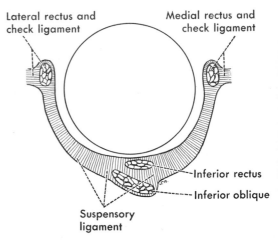

Fig. 65.   The suspensory ligament.

inferior and lateral rectus, and inferior oblique muscles; constitutes also an anterior part of the medial and lateral check ligaments; and is continuous with the inferior portion of the capsule of Tenon. The suspensory ligament is sometimes acceptably described, then, as a bandlike thickening of the lower part of the capsule of Tenon. Sutton has described it from histological studies as a thickening of the inferior orbital septum, a description which is hardly consistent with observations on its gross anatomy. The intimate relation of the dense connective tissue of the suspensory ligament to the inferior oblique and inferior rectus muscles makes recessions and advancements of the tendons of these muscles more difficult.

OTHER EXPANSIONS OF THE MUSCULAR FASCIAE

In addition to their continuity with Tenon's capsule, the fascial sleeves of the muscles of the eyeball also send out certain other expansions, which are for the most part not so well marked. The most pronounced of these are from the fasciae of the medial and lateral rectus muscles, and extend to attach to the adjacent walls

the medial attachment of the orbital septum and the medial horn of the levator palpebrae (but not to the medial palpebral ligament, as the pars lacrimalis of the orbicularis, and the lacrimal canaliculi and sac, intervene). The *lateral check ligament*, said by Sutton to be stronger than the medial, is an expansion from the lateral surface of the lateral rectus sheath to the orbital tubercle on the zygomatic

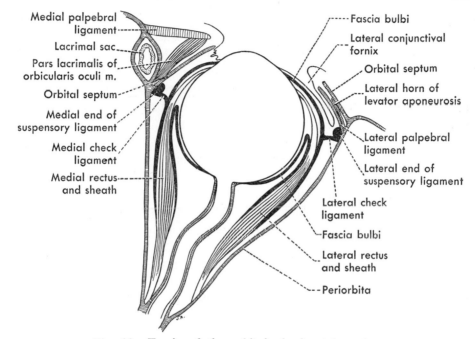

Fig. 66.   Fascia of the orbit in horizontal section.

of the orbit; because they apparently limit the action of the muscles they are named the medial and lateral check ligaments (Fig. 66). Posteriorly, where they are bordered by orbital fat, these ligaments are well defined, but anteriorly and inferiorly they are continuous with other connective tissue at the angles of the eye.

The *medial check ligament* is an expansion of the fascia on the medial surface of the medial rectus muscle, which forms a broad sheet attaching the muscle sheath to the orbital wall just behind the posterior lacrimal crest; anteriorly it is fused with

bone. At its lateral attachment it is fused anteriorly to the lateral palpebral ligament, and through this to the lateral horn of the levator. An anterior portion of each of these ligaments is sometimes described as forming the ends of the ligament of Lockwood but cannot, in fact, be separated from the remainder of the check ligaments. Whitnall notes that these ligaments may contain, occasionally, aberrant strands of voluntary muscle, and that smooth muscle has been described in them by several investigators.

Less marked superior and inferior

check ligaments are sometimes also referred to, but if present are at best ill defined. Frequently a thin expansion of fascia from the upper surface of the levator muscle may be traced upward behind the orbital septum to an attachment to the superior margin of the orbit, but this could hardly be considered a functional check ligament. Whitnall ('21a) describes the superior check ligament as a transverse, bandlike thickening of the fascia on the upper surface of the levator, attached medially to the trochlea and also to the orbital margin where it helps in bridging the supra-orbital notch, and attached laterally also to the orbital margin. The present writer has not personally observed a transverse ligament, although attachment of the aponeurosis to the trochlea is regularly seen. From the relations of the ligament described by Whitnall it would undoubtedly serve as a true check ligament; it seems, however, that the attachments of the levator aponeurosis to the trochlea and through its lateral horn to the wall of the orbit might better serve the same purpose. Since the sheaths of the superior rectus and levator muscles are fused distally, a check ligament from the levator would also serve as a check ligament for upward movements of the eyeball.

A thin expansion from the sheath of the inferior rectus is usually described as passing into the lower lid to insert on the front of the tarsal plate, in a manner similar to the attachment of the levator in the upper lid, and therefore as helping to pull the lower lid downward as the eye moves down; likewise, most of the muscles are said to send thin fascial expansions to attach to the cul-de-sac of the conjunctival fornices, but none of these finer expansions are easily demonstrable grossly. An inferior check ligament, from the inferior rectus, is not usually described, but the fusion of the fascia about this muscle with that of the inferior oblique, and its continuity with the ligament of Lockwood, apparently should afford a definite check to extreme downward movements of the eye produced by the inferior rectus.

The fascial sheath about the superior oblique muscle is continuous with the U-shaped cartilage which forms the pulley for this muscle, and with the ligaments which attach the cartilage to the wall of the orbit. The fusion of the fascia of the inferior oblique to that of the inferior rectus has already been referred to.

The expansions of the sheaths of the muscles to the eyeball and to the walls of the orbit tend to aid the orbital septum in preventing herniation of orbital fat into the eyelids.

THE EYEBALL

A DETAILED description of the anatomy of the eyeball (bulbus oculi) is beyond the scope of the present work; for this the various ophthalmological texts or detailed anatomies devoted to this subject should be consulted. In the present chapter it is possible to deal only with a few major features; the application of some of these, and of others, to surgery of the bulb has been discussed by Fralick.

The eyeball departs slightly from a perfect sphere, its horizontal and vertical diameters being about 23.5 mm. and its anteroposterior one, because of the protrusion of the cornea, about 24 mm. Its most anterior part lies about on a line drawn between the upper and lower orbital margins, but because of the indentation of the lateral margin of the orbit approximately a third of the sphere projects in front of this margin. The eyeball occupies half or more of the total depth of the orbit, which, as measured from the inferior orbital margin to the external optic foramen, is some 44 to 50 mm.

The eyeball is enclosed largely by the capsule of Tenon (fascia bulbi), which surrounds it from the point of entrance of the optic nerve almost to the sclero-

the sclera (connective tissue layer), the choroid (vascular tunic) and the retina or neural layer (Fig. 67). Toward the front of the eyeball the retina becomes rudimentary and with the choroid extends across the cavity of the eyeball, in front of the lens, to form the colored iris with its adjustable central aperture or pupil. In front of the iris and pupil the sclera

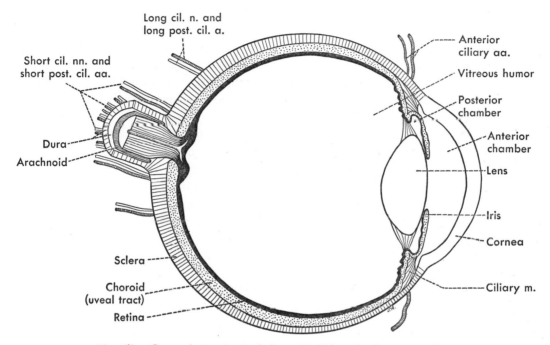

Fig. 67. General structure of the eyeball in a horizontal section.

corneal junction; it is acted upon by six voluntary muscles which pierce the capsule to insert into the outer layer of the eyeball, the sclera. The eyeball perhaps may move very slightly within the capsule of Tenon, but because of the attachment of this capsule to the sclera and to the sheaths of the muscles any appreciable movement of the bulb necessarily must involve simultaneous movement of the capsule also.

In the major portion of its circumference the eyeball consists of three layers, which are from without inward:

is modified to form the transparent cornea.

CORNEA AND SCLERA

Approximately the posterior five sixths of the outer surface of the eyeball is white and opaque and constitutes the sclera, which is continuous anteriorly with the transparent cornea; these parts together constitute the fibrous tunic of the eyeball. The region in which the transition between the sclera and cornea occurs is known as the limbus. Wiener has stated that this is the weakest part of the eyeball, and rupture of the globe, allowing the lens to protrude beneath the conjunctiva, may therefore occur here.

CORNEA

The cornea is more sharply curved than is the remainder of the eyeball, and therefore presents the appearance of a segment of a smaller transparent sphere placed upon a larger opaque one. Refraction of light takes place in the cornea, and it is largely distortions of its curvature which give rise to the condition known as astigmatism. Aside from such distortions, the cornea still does not constitute a perfect segment of a sphere, for it is said to be somewhat more flattened peripherally than centrally. The cornea is thinnest at its center, and thicker at the periphery, varying according to Wiener from 0.8 mm. at the center to 1.2 mm. peripherally; this author has also stated that the cornea becomes thinner with advancing years. Von Bahr reported markedly different findings in measurements on the living eye—an average thickness of 0.565 mm., with a normal variation of from 0.46 mm. to 0.67 mm., and no sex or age difference. The anterior surface of the cornea is covered with an epithelium which is continuous peripherally with the conjunctiva. The small blood vessels supplying the cornea are limited to the region of the limbus, so that the cornea is largely avascular, but it is supplied abundantly with sensory nerves (of pain only), which are derived from the ciliary nerves.

SCLERA

The sclera receives the attachments of the muscles of the eyeball, and is perforated posteriorly by the fibers of the optic nerve, the area of perforation being known as the lamina cribrosa. Wiener has pointed out that the sclera is about 0.6 mm. thick at the limbus, and is thinnest just behind the insertions of the recti upon the eyeball, where it is 0.3 mm. or less in thickness. Behind this point it increases again in thickness and reaches 0.6 mm. at the equator, and 1 mm. posteriorly; at the lamina cribrosa it becomes very thin. Since tendon recessions or advancements offer obvious advantages, and are apparently now preferred, to tenotomies (for instance, Peter) this varying thickness of the sclera is of considerable practical importance. Obviously, slight recessions of rectus tendons involve sewing them to the thinnest part of the sclera.

The *lamina cribrosa* is a thin portion of the sclera which is pierced by numerous holes through which pass the axons forming the optic nerve; it is situated not in the strict longitudinal axis of the eye, but above and medial to the posterior pole of the eye. Around the periphery of the lamina cribrosa the sclera is also pierced by the ciliary nerves and the short posterior ciliary arteries; slightly farther away on the medial and lateral sides of the attachment of the optic nerve the long posterior ciliary arteries pass through the sclera, and still more peripherally, in each of the four posterior quadrants of the eyeball, the venae vorticosae leave the sclera. Anteriorly, the anterior ciliary arteries enter the sclera at the attachments of the four rectus muscles.

Within the eyeball at the sclerocorneal junction lies a ring-shaped canal, the *sclerovenous sinus* or canal of Schlemm, an endothelially lined vessel which is believed to be the chief drainage of the aqueous humor from the anterior chamber of the eye, and which communicates with the anterior ciliary veins. This canal is sometimes regarded as a venous channel, and sometimes as a lymphatic one, although no other lymphatic channels have been recognized in the eyeball.

SCLEROCORNEAL JUNCTION

The sclerocorneal junction, sharply defined macroscopically though said to appear microscopically as an area of gradual

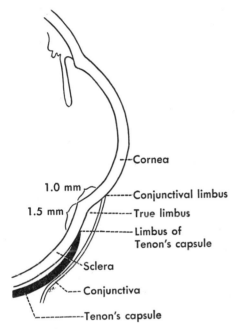

Cornea

1.0 mm — Conjunctival limbus

1.5 mm — True limbus

Limbus of Tenon's capsule

Sclera

Conjunctiva

Tenon's capsule

Fig. 68. Subdivisions of the limbus and the approximate distances between these parts. In the upper half of the figure is indicated the fashion in which the sclera participates in the formation of a part of the wall of the anterior chamber.

transition, is the true limbus. The term "limbus" is sometimes used in a broader sense to include a strip almost 3 mm. wide about the sclerocorneal junction, extending from the anterior attachment of Tenon's capsule into the sclera to the attachment of the conjunctiva on the cornea (Fig. 68); thus Tenon's capsule and the conjunctiva are both sometimes said to attach to the limbus. As the area between these attachments is of particular surgical importance in operative proce-

dures for glaucoma, confusion can be avoided by defining these attachments as the limbus of Tenon's capsule and the conjunctival limbus, respectively, and restricting the unqualified term to the macroscopic sclerocorneal junction (see also p. 100).

VASCULAR TUNIC

The middle, vascular, layer of the eyeball, often referred to as the uvea or uveal tract, consists of three continuous parts from behind forward: the choroid, the ciliary body and iris. The uvea is firmly attached to the sclera in a ring about the optic nerve, and is again attached firmly to the sclera at the sclerocorneal junction; between these two areas of attachment, however, only very delicate connective tissue unites the two layers and the resulting potential space between them is known as the perichoroidal space; it transmits the ciliary nerves and the long posterior ciliary arteries from their entrance posteriorly in the eyeball to the anteriorly situated ciliary body.

CHOROID

The choroid coat, forming approximately the posterior two thirds of the uvea, is deficient posteriorly over the lamina cribrosa, to allow for the exit of the fibers forming the optic nerve, and anteriorly blends with the ciliary body. It consists largely of a plexus of vessels, the finer vessels lying against its anterior surface, adjacent to the retina, and the larger vessels lying in its outer portion. The innermost layer of vessels is known as the choriocapillaris; it nourishes the outer portion of the retina, from which it is separated by a basement membrane (Bruch's membrane). The outer surface of the choroid, the lamina fusca, contains pigmented cells, which are also found in the connective tissue about the larger vessels; the innermost layer of the choroid is generally devoid of pigment.

CILIARY BODY

Anterior to the choroid the ciliary body represents a thickened middle portion of the uveal tract; the ciliary body and the choroid are continuous with each other at a wavy line known as the ora serrata. Like the choroid, the outer surface of the ciliary body conforms to the curvature of the sclera, but as it is traced forward it thickens internally so that in cross section it is triangular in shape. Toward its anterior border the ciliary body is continuous medially with the iris; on its inner surface, from the ora serrata forward, it is associated with the non-nervous continuation of the retina. The ora serrata therefore marks the most forward extension of the nervous elements of the retina; it lies about 8.5 mm. behind the limbus.

The bulk of the ciliary body is occupied by the *ciliary muscle,* the fibers of which run largely in an anteroposterior direction, though some inner fibers are circularly arranged. These latter are said not to be present at birth, and to become well developed only about the fifth year (they, also, have been known as Müller's muscle).

On the inner surface of its anterior portion, but behind the iris, the ciliary body presents a number of prominent longitudinally running ridges, the *ciliary processes,* to which are attached the suspensory fibers of the lens. The ciliary processes consist essentially of venous plexuses continued forward from the choroid; they constitute the most vascular region of the entire eyeball. It is through the more functionally inert posterior portion of the ciliary body (the pars plana), where neither vessels nor muscle fibers are plentiful, that incisions are often made for the removal of intra-ocular foreign bodies.

LENS AND ACCOMMODATION

The transparent lens (crystalline lens) is a biconvex body about 9 to 10 mm. in diameter and 4 to 5 mm. in anteroposterior thickness, the latter varying with focusing of the eye on near and far objects. Although it does not belong developmentally with the vascular tunic, since it arises from superficial ectoderm closely related to the primitive retina or optic cup, the lens becomes closely associated topographically with the ciliary body, and its increase in curvature during accommodation is made possible by the activity of the ciliary muscle.

The lens lies behind the iris, the central portion of its anterior surface being related to the pupil and through this to the anterior chamber of the eye; the peripheral portion of this surface forms a part of the posterior wall of the posterior chamber of the eye (see Fig. 67, p. 119). The posterior surface of the lens, more highly convex than its anterior surface, lies in a concavity of the anterior surface of the vitreous humor, a small retrolental space separating the two. In this position the lens is suspended by a complex series of fibers, collectively known as the suspensory ligament, ciliary zonule (of Zinn), or the suspensory apparatus, individually referred to as zonular or suspensory fibers; these fibers attach centrally to the capsule of the lens, peripherally to the ciliary body, including both the ciliary processes and the pars plana. Some of these fibers cross each other as they pass to their attachments upon the anterior and posterior surfaces of the lens, but they tend to form anterior and posterior lamellae, the irregular space between these lamellae and the periphery (equator) of the lens being known as the zonular spaces or canal of Petit.

The lens is of complex structure, and cannot be described in detail here. The elongated fibers of which it is largely composed have in part a laminated arrangement, but none of them completely encircles the lens; the areas of attachment of the ends of fibers to the ends of others form the lens sutures (stars, rays) visible upon inspection with a slit-lamp. New lens fibers are added to the periphery of the lens throughout life; the older, more centrally placed, fibers form a denser nucleus, while the more superficially placed fibers form the softer cortex of the lens.

Adjacent to the anterior surface of the cortex is the lens epithelium (anterior epithelium). There is no corresponding posterior epithelium, for the cells once forming such a layer are completely converted into fibers. The highly elastic capsule is the outermost layer of the lens, and although varying in its thickness in different locations, forms a complete envelope around the other elements.

Accommodation is an increase in the curvature of the lens which focuses the eye for near vision. It results from a combination of two factors, contraction of the ciliary muscle and the high elasticity of the lens capsule. The soft cortex can be molded by the pressure exerted upon it by the very elastic capsule, but during the resting condition, when the ciliary muscle is relaxed, the capsule itself is under radial tension because of the pull of the suspensory ligament upon it. The lens is then held in a more flattened state through this pull by the suspensory liga-

ment, and perhaps also because of its contact with the vitreous humor posteriorly. Contraction of the ciliary muscle relieves the tension upon the lens, which then becomes more rounded through the inherent elasticity of its capsule. Thus contraction of the ciliary muscle produces relaxation of the lens and accommodation for near vision; paralysis of the ciliary muscle incident to injury to the oculomotor nerve abolishes the power of accommodation.

The exact method by which the ciliary muscle releases the tension upon the lens is not agreed upon; its more numerous longitudinally running fibers have been thought to produce a forward displacement of the ciliary body as a whole, and thus a narrowing of the circumference of the circle from which the lens is suspended; the circular fibers may be thought of as producing the same result through their contraction in a sphincteric fashion. It has, however, been doubted that the choroid can actually be moved forward, and has been suggested that the relaxation of the tension on the ligaments of the lens is due primarily to the thickening of the longitudinal muscle fibers which occurs when they contract. It is the loss of elasticity on the part of the lens capsule or increased density of the cortex, rather than defective function of the ciliary muscle, which is responsible for the hypermetropia typically found in advancing age.

IRIS

Toward the anterior edge of the ciliary body the uvea once again changes its character, and abruptly changes its direction, to become the major portion of the iris. This latter is arranged transversely across the eyeball in the frontal plane, and presents a central diaphragmatic opening, the pupil. Beyond the attachment of the iris the ciliary body is continued forward to the sclerocorneal junction, to which it is firmly attached. The iris therefore lies distinctly behind the sclerocorneal junction. The lens and its suspensory ligament lie on the anterior surface of the vitreous humor, and therefore at the junction of the vitreous and aqueous chambers of the eye; the iris, extending in front of the lens, in turn divides the aqueous chamber into a small posterior chamber, between iris and lens, and a larger anterior chamber between iris and cornea.

The iris is usually believed to contain both circular and radially arranged muscle fibers, which are designated as the *sphincter pupillae* and the *dilator pupillae* muscles; the existence of radially arranged muscle fibers to form a dilator pupillae has been doubted, apparently because (Ingalls) the dilator muscle is composed of peculiar and atypical fibers. The sphincter pupillae is undoubtedly stronger than is the dilator, and probably most of the variations in the size of the pupil are due to variations in the contraction of the sphincter, rather than to activity of the dilator. The innervation of the sphincter pupillae is through the oculomotor nerve and the ciliary ganglion; active dilation of the pupil is controlled by fibers from the superior cervical ganglion via the carotid plexus and the ciliary nerves.

The inner surface of the ciliary body and the posterior surface of the iris are covered by a nonsensory epithelium representing the forward continuation of the retina. The pigment on the posterior surface of the iris is responsible for the blue color of many eyes; additional darkness in the color of the iris depends on the pigment present anterior to this posterior layer. The ciliary body, and sometimes also the iris, are believed to be responsible for the formation of the aqueous humor.

Blood vessels also constitute a considerable portion of the bulk of the iris, and form two circular channels from which numerous radial vessels are given off. At the base of the iris, actually in the ciliary body, is the major vascular circle of the iris (circulus arteriosus major) formed by anastomoses of the long posterior ciliary arteries with each other and with the anterior ciliary arteries. Radially directed branches from this circle run toward the free margin of the iris, close to which they anastomose to form the circulus iridis minor. The minor arterial circle is paralleled by a corresponding venous circle, but the major arterial circle is not.

RETINA

Classic descriptions of the retina usually include ten layers, but there are only three fundamental layers of nerve cells: these are, from without inward, the layer of rods and cones, the layer of bipolar cells, and the layer of ganglion cells. External to the layer of rods and cones is the pigmented epithelial layer of the retina, and internal to the ganglionic layer is the optic stratum, composed of nerve fibers of the optic nerve. Light entering the retina must therefore pass through all other layers of this structure, with the exception of the pigmented layer, in order to reach the layer of rods and cones; this circumstance, which may seem unphysiological, is brought about through the method of development of the retina (Fig. 69).

The anlage of the retina develops as an outgrowth, the optic vesicle, from the central nervous system, and like other typical parts of the central nervous system has its mantle or cellular layer located centrally, about the lumen, while its marginal layer, in which fibers will develop, lies peripherally. When the outer wall of the optic vesicle is invaginated to form the optic cup, the relationship between mantle and marginal layers is not changed, of course, so the marginal layer, even though it forms the innermost layer of the retina, is still between the mantle layer and the external source of light. Thus the rods and cones develop adjacent to the original central cavity,

thinner, there is an increase in the neuroglia, and the retina ceases as a functional layer, although it is prolonged forward over the ciliary body and the posterior surface of the iris as a two-layered epithelium. Posteriorly, at the *fovea centralis,* the retina becomes markedly thin because of the absence of ganglion cells and of most of the nerve fibers, and the rods gradually disappear to be replaced entirely by cones; thus this portion of the retina is most adapted for acute vision. Surrounding the fovea, in the macula lutea, the ganglion cell layer is particularly thick. As the nerve fibers

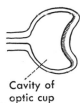

Mantle layer   Cavity of optic cup   Pigmented layer

Fig. 69. The conversion of the optic vesicle into the retina. The mantle layer is shaded; the rods and cones develop in the deeper part of this, next to the cavity of the optic cup and the pigmented layer of the retina.

which separated the neural retina from the pigmented epithelial layer, and it is the optic stratum and its associated vessels which is first presented to light entering the eyeball.

The method of development of the retina also has another consequence of practical importance. The outer, epithelial, layer of the retina becomes firmly attached to the choriocapillaris, the two sharing a basement membrane; however, the original lumen of the optic vesicle is still represented in the retina by a potential slit between the layer of rods and cones and the epithelial layer, and it is through this area of weakness that separation of the retina occurs.

At the *ora serrata* the retina becomes

of the stratum opticum converge to form the optic disc or nerve head (optic papilla), all other layers of the retina disappear, so that the disc is formed entirely of nerve fibers and hence is insensitive to light; its presence is responsible for the blind spot in the visual field. From the optic disc the nerve fibers pass through the lamina cribrosa, become myelinated, and form the optic nerve.

AQUEOUS AND VITREOUS HUMORS

The *aqueous humor* occupies the anterior and posterior chambers of the eye; it has usually been said to contain nothing not found in the blood stream (for instance, Dewey) and therefore has been held to be formed by a process of ultra-filtration from the blood vessels of the ciliary body, and perhaps also those of the iris. According to the experiments of Bárány on the rabbit, however, ultra-filtration plays a minimal role in the formation of the aqueous humor, which is formed entirely or primarily by secretion. The drainage of the aqueous humor, as already stated, is believed to be into the canal of Schlemm and hence into the veins of the eyeball. Increased pressure of the aqueous humor is designated as glaucoma.

The viscid *vitreous humor* lies behind the lens and against the inner surface of the retina. It is formed in the embryo during the stage in which the developing lens receives a branch (hyaloid artery) from the ophthalmic artery; the proximal portion of this branch forms the central artery of the retina, but the distal portion degenerates and leaves an empty canal, the hyaloid (Cloquet's) canal, through the vitreous. The anterior expanded end of this canal forms a retrolental space which may be observed in slit-lamp oph-thalmoscopy (Mann). According to Mann, however, the hyaloid canal is usually displaced inferiorly in the adult, and does not run in the median horizontal plane as so often illustrated. Since the vitreous humor cannot be replaced by the body, its loss during intra-ocular manip-ulations is to be avoided.

BLOOD VESSELS

CENTRAL ARTERY

The blood supply of the eyeball is largely from the short and long posterior ciliary arteries and from the anterior ciliary arteries, but the retina is also supplied by the central artery of the retina. This artery, with its accompanying vein, lies in the center of the distal centi-meter or more of the optic nerve and passes with this nerve through the lamina cribrosa, appearing thus at the center of the optic disc (Fig. 70). From this point the branches of the vessels pass over the retina, embedded in the inner layer of the stratum opticum, adjacent to the internal limiting membrane. The arteries here are distinctly smaller in caliber than the veins, but both sets of vessels are in such a posi-tion as to offer interference to the path of light; neither are distributed directly to the region of the fovea, however, but rather encircle it, their branches proceed-ing somewhat radially toward it. In its course the central artery of the retina gives off branches into the inner layers, but the outer layer, of rods and cones, is devoid of vessels and depends largely for its nourishment upon its close relation-ship to the exceedingly vascular chorio-capillaris of the choroid.

OTHER ARTERIES OF EYEBALL

The arteries to the choroid and the iris are the short and long posterior ciliary and the anterior ciliary arteries. Minute twigs from these also reach the sclera, which is, however, almost avascular.

The short posterior ciliary arteries, arising from the ophthalmic, penetrate the sclera in a ring about the optic nerve and immediately form a plexus in the choroid; the two long posterior ciliary arteries enter the sclera on the medial and lateral sides of the optic nerve, run forward be-tween choroid and sclera to the region of the ciliary body, and here pierce the ciliary muscle to anastomose with each other and with the anterior ciliary arteries to form the major arterial circle of the iris.

The anterior ciliary arteries arise from the muscular branches of the ophthalmic artery to the rectus muscles; according to Wolff the lateral rectus muscle usually furnishes only one anterior ciliary artery, while the remaining three muscles furnish two each. These arteries supply twigs to the sclera and the conjunctiva, and pierce the sclera at the attachment of the tendons of the muscles, subsequently joining with the long posterior ciliaries in forming the

tery of the retina may be regarded as an end artery. According to Scarlett occlusion of the central artery is usually brought about by a combination of arteriosclerosis and a thrombus, and is more apt to occur in the neighborhood of the lamina cribrosa; he has stated that digital massage is sometimes useful in restoring partial vision after such an

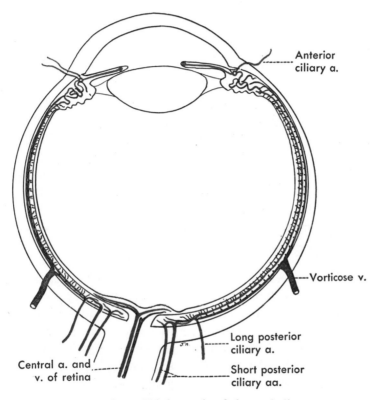

Anterior ciliary a.

Vorticose v.

Central a. and v. of retina

Long posterior ciliary a.

Short posterior ciliary aa.

Fig. 70.   Chief vessels of the eyeball.

greater arterial circle of the iris. As already described, the lesser arterial circle is formed by anastomosis of branches given off from the greater circle.

The two circulations to the eyeball, that of the central artery and that of the ciliary arteries, are completely separate from each other save for very small anastomoses which are said to be present in the region of the nerve head; for practical purposes, therefore, the central ar-

occlusion. Since the outer portion of the retina, the layer of rods and cones, is primarily dependent for its nutrition upon contact with the choriocapillaris, separation of the retina from this layer leads to nonfunction of the receptive layer of the retina; death of this layer does not immediately follow detachment, however, because of diffusion from the periphery of the detached area and from the inner, vascular, portion of the retina.

VENOUS DRAINAGE

The venous drainage from the inner portion of the retina is by means of the central vein, which accompanies the central artery through much of its course and usually ends independently in the cavernous sinus, though it normally communicates with the superior ophthalmic vein and may end by joining this.

The drainage of the choroid is by means of four veins which do not accompany the ciliary arteries, but rather pierce the sclera some considerable distance from the optic nerve; one of these veins appears in each of the four posterior quadrants of the eyeball, being formed by the convergence of veins in a radial fashion; from the manner in which they are formed, they are known as the *vorticose veins* or venae vorticosae; after penetrating the sclera they pass through Tenon's capsule, and in the intra-orbital fat the two superior vorticose veins join the superior ophthalmic vein (or the lateral one may join the lacrimal), while the inferior ones join the inferior ophthalmic vein. Anterior ciliary veins are said to parallel the arteries of the same name; some authors also describe true posterior ciliary veins, but if these are present they are minute, and the venae vorticosae represent them functionally as the drainage of the choroid, and are sometimes called posterior ciliary veins.

True *lymph vessels* have apparently not been demonstrated in the choroid, sclera, or retina, although the canal of Schlemm has sometimes been regarded as a lymphatic channel. The place of lymphatics is apparently taken by indistinct tissue spaces which pass outward along vessels and the optic nerve.

THE MUSCLES OF THE ORBIT

THE seven voluntary muscles of the orbit (Fig. 71) are the levator palpebrae; the superior, inferior, medial and lateral rectus muscles; and the superior and inferior oblique muscles. The smooth musculature of the orbit includes the orbitalis muscle, the superior and inferior palpebral muscles, and the ciliary and iridial musculature within the eyeball, all of which have already been described.

The voluntary muscles within the orbit are supplied by the third, fourth, and sixth cranial nerves: the superior oblique muscle is supplied by the fourth nerve, the lateral rectus by the sixth, while the remainder are supplied by the oculomotor nerve. The palpebral and orbital muscles of Müller are supplied by sympathetic fibers derived from the carotid plexus, and hence from the superior cervical ganglion; so likewise is the dilator pupillae; the sphincter pupillae and the ciliary muscle are supplied by parasympathetic fibers, of which the preganglionic ones traverse the oculomotor nerve to reach the ciliary ganglion, while the postganglionic ones leave the ganglion by way of the short ciliary nerves.

LEVATOR PALPEBRAE

The levator palpebrae superioris arises from the lesser wing of the sphenoid bone just above and in front of the optic foramen, and inserts into the upper lid; while it is not usually included among the muscles which arise from the annulus of Zinn, its tendon of origin is actually blended with that of the superior rectus. The levator receives its nerve supply from the superior division of the oculomotor nerve, this division first supplying the superior rectus muscle and then penetrating the medial portion of the muscle, or passing around this edge, to reach the levator. Paralysis of the levator produces a ptosis of the lid, and, since the tonus of the muscle is responsible for the superior palpebral fold, a disappearance of this fold.

From its origin the muscle extends forward above the superior rectus, lying

ligaments, respectively. Some of the fibers of the aponeurosis also pass in front of the tarsal plate to attach to it here. The two cornua of the aponeurosis blend with the medial and lateral check ligaments as they attach to the orbital wall.

The deep or posterior part of the levator in the lid constitutes the superior tarsal (palpebral) muscle of Müller, a layer of smooth muscle united proximally to the voluntary muscle of the levator, and extending downward and forward to

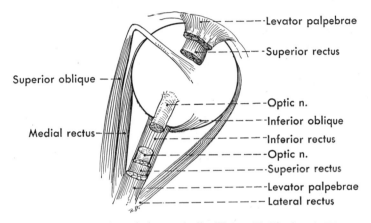

Fig. 71. Muscles of the eyeball. (From Hollinshead, W. H.: *Functional Anatomy of the Limbs and Back*. Philadelphia, Saunders, 1951.)

in close contact with this; after passing the equator of the eyeball it expands laterally and also splits to form two prominent laminae, an upper or anterior and a deeper or posterior (Fig. 50, p. 95). As described in connection with the lids, it is the anterior lamina of the muscle that represents the tendon of insertion and is known as the aponeurosis of the levator. This blends with the connective tissue of the eyelid, fibers also passing between muscle bundles of the orbicularis oculi to reach the skin, and forms a definite lateral and a somewhat less strong medial cornu, which attach in front of the lateral and behind the medial palpebral

attach to the upper border of the superior tarsal plate.

The fascial expansions from the sheath of the levator are described on page 118.

The superior tarsal (Müller's) muscle, as already noted (p. 99), is innervated through sympathetic fibers from the carotid plexus. These are said by Whitnall ('21a) probably to reach the lid by way of the oculomotor branch to the levator, but not everyone agrees that the oculomotor receives a communication from the carotid plexus; alternative routes would be by way of branches of the ophthalmic nerve, which also traverse the cavernous plexus and send sensory fibers to skin and conjunctiva of the lid, or by way of the ophthalmic artery and its branches. Paralysis of this muscle, like paralysis of the levator itself, produces a ptosis of the lid, but, in contrast to paralysis of the levator, no change in the superior palpebral fold.

Through much of its course the levator palpebrae is in direct contact below with the superior rectus muscle. Deep to or behind the lateral horn of the aponeurosis is the palpebral portion of the lacrimal gland, and above it is the orbital portion of the gland, the two parts being continuous around the posterior free edge of the aponeurosis. The trochlear nerve crosses above the levator close to the origin of this muscle, to reach the medially situated superior oblique muscle; the frontal nerve runs above the muscle for a considerable distance in gradually crossing from lateral to medial sides of the orbit; the supra-orbital artery appears on the medial side of the muscle about a third of the distance from origin to insertion, and is thereafter in relation to the upper medial border of the muscle as far as the supra-orbital notch, lying medial to the supra-orbital nerve.

SUPERIOR OBLIQUE

The superior oblique muscle, the longest and most slender of the muscles of the orbit, arises by a thin tendon above and medial to the optic foramen. It is usually described as attaching outside rather than to the annulus. The muscle is fusiform rather than ribbon-like, and becomes tendinous some distance before reaching the trochlea (Fig. 72). The trochlea itself is a small piece of fibrocartilage (Wolff) or hyaline cartilage (Whitnall) shaped like a U and attached by ligaments to the fovea on the frontal

bone; the trochlea and its ligaments are continuous both proximally and distally with the heavy connective tissue sheath of the muscle, of which the trochlea and trochlear ligaments can be regarded as a special development. Because of the necessity of free movement of the tendon over the trochlea, the space about the tendon is particularly well developed and has been said to be lined by a synovial membrane.

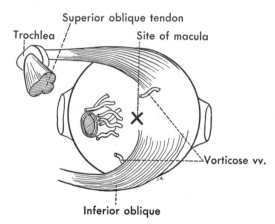

Fig. 72. Superior and inferior oblique muscles from behind and laterally. (Redrawn from Fink, W. H.: *Surgery of the Oblique Muscles of the Eye.* St. Louis, Mo., Mosby, 1951.)

The superior oblique is usually described as consisting of straight and reflected portions, the bend at the trochlea constituting the junction of these. At the trochlea the tendon of the superior oblique muscle is reflected sharply backward, outward, and downward (at an angle of about 55 degrees) toward the upper surface of the eyeball, where it pierces Tenon's capsule, passes between the superior rectus muscle and the eyeball, and spreads out in a fan-shaped insertion on the posterosuperior quadrant of the eyeball. The line of insertion into the eyeball is concave medially and forward, and is largely lateral to the longitudinal axis of the eyeball. As the tendon of the muscle pierces Tenon's capsule, the particularly thick sheath covering the reflected tendon blends with the capsule to help form it.

The superior oblique muscle is innervated by the trochlear or fourth cranial nerve, which runs along its lateral border for approximately a centimeter, giving branches into the muscle. The actions of this muscle are discussed with those of the other muscles of the eyeball.

The superior oblique is in almost direct contact with the periorbita of the roof of the medial wall of the orbit, while inferior to it are the main stem of the ophthalmic artery, after the supra-orbital branch has been given off, and the naso-ciliary nerve; consequently, the ethmoidal branches of this artery and nerve commonly pass transversely beneath the muscle to reach the ethmoidal canals. The supratrochlear nerve lies above and lateral to the muscle for most of the course of these two structures, but crosses above the reflected tendon just lateral to the trochlea.

RECTUS MUSCLES

The four rectus muscles arise from a thickening of the periosteum at the apex of the orbit, where they are placed so closely together that their tendons of origin are at first fused laterally with each other to form a common annular tendon, the annulus or common tendon of Zinn (see also p. 114). The common annular tendon surrounds the orbital end of the optic canal (the optic foramen, or external optic foramen) and a portion of the superior orbital fissure, and is somewhat oval in shape (Figs. 73 and 74). The medial portion of the oval, which is both wider and higher than the lateral, surrounds the external foramen, which it

immediately borders above and medially; below it swings somewhat away from the rim of the foramen. The lateral portion of the annulus extends across the lower portion of the superior orbital fissure, en-

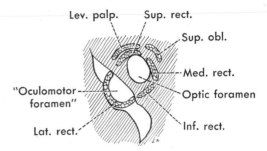

Fig. 73. Origins of the orbital muscles at the apex of the orbit.

closing a portion of this fissure (the so-called oculomotor foramen) within the annulus. From this common origin the recti diverge toward their attachments to the eyeball, thus forming a muscle cone which partially separates the orbital contents into two portions, that lying outside the cone and that lying within it (see also p. 114). The actions of the four recti will

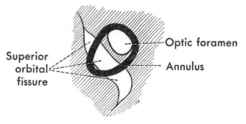

Fig. 74. Relation of the annulus of Zinn to the optic foramen and superior orbital fissure; the latter extends higher and farther laterally than is apparent from this angle. Right orbit, viewed from the front.

be discussed in connection with the actions of the orbital muscles as a whole.

SUPERIOR RECTUS

The superior rectus arises from the medial portion of the upper part of the common tendon, where this borders the upper rim of the external optic foramen; it is here firmly attached both to the periosteum at the foramen and to the sheath of the optic nerve. From its origin the muscle runs forward and somewhat laterally, covered above by the levator, at an angle of about 27 degrees to the anteroposterior axis of the eyeball; in its distal portion it, like the other muscles of the eyeball, is provided with a heavy fascial sheath which blends with Tenon's capsule at the point at which the muscle penetrates the capsule. Within the capsule the superior rectus passes above the tendon of insertion of the superior oblique, to insert into the sclera on a slightly curved, obliquely placed line. The most medial point of this insertion is anterior to the most lateral part, but its midpoint lies about 7.7 mm. behind the sclerocorneal junction.

As quoted by Wolff, the sheaths of the superior rectus and the levator palpebrae are attached by a definite band, in which a bursa may be found, this band insuring the synergistic action of the two muscles. It is usually also stated that fusion of fascia on the lower surface of the levator and the upper surface of the rectus gives rise to a slip which attaches to the superior fornix of the conjunctiva. The superior rectus muscle is supplied by the superior branch of the oculomotor nerve, which enters the inferior (deep) surface of the muscle; the muscle is usually pierced on its medial side by the continuation of this branch to the levator palpebrae.

The upper surface of the muscle is in contact from its origin to Tenon's capsule with the levator palpebrae; on its deep or inferior surface the muscle borders orbital fat, embedded in which lie the ophthalmic artery, the nasociliary nerve and branches of the superior ophthalmic vein.

LATERAL RECTUS

The lateral or external rectus muscle arises from the lateral portion of the common tendon, as this portion bridges the superior orbital fissure, and from the attachments of the tendon to the greater and lesser wings of the sphenoid across the fissure. The annulus here is on the curve of the lateral end of its oval, and from above runs laterally across the fissure to attach to the greater wing, upon which it curves down, then medially once more across the fissure to attach again to the lesser wing. Thus this portion of the annulus completely cuts off a small segment of the fissure, and it is from this part that the lateral rectus arises. The oculomotor, abducens and nasociliary nerves, usually a sympathetic branch from the carotid plexus, and sometimes the ophthalmic vein, all enter or leave the orbit through the part of the superior orbital fissure which is cut off from the more lateral part by the origin of the lateral rectus muscle, and this part is sometimes referred to as the oculomotor foramen (see Fig. 73).

As the attachment of the muscle is curved or bowed around the structures passing medial to it, the lateral rectus is sometimes described as possessing two heads, a superior and an inferior; similarly, the oculomotor nerve and the other structures listed here are sometimes described as entering the orbit between the two heads of the lateral rectus muscle. In reality, the muscle does not actually possess two heads of origin, for there is no separation between the so-called upper and lower heads; rather, the origin of the muscle is simply moulded about the lateral surface of the structures passing through this portion of the fissure.

From its origin, the lateral rectus muscle passes forward in fairly close contact with the lateral wall of the orbit, pierces Tenon's capsule (to which its sheath of course contributes) and inserts into the sclera about 7 mm. behind the limbus, on an approximately vertical line. As already described, the sheath of the lateral rectus muscle sends also an expansion to the lateral wall of the orbit to attach to the orbital tubercle and form the lateral check ligament; inferiorly, as the sheath contributes to Tenon's capsule, it also helps form the suspensory ligament of Lockwood (see p. 116). The lateral rectus is supplied by the sixth or abducens nerve, which traverses the oculomotor foramen (superior orbital fissure), passes upward and laterally between the limbs of the Y formed by the upper and lower divisions of the oculomotor nerve, and enters the lateral rectus muscle on its medial surface, almost at its middle.

RELATIONS AT ORBITAL FISSURE

At its origin, bridging the superior orbital fissure, the lateral rectus is in close relation with most of the structures entering the orbit. Above the upper portion of the tendon of origin the trochlear, frontal and lacrimal nerves enter the orbit, thus lying immediately outside the muscular cone, and usually the ophthalmic vein lies here too. Most of these structures therefore enter the orbit through the most lateral portion of the medial, wider, part of the superior orbital fissure, and lie just above and lateral to the tendon of origin of the muscle. The anastomotic branch between the lacrimal artery and the anterior branch of the middle meningeal artery lies considerably

more laterally, however, usually entering through the extreme lateral part of the fissure or a special foramen just lateral to this.

Through the oculomotor foramen, and therefore in contact with the inner surface of the lateral rectus, pass, in this order from above downward, the upper division of the oculomotor nerve, the nasociliary nerve and a branch from the sympathetic (if this latter is an independent branch), the lower division of the oculomotor nerve, then the abducens and, sometimes, the ophthalmic vein (Fig. 75). All of these structures are crowded together within such a small space that the actual order of their arrangement is really of little practical importance except to the dissector. Below the origin of the muscle, through the most medial and inferior portion of the superior orbital fissure, the inferior ophthalmic vein may occasionally leave the orbit. (The ophthalmic veins may leave the orbit separately or together, and, as indicated above, vary as to the portion of the superior orbital fissure through which they make their exit.)

In addition to the abducens nerve, close against the medial side of the muscle in its posterior third or more, the ophthalmic artery and the ciliary ganglion lie between the muscle and the optic nerve near the origin of the muscle; above the muscle through much of its length are the lacrimal artery and nerve, and more anteriorly the lacrimal gland rests upon the upper and lateral surfaces of the muscle. Below and medially, the branch of the oculomotor nerve to the inferior oblique muscle passes forward in the orbit.

MEDIAL RECTUS

The medial or internal rectus, the largest of the muscles of the eyeball, has an extensive origin from the common tendinous ring medial to and below the optic foramen. Since it arises at the border of the foramen the medial rectus is, like the superior, also closely attached to the sheath of the optic nerve; hence contraction of either of these muscles is more apt to cause pain in retrobulbar neuritis than is contraction of the other ocular muscles.

the orbit, being separated from the lamina papyracea of the ethmoid bone by only a small amount of orbital fat; the superior oblique lies above it, and between the two muscles are branches of the ophthalmic artery and the nasociliary nerve, especially the ethmoidal branches of these. The muscle is innervated by the inferior branch of the oculomotor nerve.

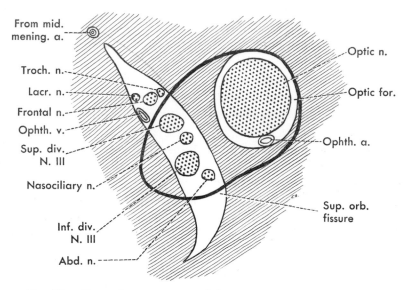

From mid. mening. a.

Troch. n.

Lacr. n.

Frontal n.

Ophth. v.

Sup. div. N. III

Nasociliary n.

Inf. div. N. III

Abd. n.

Optic n.

Optic for.

Ophth. a.

Sup. orb. fissure

Fig. 75.   General arrangement of the structures entering and leaving the back of the orbit. The ophthalmic vein is shown above the annulus, but it or a part of it may pass through or below this.

From its origin the medial rectus passes forward parallel to the medial wall of the orbit to penetrate Tenon's capsule and attach by a tendon to the sclera, the line of attachment being straight and vertical, and also closer to the cornea (5.5 mm.) than that of any of the other rectus muscles. The fascial sheath of the muscle contributes, of course, to Tenon's capsule, forms the medial check ligament (wider but less strong than the lateral check ligament) and contributes to the medial portion of the suspensory ligament of Lockwood.

On its medial aspect the medial rectus is closely related to the medial wall of

INFERIOR RECTUS

The inferior rectus arises from the annular tendon below the optic foramen and passes forward and somewhat outward (at an angle of about 27 degrees) along the floor of the orbit, paralleling the superior rectus in this regard; after penetrating Tenon's capsule it attaches to the sclera by a broad tendon, the line of attachment of which is curved with its convexity forward; like the attachment of the superior rectus, this line of attachment is also obliquely placed in respect to the sclerocorneal junction, the nasal end being farther forward than is the temporal end, but the insertion averaging about 6.5 mm. from the limbus.

The inferior rectus is innervated by the inferior division of the oculomotor nerve, which enters the upper surface of the muscle.

Through most of its course the muscle is separated from the floor of the orbit, and therefore from the roof of the maxillary sinus and the infra-orbital nerves and vessels, by a moderate amount of orbital fat. Lateral to the muscle, and also above its level, runs the branch of the inferior division of the oculomotor nerve to the inferior oblique muscle. As the muscle attains the eyeball it contributes to Tenon's capsule and passes above the inferior oblique muscle, at which point the sheaths of both muscles blend to contribute to the suspensory ligament. The anterior portion of the inferior rectus is so intimately associated with the inferior oblique through common fascial connections that only minimal recessions or resections of the tendon of this rectus muscle are possible.

INFERIOR OBLIQUE

The inferior oblique muscle is the only voluntary muscle within the orbit which does not arise from its apex; the muscle arises from the floor of the orbit just posterior to the orbital rim and lateral to the upper aperture of the nasolacrimal canal, and may arise also in part from the lacrimal fascia over the lacrimal sac. From this origin the muscle passes laterally, backward and upward, following the curve of the eyeball, to pass between the inferior rectus muscle and the floor of the orbit, and reach the posterolateral aspect of the eyeball where it inserts into the sclera under cover of the lateral rectus muscle (Fig. 76). The line of attachment

of the tendon to the sclera is convex above and laterally, its upper portion lying at about the midhorizontal plane of the eyeball, while its lateral and lower portion lies distinctly below this plane. The insertion of this muscle is an external landmark for locating approximately the macula of the eye.

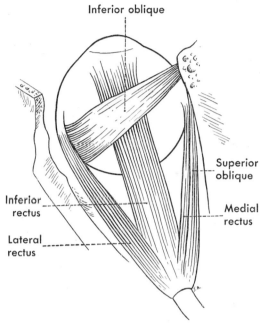

Fig. 76. The inferior oblique muscle from below. See also Figures 71 and 72. (Redrawn from Fink, W. H. *Surgery of the Oblique Muscles of the Eye.* St. Louis, Mo., Mosby, 1951.)

The inferior oblique muscle is supplied by the inferior division of the oculomotor nerve; a long branch specifically for this muscle (but usually close to its origin giving rise to the motor root of the ciliary ganglion) passes forward through the orbit; according to Wolff, it enters the muscle not at its posterior border but rather on its upper surface, near the junction of its anterior and middle thirds. This is, however, variable, for the nerve may also enter the inferior surface of the muscle, or directly into its posterior border.

The sheath of the inferior oblique muscle blends with that of the inferior rectus in contributing to Lockwood's ligament and to Tenon's capsule.

TENDONS OF THE BULBAR MUSCLES

The six extrinsic muscles of the eyeball vary considerably in the length of their tendons of insertion; the superior oblique has the longest tendon of all, extending

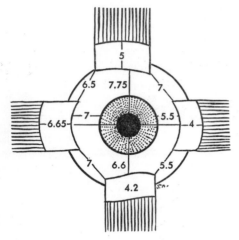

Fig. 77. Attachments of the rectus muscles to the eyeball, with the approximate length (in millimeters) of their tendons, the distance between the tendons, and the distance of the attachments from the limbus, shown on the right eyeball. (Redrawn from Duke-Elder, W. S.: *Text-book of Ophthalmology. Vol. I.* St. Louis, Mo., Mosby, 1938.)

from well behind the trochlea to the sclera, while the inferior oblique has the shortest tendinous insertion, this sometimes appearing to be actually muscular rather than tendinous. The four recti vary among themselves both in the length of their tendons (about 8.5 mm. for the lateral rectus, 5.5 mm. for the superior and inferior and 3.5 mm. for the medial) and in the relation of their lines of at-

tachment to the sclerocorneal junction; the superior rectus is attached farthest behind the sclerocorneal junction (almost 8 mm.), the medial rectus closest to the cornea (about 5.5 mm.) while the lateral rectus is slightly farther from the cornea than is the inferior one (Fig. 77). Thus, beginning with the superior rectus and proceeding laterally around the eyeball, the attachments of the recti lie progressively farther forward. This fact, and the general differences in lengths of the various tendons, are the important points, and absolute measurements should not be taken seriously, since they necessarily vary with the individual. It should be pointed out also that, as would be expected, there is some variation in the lines of attachment of any one muscle on different bulbs —these may be more or less curved than usual, or vary in their obliquity, as well as in their distance from the cornea. The oblique muscles may vary considerably in

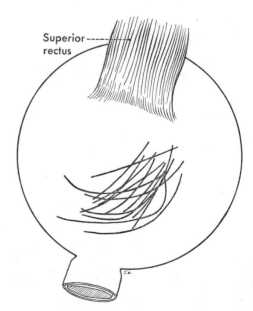

Fig. 78. Variations in the attachment of the superior oblique muscle to the eyeball. (Redrawn from Fink, W. H.: *Surgery of the Oblique Muscles of the Eye.* St. Louis, Mo., Mosby, 1951.)

their attachments to the bulb, as emphasized especially by Fink (Figs. 78 and 79).

ACTIONS OF THE BULBAR MUSCLES

The movements of the eyeball are defined in terms of the direction in which the pupil is moved. Thus "elevation" is directing the pupil upward, "depression" directing it downward; "abduction" is directing the pupil laterally, "adduction"

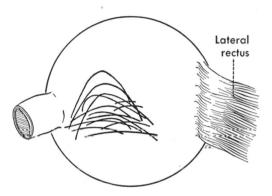

Fig. 79. Variations in the attachment of the inferior oblique muscle to the eyeball. (Redrawn from Fink, W. H.: *Surgery of the Oblique Muscles of the Eye.* St. Louis, Mo., Mosby, 1951.)

directing it medially. Finally, the eyeball may also be rotated around its longitudinal (sagittal) axis, and these movements are defined according to the direction in which the upper part of the pupil moves. Thus "inward rotation" or "inversion" is that movement in which the upper part of the pupil is rotated medially or nasally; "external rotation" or "extorsion" is, correspondingly, a rotation of the upper part of the pupil in the lateral or temporal direction.

In considering the actions of the two obliques and of the superior and inferior recti, care must be taken to distinguish between their active movements as seen

and tested clinically on the intact or partially paralyzed eye, and the slight and relatively passive action which they exert in balancing each other. Both sets of actions are frequently given equal weight in anatomical texts, and can indeed be deduced from the anatomy of the muscles themselves; in clinical practice, however, one rarely observes the action of a single eye muscle, and one naturally tests in the direction of the strongest movement. It is this latter, therefore, that is of prime importance.

ACTION OF SUPERIOR OBLIQUE

The chief action of the superior oblique is to turn the pupil downward. Since the line of pull of this muscle is from the trochlea to the posterolateral aspect of the eyeball, adduction, which turns this aspect of the eyeball farther laterally, increases the distance between trochlea and insertion and therefore increases the strength of the downward movement. Abduction, on the other hand, decreases the distance between trochlea and insertion, and therefore decreases the strength of a downward movement; marked abduction of the eye abolishes the depressor action of the superior oblique. Hence this muscle is always tested by having the patient attempt to look downward *while the pupil is directed nasally*.

ACTION OF INFERIOR OBLIQUE

The chief action of the inferior oblique is to elevate the pupil, or turn it upward. Since the line of pull of this muscle, like that of the superior oblique, is from an anteromedial position on the orbital wall to a posterolateral one on the eyeball, the strength of the movement of this muscle also is increased by adduction, and decreased or abolished by abduction. Hence both obliques are tested by requesting the appropriate upward and downward movements *with the eye in the adducted position.*

BALANCING ACTIONS OF OBLIQUE MUSCLES

Both obliques have additional, minor, actions of abduction and rotation, which are primarily concerned with counterbalancing opposite tendencies upon the part of the superior and inferior recti, and counterbalancing the rotational movements of each other. These are, therefore, actions that would be apparent only if the action of the muscle were unopposed because of widespread paralysis of the other bulbar muscles. Thus the superior oblique tends to produce slight abduction, while the inferior rectus with which it may act in depression tends to produce slight adduction; also, the superior oblique tends to produce internal rotation, while the inferior rectus tends to produce external rotation. The rotatory movement on the part of the superior oblique can be demonstrated in cases of paralysis of the oculomotor nerve (p. 144); the tendency toward abduction is usually masked by the activity of either the medial or lateral recti, and would become fully apparent only when both these muscles are paralyzed—that is, in the theoretically possible case of paralysis of both oculomotor and abducens nerves, with sparing of the trochlear. Since the tendency to abduction markedly lowers the effectiveness of the superior oblique in directing the pupil downward, isolated action of this muscle is largely ineffective in regard to both movements simultaneously, as can be noted in paralysis of the lateral rectus muscle.

The same statements hold true in regard to the inferior oblique, except that it tends to produce abduction and external rotation to counterbalance the tendency to adduction and internal rotation on the part of the superior rectus. In the case of the inferior oblique, even more than in that of the superior, these facts have little clinical application, since it is difficult to imagine an actual case in which only the inferior oblique is spared. So far as clinical observations are concerned, it must be remembered only that adduction increases, and abduction decreases or abolishes, the action of the inferior oblique in turning the pupil upward.

ACTION OF RECTI MUSCLES

Of the four recti muscles, the medial and lateral direct the pupil only medially and laterally; since they are usually symmetrically attached to the eyeball, they have no subsidiary actions. The superior rectus has its chief action in directing the pupil upward, and the inferior rectus likewise has its chief action in directing the pupil downward. Like the obliques, these recti really run somewhat obliquely (in regard to the sagittal plane) and insert obliquely upon the eyeball, and both tend to produce adduction and rotation—the superior rectus tending to produce internal rotation, the inferior, external rotation. It is in these subsidiary actions that the recti are counterbalanced by the obliques. Abduction increases, and adduction decreases, the power of movement of the superior and inferior recti; thus these two muscles are always tested by upward and downward movements *while the eye is well abducted.* In this position the obliques are so shortened that they have no action, and the recti, which are correspondingly lengthened, are the only muscles that can produce these movements.

Similarly, in the adducted position used for testing the obliques, these latter are the only muscles that can produce upward and downward movements, since the action of the superior and inferior recti is obviated by the adduction. Thus it is possible to test inferior oblique and superior rectus (elevators), and superior oblique and inferior rectus (depressors), independently of each other, although both elements composing a pair have exactly the same chief action.

In addition to their actions on the eyeball, the superior rectus presumably aids the levator in elevation of the upper lid and of the conjunctival fornix, through the attachment of its fascial sheath to that of the levator, while the inferior rectus is said to attach to the lower lid and conjunctiva and depress this.

VARIATIONS

Slight variations in the attachments of the muscles of the eyeball are probably fairly common, but major anomalies are at least infrequent. Whitnall ('21b) has recorded variations in a number of muscles, and noted that there may be complete absence of a muscle, absence of the medial rectus being sometimes a cause of divergent strabismus and that of the lateral rectus the cause of some cases of medial strabismus. The levator palpebrae and the superior rectus, associated in action, also are closely associated in their development, and therefore tend to be defective simultaneously. Insertion of the levator into the trochlea, forming a tensor trochleae, is probably the most common anomalous development of the muscles of the orbit, and has been reported a number of times. The levator may also have a transverse belly, and in a case reported by Whitnall ('21b) had a slip inserted into the lacrimal gland. MacEwen described a separate levator of the fornix and other anomalous muscles in an orbit, including an attachment to the lacrimal gland; he also described a case of continuity between the superior rectus and superior oblique muscles at their insertions. Rex described an accessory inferior oblique muscle, and MacEwen stated that he also had seen doubling of this muscle. Whitnall ('11) described a case of a retractor bulbi, a remnant of a cone of muscle attached to the eyeball within the cone of the recti in some mammals, but not frequently found in man; the writer saw such a case during the first dissection of the human orbit he ever made, but has not seen one since. Posey reviewed much of the early literature upon anomalies of the extrinsic bulbar muscles, and reported cases which he himself observed.

NERVES

OPTIC NERVE

SINCE the retina is embryologically an outgrowth from the diencephalon, the optic nerves are not strictly speaking peripheral nerves but rather tracts connecting two portions of the brain, and show this in their morphology. Thus they, unlike any of the other cranial or spinal nerves, contain neuroglia throughout their entire lengths, and are surrounded, from the lamina cribrosa of the sclera inward, by the typical three layers of cerebral meninges and by a cerebrospinal space.

The fibers forming the optic nerve arise from the ganglionic cells which form the innermost cellular layer of the retina and converge upon a point situated slightly above and internal to the longitudinal axis of the eyeball, where they form the optic disc (blind spot, papilla of the optic nerve, nerve head) and leave the eyeball through the lamina cribrosa. As they emerge from this plate they acquire myelin sheaths and become grouped together to

tion in the orbit, running obliquely from the back of the eyeball to the optic canal; after traversing this it converges toward the opposite optic nerve intracranially to form the optic chiasma. At the chiasma, it will be remembered, the fibers from the

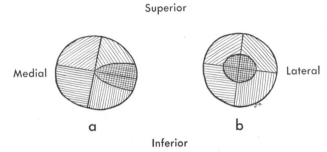

Fig. 80. Positions of the fibers from the macula and the four quadrants of the retina in the optic nerve. *a*. Close to the eyeball. *b*. Well behind the eyeball.

form the optic nerve. Close behind the eyeball, the fibers from the macula lie superficially on the lateral side of the nerve, but proximally they run deeper into the nerve so that they come to occupy the center of it (Fig. 80).

The optic nerve occupies a central posi-

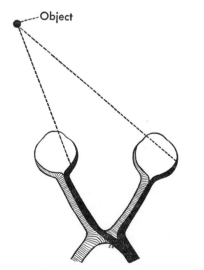

Fig. 81. Illustrating the manner in which visual stimulation from one side of the visual field induces contralateral conduction in the optic tract.

medial or nasal half of each retina cross to the opposite side, joining those from the lateral or temporal half of the other retina, which do not cross, to form the optic tract. It is through this decussation of only the fibers from the medial portion of each retina that it comes about that the optic tracts are physiologically similar to other tracts of the brain, in that they are carrying impulses set up by stimuli originating from the opposite side of the body. For example, pain originating from one side of the body is conducted at least primarily contralaterally in the cord; in a strictly similar fashion, light impulses originating to the right side of the body impinge upon the nasal half of the right retina and the temporal half of the left retina, and it is the fibers from these parts of both retinae that run in the left optic tract (Fig. 81).

SHEATH

As the optic nerves are traced forward toward the eyeball from the optic chiasma they lie at first in the subarachnoid space at the base of the brain, and as each nerve enters and traverses the optic canal it is accompanied by pia, arachnoid, and dura. As on the brain itself, the pia is closely attached to the outer surface of the optic nerve, while the arachnoid forms a looser sleeve about both, being continuous with the pia through arachnoid trabeculae but also partially separated from it by the subarachnoid space.

The dura about the optic nerve within the optic canal is like cranial dura elsewhere in consisting of two layers, an inner dura proper and an outer periosteum for the bone against which it lies; as it emerges from the anterior end of the optic canal, however, its two layers separate; the periosteal layer continues over the walls of the orbit as the periorbita, while the dural layer proper continues forward as a sleeve about the optic nerve, and is usually termed the sheath of the optic nerve. Obviously, the sheath of the optic nerve and the periorbita are continuous at the anterior end of the optic canal, since it is here that they are formed by a splitting of the cranial dura; where the superior and medial rectus muscles attach about the margin of the optic canal these two layers are also continuous with the annulus of Zinn, which arises in the cleft between them. The inferior rectus and the lateral rectus muscles are not attached to the margin of the optic foramen, however, for the inferior rectus attaches both below and in large part lateral to it, while the lateral rectus bridges the medial end of the superior orbital fissure; the line of attachment of the annulus thus corresponds only in part to the point of separation of the nerve sheath and the periorbita, and the inferior and lateral rectus muscles are attached only to periorbita, not to the nerve sheath. Pia, arachnoid, and dura continue forward about the optic nerve throughout its intra-orbital course, ending only at the cribriform lamina of the eyeball, where pia and arachnoid become continuous with each other, and the dura fuses with the sclera and Tenon's capsule.

VASCULAR SUPPLY

The optic nerve is supplied by tiny filaments from the central artery of the retina, from the ophthalmic artery directly, and from the anterior cerebral and internal carotid arteries. The latter two vessels, and intracranial branches of the ophthalmic, are said to supply the intracranial and canalicular portions of the nerve; the proximal portion of the nerve within the orbit is supplied by twigs from various branches of the ophthalmic, while the distal portion is supplied primarily by twigs given off from the central artery of the retina as it pierces the dura, and perhaps from the ciliary arteries. One of the branches of the central artery is regularly described as running retrogradely in the optic nerve to supply this as far back as the external optic foramen.

RELATIONS

The relations of the optic chiasma are discussed in the chapter on the cranium (p. 49). As the optic nerve traverses the optic canal it is accompanied by the ophthalmic artery; this arises from the internal carotid artery just as the latter vessel penetrates the dura, and thus lies inferior to the optic nerve. As the artery runs forward beneath the optic nerve it gradually sinks into the dural floor of the canal, and at the distal end of the canal emerges into the orbit, lying here at first inferior and somewhat lateral to the optic nerve.

Within the orbit the optic nerve is at first closely related to the superior and medial rectus muscles especially, and to a less extent to the inferior rectus, but not at all closely to the lateral rectus. Close to the apex of the orbit the optic nerve is normally (85 per cent) crossed above by the ophthalmic artery which turns upward and medially after having given off its lacrimal branch; only slightly beyond this, it is crossed above, in a lateral to medial position, by the nasociliary nerve, and still farther distally the larger medial branch of the superior ophthalmic vein crosses in the fat between the superior rectus and the nerve. The trochlear nerve, passing from the apex of the orbit to the medial side, is separated from the optic nerve by the levator palpebrae and the superior rectus muscles; the oculomotor nerve, however, is in closer relation at the apex, since it lies only slightly lateral to the optic nerve, separated from it by the ophthalmic artery. The superior and inferior divisions of the oculomotor nerve then separate to run above and below the optic nerve.

Not far distal to this, and still well back toward the apex of the orbit, the ciliary ganglion lies against the lateral surface of the optic nerve, between it and the lateral rectus muscle; from this point forward the optic nerve is surrounded by numerous ciliary nerves and arteries which approximately parallel its course to reach the eyeball. During about the last centimeter or so of its course the optic nerve contains the central artery and vein of the retina, more or less in its middle; proximal to the point of entrance of the artery through the dural sheath the vessel lies in contact with the sheath for some distance along its lower surface, mingled with the ciliary vessels.

In head injuries in which the optic nerve is injured indirectly, it is usually the intracranial portion of the nerve, or that within the optic canal, which is so affected according to Turner. He has said that hemorrhage into the subarachnoid space about the nerve is not a factor, but that it is intraneural hemorrhage or thrombosis which is the usual cause of damage in such cases. Within the orbit the nerve is protected both by the surrounding soft tissues and by its laxity. It is approximately 5 mm. longer intraorbitally than the distance (about 2.5 cm.) between the back of the eyeball and the external optic foramen. Physiologically, this excess length allows unimpeded movement of the globe; surgically, it allows a considerable forward displacement of the globe, in retrobulbar operations, before undue tension is exerted on the nerve.

Because of the close association of the optic canal with the sphenoid sinus and posterior ethmoid cells (p. 112), and the thinness of the bony wall which may intervene between the nerve and the mucosa of the sinus, the optic nerve has been said to be vulnerable to infection from these sources. Strauss and Needles stated that sinus infections have been held responsible for about 15 per cent of cases of retrobulbar neuritis, and Vail quoted a study of 500 cases of disease of the sinuses in which 2.6 per cent presented definite characteristics of retrobulbar neuritis. Ellett also pointed out the relationship between optic neuritis and disease of the sinuses, but emphasized that there are, of course, many causes of this neuritis. Many workers now believe that there is practically never a causal relationship between sinusitis and optic neuritis.

MOTOR NERVES OF THE ORBIT

The three motor nerves to the voluntary muscles of the orbit all enter the orbit through the superior orbital fissure (see Fig. 75, p. 134), but while the oculomotor and abducens nerves enter through that portion (the oculomotor foramen) cut off by the tendinous ring, and therefore lie within the muscle cone, the trochlear nerve enters above the ring and throughout its course lies outside the muscle cone. The trochlear and abducens nerves supply only one muscle each, the superior oblique and lateral rectus muscles respectively, while the oculomotor supplies the remainder. The origins and intracranial courses of these nerves have already been described in the preceding chapter, and need only be summarized here. Their orbital courses and distributions are discussed in more detail.

of course, indicates the very delicate control of eye movements, probably matched by no other muscles of the body.

OCULOMOTOR NERVE

The oculomotor nerve arises from the base of the midbrain, passes between the posterior cerebral and the superior cerebellar arteries, and, running forward and downward through the subarachnoid space, passes lateral to the posterior clinoid process to reach the medial side of the middle cranial fossa and penetrate the dura not far from the posterior clinoid process; having done so, it comes to lie in the lateral wall of the cavernous sinus (Fig. 82). It is at first the most superior

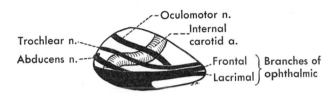

Fig. 82. Arrangement in the cavernous sinus of the nerves of the orbit which traverse this, as seen from above and laterally. The nasociliary branch of the ophthalmic lies medial to the other branches of this nerve, and is not shown.

The nerves to the muscles of the eyeball are remarkable for their relatively enormous sizes in proportion to the sizes of the muscles which they innervate. The abducens nerve, for instance, is said to be the largest nerve in the body in this relationship. Counts and estimates of the total numbers of nerve fibers in the motor nerves to the eyeball, and of the muscle fibers supplied by them, indicate a ratio of approximately one nerve fiber to every three muscle fibers. Even though this comparison necessarily includes sensory fibers in the nerves, since these have never been eliminated experimentally, it nevertheless indicates an exceedingly high proportion of nerve fibers to muscle fibers, and therefore a very small motor unit; this in turn,

of the several nerves running in the lateral wall of the sinus, as the fourth nerve and the upper two divisions of the fifth nerve lie below it here. At the anterior part of the cavernous sinus the oculomotor nerve separates into a small superior and a large inferior division, just before it passes through the superior orbital fissure. At about this point the nerve is crossed on its lateral side by the trochlear nerve, which then passes above it to lie more medially; just distal to this crossing by the trochlear, the oculomotor nerve is also crossed by the ophthalmic division of the fifth, which runs from below upward lateral to the oculomotor and usually here divides into its three major branches.

The trochlear nerve, and the frontal

and lacrimal branches of the ophthalmic, pass above the annulus and are therefore separated from the oculomotor by the lateral rectus muscle, but the nasociliary branch of the ophthalmic passes to a medial position between the two branches of the oculomotor and maintains this relationship to them as it enters the orbit through the oculomotor foramen. At the anterior end of the cavernous sinus the oculomotor nerve also comes in closer relationship to the abducens, which had been lying more deeply in the sinus; the oculomotor nerve at first lies above the abducens, but as the nerves pass through the oculomotor foramen the abducens runs upward and then turns laterally between the two divisions of the oculomotor nerve to reach the lateral rectus muscle.

COURSE WITHIN ORBIT

Within the orbit the *superior division* of the oculomotor nerve passes upward and medially above the optic nerve, paralleling but proximal to the nasociliary nerve, and enters the superior rectus muscle at the junction of about its middle and posterior thirds; the branch to the levator palpebrae continues farther, reaching this muscle either through or around the medial border of the superior rectus.

The larger *inferior division* of the oculomotor divides into three branches to supply medial and inferior recti and the inferior oblique. The branch to the medial rectus passes beneath the optic nerve to enter the muscle on its lateral side at about the junction of middle and posterior thirds; that to the inferior rectus runs forward to enter this muscle on its upper surface in about the corresponding position; the nerve to the inferior oblique is of necessity much longer, and runs forward close to the floor of the orbit, lateral to and slightly above the inferior rectus muscle. Wolff has emphasized that this nerve does not actually enter the posterior border of the inferior oblique, but rather runs across this border to enter the upper surface of the muscle; this relationship is, however, variable (p. 135).

Close to its origin the nerve to the inferior oblique gives rise to the short but stout motor root of the ciliary ganglion (Fig. 83), containing the parasympathetic fibers of the oculomotor nerve; details of this connection will be found in a following section (p. 154). The oculomotor nerve thus innervates all of the voluntary muscles of the orbit except the superior oblique and the lateral rectus, and also, through its branch to the ciliary ganglion, innervates the sphincter pupillae and the ciliary muscle.

INTRACRANIAL INJURY

In its intracranial course the oculomotor nerve is subject to damage through sclerosis or aneurysm of the several arteries related to it—particularly the posterior cerebral and the superior cerebellar, but also the basilar, the posterior communicating, or the internal carotid itself (p. 86). Paralysis of this nerve results in the pupil of the eye being turned laterally, as a result of the unopposed actions of the superior oblique and lateral rectus muscles; the downward movement usually imparted by the superior oblique is minimized in this case by the abduction of the eye.

An individual so affected is unable to look downward, upward, or inward beyond the midline with the affected eye, but if the superior oblique is still intact the eye can be intorted. (Movement of a paralyzed eye to about the midline, owing to reciprocal innervation of the extraocular muscles, has been often affirmed and sometimes denied; as pointed out by Adler, it is useless to study late cases of paralysis to demonstrate such reciprocal innervation, since by that time the unparalyzed muscles have contracted too far to allow proper relaxation.) Also, because of its parasympathetic fibers, paralysis of the oculomotor nerve produces a somewhat dilated pupil which is "fixed," reacting neither to light nor accommodation.

TROCHLEAR NERVE

The fourth or trochlear nerve supplies only the superior oblique muscle, and is

As the trochlear nerve leaves the cavernous sinus and enters the superior orbital fissure (above the annulus) it crosses the oculomotor nerve, passing lateral to and then above it and, as it enters the orbit, bending sharply medially. It courses above the levator palpebrae and enters the upper border of the superior oblique muscle, usually by several branches which are distributed over the muscle for almost a centimeter of its length.

The trochlear nerve may be subjected to pressure from the same vessels as the oculomotor (p. 144). Because of their higher positions in the cavernous sinus, both oculomotor and trochlear nerves are

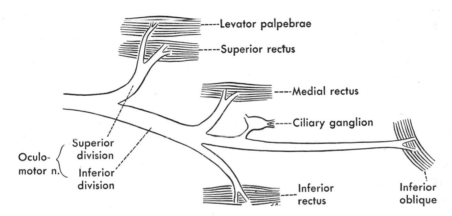

Fig. 83. Schema of the distribution of the oculomotor nerve.

the longest and most slender of the three eye muscle nerves. Arising from the roof of the brain just behind the mesencephalon it runs forward below the level of the tentorium cerebelli to become associated with the inferior surface of this, which it penetrates a little behind the posterior clinoid process. It then runs forward intradurally, thus coming to lie in the lateral wall of the cavernous sinus. In this position the oculomotor lies above and slightly medial to it, while the ophthalmic division of the fifth lies below and slightly lateral to it.

more apt to be affected by enlargements of the hypophysis than is the abducens nerve, which lies in a lower position and is also protected by the presence of the internal carotid artery.

The greatest limitation of movement produced by paralysis of the trochlear nerve is seen when the patient is asked to look downward with the eye adducted; in this position the action of the inferior rectus is minimal, while that of the superior oblique should be maximal. The nerve is not often paralyzed alone, however.

ABDUCENS NERVE

The abducens nerve, like the trochlear, supplies a single muscle, the lateral rectus. It leaves the base of the brain stem at the lower border of the pons and passes forward and slightly laterally to enter the cranial dura over the basal portion of the occipital bone, and then run upward and forward between the two layers of dura. It passes over the anterior end of the petrous portion of the temporal bone (petrous tip), usually crossing superficial to the inferior petrosal sinus to lie lateral to this, and passing with the sinus through Dorello's canal. This canal is the foramen formed by the attachment of the petrosphenoidal or petroclinoid ligament (of Gruber) across the notch at the petrosphenoid joint.

The abducens makes a sharp, almost right-angle, turn over the petrous tip to enter the cavernous sinus and lie against the lateral aspect of the internal carotid artery (not, therefore, in the lateral wall of the sinus). It crosses the vertical portion of the carotid artery in the cavernous sinus, and more anteriorly lies approximately parallel to the horizontal portion of this vessel; as it enters the superior orbital fissure it lies at first below the two divisions of the oculomotor nerve, but immediately passes upward and laterally to run between these two divisions and reach the medial surface of the lateral rectus muscle.

INTRACRANIAL INJURY

The well-known vulnerability of the abducens nerve, evidenced by the fact that an isolated paralysis of the lateral rectus (resulting in an internal strabismus) is a relatively common concomitant of intracranial lesions, especially those accompanied by increased intracranial pressure, is probably due to several different fac-

tors. These have been for the most part discussed in the preceding chapter (p. 85). It was there mentioned that at the point at which the abducens lies in Dorello's canal, it may be subject to injury as a result of infection of the air spaces: if the petrous tip cells are well developed, the nerve may obviously lie in direct contact with the outer wall of such cells and therefore be involved easily in middle ear infections extending to these. The incidence of pneumatization of the petrous tip is not known, but has been reported to be as high as 34 per cent (Hagens) or as low as 11 per cent (Myerson, Rubin and Gilbert).

In Dorello's canal, also, the abducens may be relatively close to the sphenoid sinus; according to Houser this distance may be no more than 2 mm., though it may be as much as 22 mm. In the series of cases in which he measured the distance between the mucosa of the sphenoid sinus and the abducens nerve he found a distance of 2 mm. or less in 5.2 per cent of sinuses and 10.5 per cent of heads, and a distance of 3 mm. or less in 10.5 per cent of sinuses and 15.7 per cent of heads.

Finally, as pointed out by Bucy and Weaver, the abducens nucleus is so located that it is subject to pressure from a cerebellar abscess; in 3 out of 7 cases of such abscess they found paralysis of lateral conjugate movement toward the side of the abscess, due apparently to implication of both the abducens nucleus and the posterior longitudinal bundle. Obviously, there are a number of factors which may account for injury to this nerve.

SENSORY FIBERS IN THE EYE MUSCLE NERVES

While it is perhaps not universally accepted clinically that the third, fourth, and sixth nerves contain proprioceptive fibers from the eye muscles, there is a considerable bulk of uncontroverted anatomical and physiological evidence indicating the existence of such fibers. Endings of sensory type at the musculotendinous junctions of the eye muscles have been described by many authors (for instance, Tozer and Sherrington, Woollard, Tark-

Distal End (Insertion)

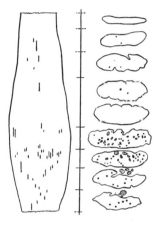

Proximal End (Origin)

Fig. 84. Locations of muscle spindles in the inferior rectus muscle. The nerves in the cross sections are shaded, and in the fourth section up are easily confused with the spindles; comparison with the surface view of the muscle at this level shows that it contains few spindles, however. (Redrawn from Cooper, Sybil, and Daniel, P. M.: *Brain 72*:1, 1949.)

han) and shown to be terminations of the fibers of the eye muscle nerves rather than of the trigeminal.

Daniel has described, in addition to these, a spiraling of nerve fibers about single small muscle fibers, which apparently represents a simple type of muscle spindle, and Cooper and Daniel, in careful studies of human eye muscles, have found numerous typical muscle spindles (Fig. 84). Merrillees, Sunderland and Hayhow have confirmed this finding. Actually,

there seems to be little doubt upon the part of those who have studied this question that fibers of proprioceptive character form sensory endings in the muscles of the eyeball and enter the brain stem as a component of the motor nerves to the orbit; the point of disagreement lies not in their presence, but in the location of their cells of origin.

There are apparently, also, numerous nerve fibers for pain associated with the orbital muscles, for they are very sensitive to stretching—a muscle anesthetized with procaine so that it may be cut without pain may still produce exquisite pain when it is pulled upon. Nothing is known definitely concerning the course of pain fibers from the orbital muscles, but the fact that Abd-Él-Malek produced a rise in blood pressure by stimulation of the central ends of the three motor nerves to the eyeball indicates that pain fibers, like the proprioceptive ones, probably enter the brain stem with the so-called motor nerves of the orbit.

It has long been known that occasional scattered cells may be found along the rootlets of these nerves, and Nicholson has also reported the presence of tiny ganglia on the sixth and third nerves (of man) within the orbit; the largest such ganglion contained about thirty cells and lay on the sixth nerve, while the largest one in connection with the oculomotor contained thirteen cells. Although these cells are probably sensory, they are by no means numerous enough to account for the endings of sensory type demonstrated in the muscles, and therefore it is believed that the majority of ganglion cells associated with these nerves lie intracranially.

It has generally been assumed that the most probable locus of origin for the fibers is in cells of the mesencephalic nucleus of the fifth nerve: this nucleus consists of primary sensory cells which admittedly furnish proprioceptive fibers to the muscles of mastication, and not only does it lie close to the motor nuclei supplying the eye muscles but cells of the type which it contains are also found within the brain stem along the intracerebral course of the trochlear nerve (Pearson, Tarkhan). Tarkhan expressed the belief that he could trace, histologically, large numbers of fibers from cells of the mesencephalic nucleus into both the third and fourth nerves. However, Corbin, Corbin and Oliver, and Corbin and Harrison, were not, in their various experiments, able to obtain evidence to confirm such a localization for the sensory cells to the eye muscles; their evidence indicated, rather, that in the case of the oculomotor nerve at least, the cells of origin of the sensory endings are located close to or in the oculomotor nucleus itself and not in the mesencephalic nucleus.

While it must be admitted that too little is known concerning sensory fibers to the muscles of the eyeball, their presence has thus apparently been demonstrated by everyone who has studied the question. Although it is difficult to believe that the precise adjustments required in the movements of the eyeball could be so nicely carried out in the absence of proprioceptive fibers from the muscles, the practical physiology of these fibers has not been demonstrated experimentally, probably because of the difficulty in separating the motor and sensory fibers in the nerves concerned. In addition to guiding the movements of the eyeball, it may be, as Sherrington suggested, that the proprioceptive fibers may play a part in the perception of depth and space, and it is also conceivable that they may be involved in the initiation of the accommodation accompanying convergence.

OTHER CONNECTIONS OF THE EYE MUSCLE NERVES

In their courses through the cavernous sinus and within the orbit itself the motor nerves to the eyeball are related both to the sympathetic plexus on the internal carotid artery and to various sensory branches of the ophthalmic portion of the fifth nerve. Thus both the fourth and the sixth nerves have been said to receive twigs from the carotid sympathetic plexus in the cavernous sinus, although Koch has stated that only the sixth nerve contains unmyelinated fibers; similarly, fine filaments from some portion of the ophthalmic may reach any of the motor nerves, or there may be an anastomosis peripherally within the orbit with some ophthalmic branch. The physiological importance of such connections is not known; it has, however, apparently been shown that these connections do not furnish sensory fibers which end on the muscles of the eyeball, as was formerly believed to be the case.

VARIATIONS

Variations in the nerves to the muscles of the orbit are apparently rare, but several have been described including occasional penetration of a muscle by a branch of a nerve on its way to some other distribution, communications between the third and sixth nerves, and such anomalous distribution of the nerves as partial supply of the superior oblique from the oculomotor, or replacement of the innervation of the lateral rectus by the oculomotor with absence of the abducens nerve.

OPHTHALMIC NERVE

All three branches of the ophthalmic nerve, a purely sensory branch of the trigeminal, traverse the orbit and have a cutaneous distribution to the face, but only two of these, the lacrimal and the nasociliary, are important in the innervation of the orbital contents. After leaving the semilunar ganglion the ophthalmic nerve passes forward in the lateral wall of the cavernous sinus, between the maxillary nerve below and the trochlear and oculomotor nerves above; just before it

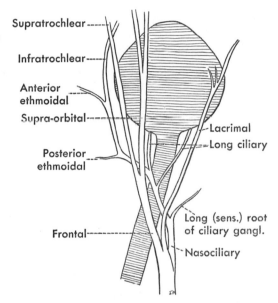

Supratrochlear

Infratrochlear

Anterior ethmoidal

Supra-orbital

Posterior ethmoidal

Frontal

Lacrimal

Long ciliary

Long (sens.) root of ciliary gangl.

Nasociliary

Fig. 85. Course and branches of the ophthalmic nerve in the orbit.

enters the superior orbital fissure the ophthalmic nerve divides into its three main branches (the nasociliary, the lacrimal and the frontal), the nasociliary usually being the first to be given off and the remainder of the nerve then dividing to form the frontal and lacrimal (Fig. 85). At about this point the ophthalmic or its branches cross lateral to the oculomotor nerve to lie above it.

All three of these branches of the ophthalmic then enter the orbit through the superior orbital fissure, but the frontal and lacrimal do so above the common

annular tendon and thus lie outside of the muscle cone, while the nasociliary passes through the so-called oculomotor foramen within the annulus of Zinn. Since the larger terminal branches of both the ophthalmic nerve and the ophthalmic artery leave the orbit through the medial portion of the superior orbital septum, it is in operations in and around the upper nasal quadrant of the orbit that one must be especially alert for these structures.

LACRIMAL BRANCH

The lacrimal branch of the ophthalmic passes through the superior orbital fissure above the upper portion of the lateral rectus muscle and in this position lies lateral to the frontal and trochlear nerves, and above and medial to the ophthalmic vein. It runs forward along the lateral or upper border of the lateral rectus muscle, and in the distal two thirds of this course is joined by the lacrimal artery, the two running together to reach the lacrimal gland. Like the artery, branches of the lacrimal nerve are continued beyond the gland to supply the conjunctiva and, usually, the skin of the lateral corner of the eyelids, where it anastomoses with branches of the zygomaticofacial. Through the anastomosis which the lacrimal nerve receives from the zygomaticotemporal branch of the maxillary nerve, before this leaves the orbit, the lacrimal nerve receives secretory fibers for the supply of the lacrimal gland.

It seems to be generally agreed that, as reviewed by Ruskin, the preganglionic parasympathetic fibers concerned with tear secretion run at first with the facial nerve, and leave this at the geniculate ganglion to form a part of the greater superficial petrosal nerve by which they reach the sphenopalatine ganglion. Postganglionic fibers originating from this ganglion then join the maxillary nerve, leave it by way of the zygomatic and the zygomaticotemporal, and, through the anastomosis with the lacrimal nerve, reach the lacrimal gland. Ruskin has noted that sympathetic fibers from the deep petrosal nerve are also distributed to the lacrimal gland, but whether they are secretory or purely vasomotor is not known. He has also stated that blocking of the spheno-palatine ganglion does not abolish tear secretion entirely, but does markedly reduce it.

Whitnall stated that the anastomotic branch from the zygomaticotemporal has been reported as sometimes missing; however, there are anatomical alternative routes available between the sphenopalatine ganglion and the lacrimal gland, and in such a case one of these may be used. One such route would be via the zygomaticofacial nerve to its cutaneous branches at the lateral corner of the eye, and thence, by way of the anastomosis between this and the lacrimal nerve, recurrently in this latter nerve to the gland.

FRONTAL BRANCH

The frontal nerve, the largest branch of the ophthalmic, enters the orbit through the superior orbital fissure above the lateral rectus muscle where it lies between the trochlear and the lacrimal nerves, the trochlear being above and medial, and the lacrimal inferior and lateral. The frontal nerve passes forward above the levator palpebrae, and close to the roof of the orbit, to divide into its two terminal branches, the supratrochlear and the supra-orbital nerves.

Of these the *supra-orbital* is by far the larger, and continues the direction of the frontal nerve to pass through the supra-orbital notch or foramen and be distributed to the skin of the forehead and of the upper eyelid. As it passes through the supra-orbital notch it supplies a twig to the frontal sinus through the aperture for the frontal diploic vein in the notch. The supra-orbital nerve may divide into two branches before it crosses the orbital rim, in which case these branches are sometimes called the supra-orbital and the frontal, the supra-orbital lying lateral to the frontal according to this terminology.

Upon leaving the frontal nerve the *supratrochlear* passes more medially, toward the medial angle of the orbit; it passes above the trochlea of the superior oblique muscle, usually communicating at about this point with the infratrochlear nerve, and then pierces the orbital septum with the frontal or frontonasal artery to curve upward with the frontal artery and supply skin and conjunctiva of the upper lid, and skin on the lower medial portion of the forehead. At their points of exit from the orbit both supra-orbital and supratrochlear nerves lie deep to the orbicularis and frontalis muscles, and their terminal cutaneous branches pierce these muscles.

NASOCILIARY BRANCH

The nasociliary (nasal) nerve arises from the medial and inferior portion of the ophthalmic; it is intermediate in size between the lacrimal and the frontal and is usually the first of the three branches to be given off. It enters the orbit within the annulus of Zinn, being therefore the only branch of the ophthalmic to lie within the muscle cone; lying first lateral to the oculomotor nerve, between this and the remainder of the ophthalmic, it passes medially between the two divisions of the former nerve at about the level of the oculomotor foramen. Upon entering the orbit it lies lateral and superior to the optic nerve, and in this position is associated with the ophthalmic artery. As the ophthalmic artery crosses above the optic nerve to attain a more medial position the nasociliary nerve does likewise, passing between the superior rectus and the optic nerve, and then running along the medial wall of the orbit between the superior oblique and medial rectus muscles.

Before or after the nasociliary nerve enters the orbit it gives off the *long or sensory root of the ciliary ganglion,* which within the orbit runs along the lateral surface of the optic nerve to reach the upper and posterior part of the ganglion; as the nasociliary crosses the optic nerve it gives off the posterior ethmoidal nerve and the long ciliary nerves.

The *posterior ethmoidal nerve,* which is often lacking (in 4 out of 6 cases, as quoted by Whitnall), runs transversely across the orbit to enter the posterior ethmoidal foramen with the corresponding branch of the ophthalmic artery, and supplies posterior ethmoidal cells and the sphenoid sinus.

There are typically two *long ciliary nerves,* which run forward, usually one along the medial side of and one above the optic nerve, to pierce the sclera medial and lateral to the nerve and be distributed to the eyeball. The long ciliary nerves are largely sensory, but may also contain sympathetic fibers derived from the carotid sympathetic plexus. After giving off these branches, and passing forward along the medial wall of the orbit, the nasociliary divides into its two terminal branches, the infratrochlear and the anterior ethmoidal.

The *infratrochlear nerve* continues the direction of its parent branch to pass beneath the pulley of the superior oblique, and divide into two branches which pierce the orbital septum and the orbicularis oculi to be distributed to the medial portion of the upper and lower lids, to the lacrimal sac, and to the upper part of the lateral aspect of the nose.

The *anterior ethmoidal nerve,* a large and constant branch, leaves the parent stem at almost a right angle to pass through the anterior ethmoidal foramen in company with the corresponding branch of the ophthalmic artery. Through this foramen it gains access to the anterior cranial fossa, where it runs forward along the cribriform plate of the ethmoid bone, outside the dura; it then enters the nasal cavity through the slitlike ethmoidal fissure at the side of the crista galli, and within the nose divides into internal and external nasal branches.

The internal nasal branches are distributed to the upper part of the septum and of the lateral wall of the nose; the external nasal branch runs downward on the inner surface of the nasal bone, passes between the nasal bone and the lateral nasal cartilage, and supplies skin over the lower part of the dorsum of the nose. As the anterior ethmoidal nerve and artery leave the orbit, they are at the level of the cribriform plate, and therefore serve as a landmark for this; they thus indicate the division between that part of the medial orbital wall adjacent to the anterior cranial fossa, and that part adjacent to the nasal cavity.

MAXILLARY NERVE

The major portion of the maxillary nerve, the second division of the trigeminal, also has a close relationship to the orbit. This branch leaves the skull by way of the foramen rotundum to enter the pterygopalatine (sphenomaxillary) fossa, where it has suspended from it the sphenopalatine ganglion; through the ganglion it gives off branches to the nose and pharynx, and the posterior superior alveolar nerves, and it also receives branches from the ganglion. The zygomatic nerve usually also arises in the fossa to run forward parallel to the continuation of the maxillary, hereafter known as the infra-orbital because of its position.

The infra-orbital and zygomatic nerves leave the pterygopalatine fossa by the inferior orbital fissure, and attain the infra-orbital sulcus in the floor of the orbit; they are separated from the orbital contents by the periorbita and the inferior orbital muscle, which bridge the fissure and sulcus. While it lies in the sulcus the *infra-orbital nerve* gives off the middle superior alveolar branch (when this is present) and becomes separated from the zygomatic nerve as this latter diverges laterally. The infra-orbital continues forward to enter the infra-orbital canal, within which it gives off the anterior superior alveolar branches, and then divides into terminal cutaneous branches as it emerges from the infra-orbital foramen. This foramen may often be located, for purposes of local anesthesia, by dropping a vertical line from the palpable supraorbital notch; the infra-orbital foramen usually lies on or just lateral to this line.

The infra-orbital nerve is accompanied in its course by the infra-orbital artery, one of the terminal branches of the internal maxillary; in the pterygopalatine fossa, the artery arises lateral to the nerve; in their infra-orbital courses the relationship varies, for the artery may at first lie lateral but subsequently pierce or cross the nerve to lie medial to it, or may lie medial to it throughout the whole of their infra-orbital courses. In the floor of the orbit the infra-orbital nerve is also in the roof of the maxillary sinus, and the position of the canal may be marked by a ridge on this roof; sometimes the bone below the nerve is deficient, the nerve then lying in contact with the mucous membrane of the sinus.

The *zygomatic branch* of the maxillary nerve, leaving the infra-orbital nerve soon after the two have passed through the inferior orbital fissure, enters the orbit and runs anteriorly and laterally beneath the periosteum, at first just anterior to and about parallel with the lateral limb of the inferior orbital fissure; low on the lateral wall it divides into its two terminal branches, the zygomaticofacial and zygomaticotemporal nerves, which leave the orbit by minute foramina to become cutaneous. While it is within the orbit the zygomaticotemporal nerve gives a branch of communication to the lacrimal nerve along the lateral wall of the orbit (Fig. 86); this branch contains the secretory fibers, derived from the sphenopalatine ganglion, for the lacrimal gland (p. 149).

AUTONOMIC NERVES OF ORBIT

CILIARY GANGLION

Associated with both the oculomotor and the nasociliary nerves is the ciliary ganglion, the parasympathetic ganglion connected with the eyeball. This small ganglion, usually about the size of the head of an ordinary pin, but according to Devos and Marcelle varying in size from about 1×1 mm. to 3×4 mm., lies well back in the orbit (3.5 to 4 cm. from the superolateral orbital brim) between the optic nerve and the lateral rectus muscle, closely associated with the ophthalmic artery or its branches as these lie also lateral to the nerve. It is said to be supplied by a special artery, from a posterior ciliary or other branch. The ganglion is described as receiving typically three

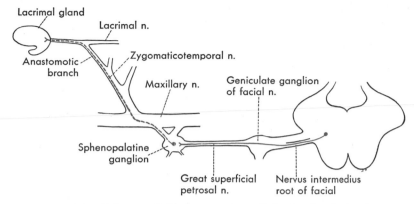

Fig. 86.   Schema of the innervation of the lacrimal gland.

roots, a long, superior, or sensory root (communicating branch) from the nasociliary, a short, inferior, or motor root from the oculomotor, and an intermediate, sympathetic root from the carotid plexus (Fig. 87). Devos and Marcelle, however, found more than three roots in 35 per cent of the specimens which they dissected, owing usually to doubling of the inferior root.

In spite of its several roots the ciliary ganglion is a purely parasympathetic one, which like the other parasympathetic ganglia in the head is traversed by sensory

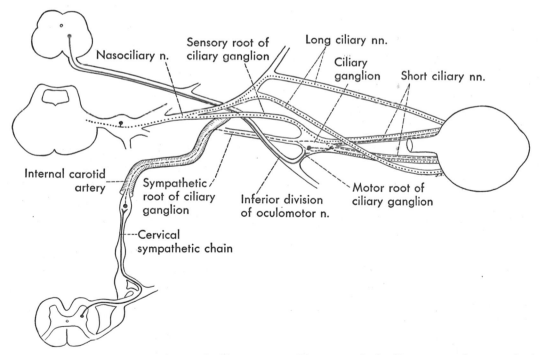

Fig. 87.   The ciliary ganglion and ciliary nerves. Parasympathetic fibers are red, sympathetic ones black, the preganglionic fibers being indicated in each case by solid lines, the postganglionic ones by broken lines. Sensory fibers are indicated by the black dotted lines. To avoid further complications in the diagram, the fact that sympathetic fibers may reach the eyeball by the long ciliary nerves or some other route (see text) is not shown.

and sympathetic fibers so that its branches of distribution (short ciliary nerves) contain both these and the fibers from the ganglion. Scattered ganglion cells or small ganglia may be found along the course of the short ciliary nerves, but beyond these all the parasympathetic fibers are postganglionic.

SENSORY ROOT

The long or sensory root of the ciliary ganglion is derived from the nasociliary nerve either before or after it enters the orbit, and may probably, exceptionally, even take origin directly from the semilunar ganglion (Smith). It may contain sympathetic fibers derived from the carotid plexus by the nasociliary nerve in passing through the cavernous sinus, or may be joined by the sympathetic root of the ciliary ganglion, but otherwise consists of sensory fibers; it enters the ciliary ganglion at its posterosuperior angle. The fibers of this root do not, however, end in the ganglion; since they are sensory or postganglionic sympathetic ones, they traverse the ganglion without synapse and help to form the short ciliary nerves arising from it.

MOTOR ROOT

The motor root of the ciliary ganglion consists of preganglionic fibers which arise from the nucleus of Edinger-Westphal close to the voluntary nucleus of the oculomotor nerve and leave the brain stem with this nerve to make synapse in the ganglion. Sunderland and Hughes expressed the belief that these fibers are often grouped superficially on the superior surface of the oculomotor nerve as it traverses the cavernous sinus. The fibers then run in the inferior division of the nerve; they separate from the branch to the inferior oblique muscle, to form the short motor root to the ganglion. This has been described as absent only when the ganglion was located directly on the nerve to the inferior oblique, and in the real sense is therefore apparently never absent. Devos and Marcelle found it to be double in about a third of the specimens which they dissected, and occasionally triple.

The postganglionic fibers derived from the cells of the ciliary ganglion join the sympathetic and sensory fibers which traverse the ganglion, to form the short ciliary nerves. Within the eyeball they are distributed to the sphincter pupillae and the ciliary muscle; hence, activity of this system produces constriction of the pupil and accommodation of the lens for near vision.

SYMPATHETIC ROOT

The classic description of the sympathetic root of the ciliary ganglion is that it leaves the internal carotid artery in the cavernous sinus, enters the orbit through the annulus of Zinn just below the nasociliary nerve, and joins the posterior border of the ganglion between the upper and lower roots. This root is the most variable of the three in its gross anatomy, and is often not seen in dissections; Devos and Marcelle expressed the belief that it is nevertheless constantly present. Since it arises from fibers of the carotid plexus, it may in some cases join the ophthalmic nerve directly and hence be contained in the long or sensory root of the nasociliary; it is not infrequently found to join this root at a greater or lesser distance from the ganglion.

Devos and Marcelle have also reported that the sympathetic root may not arise within the cavernous sinus at all, but instead may leave the carotid plexus later. They have found it passing through the optic foramen medial and inferior to the ophthalmic artery; they said also that the fibers representing it may form a part of the plexus about the ophthalmic artery, passing to the ganglion where these two are in close apposition; in this case, obviously, the sympathetic root as a gross anatomical entity is lacking, but the fibers are present nevertheless. Like the fibers of the sensory root, those of the sympathetic root merely traverse the ganglion, and make no functional connections with it; upon leaving the ganglion they too help to form the short ciliary nerves.

SHORT CILIARY NERVES

From the anterior end of the ciliary ganglion arise the short ciliary nerves, somewhat variable in number (about four to twelve). These pass forward above and below the optic nerve, mingled with the short ciliary arteries, and diverge slightly so that nerves and arteries practically surround the optic nerve at the eyeball, and pierce the sclera in a circle about this nerve. The short ciliary nerves may have delicate anastomoses with each other and with the long ciliaries. Within the eyeball the fibers of the ciliary nerves run forward between the choroid and the sclera, to reach and supply the ciliary muscles, the iris, and the cornea. The central artery of the retina also brings fibers (forming a plexus, the so-called Tiedemann's nerve) from the ciliary nerves into the bulb.

From the above statements, it should be apparent that while the long ciliary nerves contain only sensory fibers, or sensory and sympathetic ones, the short ciliary nerves contain sensory, sympathetic, and parasympathetic fibers. The sensory fibers of both sets of nerves are derived from sensory cells located in the semilunar ganglion; the fact that they may traverse the ciliary ganglion on their way to the eyeball has therefore no functional significance.

SYMPATHETIC FIBERS

The sympathetic fibers to the eyeball constrict the blood vessels and dilate the pupil; they are derived from the superior cervical ganglion, or perhaps also from smaller ganglia which are known to be located in the sympathetic plexus on the carotid artery while it lies in the cavernous sinus (Gellért), and are therefore already postganglionic fibers as they enter the orbit. While most of them traverse the ciliary ganglion, their connection with this is purely adventitious.

SEGMENTAL ORIGIN

The preganglionic sympathetic fibers for the innervation of the orbit are derived from the upper thoracic segments of the spinal cord, and occasionally also from the eighth cervical segment. In so far as the pupil is concerned, at least, there is apparently considerable variation in the segmental origin of these fibers. Ray, Hinsey, and Geohegan stimulated the anterior roots of the eighth cervical and first five thoracic nerves in 10 patients at operation, and recorded the effects upon the pupil. In 1 case, pupillary dilation was produced by stimulation of each of the anterior roots from C-8 to T-3 inclusive, in 2 cases by stimulation of T-1 through T-4, in 1 case by stimulation of T-1 through T-3, in 4 by stimulation of T-1 and T-2, and in 2 by stimulation of T-1 only. In all of these cases, then, T-1 definitely supplied dilator fibers to the pupil, and T-4 was the lowest nerve so contributing. Whether these observations hold only for the pupil or are true also of the sympathetic innervation of all orbital smooth muscle is not known; according to Hyndman and Wolkin the highest origin of sympathetic fibers to the skin of the face (presumably including that of the lids) is the second thoracic nerve.

DISTRIBUTION

The preganglionic sympathetic fibers to the orbit synapse, for the most part at least, in the superior cervical ganglion, whence postganglionic fibers follow the internal carotid artery into the skull. It is possible, as already stated, that some fibers may pass through the superior cervical ganglion to synapse upon ganglion cells located in the internal carotid plexus; the functional connections of these cells are not known, however, and it has been suggested that some of them may be parasympathetic rather than sympathetic (p. 41). Most of the postganglionic fibers to the orbit leave the internal carotid plexus as the sympathetic root of the ciliary ganglion and are distributed to the blood vessels and the dilator pupillae muscle of the eyeball.

In addition to the sympathetic fibers in the ciliary nerves which are distributed to the bulb, sympathetic fibers from the carotid plexus are also distributed to the smooth muscle of the lids and to the orbitalis muscle. The details of this distribution are not known, but the fibers obviously run in part through the plexus along the ophthalmic artery or by way of some of the connections existing between the carotid plexus and the orbital nerves. Sunderland and Hughes, for instance, described the sympathetic twig to the sixth nerve as running with this for only a short distance, and then leaving it to divide and join the ophthalmic and maxillary nerves—from which sympathetic fibers might reach both lids and the floor of the orbit. The pathway may be quite variable. The orbitalis has been said to be supplied from its inferior surface by a branch from the sphenopalatine ganglion (presumably sympathetic fibers which traverse the ganglion).

Of clinical importance is the innervation of the superior tarsal muscle by the sympathetic, since interruptions of the cervical sympathetic chain produce both a ptosis of the lid and a myosis of the pupil, two of the characteristics of Horner's syndrome. Evidence of paralysis of the inferior palpebral muscle has apparently not been reported.

Interruption of the cervical sympathetic chain has been said also to produce an enophthalmos, due to paralysis of the orbitalis muscle, but this is apparently a false impression caused by the ptosis which does occur. Likewise, stimulation of the orbitalis, through the cervical sympathetic chain or otherwise, was once seriously considered as a cause of exophthalmos. Naffziger has pointed out that cervical sympathetic stimulation in man does not produce exophthalmos, and it is now rather generally agreed that exophthalmic goiter produces its effects through edematous and degenerative changes in the orbital contents (see also p. 114).

BLOOD VESSELS

OPHTHALMIC ARTERY

The ophthalmic artery is the chief blood supply to the contents of the orbit, but is supplemented by orbital branches from the middle meningeal and infraorbital arteries, and through its connection with the facial or external maxillary artery at the inner corner of the eye can supply the orbit when that portion of the internal carotid from which it takes origin is occluded.

It normally arises from the internal carotid just as this vessel leaves the cavernous sinus, therefore just medial to the anterior clinoid process. At this point the artery lies beneath the optic nerve, and runs forward in the dural sheath of this; it may also be at first slightly medial

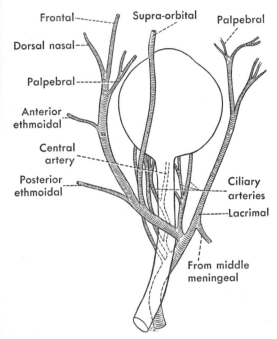

Fig. 88. Course and branches of the ophthalmic artery in the orbit. The variable muscular branches are not shown.

to the nerve, but if so proceeds slightly laterally, gradually pierces the dural sheath, and emerges from the optic canal to lie outside the sheath of, and lateral and inferior to, the optic nerve (Fig. 88). After its entrance into the orbit the ophthalmic artery lies between the optic nerve and the lateral rectus muscle; in this position it gives off numerous small branches which include muscular ones, posterior ciliary arteries, and the central artery of the retina.

POSTERIOR CILIARY ARTERIES

The posterior ciliary arteries are divided into two sets, short and long. The short ciliary arteries are some ten to twenty in number as they reach the eyeball, but may arise from only a few stems. They gradually surround the optic nerve to become intermingled with the short ciliary nerves; running forward with these they pierce the sclera close to the entrance of the optic nerve to ramify in the choroid. The long posterior ciliary arteries, typically two in number but sometimes multiple, also parallel the optic nerve, and pierce the sclera medial and lateral to it, but outside of the circle of the short ciliaries; before or after penetrating the sclera they break up into multiple branches which run forward between sclera and choroid as far as the ciliary body, where they anastomose with the anterior ciliary arteries (p. 126).

CENTRAL ARTERY OF RETINA

The central artery of the retina arises in company with the posterior ciliary arteries from the ophthalmic while this lies inferolateral to the optic nerve, or may arise in common with some of the other branches here; it runs forward beneath the optic nerve and some 10 to 15 mm. behind the eyeball turns upward to penetrate the dura and arachnoid, pass through the subarachnoid space in a short oblique course, and then turn abruptly upward to penetrate the optic nerve and pass (usually) to the center of this. During this course it gives off tiny twigs to the meninges about the nerve.

According to Deyl the central artery of the retina always enters the lower medial surface of the nerve, and not the lateral surface as frequently described; proximal to its entrance, however, it lies more laterally than medially, and can hence frequently be most readily demonstrated in dissections by so rotating the optic nerve as to throw its inferior surface laterally. The course of this artery within the optic nerve and the eyeball has already been noted (pp. 126 and 142).

After giving off these multiple small branches in the posterior part of the orbit, the ophthalmic artery typically turns upward and sharply medially to cross above the optic nerve, thus usually passing between the optic nerve and the superior rectus muscle; in about 15 per cent of cases the artery crosses below the nerve. Before or as it crosses the nerve it gives off the lacrimal artery which runs along the lateral wall of the orbit, and after crossing the nerve gives off a supraorbital branch which accompanies the corresponding branch of the frontal nerve to the forehead. The main stem of the ophthalmic then runs along the medial wall between superior oblique and medial rectus muscles. In this position it is paralleled by the nasociliary nerve, and like this nerve usually gives off branches, the posterior and anterior ethmoidal arteries, which leave the orbit through the similarly named canals. As it passes beneath the trochlea of the superior oblique muscle the ophthalmic artery gives off the medial palpebral branches to the lid, and then divides into its two terminal branches, the frontal (supratrochlear) and dorsal nasal arteries.

LACRIMAL ARTERY

The lacrimal artery usually arises close to the apex of the orbit before or as the ophthalmic crosses the optic nerve; it runs forward along the lateral wall of the orbit, at first within the muscle cone but later leaving this to accompany the lacrimal nerve in the distal part of its course and lie above the lateral rectus muscle; it ends largely in the lacrimal gland. In its course the lacrimal artery supplies small branches to other structures in the orbit, and beyond the lacrimal gland sends twigs (lateral palpebral arteries) to the lateral angle of the eye which may complete the palpebral arterial arches. The lacrimal artery is usually the origin of the muscular branch to the lateral rectus muscle, and may give rise to some of the short posterior ciliary arteries.

The lacrimal artery is connected to the anterior branch of the middle meningeal artery by an anastomotic channel of varying size, which is sometimes referred to as the orbital branch of the middle meningeal and sometimes as the meningeal branch of the lacrimal; this connecting vessel passes through the superior orbital fissure as the most lateral structure traversing this fissure, or through a special foramen lateral to the upper end of the fissure; when it is large it may form the major or the sole stem of the lacrimal artery, which may then be a branch of the middle meningeal rather than of the ophthalmic. More rarely, this connection from the middle meningeal may give rise to the entire ophthalmic artery (Fig. 89) or its major portion (for instance, Musgrove, Chanmugam, and Harvey and Howard).

An anomalous ophthalmic artery may give rise to all of the branches of a normal ophthalmic artery, as seen in a recent dissection by the author; in this case the only trace of a connection between the ophthalmic and the internal carotid consisted of a recurrent twig from the ophthalmic that was lost posteriorly in the dura of the optic canal. In other cases the ophthalmic of carotid origin may be somewhat larger and distribute ciliary branches and the central artery of the retina, while the anomalous vessel gives rise to the larger branches. Except for its lack of relationship to the optic nerve in the optic canal, the relationships of an anomalous ophthalmic artery may otherwise be entirely normal; since it enters the superior orbital fissure it quickly assumes a position lateral to the optic nerve, corresponding to that assumed by a normal ophthalmic artery after it enters the orbit.

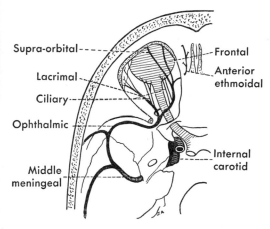

Fig. 89. Anomalous origin of the ophthalmic artery from the middle meningeal. (Adapted from Harvey J. C., and Howard, L. M.: *Anat. Rec.* 92:87, 1945.)

ETHMOIDAL ARTERIES

The posterior ethmoidal artery leaves the ophthalmic to pass medially between the superior oblique and medial rectus muscles (occasionally above the superior oblique) and enter the posterior ethmoidal foramen. It supplies twigs to the posterior ethmoidal cells and to the dura mater over the cribriform plate, and then leaves the cranial cavity to enter the nose and be distributed to the posterior portion of the superior meatus. The anterior ethmoidal artery, typically larger than the posterior but sometimes replaced by it, leaves the orbit by way of the anterior ethmoidal canal to enter the cranial cavity. It supplies branches to the anterior ethmoidal cells, and usually an anterior meningeal artery to the dura of the anterior cranial fossa. It leaves the cranial cavity in company with the anterior ethmoidal nerve and enters the nasal cavity, where its branches supply the more anterior parts of the superior and middle meatuses of the nose, and help to supply the frontal sinus; finally, its terminal branch passes with the external nasal branch of the nasociliary nerve to end in the skin of the nose.

MEDIAL PALPEBRAL ARTERIES

The superior and inferior medial palpebral arteries arise from the ophthalmic by separate stems or by a common trunk at about the level of the trochlea, penetrate the orbital septum (the superior above, the inferior below the medial palpebral ligament) and run across the lids to form the palpebral arches (p. 103); twigs from those vessels also supply the conjunctiva, and the lacrimal sac and nasolacrimal duct.

FRONTAL AND NASAL ARTERIES

The terminal branches of the ophthalmic artery are the frontal (supratrochlear) and nasal (or dorsal nasal) arteries, and the stem of the ophthalmic from which they arise is therefore sometimes referred to as the frontonasal artery. These vessels usually separate from each other behind the orbital septum to penetrate this individually, but may divide after penetrating the septum. The frontal artery passes upward over the superior margin of the orbit to supply the forehead, while the dorsal nasal artery passes above and then downward in front of the medial palpebral ligament to descend along the side of the nose, which it helps to supply, giving off also twigs to the lacrimal sac, and anastomosing with the facial artery.

One or more of the branches of the ophthalmic emerging at the medial angle of the eye (usually the dorsal nasal or the inferior palpebral or both) anastomose broadly with the angular or the angular and nasal branches of the facial (external maxillary) artery. In addition to this larger anastomosis, the smaller branches of the ophthalmic on the lids and the forehead anastomose especially with the transverse facial, the anterior branch of the superficial temporal and with smaller branches of the external maxillary artery and vessels of the opposite side. These numerous anastomoses with branches of the external maxillary account for the excellence of the collateral circulation to the orbit.

Variations in the branches of the ophthalmic artery are frequent, but of no particular importance clinically. In addition to those already cited, they consist primarily in the origin of several arteries from a common stem, or in the separate origin of these from the ophthalmic artery.

INFRA-ORBITAL ARTERY

Also in relation to the orbit is the infra-orbital artery, a terminal branch of the internal maxillary. This artery arises from the internal maxillary in the pterygo-palatine fossa, where it is therefore in close relation to the maxillary nerve. It accompanies the continuation of the maxillary nerve, the infra-orbital, through the inferior orbital fissure and the infra-orbital groove and canal in the floor of the orbit.

It usually lies at first lateral to the nerve, to cross and lie medial to it as they approach the orbital brim, but may lie medial to the nerve even as they enter the fissure. In the floor of the orbit the infra-orbital artery usually gives off small branches which help to supply the fat of the orbit and the inferior rectus and inferior oblique muscles, and may also help to supply the lacrimal gland.

VEINS OF THE ORBIT

The superior and inferior ophthalmic veins, the two major vessels draining the orbit, show even wider anastomoses with the veins of the face than occur on the arterial side; the anastomoses of the superior vein are so well developed that it is frequently said to begin as branches of the angular vein (Fig. 90). These communications are of particular importance since neither the ophthalmic nor the facial veins contain valves, and therefore the ophthalmic may readily conduct infected thrombi from a superficial position in the face, with resultant cavernous sinus thrombosis. The flow of blood from the orbit is probably normally both to the cavernous sinus and to the facial vein (Whitnall). The communications between the angular and ophthalmic veins at the medial corner of the eye are also of obvious importance to the surgeon, as they may be of considerable size.

At the upper medial corner of the eye the frontal vein from the forehead, paralleling the corresponding artery, usually receives the supra-orbital vein which runs transversely along the upper orbital margin; the common stem thus formed then unites with the angular vein, and from this union a branch turns backward through the orbital septum to pass above the trochlea. The angular vein commonly also has a branch which perforates the superior septum to pass into the orbit beneath the trochlea, and the union of these two branches forms the largest stem of the superior orbital vein, which is then joined by tributaries within the orbit.

SUPERIOR OPHTHALMIC VEIN

The superior ophthalmic vein is the larger of the two ophthalmic veins, and, accompanying the ophthalmic artery above the optic nerve and below the superior rectus muscle, surrounded by orbital fat, it receives most of the branches corresponding to the branches of this artery. Close to its origin it receives and in leaving the eyeball at some distance from the optic nerve.

As the superior ophthalmic vein nears the apex of the orbit it usually receives the inferior ophthalmic vein, so that the two veins open together into the cavernous sinus; more commonly the united veins pass through the superior orbital fissure above the lateral rectus muscle, and therefore outside of the annulus (usually lying here lateral to and below the nerves which pass through this portion of the superior orbital fissure) but

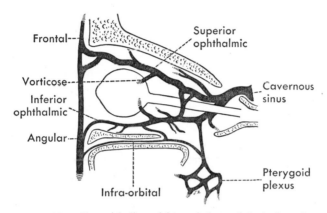

Fig. 90. General disposition of the ophthalmic veins and their chief connections.

a communication from the supra-orbital vein, which in passing through the supra-orbital notch receives the frontal diploic vein. After this, the superior ophthalmic vein receives the anterior and posterior ethmoidal veins, the lacrimal vein, and most of the muscular branches. It also communicates with the central vein of the retina, which is, however, said to open usually also directly into the cavernous sinus. The superior ophthalmic vein also receives the venae vorticosae from the upper half of the eyeball. As described in connection with the eyeball, the venae vorticosae represent posterior ciliary veins, but differ from the corresponding arteries in being less numerous the position of the common vein is somewhat variable and it may pass through the annulus or pass through the lower portion of the superior orbital fissure below the annulus. Also, the superior and inferior ophthalmic veins may empty separately into the cavernous sinus, and may then have different relations to the annulus as they leave the orbit.

CENTRAL VEIN OF RETINA

The central vein of the retina accompanies the central artery through the subarachnoid space, and is here subject to the effects of increased pressure from the cerebrospinal fluid during elevation of the general intracranial pressure. It is generally taught that this is a matter of considerable clinical importance, following the statement by Paton and Holmes, many years ago, that papilledema or "choked disc" associated with increased intracranial pressure is probably due in large part to venous engorgement of the nerve head resulting from a rise of intravenous pressure sufficient to maintain the circulation through the central vein. These investigators also suggested that a second factor in papilledema is obstruction of lymphatic drainage (or, more modernly, tissue fluid drainage) as a result of the increase in pressure within the nerve sheath.

In the dog and cat Gibbs found that the basic pressure in the veins of the nerve head is about 18 mm. of mercury, and showed that alterations of cerebrospinal pressure below this level did not affect the pressure in the veins on the nerve head; when the cerebrospinal pressure was raised above 18 mm., however, venous pressure rose step by step with this, remaining from 2 to 4 mm. of mercury above it. Thus increased cerebrospinal pressure does apparently lead to increased venous pressure.

The problem of papilledema is more complicated than would appear to be indicated by these simple anatomical and physiological facts, however, and is not clearly understood. Thus Dandy has described cases of papilledema, even with hemorrhage into the eyegrounds, that were associated with no increase in intracranial pressure, and Watkins, Wagener, and Brown described papilledema accompanying certain blood dyscrasias.

The central vein of the retina is often described as ending by joining the superior ophthalmic vein at the apex of the orbit, but according to both Whitnall and Wolff it usually ends independently in the cavernous sinus, although regularly communicating with the superior ophthalmic vein. As pointed out by Whitnall, this communication with the superior ophthalmic provides a collateral channel from the retina in cases of thrombosis of the cavernous sinus.

INFERIOR OPHTHALMIC VEIN

The inferior ophthalmic vein lies below the optic nerve and begins by the confluence of small vessels on the floor of the orbit; these in turn may communicate with the facial vein across the orbital rim. It passes backward along the floor of the orbit in the orbital fat, usually having communications with the superior ophthalmic vein, and receives the two inferior vorticose veins and branches from the lower muscles of the orbit. As it passes across the inferior orbital fissure it communicates with the pterygoid plexus. It usually ends, as already noted, by joining the superior ophthalmic, but if it fails to do so it may pass alone through the oculomotor foramen, or lie outside of and below the annulus.

INFRA-ORBITAL VEIN

The infra-orbital vein, when present (it often cannot be found upon dissection), accompanies the infra-orbital nerve and artery in the floor of the orbit, and communicates externally with the anterior facial vein, and posteriorly with the pterygoid plexus. It may also have communications with the inferior ophthalmic vein, and assist in draining structures in the floor of the orbit.

REFERENCES

ABD-ÉL-MALEK, S. On the presence of sensory fibres in the ocular nerves. *J. Anat.* 72:524, 1938.

ADLER, F. H. Reciprocal innervation of the extraocular muscles. *Tr. Am. Acad. Ophth.* p. 205, 1929.

VON BAHR, G. Measurements of the thickness of the cornea. *Acta ophth.* 26:247, 1948.

BÁRÁNY, E. H. The relative importance of ultrafiltration and secretion in the formation of aqueous humour as revealed by the influence of arterial blood pressure on the osmotic pressure of the aqueous. *Acta physiol. Scandinav.* 13:81, 1947.

BUCY, P. C., and WEAVER, T. A., JR. Paralysis of conjugate lateral movement of the eyes in association with cerebellar abscess. *Arch. Surg.* 42:839, 1941.

BURCH, G. E. Superficial lymphatics of human eyelids observed by injection in vivo. *Anat. Rec.* 73:443, 1939.

CHANMUGAM, P. K. Note on an unusual ophthalmic artery associated with other abnormalities. *J. Anat.* 70:580, 1936.

COOPER, SYBIL, and DANIEL, P. M. Muscle spindles in human extrinsic eye muscles. *Brain.* 72:1, 1949.

CORBIN, K. B. Observations on the peripheral distribution of fibers arising in the mesencephalic nucleus of the fifth cranial nerve. *J. Comp. Neurol.* 73:153, 1940.

CORBIN, K. B., and HARRISON, F. Further attempts to trace the origin of afferent nerves to the extrinsic eye muscles. *J. Comp. Neurol.* 77:187, 1942.

CORBIN, K. B., and OLIVER, R. K. The origin of fibers to the grape-like endings in the insertion third of the extra-ocular muscles. *J. Comp. Neurol.* 77:171, 1942.

COSTEN, J. B. Anatomic phases involved in the surgery of the naso-antral wall and the floor of the mouth. *Ann. Otol., Rhin. & Laryng.* 41:820, 1932.

DANIEL, P. Spiral nerve endings in the extrinsic eye muscles of man. *J. Anat.* 80:189, 1946.

DANDY, W. E. Papilledema without intracranial pressure (optic neuritis). *Ann. Surg.* 110:161, 1939.

DEVOS, L., and MARCELLE, R. Variations morphologiques du ganglion et des nerfs ciliaires. *Arch. d'anat., d'histol. et d'embryol.* 27:277, 1939.

DEWEY, KAETHE W. A contribution to the study of the lymphatic system of the eye. *Anat. Rec.* 19:125, 1920.

DEYL, J. Ueber den Eintritt der Arteria centralis retinae in den Sehnerv beim Menschen. *Anat. Anz.* 11:687, 1896.

DIXON, F. W. A comparative study of the sphenoid sinus: A study of 1600 skulls. *Ann. Otol., Rhin. & Laryng.* 46:687, 1937.

DUKE-ELDER, W. S. *Text-Book of Ophthalmology.* St. Louis, Mosby, 1938, vol. 1.

ELLETT, E. C. The relative importance of disease of the nasal sinuses as a cause of disease of the optic nerves. *Arch. Otolaryng.* 10:49, 1929.

FINK, W. H. *Surgery of the Oblique Muscles of the Eye.* St. Louis, Mosby, 1951.

FRALICK, F. B. Surgical anatomy of the eye. *Surg. Gynec. & Obst.* 74:589, 1942.

GEDDES, A. C. An abnormal nasal duct. *Anat. Anz.* 37:5, 1910.

GELLÉRT, A. Ganglia of the internal carotid plexus. *J. Anat.* 68:318, 1934.

GIBBS, F. A. Relationship between the pressure in the veins on the nerve head and the cerebrospinal fluid pressure. *Arch. Neurol. & Psychiat.* 35:292, 1936.

GOODYEAR, H. M. Ophthalmic conditions referable to diseases of the paranasal sinuses. *Arch. Otolaryng.* 48:202, 1948.

HAGENS, E. W. Anatomy and pathology of the petrous bone: Based on a study of fifty temporal bones. *Arch. Otolaryng.* 19:556, 1934.

HARVEY, J. C., and HOWARD, L. M. A rare type of anomalous ophthalmic artery in a Negro. *Anat. Rec.* 92:87, 1945.

HINTON, J. W. Unilateral exophthalmos. *Ann. Surg.* 100:1184, 1934.

HOLLINSHEAD, W. H. *Functional Anatomy of the Limbs and Back: A Text for Students of Physical Therapy and Others Interested in the Locomotor Apparatus.* Philadelphia, Saunders, 1951.

HOUSER, K. M. Anatomic relation of the sphenoid sinus to Dorello's canal: Abducens paralysis. *Arch. Otolaryng.* 16:488, 1932.

HYNDMAN, O. R., and WOLKIN, J. Sympathectomy of the upper extremity: Evidence that only the second dorsal ganglion need be removed for complete sympathectomy. *Arch. Surg. 45:*145, 1942.

INGALLS, N. W. The dilatator pupillae and the sympathetic. *J. Comp. Neurol. 35:*163, 1923.

KOCH, S. L. The structure of the third, fourth, fifth, sixth, ninth, eleventh and twelfth cranial nerves. *J. Comp. Neurol. 26:*541, 1916.

MACEWEN, E. M. Orbital variations. *Anat. Rec. 46:*223, 1930.

MAHONEY, W., and SHEEHAN, D. Experimental ptosis in primates. *Arch. Neurol. & Psychiat. 35:*99, 1936.

MANN, IDA C. The relations of the hyaloid canal in the foetus and in the adult. *J. Anat. 62:*290, 1928.

MERRILLEES, N. C. R., SUNDERLAND, S., and HAYHOW, W. Neuromuscular spindles in the extraocular muscles in man. *Anat. Rec. 108:*23, 1950.

MOST, A. Ueber die Lymphgefässe und die regionären Lymphdrüsen der Bindehaut und der Lidder des Auges. *Arch. f. Anat. u. Physiol.,* p. 96, 1905.

MUSGROVE, J. Origin of ophthalmic artery from the middle meningeal. *J. Anat. & Physiol. 27:*279, 1893.

MYERSON, M. C., RUBIN, H., and GILBERT, J. G. Anatomic studies of the petrous portion of the temporal bone. *Arch. Otolaryng. 20:*195, 1934.

NAFFZIGER, H. C. Progressive exophthalmos associated with disorders of the thyroid gland. *Ann. Surg. 108:*529, 1938.

NICHOLSON, HELEN On the presence of ganglion cells in the third and sixth nerves of man. *J. Comp. Neurol. 37:*31, 1924.

PATON, L., and HOLMES, G. The pathology of papilloedema: A histological study of sixty eyes. *Brain. 33:*389, 1910.

PEARSON, A. A. The trochlear nerve in human fetuses. *J. Comp. Neurol. 78:*29, 1943.

PETER, L. C. Present status of tendon transplantation of the ocular muscles. *Am. J. Surg. n.s. 42:*30, 1938.

PORTER, C. T. The etiology and treatment of orbital infection. *Ann. Otol., Rhin. & Laryng. 41:*1136, 1932.

POSEY, W. C. Concerning some gross structural anomalies of the muscles of the eye and its adnexa. *Tr. Am. Acad. Ophth. 28:* 243, 1923.

RAY, B. S., HINSEY, J. C., and GEOHEGAN, W. A. Observations on the distribution of the sympathetic fibers to the pupil and upper extremity as determined by stimulation of the anterior roots in man. *Ann. Surg. 118:* 647, 1943.

REX, H. Über einen abnormen Augenmuskel (Musc. obliquus accessorius inferior). *Anat. Anz. 2:*625, 1887.

RUEDEMANN, A. D. Exophthalmos. *Ann. Otol., Rhin. & Laryng. 50:*1064, 1941.

RUSKIN, S. L. Control of tearing by blocking the nasal ganglion. *Arch. Ophth. n.s. 4:* 208, 1930.

RYCHENER, R. O. The present status of surgery of the lacrimal sac. *Surg., Gynec. & Obst. 68:*414, 1939.

SCARLETT, H. Occlusion of the central artery of the retina. *Ann. Surg. 101:*318, 1935.

SCHAEFFER, J. P. The genesis and development of the nasolacrimal passages in man. *Am. J. Anat. 13:*1, 1912a.

SCHAEFFER, J. P. Types of ostia nasolacrimalia in man and their genetic significance. *Am. J. Anat. 13:*183, 1912b.

SCHAEFFER, J. P. *The Nose, Paranasal Sinuses, Nasolacrimal Passageways, and Olfactory Organ in Man: A Genetic, Developmental, and Anatomico-Physiological Consideration.* Philadelphia, Blakiston, 1920.

SHERRINGTON, C. S. Observations on the sensual rôle of the proprioceptive nerve-supply of the extrinsic ocular muscles. *Brain 41:*332, 1918.

SMITH, W. R. On the long sensory root of the ciliary ganglion as figured by Cloquet. *J. Anat. & Physiol. 28:*408, 1894.

STRAUSS, I., and NEEDLES, W. Optic nerve complications of accessory nasal sinus disease. *Ann. Otol., Rhin. & Laryng. 47:*989, 1938.

SUNDERLAND, S., and HUGHES, E. S. R. The pupillo-constrictor pathway and the nerves to the ocular muscles in man. *Brain 69:* 301, 1946.

SUTTON, J. E., JR. The fascia of the human orbit. *Anat. Rec. 18:*141, 1920.

TARKHAN, A. A. The innervation of the extrinsic ocular muscles. *J. Anat. 68:*293, 1934.

TOZER, FRANCES M., and SHERRINGTON, C. S. Receptors and afferents of the third, fourth and sixth cranial nerves. *Proc. Roy. Soc., London. s.B. 82:*450, 1910.

TURNER, J. W. A. Indirect injuries of the optic nerve. *Brain 66:*140, 1943.

VAIL, H. H. Retrobulbar optic neuritis originating in the nasal sinuses: A new method of demonstrating the relation between the sphenoid sinus and the optic nerve. *Arch. Otolaryng. 13:*846, 1931.

VAN ALYEA, O. E. Sphenoid sinus: Anatomic study, with consideration of the clinical significance of the structural characteristics of the sphenoid sinus. *Arch. Otolaryng. 34:*225, 1941.

WATKINS, C. H., WAGENER, H. P., and BROWN, R. W. Cerebral symptoms accompanied by choked optic discs in types of blood dyscrasia. *Am. J. Ophth. 24:*1374, 1941.

WHEELER, J. M. The use of the orbicularis palpebrarum muscle in surgery of the eyelids. *Am. J. Surg. n.s. 42:*7, 1938.

WHITNALL, S. E. An instance of the retractor bulbi muscle in man. *J. Anat. & Physiol. 46:*36, 1911.

WHITNALL, S. E. *The Anatomy of the Human Orbit and Accessory Organs of Vision.* New York, Oxford, 1921a.

WHITNALL, S. E. Some abnormal muscles of the orbit. *Anat. Rec. 21:*143, 1921b.

WIENER, M. Applied anatomy in eye surgery. *Surg., Gynec. & Obst. 84:*777, 1947.

WOLFF, E. *The Anatomy of the Eye and Orbit: Including the Central Connections, Development, and Comparative Anatomy of the Visual Apparatus.* (ed. 3) Philadelphia, Blakiston, 1948.

WOOLLARD, H. H. The innervation of the ocular muscles. *J. Anat. 65:*215, 1931.

CHAPTER 3

The Ear

THE ear is conveniently divided for purposes of discussion into three portions (Fig. 91): (1) the external ear, consisting of the auricle or pinna, the external auditory meatus, and the tympanic membrane at the medial, blind, end of the meatus; (2) the middle ear cavity with its contained bones, its connection with the pharynx by way of the auditory or Eustachian tube, and its expansions in the form of air cells in the temporal bone;

and (3) the internal ear, embedded in the petrous portion of the temporal bone and consisting of a membranous (otic) labyrinth which lies within the particularly dense bone (otic capsule) that is excavated to form the osseous or periotic labyrinth. The internal ear is the sense organ, both for hearing and balance; the external and middle ears represent simply accessory sound-conducting apparatus for the auditory part of the internal ear.

THE EXTERNAL EAR

AURICLE AND MEATUS

AURICLE

The skeleton of the auricle or pinna consists of a single plate of yellow elastic cartilage which conforms closely to the shape of the ear as seen in the living (Fig. 92) except for the lobule, which is obviously devoid of skeletal support. The cartilage of the auricle is continuous with that of the external meatus; it is attached to the bony skull by anterior, superior, and posterior ligaments, and is also anchored through its continuity with the cartilage of the meatus, and through the skin and extrinsic muscles. Perhaps

the most important ligament is the fibrous band stretching between the cartilage of the tragus and that of the helix, to complete the front of the external meatus.

The auricle consists essentially of the elastic cartilaginous plate and its covering skin, the latter being more loosely attached on the medial or posteromedial aspect of the ear than it is on the lateral aspect. Some six or more small and rudimentary intrinsic muscles have been described in connection with the cartilage of the external ear, but they are of no apparent importance. The extrinsic muscles of the ear—anterior, su-

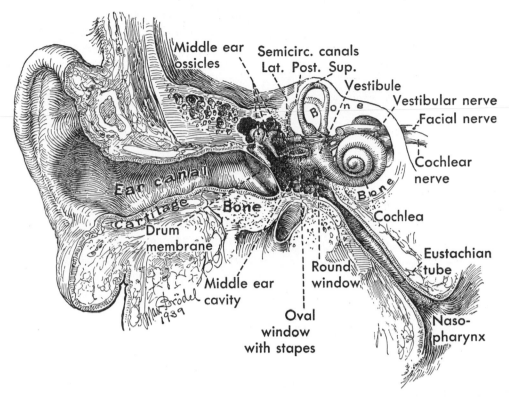

Fig. 91. Diagram of the external, middle, and internal ears. (From Brödel, M.: *Three Unpublished Drawings of the Anatomy of the Human Ear.* Philadelphia, Saunders, 1946.)

perior, and posterior auricular muscles —are distinctly better developed than the intrinsic, and, although usually functionless in man, are sometimes subject to voluntary control as in "wiggling" the ears. Both extrinsic and intrinsic muscles of the ear are supplied by the facial nerve.

MEATUS

The external auditory (acoustic) meatus, or auditory canal, extends from the concha to the tympanic membrane. The lateral portion of its wall consists of cartilage and connective tissue, the medial portion of bone. Laterally, the cartilage of the external meatus is continuous with that of the body of the auricle through a narrow cartilaginous band, the isthmus, and in turn bears the cartilage of the tragus; thus the cartilage of the tragus is

continuous with that of the auricle proper only through the meatus, and a gap (the anterior or trago-helicine incisure) exists anterosuperiorly between the cartilage of the helix and that of the tragus (Fig. 93). The incision for the endaural approach to the ear is made between tragus and helix, and thus avoids cutting cartilage.

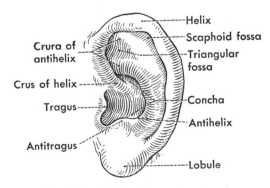

Fig. 92. Parts of the external ear.

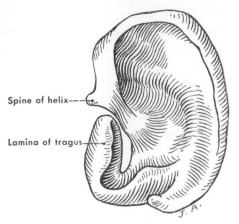

Spine of helix‑‑‑

Lamina of tragus‑‑‑

Fig. 93. Cartilage of the left ear, lateral view, showing the gap between the cartilaginous support of the helix and tragus.

Medially, the meatal cartilage is firmly attached to the outer lip of the bony meatus (Fig. 94). The cartilage of the meatus does not form a tube, as one might assume, but rather a trough with its opening directed superiorly and posteriorly; this trough is bridged by dense connective tissue which completes the wall of the canal.

The *cartilaginous part* of the meatus constitutes somewhat less than half its total length. Inconstant fissures (fissures of Santorini) filled with connective tissue occur in the cartilage, and may transmit infections from the meatus to the parotid and superficial mastoid regions, or vice versa. The cartilaginous meatus is slightly concave anteriorly, so that this portion of the meatus may be somewhat straightened and the insertion of a speculum made easier by drawing the auricle posteriorly and upward.

The *bony meatus,* a tunnel into the temporal bone, is in turn slightly concave

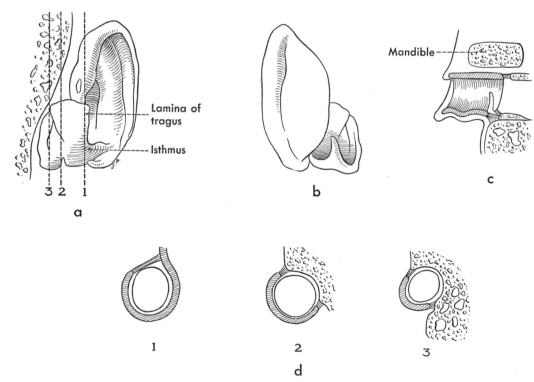

Lamina of tragus

Isthmus

3 2 1

a

b

Mandible‑‑‑

c

1

2

3

d

Fig. 94. Cartilage of the left ear and its relation to the external auditory meatus. *a.* From the front. *b.* From behind. *c.* From above in a horizontal section through the meatus. *d.* Indicates the relationship between cartilage and bone in the planes indicated in *a.*

posteriorly, so that the meatus as a whole is slightly S shaped. In the child up to the age of about 4 years, and sometimes in the adult, the bony meatus is deficient antero-inferiorly, and through this gap (foramen of Huschke) infections may pass between the adjacent parotid gland and the meatus. The entire meatus is lined by a reflection inward from the skin.

Because of the downward and inward slope of the tympanic membrane, the posterosuperior wall of the external meatus measures only about 25 mm. in length, while the antero-inferior wall is about 6 mm. longer. The anterior and inferior walls of the meatus are related closely to the parotid gland; the anterior wall of the bony meatus is also closely related to the condyle of the mandible, but the more important relations of the meatus are that of the posterior wall to the mastoid cells and that of the medial portion of the superior wall to the epitympanic recess—these air cavities being separated from the meatus by relatively thin bone. Lateral to the epitympanic recess thicker bone, which however often contains extensions of the mastoid air cells, intervenes between the meatus and the middle cranial fossa.

VESSELS AND NERVES

The auricle has a rather abundant blood supply derived from branches of the posterior auricular and superficial temporal arteries (branches of the external carotid); however, as the vessels are necessarily superficially located and are not embedded in any appreciable amount of fat, the ear is particularly subject to frost bite in spite of its vascularity.

The blood supply to the external auditory meatus is the same as that to the auricle, but in addition the meatus also receives twigs from the *deep auricular artery,* a branch from the first part of the internal maxillary. The deep auricular artery passes through the parotid gland and behind the capsule of the temporomandibular joint to penetrate either the cartilaginous or bony part of the meatus, and supply the deeper part of the meatus and the external surface of the tympanic membrane.

The *veins* from the auricle drain into the superficial temporal and posterior auricular veins; the former joins the posterior facial vein and hence contributes primarily to the internal jugular vein; the latter joins the external jugular but sometimes connects also with the transverse sinus through the mastoid emissary vein.

The *lymphatics* of the external ear empty into neighboring auricular lymph nodes; some of those from the meatus apparently pass through the fissures of Santorini to the posterior auricular (mastoid) nodes, and enlargement of these has in the past been a cause of some confusion between the diagnoses of external otitis and acute mastoiditis. The veins and lymphatics from the auditory canal join those of the auricle itself.

The external ear represents a region of juncture between skin originally over the branchial region and postbranchial skin, and this is reflected in its *nerve supply* (Fig. 95). Because of the usual overlap between the sensory distribution of adjacent cutaneous nerves, and probably also because of a good deal of variation in the contribution that the rudimentary cutaneous branches of the seventh and ninth nerves make to the innervation of the external ear, the exact distribution of the various components to the auricle and the external meatus is not known. However, the approximate distribution is as follows.

The auriculotemporal branch of the

mandibular division of the trigeminal nerve is distributed to only the most anterior portion of the auricle, including the anterior limb of the helix and a portion of its crus, and the tragus; it also supplies the anterior and upper walls of the external auditory meatus and a corresponding portion of the external surface of the tympanic membrane (Cushing). In some of the individuals studied by Cushing, however, the deeper (medial) portion of the posterior wall, and the

the second and third cervical nerves through the cervical plexus. The small occipital also supplies the skin on the upper medial portion of the pinna, overlapping here with the nerve supply from the great auricular.

The concavity of the concha, between the area supplied by the fifth cranial and that supplied by cervical nerves, is supplied by the auricular branches of the ninth and tenth nerves, and apparently also (Hunt, '09, '10, '15; Maybaum and

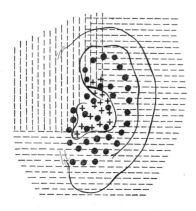
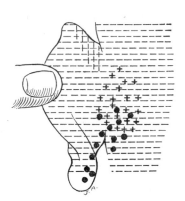

Fig. 95. Cutaneous innervation of the ear on the lateral and posterior aspects. The former is adapted from Cushing (*Bull. Johns Hopkins Hosp. 15:* 213, 1904), the latter from Graves and Edwards (*Arch. Otolaryng. 39:359,* 1944.) The outlines of the areas of distribution undoubtedly vary with the individual, and so do the zones of overlap. Vertical broken lines indicate the trigeminal field (auriculotemporal), horizontal lines the cervical field (C-2 and C-3); the area of distribution of the ninth and tenth cranial nerves is indicated by crosses, the probable distribution of the seventh by circles.

entire drum, seemed to be supplied by the fifth (that is, auriculotemporal) nerve.

The greater portion of the posterior or medial surface of the auricle, and the more posterior portion of the lateral surface (including most of the helix, and the antihelix and lobule, but not dipping into the concha proper) is supplied by cutaneous branches of the cervical plexus, primarily the great auricular nerve from C-2 and C-3. The skin over most of the mastoid region is supplied by the lesser occipital nerve, also receiving fibers from

Druss; Rosenberger; Johnson and Zonderman) by fibers of the seventh nerve. The tenth or ninth and tenth nerves, and the facial nerve, also supply the posterior portion of the external auditory meatus and usually the posterior portion of the external surface of the drum; according to Hunt, these nerves also are distributed, individually or together, to a small area of skin on the posteromedial aspect of the auricle and adjacent mastoid region.

The auricular branch of the vagus (nerve of Arnold) arises from the jugular ganglion and enters the temporal bone through a foramen in the lateral wall of the jugular fossa, parallels the facial nerve as far as the stylomastoid foramen, through which it usually emerges, and supplies skin on the posterior aspect of the auricle, the posterior and inferior part of the external auditory meatus, and the lower part of the outer surface of the tympanic membrane. It is normally joined by the auricular branch of the ninth (not to be confused with the tympanic branch of this nerve), but the two branches vary inversely in size and one may entirely replace the other. The auricular branch of the tenth may also receive a filament from the seventh nerve in the facial (Fallopian) canal, and a communication from the posterior auricular branch of the facial.

While it is impossible anatomically to differentiate between the distributions of the auricular branches of the ninth and tenth, or even demonstrate by dissection the distribution of the seventh to skin, Hunt's observations on the location of the eruptions in herpes zoster of the seventh, ninth, and tenth ganglia have indicated that all three nerves participate in the innervation thus outlined, although there may be considerable variation from individual to individual.

TYMPANIC MEMBRANE

The tympanic or drum membrane, sometimes also referred to as the ear drum or tympanum (confusingly, since these terms are more properly applied to the middle ear as a whole) is a fibrous sheet interposed between the external auditory meatus and the middle ear cavity; it is covered on its lateral side by a thin layer of skin continuous with that lining the meatus, and on its medial sur-

face by mucosa continuous with that lining other surfaces of the middle ear cavity. The connective tissue interposed between these two layers consists largely of radiating fibers attached to the manubrium of the malleus, but these are reinforced peripherally by circular fibers, which are thickened at the margin of the

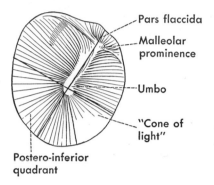

Fig. 96.   Lateral view of the right tympanic membrane. The positions of the malleolar folds, bounding the pars flaccida, are indicated by the lines diverging from the malleolar prominence (produced by the lateral process of the malleus). The positions of the manubrium of the malleus (ending at the umbo) and of the long limb of the incus, and the division of the membrane into quadrants, are also indicated.

drum membrane to form a fibrocartilaginous ring that attaches the membrane to the tympanic sulcus of the temporal bone. In a limited upper portion, where the pars flaccida occurs, these connective tissue fibers are wanting; in this area also the ringlike tympanic portion of the temporal bone (sometimes referred to as the annulus) is deficient, and in this gap (the tympanic incisure, or notch of Rivinus) the membrane attaches to the squamous portion of the temporal bone.

The tympanic membrane (Fig. 96) is set obliquely at the end of the external auditory meatus, so that it slopes medially both from above downward and from behind forward. Its outer aspect is slightly concave, the center of this concavity being known as the *umbo*; this latter marks the strong attachment of the manubrium of the malleus to the tympanic membrane. In the anterosuperior portion of the membrane the lateral process of the malleus is also attached to it, and from this point of attachment stretch the anterior and posterior malleolar (a corruption from mallear?) folds which enclose the pars flaccida (Shrapnell's membrane) of the drum. The "*cone of light*," seen in otoscopic examination of the tympanic membrane, is a bright area of reflection that extends downward and forward from the umbo.

VESSELS AND NERVES

The vessels and nerves of the tympanic membrane are, as might be expected, derived in part from those supplying the external auditory meatus and in part from those supplying the middle ear cavity, and

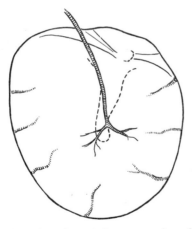

Fig. 97.   Arteries of the external surface of the right tympanic membrane, with the manubrial artery descending from above.

may thus be divided into external and internal branches. Most of the arterial twigs to the external surface of the membrane are from the deep auricular branch of the internal maxillary and enter the membrane radially from below, in front and behind; the largest artery (the manubrial) is derived usually from the same source but descends (sometimes duplicated) from above, at first slightly poste-

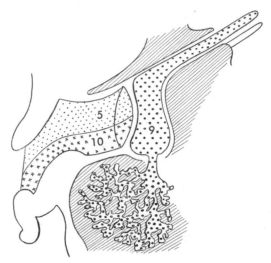

Fig. 98.   Distribution of sensory nerves to the meatus, tympanic membrane and middle ear. The numbers refer to the corresponding cranial nerves. (Redrawn from Graves, G. O., and Edwards, L. F.: *Arch. Otolaryng. 39*:359, 1944.)

rior to, then upon, the manubrium mallei (Fig. 97). The arterial twigs to the mucous surface are from the anterior tympanic branch of the internal maxillary artery and from the stylomastoid branch of the posterior auricular.

The innervation of the external surface of the drum membrane, as already noted, is usually described as being from the auriculotemporal branch of the fifth and the auricular branch of the tenth (or seventh, ninth and tenth) nerves, thus corresponding to the innervation of the external meatus (Fig. 98); the innervation of its inner surface is believed to be entirely from the tympanic plexus, therefore from the ninth nerve (with possibly, according to Hunt, some participation also by the seventh).

The majority of the nerve fibers in the human tympanic membrane (Wilson, '11), as in that of the dog, cat and monkey (Wilson, '07), descend from posterosuperiorly across the flaccid portion toward the umbo, accompanying the principal artery of the membrane, and lying just behind the level of the manubrium of the malleus (Fig. 99). The pars flaccida has a particularly rich innervation, the pars tensa a poorer one.

Fig. 99. Nerves of the external surface of the right tympanic membrane. (Redrawn from Wilson, J. G.: *Am. J. Anat. 11*:101, 1911.)

While numerous small branches enter the membrane around its periphery, most of these are derived from the nerves of the meatus, and relatively few enter it from the tympanic cavity. Wilson was unable to distinguish the origin of the nerves to the external surface in man, but found that after section of the auriculotemporal nerve in the monkey almost all of the fibers on the membrane disappeared; the few fibers still remaining, which crossed the flaccid portion and were irregularly distributed over the tense portion, were presumably derived from the seventh-ninth-tenth complex (see also p. 170).

The fact that its chief arterial and nerve supply enter the tympanic membrane from above is one of several factors influencing the site of incision of it (myringotomy) in middle ear infections. A preferable location for this is the postero-inferior quadrant. Since the distance between the tympanic membrane and the inner wall of the middle ear cavity may be no more than from 2 to 4 mm., the relations of the membrane to structures in the middle ear cavity must also be considered. Druss has pointed out that its anterosuperior quadrant is closely related to the tympanic opening of the Eustachian tube, its antero-inferior quadrant to the carotid canal (the bony wall of which may be deficient), its posterosuperior quadrant to the long process of the incus and to the stapes and oval window, and its postero-inferior quadrant to the promontory.

The chief danger in incisions of the postero-inferior quadrant of the membrane, but a relatively remote one according to Druss (although cases have been reported in the older literature), is that of wounding the internal jugular vein (jugular bulb); the bony canal for this vein occasionally protrudes into the lower portion of the middle ear cavity, and there are sometimes dehiscences between the canal for the vein and the middle ear cavity.

In performing a myringotomy it is customary to turn the point of the knife upward, as close to the medial surface of the tympanic membrane as possible, in order to open Prussak's space (p. 177), which lies medial to the pars flaccida; this has poor or no natural gravity drainage, and therefore may continue to harbor infection and pus in spite of the incision in the drum.

VARIATIONS AND ANOMALIES

Wolff ('33) has pointed out that in the 6-month fetus the tympanic membrane is almost horizontal, and lies below rather than lateral to the otic capsule; the subsequent shift to the lateral and more nearly vertical position may be more or less complete, thus accounting for the *variations in slope* of the tympanic membrane commonly encountered. In the infant, also, the bony portion of the external meatus has little depth. The meatus is developed largely from a separate element of the temporal bone, the tympanic ring, which is actually somewhat less than a ring as it is incomplete superiorly; in the newborn this has little depth in the lateromedial direction, and further growth both of the ring and of the squamous portion of the temporal bone (which forms the roof and posterosuperior part of the meatus) is necessary to produce a real bony canal.

In the process of growth of the ring, the floor lags behind the anterior and posterior walls; thus there is left in the floor a gap (the foramen of Huschke—p. 169), which is gradually shifted to the anterior wall but usually is closed by about the fifth year; it may, however, remain throughout adult life. Retraction and calcification of the tympanic membrane are mentioned on page 198.

Congenital atresia of the external auditory meatus has, according to Richards, been estimated to occur in about 1 in 2000 patients suffering from aural disease, and to be bilateral in about 1 in every 6 of these. Cohen and Fox have found a higher percentage in their own practice, about 1 in 1000 patients, but the incidence in the general population must, of course, be very low. Cohen and Fox found males to be more frequently affected than females, as did also Fraser, who stated that the condition occurs much more often on the right than on the left side. Maldevelopment of the middle ear and its associated bones is commonly associated with atresia of the external meatus, but the internal ear may or may not be affected, and deafness may be solely of the conduction type (Richards).

Cohen and Fox expressed the belief that the unilateral condition is perhaps best left alone, but that in bilateral atresia operation should be done in early life, even before the third month; they and Pattee have outlined operations for this condition. It should be remembered that in distorted and anomalous formations of the ear the facial nerve may also have an anomalous course.

Calcification and ossification of the external ear have been occasionally reported, and have been discussed by Scherrer. "Supernumerary external ears," which usually do not particularly resemble a normal ear and are often therefore termed *"preauricular appendages"* or "preauricular nodules," also occur occasionally anterior to the normal ear (Fig. 100); Wood-Jones and I-Chuan, and Costello and Shepard, have stated that 33 such cases were found in a series of 50,-000 children. Costello and Shepard have pointed out that the nodules have been mistaken for fibromas, and that the anomaly is usually solitary and unilateral but may be multiple. They stated that the literature indicates that the condition may be inherited, and is more frequent in males than females.

Preauricular cysts, fossae, sinuses and fistulas also occur in the same area in which nodules are found, and like these have a low incidence: Wood-Jones and I-Chuan quoted an occurrence of about 2 per 1000 births, but Pastore and Erich noted that 12 such cases were reported among 2000 children in one study, 48 cases among 3200 in another, and that the incidence among members of the Oriental race has been said to be as much as 4 to 6 per cent.

Most of the so-called fistulas are apparently really blindly ending sinuses (Becker and Brunschwig), and are of no clinical importance unless they become infected. They are congenital and apparently hereditary (Pastore and Erich)

don, Rowhanavongse and Varamisara). Congdon and his co-workers found that while about 90 per cent of juxta-auricular fossae (of a series of 470) were close to the anterior border of the helix, the remainder were in various locations on the

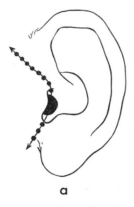 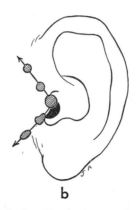

Fig. 100. Distribution of preauricular fistulae, *a,* and appendages, *b.* (Redrawn from Wood-Jones, F., and I-Chuan, Wen: *J. Anat. 68:* 525, 1934.)

and, depending upon one's interpretation of the development of the ear, are sometimes regarded as remnants of the first branchial cleft (Wood-Jones and I-Chuan; Becker and Brunschwig) or as due to incomplete fusion of the tubercles described by His as contributing to the auricle (for instance, Stammers; Cong-

ear itself, or even behind it; they expressed the belief that these variations in position could not be compatible with a development from the first branchial cleft. Neither Streeter ('22) nor Wood-Jones and I-Chuan agreed entirely with His' description of the development of the external ear.

THE MIDDLE EAR

THE middle ear cavity consists of a central air-filled space, the tympanic cavity; its connection to the pharynx, the auditory tube; and its extensions into neighboring parts of the temporal bone. These extensions, outgrowths from the central cavity, are likewise normally filled with air and are known as air cells.

TYMPANUM

The tympanic cavity (tympanum proper, cavum tympani, middle ear cav-

ity) lies in the temporal bone, between the tympanic membrane, tympanic ring and a process of the squamous portion of the temporal bone laterally, and the base of the petrous pyramid or petrous portion of the temporal bone, surrounding the internal ear, medially. It communicates anteriorly with the pharynx by way of the auditory or Eustachian tube, and posteriorly with the mastoid air cells by way of the aditus and tympanic antrum (Figs. 101 and 102). In it lie, covered by mucous membrane, the three bones

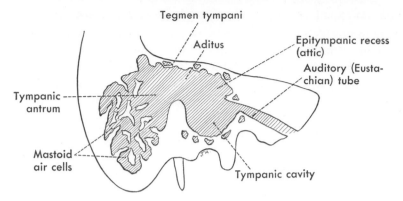

Fig. 101. Schema of the tympanic cavity and its associated air spaces.

of the middle ear cavity, their ligaments, and the tendons of their associated muscles, and through it (also covered by mucous membrane) runs the chorda tympani from the facial nerve.

SUBDIVISIONS OR POUCHES

Since the structures in and traversing the middle ear cavity are all covered by reflections of mucous membrane, they and the folds of mucosa associated with them tend to partially subdivide the tympanum into various "pouches." Most of these communicate widely with the rest of the tympanum and with each other, and are of little import: for instance, the anterior pouch of the malleus is simply that portion of the tympanum

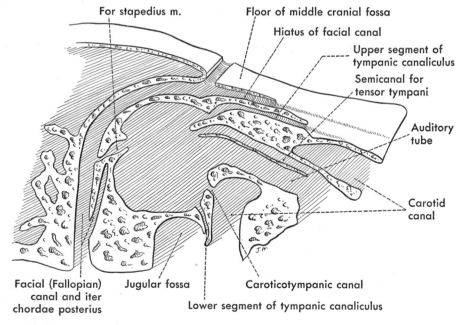

Fig. 102. Some relationships of the tympanic cavity. All those indicated do not actually lie in the same plane, but are at varying depths from the lateral wall.

lying between the head of the malleus, the anterior tympanic wall, and the superior and anterior malleolar ligaments; similarly, the superior and inferior "pouches" of the incus are the areas lying above and below the short process of the incus (Fig. 103).

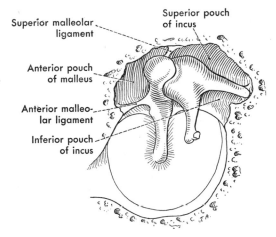

Fig. 103. Malleus and incus from the medial side, to illustrate the larger "pouches" associated with them.

The one subdivision of clinical importance is the pouch of Prussak, or upper tympanic pouch. This is bounded laterally by the pars flaccida of the tympanic membrane, medially by the neck of the malleus, above by the lateral malleolar ligament, and below by the short process of the malleus (Fig. 104). The

mucosal folds reflected upon the ligament and short process may convert this space into one which has only relatively small anterior and posterior openings, and therefore no good gravity drainage. On the other hand, the anterior and posterior pouches of von Tröltsch (anterior and posterior recesses of the tympanic membrane), which lie between the tympanic membrane and the anterior and posterior malleolar folds, respectively, open downward and therefore do not tend to harbor pus.

LATERAL WALL

The tympanum extends well above the level of the tympanic membrane, and the portion of the cavity above this level is known as the epitympanic recess (attic); in it lie the head of the malleus and the body and short process of the incus. The epitympanic recess projects laterally above the external auditory meatus, and it is this portion of the tympanum which has as its lateral wall a part of the squamous portion of the temporal bone; below this level the lateral wall of the tympanum is composed of the tympanic membrane and ring.

ROOF

The roof of the tympanic cavity, or, more properly speaking, of the epitym-

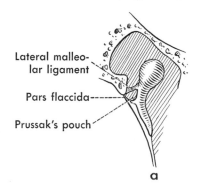

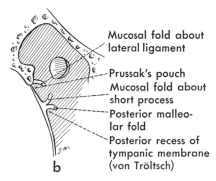

Fig. 104. Some "pouches" related to the tympanic membrane in frontal section through the ear. *a*. Through the malleus. *b*. Posterior to the malleus.

panic recess, is a thin plate of bone known as the *tegmen tympani*, which separates the middle ear cavity from the cranial cavity; prolonged backward it separates the tympanic antrum from the cranial cavity and prolonged forward it forms the roof of the canal for the tensor tympani muscle. In children the unossified petrosquamous suture in the tegmen tympani may allow the direct passage of infection from the tympanum to the meninges of the middle cranial fossa, and even in the adult veins from the middle ear perforate this suture to end in the petrosquamosal sinus (present in about 50 per cent of cases) and the superior petrosal sinus, and thus may transmit infection directly to the cranial venous sinuses.

FLOOR

The floor of the middle ear cavity, lying slightly below the level of that of the meatus, is usually a thin plate of bone which separates the cavity from the internal jugular vein; if the superior bulb of the vein is particularly small, the floor may be even as much as a centimeter thick, and may contain air cells (hypotympanic cells) intervening between the middle ear cavity and the vein; if the bulb is large, it bulges upward into the middle ear and the wall is very thin, and may present dehiscences (Maybaum and Goldman). The major portion of the epitympanic recess has of course no floor, as it is simply an upward extension of the main portion of the tympanic cavity, but the laterally projecting portion has as its floor the roof of the external meatus. In this also there may be air cells (cells of Kirchner). The hypotympanic cells in the floor of the tympanum may extend also below the labyrinth to lie adjacent to "petrous apex" cells; in this case, they afford a good surgical approach to the more anterior cells of the petrous pyramid.

POSTERIOR WALL

The posterior wall of the tympanum is deficient above where it opens through a narrowed aditus into a wider cavity in the mastoid process known as the tympanic antrum; below the aditus a relatively thin bony wall intervenes between the tympanic cavity and the antrum with its connecting mastoid air cells. From this posterior wall the pyramidal eminence or pyramid projects, and at its apex has an aperture transmitting the tendon of the stapedius muscle; just above and behind the base of the pyramidal eminence the facial nerve, in the medial wall of the tympanum, curves downward to change its course from an almost horizontal to an almost vertical one. The chorda tympani, arising from the facial, then enters the tympanic cavity through a foramen in the posterior wall.

ANTERIOR WALL

The lower part of the anterior wall of the tympanic cavity consists of a thin plate of bone, which may be incomplete or may contain air cells, between this cavity and the carotid canal, housing the internal carotid artery. In the Ramadier approach to "petrous apex" cells, the exact position of the carotid canal is of major importance; the technic involves apicotomy through the anteromedial aspect of the tympanic wall between the carotid canal and the promontory, and the space between these two varies considerably. The upper part of the wall, like the corresponding part of the posterior wall, is deficient, as the canal containing the tensor tympani muscle opens here and immediately below this is the tympanic orifice of the auditory tube. Through the auditory tube the tympanic cavity proper, the tympanic antrum, and the mastoid and other air cells connected with the middle ear cavity are in continuity with the nasopharynx.

MEDIAL WALL

The medial wall of the tympanic cavity is the petrous portion of the temporal bone surrounding the internal ear and here separating the cavities of the middle

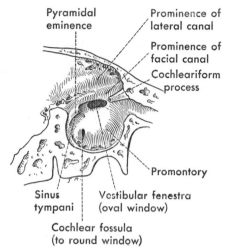

Fig. 105. Medial wall of the tympanic cavity.

and internal ears. It presents on its surface, more or less clearly, several *markings* of particular importance (Fig. 105). Posteriorly and above is the broad prominence produced by the anterior end of the lateral semicircular canal; below this, and also extending more anteriorly, is the less marked prominence of the facial (Fallopian) canal, produced by the horizontal portion of the facial nerve as it passes in the relatively thin bony wall between internal and middle ears. Anterior to the prominence of the facial canal the hollow cochleariform process, transmitting the tendon of the tensor tym-

pani muscle, projects posteriorly along the medial wall from the junction of this with the anterior one; its apex, at which the tensor tympani muscle turns sharply laterally, is the landmark for the position of the turn (external genu) between the anterolaterally and the posteriorly directed horizontal portions of the facial nerve.

Immediately below the facial canal is a depression which leads to the oval window, or vestibular fenestra, closed by the base of the stapes. Below the vestibular window is the rounded bulge of the promontory, formed by the basal turn of the cochlea; the tympanic nerve plexus lies upon the promontory, covered by its mucous membrane. Below the back part of the promontory is a depression, the cochlear fossula or round window niche, the inferior border of which is deepened and leads to the round window or fenestra cochleae; this window is closed by a fibrous membrane, the secondary tympanic membrane. Depending upon the bulge of the promontory, and therefore the depth of the groove leading to the round window, the round window may present itself inferiorly on the promontory or may actually face somewhat medially, completely covered by the bulge of the promontory.

Behind the promontory, medial and inferior to the pyramidal eminence and immediately below the ridge of the facial canal, is a depression, the sinus tympani (recessus tympanicus subcanalis Fallopii); the depth to which this extends into the petrous portion of the temporal bone varies greatly, but it may harbor infections, and when it extends deeply enough to lie close to the ampullary end of the posterior canal and the posterior end of the lateral canal it may transmit infections to these. Its opening, which lies approximately midhorizontally between the oval and round windows, may look forward rather than laterally and therefore be quite inconspicuous.

BONES OF MIDDLE EAR

Of the three bones of the middle ear, the *malleus* is closely attached to the tympanic membrane by both its manubrium (handle) and its lateral process, while its head projects somewhat above the membrane into the epitympanic recess to articulate with the body of the incus (Fig. 106). The anterior process ("long"

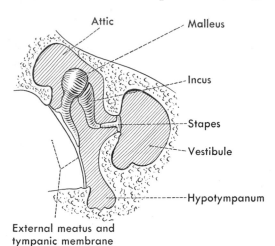

Fig. 106. Middle ear cavity in diagrammatic frontal section.

process, processus gracilis) of the malleus is a slender spicule extending obliquely downward from the neck toward the petrotympanic fissure; in the infant it may reach this fissure but in the adult the process is usually largely converted into connective tissue which forms the anterior malleolar ligament, and the bony process itself is short. The malleus is also attached to the tympanic wall by a superior and a lateral malleolar ligament: the superior malleolar ligament descends almost straight down from the roof of the epitympanic recess, while the broad but short lateral malleolar ligament attaches the neck of the bone to the margin of the tympanic notch. The articular cavity between the incus and the head of the malleus is bounded by a thin capsular ligament.

The body of the *incus*, fitted against the head of the malleus, lies also in the epitympanic recess, and the short limb of this bone rests in a depression, the fossa of the incus, situated at the base of the epitympanic recess where it goes into the aditus, and below the prominence of the lateral semicircular canal. The long limb of the incus descends parallel and slightly posteromedial to the manubrium of the malleus, but at its lower end turns medially at almost right angles to articulate with the stapes. The incus is held in place by a posterior ligament attaching to its short limb, and by a superior ligament which descends from above to attach to the body. The articulation between the incus and stapes is usually described as a diarthroidial joint.

From its articulation with the incus, the *stapes* passes almost horizontally to the oval window. The edge of the footplate or base of the stapes is covered with cartilage, as is also the rim of the vestibular window, and the two are united by an annular ligament; this is a ring of elastic fibers which allows movement of the stapes and yet seals the potential space between its footplate and the edges of the oval window.

In addition to their ligaments, the stapes and the manubrium of the malleus also have muscles attached to them. The *stapedius muscle* lies within the hollow of the pyramidal eminence in the posterior wall of the tympanic cavity; its tendon, emerging through the opening at the apex of the eminence, turns rather sharply inferiorly to insert on the neck of the stapes. This muscle is believed to diminish the excursion of the base of the stapes by drawing it laterally, and through its reflex contraction is supposed to protect the internal ear from excessive sound. The stapedius muscle is innervated by a branch of the facial nerve, which leaves this nerve within the facial (Fallopian) canal at about the level of the muscle.

The *tensor tympani muscle*, like the stapedius, enters the tympanum through a bony canal, but is much larger than the latter. The muscle takes origin outside the skull, from the upper surface of the cartilaginous portion of the Eustachian tube; it then enters its bony canal (termed the semicanal for the tensor tympani) which lies directly above the bony Eustachian tube, a very thin wall of bone separating the lumina of the two canals. At its emergence from the canal, the tendon of the tensor tympani turns sharply laterally across the tympanic cavity to attach to the manubrium of the malleus close to the neck. The muscle is innervated by a branch of the mandibular nerve which usually traverses the otic ganglion; by its contraction it draws the manubrium medially and thus tightens the tympanic membrane.

It might be pointed out that the stapes represents a portion of the hyoid arch which has been enclosed within the middle ear, and its muscle, the stapedius, is therefore innervated by the nerve of the hyoid arch—the facial nerve. On the other hand, the malleus and the incus represent a backward projecting portion of the original cartilage of the lower jaw, and the muscle of the malleus, the tensor tympani, is therefore innervated by the nerve to the musculature of the lower jaw—the mandibular. The course of the migration of the malleus (and incus) from the jaw to the middle ear cavity is evidenced in the adult by the anterior ligament of the malleus, extending to the petrotympanic fissure, and the sphenomandibular ligament which extends from just outside the fissure to the mandible. Both of these ligaments represent degenerated remains of the mandibular (Meckel's) cartilage, the original skeleton of the lower jaw from which the incus and malleus are derived.

NERVES AND VESSELS

TYMPANIC PLEXUS

The nerves of the middle ear cavity (Fig. 107) are represented by the tympanic plexus which lies on the promontory beneath the mucosa, in grooves or even actual canals (Frenckner) in the bone. This plexus is formed chiefly by the tympanic branch of the ninth cranial nerve (nerve of Jacobson), but is reinforced by one or more caroticotympanic nerves derived from the internal carotid plexus. The tympanic branch of the ninth nerve supplies sensory fibers to the mucosa of the middle ear, while the sympathetic fibers are presumably vasomotor. Lempert ('46) has stated that there are ganglion cells in the plexus.

The sympathetic filaments from the carotid plexus enter the tympanic cavity inferiorly, penetrating the thin bone between the middle ear cavity and the carotid canal in company with the caroticotympanic branch of the internal carotid artery. The tympanic branch of the glossopharyngeal nerve arises from the petrosal ganglion and traverses the tympanic canaliculus in the thin lamina of bone between the carotid canal and the jugular fossa to enter the tympanic cavity inferiorly or antero-inferiorly. Hunt ('15) has suggested that sensory branches from the facial nerve also may join the tympanic plexus to be distributed to the middle ear cavity, reaching this by connections between the facial and the lesser superficial petrosal nerve, which arises from the plexus. This is, of course, anatomically possible, but has apparently been demonstrated neither clinically nor anatomically.

From the tympanic plexus branches are given off not only to the tympanum proper, but also to the mastoid air cells and to the Eustachian tube; a connection

ficial petrosal, with which it may exchange branches, and then, like this latter, leaves the middle cranial cavity. The point of exit of the lesser superficial petrosal nerve is variable but is through or close to the foramen ovale; immediately outside the foramen ovale the nerve ends in the otic ganglion. The fibers in this nerve are said to be preganglionic ones destined for the innervation of the parotid gland.

Tumors said to be histologically identi-

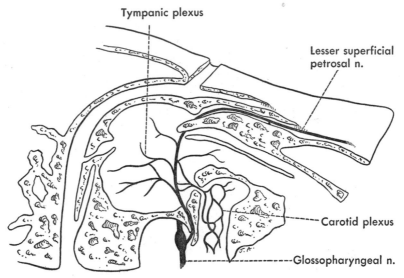

Fig. 107.   Formation of the tympanic plexus and the lesser superficial petrosal nerve.

to the cochlear nerve has been suspected (for example, Frenckner) but not proved. From the upper border of the plexus arises the *lesser superficial petrosal nerve*. This nerve is believed to be formed by preganglionic fibers of the ninth nerve which traverse the plexus and upon leaving it run through a canal in the petrous portion of the temporal bone (beneath and medial to the canal of the tensor tympani) to enter the middle cranial fossa. Here the lesser superficial petrosal parallels but lies lateral to the great super-

cal with carotid body tumors (p. 482) and usually termed "glomus jugulare" tumors, apparently arise from cell groups associated with the nerves to the ear. Winship and Louzan, for instance, have reported one arising on the promontory of the middle ear, and have quoted Guild as having found such cell groups in the normal ear associated with the tympanic branch of the ninth nerve even beyond the promontory, and also along the auricular branch of the vagus—thus not always adjacent to the jugular bulb, where the tissue of this type related to the ear was first found, and hence obtained its name.

The chorda tympani traverses the middle ear cavity, but is not a source of innervation to this cavity; its course is described in connection with that of the facial nerve (p. 196).

ARTERIES

There are several arteries supplying the tympanum, most of them derived from tympanic branch of the ninth nerve through the tympanic canaliculus between carotid and jugular vessels, to enter the cavity inferiorly and anastomose with the other vesels. The *stylomastoid branch of the posterior auricular artery* (from the external carotid directly or from the occipital) follows the facial nerve retrogradely within the facial (Fallopian) canal, helps to supply the mastoid cells, and, leaving the facial canal with the chorda tympani, attains the middle ear

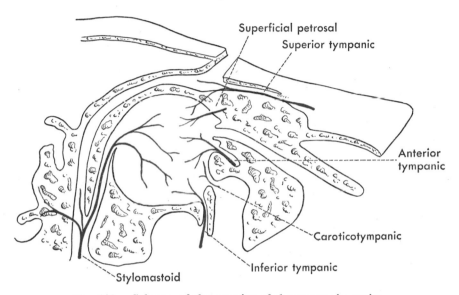

Fig. 108. Schema of the arteries of the tympanic cavity.

the external carotid. The majority reach the tympanum by accompanying the nerves which enter or leave this cavity (Fig. 108). The *anterior tympanic artery*, a small branch of the internal maxillary, accompanies the chorda tympani nerve (retrogradely) through the petrotympanic fissure to be distributed to the more anterior part of the middle ear cavity, including a portion of the tympanic membrane; it and the other branches to the middle ear anastomose freely. The *inferior tympanic artery*, derived from the ascending pharyngeal, accompanies the cavity to supply the posterior part of the tympanic membrane, the promontory and much of the rest of the medial wall.

The *middle meningeal artery* (from the internal maxillary) furnishes two branches to the middle ear, a superficial petrosal which enters the facial canal by way of the hiatus through which the greater superficial petrosal nerve emerges, and a superior tympanic artery which enters the middle ear through the petrosquamous fissure.

Finally, the internal carotid artery supplies a *caroticotympanic branch* which accompanies the nerve of the same name, arising from the carotid artery within the canal and entering the middle ear cavity to supply its anterior wall.

VEINS AND LYMPHATICS

The veins of the middle ear roughly parallel the arteries and empty into the pterygoid plexus of veins or into the superior petrosal sinus. The lymphatics end in the retropharyngeal and parotid lymph nodes.

EUSTACHIAN TUBE

The auditory, pharyngotympanic, or Eustachian tube extends from its tympanic orifice high on the anterior wall of the tympanic cavity to a pharyngeal orifice situated just posterior to the inferior nasal concha. In the adult the tympanic orifice of the tube is approximately 2 to 2.5 cm. higher than is the pharyngeal end, and the tube thus runs downward, medially, and anteriorly toward the pharynx. It is, however, not straight, but slightly S shaped. In the infant the tube is shorter, relatively wider, and more nearly horizontal in position than in the adult, and therefore affords an easier pathway for infections ascending from the pharynx to the tympanic cavity; on the other hand, however, the tube also opens relatively and actually lower in the tympanic cavity, so that it affords better drainage from the tympanum. The length of the entire tube in the adult varies from 31 to 38 mm. (Graves and Edwards); of this the lateral or tympanic third has a bony wall and is therefore referred to as the osseous portion, while the anteromedial two thirds has a cartilaginous and connective tissue wall and is referred to as the cartilaginous portion of the tube.

OSSEOUS CANAL

The osseous canal, usually referred to as the semicanal of the auditory tube, is separated by a very thin lamina of bone from the similar canal of the tensor tympani muscle lying above it; medially it is related to the lateral aspect of the carotid canal, and inferiorly a lamina of bone of varying thickness, which may contain air cells, separates it from the jugular fossa. The osseous canal is widest at its tympanic orifice and gradually narrows throughout its length; its anteromedial end forms the narrowest part, or isthmus, of the entire tube. At the isthmus the cartilage of the tube is firmly attached to the bony tube (and may extend posteriorly as a part of the roof of this), and from this point to the pharynx the tube gradually widens again. The cartilaginous and bony tubes meet at an obtuse angle.

CARTILAGINOUS CANAL

Unlike the bony tube, which is complete and consequently remains permanently open, the cartilaginous portion of the tube is not completely surrounded by cartilage, and in the resting condition is converted into a closed, slitlike cavity. The cartilage of the tube is essentially hooklike in section, being applied to the entire medial wall and turning over the superior aspect to descend slightly on the lateral wall; fibrous connective tissue (the lamina membranacea or the salpingopharyngeal fascia) completes the lateral wall of the tube. In addition to the single twisted sheet of cartilage forming the main support of the tube, accessory cartilages may occur about the pharyngeal orifice.

It is usually stated that the tensor veli palatini muscle, which is described as attached in part to the lateral wall of the tube, opens the tube by pulling on this wall (for instance, Graves and Edwards; Lierle and Potter). Eggston and Wolff stated, however, that in their histological studies they found no attachment of the tensor to the wall of the auditory tube. Less frequently, it is stated that the salpingopharyngeus, through its attachment to the pharyngeal orifice, may assist in opening this orifice. Simkins expressed the belief, however, that the tube opens passively upon release of the tension on the cartilage, and that this tension is released by elevation of the pharyngeal portion of the tube. He therefore regarded the levator veli palatini as being the chief opener of the tube through its elevation of the cartilage, and spoke of the tensor palatini as a passive closer of the tube. These muscles are described on page 351.

The tube is lined throughout its length with a low columnar ciliated epithelium, except at its pharyngeal end where it forms a pseudostratified epithelium containing many goblet cells. In its cartilaginous portion it contains also mucous glands; it is often described as containing lymphoid (adenoid) tissue—"Gerlach's tubal tonsil"—near its pharyngeal end, but Eggston and Wolff found such tissue in only 1 of 47 Eustachian tubes examined. According to Wolff ('34a), the air cells opening into the osseous portion of the tube are not originally outgrowths from this tube, but rather of the tympanic cavity itself; only secondarily do they come to empty into the tube.

BLOOD SUPPLY

The blood supply to the Eustachian tube is through twigs from the pharyngeal branches of both the internal maxillary and ascending pharyngeal arteries, from the ascending palatine branch of the facial (external maxillary) artery, the su-

perior tympanic branch of the middle meningeal, and the artery of the pterygoid canal (a branch of the sphenopalatine from the internal maxillary). The veins drain into the pterygoid venous plexus. The lymphatics drain into the retropharyngeal and deep cervical nodes; the several courses described for them have been summarized by Graves and Edwards.

INNERVATION

The sensory supply to the Eustachian tube is largely by way of the tympanic

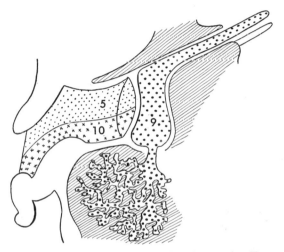

Fig. 109. Sensory nerve supply to the Eustachian tube, mastoid cells, and middle ear. (Redrawn from Graves, G. O., and Edwards, L. F.: *Arch. Otolaryng. 39:*359, 1944.)

plexus, and therefore through the ninth nerve (Fig. 109). Cushing reported some anesthesia of the pharyngeal orifice of the tube following destruction of the fifth nerve, while Dandy ('27) included the orifice in the area of distribution of the pharyngeal branch of the ninth nerve. According to Graves and Edwards, the reports of various workers indicate that the pharyngeal orifice is probably innervated through the ninth nerve in about 50 per cent of cases, and through the maxillary portion of the trigeminal (via branches of the sphenopalatine ganglion) in the other 50 per cent.

The relation of the tube to infections of the middle ear cavity is obvious, as it forms an easy pathway for ascending infections from the pharynx. The close association between the pharyngeal orifice and the fossa of Rosenmüller (pharyngeal recess), which contains the lymphoid tissue of the pharyngeal tonsil or adenoid, renders the tube particularly susceptible to occlusion from overgrowth of this tissue.

CONDUCTION OF SOUND THROUGH THE MIDDLE EAR

CONDUCTION BY AIR

As is true of other phases of hearing, the physiology of the middle ear is not too well understood. Pohlman ('31, '41), in discussing this question, pointed out that it has been held that the vibrations of the drum might pass entirely by air conduction to the round window, so that the ossicles could be regarded as completely unnecessary, and that it has also been suggested that high frequencies alone might pass directly to the round window while the low frequencies pass through the ossicles. Pohlman expressed the belief that sound vibrations impinging on the tympanic membrane are usually transmitted to the cochlea both by the ossicular chain and through the air of the tympanic cavity, but that the bony route is much more efficient; he stated that whenever the ossicular chain no longer functions, the air route becomes operative but that the deafness when this route alone is used is about 40 decibels. He pointed out, also, that since large perforations of the membrane much depress the acuity of hearing at all tonal

ranges, all tones apparently normally employ the ossicular chain.

The role of air conduction as compared with conduction by the bones of the middle ear has been further analyzed by Wever, Lawrence, and Smith. They found in experimental animals that breaking the ossicular chain between the incus and stapes produced a great loss of sensitivity, amounting to 60 decibels in the middle range of tonal frequencies and a little less for lower and higher frequencies; subsequent removal of the drum membrane and the ossicles moderated the loss, for these then useless parts apparently interfered with the entrance of the sound waves to the middle ear. Wider opening of the middle ear to the outside by removal of bone decreased the loss still more, until it amounted to only about 28 decibels.

CONDUCTION BY THE OSSICULAR CHAIN

Under normal conditions, the tympanic membrane is obviously set in motion by the sound waves impinging upon it. It is usually believed that the effects of such sound waves would be to produce an initial inward movement of the membrane, and therefore an inward movement of the ossicular chain; MacNaughton-Jones has, however, argued that the effect of sounds within physiological limits is to produce a rounding of the membrane, with therefore a diminution in the height of its conelike form—thus drawing the umbo and the attached ossicular chain outward as the first phase in the vibratory movement.

The ossicular chain has been regarded as a lever system which converts the vibrations of the tympanic membrane into intensified movements of the stapes against the perilymph; Wever, Lawrence, and Smith interpreted their results to indicate not so much a lever mechanism as an "hydraulic mechanism," through which the vibrations of the air can impart their energy more efficiently to the heavier perilymph; in this transmission the important factor is the ratio of the area of the drum membrane to that of the stapedial footplate. As summarized by Lawrence the ratio is such that in the cat about 54 per cent of the vibrations from the air reach the perilymph—and the energy imparted to the perilymph by the drum-ossicle route is at least 1000 times that of the energy of vibrations entering through the round window.

The effect of contraction of the tensor tympani upon sound conduction through the ossicular chain has been variously interpreted as increasing the efficiency of transmission, decreasing it, preventing excessive vibration of the tympanic membrane, or changing the natural frequency of vibration of the bones so that some tones are favored over others in transmission; it has also been believed that it simply maintains the membrane and the ossicles in a constant state of tension and therefore aids in the transmission process in this fashion. Crowe, Hughson, and Witting reported that section of the tensor tympani in the cat results in a relaxation of the ossicular chain with marked impairment of the transmission of higher tones but practically no effect upon low tones; tension on the tensor tympani tendon, on the other hand, was reported to increase the rigidity of the ossicular chain and impair the transmission of all low tones. They inferred that impairment of tensor tympani function may be a common cause of impairment of hearing for high tones in patients. Wever and Bray did not completely agree with this; they reported that tension on the tensor tympani tendon of the cat produced a diminu-

tion of hearing (as recorded from the electrical responses of the cochlea) of all sounds except those of high intensity, which showed many variations. From their results, they concluded that contraction of the muscle both reduces sound conduction as a whole and at the same time raises the natural frequency of the transmission system of the chain.

The action of the stapedius muscle, producing a lateral movement of the base of the stapes, is generally interpreted as a reflex contraction to sound which prevents undue excursion of the base of the stapes. Lindsay, Kobrak, and Perlman have observed the stapedius tendon in patients with perforations of the tympanic membrane, and reported that the reflex varies with the acuity of hearing of the patient—that is, that its afferent pathway is apparently only the eighth nerve itself. They found that when the patient had good air-conduction hearing there was a good stapedial reflex to sounds conducted by air, but if hearing with bone conduction only was present then there was no reflex with air conduction, but there was with bone conduction.

ROUND WINDOW

The function of the round window has been variously interpreted. Wever, Lawrence, and Smith have supported the concept that air vibrations in the middle ear cavity may reach the cochlea directly through the round window, as they have stated that in the cat the cochlea may be stimulated almost as readily by way of the round window as by way of the oval window, when the middle ear mechanism is absent.

MacNaughton-Jones has argued that there must be differences in the pressure exerted upon the round and oval windows in order to produce movements of the perilymph, and suggested that in the absence of the tympanic membrane the sound waves are concentrated upon the round window. According to his concept, therefore, the first movement of the membrane of the round window is inward, being either drawn inward by an outward movement of the stapes, or, in the absence of the tympanic membrane, pushed inward by the greater pressure exerted upon it as compared with the oval window. Crowe, Hughson, and Witting stated that pushing in the round window membrane (in the cat) after section of the tensor tympani tendon increases sensitivity to high tones. Kobrak ('49) has noted that the round window membrane has been shown to execute larger excursions than has the stapes itself, and apparently regarded it both as a point for entrance of sound into the cochlea and as a compensating area for the vibrating fluid in the cochlea. He has found that in the intact round window the inward movement of the membrane is greater than the outward movement.

Hughson and Crowe reported that occlusion of the round window in the cat, by cotton or a periosteal graft, produced a great increase in the intensity of the electrical activity of the cochlea in response to the spoken voice; Hughson ('40) subsequently used similar grafts in man to immobilize the round window, and reported that they produced an increase in the acuity of hearing. This has apparently not been confirmed, and how it can be so is not clear. Wever and Lawrence reported that attempts to block the round window in the cat produced a reduction rather than an increase in the response to tones.

Most workers would probably agree with Sullivan and Hodges, who reasoned that movement of the round window increases the acuity of hearing, and that deafness may be expected to result from immobility of the window; they suggested that deafness after a fenestration, for example, may be due to scar tissue filling in the niche of the round window.

CHANGES OF PRESSURE

Loch ('42a and b) has reported that decreased pressure in the middle ear cavity, due to absorption of air following occlusion of the Eustachian tube, produces an impairment for high tones which gradually increases and eventually involves also additional lower tones. He suggested, therefore, that tubal occlusion should be considered as one of the causes of impaired hearing for high tones.

In the opposite experiment, producing increasing pressure in the middle ear, he found that a slight positive pressure here improved the acuity of hearing for the highest tones; a moderate increase in pressure caused impairment of the thresholds for low and middle tones; a marked positive middle ear pressure impaired all frequencies below 2048 cycles by some 20 to 30 decibels. With increased pressure part of the improvement in hearing for the highest frequencies usually was lost.

Obviously, these experiments can be interpreted as demonstrating the effects of alterations of pressure on the tympanic membrane, on the mobility of the round window membrane directly, or on the pressure within the cochlea itself. Kobrak ('35) has reported that changes in the pressure in the middle ear cavity (of the rabbit) are transferred to the labyrinth, and if sufficiently great produce also a decrease in the contraction of the tensor tympani muscle.

BONE CONDUCTION

In contrast to hearing by air conduction, hearing by bone conduction does not involve the osseotympanic pathway, but a purely osseous one (Fig. 110). Guild ('36), in discussing this question, has pointed out that the most important part of this path is the osseous trabeculae connecting the medial part of the posterior wall of the external auditory canal to the inferolateral aspect of the horizontal semicircular canal; he has stated that this is of more importance than the other ones

not necessarily indicate so-called nerve deafness.

PNEUMATIZATION OF THE TEMPORAL BONE

The tympanic antrum communicates through the aditus with the upper part of the posterior portion of the epitympanic recess; it extends somewhat lateral to the

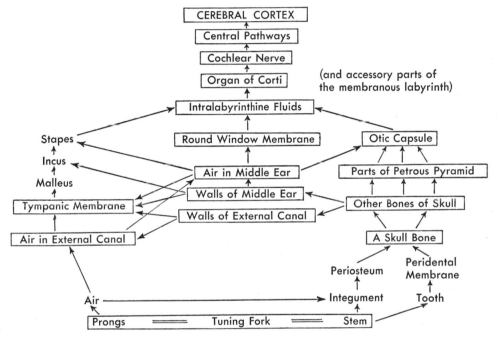

Fig. 110. Conduction of sound to and through the ear. (Redrawn from Guild, S. R.: *Ann. Otol., Rhin. & Laryng. 45:*736, 1936.)

because of the direction from which and the place at which the sound waves enter the intralabyrinthine fluids, and noted that lesions of this important pathway cause an impairment of the threshold of hearing by bone conduction. This emphasizes the fact, sometimes overlooked but also pointed out by Hughson ('38), that impairment of hearing by bone conduction is not necessarily due to a lesion of the inner ear or of the nerve itself—that is, that impairment of bone conduction does

tympanic cavity, and communicates in turn with the mastoid air cells. Since it is a relatively large cavity, it is the key to surgery of this region; both the mastoid air cells and the middle ear cavity proper may be approached from it.

The older surgical approach to the tympanic antrum is just behind the posterosuperior quadrant of the external meatus, through the so-called suprameatal triangle. In the adult, in whom the bony markings are best developed, the superior boundary of this triangle is the continuation backward above the meatus of the root of the zygoma; its anterior border is the posterosuperior segment of the bony external meatus, and its postero-inferior border is an imaginary line joining these two parts. In the endaural approach to the antrum, in which the incision is made between the tragus and helix and the skin is reflected from the bony meatus, the antrum is entered through its anterior wall, from the meatus. In opening the antrum or the mastoid air cells in the postaural approach the sigmoid sinus and the facial nerve are in particular danger, but can best be avoided by making the original opening as close to the angle of union between the root of the zygoma and the posterior wall of the meatus as possible, and carefully enlarging downward and backward from this. From the lateral aspect, the facial nerve lies approximately on the line of the groove between the tympanic and mastoid parts of the temporal bone (p. 195). In the endaural approach, the tympanic ring serves as a landmark for the depth of the facial nerve from the external surface; the vertical portion of the nerve lies only slightly deeper than this.

MASTOID PORTION

The mastoid portion of the temporal bone is constantly pneumatized in the adult (though not in the infant) but varies very considerably in the extent of its pneumatization and in the arrangement of the air cells. These cells grow out not only from the antrum, but also from each other, so that they form complex interlocking chains of thin-walled cavities opening into each other (Fig. 101, p. 176). While there are apparently always air cells in the region of the antrum, the mastoid process as a whole is usually de-scribed as being of one of several types: pneumatized, diploic (containing marrow rather than air cells), mixed (containing both marrow and air cells), or sclerotic (very dense bone). Tremble reported that about 80 per cent of mastoids are well pneumatized by the age of 3 or 4 years, but that in 20 per cent normal pneumatization fails to appear.

The *terminology* describing the cell groups in the mastoid is complex and variable. The cell groups within the body of the mastoid may be along the posterior aspect of the facial canal (retrofacial cells of Broca), over the lateral surface of the sigmoid sinus, behind the sinus (marginal cells), or at the tip of the mastoid process (mastoid tip cells). Meltzer has considered them in three major groups: a superior group, an antero-inferior group, and a medioposterior group, according to their relations to the sigmoid portion of the lateral sinus. He has pointed out that the position of the lateral sinus in relation to the mastoid process (a variable relationship, since the lateral sinus shows variations in both its course and size) determines to what extent pneumatization by these various cell groups will occur and causes definite variations in their development (Fig. 111). He called attention to the fact that when the sinus plate (the harder bone surrounding the sinus) is in contact with the cortex of the squama, cells cannot develop posterior to the sinus and the medioposterior group is therefore missing; if the sinus plate is deep and close to the floor of the antrum and the facial ridge, cells develop freely both antero-inferiorly and medioposteriorly; if it is in contact with the posterior wall of the external auditory canal and with the lateral surface of the mastoid process then cells cannot develop either antero-inferiorly or medioposteriorly.

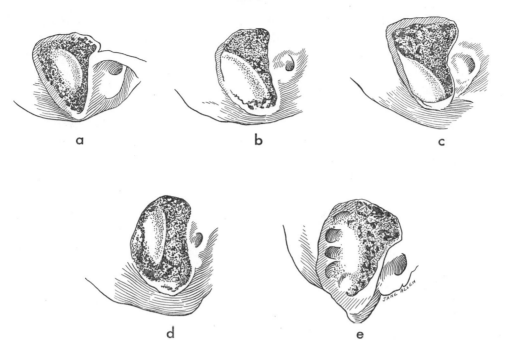

a b c

d e

Fig. 111. Various relations of the sigmoid sinus in the mastoid process, indicating the fashion in which the size and placement of this sinus affects the development of cell groups in the mastoid. (Redrawn from Meltzer, P. E.: *Arch. Otolaryng. 19*:326, 1934.)

"FALSE BOTTOM"

As the mastoid process develops from two different portions of the temporal bone (squamous and petrous), the cells growing downward from the antrum are, at least at first, divisible into two groups, squamous and petrous, separated from each other by the petromastoid (petrosquamous) suture. The suture itself is usually obliterated in adult life, though it may be marked on the surface of the mastoid process by a line at which the periosteum is firmly attached. Internally, the plane of the suture may divide the mastoid cells into a superficial and upper (squamous) group and a deeper (petrous) group which extends downward into the mastoid tip. These two cell groups may differ in the degree of their development; moreover, it sometimes happens that they are separated by an appreciably heavy plate of bone along the petromastoid suture. If this is well developed, it is called the "false bottom" or Korner's septum (Fig. 112), and is of special significance in operations upon the mastoid cells.

The postaural approach to the mastoid

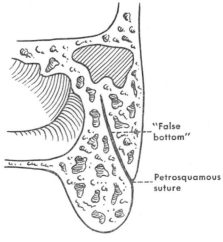

"False bottom"

Petrosquamous suture

Fig. 112. Diagram of the "false bottom."

leads to the superficial and upper group of cells; if these are poorly developed, difficulty may be experienced in reaching the deeper cells through the more dense bone. Moreover, if the "false bottom" is well developed, it may mislead the inexperienced surgeon into believing that the cellular portion of the mastoid has been entirely explored, while in fact the petrous cells, deep to the false bottom, are apt to be larger and better developed than are the superficial cells. It is the deep

accessory cells derived from the mastoid may also extend into the root or body of the zygomatic arch, into the squamous portion of the temporal bone, and into the floor of the middle cranial cavity as *epitympanic cells* (both above the otic capsule and, as cells of Kirchner, in the roof of the external meatus). From examinations of gross sections of the temporal bone the cells extending forward in the petrous pyramid have also been classed as a part of the mastoid group,

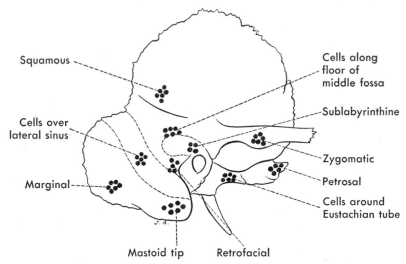

Fig. 113.   The chief groups of air cells in the temporal bone. (Redrawn from Tremble, G. E.: *Arch. Otolaryng. 19:*172, 1934.)

cells, also, that lead to the lowest cells in the mastoid, those at the tip.

but are apparently not so derived (see the following paragraph).

ACCESSORY CELL GROUPS FROM MASTOID

The air cells developed in connection with the mastoid process are not necessarily confined to this process, but may also invade other parts of the temporal bone to form accessory cell groups (Fig. 113). Thus cells from the mastoid may also extend below the labyrinth and into the floor of the tympanic cavity, between this and the jugular bulb, where they are usually referred to as *hypotympanic cells*, or as the jugular bulb group. Similarly,

PETROUS PORTION

The petrous portion of the temporal bone anterior to the tympanum and the labyrinth (petrous apex) is also subject to pneumatization, varying markedly however from one individual to another. The cells in the *petrous apex*, once regarded as extensions of the mastoid cells, are now accepted as being independent outgrowths from the tympanic cavity near the orifice of the auditory tube. Subtubal air cells are said to be present in 90 per cent of infants up to the age of 6 years, and may or may not spread widely through the petrous pyramid. Hagens reported that approximately 34 per cent of the temporal bones which he studied showed air cells in the petrous tip; Myerson, Rubin, and Gilbert reported that only 11 per cent of the bones they studied had well-pneumatized petrous pyramids, and that none of these occurred in individuals below the age of 15 years. As noted by the last-named authors and by Ziegelman the cellular character of the mastoid does not necessarily indicate the extent of pneumatization of the petrous pyramid.

The cells extending into the petrous apex are necessarily related both to the Eustachian tube and to the carotid canal, and have been variously termed peritubal cells, petrous cells, angle cells, and cells of the petrous tip, but this latter term should be reserved for those cells located in the anterior end of the pyramid. Dearmin has stated that the petrous tip cells always lie posterior and superior to the carotid artery.

According to Anson, Wilson, and Gaardsmoe, the cell groups of the petrous pyramid have essentially a simple pattern related chiefly to the carotid canal. Four chief groups of cells, originating anterolateral to the canal and tending to encircle it, were distinguished: one group extends posterolaterally (backward) along the carotid canal, as far as the apical turn of the cochlea; another and larger group extends upward, spreading above the carotid canal and then downward on its posteromedial aspect; a third group extends forward lying anteromedially along the course of the auditory canal and beneath the turn of the carotid canal to extend into the walls of the jugular and mandibular fossae; and a more posterior group extends almost as far as the basal turn of the cochlea and the internal auditory meatus, but not above or below the labyrinth. Although the cell groups of the petrous pyramid may be directly adjacent to mastoid cells of the epitympanic and hypotympanic groups, these workers found no continuity between the mastoid and petrous groups. In this study they also found no cells arising from the auditory tube itself; rather the cells merely extended along the tube from an origin on the tympanic wall. Wolff ('34a) has similarly stated that the peritubal cells in the fetus are derivatives of the tympanic cavity and not of the Eustachian tube itself, but stated that secondarily they may open into the tube.

The most evident pathway for *infection of the petrous pyramid,* in addition to those furnished by the pathways of the nerves and vessels of this region, is by direct extension from the middle ear cavity, and Lindsay ('45) has stated that osteomyelitis of the pyramid is usually due to such an extension. Earlier workers stressed especially the possibility of extension from the mastoid along either an epitympanic or a hypotympanic route; while this is of course a possibility, it is lessened by the apparent fact that the mastoid and petrous pyramid cells, while they may be contiguous, are not, as once thought, continuous with each other.

Dearmin, Jones, and Ziegelman have each discussed the surgery of these cell groups. In essence, it obviously depends upon following closely the carotid canal in order to remove the cells about it. Farrior ('49) has emphasized that the hypotympanic cells may come into contiguity with peritubal and petrous apex cells, and should be explored in all radical mastoidectomies. He described a technic for complete exenteration of cells in the hypotympanum and about the carotid artery and auditory tube in a radical mastoidectomy; earlier ('42) he described a sublabyrinthine approach to the petrous apex, which can be developed, after a simple mastoidectomy, through the sublabyrinthine cells. He stated that this route could be developed even when sublabyrinthine cells are not present, but surely in many of these cases the available space must be severely limited by the sigmoid sinus.

point of considerable importance to the aural surgeon.

The facial nerve traverses the internal auditory meatus, within the petrous portion of the temporal bone, in company with the auditory nerve and the internal auditory artery; at the outer end of this canal the facial lies above the other elements, and pierces the arachnoid and dura to enter its own bony canal, the facial canal (aqueduct of Fallopius, Fallopian canal). Occasionally, the subarachnoid

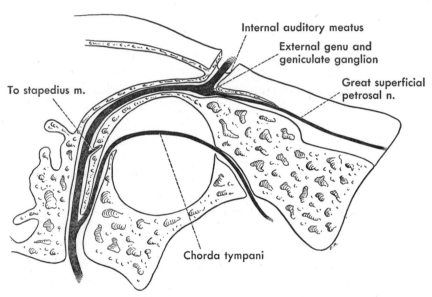

Fig. 114. The facial nerve in the temporal bone. The chorda tympani actually passes between the malleus and incus, not shown, in its course across the tympanic membrane.

COURSE OF THE FACIAL NERVE THROUGH THE TEMPORAL BONE

FACIAL NERVE

The orgin of the facial nerve is discussed in the chapter on the cranium, and its more specific relations and distributions are described in connection with the external ear, the face, the nose, and the mandibular and lingual regions. The only concern here is the relationships of the nerve within the temporal bone, a

space may accompany the facial nerve into the canal, even as far as the geniculate ganglion (Perlman and Lindsay, '39). This canal continues for a short distance the lateral direction of the internal meatus, and the facial nerve thus comes to lie just above the base of the cochlea (therefore above and medial to the promontory), where it bears the geniculate ganglion (Fig. 114). From the geniculate ganglion is given off the greater superficial petrosal nerve, which passes anteriorly and slightly medially to enter the middle cranial fossa (pp. 252 and 66).

Immediately beyond the geniculate ganglion the course of the facial nerve is altered abruptly, as the nerve here forms its external genu, a sharp turn laterally and posteriorly around the front of the vestibule of the internal ear, between this and the cochlea. The position of the genu may be located from the middle ear by the emerging tendon of the tensor tympani muscle, as the genu lies just deep to the tip of the processus cochleariformis. As it runs backward in the bone of the lateral wall of the vestibule, which is also the medial wall of the tympanic cavity, the facial nerve also inclines slightly downward and laterally; here the bone about it forms a projection (the prominence of the facial canal) into the latter cavity, so that the course of the facial canal beneath the prominence of the lateral (horizontal) semicircular canal and above the vestibular or oval window can be seen upon inspection of the middle ear cavity. In the posterior part of its short "horizontal" course the facial nerve, although it lies below the prominence of the lateral semicircular canal, may come to lie lateral and then posterior to the posterior end of this canal, and also just lateral to and above the ampullary end of the posterior vertical canal.

In this position, behind the base of the pyramidal eminence, the facial nerve makes a rather broad curve downward to run almost vertically, but inclining slightly outward, through the mastoid process to the stylomastoid foramen; here the facial canal ends, and the nerve finally emerges from the skull. The position of the stylomastoid foramen is located in mastoidectomy by the anteromedial end of the digastric crest, the upward projection of cortical bone formed by the di-gastric or mastoid notch on the inferior surface of the mastoid. As it passes behind the pyramidal eminence the nerve gives off a filament for the innervation of the stapedius muscle, and shortly before leaving the stylomastoid foramen it gives off the chorda tympani, the course of which is described later in this section.

As it runs downward through the mastoid process behind the tympanic cavity the facial nerve may have a straight course or may be slightly concave anteriorly; the course of the nerve in relation to the exterior of the skull corresponds approximately to the suture groove between the tympanic and mastoid portions of the temporal bone, though the nerve lies, of course, medial to this. Kettel ('46) quoted Batson as having found the nerve never lying posterior to this line, but sometimes slightly anterior to it; among 125 operations on the nerve within the canal, however, Kettel reported 3 cases in which there was a marked deviation from this course, and the nerve lay posterior to its usual line. In 2 of these 3 cases the nerve emerged from the anterior aspect of the mastoid process rather than from between the mastoid and styloid processes (Fig. 115). In the infant, in whom the mastoid process has not yet developed, the facial nerve lies quite superficially in the bone behind the external meatus, and upon its emergence through the stylomastoid foramen is almost subcutaneous, since it is not protected by a mastoid process.

INJURIES IN THE TEMPORAL BONE

Because of its relationship to the middle ear cavity and the mastoid cells, the facial nerve during its intratemporal course is subject to damage both from infections of the middle ear and the mastoid, and from operations upon the mastoid. Bunnell ('37) has estimated that in not more than 7 per cent of cases is facial paralysis due to infections of the middle ear cavity; the incidence of surgical injury is of course unknown. So-called idiopathic paralysis of the facial nerve within the canal also occurs, as described originally by Bell; it has been thought to be due to edema of the nerve with compression by the bony canal.

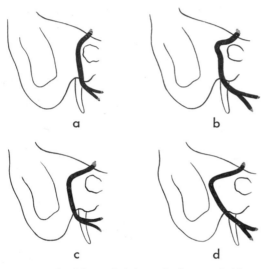

Fig. 115. Normal (*a*) and abnormal (*b*, *c*, *d*) courses of the facial nerve. (Redrawn from Kettel, K.: *Arch. Otolaryng. 44:*406, 1946.)

Kettel ('47) concluded that the primary change is one of ischemia, due to malfunction of the vasa nervorum, and has reported and discussed a number of cases in which decompression of the nerve was carried out by opening the Fallopian canal from the stylomastoid foramen to the lateral semicircular canal.

The diagnosis of the level of injury in cases of lesions of the facial nerve, dependent upon the level at which various branches leave it, has been discussed by Bunnell, and by Tschiassny; it should be mentioned, however, that some of the conclusions of this latter worker as to the

anatomy of the facial nerve are not widely accepted. Ballance and Duel pointed out the possibility of the use of a nerve graft to fill the gap produced by destruction of a portion of the nerve in the Fallopian canal, and said that such a graft is preferable to freeing the nerve from its normal location and displacing it so that the ends may be brought together by primary suture. Bunnell ('27) first described this latter technic, and reported the first successful case of intratemporal repair of the facial nerve; he has emphasized the advantages of intratemporal repair, pointing out that anastomosis with other nerves does not restore emotional facial expression.

Chorda Tympani

The chorda tympani is composed of sensory and preganglionic motor fibers, both of these running proximally in the pars intermedia (nerve of Wrisberg) of the facial nerve. Beyond the geniculate ganglion, the fibers destined for the chorda tympani are an intrinsic part of the facial trunk until it reaches a point shortly above the stylomastoid foramen; here the chorda tympani leaves the facial trunk and takes a recurrent course upward and forward in the iter chordae posterius, to enter the tympanic cavity through its posterior wall. Within the cavity it lies at first close to the posterior border of the tympanic membrane, but diverges somewhat to pass between the malleus and the incus, as it crosses the upper aspect of the membrane; it leaves the tympanic cavity by way of the iter chordae anterius and emerges from the skull through the petrotympanic fissure. It then joins the lingual nerve to be distributed to taste buds of the anterior two thirds of the tongue, and to the submaxillary ganglion, through which postganglionic fibers reach the submaxillary and sublingual salivary glands. After its emergence from the skull it has a twig of communication with the otic ganglion; it is believed by some workers that through this communication the facial nerve also supplies secretory fibers to the parotid gland, which is generally admitted to be supplied also or exclusively by the ninth nerve.

In spite of its theoretical importance as indicated by the above statements, *injuries* to the chorda tympani are not necessarily associated with any marked symptoms. The chorda tympani may be destroyed by disease in chronic mastoiditis, removed in radical mastoidectomy, or occasionally accidentally torn in fenestration operations, yet the patient does not necessarily complain of the loss of taste on the anterior two thirds of the tongue. Likewise, the reduction in salivation which would be expected to be produced by injury to this nerve is apparently not marked, either because of autonomous activity on the part of the denervated glands, or because, as suggested by several authors, the glands may likewise be innervated through the glossopharyngeal nerve.

In its course through the iter posterius toward the middle ear the chorda tympani is accompanied by a branch of the stylomastoid artery to the middle ear, and through the anterior iter it is accompanied by the anterior tympanic branch of the internal maxillary artery. The nerve is of course subject to damage through anything affecting the intracranial portion of the facial nerve as a whole, and may be injured by any injury to the upper part of the tympanic membrane. Like the other structures in the middle ear cavity, the chorda tympani is covered by a reflection of the mucous membrane of this cavity and therefore does not actually traverse this space.

ANOMALIES AND PATHOLOGY

Variations in the middle ear due to varying arrangements of air cells are of course numerous and are discussed briefly in the section on pneumatization of the temporal bone.

Atresia of the external auditory meatus (p. 174) is usually accompanied by deformations of the middle ear cavity and of the ossicular chain, and the bones may be so deformed as to be hardly recognizable.

Other purely anatomical anomalies of the middle ear are also occasionally found. Walls has described 3 specimens in which a muscle arising from the spine of the sphenoid bone had a tendon of insertion that passed through the petrotympanic fissure to join the anterior or long process of the malleus. Describing this under the name of the *laxator tympani muscle,* he has noted that it has been previously described as the major laxator, but that it is now generally agreed that the so-called minor laxator is actually a ligament rather than a muscle.

Druss and Allen have described a rare case of *fistula* communicating with the middle ear cavity; as already noted, the so-called preauricular fistula and others of that nature usually do not communicate with the middle ear. The auricle on the involved side was markedly abnormal; a fistula began on the upper part of the auricle close to the external auditory meatus and opened into the neck immediately behind the lower margin of the auricle, but from this lower opening a second fistula extended medially and forward deep into the neck, and one part of it communicated with the lower part of the tympanic cavity. They found only 1 similar case previously reported.

Polvogt has described a number of abnormalities of the tympanic membrane and other parts of the middle ear in persons who had, before death, been shown to have had apparently normal hearing. A number of these ears showed pathological variations of the membrane ranging from slight thickening to marked calcification, and variations in its position ranging from moderate to extreme retraction, in the latter cases with the drum even adherent to the promontory. He found that in such cases the region of the oval window and the niche of the round window were seldom free from strands of embryonic tissue, these strands being sometimes small and delicate and sometimes broad and fibrous. In 16 of 63 ears the mucous membrane over the promontory was abnormally thickened, probably as a result of old infections. He also noted that in some cases the malleus and incus were composed of dense bone with few marrow spaces, while in others there were large marrow spaces with a thin bony cortex. None of these variations had apparently any effect upon hearing.

The rare "glomus jugulare" tumors of the middle ear have already been commented upon (p. 182).

OTOSCLEROSIS

The most common and serious anatomicopathological change of the middle ear is otosclerosis. This was said by Davenport, Milles, and Frink to occur probably in about 0.2 per cent of the white population of the United States, but Guild ('44) pointed out that a sharp distinction should be made between clinical otosclerosis and histological otosclerosis; in a large series of ears which he investigated the incidence of histological otosclerosis was 1 in 8 for white females and 1 in 15 for white males above the age of 5 years. From Guild's study it appears that factors of race, sex, and age all influence the incidence of the disease. While Davenport, Milles, and Frink concluded that there was a genetic factor involved, Guild's study indicates the impossibility of drawing valid conclusions concerning this from purely clinical studies.

Wilson and Anson, among others, have described the histological characteristics of otosclerosis, noting that the diseased bone is richly vascularized by large thin-walled vessels, and usually restricted to certain portions of the capsule; Davenport, Milles, and Frink, in discussing this disease, pointed out that the first marked changes are an ossification of the annular ligament, between the fenestra ovalis and the base of the stapes, but that this is apparently not dependent upon inflammatory changes; Wilson and Anson likewise found no evidence of inflammatory reaction in the cases which they studied.

Bast ('33), Anson and Martin, Bast ('40), and Anson, Cauldwell and Bast have all emphasized that the otic capsule, even in the adult, may not be completely ossified but may contain, rather, islands of cartilage, and have said that these islands, which may show calcification, are foci for the origin and spread of otosclerosis. Bast suggested that attempts to repair these bony defects later in life, when ossification of the capsule is normally completed, might be the initiating cause. These writers have especially stressed the relationship of the fissula ante fenestram (p. 204) to the onset of otosclerotic changes, since this opens usually close to the oval window and regularly contains cartilage at its vestibular end with islands of calcified cartilage scattered elsewhere within it. Guild, in his extensive study, found no support for this concept. Bast ('40) found defective ossification of residual cartilage about the fossula post fenestram in only about 5 per cent of the cases which he studied, and found that otosclerotic bone formation here was rare; on the other hand, he found defective development of the petrous bone in the region of the fissula ante fenestram in a large percentage of the ears of fetuses and young children. He also reported finding cartilage and defective bone in the infracochlear region, the base of the styloid process, the region of the petrosquamous suture (and the capsule beneath the suture), and the region of the semicircular canals.

Wittmaack concluded that venous stasis may be a factor in the onset of otosclerosis; upon producing such stasis in the hen he found that changes similar to those in human clinical otosclerosis occurred. Noting that otosclerotic changes are more common near the oval window, he has pointed out that the chief drainage from this region is a vein running with the lesser superficial petrosal nerve to join the pterygoid plexus. Lempert and Wolff have regularly found pathological changes in the blood vessels of the bones of otosclerotic ears, and expressed the belief that these changes precede and probably initiate the changes in the bones; as further discussed by Wolff ('50), they have interpreted their observations to mean that otosclerosis has no specific etiologic agent, but is the result of damage to the peripheral blood supply, of whatever cause—chemical, vasomotor, or allergic.

The recognized operation at present,

perfected especially by Lempert (for instance, '38, '40, '41, '47, '48a), is that commonly referred to as "*fenestration.*" This involves exposing the lateral wall of the otic capsule by an approach to the middle ear, removing the useless incus and excising the head of the malleus, and removing bone and external and internal periostea between the internal and middle ears so as to make a new opening or window into the perilymphatic cavity. The rationale of the operation is to provide two movable windows, so that differences in the pressure upon these may set up movements in the perilymph. The opening could conceivably be made in several locations, but has become standardized over the ampullary (anterior) end of the lateral (horizontal) canal; the landmarks here are clearest, and an opening so made in the bony labyrinth leads directly into the vestibule. The new window thus made is covered with a viable graft to serve as a membrane; this graft is commonly a skin flap from the external auditory meatus.

In addition to the usual necessity for careful selection of cases for operation, and precise surgical technic, another factor also influences the permanent success of this operation: following the formation of a new window, new bone formation may occur around its edge so that the window becomes narrowed or indeed entirely closed once more. Lindsay ('46) has emphasized the importance of the removal of all bony fragments from the region of the window; he said also that prevention of regeneration of bone depends upon an adequate fibrous union between the flap and the membranous canal, to prevent the ingrowth of osteogenic tissue (periosteum or endosteum).

THE INTERNAL EAR

THE internal ear consists of two fundamental parts: complex cavities (perilymphatic or periotic spaces) hollowed out within the petrous portion of the temporal bone (petrous pyramid) and referred to, with the surrounding bone, as the osseous labyrinth; and, within the osseous labyrinth, the delicate and slightly more complex membranous (otic) labyrinth.

various connections are formed (Fig. 116). The membranous labyrinth, being essentially tubular and saccular in nature, contains a cavity termed the endolymphatic space, which in turn is filled with fluid, the endolymphatic fluid.

Since the early development of the membranous labyrinth takes place in mesenchyme, and subsequently even in

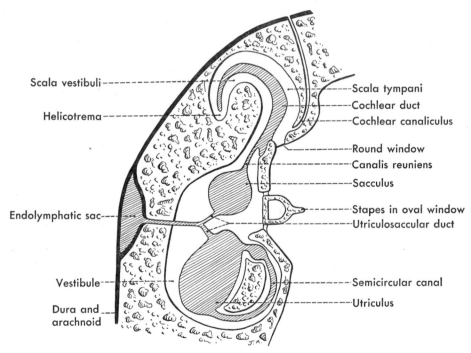

Fig. 116. Highly schematic representation of the perilymphatic and endolymphatic systems. The endolymphatic system is shaded.

EMBRYOLOGY

The membranous labyrinth is developed from a placodal thickening of the ectoderm, which subsequently sinks beneath the surface ectoderm to become a closed vesicle. By differential growth of this tiny vesicle and fusion of portions of its walls three semicircular canals, a utricle and a saccule, a cochlear duct, an endolymphatic (otic) sac, and their

the cartilage destined to form the petrous portion of the temporal bone, it is obvious that the membranous labyrinth must lie in cavities excavated from this mesenchyme or cartilage (later transformed to bone). The cavities of the temporal bone surrounding the membranous labyrinth are larger than is necessary for the accommodation of this latter, and the excess space thus existing between the inner surface of the bony wall and the outer surface of the membranous labyrinth is the perilymphatic (periotic) space; this space is in most locations traversed by numerous fibrous trabeculae, between which are interstices filled with fluid, termed the perilymphatic fluid. In other locations, notably the cochlea, the trabeculae are reduced or absent and fluid alone occupies the perilymphatic space.

The perilymphatic spaces develop around the membranous labyrinth by a process of fusion of mesenchymal spaces to form larger ones, eventually almost completely surrounding the membranous portion; as the petrous portion of the temporal bone is represented in cartilage for some time before the membranous labyrinth has completed its growth, further growth of this portion is allowed for by a constant dedifferentiation of the cartilage surrounding the membranous labyrinth and subsequent enlargement of the perilymphatic spaces following degeneration of this cartilage.

The essential steps in the formation and growth of the membranous labyrinth and the perilymphatic spaces have been described by Streeter ('17a and b); further details have more recently been contributed by Foley. The development of the bony capsule has been analyzed especially by Bast; references on this subject will be found in his paper of 1942, and in the text of Bast and Anson.

OSSEOUS LABYRINTH

The shape of the bony labyrinth in the adult may be determined by casts of the perilymphatic cavity (periotic cistern), or, because the bone adjacent to the perilymphatic cavity is usually more dense than bone elsewhere, may be outlined by dissections to the surface of this denser bone (the otic capsule). In the infant, this latter procedure is said to be especially accurate.

The cavity of the bony labyrinth is lined by a thin layer of internal periosteum or endosteum, and most of it is crossed, as already mentioned, by a spongelike arrangement of delicate trabeculae somewhat similar to the arachnoid trabeculae of the subarachnoid space. According to Lempert, Wever, Lawrence, and Meltzer this spongelike tissue is so dense that it prevents the free escape of perilymph from the trephine opening of a fenestration; however, they found this tissue to be lacking in the immediate neighborhood of the footplate of the stapes, and throughout the bony cochlea (scala vestibuli and scala tympani). The periosteum and the trabeculae lying within the bony otic capsule can properly be referred to as the periotic labyrinth (Bast and Anson), a term that distinguishes between these soft tissues and the bone that surrounds them —either or both may be implied by the term "osseous labyrinth." The periotic labyrinth and the perilymphatic (periotic) fluid in turn surround the membranous (otic) labyrinth except in certain locations where the membranous labyrinth is fused to the periosteum lining the bony labyrinth.

VESTIBULE

The central portion of the cavity of the bony labyrinth is the vestibule, a relatively large ovoid perilymphatic space (about 4 mm. in diameter) containing both the sacculus and the utriculus of the membranous labyrinth. In the floor of the bony vestibule may be seen an elliptical recess for the anterior end of the utriculus, and anterior and slightly lateral to this a spherical recess for the sacculus. In the lateral wall of the vestibule is the oval window, housing the footplate of the stapes. Through the stapes the perilymph of the vestibule receives the vibrations of the tympanic membrane and ossicular chain set up by sound waves reaching the tympanic membrane. On the medial wall and floor of the vestibule, where it abuts on the lateral end of the internal auditory meatus, are minute openings for the entrance of the nerve branches to the vestibular portion of the ear.

SEMICIRCULAR CANALS

The vestibule is continuous with the three bony semicircular canals; the cavities within these are markedly larger than the membranous canals which they contain. A portion of the superior bony semicircular canal may form a ridge (arcuate ridge) on the floor of the middle cranial fossa, and the posterior canal may form a projection in the anterior wall of the posterior cranial fossa (posterior surface of the petrous ridge). The lateral ("horizontal") semicircular canal projects, as already described, as a ridge on the medial wall of the tympanic cavity, and it is here, toward the anterior end of this canal, that the perilymphatic space is opened in the operation of fenestration. The cavities (periotic or perilymphatic spaces) of all three bony semicircular canals open into the vestibule at both their ends.

The superior (anterior) and posterior semicircular canals (sometimes referred to together as the vertical canals) are both arranged in the vertical plane, but their long axes are at approximate right angles to each other. The superior semicircular canal is directed anterolaterally at an angle of about 45 degrees to the midsagittal plane, and the posterior canal is directed posterolaterally at a corresponding angle. The posterior end of the superior canal and the anterosuperior end of the posterior canal join together before entering the vestibule, to form a common crus. The lateral canal lies only approximately in the horizontal plane, for its anterior end is higher than its posterior one so that it makes an angle of about 30 degrees with this plane; both its anterior and posterior ends open independently into the vestibule.

COCHLEA

The perilymphatic (periotic) cavity of the vestibule is also continuous with that of the other functional division of the inner ear, the cochlea (see Figs. 91, p. 167, and 116, p. 200). The bony cochlea, a part of the otic capsule, is named from its resemblance to a snail shell; it is a hollowed spiral of about two and three fourths turns which diminishes in size from a relatively broad base to a pointed apex or cupula. The base lies against the anteromedial surface of the vestibule, and abuts also on the anterior surface of the lateral or blind end of the internal auditory meatus. The large basal coil of the cochlea forms the promontory where it projects into the middle ear cavity. From the vestibule the cochlea is directed anterolaterally and slightly upward. A central core of bone, the modiolus, runs forward in the cochlea, but fails to reach the apex; it is about this central core that the spiral channels (perilymphatic and endolymphatic) of the cochlea are arranged. A layer of bone, arranged in a spiral fashion, unites the modiolus to the peripheral wall of the bony cochlea, and separates the successive spiral cavities from each other.

The modiolus is hollow; its base lies against the lateral end of the internal auditory meatus, from which it receives and transmits in its center the cochlear nerve. From the outer surface of the modiolus, like the flanges of a screw, an osseous spiral lamina projects into the perilymphatic space and partially divides it into two parts. This is also hollow, and transmits the branches of the cochlear nerve to the end organ, the organ of Corti of the membranous cochlear duct. The membranous cochlear duct or scala media is attached to the osseous spiral lamina,

ing to describe this spiral structure; hence it is customary to describe the cochlea as if it were sitting on its base with the apex pointing upward. The true directions can be somewhat approximated if, in the present account, the word "anterior" is substituted for "above," and "posterior" is substituted for "beneath.") The scala vestibuli is separated from the descending spiral, the scala tympani, both by the spiral lamina and by the membranous cochlear duct itself (Fig. 117).

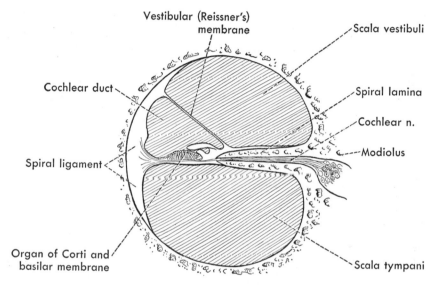

Fig. 117. Section through a single turn of the cochlea.

and extends from this central core of bone across the perilymphatic space, to attach to the outer wall of this space; thus the spiral lamina and the membranous cochlea divide the perilymphatic space into its two portions, an ascending and a descending spiral.

The ascending spiral of the bony labyrinth is the scala vestibuli, which lies "above" the spiral lamina of the cochlea. (Since the cochlea points anteriorly, laterally, and slightly upward, the usual anatomical terms indicating position become hopelessly complicated in attempt-

At the apex of the cochlea the cochlear duct, like the modiolus, ends blindly, without coming in contact with the apex of the bony wall, and around these blind ends the scala vestibuli becomes continuous with the descending scala tympani, this communication being known as the helicotrema. The scala vestibuli begins at the base of the cochlea as a large opening from the vestibule; from the helicotrema the descending osseous labyrinth, the scala tympani, runs backward and downward "beneath" the spiral osseous lamina and the cochlear duct to end blindly at its lower end, being provided here with a membranous round window by which the perilymphatic space is separated from the middle ear cavity.

CONNECTIONS OF PERILYMPHATIC SPACES

The perilymphatic (periotic) spaces of the osseous semicircular canals are continuous with the perilymphatic space of the vestibule, and this space is continuous widely with that of the scala vestibuli, which is then in turn continuous with that of the scala tympani at the helicotrema. All the perilymphatic spaces, therefore, open widely into each other. While these perilymphatic spaces lie within the compact bone of the petrous portion of the temporal bone, this bone is deficient in certain locations, and therefore presents regions of actual or potential communication between the perilymphatic space and other cavities. Thus, in addition to the oval and round windows which form potential communications between the middle and internal ears, the fissula (fissura) ante fenestram, and sometimes the fossula post fenestram, are likewise defects in the bony wall between these two parts, while the cochlear and vestibular canaliculi, and the foramina for the nerves and vessels of the internal ear, are channels between the inner ear and the cranial cavity. Of these channels, all except possibly one are normally obstructed.

At the *oval window* the vestibule is of course sealed off from the middle ear cavity by the footplate of the stapes and its retaining ligament, while the *round window* is similarly sealed by its membrane. The *fissula ante fenestram* and the *fossula post fenestram* are irregular clefts in the lateral wall of the internal ear, extending from the vestibule toward the tympanic cavity; the fissula usually extends completely through the bony lateral wall of the vestibule, while the fossula usually has a vestibular end only, but in about 25 per cent of cases extends to the tympanic cavity. In any case, however, these fissures contain no marked extension of the perilymphatic space since they are obliterated by connective tissue (Anson, Cauldwell, and Bast).

The cochlear canaliculus, however, does contain a perilymphatic channel, the *cochlear aqueduct* or the *perilymphatic* or *periotic duct,* which according to most descriptions opens at one end into the perilymphatic space (at the lower end of the scala tympani) and at the other end into the subarachnoid cavity (but see p. 205). In addition to the cochlear aqueduct, the cochlear canaliculus is usually said to transmit also a vein, known as the vein of the cochlear canaliculus; according to Bast ('46), however, this vein lies in a separate canal after ossification of the otic capsule has occurred.

The *vestibular canaliculus* likewise extends through the otic capsule, from the vestibule to the posterior cranial fossa; its periosteal lining forms the vestibular aqueduct, which transmits the *endolymphatic (otic) duct* and an accompanying vein. The duct and its terminal dilation end blindly beneath the dura; moreover, although the vestibular aqueduct is usually described and diagrammed as containing, around the endolymphatic duct, a perilymphatic space continuous with that of the vestibule and ending blindly subdurally, Bast and Anson have emphasized that this is not correct, as the endolymphatic duct and its associated connective tissue and vein completely fill the canaliculus. Thus the perilymphatic space of the vestibule is not brought here into close contact with other cavities.

Finally, the channels transmitting the nerves and vessels, while forming routes by which infections may reach the internal ear, are normally closed by the structures which traverse them, and therefore do not actually open into the perilymphatic space.

Circulation of the Perilymph

It has been commonly believed that there may be a constant interchange between the cerebrospinal and the perilymphatic fluids, or that indeed the perilymph arises from the cerebrospinal fluid. Thus Perlman and Lindsay ('39), in discussing the communications, potential or actual, between the meningeal spaces and those of the internal ear, have described extensions of pus, or of red blood cells following a subarachnoid hemorrhage, as passing outward from the subarachnoid space through the cochlear aqueduct, to accumulate in the basal turn of the scala tympani. Perlman and Lindsay said that there was probably little circulation of perilymph within the cochlea, but concluded that the observations reported above indicated that such circulation as is present is from the subarachnoid space to the cochlea.

Altmann and Waltner ('47), working on the rabbit (in which the cochlear aqueduct is apparently much wider than in man), found that substances injected into the subarachnoid space reached the perilymph very rapidly, even within five minutes, and expressed the belief that there was a strong current from the subarachnoid to the perilymphatic space. Later (Altmann and Waltner, '50) they reported similar experiments on monkeys, in which the cochlear aqueduct is narrower, and concluded that the spread was by diffusion, that there are probably no active currents in the perilymph, and that the cerebrospinal fluid is not an essential source of perilymph. In tracing the "flow" of the perilymph by means of a Prussian blue solution injected into the subarach-

noid space, these authors found it spreading up the scala tympani and down the scala vestibuli to the vestibule, but it also penetrated the thin roof (Reissner's membrane) of the membranous cochlea; most of it was apparently absorbed into the blood stream in the membranous cochlea (in the area of the spiral ligament), but they said some was probably absorbed also from the endolymphatic sac.

COCHLEAR AQUEDUCT

Waltner has stated that the cochlear aqueduct (perilymphatic duct) does not form an actual open communication between the scala tympani and the subarachnoid cavity in the human ear. He has described in animals and in the adult human being, as well as in the fetal one, a thin membrane (the barrier membrane of the cochlear aqueduct) which he said completely occludes the cochlear aqueduct at the point at which it is supposed to open into the scala tympani. He expressed the belief that this membrane is normal, and that it therefore prevents interchange between the perilymphatic and subarachnoid fluids except by a process of diffusion. The invasion of the internal ear through the cochlear aqueduct, by pathological processes originating in the subarachnoid space, can of course be explained under these circumstances as being due to injury to this thin layer.

There is, however, even less agreement upon the structure and function of the cochlear aqueduct than is indicated by the opinions quoted above. Mygind ('48a) has noted that the osmotic pressure and the albumen content of the perilymph have been shown to be higher than those of the cerebrospinal fluid, and pointed out also that increased intracranial pressure is rarely accompanied by evidence of increased labyrinthine pressure. He said this was due to the meshwork of tissue in the periotic space of the cochlear aqueduct, which he conceived of as being so dense as to allow no actual flow of fluid, but rather only a gradual soaking through, as through a piece of cotton. Finally, Meurman has described the periotic duct or cochlear aqueduct as becoming a solid fibrous thread at its vestibular end, so that it cannot possibly transmit fluid freely under normal conditions.

OSMOTIC PRESSURE

Whatever may be the facts, the weight of evidence appears to indicate that there is not a free interchange between the cerebrospinal and the perilymphatic fluids, as has usually been assumed in the past. Aldred, Hallpike, and Ledoux, through their studies of the osmotic pressure of the endolymph, perilymph, and cerebrospinal fluid, have apparently shown that the perilymph is formed by free diffusion of the endolymph through Reissner's membrane, as the osmotic pressure of the two is usually identical; on the other hand, the higher osmotic pressure of the perilymph over that of the cerebrospinal fluid does not indicate a contribution of cerebrospinal fluid to the perilymph. It seems very probable that the perilymph has a common origin with the endolymph, and is either absorbed with that or into the small vessels which cross the perilymphatic space in the trabeculae. Altmann and Waltner ('50) expressed preference for the concept that the perilymph originates largely from the perilymphatic blood vessels.

LYMPHATICS?

The interesting experiments and observations of Young ('49, '50) suggest still another possibility for normal absorption of the perilymph. This worker diffused dye into the perilymph, and found it later not in the subarachnoid fluid but rather in retropharyngeal lymphatics and nodes; by this technic and other means he has apparently demonstrated lymphatic channels which drain the labyrinth and join the lymphatics of the middle ear to pass along the Eustachian tube, or which pass through channels in the bone to emerge close to the temporomandibular joint.

MEMBRANOUS LABYRINTH

It is the growth of the membranous (otic) labyrinth which gives rise to the form of the osseous one, since the osseous labyrinth consists simply of periosteum-lined spaces surrounding and enclosing the membranous labyrinth. The differentiation of the membranous labyrinth leads to the formation of a superior, a posterior, and a lateral semicircular canal, pinched off from the central vesicle except at their ends; a spiral cochlear duct, an outgrowth from the central vesicle; and an endolymphatic duct and sac, likewise an outgrowth. Finally, the remainder of the vesicle, lying in the vestibule, becomes subdivided into two parts, utricle and saccule, united only by a narrow duct. The interconnecting spaces of the membranous labyrinth constitute the endolymphatic cavity (Fig. 116, p. 200).

CANALS

The superior or anterior membranous canal, like its surrounding bony one, is of course directed anterolaterally, while the posterior canal is directed posterolaterally, and the two canals form a laterally directed angle of approximately 90 degrees between themselves. At the corner or angle formed by them they, like the bony ones, join to form a common crus which leads into the utricle; from this common crus the superior or anterior canal curves upward, while the posterior canal curves backward and then downward, so that the major portion of the anterior canal comes to lie largely above the level of the posterior one.

At their other ends, that is at the anterior end of the superior canal and the inferior end of the posterior one, these canals are marked by enlargements, the ampullae, which contain the functional sensory endings of the canals. The ampullary ends of the superior and posterior semicircular canals empty by short, wide continuations of the canals into the utricle. The lateral semicircular canal sits only approximately, like the bony one (p. 202), in the horizontal plane, both of its ends being also connected with the utricle, and the anterior end bearing the ampulla. The membranous canals, much smaller than the osseous ones, are situated eccentrically in the perilymphatic space, so that they lie against the outer or convex surface of the lining periosteum of the bony canals, to which they are united by denser connective tissue than the trabeculae which elsewhere bridge the perilymphatic spaces of the bony canals.

UTRICLE

The utricle or utriculus is an elongated portion of the membranous labyrinth, larger in diameter than the semicircular canals and receiving both ends of each semicircular canal (five in all, since the superior and posterior canals have a common opening). It and the saccule, another large part of the membranous labyrinth, lie in close association in the larger chamber of the perilymphatic space, the vestibule. On the inferior surface of the utricle and extending also slightly onto its lateral surface lies the *macula,* which is provided with sensory endings; from the utricle arises usually a utriculosaccular duct, which communicates with the endolymphatic duct and also connects the utriculus to the sacculus.

SACCULE

The saccule is more rounded than is the utricle, and is situated somewhat anteromedial to the upper end of this latter. It is continuous with the utricle through the angulated utriculosaccular duct, and with the cochlear duct (membranous cochlea) by the tiny *canalis reuniens*. The macula of the saccule is an oval thickening on its lateral wall, containing the sensory nerve endings of this portion of the internal ear.

UTRICULOSACCULAR DUCT

The utriculosaccular duct is frequently described in textbooks as being only that portion which joins the utriculus to the endolymphatic duct, and the continuation to the sacculus is then described as the proximal portion of the endolymphatic duct, but this terminology is obviously not logical. Rather the utriculosaccular duct should be regarded as consisting of two portions, a utricular and a saccular one, which meet usually at an acute angle; from this angle the endolymphatic duct is given off. Occasionally (14.1 per cent according to Bast, '37) the utricular part (between the utriculus and the endolymphatic duct) is very short or may be lacking, so that the endolymphatic duct leads directly from the utricle.

ENDOLYMPHATIC DUCT AND SAC

The endolymphatic duct is usually described as a slender duct extending medially through the petrous bone in the periosteum-lined channel of the vestibular aqueduct (which apparently contains no perilymphatic space—p. 204), and, after emerging from the vestibular aqueduct through an aperture situated just postero-lateral to the opening of the internal acoustic meatus, expanding to form the endolymphatic sac. Anson and Wilson ('36), and Anson and Nesselrod, how-ever, made reconstructions of the endo-lymphatic duct and sac of children and adults, and found that the duct differs con-siderably from this. According to their description the first part of the endo-lymphatic duct is not a narrow duct but a sinus-like dilatation lying medial to the utriculus, with the utricular duct appear-ing to be a narrow lateral extension of this; this dilatation is said to attain some-times a size almost equal to that of the utricle, but to be more elongated. Its wall was mostly smooth, but occasionally the distal portion was found to be plicated.

Following this dilated portion they found a constricted section (isthmus) and then a second sinus-like dilatation. This second dilatation they described as having extensive folds of epithelium con-taining cones of vascular connective tissue; beyond this there was another narrowing followed by the terminal dilata-tion commonly referred to as the *endo-lymphatic sac*.

Anson and Nesselrod called these dila-tations in order Sinus I, Sinus II, and Sinus III; they concluded that Sinus II, with its concentration of vessels, was the site of greatest physiological activity of the endolymphatic duct and sac.

This description sounds somewhat complicated; the important part seems to be that the peripheral dilatation of the endolymphatic duct—the endolymphatic sac—may be divided histologically into two portions, a proximal (Sinus II), apparently physiologically active portion, and a more distal (Sinus III), less active or inactive portion.

The endolymphatic sac may be found within the dura on the posterior surface of the petrous pyramid, about halfway between the internal auditory meatus and the lateral wall of the skull. According to Anson and Davis the part of the endo-lymphatic sac within the cranial cavity varies from 4 to 19 mm. in length, as measured by the shallow fovea in which it lies on the skull. The upper margin of this fovea lies approximately halfway between the sigmoid sinus and the petrous ridge, or (Anson and Davis) from 4 to 12 mm. below the sulcus of the superior petrosal sinus.

MEMBRANOUS COCHLEA

The membranous cochlea (cochlear duct or scala media) is, as already men-tioned, united to the sacculus by the canalis or ductus reuniens; it has a short blind end, the vestibular cecum, before it is joined by the ductus reuniens, and then spirals forward within the osseous cochlea, to end blindly below the apex of this. Hardy ('38) measured the length of the organ of Corti (therefore essen-tially of the membranous cochlea) from 68 cochleae of individuals of from 10 weeks to 85 years of age, and found that the average total length of this organ is 31.52 mm., with a range of from 25.26 to 34.45 mm. Of this length, the basal turn usually involved an average of 57.9 per cent, the middle one of 29.4 per cent and the apical 12.8 per cent. She found the number of turns to vary between two and one half and two and three fourths in 59 cases, or 87 per cent of the total; of these, 9 had exactly two and one-half turns. Eight had more than two and three-fourths but less than three turns, and 1 had only two and one-sixth turns.

The cochlear duct (scala media) is roughly triangular in cross section, the apex of the triangle being sharply pointed and attached to the osseous spiral lamina from the modiolus (Fig. 118); from this attachment the cochlear duct extends across the bony labyrinth, separating the scala vestibuli from the scala tympani except at the apex of the cochlea.

The fibrous *basilar membrane* stretches from the spiral lamina to a basal project-

sory organ of hearing, lies upon the basilar membrane and consists of a thickened specialized epithelium; the tectorial membrane, a fibrogelatinous membrane with its base attached to the periosteum of the spiral lamina, projects laterally to lie "upon" (really anterior to) the epithelial hair cells of the organ of Corti, to which it is firmly attached by the stiff hairlike processes, or phalanges, of these cells.

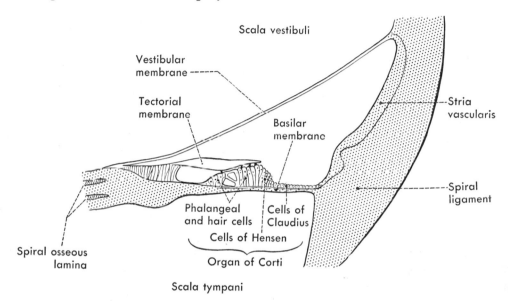

Fig. 118. Cross section of the cochlear duct.

ing portion of the spiral ligament of the cochlea, and forms the floor of the cochlear duct, separating the endolymph of this duct from the perilymph of the scala tympani. The spiral ligament is a thickened, modified portion of the periosteum (endosteum) of the bony cochlea, which forms the outer, curved wall of the cochlear canal. The very thin *vestibular membrane* (of Reissner) forms the roof of the cochlear duct, separating its cavity from that of the scala vestibuli, and passing from the upper border of the spiral ligament to the osseous spiral lamina.

The *spiral organ* (of Corti), the sen-

In the outer wall of the cochlear duct, and therefore on the inner surface of the spiral ligament, is the vascular area known as the *stria vascularis*; the stria is supplied by some thirty to thirty-five small arteries which originate in the modiolar region of the scala vestibuli and pass outward to the lateral wall of the osseous labyrinth (Belemer) and it is generally believed that it is the source of the endolymphatic fluid (Guild, '27). Altmann and Waltner have produced evidence that tissue spaces of the spiral ligament also serve as a site of absorption of perilymph which passes through the vestibular membrane to mix with the endolymph; apparently, therefore, the spiral ligament may be the site of both formation and absorption of the endolymph.

FINER STRUCTURE OF THE MEMBRANOUS LABYRINTH

Any theory of the mechanism of vestibular function or of hearing, to be at all tenable, must take into account the known structure of the parts concerned; therefore, a brief review of some of these facts and the ways in which they have been interpreted seems not out of place. The following incomplete account takes into consideration recent observations and interpretations of the anatomy of the ear which have especially influenced physiological concepts.

The membranous labyrinth, as already described, consists of epithelium-lined channels surrounded by connective tissue and largely suspended in the perilymphatic cavity. However, nerves and vessels must reach the membranous labyrinth, and the points of entrance are chiefly through areas of adhesion between the connective tissue of the membranous labyrinth and that of the periosteum lining the perilymphatic cavity. Thus the membranous semicircular canals are situated eccentrically in the perilymphatic space, and are attached along their greater curvatures by tissue stronger than the trabeculae which elsewhere unite the membranous and perilymphatic canals. The attachments are especially strong at the ampullae, where the nerves enter. Similarly, the utriculus and sacculus are firmly attached to the floor and medial wall of the vestibule, through which their nerves reach them. Finally, the cochlear duct is of course attached to the spiral lamina, through which it receives its nerves, and its peripheral border is firmly

fused with the periosteum of the osseous labyrinth.

SENSORY ORGANS

The three basic divisions of the membranous labyrinth—the semicircular canals, the utriculus and sacculus, and the cochlear duct—have an essentially similar structure: the sensory organ of each of these parts consists of a specialized thickened epithelium which is surmounted by and has attached to it a gelatinous mass. The specialized epithelium consists of at least two kinds of cells: supporting cells and hair cells; these latter, which have about them the endings of the eighth nerve, are provided with processes ("hairs") which project from the free edge of the cells and are embedded in or attached to the gelatinous mass.

The sensory endings in the semicircular canals are located in the ampulla of each canal, and are designated as *cristae*. Each crista consists of thickened epithelium surmounted by a gelatinous cupula. The hairs of the epithelial hair cells project into the base of the cupula. As shown first by Steinhausen and confirmed by Dohlman the cupula so fills the ampulla that actual flow of fluid past it is impossible; since the cupula is gelatinous, however, it may be bent by the pressure of the endolymph, and it is this bending which apparently stimulates the hair cells and therefore the nerve endings of the cristae. The physiology of the semicircular canals is discussed beginning with page 214.

The sensory areas of the utriculus and sacculus, known as *maculae,* are identical in structure with each other, and fundamentally similar also to the cristae of the semicircular canals. The epithelium consists of supporting and hair cells, and the hair cells have stiff, nonmotile projections which are embedded in gelatinous material designated as the otolithic membrane. In the otolithic membrane are also embedded numerous crystalline bodies containing calcium carbonate (the otoconia or otoliths). It is usually stated that these lie close to the free surface of the membrane, but Ulrich has apparently shown that in the living ear (of the pike) there is an extensive gelatinous membrane covering the otoliths. It is only in the occurrence of otoliths that the maculae differ sharply from the other sensory areas of the ear; their presence is presumably correlated with the fact that the essential stimulus to the maculae is probably gravity (p. 215).

The sensory part of the cochlear duct, the *organ of Corti,* is of course arranged in a spiral like the duct itself, and is supported by the spiral basilar membrane (Fig. 118, p. 209). It, also, consists of supporting cells and hair cells. The supporting cells are of several different types, but all contain stiffening fibrils within their cytoplasm, and their free edges expand to form a cuticular membrane against which the gelatinous tectorial membrane rests. Possibly among the most important of the supporting cells are the phalangeal cells, arranged in two groups: the inner group is a single row of cells while the outer (outer phalangeal cells, cells of Deiters) is said to form from three to five rows, depending upon the level of the cochlea investigated (fewer rows toward the base, more toward the apex). The inner row of phalangeal cells is associated with a single row of hair cells, while the outer rows of phalangeal cells alternate with rows of hair cells—each phalangeal cell apparently being closely associated with a hair cell. The phalangeal cells get their names from the shape of the stiff processes which project from the cells and are believed to form the cuticular membrane on the free surface of the organ of Corti. Mygind ('48a) suggested that deformation of the phalanges by pressure of the tectorial membrane aids in deforming the hair cells, and thus in initiating nerve impulses in response to hearing.

Peripheral to the outer phalangeal cells—that is, toward the attachment to the spiral ligament—are some tall cells (cells of Hensen) and still more peripherally shorter cells (of Claudius); their functions are completely unknown, but Mygind suggested that the cells of Hensen act as an elastic pillow which keeps the tectorial membrane firmly applied to the organ of Corti.

Intercellular spaces have been described among the cells of the organ of Corti, and are believed to be filled with a gelatinous intercellular substance. The largest of these spaces is one which runs the entire length of the organ of Corti between the inner and outer rows of phalangeal and hair cells, and is known as the tunnel, inner tunnel, or canal of Corti; this is bounded by special supporting cells, the inner and outer pillars (Corti's rods). The canal and its pillars together form Corti's arch. Mygind suggested that the organ of Corti might make seesaw movements at Corti's arch, swinging on this somewhat as on a hinge.

The hair cells of the organ of Corti have numerous (from about 40 to 100 per cell) "hairs" projecting from their cuticular surface, and in the better histological preparations the tectorial membrane may be seen to be attached to these hairs. In all theories of hearing this fact is fundamental, for regardless of the exact mechanism it seems obvious that stimulation of the hair cells must be brought about by a push or pull between the cells and the tectorial membrane. The inner hair cells are long, but the outer hair cells are short and wedged between the apices of the phalangeal cells, so that they do not reach the basilar membrane.

Since the organ of Corti is supported by the *basilar membrane* and in turn has the *tectorial membrane* attached to it, one or both of these would seem to be particularly important in the stimulation of this organ, and most of the theories of the mechanism of hearing have been built around the supposed facts of their structure. The outstanding element in the basilar membrane is its fibers (basilar fibers, auditory strings) which pass from the spiral lamina to the spiral ligament. There are said to be some 24,000 of these in the human ear, and they increase in length from the basal to the apical coil. The presence of these fibers, and their varying lengths, has been held as evidence for a resonator action on the part of the basilar membrane, or at least as evidence that the basilar membrane vibrates. This has been protested against at various times, most recently by Mygind ('48a), who quoted von Békésy as having shown that the basilar membrane has no tension in any direction; Mygind also said that the base of the membrane is too thick, and its attachment to the spiral ligament too unstable, to allow this membrane to act as a vibrator.

The tectorial membrane is generally described as a gelatinous structure, but numerous fine fibers have been described in it also; it, like the basilar membrane, increases in size from base to apex of the cochlea, and it also, therefore, has been regarded as the vibrator which affects the hair cells. It has been described in considerable detail by Hardesty ('08, '15).

The possible functions of the various parts of the cochlear duct in the perception of sound are discussed beginning with page 216.

CIRCULATION OF THE ENDOLYMPH

The endolymphatic sac has been regarded as the source of the endolymphatic fluid, but following the work of Guild ('27) it has been generally accepted as being rather a chief locus of absorption of the fluid. According to this work the endolymph is formed in the stria vascularis, flows toward the basal end of the cochlear duct, from this through the canalis reuniens into the sacculus, and from the sacculus through the saccular duct into the endolymphatic duct and the endolymphatic sac; endolymph is then supposed to leave the membranous labyrinth by passing through the wall of the pars intermedia of the endolymphatic sac into numerous small blood vessels of this region. The pars intermedia of Guild presumably corresponds to Sinus II of Anson and Nesselrod.

The *formation* of the endolymph is probably not through filtration from the blood vessels only, for some of the epithelium of the cochlear duct, as described by Shambaugh as early as 1908, is such as strongly to suggest secretory activity; further, the work of Aldred and his associates on the comparative osmotic pressure of the endolymph and the blood has apparently shown that the endolymph must be formed in part by secretion.

The same is true also of its *absorption* —the structure of the pars intermedia suggests activity upon the part of the cells here, and Aldred and his co-workers expressed the belief that a process of excretion must be involved in the removal of the fluid from the cavity of the endolymphatic sac.

While this view of the circulation of the endolymph is usually accepted, Lindsay ('47) has produced evidence that the vascular portion of the sac, Sinus II, may not be the only area from which endolymph can be absorbed; apparent destruction of this area in several monkeys failed to increase the fluid pressure (that is, to produce hydrops) of the labyrinth. From Altmann and Waltner's work on absorption of perilymph (pp. 205, 209) into the tissue spaces of the spiral ligament, it seems obvious that this area should also be a site of absorption of endolymph.

At the junction of the utricular duct and the utriculus itself there is a valvelike folding of the wall referred to as the *utriculo-endolymphatic valve* (Bast, '28; Anson and Wilson, '29; and others). Bast ('34) suggested that it is so placed that a sudden pressure disturbance in the utricle would close the valve and thus prevent fluid from flowing out into the endolymphatic duct. He indicated that the usual flow of endolymph is from the utricular duct into the utricle, but that a slow movement in the opposite direction should be possible. He observed 2 cases in which a rupture of the cochlear duct and the sacculus had occurred without damage or collapse of the utricle and the semicircular canals, the pressure within these having apparently been maintained at approximately normal by the utriculo-endolymphatic valve.

Perlman and Lindsay have also regularly observed the utriculo-endolymphatic valve in their preparations of the ear, and have expressed the belief also that it may function as a valve presenting a barrier to the outflow from the utricle into the utricular duct. Wolff ('34b) found this fold to be usually quite small in the late fetus, and expressed doubt that it could actually function as a valve.

MÉNIÈRE'S DISEASE

Subjective symptoms of dizziness and of tinnitus, which may eventually be followed by deafness, constitute a syndrome known as Ménière's disease. Its cause is not certainly known. Dandy ('33) suggested that the lesion was probably not within the inner ear itself but rather on the eighth nerve, but this concept is not consonant with the findings of otolaryngologists, who have reported (for instance Altmann and Fowler) that the chronic symptoms of Ménière's disease are accompanied by a dilation of the endolymphatic system. It is now believed, therefore, that these symptoms are due to excessive accumulation of endolymph, which exerts pressure upon the nerve endings; this disease is therefore frequently referred to as endolymphatic hydrops. The extent of the dilation of the endolymphatic duct system varies, but the cochlear duct is apparently always dilated and the sacculus and utriculus are usually affected, while the semicircular canals remain free of dilation.

The cause of the hydrops might obviously be either decreased absorption or increased secretion of the endolymph, or both; a fibrosis of the connective tissue about the endolymphatic sac has been noted (Altmann and Fowler) and has been thought (for example Cawthorne) to play a part in the onset of the disease, but it is now more widely believed that the essential fault is more probably an overproduction of fluid (Atkinson, Altmann and Fowler; and others). This view would seem to be supported by Lindsay's ('47) experiments on ablation of the endolymphatic sac in the monkey, which should have interfered with absorption of the fluid and yet produced no evidence of hydrops.

It should be noted, however, that a mere overproduction of endolymph should not be expected to produce dilation of the membranous labyrinth if, as the evidence indicates, there is normally rather free mixing of endolymph and perilymph through Reissner's membrane; rather there would have to be a production of abnormal endolymph, elements of which could not permeate Reissner's membrane, in order to produce a differential pressure from within the membranous labyrinth.

Williams ('47a) has pointed out that, while degenerative changes may be found in the organ of Corti and at times in the stria vascularis, inflammatory changes in the ear are conspicuously lacking in Ménière's disease; he has expressed the belief that it is not of inflammatory origin, but rather represents an extracellular edema. He (Williams, '47a and b; '52) has attributed this to a physical allergy in which dysfunction of the autonomic system produces a labyrinthine ischemia and increases capillary permeability. Atkinson, also, wrote that Ménière's disease is a syndrome due to vascular abnormalities in the ear.

Atkinson, Williams ('47a), and Cawthorne have all remarked upon the beneficial results to be obtained in this disease by conservative treatment (such as limitation of intake of salt and fluids, and administration of nicotinic acid); Williams has reported that such conservative measures may relieve patients of their symptoms in about 80 per cent of cases. The earlier surgical treatment of the disease consisted in sectioning the anterior or vestibular portion of the auditory nerve, as much as three fourths of this being sectioned (Dandy, '41); this may

eliminate the symptoms, but obviously does nothing toward checking the destruction of the labyrinth and the gradual loss of hearing. Other surgical technics for relief from this disease include Putnam's subtemporal approach to the internal ear with coagulation of the vestibular ganglion, Day's coagulation of the internal ear by means of a needle inserted through the horizontal canal into the vestibule, and Lempert's ('48b) decompression of the labyrinth by removal of the stapes and the membrane of the round window. The two latter operations are apparently followed by degeneration of the entire endolymphatic labyrinth, including the organ of Corti; they seem logical approaches for relief of the hydrops, and the loss of hearing attending them is said actually to be desired, because of the tinnitus. However, it is to be hoped that such necessarily crude surgical methods may be supplanted in most cases by medical ones which can actually relieve the cause of the condition and restore the function of the ear.

VESTIBULAR FUNCTION

The sensory areas of the vestibular apparatus consist, as already described, of the cristae in the ampullae of the semicircular canals, and the maculae of the utriculus and of the sacculus.

SEMICIRCULAR CANALS

It seems to be generally granted that the semicircular canals are stimulated by movement, and not by position—that is, that they are organs responding to acceleration. It is frequently stated that the cristae of the semicircular canals are most stimulated when the flow of endolymph is toward the ampulla, and least stimulated when the flow of endolymph is away from the ampulla; McNally, in discussing this question, has stated, however, that it has been shown in pigeons that flow toward the ampulla in the horizontal canal is the maximal stimulus in this canal, but flow away from the ampulla is the maximal stimulus in the vertical canals. He pointed out that this does not necessarily apply to man, however, and from an analysis of the literature and the results of vestibular tests concluded that there was some evidence that flow in the horizontal canal may produce an equal stimulus whether it is toward or away from the ampulla, and that the question deserved further investigation.

Hyndman has emphasized, as have others, that the semicircular canals are responsible for nystagmus; he has stated that when a canal is maximally stimulated the nystagmus is to the ipsilateral side, while minimal stimulation causes nystagmus toward the opposite side (the direction of a nystagmus is given as that of its quick component). Favill has analyzed the supposed effect of movements in each of the canals in relation to the eye muscles and nystagmus, but Hyndman expressed doubt that the various canals can be correlated with specific eye muscles.

It is customary to speak of flow of fluid within a canal, the original concept being that movements produced an actual streaming of the endolymph within the membranous canals: thus as the head moved in a given direction, carrying of course the attached membranous canals with it, the inertia of the endolymph was supposed to produce, in one or more canals, a relative drag in the opposite direction; continued acceleration overcame the inertia of the endolymph so that it moved with rather than in the canals, and the drag between fluid and membrane therefore ceased; when the movement of the head and canals was stopped, the momentum of the endolymph continued to carry it briefly in the original direction of movement. The basic concept is still held, but rather than actual flow of endolymph it is now believed that these results are brought about by changes in pressure. Morgan, Summers, and Reimann have pointed out that normal responses in the canals are not prevented by section, ligation or plugging; moreover, both Steinhausen and Dohlman have shown by actual observation on the ears of animals that the cupula completely occludes the ampulla, so that fluid cannot pass it; they have apparently shown that it is a bending of the cupula in response to pressure, this bending in turn presumably exerting pressure upon some hair cells and tension on others, that produces stimulation of the sensory endings.

UTRICLE AND SACCULUS

It is also generally stated that the macula of the utricle does not respond to acceleration or movement per se, but responds only to position; that is, the utricle is an organ of static equilibrium controlling posture and righting reflexes, and is stimulated not by the pressure but by the pull of the otoliths; since the macula of the utricle is in almost the horizontal plane, it would then be maximally stimulated in bending toward the floor.

The macula of the sacculus, lying largely at right angles (that is, in the sagittal plane) to that of the utricle, has also been held to be responsible for reflexes of static equilibrium, but many authors, including Hyndman and McNally, have stated their belief that the sacculus has not been shown to be vestibular or equilibratory in function.

Mygind ('48b) interpreted both the

utriculus and the sacculus as strictly vestibular organs, but stated that they both probably react not only to position but also slightly to acceleration—the otoliths exerting pressure upon one part of the macula, pull upon another part, with increase or decrease in acceleration. The relation of the sacculus to the development of the cochlear duct, and the comparative anatomy of the internal ear, have led to the suggestion that the sacculus may be connected with hearing, but it must be concluded that this has not been demonstrated; its similarity to the utriculus implies that it functions similarly.

COCHLEAR FUNCTION

The literature on the physiology of hearing is extremely voluminous, but there are so many points that are not clearly understood that it seems fair to state that we do not yet know the basic mechanism, and that all theories of hearing are actually only theories. The subject can be reviewed only briefly here. Conduction of sound through the middle ear has already been discussed (p. 186).

MOVEMENTS OF PERILYMPH

It is generally agreed that movements of the stapes, brought about by sound waves impinging upon the tympanic membrane, and the transmission of the vibrations of this through the ossicular chain, produce in turn movements, vibrations, or eddies of the perilymph. Vibrations of the perilymph can also be set up by sound waves reaching the round window, or by vibrations transmitted directly to the walls of the bony labyrinth through purely osseous channels. Normally, therefore, the vibrations in the perilymph are set up primarily in the vestibule but spread readily into the scala vestibuli; sound waves entering through the round window first affect, of course, the perilymph in the scala tympani.

Varying views as to the function of the round window membrane have been discussed on page 187; they are of interest here in regard to the question as to whether movement of the stapes produces an actual mass displacement of the perilymph, or whether it merely sets up vibrations in this. Pushing and pulling upon the stapes have been shown to produce outward and inward bulging of the round window, but Pohlman ('41) has expressed the belief that such a mass movement of the cochlear fluid cannot be regarded as necessary to hearing, in view of the immediate improvement in hearing produced by the Lempert fenestration operation, in which perilymphatic fluid, he said, is necessarily lost (but see p. 201 —Lempert, Wever, Lawrence, and Meltzer). Sullivan and Hodges have argued, however, that inward motion of the oval window can be compensated for only by outward motion of the round window and downward displacement of the basilar membrane. As already stated, they indicated that deafness may be expected to result from immobility of the window.

VIBRATORY MECHANISM

It is generally agreed that vibrations in the perilymph in turn affect the membranous cochlea, which lies between the scala vestibuli and the scala tympani, and that the varying strength of impingement of the hair cells of the spiral organ on the attached tectorial membrane sets up nerve impulses concerned with sound. While various views as to the vibratory mechanism of the internal ear have been favored at different times, the main argument being whether the tectorial membrane or the basilar membrane was the vibratory mechanism, it has been widely assumed in recent years that the basilar membrane serves as the resonator of the internal ear.

Shambaugh ('07) and Hardesty pointed out that the spiral organ of Corti becomes larger as it passes from the basal to the apical end of the cochlea, and that the tectorial membrane is also widest and thickest at its apical end, and they expressed the belief that this membrane was the vibrating mechanism of the cochlea; they maintained that the basilar membrane is entirely too rigid and too firmly attached to allow it to vibrate. Most recent workers, however, have regarded the basilar membrane as the vibratory mechanism. Lurie reviewed the evidence indicating that damage to the basilar membrane alone definitely affects hearing, and found all evidence in favor of the resonance theory.

Although the bony canal of the cochlea gets smaller as it is traced toward its apex, and the basilar membrane therefore might also be expected to get narrower, this membrane, like the tectorial membrane, actually increases in width as it is traced to the apex because of a disproportionate decrease in the width of the osseous spiral lamina. Wever reported the measurements of twenty-five basilar membranes; he found that while these did, as generally stated, increase in width as they were traced from the basal toward the apical turns, they attained a maximal width at a point about one-half turn before the apex, and then decreased rapidly (Fig. 119); the average maximal width of the basilar membrane was found to be 498 microns, while the minimum was about 80 microns. He noted also that while measurements of the various membranes were in good agreement in the basal part

of the cochlea they tended to show wide variations in the apical part.

The common concept of the anatomy and the role of the basilar membrane is not, however, accepted by all modern students of the question (p. 212). Mygind ('48a) has argued, like Shambaugh and Hardesty, that the basilar membrane cannot be a vibrator; he followed von Békésy (p. 218) in the belief that this is indicated not by its rigidity

Fig. 119. The basilar membrane. Note the steady increase in width from the base of the cochlea almost to the apex, and then its decrease. (From Wever, E. G.: *Am. Otol., Rhin. & Laryng. 47*:37, 1938.)

and firmness of fixation, as stated by Shambaugh and Hardesty, but rather by the fact that it is not under tension and that the spiral ligament is not a firm enough area of fixation. He has therefore accepted the tectorial membrane as the "vibrator," and has suggested that it exerts its effects by a change in shape which allows it alternately to push and pull upon the inner and outer hair cells and the associated phalangeal cells.

In summary, while the mechanism of cochlear stimulation is still not known, there is at present a tendency to concede that both the basilar membrane and the tectorial membrane move, one acting as the vibrator and the other as a damper, though which of the membranes does which is not agreed.

LOCALIZATION IN COCHLEA

The supposed relation of the basilar membrane to the perception of tones has been variously interpreted; some authors, pointing out that the basilar membrane may be regarded as a series of strings which are shorter at the base and longer at the apex, have contended that there was a precise localization of tones of various frequencies within the membrane, the low tones being localized, of course, toward the apex of the cochlea where the strings are longer, and high tones being localized in the base of the cochlea where the strings are shorter. Other writers have felt that there was no good evidence for strict localization of any tones within the cochlea.

Bast and Shover pointed out in 1943 that there were two main theories of hearing: one, the place theory, states that a specific tone activates a particular region of the basilar membrane and that there is a corresponding specificity of nerve action, so that high tones stimulate areas in the basal turn of the cochlea and low tones areas of the apical region; the other theory, that of Wever and Bray, holds that only high tones are represented purely by place, that low tones are represented by frequencies, and that tones between the two are represented by a combination of both place and frequency. According to the latter theory, then, high tones are localized specifically in the cochlea and place alone serves for them; frequency alone serves for the lowest tones because they spread so widely in the cochlea.

While Fowler and others have said that there was sufficient evidence to indicate that small and limited lesions in the basilar membrane may account for narrow deafened areas in the ear, the general conclusion reached by the symposium of the American Otological Society in 1935 seems to be that only the high tones are definitely localized and that low frequency tones are apparently not definitely localized in the cochlea. Wever has pointed out that any theory postulating a differentiating role for the basilar membrane must allow for a wide range of normal variation in width in the apical region.

Von Békésy apparently demonstrated that the basilar membrane is not under tension, and therefore cannot serve as a string resonator; he said that specific tones produce widespread vibrations of the basilar membrane, and that differentiation occurs not in the membrane but rather as the nerve impulses are transmitted to higher centers. Mygind ('48a) also has rejected the idea that there can be any fundamental difference between the ways in which high and low tones affect the cochlea, and has concluded that a single tone is represented maximally over about a fifth of the total length of the organ of Corti. There thus seems to be a growing belief that localization in the cochlea is at best only approximate, various tones overlapping widely.

The finer aspects of hearing, such as the resolution of harmonies, appreciation of intensity of sounds, and the like, are really not at all understood, and a discussion of them lies much beyond the scope of the present work. It may be mentioned that Lurie expressed the belief that the external hair cells of the organ of Corti are responsible for detection of very faint sounds, while the internal hair cells are concerned with the fine discrimination of pitch, but this cannot be regarded as demonstrated.

ANOMALIES

Polvogt and Crowe, in an investigation of the internal ears of individuals who had been shown before death to have normal hearing, found among 17 cochleae 1 which had only two turns and another that had three full turns; they concluded that the number of turns of the cochlea is apparently of little importance provided the length of the basilar membrane (see p. 208) is within normal limits.

Among these 17 apparently normally functioning cochleae, they also found several marked anomalies. In 6 of these there was a gap in the bony septum between the middle and apical turns, so that there was a free communication between the scala vestibuli and the scala tympani, forming what is termed a scala communis cochleae; they said that there should be in this condition, theoretically, an impairment for low tones but no such impairment had been found. The ears of 2 individuals showed arrested bony development at the apex of the modiolus, so that the nerve in the apical turn was supported purely by a fibrous band; although the lesion was unilateral in both, hearing had been equally acute on the two sides. In another patient there was a defect on one side in the bony wall of the middle turn of the cochlea, and some of the fibers of the facial nerve passed through a portion of the spiral ligament. Polvogt has even noted atrophy of the nerve in a portion of the basal coil of the cochlea, with no apparent effect upon the hearing; he has stated that it is common to observe atrophy of the stria vascularis over short distances of any level of the cochlea, with no apparent effect upon hearing.

VESSELS AND NERVES

ARTERIES

The chief artery of the internal ear is the internal auditory (labyrinthine) artery, usually given as a branch of the basilar artery, but according to Sunderland arising in only 17 per cent of 264 cases from the basilar artery and in the remaining 83 per cent from the anterior inferior cerebellar artery. The internal auditory artery, which may be double (in perhaps almost 10 per cent, according to Watt and McKillop) accompanies the seventh and eighth nerves through the internal auditory meatus; its main branches run in the inner periosteum of the bony labyrinth, and through the trabeculae between the membranous and bony labyrinths are distributed to the membranous labyrinth (Fig. 120). There are apparently no functional anastomoses between the vessels supplying the membranous labyrinth and those to the otic capsule itself.

According to Shambaugh ('23) the internal auditory artery typically gives off the posterior vestibular (or vestibulo-cochlear) artery which supplies the macula of the sacculus, the ampulla and entire length of the posterior canal, the common crus and adjacent posterior portion of the superior canal, the posterior portion of the horizontal canal, and, frequently, a branch to the base of the cochlea. After giving off its posterior vestibular branch the internal auditory artery then divides into the artery of the cochlea and the anterior vestibular (frequently termed simply the vestibular) artery. This latter artery supplies the macula of the utricle and the anterior portions of the superior and horizontal canals, including their maculae. The artery of the cochlea runs up the modiolus to the apex; it anastomoses with the branch to the basal part and distributes radial branches to the organ of Corti and the stria vascularis. Considerable variation apparently exists, however, in the exact manner of branching and distribution of these branches of the internal auditory artery; Hilger, for

VEINS

Shambaugh described only two veins as draining the labyrinth, one running by way of the cochlear aqueduct and the other by way of the vestibular aqueduct. He stated that the vein of the cochlear aqueduct drains the entire cochlea and part of the vestibular apparatus, including the maculae of the sacculus and utriculus and the cristae of the superior and

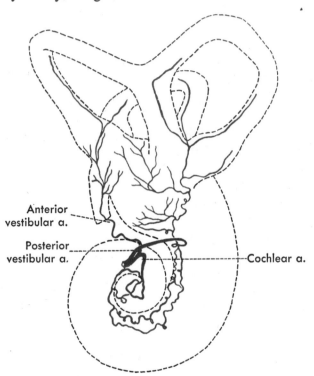

Anterior
vestibular a.

Posterior
vestibular a.

Cochlear a.

Fig. 120. The arterial supply to the labyrinth. (Adapted from Shambaugh, G. E.: *Am. J. Anat. 32:* 189, 1923.)

instance, in summarizing the usual manner of branching of this artery, described two patterns, neither of which agrees exactly with that given above. A common description is that which designates the vestibular (anterior vestibular) as the first branch, the remaining common cochlear artery then dividing into vestibulocochlear (posterior vestibular) and cochlear artery proper.

horizontal canals, while the vein of the vestibular aqueduct drains only a limited area, namely, the remainder of the superior and horizontal canals, and the posterior canal including its crista (Fig. 121).

The vein of the cochlear aqueduct joins the inferior petrosal sinus or the superior bulb of the internal jugular vein, while the vein of the vestibular aqueduct joins the superior petrosal sinus. Most texts also describe these veins as joining to form an internal auditory vein, which is said to be the chief drainage from the inner ear and to open into the inferior petrosal sinus, but Shambaugh specifically denied that it is usually present in the human ear.

meatus the trunk divides into three parts, two vestibular and one cochlear.

The fibers of the *vestibular nerve* arise from the vestibular ganglion (Scarpa's ganglion), which is situated at the lateral end of the internal auditory (acoustic) meatus; centrally, the fibers become asso-

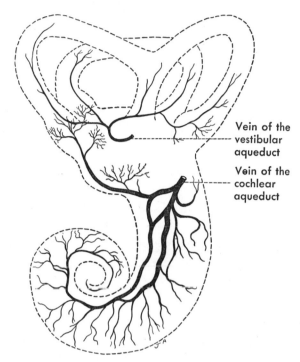

Vein of the vestibular aqueduct

Vein of the cochlear aqueduct

Fig. 121. The venous drainage of the labyrinth. (Adapted from Shambaugh, G. E.: *Am. J. Anat.* 32:189, 1923.)

LYMPHATICS

Lymphatics from the internal ear are not usually described, but recently Young has apparently demonstrated such channels (p. 206); a detailed report of these is not yet available.

NERVES

The nerve to the internal ear is the acoustic, auditory, or eighth cranial nerve, consisting functionally of vestibular and cochlear divisions (Fig. 122). In the internal meatus these two parts are closely associated, but at the lateral end of the

ciated with the cochlear division of the nerve, from which they are separable grossly with difficulty or not at all; at the brain stem, however, they lie anterior (ventral) to the cochlear fibers. Peripherally, the vestibular nerve divides into two main divisions, a superior and an inferior; the superior division of the nerve is said to be distributed to the ampullae of the horizontal and anterior canals, and to the maculae of both the utriculus and the sacculus. The inferior division of the nerve is distributed largely to the macula of the sacculus and to the posterior ampulla; it usually gives also a small division (Oort's nerve) to anastomose with the cochlear nerve. Hardy ('34) has described the macula of the saccule as being innervated not only by both divisions of the vestibular nerve, but also by the cochlear nerve through a branch passing from the base of the cochlea to the sacculus.

eighth nerve is usually connected by two filaments to the facial; it has been thought that through such communications the facial nerve may distribute fibers to the internal ear, though the communications more probably represent simply a short aberrant course of facial fibers with the eighth.

Little is known concerning the trans-

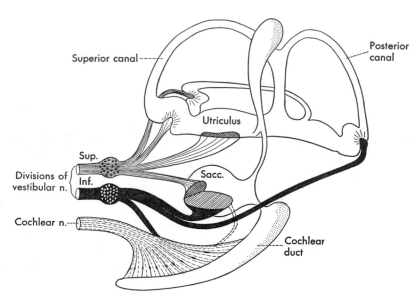

Fig. 122. Schema of the innervation of the labyrinth. Redrawn from Hardy (*Anat. Rec. 59:*403, 1934), after De Burlet. The nerve of Oort is the branch between vestibular and cochlear nerves.

The cells of origin of the *cochlear nerve* form the spiral ganglion, situated in the coils of the modiolus at the base of the attachment of the spiral lamina; the peripheral fibers pass through the lamina to perforate its free edge and end in the organ of Corti. According to Rasmussen the fibers which the cochlear nerve receives from the vestibular by way of the nerve of Oort do not arise from the vestibular ganglion, but represent efferent fibers derived from the superior olive which leave the brain stem with the vestibular nerve.

Within the internal auditory meatus the

mission of *autonomic impulses* to the internal ear; sympathetic fibers presumably reach it along the vessels, and should be derived from the inferior cervical ganglion by way of the vertebral plexus. Murphy, noting that sympathetic stimulation has been said to produce a hyperexcitability of the labyrinth on the affected side, investigated 5 individuals in regard to the threshold of caloric excitability after interruption of the cervical sympathetic on one side. He found no abnormal variations in the threshold of excitation, and speculated that parasympathetic stimulation is necessary to produce vasodilation in the inner ear.

The origin and course of parasympathetic fibers to the internal ear have apparently not been demonstrated, nor is there even definite confirmation of their presence, but Rasmussen has suggested that the efferent fibers derived from the superior olive may represent preganglionic fibers associated with the blood vessels and secretory epithelium.

REFERENCES

ALDRED, P., HALLPIKE, C. S. and LEDOUX, A. Observations on the osmotic pressure of the endolymph. *J. Physiol. 98:*446, 1940.

ALTMANN, F., and FOWLER, E. P. JR. Histological findings in Ménière's symptom complex. *Ann. Otol., Rhin. & Laryng. 52:*52, 1943.

ALTMANN, F., and WALTNER, J. G. The circulation of the labyrinthine fluids: Experimental investigations in rabbits. *Ann. Otol., Rhin. & Laryng. 56:*684, 1947.

ALTMANN, F., and WALTNER, J. G. New investigations on the physiology of the labyrinthine fluids. *Laryngoscope 60:*727, 1950.

ANSON, B. J., and DAVIS, R. A. On the form and size of the intracranial fovea for the endolymphatic sac. (Abstr.) *Anat. Rec. 106:*169, 1950.

ANSON, B. J., and MARTIN, J., JR. Fissula ante fenestram: Its form and contents in early life. *Arch. Otolaryng. 21:*303, 1935.

ANSON, B. J., and NESSELROD, J. P. Endolymphatic and associated ducts in man. *Arch. Otolaryng. 24:*127, 1936.

ANSON, B. J., and WILSON, J. G. The utricular fold in the adult human ear. *Anat. Rec. 43:*251, 1929.

ANSON, B. J., and WILSON, J. G. The form and structure of the endolymphatic and associated ducts in the child. *Anat. Rec. 65:*485, 1936.

ANSON, B. J., CAULDWELL, E. W., and BAST, T. H. The fissula ante fenestram of the human otic capsule: I. Developmental and normal adult structure. *Ann. Otol., Rhin. & Laryng. 56:*957, 1947.

ANSON, B. J., WILSON, J. G., and GAARDSMOE, J. P. Air cells of petrous portion of temporal bone in a child four and a half years old: A study based on wax plate reconstruction. *Arch. Otolaryng. 27:*588, 1938.

ATKINSON, M. Ménière's syndrome: The basic fault? *Arch. Otolaryng. 44:*385, 1946.

BALLANCE, C., and DUEL, A. B. The operative treatment of facial palsy by the introduction of nerve grafts into the Fallopian canal and by other intratemporal methods. *Arch. Otolaryng. 15:*1, 1932.

BAST, T. H. The utriculo-endolymphatic valve. *Anat. Rec. 40:*61, 1928.

BAST, T. H. Development of the otic capsule: II. The origin, development and significance of the fissula ante fenestram and its relation to otosclerotic foci. *Arch. Otolaryng. 18:*1, 1933.

BAST, T. H. Function of the utriculo-endolymphatic valve: Two cases of ruptured saccules in children. *Arch. Otolaryng. 19:*537, 1934.

BAST, T. H. The utriculo-endolymphatic valve and duct and its relation to the endolymphatic and saccular ducts in man and guinea pig. *Anat. Rec. 68:*75, 1937.

BAST, T. H. Development of the otic capsule: V. Residual cartilages and defective ossification and their relations to otosclerotic foci. *Arch. Otolaryng. 32:*771, 1940.

BAST, T. H. Development of the otic capsule: VI. Histological changes and variations in the growing bony capsule of the vestibule and cochlea. *Ann. Otol., Rhin. & Laryng. 51:*343, 1942.

BAST, T. H. Development of aquaeductus cochleae and its contained periotic duct and cochlear vein in human embryos. *Ann. Otol., Rhin. & Laryng. 55:*278, 1946.

BAST, T. H., and ANSON, B. J. *The Temporal Bone and the Ear.* Springfield, Ill., Thomas, 1949.

BAST, T. H., and SHOVER, JAYNE A historical survey of the structure and function of the cochlea. *Ann. Otol., Rhin. & Laryng. 52:*281, 1943.

BECKER, S. W., and BRUNSCHWIG, A. Sinus preauricularis (fistula preauricularis congenita). *Am. J. Surg. n.s. 24:*174, 1934.

VON BÉKÉSY, G. V. Über die Frequenzauflösung in der menschlichen Schnecke. *Acta oto-laryng.* 32:60, 1944.

BELEMER, J. J. The vessels of the stria vascularis: With special reference to their function. *Arch. Otolaryng.* 23:93, 1936.

BRÖDEL, M. *Three Unpublished Drawings of the Anatomy of the Human Ear.* Philadelphia, Saunders, 1946.

BUNNELL, S. Suture of the facial nerve within the temporal bone with a report of the first successful case. *Surg., Gynec. & Obst.* 45:7, 1927.

BUNNELL, S. Surgical repair of the facial nerve. *Arch. Otolaryng.* 25:235, 1937.

CAWTHORNE, T. Ménière's disease. *Ann. Otol., Rhin. & Laryng.* 56:18, 1947.

COHEN, L., and FOX, S. L. Atresia of the external auditory canal. *Arch. Otolaryng.* 38:338, 1943.

CONGDON, E. D., ROWHANAVONGSE, S., and VARAMISARA, P. Human congenital auricular and juxta-auricular fossae, sinuses and scars (including the so-called aural and auricular fistulae) and the bearing of their anatomy upon the theories of their genesis. *Am. J. Anat.* 51:439, 1932.

COSTELLO, M. J., and SHEPARD, J. H. Supernumerary external ears. *Arch. Otolaryng.* 29:695, 1939.

CROWE, S. J., HUGHSON, W., and WITTING, E. G. Function of the tensor tympani muscle: An experimental study. *Arch. Otolaryng.* 14:575, 1931.

CUSHING, H. The sensory distribution of the fifth cranial nerve. *Bull. Johns Hopkins Hosp.* 15:213, 1904.

DANDY, W. E. Glossopharyngeal neuralgia (tic douloureux): Its diagnosis and treatment. *Arch. Surg.* 15:198, 1927.

DANDY, W. E. Ménière's disease: Diagnosis and treatment (report of thirty cases). *Am. J. Surg.* n.s.20:693, 1933.

DANDY, W. E. The surgical treatment of Ménière's disease. *Surg., Gynec., & Obst.* 72:421, 1941.

DAVENPORT, C. B., MILLES, BESS L., and FRINK, LILLIAN B. The genetic factor in otosclerosis: Part I. Problem, method of study and results; Part III. General *Arch. Otolaryng.* 17:135;503, 1933.

DAY, K. M. Labyrinth surgery for Ménière's disease. *Laryngoscope* 53:617, 1943.

DEARMIN, R. M. A logical surgical approach to the tip cells of the petrous pyramid. *Arch. Otolaryng.* 26:314, 1937.

DOHLMAN, G. Investigations in the function of the semicircular canals. *Acta oto-laryng.* Suppl. 51:211, 1944.

DRUSS, J. G. Incisions of drum membrane in otitis media. *Am. J. Surg.* n.s.36:102, 1937.

DRUSS, J. G., and ALLEN, B. Congenital fistula of the neck communicating with the middle ear. *Arch. Otolaryng.* 31:437, 1940.

EGGSTON, A. A., and WOLFF, DOROTHY. *Histopathology of The Ear, Nose and Throat.* Baltimore, Md., Williams & Williams, 1947.

FARRIOR, J. B. The sublabyrinthine exenteration of the petrous apex. *Ann. Otol., Rhin. & Laryng.* 51:1007, 1942.

FARRIOR, J. B. The radical mastoidectomy: Anatomical considerations in surgical technique. *Surg., Gynec. & Obst.* 89:328, 1949.

FAVILL, J. An explanation of the mechanism of induced rotary and vertical nystagmus. *Arch. Neurol & Psychiat.* 13:479, 1925.

FOLEY, J. O. The cytological processes involved in the formation of the scalae of the internal ear. *Anat. Rec.* 49:1, 1931.

FOWLER, E. P. Limited lesions of the basilar membrane. *Arch. Otolaryng.* 10:624, 1929.

FRASER, J. S. Maldevelopments of the auricle, external acoustic meatus and middle ear: Microtia and congenital meatal atresia. *Arch. Otolaryng.* 13:1, 1931.

FRENCKNER, P. Observations on anatomy of the tympanic plexus and technique of tympanosympathectomy. *A.M.A. Arch. Otolaryng.* 54:347, 1951.

GRAVES, G. O., and EDWARDS, L. F. The Eustachian tube: A review of its descriptive, microscopic, topographic and clinical anatomy. *Arch. Otolaryng.* 39:359, 1944.

GUILD, S. R. The circulation of the endolymph. *Am. J. Anat.* 39:57, 1927.

GUILD, S. R. Hearing by bone conduction: The pathways of transmission of sound. *Ann. Otol., Rhin. & Laryng.* 45:736, 1936.

GUILD, S. R. Histologic otosclerosis. *Ann. Otol., Rhin. & Laryng.* 53:246, 1944.

HAGENS, E. W. Anatomy and pathology of the petrous bone: Based on a study of fifty temporal bones. *Arch. Otolaryng.* 19:556, 1934.

HARDESTY, I. On the nature of the tectorial membrane and its probable role in the anatomy of hearing. *Am. J. Anat. 8:*109, 1908.

HARDESTY, I. On the proportions, development and attachment of the tectorial membrane. *Am. J. Anat. 18:*1, 1915.

HARDY, MARY Observations on the innervation of the macula sacculi in man. *Anat. Rec. 59:*403, 1934.

HARDY, MARY The length of the organ of Corti in man. *Am. J. Anat. 62:*291, 1938.

HILGER, J. A. Vasomotor labyrinthine ischemia. *Ann. Otol., Rhin. & Laryng. 59:* 1102, 1950.

HUGHSON, W. The inner ear from an experimental and clinical standpoint. *Ann. Otol., Rhin. & Laryng. 47:*68, 1938.

HUGHSON, W. A summary of round window graft operations performed for deafness. *Ann. Otol., Rhin. & Laryng. 49:*384, 1940.

HUGHSON, W., and CROWE, S. J. Immobilization of the round window membrane: A further experimental study. *Ann. Otol., Rhin. & Laryng. 41:*332, 1932.

HUNT, J. R. The sensory system of the facial nerve and its symptomatology. *J. Nerv. & Ment. Dis. 36:*321, 1909.

HUNT, J. R. The symptom-complex of the acute posterior poliomyelitis of the geniculate, auditory, glossopharyngeal and pneumogastric ganglia. *Arch. Int. Med. 5:*631, 1910.

HUNT, J. R. The sensory field of the facial nerve: A further contribution to the symptomatology of the geniculate ganglion. *Brain 38:*418, 1915.

HYNDMAN, O. R. Physiology of the vestibular labyrinth. *Arch. Otolaryng. 29:*759, 1939.

JOHNSON, L., and ZONDERMAN, B. Herpes zoster oticus ("Ramsay Hunt syndrome"): Report of a case. *Arch. Otolaryng. 48:*1, 1948.

JONES, M. F. Pathways of approach to the petrous pyramid. *Ann. Otol., Rhin. & Laryng. 44:*458, 1935.

KETTEL, K. Abnormal course of the facial nerve in the Fallopian canal. *Arch. Otolaryng. 44:*406, 1946.

KETTEL, K. Bell's palsy: Pathology and surgery; a report concerning fifty patients who were operated on after the method of Balance and Duel. *Arch. Otolaryng. 46:*427, 1947.

KOBRAK, H. Influence of the middle ear on labyrinthine pressure. *Arch. Otolaryng. 21:* 547, 1935.

KOBRAK, H. G. Round window membrane of the cochlea: Experiments demonstrating its physical responses. *Arch. Otolaryng. 49:* 36, 1949.

LAWRENCE, M. Recent investigations of sound conduction: Part I. The normal ear. *Ann. Otol., Rhin. & Laryng. 59:*1020, 1950.

LEMPERT, J. Endaural, antauricular surgical approach to the temporal bone: Principles involved in this new approach; summary report of 1,780 cases. *Arch. Otolaryng. 27:* 555, 1938.

LEMPERT, J. Endaural fenestration of external semicircular canal for restoration of hearing in cases of otosclerosis: Summary report of one hundred and twenty cases. *Arch. Otolaryng. 31:*711, 1940.

LEMPERT, J. Fenestra nov-ovalis: A new oval window for the improvement of hearing in cases of otosclerosis. *Arch. Otolaryng. 34:* 880, 1941.

LEMPERT, J. Tympanosympathectomy: A surgical technic for the relief of tinnitus aurium. *Arch. Otolaryng. 43:*199, 1946.

LEMPERT, J. Symposium of fenestration of the labyrinth: Lempert fenestra nov-ovalis operation for the restoration of serviceable unaided hearing in patients with clinical otosclerosis; its present evolutionary status. *Arch. Otolaryng. 46:*478, 1947.

LEMPERT, J. Bone-dust-free Lempert fenestra nov-ovalis: A new evolutionary development of the surgical treatment of clinical otosclerosis. *Arch. Otolaryng. 47:*280, 1948a.

LEMPERT, J. Lempert decompression operation for hydrops of the endolymphatic labyrinth in Ménière's disease. *Arch. Otolaryng. 47:*551, 1948b.

LEMPERT, J., and WOLFF, DOROTHY. Otosclerosis: Theory of its origin and development. *Arch. Otolaryng. 50:*115, 1949.

LEMPERT, J., WEVER, E. G., LAWRENCE, M., and MELTZER, P. E. Perilymph: Its relation to the improvement of hearing which follows fenestration of the vestibular labyrinth in clinical otosclerosis. *Arch. Otolaryng. 50:*377, 1949.

LIERLE, D. M., and POTTER, J. J. Physiology and histopathology of the middle ear. *Ann. Otol., Rhin. & Laryng. 50:*235, 1941.

LINDSAY, J. R. Osteomyelitis of the petrous pyramid of the temporal bone. *Ann. Surg. 122:*1060, 1945.

LINDSAY, J. R. Histologic observations on the healing of labyrinthine fistulas in monkeys. *Arch. Otolaryng. 43:*37, 1946.

LINDSAY, J. R. Effect of obliteration of the endolymphatic sac and duct in the monkey. *Arch. Otolaryng. 45:*1, 1947.

LINDSAY, J. R., KOBRAK, H., and PERLMAN, H. B. Relation of the stapedius reflex to hearing sensation in man. *Arch. Otolaryng. 23:*671, 1936.

LOCH, W. E. The effect on hearing of experimental occlusion of the Eustachian tube in man. *Ann. Otol., Rhin. & Laryng. 51:*396, 1942a.

LOCH, W. E. Effect of experimentally altered air pressure in the middle ear on hearing acuity in man. *Ann. Otol., Rhin. & Laryng. 51:*995, 1942b.

LURIE, M. H. How does the organ of Corti distinguish pitch? *Ann. Otol., Rhin. & Laryng. 45:*339, 1936.

MacNAUGHTON-JONES, H. *Hearing and Equilibrium.* Baltimore, Md., Williams & Wilkins, 1940.

McNALLY, W. J. The physiology of the vestibular mechanism in relation to vertigo. *Ann. Otol., Rhin. & Laryng. 56:*514, 1947.

MAYBAUM, J. L., and DRUSS, J. G. Geniculate ganglionitis (Hunt's syndrome): Clinical features and histopathology. *Arch. Otolaryng. 19:*574, 1934.

MAYBAUM, J. L., and GOLDMAN, J. L. Primary jugular bulb thrombosis: A study of twenty cases. *Arch. Otolaryng. 17:*70, 1933.

MELTZER, P. E. The mastoid cells: Their arrangement in relation to the sigmoid portion of the transverse sinus. *Arch. Otolaryng. 19:*326, 1934.

MEURMAN, Y. Zur Anatomie des Aquaeductus Cochleae nebst einigen Bermerkungen über dessen Physiologie. *Acta Soc. med. fenn. doudecim. s.B. 13:*1, 1930.

MORGAN, R., SUMMERS, R. D., and REIMANN, S. P. Effects of various types of motion on differences in hydrostatic pressure between ends of a semicircular canal: A theoretic analysis. *Arch. Otolaryng. 36:*691, 1942.

MURPHY, A. B. The influence of the sympathetic nervous system on the internal ear. *Ann. Otol., Rhin. & Laryng. 42:*166, 1933.

MYERSON, M. C., RUBIN, H., and GILBERT, J. G. Anatomic studies of the petrous portion of the temporal bone. *Arch. Otolaryng. 20:*195, 1934.

MYGIND, S. H. Further labyrinthine studies: I. Affections of the humoral system of the labyrinth; II. On the labyrinthine transformation of the acoustic vibrations to pitch-differentiated nervous impulses. *Acta otolaryng. Suppl.68,* 1948a.

MYGIND, S. H. Static function of the labyrinth: Attempt at a synthesis. *Acta otolaryng. Suppl.70,* 1948b.

PASTORE, P. N., and ERICH, J. B. Congenital preauricular cysts and fistulas. *Arch. Otolaryng. 36:*120, 1942.

PATTEE, G. L. An operation to improve hearing in cases of congenital atresia of the external auditory meatus. *Arch. Otolaryng. 45:*568, 1947.

PERLMAN, H. B., and LINDSAY, J. R. The utriculo-endolymphatic valve. *Arch. Otolaryng. 24:*68, 1936.

PERLMAN, H. B., and LINDSAY, J. R. Relation of the internal ear spaces to the meninges. *Arch. Otolaryng. 29:*12, 1939.

POHLMAN, A. G. The conduction of air sounds to the cochlea. *Ann. Otol., Rhin. & Laryng. 40:*717, 1931.

POHLMAN, A. G. The reactions in the ear to sound. *Ann. Otol., Rhin. & Laryng. 50:*363, 1941.

POLVOGT, L. M. Histologic variations in the middle and inner ears of patients with normal hearing. *Arch. Otolaryng. 23:*48, 1936.

POLVOGT, L. M., and CROWE, S. J. Anomalies of the cochlea in patients with normal hearing. *Ann. Otol., Rhin. & Laryng. 46:*579, 1937.

PUTNAM, T. J. Treatment of recurrent vertigo (Ménière's syndrome) by subtemporal destruction of the labyrinth. *Arch. Otolaryng. 27:*161, 1938.

RASMUSSEN, G. L. The olivary peduncle and other fiber projections of the superior olivary complex. *J. Comp. Neurol. 84:*141, 1946.

RICHARDS, L. Congenital atresia of the external auditory meatus. *Ann. Otol., Rhin. & Laryng. 42:*692, 1933.

ROSENBERGER, H. C. Herpes zoster oticus with facial paralysis and acoustic symptoms:

A subjective experience. *Ann. Otol., Rhin. & Laryng. 50:*271, 1941.

SCHERRER, F. W. Calcification and ossification of the external ears. *Ann. Otol., Rhin. & Laryng. 41:*867, 1932.

SHAMBAUGH, G. E. A restudy of the minute anatomy of structures in the cochlea, with conclusions bearing on the solution of the problem of tone perception. *Am. J. Anat. 7:*245, 1907.

SHAMBAUGH, G. E. On the structure and function of the epithelium in the sulcus spiralis externus. *Arch. Otology 37:*538, 1908.

SHAMBAUGH, G. E. Blood stream in the labyrinth of the ear of dog and of man. *Am. J. Anat. 32:*189, 1923.

SIMKINS, C. S. Functional anatomy of the Eustachian tube. *Arch. Otolaryng. 38:*476, 1943.

STAMMERS, F. A. R. Pre-auricular fistulae. *Brit. J. Surg. 14:*359, 1927.

STEINHAUSEN, W. Neuere Untersuchungen zur Anatomie und Physiologie der Cupula terminalis in den Bogenausgangsampullen des inneren Ohres. *Ztschr. f. Laryng., Rhin., Otol. 26:*29, 1935.

STREETER, G. L. The factors involved in the excavation of the cavities in the cartilaginous capsule of the ear in the human embryo. *Am. J. Anat. 22:*1, 1917a.

STREETER, G. L. The development of the scala tympani, scala vestibuli and perioticular cistern in the human embryo. *Am. J. Anat. 21:*299, 1917b.

STREETER, G. L. Development of the auricle in the human embryo. *Contr. Embryol. 14:*111, 1922.

SULLIVAN, J. A., and HODGES, W. E. Effect of differential mobility of the windows of the cochlea on the mechanism of hearing. *Arch. Otolaryng. 49:*63, 1949.

SUNDERLAND, S. The arterial relations of the internal auditory meatus. *Brain 68:*23, 1945.

Symposium before the American Otological Society, Toronto, May 27, 1935. Subject: Is there localization in the cochlea for low tones? Is impaired hearing for the tones below 1000 D.V. ever due to a cochlear or inner ear lesion; if so, where is the lesion located and how is it recognized clinically? *Ann. Otol., Rhin. & Laryng. 44:*736.

TREMBLE, G. E. Pneumatization of the temporal bone. *Arch. Otolaryng. 19:*172, 1934.

TSCHIASSNY, K. The site of the facial nerve lesion in cases of Ramsay Hunt's syndrome. *Ann. Otol., Rhin. & Laryng. 55:*152, 1946.

ULRICH, H. Die Funktion der Otolithen, geprüft durch direkte mechanische Beeinflussung des Utriculusotolithen am lebenden Hecht. *Arch. f. d. ges. Physiol. 235:*545, 1935.

WALLS, E. W. The laxator tympani muscle. *J. Anat. 80:*210, 1946.

WALTNER, J. G. Barrier membrane of the cochlear aqueduct: Histologic studies on the patency of the cochlear aqueduct. *Arch. Otolaryng. 47:*656, 1948.

WATT, J. C., and MCKILLOP, A. N. Relation of arteries to roots of nerves in posterior cranial fossa in man. *Arch. Surg. 30:*336, 1935.

WEVER, E. G. The width of the basilar membrane in man. *Ann. Otol., Rhin. & Laryng. 47:*37, 1938.

WEVER, E. G., and BRAY, C. W. The tensor tympani muscle and its relation to sound conduction. *Ann. Otol., Rhin. & Laryng. 46:*947, 1937.

WEVER, E. G., and LAWRENCE, M. The functions of the round window. *Ann. Otol., Rhin. & Laryng. 57:*579, 1948.

WEVER, E. G., LAWRENCE, M., and SMITH, K. R. The middle ear in sound conduction. *Arch. Otolaryng. 48:*19, 1948.

WILLIAMS, H. L. Diagnosis and treatment of endolymphatic hydrops (Ménière's disease). *J. Iowa State Med. Soc. 37:*1, 1947a.

WILLIAMS, H. L. The present status of the diagnosis and treatment of endolymphatic hydrops (Ménière's disease). *Ann. Otol., Rhin. & Laryng. 56:*614, 1947b.

WILLIAMS, H. L. *Ménière's Disease.* Springfield, Ill., Thomas, 1952.

WILSON, J. G. The nerves and nerve-endings in the membrana tympani. *J. Comp. Neurol. 17:*459, 1907.

WILSON, J. G. The nerves and nerve endings in the membrana tympani of man. *Am. J. Anat. 11:*101, 1911.

WILSON, J. G., and ANSON, B. J. Form and structure of an area of otitic sclerosis in the temporal bone of an adult. *Arch. Otolaryng. 18:*291, 1933.

WINSHIP, T., and LOUZAN, J. Tumors of the glomus jugulare not associated with the jugular vein. *A.M.A. Arch. Otolaryng. 54:*378, 1951.

WITTMAACK, K. The pathogenesis of otosclerosis. *Arch. Otolaryng. 14:*186, 1931.

WOLFF, DOROTHY Significant anatomic features of the auditory mechanism with special reference to the late fetus. *Ann. Otol., Rhin. & Laryng. 42:*1136, 1933.

WOLFF, DOROTHY The microscopic anatomy of the Eustachian tube. *Ann. Otol., Rhin. & Laryng. 43:*483, 1934a.

WOLFF, DOROTHY Significant anatomic features of the auditory mechanism with special reference to the late fetus. *Ann. Otol., Rhin. & Laryng. 43:*193, 1934b.

WOLFF, DOROTHY Otosclerosis: Hypothesis of its origin and progress. *Tr. Am. Acad. Ophth. Suppl.,* p. 11, 1950.

WOOD-JONES, F., and I-CHUAN, W. The development of the external ear. *J. Anat. 68:*525, 1934.

YOUNG, M. W. The drainage of the perilymph in Macacus rhesus. (Abstr.) *Anat. Rec. 103:*524, 1949.

YOUNG, M. W. Anatomical basis for labyrinthine disturbances resulting from dental deformities. (Abstr.) *Anat. Rec. 106:*296, 1950.

ZIEGELMAN, E. F. The cellular character of one hundred temporal bones: Clinical and surgical significance. *Ann. Otol., Rhin. & Laryng. 44:*3, 1935.

{CHAPTER 4}

The Nose
and Paranasal Sinuses

THE EXTERNAL NOSE

THE external nose has a roughly pyramidal shape, and for this reason is frequently referred to as the nasal pyramid. The upper attachment of the nose at the forehead is defined as the root, and the free lower angle as the apex or tip; the rounded ridge connecting these two parts is the dorsum nasi, the upper part of which, supported by the nasal bones, is the bridge (Fig. 123). The lateral surfaces of the nose are referred to simply as the sides, while the blendings of these sides with the tissues of the face proper form the margins of the nose (nasofacial angles). The sides are expanded below to form the rounded alae, uniting with the upper lip at the nasolabial sulci. The alae and the septum bound the two external openings (nostrils, nares, or anterior or external nares) at the base of the nasal pyramid.

Both the dorsum and the tip of the nose vary in shape as seen in profile; thus the former may be straight ("Grecian nose"), or present a projecting angle ("Roman nose") or a depression ("pug nose"); a prominent tip is characteristic of the "Roman" and "pug" noses; a downwardly turned tip converts the "Roman" into the "Jewish" or "aquiline" nose. These variations in the shape of the nose are familial and individual; the width of the nose at the alae, as compared with the length of the nose (given as the nasal index, the greatest width times 100, divided by the greatest length) varies racially, however —the white races have the lower nasal index (longer, higher noses), the black the higher index (short, broad noses), and the yellow races are intermediate in this regard.

The muscles about the nose are described in connection with the other facial muscles (p. 311).

Skeleton of Nasal Pyramid

NASAL BONES

The skeleton of the external nose is partly cartilaginous and partly bony. The upper, bony, part consists largely of the

229

paired nasal bones, supplemented by processes from the frontal and maxillary bones. The nasal bones are usually narrower and thicker above, wider and thinner below; they articulate firmly above with the nasal part of the frontal bone, which extends downward behind and beneath the nasal bones and the

of the maxilla, while the lower part is locked behind this process.

The medial articular surfaces of the nasal bones, where the two come together, are wider, for each projects downward and backward into the nasal cavity so that the two projections together form a crest, tapering from above downward;

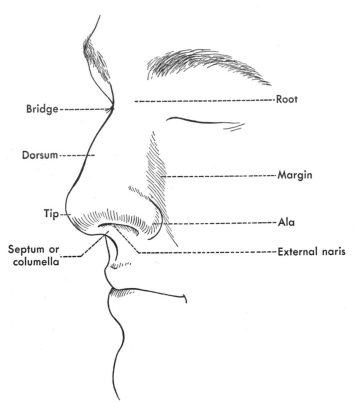

Fig. 123. Parts of the external nose.

frontal processes of the maxillae to form a shelflike support to these, thus adding strength to the bridge of the nose. The lateral border of each nasal bone is bevelled—in about the upper half of this border the bevel is on the inner surface of the bone, while in the lower part the bevel is on the outside. Thus the lateral articulation is also particularly firm, for the upper part of this border rests upon the anterior surface of the frontal process

this crest contributes to the nasal septum, and articulates with the spine of the nasal process of the frontal bone, the perpendicular plate of the ethmoid bone and the septal cartilage of the nose. Even without the bracing action of the septum in the middle, the bridge of the nose possesses considerable structural strength, because of its arched form and the strength of its articulations.

In the dried and prepared skull the free

lower edges of the nasal bones form the borders of the piriform aperture, but in the fresh condition these borders have attached to them the thin upper edges of the lateral nasal cartilages.

Exceptionally, the nasal bones may be fused in the midline, or they may even be completely absent, their place being taken by enlarged frontal processes of

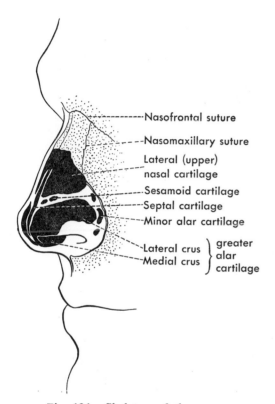

Nasofrontal suture

Nasomaxillary suture

Lateral (upper) nasal cartilage

Sesamoid cartilage

Septal cartilage

Minor alar cartilage

Lateral crus } greater
Medial crus } alar cartilage

Fig. 124. Skeleton of the nose.

the maxilla. Minor variations in their shape and size are common. It should be remembered also, in examining roentgenograms of the face for possible fracture of the nasal bones, that the nasal bones may be multiple—that is, a bone may be naturally divided into two parts —and that accessory bones may occur at their lines of articulation.

NASAL CARTILAGES

The lower part of the nasal pyramid, largely cartilaginous, is usually described as being formed by five major cartilages and a variable number of smaller ones (Fig. 124). The major cartilages are the two lateral (upper nasal, or triangular) cartilages above, the greater alar (lower nasal) cartilages below, and the median unpaired septal (quadrangular) cartilage. In their upper portions, the lateral nasal cartilages are continuous with each other across the midline, and also with the septal cartilage; therefore the lateral nasal and septal cartilages are frequently described together as a single cartilage, the nasoseptal cartilage.

The *lateral nasal cartilage* is somewhat triangular in shape: its upper edge, the base of the triangle, is thin, and articulates closely with the nasal and maxillary bones; its lateral and inferior border, the hypotenuse of the triangle, likewise thin, is bound by dense connective tissue (in which minor alar and sesamoid cartilages may be embedded) to the upper border of the greater alar cartilage; its medial border is however thick, both above where it is continuous with the septal cartilage and below where it forms a free edge lateral to the midline of the nose. As in the case of the bridge of the nose, the part of the nasal pyramid formed by the lateral nasal cartilages possesses a certain intrinsic strength of its own, since the cartilages of the two sides are continuous with each other above, and therefore actually form a single, highly curved piece of cartilage (Fig. 125); in addition, this arch is supported at its middle by its continuity with the septal cartilage. The *septal cartilage* is discussed with other elements of the nasal septum on page 238.

The *greater alar cartilages* are thin curved plates which bound and hold open the nasal apertures. They are thus responsible for the shape of the tip of the nose, and plastic surgery involving them has become relatively common. Some of the numerous variations of these cartilages have been discussed by Daley.

Each greater alar cartilage consists of a medial and a lateral crus. The lateral crus is the broader, and extends from

and closely approaches the maxilla, this membrane forms the most posterolateral part of the ala and has embedded in it several minor (lesser) alar cartilages. Variations in the numbers and relative sizes of the cartilages of the nose are easily accounted for by their development —they form at first one continuous cartilaginous mass, in which separate elements are produced by disappearance of cartilage in certain areas and its replacement

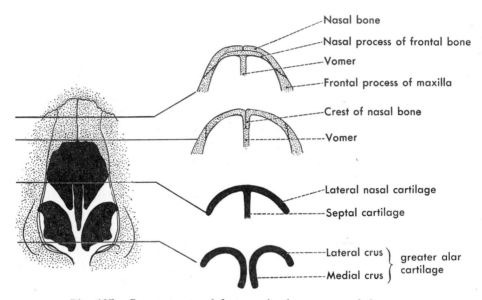

Nasal bone

Nasal process of frontal bone

Vomer

Frontal process of maxilla

Crest of nasal bone

Vomer

Lateral nasal cartilage

Septal cartilage

Lateral crus } greater alar

Medial crus } cartilage

Fig. 125.   Some structural features in the support of the nose.

the tip into the ala of the nose; it is united by dense connective tissue to the lateral nasal cartilage above, and to the lower part of the septal cartilage; toward the midline these cartilages are usually close together, but more laterally the fibrous membrane uniting lateral nasal and alar cartilages is broader, and usually contains one or more small sesamoid cartilages within it. The lateral crus varies in the extent to which it continues posterolaterally into the ala, but is in all cases united to the maxilla by a lateral continuation of the fibrous membrane; except when the lateral crus is unusually large

by connective tissue; it is this tissue that forms the fibrous membrane uniting the cartilages.

The medial crus of the greater alar cartilage, more slender than the lateral, is continuous with the lateral at the apex of the nose, the curve between the two forming the lateral portion of the apex; the medial crus runs downward and backward in the free edge of the nasal septum. The two medial crura are, at the very tip of the nose, separated from each other by a rather wide groove, which can easily be palpated. As they run into the septum, however, they become closely associated, and together form the support of the mobile septum (columna nasi, columella), which lies below or distal to the cartilage of the nasal septum. The medial crura are loosely united to each other, and to the lower edge of the septal cartilage, by connective tissue; the mobile septum may thus easily be pushed to one side, so that the firm lower edge of the

septum above the medial palpebral ligament and runs downward on the side of the nose to anastomose with the nasal branch of the facial (external maxillary) artery, giving off in its course a branch to the lacrimal sac. These vessels, which may vary inversely in size, are supplemented laterally by twigs from the infraorbital branch of the internal maxillary

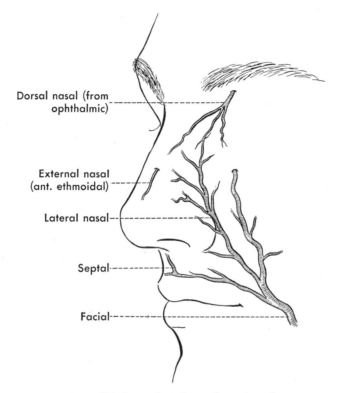

Dorsal nasal (from ophthalmic)

External nasal (ant. ethmoidal)

Lateral nasal

Septal

Facial

Fig. 126. Chief arteries about the external nose.

septal cartilage can be felt. At their posterior free edges, the medial crura turn slightly outward again.

BLOOD SUPPLY

The arteries on the external surface of the nose are primarily the nasal branch of the facial (external maxillary), running over the ala to supply the lower portion of the nose, and the nasal or dorsal nasal branch of the ophthalmic artery (Fig. 126); this latter perforates the orbital

artery, and inferiorly, over the nasal septum, by twigs from the arteries of the nasal septum (which largely, however, supply the interior of the nose, and are a common source of nosebleed). At the junction between nasal bone and nasal cartilage, the small external nasal branch of the anterior ethmoidal artery emerges to supply skin along the dorsum to the apex. The chief veins of the nose end in the anterior facial and ophthalmic veins.

INNERVATION

The skin of the root of the nose and over the bridge and the upper part of the side of the nose is supplied by branches from the frontal and nasociliary portions of the ophthalmic nerve, the particular branches concerned being the supratrochlear and infratrochlear nerves (Fig. 127). The skin on the side of ap-

proximately the lower half of the nose is supplied through twigs from the infra-orbital branch of the maxillary nerve; the external nasal branch of the anterior ethmoidal nerve (from the nasociliary) emerges between the nasal bone and the lateral nasal cartilage to supply skin over the dorsum of this part of the nose down to the tip.

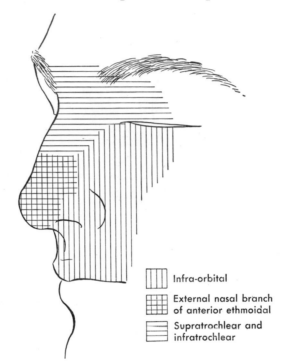

Infra-orbital

External nasal branch of anterior ethmoidal

Supratrochlear and infratrochlear

Fig. 127. Innervation of the skin of the nose.

THE INTERNAL NOSE

THE paired cavities of the nose, divided from each other by the nasal septum, are also known as the nasal fossae; in frontal section they are roughly triangular in shape, being narrow above and wider below. Their external openings are the nares or external nares, while their posterior or pharyngeal openings are the choanae or internal nares. The major *walls* of each nasal fossa consist of a medial wall, formed by the nasal septum, a lateral

wall, and an inferior wall or floor. The medial and lateral walls are partly cartilaginous and membranous, partly bony, but the floor is entirely bony. The roof of the nasal fossa is formed by the cribriform plate, and is quite narrow—about 5 mm. at its widest, or posterior, end.

The portion of the nasal fossa corresponding to the ala of the nose is known as the *vestibule*; it is lined with skin which contains the vibrissae or hairs, and sweat and sebaceous glands; along the nasal septum there is no distinct demarcation between the vestibule and the remainder of the nasal fossa, but on the lateral wall there is a ridge, the limen vestibuli, which separates the two and marks both the lower end of the lateral (upper) nasal cartilage and the point at which the skin lining the vestibule passes over into the mucous membrane of the remainder of the nasal fossa.

Except in the vestibule, each nasal fossa is lined by *mucous membrane* which is tightly attached to the periosteum and perichondrium of its walls. The greater part of this mucous membrane is highly vascular, contains numerous mucous and serous glands, and is covered by pseudostratified columnar ciliated epithelium. This constitutes the respiratory mucosa (Schneiderian membrane). A limited upper part of the nasal fossa bounded largely by the superior nasal concha and the lateral wall above this, and by a corresponding part of the septum, is lined by the olfactory mucous membrane, which is less vascular (yellowish rather than pink in color), covered by a nonciliated epithelium, and contains the modified nerve-cell bodies which give rise to the olfactory nerve fibers; its glands are apparently of the serous type. The mucosa of the paranasal sinuses is similar to respiratory mucosa, but less vascular, thinner, and more loosely attached to the bony walls.

The presence of the large inferior and middle conchae much increases the area of the respiratory mucosa, so that air drawn into the nose may be warmed and humidified before reaching the trachea. The marked vascularity of the respiratory mucosa, and its abundant glands, adapt it especially for this purpose, and in quiet respiration the air currents are primarily through the inferior and middle meatuses, therefore against this mucosa. The thinner olfactory mucosa is adapted for the reception of odoriferous stimuli, and is above the main stream of air flow —hence the necessity to sniff, and thus create eddies toward the roof of the nasal cavities, in attempting to recognize or appreciate odors.

Irritation of the nasal mucous membrane leads to reflex vasodilation of the vessels within it, and increased secretion by its glands, and may be followed by sneezing, also a reflex act. Since sneezing involves voluntary muscles, however, this (but not the turgescence and increased secretion of the mucous membrane) may often be voluntarily inhibited; it is also well known that pressure upon the mobile part of the nasal septum tends to inhibit sneezing.

CILIARY ACTIVITY

As observed in the monkey (Lucas) the ciliated epithelium of the respiratory mucosa and the paranasal sinuses as a whole has a beat so directed that mucus is propelled from smaller toward larger cavities and carried away from the margin of the olfactory epithelium; in general, therefore, the beat of the cilia is downward and backward toward the nasopharynx. Hilding ('32) found this direction to prevail also in man (Figs. 128 and 129).

While Lucas described the ciliary activity as increasing from the roof to the floor of the nose, Hilding has divided the respiratory mucous membrane into anterior and posterior parts on the basis of its activity: He found that the anterior third of the nose is relatively inactive in regard to ciliary action, and drains slowly, requiring an hour or more for droplets of ink placed here to enter the inferior

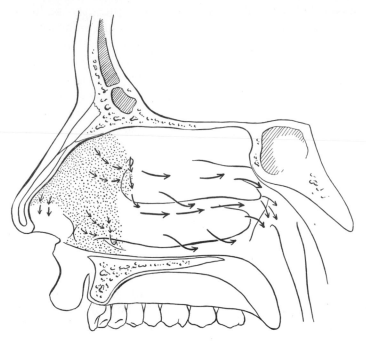

Fig. 128. Direction of flow of mucus (direction of ciliary beat) on the lateral wall of the nose. The area of less active ciliary movement is stippled. (Adapted from Hilding, A.: *Arch. Otolaryng. 15:*92, 1932.)

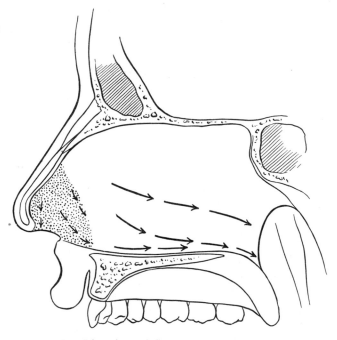

Fig. 129. Direction of flow of mucus (ciliary beat) on the nasal septum, the area of less active ciliary action being stippled. (Adapted from Hilding, A.: *Arch. Otolaryng. 15:* 92, 1932.)

and middle meatuses. On the other hand, the posterior two thirds is a region of active ciliary action, and may drain into the nasopharynx in from three to ten minutes. Hilding noted that mucus is moved apparently not only by ciliary activity directly, but also by gravity and by the traction resulting either from ciliary movements or from the pharynx as in swallowing; the greatest rate of movement produced by these combined factors was in the inferior and middle meatuses.

more rapid than at the beginning of the experiments, reaching as much as ten or more beats per second. In contrast, the cilia exposed to excessive heat did not resume their function even after several hours at more nearly normal temperatures. This work, carried out both upon the rabbit and upon man, apparently indicates that while inspiration of cold air does not actually damage the cilia, nasal douches exceeding 40° C. may produce severe damage. Drugs introduced into the

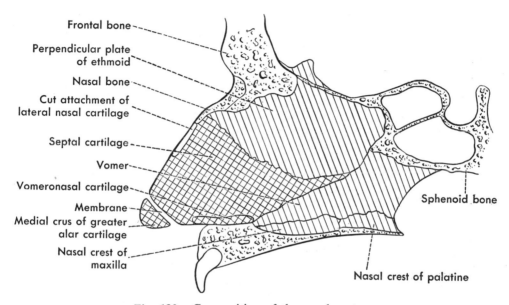

Frontal bone
Perpendicular plate of ethmoid
Nasal bone
Cut attachment of lateral nasal cartilage
Septal cartilage
Vomer
Vomeronasal cartilage
Membrane
Medial crus of greater alar cartilage
Nasal crest of maxilla
Sphenoid bone
Nasal crest of palatine

Fig. 130.   Composition of the nasal septum.

Ciliary activity may be drastically affected by extremes of temperature and by various chemicals. Proetz found that temperatures of 40° C. greatly retard, and those of 43° or 44° completely inactivate ciliary movement; temperatures below 18° C. were found also to decrease ciliary movement, and all movement ceased when the temperature was lowered to between 12° and 7°; upon warming the mucous membrane again, however, the ciliary action was resumed and at 18° C. was found to be much

nasal cavity for various purposes may also have a deleterious effect on ciliary action.

NASAL SEPTUM

The larger part of the nasal septum (Fig. 130) is formed by the perpendicular plate of the ethmoid bone posteriorly, and the septal cartilage anteriorly; the vomer forms a postero-inferior portion of the septum, while the medial crura of the greater alar cartilages and the low nasal process (crest) of the maxilla complete the septum anteriorly.

The *perpendicular plate of the ethmoid* forms the upper third or more of the nasal septum; it is continuous above with the horizontal portion of the ethmoid bone, thus dividing the nasal roof into right and left sides. It articulates anteriorly and above with the frontal and nasal bones, posteriorly with the crest of the sphenoid, postero-inferiorly with the vomer, and antero-inferiorly with the septal cartilage.

The extent of the perpendicular plate anteriorly and inferiorly, that is, the level

bones. Its anterior border is grooved for the reception of the septal cartilage.

The nasal spine of the frontal and the crests of the maxillary, palatine, and nasal bones contribute little to the nasal septum; they serve as points of articulation for the other elements of the septum, and hence help to complete it about its edges.

SEPTAL CARTILAGE

The septal (quadrangular) cartilage, continuous with the lateral nasal cartilages toward the bridge of the nose but separate from their diverging lower ends, forms the cartilaginous portion of the

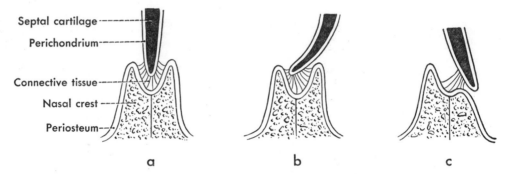

Fig. 131. Method of articulation of the septal cartilage so as to allow flexion of it as shown in *b*; *c* indicates how dislocation is favored by defective development of the nasal crest.

of its junction with the septal cartilage, varies; its lowest point may be a centimeter or so above the lower free edge of the nasal bones, but it may extend to the edge of these bones, or actually not articulate with them at all, but only with the nasal spine of the frontal bone (Schaeffer, '20). The septal cartilage varies inversely with the size of the perpendicular plate of the ethmoid.

The *vomer* completes the nasal septum posteriorly and inferiorly; it articulates above with the body of the sphenoid bone and with the perpendicular plate of the ethmoid, and below with the nasal crests (processes) of the maxillary and palatine

septum. Its articulations are peculiar anatomically, for cartilage does not usually articulate directly with bone, and important clinically because they allow movement. Posteriorly, the thin edge of the septal cartilage is received into a groove on the edge of the perpendicular plate of the ethmoid, and its inferior edge also fits into a similar groove on the nasal crest (Fig. 131). While the periosteum of the bones with which it articulates and the perichondrium of the septal cartilage are united by connective tissue, they are not otherwise directly continuous with each other; the periosteum of each bone passes across the groove for reception of the cartilage, to become continuous with the periosteum on the other side of the bone, and the perichondrium of the cartilage likewise turns around the edge of the cartilage. Thus the cartilage and the bone are united by connective tissue external to the periosteum and perichondrium, this tissue forming a sort of ligament which unites the two elements, yet allows movement between them; there may even be fat interposed between the cartilage and bone (Aymard).

The mobility of the joints thus formed, and especially that with the maxilla, is of physiological importance, since it allows the base of the cartilage to rotate as the cartilage is flexed, thus minimizing the danger of fracture of it from pressure upon the dorsum of the nose. Anatomically, it also allows marked deviation of the septum without dislocation; if the tissue is loose, and particularly when one side of the groove into which the cartilage fits is not properly developed, this mobility also accounts for the occurrence of dislocations of the septal cartilage. Marked dislocations may be accompanied by distortion of the whole lower cartilaginous portion of the nose (Cohen).

MOBILE SEPTUM

The mobile septum, columna or columella, sometimes referred to also as the membranous septum, actually also contains cartilage, as it is supported by the medial crura of the alar cartilages (p. 232). As already described, the mobile septum is not closely connected to the free lower edge of the septal cartilage, and advantage is taken of this fact in submucous resections of deviated septa; properly speaking, it is this gap that should be referred to as the membranous septum.

SUBMUCOUS RESECTION

The entire septum, bony and cartilaginous (and membranous), is covered by a continuous layer of mucosa, changing to skin at the vestibule; in submucous resections this can be incised at the lower edge of the septal cartilage, by pushing the mobile septum to one side. Deviated septa usually involve the septal cartilage and perpendicular plate of the ethmoid, and sometimes the nasal process of the maxilla and palatine bone, but the vomer is less often affected. In spite of the fact that the union of the two lateral nasal cartilages in a curve on the dorsum of the nose gives added strength to this region, the support to the dorsum of the nose here, and to a much greater extent below, where the lateral nasal cartilages have freely projecting apices, must depend upon the septal cartilage; a depressed area of the dorsum ("saddle nose") may follow too great removal of the septal cartilage, although it has been denied, and affirmed, that this is due entirely to the removal of support. The argument on this point seems to be the extent to which some support from the nasal cartilage is necessary to support the soft tissues of the dorsum below the union of the lateral nasal cartilages, and is therefore one concerning relative strength following an operation. Several writers have emphasized the role that scar tissue and its retraction may play in the formation of "saddle nose"; while the columella, after submucous resection, adequately supports the tip of the nose, it also may be involved by scar tissue and drawn inward and upward.

VOMERONASAL CARTILAGE

On either side of the septal cartilage along its inferior border there may be a small bar of cartilage, the vomeronasal cartilage; this is associated with a small opening which leads into the rudimentary vomeronasal organ (of Jacobson); in some animals this organ gives rise to a branch of the olfactory nerve and is highly specialized, but in man it is usually simply a short tubular sac, from 2 to 6 mm. in length, lined by epithelium continuous with that of the nasal cavity proper.

LATERAL NASAL WALL

In contrast to the simple medial wall, the lateral nasal wall is complicated in its anatomy. It bounds most of the paranasal sinuses and receives the openings from these, and bears three or four nasal conchae or turbinates, delicate projecting scrolls of bone covered by mucous membrane (Fig. 132). These conchae are named, from below upward, the in-

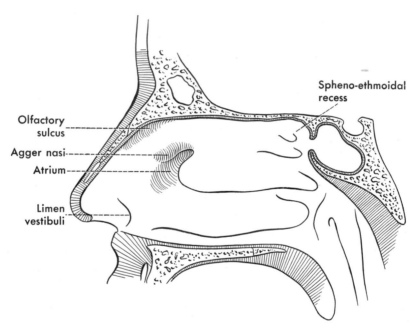

Fig. 132. Lateral nasal wall.

INNERVATION AND BLOOD SUPPLY

The chief nerves of the nasal septum are from the anterior ethmoidal and maxillary nerves, the latter via branches of the sphenopalatine ganglion; they are described in connection with the innervation of the nasal fossa as a whole (p. 245). The arteries of the nasal septum include branches from the sphenopalatine artery, from both ethmoidal arteries, and from the facial (pp. 254 ff.).

ferior, middle, and superior conchae; when a fourth one is present (in about 60 per cent of bodies) it lies above the others, is the smallest of all, and is known as the supreme concha.

The air spaces, or meatuses, beneath and lateral to the conchae are named according to the conchae to which they are related: thus the inferior meatus lies beneath the root of attachment of the inferior concha, and lateral to its freely projecting portion, between this and the lateral wall of the nose; similarly, the middle meatus lies beneath and lateral to the middle concha, and above the root of attachment of the inferior concha, and the superior lies beneath and lateral to the superior concha. The supreme meatus, when present, is usually a barely perceptible furrow beneath the supreme concha.

The *inferior and middle conchae,* the prominent projections of the lateral wall, both begin anteriorly at approximately the level of the vertical plane of the forehead, and extend, one below the other, almost to the choanae. Anterior to these two conchae the lateral wall of the nose above the limen vestibuli is more delicately marked. About halfway between the anterior end of the middle turbinate and the dorsum of the nose is a slight projection, the *agger nasi,* said to be the remnant of an additional turbinate found in lower animals, but important in man as marking the location of ethmoidal air cells frequently designated the agger nasi cells; the passageway above the agger nasi, leading to the uppermost part of the nasal fossa, is known as the olfactory sulcus, and aids in conducting air to the upper, olfactory, portion of the nasal fossa; below and posterior to the agger nasi, in front of the middle meatus and above and anterior to the attached end of the inferior concha, is a shallow depression known as the atrium of the middle meatus.

The *superior concha,* about half the length of the other two, begins at about the middle of these and extends backward to become about coterminous with them. Above the uppermost concha, superior or supreme as the case may be, the part of the nasal fossa between this and the anterior surface of the body of the

sphenoid bone is known as the *sphenoethmoidal recess*; the opening of the sphenoid sinus is typically through the posterior wall of this recess.

The three conchae converge somewhat toward each other posteriorly, and after they blend with the lateral nasal wall the remaining posterior portion of the nasal fossa, between the ends of the conchae and the posterior nasal sulcus, forms the nasopharyngeal meatus.

INFERIOR NASAL CONCHA AND INFERIOR MEATUS

The inferior nasal concha is an independent bone, covered with thick mucous membrane which contains an especially dense venous plexus. It is so arched that the inferior meatus, lying beneath and lateral to it, is narrowed both anteriorly and posteriorly, but is both wider and higher at its middle.

The only structure of importance in the inferior meatus is the opening of the nasolacrimal duct (Fig. 133). This ostium is usually in the anterior portion of the lateral wall of the inferior meatus; it has been variously described as being placed more commonly quite high, just below the attached border of the lower turbinate, or more commonly somewhat below this level. Costen ('32) has stated that it is more commonly high and well forward, and pointed out that accessory openings into the antrum through the inferior meatus should therefore be made as far back as possible in order to avoid scarring or destruction of the nasolacrimal ostium.

The shape of the opening varies considerably, from rounded to slitlike; it may open upon a papilla-like formation, or into a shallow fossa or deep groove (Fig. 134), and occasionally the opening may be duplicated (Schaeffer, '12). It has

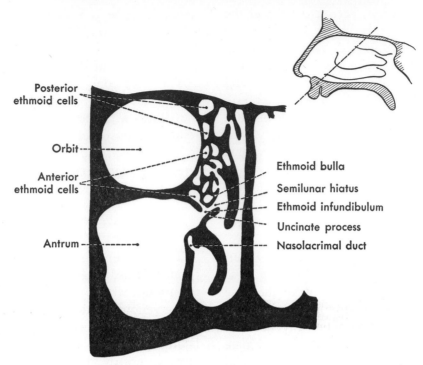

Fig. 133. A hypothetical section through the lateral nasal wall, slanted as indicated in the smaller diagram, indicating some of its relations.

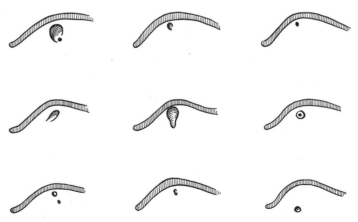

Fig. 134. Variations in the size, shape, and position of the opening of the nasolacrimal duct. The cut base of the inferior concha is indicated. (Adapted from Schaeffer, J. P.: *Am. J. Anat. 13:*183, 1912.)

been stated that when the opening is high it tends also to be wide, while when it is located lower it is more apt to be slitlike. When the opening is slitlike the nasolacrimal duct runs obliquely through the mucous membrane and is usually then protected by a fold of mucous membrane known as the plica lacrimalis or valve of Hasner. The lacrimal sac and the nasolacrimal duct are described in connection with the orbit.

the genu and is known as the *frontal recess*. The frontal recess may receive directly the nasofrontal duct from the frontal sinus, and the openings of some of the anterior ethmoidal cells. From the frontal recess the middle meatus runs downward and backward, and this portion is then referred to as the descending ramus; it is marked by the ethmoidal bulla, the uncinate process, and the semilunar hiatus.

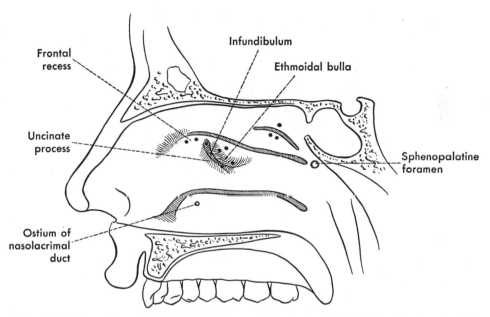

Fig. 135. Lateral nasal wall with the conchae removed. Variable locations of the ostia of the ethmoid cells are indicated by the black dots—anterior ethmoid cells may open into the frontal recess, the ethmoidal infundibulum, the suprabullar furrow, or on the bulla itself; posterior cells into the superior or supreme meatus.

MIDDLE NASAL CONCHA AND MIDDLE MEATUS

The middle nasal concha, also quite large, is a part of the ethmoid bone, and overhangs the important and complicated middle nasal meatus (Fig. 135). The anterior end of the middle concha has its line of attachment running almost vertically upward, to join the remainder of the concha at an angle or genu; the highest part of the middle meatus lies beneath

ETHMOIDAL BULLA

The ethmoidal bulla, a rounded projection of the lateral wall of the middle meatus beneath the middle concha, contains one or more anterior ethmoidal cells (also known as middle ethmoidal cells, or as bullar cells); these cells open into the middle meatus upon or above the bulla. Above the bulla, between it and the attached base of the middle concha, is the suprabullar recess or furrow.

The ethmoidal bulla is bordered below by an aperture termed the semilunar hiatus, which lies between the bulla above and a sharp ridge of bone, the uncinate process, below; the semilunar hiatus is the opening of a groove known as the ethmoidal infundibulum (uncinate or unciform groove).

ETHMOIDAL INFUNDIBULUM

From the semilunar hiatus the ethmoidal infundibulum extends downward, thus intervening between the lateral nasal wall and the ledge of bone forming the uncinate process. The ethmoidal infundibulum varies in depth (from 0.5 to 10 mm., averaging about 5 mm.) and therefore the upwardly projecting uncinate process varies in its height. Anterior ethmoid cells (infundibular cells) open into the ethmoidal infundibulum, and so also does the maxillary sinus; the accessibility of the ostium of the antrum therefore depends primarily upon the depth of the ethmoidal infundibulum and upon the closeness with which the uncinate process hugs the lateral wall—that is, also upon the width of the infundibulum. These factors are discussed on page 274.

Posteriorly, the ethmoidal infundibulum becomes continuous with the middle meatus; anteriorly, it either ends blindly at the ostia of anterior ethmoid cells, or is prolonged upward to groove the frontal recess and is then directly continuous with the ostium of the frontal sinus. It is the funnel-shaped anterior end of the infundibulum which earns it its name, and in some texts the name is restricted to this part; the remainder of it is then referred to as the semilunar hiatus, a term otherwise used to denote only the opening rather than the groove itself. The *medial wall* of the infundibulum is, of course, the bony uncinate process; the *lateral wall*, a part of the lateral nasal wall, is in places entirely membranous, and in perhaps as many as 40 per cent of cases presents accessory ostia leading into the maxillary sinus.

SUPERIOR NASAL CONCHA AND SUPERIOR MEATUS

The superior nasal concha is short, only about half the length of the middle, and is a much less prominent projection; its mucous membrane is thinner and less vascular than that of the other conchae, and, unlike those, is covered with olfactory epithelium containing the sensory cells of the olfactory nerve. Correspondingly, the superior meatus is a narrow channel between the superior concha and the posterior half of the middle concha; the majority of the posterior ethmoid cells open into this meatus.

SUPREME NASAL CONCHA

The supreme concha is said to be present unilaterally or bilaterally in about 60 per cent of bodies, but even when present is usually a rather slight fold of the lateral nasal wall. The shallow groove beneath it is then spoken of as the supreme meatus, and is said to receive the ostium of a posterior ethmoid cell in about 75 per cent of the cases in which it is present.

NERVES

OLFACTORY MUCOUS MEMBRANE

The olfactory mucous membrane, containing the cells of origin of the olfactory nerve fibers, is limited to approximately the upper third of the nasal mucous membrane, thus primarily to the superior concha, a corresponding portion of the septum, and the roof of the nasal fossa; because of the greater length of the nasal fossa inferiorly, the olfactory mucous membrane actually occupies much less than a third of the entire epithelium (Fig. 136). Smith ('41, '42) has shown that the number of fibers in the olfactory nerve begins to decrease shortly after birth, and continues to do so at the rate of about 1 per cent a year; he found that 55 per

to pathological changes in the nasal mucosa.

GENERAL SENSATION

The general sensory supply to the mucous membrane of the nose is derived from both the ophthalmic and maxillary branches of the fifth nerve, and probably

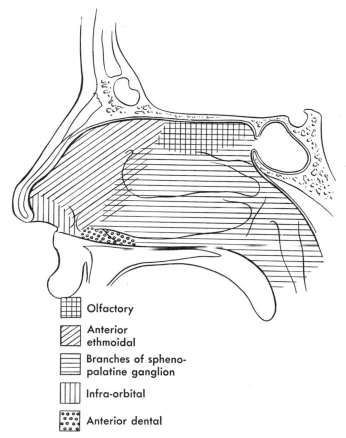

Olfactory

Anterior ethmoidal

Branches of spheno-palatine ganglion

Infra-orbital

Anterior dental

Fig. 136. General distribution of nerves to the lateral nasal wall.

cent of adults had lost more than three fifths of their complement of olfactory nerve fibers, and 13 per cent had lost all of them; only 29 of 163 noses of adults which he examined seemed to have a normal number of fibers, some 10,000 or more. He concluded that the marked reduction observed in adults is due in part to the aging factor, but much more

also from the great superficial petrosal branch of the seventh (p. 248); the fibers from the latter two branches reach the nose largely through the sphenopalatine ganglion and its branches.

NASOCILIARY NERVE

The branch of the ophthalmic division of the fifth nerve concerned with the innervation of the nasal mucous membrane is the nasociliary (nasal). The origin, course and branches of this nerve have been described on page 150, in connection with the orbit; briefly summarized, the nasociliary nerve arises from the ophthalmic nerve while this lies in the lateral wall of the cavernous sinus, enters and traverses the orbit, giving off branches to structures here, and divides into two limited dorsal and anterior portion of this (Figs. 137 and 138), including especially on the lateral wall the area anterior to the superior concha and above the attached border of the middle concha, the atrium, and the anterior ends of the middle and inferior conchae; these internal nasal branches are also distributed to a corresponding portion of the nasal septum. After giving off its internal nasal

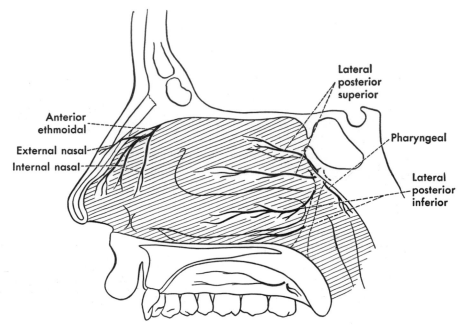

Fig. 137. Major nerve branches on the lateral nasal wall, the olfactory not being shown. The pterygopalatine canal and the position of the sphenopalatine ganglion at its upper end are indicated by broken lines.

terminal branches, the infratrochlear nerve (to skin at the medial angle of the eyelids) and the anterior ethmoidal nerve.

The anterior ethmoidal nerve leaves the orbit through the anterior ethmoidal foramen, typically in company with the anterior ethmoidal artery, and enters the cranial cavity to run forward along the lateral margin of the cribriform plate; it leaves the cranium through the ethmoidal slit at the side of the crista galli to enter the nasal cavity and supply a branches, the anterior ethmoidal nerve leaves the nasal cavity between the nasal bone and the lateral nasal cartilage to supply skin on the dorsum and tip of the nose.

Littell has stated that defects at the olfactory fissure may produce chronic infection in this area, and that the membrane here, which is innervated through the nasociliary nerve, is much more sensitive for pain than that within the paranasal sinuses; he inferred that pain from this region has often been mistaken for chronic ethmoiditis. Burnham ('49) also recognized that referred pain from the anterior ethmoidal nerve may resemble that of sinusitis, but expressed the belief that in some cases the nerve is affected by pressure from dilation of surrounding veins.

MAXILLARY NERVE

The terminal or infra-orbital branch of the maxillary nerve supplies a portion of the lining of the vestibule, through branches which enter by way of the external nares, and the anterior superior alveolar (dental) nerve gives off a nasal branch which pierces the lateral wall of the nasal fossa to supply an anterior part of the inferior meatus and a corresponding part of the floor of the fossa. However, the chief supply from the maxillary nerve to the nasal cavity is through the sphenopalatine ganglion. As the maxillary nerve traverses the pterygopalatine (sphenomaxillary) fossa, after having left the cranial cavity by way of the foramen rotundum, it has suspended from it the *sphenopalatine ganglion,* one of the four major parasympathetic ganglia of the head.

The connection between the maxillary nerve and sphenopalatine ganglion is through the sphenopalatine or ganglionic branches of the maxillary, usually two in number; the fibers forming these branches are sensory, and therefore do not synapse in the ganglion. The majority pass medial to the ganglion while others traverse it, to be distributed however with the motor fibers from the ganglion in the so-called branches of the sphenopalatine ganglion. The branches of distribution of the ganglion, therefore, contain not only vasomotor and secretory fibers but also a very large proportion of sensory ones. These branches of distribution are enumerated on page 253, and some of them are described in more detail in connection with the mouth and pharynx; it is the branches to the nasal fossa that are important here.

The internal or *nasal branches of the sphenopalatine ganglion* pass through the sphenopalatine foramen, located just behind the posterior end of the middle nasal concha, and are divisible into two sets, the lateral posterior superior (short sphenopalatine, superior nasal) and the medial posterior superior (septal) branches.

The lateral posterior superior nasal branches are a number of small twigs which are distributed to the mucous membrane over the larger posterior part of the superior and middle nasal conchae, helping also to supply the posterior ethmoidal cells; the medial posterior superior nasal branches (Fig. 138) are distributed to the nasal septum, crossing the roof of the nasal fossa as it is formed by the antero-inferior face of the sphenoid bone. The largest of this group is the nasopalatine (long sphenopalatine) nerve; this runs downward and forward on the nasal septum, between the periosteum and the mucous membrane, to reach the incisive or anterior palatine canal. Here it anastomoses with the nasal branch of the anterior superior alveolar nerve; the two nasopalatine nerves then pass through the foramina in the intermaxillary suture (foramina of Scarpa), the left nerve usually anterior to the right, to be distributed to the anterior portion of the hard palate behind the incisor teeth, where they communicate with the anterior palatine branches of the sphenopalatine ganglion.

The lower part of the nasal cavity is also supplied by branches of the sphenopalatine ganglion, but less directly; as the great or anterior palatine nerve passes downward in the pterygopalatine canal within the lateral nasal wall it gives off small posterior nasal branches which pass through the perpendicular plate of the palatine bone to supply the mucous membrane over the posterior part of the inferior nasal concha and the adjacent portions of the middle and inferior meatuses of the nose.

nasal mucosa. The plexus which they form in this location also contains nerve cells.

The function of the nervus terminalis is not known; it has been regarded both as sensory and as having an autonomic function. According to Pearson the ganglion cells of the nervus terminalis are derived at least in part by migration of cells from the olfactory placode, and per-

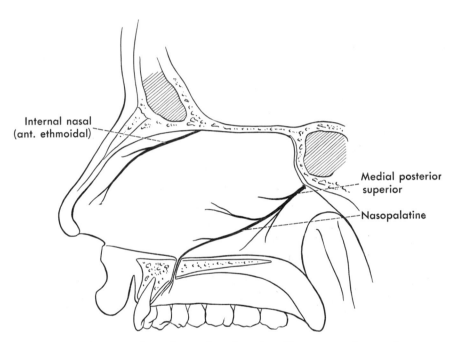

Fig. 138.   Major nerve branches, other than the olfactory, on the nasal septum.

NERVUS TERMINALIS

In addition to the branches already described, the nasal mucous membrane also receives the fibers of the nervus terminalis. According to Brookover ('14, '17) the ganglion cells of this nerve lie largely embedded in the dura between the crista galli and the olfactory bulb; its branches emerge into the nose through the cribriform plate to lie against the cartilaginous septum, deep to most of the vessels and other structures of the

haps also from migration of cells from the forebrain.

GREAT SUPERFICIAL PETROSAL NERVE

Since the great superficial petrosal nerve, the motor root to the sphenopalatine ganglion, contains in addition to its preganglionic fibers a goodly number of sensory ones, it is obvious that these fibers must be distributed through the branches of the ganglion. The great superficial petrosal nerve is derived from the seventh nerve, and the sensory fibers in it have their cells of origin in the geniculate ganglion of the facial. (Foley, Pepper, and Kessler found about 2000 sensory fibers in the facial nerve of the cat, of which from 27 to 40 per cent, according to Foley and DuBois, go into the great superficial petrosal nerve.) The exact distribution of these sensory fibers of the facial nerve is not known, nor are their functions clearly understood.

SENSATION AND ANESTHESIA OF NOSE

Cushing described the nasal mucous membrane as being completely anesthetic, even to such irritating stimuli as ammonia, following interruption of the fifth nerve. Lederer and Dinolt studied the noses of 10 patients in whom the sensory root of the trigeminal nerve had been sectioned, and reported that they found anesthesia of the affected side in 9 patients and hypoesthesia in 1; they concluded that the first and second branches of the trigeminal nerve provide all the sensory innervation of the nose except perhaps that of a small area of the septum which receives branches of the nervus terminalis. Higbee, from an examination of 16 patients with section of the root of the fifth nerve, concluded likewise that the fifth nerve is the sole sensory supply to the nose.

These clinical reports are not, however, in complete agreement with the known anatomy; it seems possible that residual sensation in the more posterior part of the nose, to which sensory fibers of the facial nerve are apparently distributed, may have been overlooked—or that the great superficial petrosal nerve had been interrupted, as may easily occur, in the approach to the sensory root of the fifth nerve.

While some of the sensory fibers of the facial passing through the spheno-palatine ganglion may, as stated by Rowbotham, be gustatory fibers distributed by way of the palatine nerves to the soft palate, pain in the deeper nasal region and the sinuses has been described as a symptom of geniculate ganglion neuralgia (Hunt), and Fenton has pointed out that reference of pain of apparent nasal origin to the auditory and mastoid regions can best be explained as due to the sensory distribution of the facial nerve to the nose. Christensen has stated that not only do the lateral nasal and nasopalatine branches of the sphenopalatine ganglion contain sensory fibers from the seventh nerve as well as the fifth, but that these branches and the nasociliary nerve apparently also include some afferent components derived from the vagus and upper thoracic spinal nerves. Larsell and Burns have pointed out that myelinated fibers (therefore presumably afferent ones) leave the internal carotid plexus by way of the deep petrosal to reach the sphenopalatine ganglion, and suggested that they may have to do with the muscle pain sometimes present in the neck when the region of the sphenopalatine ganglion is diseased. The fifth nerve, therefore, probably cannot be regarded as the sole sensory supply to the nose; since, however, the other nerves concerned run with fifth nerve fibers as branches of the sphenopalatine ganglion, cocainization of the ganglion affects all of the nerve supply to the posterior part of the nose.

Because of the complexity of the nasal cavity, cocainization of the mucosa usually produces only partial anesthesia of the fossa; Hill has therefore advocated injection through the infra-orbital foramen to infiltrate the maxillary nerve and the sphenopalatine ganglion and its branches (which have also been anesthetized through a lateral approach, anterior to the mandible or between its coronoid and condyloid processes) and injection along the nasal wall of the orbit to block the nasociliary nerve at the anterior ethmoid foramen. These two injections, properly carried out, should effectively interrupt all sensory fibers to the nasal fossa, regardless of their origin

The facial nerve supplies the parasympathetic fibers to the nose. The preganglionic fibers pass through the nervus intermedius portion of the facial nerve with the sensory fibers, leave the facial at its external genu to form a part of the greater superficial petrosal nerve, and end in the sphenopalatine ganglion. The postganglionic fibers, arising from the cells

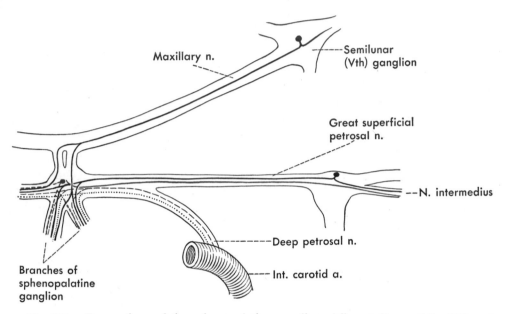

Fig. 139.   Connections of the sphenopalatine ganglion. Afferent fibers of the fifth and seventh (nervus intermedius portion) cranial nerves and from the carotid plexus, solid black lines; postganglionic sympathetic fibers, broken black lines; preganglionic parasympathetic fibers, solid red lines; and postganglionic parasympathetic fibers, broken red lines.

(and also fibers to most of the paranasal sinuses).

Autonomic Innervation

Some sympathetic fibers may enter the nose with the nasociliary nerve (Christensen), and the nervus terminalis may have an autonomic function, but the chief autonomic innervation of the nose, both sympathetic and parasympathetic, is through the sphenopalatine ganglion and its branches of distribution (Fig. 139).

of the ganglion, are then distributed with the sympathetic and sensory fibers through the branches of the ganglion. The great superficial petrosal nerve contains both vasodilator and secretory fibers.

The sympathetic fibers to the nose undoubtedly arise, like the fibers to other parts of the head, from the upper thoracic segments of the cord, and perhaps occasionally from the eighth cervical segment; these preganglionic fibers then ascend to reach the superior cervical ganglion in which they synapse. Postganglionic fibers from the superior cervical ganglion pass along the internal carotid artery as the chief component of the internal carotid plexus, and those destined for the nose leave this plexus as the deep petrosal nerve, which joins the great superficial petrosal to form the Vidian nerve; the sympathetic fibers pass through the sphenopalatine ganglion without synapse to be distributed with its branches. These fibers are primarily vasoconstrictors, but according to Larsell and Fenton they have been said to include also some vaso-dilators.

SPHENOPALATINE GANGLION

The sphenopalatine (*nasal or Meckel's*) ganglion lies very deeply in the pterygopalatine (sphenomaxillary) fossa; it is immediately adjacent to the sphenopalatine foramen in the lateral nasal wall, and thus just posterior to and perhaps slightly above the posterior end of the middle nasal concha. It is usually beneath the floor of the sphenoid sinus, but if this is small or narrow it may lie lateral to the sinus. Since its posterior superior nasal branches pass through the sphenopalatine foramen, these may be blocked by the application of a cocainized pledget of cotton to the lateral wall of the nose behind the middle concha.

Injection about the ganglion, and presumably therefore about all the sensory fibers passing through it, has been carried out through the foramen or the thin bone about it; by injecting deeply backward along the infra-orbital foramen; by the lateral, paramandibular, approach to the pterygopalatine fossa; and by injecting upward through the greater (posterior) palatine foramen and the pterygopalatine canal. Both the infra-orbital and posterior palatine approaches are especially at-tended by danger, for in the first the needle may penetrate the often very thin roof of the infra-orbital canal and enter the orbit, while in the second the needle may miss the bony landmark, the face of the sphenoid bone, and pass through the inferior orbital fissure into the orbit, or even through this and the superior orbital fissure into the cranial cavity. So-called injections of the ganglion have largely been carried out for relief of "sphenopalatine ganglion neuralgia" (p. 254), as have also surgical approaches to the ganglion.

Anatomically, the ganglion is easily accessible in the cadaver after making a sagittal section of the head, through the removal of the thin bone around the sphenopalatine foramen, but surgically this approach is difficult because of the very limited intranasal space here, and dangerous because of the presence of the terminal branches of the internal maxillary artery in the fossa. Averbukh, Brevda, Lubotsky, and Semenova have described a *palatine approach* to the ganglion: they have advocated removing a posterior portion of the hard palate, dissecting the nasal mucous membrane loose from the lateral nasal wall, and following this bony wall up to the inferior surface of the body of the sphenoid; here they have removed the upper and inner wall of the sphenopalatine canal to expose the Vidian nerve, and then followed this to the ganglion. They stated that they themselves had carried out this procedure only on the cadaver but that their surgical friends have found it to be an appropriate approach.

Sewall has advocated a *transantral approach*, pointing out that this offers access not only to the ganglion but to the maxillary nerve, the branches of the internal maxillary artery, and even to the sphenoid sinus and the orbit. In this approach he opened the antrum through the canine fossa, removed the mucosa and the bone in the posterior wall of the antrum, and incised the periosteum to expose the contents of the fossa.

The *roots* of the sphenopalatine ganglion, motor, sympathetic, and sensory, have necessarily been discussed in part with the branches of distribution of the ganglion; the following is a summary of these roots, and a description of their courses. The *motor root* of the sphenopalatine ganglion is the great superficial petrosal nerve; after leaving the geniculate ganglion this nerve passes through the hiatus of the facial canal (Fallopian hiatus, hiatus for the greater superficial petrosal nerve) into the middle cranial fossa, where it lies in a groove on the anterolateral surface of the petrous portion of the temporal bone and passes forward and medially beneath the semilunar ganglion to leave the skull by way of the foramen lacerum. At the foramen lacerum the great superficial petrosal nerve lies immediately lateral to the internal carotid artery, and in this location is joined by the deep petrosal nerve consisting of fibers derived from the carotid plexus. The union of the great superficial and deep petrosal nerves forms the Vidian nerve, or nerve of the pterygoid canal, which then passes forward in the base of the pterygoid process, and usually in the floor of the sphenoid sinus, to enter the pterygopalatine fossa and end in the ganglion.

The *sympathetic root* of the sphenopalatine ganglion is the deep petrosal; this conducts postganglionic sympathetic fibers to the Vidian nerve and thence to the branches of the sphenopalatine ganglion. Obviously, motor and sympathetic

roots of the ganglion are combined from about the foramen lacerum forward.

The *sensory "root"* of the sphenopalatine ganglion is actually multiple, as it consists not only of the usually named sphenopalatine branch or branches from the maxillary nerve, but of the divers sensory fibers contained in the Vidian nerve. As already noted, the majority of these latter fibers are of geniculate ganglion origin, but some are said to be derived from the tenth nerve (for example, Christensen), and nerve fibers of afferent type have also been seen in the deep petrosal nerve (Larsell and Fenton); it has been stated that the latter may represent sensory fibers from upper thoracic spinal nerves.

The Vidian nerve itself, and the sensory roots attaching the ganglion to the maxillary nerve, are obviously accessible surgically by the various routes used to expose the sphenopalatine ganglion; the Vidian nerve alone could probably be sectioned most easily through the palatine approach already referred to. Within the pterygoid canal, the Vidian nerve often raises a ridge on the floor of the sphenoid sinus, and the intervening bone is quite thin and may be deficient, so that the nerve lies directly against the mucous membrane of the sinus.

Ziegelman has described surgical approaches to the great superficial petrosal nerve; he expressed the belief that the marked swelling of the nasal mucous membrane sometimes observed in head injuries is due to vasodilation by way of this nerve. The easiest approach would appear to be the subtemporal one, with section of the nerve as it enters the dura of the cranial floor; this is, of course, quite similar to the subtemporal approach to the semilunar (Gasserian) ganglion, but can be carried out behind the foramen spinosum so that the middle meningeal artery may be avoided. Ziegelman has also suggested that the nerve may be sectioned by exposing the geniculate ganglion through the tegmen tympani, and cutting the nerve close to the ganglion, but points out that this is more difficult.

The *branches of distribution* of the sphenopalatine ganglion are to the sphenoidal sinus and the posterior ethmoidal cells, to the nose, to the hard and soft palates, to the choanae, and to the uppermost part of the pharynx. The nasal branches of the sphenopalatine ganglion have already been described (p. 247), but the other branches will be described briefly here.

The *orbital (ascending) branches* of the sphenopalatine ganglion are tiny twigs, two or three in number, which are described as entering the orbit through the inferior orbital (sphenomaxillary) fissure, to pass upward in the periosteum on the inner wall of the orbit to the posterior ethmoidal foramen; they leave the orbit by way of this foramen and are distributed to the mucous membrane of the posterior ethmoidal cells and the sphenoidal sinus.

In addition to the nasopalatine nerve, which supplies an anterior portion of the hard palate, three palatine nerves proper are usually described: these are the great or anterior palatine nerve, the posterior or small palatine nerve, and the middle or external palatine nerve. The *great palatine nerve* leaves the inferior border of the sphenopalatine ganglion and passes downward in the pterygopalatine fossa, which it leaves by way of the pterygopalatine canal. It emerges from the canal at the greater or posterior palatine foramen and divides into several branches which pass forward on the hard palate to supply its mucous membrane and the gums on the inner aspect of the upper jaw. It is accompanied in its course by the descending palatine artery; within the pterygopalatine canal it gives off the posterior nasal nerves to the posterior portion of the middle and inferior meatuses and the inferior concha. The great palatine nerve is said to derive its sensory fibers both from the maxillary and the great superficial petrosal nerves; its autonomic fibers are distributed to the glands and blood vessels of the palate.

The *posterior or small palatine nerve* passes downward parallel to the greater palatine and emerges on the palate through a lesser palatine foramen, lying behind the greater; it turns backward into the soft palate to supply this and possibly sends branches also downward as far as the tonsil. Its sensory fibers are said to be derived from the facial nerve, by way of the great superficial petrosal. It is this branch which was at one time believed to contain also voluntary motor fibers from the facial, and to innervate some of the muscles of the soft palate (but see p. 353).

The *middle or external palatine nerve* emerges with or close to the posterior palatine to supply a lateral portion of the soft palate and a few twigs to the tonsil. It, also, is said to contain sensory nerve fibers derived from the facial nerve.

The *pharyngeal branch* of the sphenopalatine ganglion is a small branch which passes backward and somewhat medially, in company with the corresponding branch of the sphenopalatine artery, to be distributed to the upper portion of the pharynx and the upper posterior part of the choanae, perhaps to the opening of the Eustachian tube, and to the lining of the sphenoidal sinus. Its sensory fibers are said to be derived from the maxillary nerve; according to Graves and Edwards the available evidence indicates that the opening of the Eustachian tube is supplied in about 50 per cent of cases through the fifth nerve (that is, this branch of the maxillary), while in other cases it is supplied by the pharyngeal branch of the glossopharyngeal nerve.

The distribution of the sensory fibers believed to be derived from the tenth cranial and upper spinal nerves is said to be to the nose (p. 249).

SPHENOPALATINE GANGLION NEURALGIA

From the foregoing description it is obvious that sensory fibers from the posterior portion of the nose, from the sphenoid and posterior ethmoidal sinuses, and from the hard and soft palates and a limited portion of the pharynx all pass through or immediately adjacent to the sphenopalatine ganglion. Sluder (for instance, '22a, '22b, '23) described a number of referred pains which apparently arose in this region of distribution and which he found to be controllable through anesthetization or destruction of the sphenopalatine ganglion. These have been generally grouped together under the term "sphenopalatine ganglion neuralgia," which has, however, been variously defined.

In recent years there has been a tendency to discard the term completely, since it is obvious that many diverse conditions have been described under this heading. From the anatomical point of view, it would seem that the term should be used to describe only a neuralgia which is due to an affection of the sphenopalatine ganglion itself, concerning the existence of which this author has seen no proof. Some of the symptoms which have been said to be those of sphenopalatine ganglion neuralgia can obviously

be explained much more easily as due to a direct involvement of the sensory fibers to the nose (many of which, of course, do pass through or close against the ganglion, and can therefore be blocked by anesthetization of the ganglion); other symptoms which cannot be explained upon the basis of the known anatomy have also been reported. Larsell and Fenton, and later Fenton, have described and discussed some of the nerve pathways that may be involved in certain cases of referred pain from the nose and sinuses, or of "sphenopalatine ganglion neuralgia."

Much of the confusion surrounding this question in the clinical literature has apparently been based upon a failure to appreciate fully that the sphenopalatine ganglion is an autonomic one, and that none such has ever been shown to contain sensory nerve cells. In so far as "sphenopalatine ganglion neuralgia" is due to affections of the sensory fibers distributed with the postganglionic fibers from the ganglion, it differs from no other peripherally induced pain in its anatomy and physiology, and can undoubtedly be alleviated by correcting, for instance, the nasal deformity which may have caused it, or by interrupting the sensory pathways back to the brain stem. Operations upon the ganglion, and alcohol injections of it, actually accomplish the latter; since they are both difficult and dangerous, it appears obvious that every effort should be made to find a cause of peripheral nerve involvement before undertaking these.

VESSELS

The arterial supply to the nasal fossa is, like the nerve supply which it parallels, derived from several sources and enters the nose in various locations. The internal maxillary artery, especially through its important sphenopalatine branch, supplies the larger posterior part of the nose; anterior and posterior ethmoid arteries, from the ophthalmic and therefore the internal carotid, supply an upper and anterior portion; branches of the external maxillary (facial), like the internal maxillary a branch of the ex-

The sphenopalatine artery also has a nasopalatine or septal branch, which parallels the corresponding nerve to run across the roof of the fossa to the septum and supply the posterior and inferior portions of this.

DESCENDING PALATINE

Another branch of the internal maxillary artery, the descending palatine, ac-

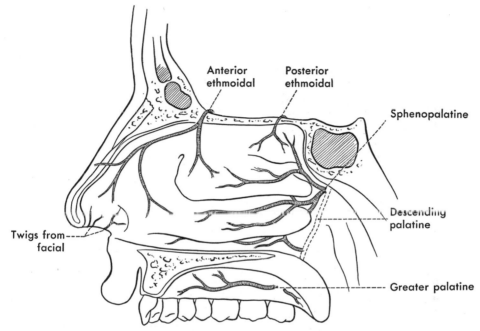

Fig. 140. Arteries of the lateral nasal wall.

ternal carotid, supply especially the vestibule of the nose.

SPHENOPALATINE ARTERY

The posterior nasal branches of the sphenopalatine artery pass with the nerves through the sphenopalatine foramen and supply the major portion of the conchae (Fig. 140); it is these branches which are more commonly involved in postoperative bleeding, making it necessary to pack the area behind the middle turbinate, or even occasionally to ligature the external carotid artery.

companies the great palatine nerve downward in the pterygopalatine canal, and like the nerve supplies twigs to the lower posterior portion of the nasal fossa. Upon emerging onto the oral surface of the hard palate through the greater palatine foramen this artery gives off minor palatine vessels that pass backward to the soft palate, but the major portion turns forward as the major palatine artery; this supplies the mucosa of the hard palate and the inner gums of the upper teeth, and through the incisive foramen and its lateral subdivision, the foramen of

Stensen, anastomoses with the naso-palatine branch of the sphenopalatine artery to help supply a portion of the floor of the anterior part of the nasal fossa.

ANTERIOR AND POSTERIOR ETHMOIDAL ARTERIES

The anterior and posterior ethmoidal arteries enter the nasal cavity through its

(external nasal branch) runs in a groove on the internal surface of the nasal bone, and leaves the nasal cavity between this bone and the lateral nasal cartilage to run on the dorsum of the nose down to its tip. The posterior ethmoidal artery is limited largely in its distribution to the region of the superior concha and a corresponding portion of the septum.

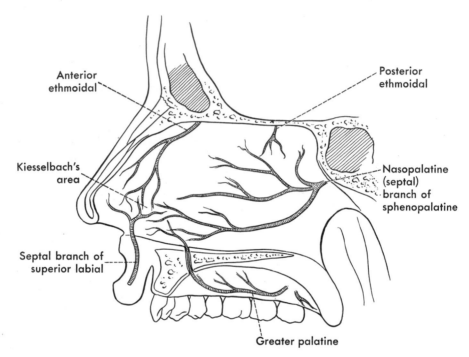

Fig. 141. Arteries of the nasal septum.

roof (Fig. 141); they leave the ophthalmic artery within the orbit, course through the anterior and posterior ethmoidal canals, respectively, to obtain an intracranial course and then turn downward at the lateral border of the cribriform plate (p. 159). The anterior ethmoidal artery is normally much the larger; it is distributed to about the anterior third of the lateral wall of the nose and to a similar portion of the septum, and anastomoses with the sphenopalatine artery; the terminal branch of the artery

ARTERY OF THE NASAL SEPTUM

The important branch of the external maxillary artery to the vestibule is the artery of the nasal septum, derived from the superior labial branch of the facial. On the anterior portion of the septal cartilage this vessel anastomoses with the nasopalatine branch of the sphenopalatine artery; the anastomosing branches between these vessels (probably joined variably by branches from the greater palatine and anterior ethmoidal arteries) are situated superficially in the mucosa, and the site at which they occur is known as *Kiesselbach's (or Little's) area.*

EPISTAXIS

According to Trible, it has been stated that from 90 to 99 per cent of all bleeding from the nose is due to a local vascular defect, and that 90 per cent of this is from Kiesselbach's area. Since this area is easily accessible, such bleeding can frequently be stopped with simple packs, or even by pressure upon the septal artery. More drastic measures have included the use of silver nitrate, and cutting through the (nasopalatine) vessels about a centimeter posterior and above the bleeding point and applying packs.

Unfortunately, however, as Roy has emphasized, the majority of nasal hemorrhages in elderly people and in individuals with arteriosclerosis arise from the neighborhood of the middle turbinate or from the attic of the nose—that is, from the sphenopalatine or ethmoidal vessels. If ordinary methods fail to control severe bleeding from these locations, surgical ligation is usually undertaken. Of 100 patients in a series reported by Spar and Hallberg requiring hospitalization for severe nosebleed, more than half of these bled from the anterior portion of the nasal septum, but nearly a third bled from a point high and posteriorly in the nose, usually from the sphenopalatine artery.

These workers found that this bleeding also was usually controllable by packs, but 11 patients required ligation of the external carotid artery. As in the case reported by Johnson and Foster, however, ligation of the external carotid cannot be expected always to control bleeding from the sphenopalatine artery; in their case severe nasal hemorrhage recurred five days after such ligation, apparently because of the establishment of a part of the potentially abundant collateral circulation. Hirsch concluded that external carotid ligation produces too uncertain results, and therefore advocated the transantral approach to the pterygopalatine fossa, through which the sphenopalatine artery can be ligated quite near the foramen. Obviously, this technic is much more difficult than is ligation of the external carotid itself.

Bleeding from high in the nose is not necessarily from the sphenopalatine artery, however; as in a case reported by Fitz-Hugh and Risher, such bleeding may be from an ethmoidal artery (from the internal carotid) and therefore be not at all checked by ligation of the external carotid. Surgical interruption of one or both of the ethmoid arteries is then a logical procedure.

Weddell, Macbeth, Sharp, and Calvert have reviewed the blood supply of the nose and the methods available for checking bleeding from this organ; they pointed out that ligation of the common carotid artery, which has been carried out to check bleeding high in the nose, actually may not halt the bleeding (because of the anastomoses with the vessels of the other side) but only reduce its flow. (Also, ligation of the common carotid is not to be taken lightly, since it greatly reduces the blood flow in the internal carotid—page 476.) They have reported 7 cases in which nosebleed was not controlled until the ethmoidal arteries of the affected side had been occluded; for this they used the orbital route, usually placing a clip upon the anterior ethmoidal artery before it enters its canal, and coagulating the usually smaller posterior ethmoidal artery as it approaches the medial orbital wall.

VEINS

The veins of the nose begin in venous plexuses, which are so well developed on the inferior nasal concha, the inferior meatus, and the back part of the septum as to resemble erectile tissue; the definitive veins of the nose correspond approximately to the arteries. The sphenopalatine veins drain through the sphenopalatine foramen into the pterygoid plexus; the anterior and posterior ethmoidal veins run with their arteries to join the superior ophthalmic vein; other small vessels pass downward into the superior labial vein, or through the wall of the external nose to join the anterior facial vein as it lies at the lateral border of the nose.

LYMPHATICS

The larger lymphatics from the nose apparently flow posteriorly (Most); some are said to pass to the tonsillar region and hence to the deep cervical lymph nodes directly, while the greater number are said to join the posterior pharyngeal plexus and hence reach the lateral pharyngeal ("retropharyngeal") node or nodes. Lymphatics from the more anterior part of the nose communicate also through the external nares with lymphatics of the skin, or pass outward between cartilages of the nose.

THE PARANASAL SINUSES

THE paranasal or accessory nasal sinuses, with the exception of the sphenoid sinus, begin their development as evaginations of the mucosa of the nasal fossa during the third and fourth fetal months. While all of the sinuses undergo their major expansion after birth, the maxillary sinuses and the ethmoid air cells are of appreciable size at birth, even though, as pointed out by Wasson, they are of course not filled with air. Aeration of the sinuses developed at birth seems to take place quite slowly, and Wasson has stressed that great care must be exercised in attempting to diagnose from roentgenograms the conditions of the nasal accessory sinuses during the early weeks of life. The frontal sinus is a very small diverticulum at birth and undergoes almost all of its development thereafter; the sphenoid sinus at birth can hardly be said to exist as an entity, since it is represented merely by a posterosuperior part of the nasal fossa; it is not until about the third year of life that it actually invades the sphenoid bone.

Like the nasal fossa, the sinuses typically are lined by a pseudostratified columnar ciliated epithelium; as reported by Hilding ('44) the direction of flow induced by the ciliary beat in all of the sinuses seems to be a spiral which centers at the ostium, material anywhere within the sinus tending therefore to be carried to the nose. McMurray has stressed also the effect of negative air pressure as an aid to ciliary drainage; he has reported that inspiration produces a negative pressure in the antrum, and that in the absence of the inspiratory air current the ciliary action alone is not sufficient to drain the antrum in the upright position, judging from the movement of iodized oil.

Latta and Schall have pointed out that in acute irritation the basal cells of the epithelium lining the paranasal sinuses undergo hyperplasia, and that this may continue until a true stratified columnar epithelium is present. Regeneration following degeneration and sloughing of an injured epithelium is said to be probably from the basal cells, which are not usually involved in such degeneration. Brownell reviewed the literature up to 1936 upon regeneration of the mucous membrane of the paranasal sinuses.

All of the sinuses typically show variations, from one individual to another, in their sizes and therefore in the extent to which they have invaded the neighboring bones; these, and the varying positions and sizes of their ostia, are of some importance to the rhinologist.

partially subdivide its cavity, and may be so placed as to interfere seriously with its drainage. Aside from these, however, the sinus varies markedly in its development. It normally extends upward into the vertical portion of the frontal bone, and also backward in the orbital part of this bone, between the inferior surface of the frontal lobe and the orbital contents (Fig. 143). Either the vertical or the horizontal portions of the sinus may be unusually developed and invade adjacent

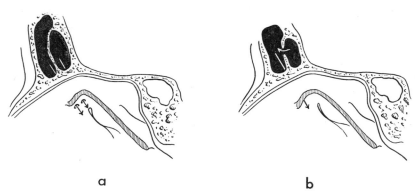

a   b

Fig. 142. Anteroposterior duplication of the frontal sinus, indicating the two types that may occur. In *a* are two separate sinuses; in *b* one is a diverticulum of the other.

FRONTAL SINUS

The frontal sinus develops as one of several outgrowths from the region of the frontal recess, other similar outgrowths here representing anterior ethmoid cells. Two, three, or even more frontal sinuses on a side have been reported, though a source of confusion is the fact that anterior ethmoid cells may invade the territory of the frontal sinus, and whether or not they should then be called frontal sinuses has been disputed. It makes no practical difference; the point is that several separate sinuses may occur in the frontal bone on one or both sides. They may lie one lateral to another, or one behind the other (Fig. 142). The frontal sinus likewise often contains septa, which

bones, or may be poorly developed (Figs. 144 and 145); failure of the sinus to invade the vertical portion of the frontal bone has undoubtedly often been mistaken for agenesis of the sinus, which is

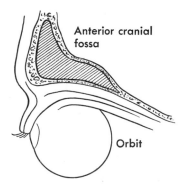

Anterior cranial fossa

Orbit

Fig. 143. Relations of the frontal sinus in a parasagittal section.

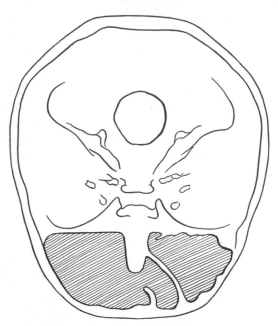

Fig. 144. Extreme supra-orbital development of the frontal sinuses. (Adapted from Schaeffer, J. P.: *The Nose, Paranasal Sinuses, Nasolacrimal Passageways, and Olfactory Organ in Man*. Philadelphia, Blakiston, 1920.)

it is possible to open a normal sinus of the other side in attempting to reach a diseased one.

The important relations of the frontal sinus are to the anterior cranial fossa and the orbit. The bone separating the frontal sinus from the roof of the orbit and from the floor of the cranial cavity is often particularly thin; an operative perforation of it can easily occur. Wickliffe has reported a case of abscess of the frontal lobe due to acute frontal sinusitis.

FRONTONASAL CONNECTION

As noted by Schaeffer ('16) the frontal sinus is usually a derivative of the frontal recess directly, or of one or more anterior ethmoidal cells arising in frontal pits, but occasionally it arises from the frontal extremity of the ethmoidal infundibulum. In Kasper's investigation of 100 frontal sinuses he found that the frontonasal connection led to the frontal recess rather than to the ethmoidal infundibulum in 62 per cent; in 4 per cent of his cases the ethmoidal infundibulum and the frontal sinus were in direct anatomical continuity; in 34 per cent more, however, he concluded that the

apparently quite rare (Schaeffer, '20). The two frontal sinuses are frequently asymmetrical, one being larger than the other, and the larger sinus may in such cases pass across the midline, and even overlap the other. Because of the latter,

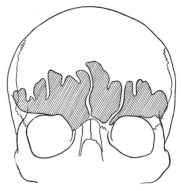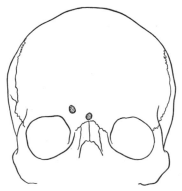

Fig. 145. Some extremes in the development of the frontal sinuses. In the figure on the left, the left sinus is double. (Adapted from Schaeffer, J. P.: *The Nose, Paranasal Sinuses, Nasolacrimal Passageways, and Olfactory Organ in Man*. Philadelphia, Blakiston, 1920.)

sinus had arisen from an anterior eth-moidal cell located in the infundibulum, and thus in 38 per cent the frontal sinus actually drained, directly or indirectly, into the infundibulum. Schaeffer ('16) has stated that in approximately 50 per cent of adults the ethmoidal infundibulum may act as a channel for carrying secre-tion or infection from the frontal sinus and some of the anterior ethmoid cells to the maxillary sinus, either because of continuity of the frontal sinus and the infundibulum or their intimate relation.

Van Alyea concluded that in many in-stances such cells must influence drainage from the frontal sinus, and that their presence is sometimes the sole reason for the maintenance of chronic infection in the sinus. According to Van Alyea, an-other anatomical factor interfering with drainage of the frontal sinus is a blocked middle meatus, usually caused by im-pingement of the middle turbinate against the lateral nasal wall.

From Van Alyea's findings (Fig. 148), it appears that the frontal ostium should

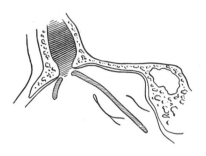 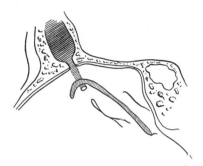

Fig. 146. The two chief types of drainage of the frontal sinus—by an ostium directly into the nose, and by a nasofrontal duct.

The connection of the frontal sinus with the nasal cavity may be by means of a narrowed nasofrontal duct, or the sinus may open directly through an ostium (Fig. 146). Lillie and Simonton re-ported a case in which at operation an anterior ethmoid cell was found to have invaded the frontal sinus so as to interfere with its ventilation and drainage, and Van Alyea ('41a, '44) has stated that in ap-proximately 50 per cent of persons there are extra air cells (anterior ethmoidal cells) which impinge upon the frontal sinuses, about one third of them in the region of the frontal ostium. If the floor of the sinus is pushed up, the bulge is known as a frontal bulla; such a bulla may be due to encroachment by the other frontal sinus, but more frequently is formed by an ethmoid cell (Fig. 147).

be relatively accessible for irrigation in about 85 per cent of cases; he has stated ('46a) that in about 55 per cent the frontal sinus drains directly into the frontal recess, and in another 30 per cent opens above but not into the infundibu-lum, so that the ostium can be reached

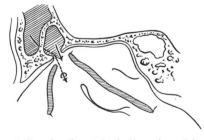

Fig. 147. A frontal bulla, in this case formed by an ethmoid cell, encroaching on the frontal sinus and frontonasal duct. (Adapted from Van Alyea, O. E.: Arch. Otolaryng. 34: 11, 1941.)

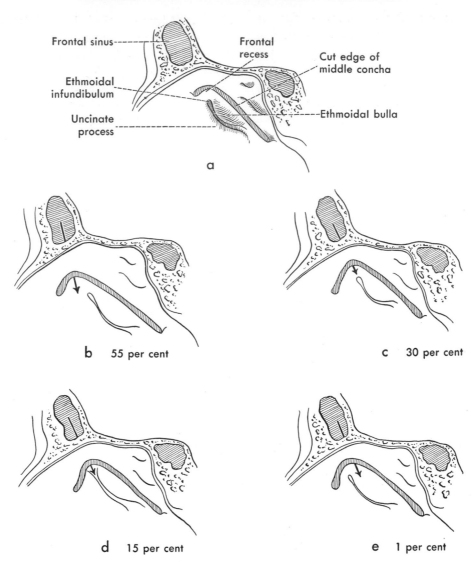

Fig. 148. Variations in the location of the opening of the frontal sinus. *a* shows the general anatomy depicted in these diagrams; in the remainder, which are adapted from Van Alyea (*Ann. Otol., Rhin. & Laryng. 55:*267, 1946), the drainage of the sinus is indicated by the arrow. Approximate percentages of the various types, as given by Van Alyea, are noted. *b* shows drainage into the frontal recess anterior to the infundibulum; *c*, drainage above but not into the infundibulum; *d*, drainage into the infundibulum; *e*, drainage above the bulla.

by a cannula. In 15 per cent, however (his figures differ somewhat from those of Kasper), he found the frontal sinus to be continuous with the ethmoidal infundibulum, and in about 1 per cent to open above the ethmoid bulla; in these cases the opening is apt to be inaccessible.

BLOOD SUPPLY AND INNERVATION

The chief blood and nerve supply to the frontal sinus reaches it through one or more small openings in the roof of the supra-orbital notch. The supra-orbital artery, as it passes from the orbit to the forehead, gives off a diploic branch which enters the diploë and supplies also the frontal sinus. The venous drainage corresponds to the arterial supply, being represented by a small vein which passes into the anastomosis between the supraorbital and superior ophthalmic veins. The connections of the venous drainage of the frontal sinus with other diploic

with the distribution of the ophthalmic nerve to the forehead and to the dura of the anterior cranial fossa. Reference of pain from the nose and the more posterior sinuses to the region of the ear and mastoid process, said to occur, has likewise been explained by the distribution of the fifth and seventh nerves to these regions.

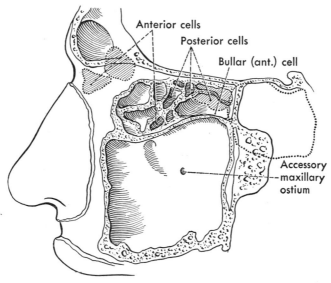

Fig. 149.   Ethmoid cells from the lateral side. (Redrawn from Van Alyea, O. E.: *Arch. Otolaryng. 29:*881, 1939.)

veins, and of the latter with the veins of the scalp and dura, probably account for the spread of osteomyelitis in the frontal bone subsequent to disease of the frontal sinus (for instance, Williams and Heilman). Similarly, the supra-orbital branch of the ophthalmic nerve, as it passes across the supra-orbital notch, gives off a branch to the diploë and the mucous membrane of the frontal sinus.

Fenton expressed the belief that referred pain from the ophthalmic division of the fifth nerve is probably dependent upon both the cutaneous distribution of this nerve and that to the dura; frontal sinusitis has been said to give rise to supra-orbital pain, which is consonant

ETHMOID AIR CELLS

The ethmoid sinuses or ethmoid air cells (Figs. 149, 150, 151) honeycomb the ethmoid bone, and thus lie between the upper part of the lateral nasal wall and the medial wall of the orbit. There may be as few as three or as many as eighteen; the greater the number, the smaller the cells. Mosher has discussed various phases of the surgical anatomy of the ethmoid region; he noted that while the ethmoid cells typically together form a pyramid, with the wider base located posteriorly, the ethmoid labyrinth as a whole may form a relatively thin plate. He gave the average dimensions as

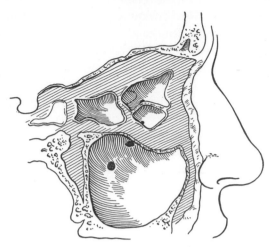

Fig. 150. Ethmoid cells limited to four; the more posteriorly located one opened on the bulla, the two larger anterior ones into the infundibulum, and the smaller one above the infundibulum; thus all are actually anterior cells. (Redrawn from Van Alyea, O. E.: *Arch. Otolaryng.* 29:881, 1939.)

4 to 5 cm. in length (anteroposterior), 2.5 to 3 cm. in height, and about 0.5 cm. in width anteriorly, 1.5 cm. posteriorly.

The ethmoid cells show great variety

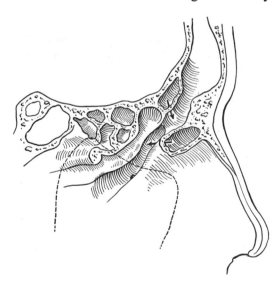

Fig. 151. Ethmoid cells seen from the nasal side. Only three anterior cells are shown here, opening respectively above the infundibulum, above the bulla and (an agger nasi cell) into the infundibulum. (Redrawn from Van Alyea, O. E.: *Arch. Otolaryng.* 29:881, 1939.)

in their *openings,* as they may have arisen as diverticula above, upon or below the bulla, or from any portion of the middle meatus, from the frontal recess, from the superior meatus, or from above and behind the superior nasal concha. On the basis of their openings, they are commonly divided into anterior ethmoid cells, which open into the middle meatus, and posterior ethmoid cells which open into the superior or supreme meatus.

ANTERIOR ETHMOID CELLS

The anterior ethmoid cells are in turn classified into subgroups upon the basis of their location or that of their ostia; since, however, cells of a given origin frequently invade the territory usually occupied by cells of another origin, they are most easily classified by the location of their ostia. On this basis the anterior ethmoid cells are classified into frontal recess ethmoidal cells, opening into the frontal recess of the middle meatus; infundibular ethmoidal cells, opening into the ethmoidal infundibulum; and bullar ethmoidal cells, opening directly into the middle meatus either upon or above the ethmoidal bulla.

The *frontal recess ethmoidal cells* are genetically related to the frontal sinus, and number usually three or four; it is especially one of these which may encroach upon the frontal sinus, either upon its wall or at its ostium, although infundibular or bullar cells often also reach this region. Van Alyea ('41a) found 100 specimens in which ethmoid cells encroached upon the frontal sinus (frontal ethmoid or ethmofrontal cells) in 242 specimens examined; 56 of these were frontal recess cells, and 63 cells were of other origin (both types being present in 19 cases).

Van Alyea ('39) reported that in 100

specimens there was an average of three *infundibular cells*, the number varying from one to seven; the most constant which he found was the cell in the agger nasi, which was encountered in 89 of 100 specimens, being represented in 12 of these by two cells. It is an agger nasi cell which is most frequently opened in the endonasal approach to the lacrimal sac. In 34 cases the cell of the agger nasi formed the upper blind termination of the infundibulum.

The number of *bullar cells* was also reported to average three, with a variation of from one to six; Van Alyea regarded them as the most constant of any of the ethmoid group.

As already stated, anterior ethmoid cells of one origin may encroach upon the territory of those of another origin; the most frequent example of this found by Van Alyea was the extension of a "tip cell" (from the anterior end of the infundibulum) into the bulla (16 per cent). Cells of either the anterior or the posterior group may also encroach upon the maxillary sinus. Ethmoid cells may also extend into the middle or superior nasal conchae or into the uncinate process (Schaeffer, '10a); they open into the infundibulum, the middle meatus directly or into the superior meatus, and appear therefore to be sometimes anterior and sometimes posterior ethmoid cells.

POSTERIOR ETHMOID CELLS

The posterior ethmoid cells are usually stated to vary from one to seven in number; in his dissections Van Alyea found from none to six, but one or more were present in 96 per cent of his specimens; in 67 of his 100 specimens there was a supreme concha present and in 38 of these there was one or more cells (postreme cells) which opened into the supreme meatus.

The bullar ethmoidal cells and the posterior ethmoidal cells may encroach upon each other, the bullar cells spreading backward or the posterior ethmoidal cells spreading forward so that these groups overlap; less frequently, infundibular and posterior ethmoidal cells are in contact. The posterior cells may also encroach upon the sphenoid sinus. Riggle reported 3 cases in which a posterior ethmoidal cell had grown back into the body of the sphenoid bone and practically taken the place of the sphenoid sinus, the latter being a rudimentary cell rather than a large sinus. In 55 of 1600 specimens examined Dixon found posterior ethmoid cells which had invaded the superior part of the sphenoid bone to partially surround the optic canal; Van Alyea ('44) found a similar relation in 5 of 100 sides which he examined. In contrast to the tendency of ethmoid cells to invade the territory of the neighboring sinuses, these cells are relatively free from interference with their growth, except by each other, since they develop early.

Since the ethmoid cells as a whole are separated from the orbit only by the very thin lamina papyracea, severe infections of them spread fairly readily to the orbit, and infections of the ethmoids have been said to be the most common cause of orbital cellulitis. One or more posterior ethmoid cells may be in close contact with the optic nerve as this traverses the optic canal and infections of these or of the sphenoid sinus, also closely related to the optic canal (p. 269), have been held to be responsible for a number of cases of retrobulbar neuritis. This has been discussed on page 142.

Regardless of whether there is such a

causal relationship or not, the anatomical relations are of importance to the surgeon. Goodyear ('48) has expressed the belief that the sinuses should be carefully examined in all ophthalmic lesions, but has, in addition, pointed out that he has seen total blindness of an eye follow surgical opening of posterior ethmoid cells and of the sphenoid sinus; he described and illustrated a case in which the optic nerve passed through the middle of a posterior ethmoid cell, being completely surrounded by this and separated from the ethmoid mucosa by only a very thin cylinder of bone. In such cases as this, the danger of operative injury to the optic nerve during the process of opening and cleaning infected sinuses is obviously quite considerable, and in all cases it should be realized that the bony lamina about the optic canal may be very thin, even presenting dehiscences.

BLOOD SUPPLY AND INNERVATION

The arterial supply of the ethmoidal air cells is through the posterior lateral nasal branches of the sphenopalatine artery; in addition, the anterior ethmoidal cells are supplied by twigs from the anterior ethmoidal artery (and in the case of some frontal ethmoidal cells, probably also by the frontal branch of the supra-orbital artery), while the posterior ethmoidal cells are supplied by branches from the posterior ethmoidal artery. Thus the ethmoid sinuses receive blood from both the internal and external carotid systems.

The veins from the ethmoid sinuses presumably join those of the nasal cavity proper, thus draining into the ophthalmic vein or the pterygoid plexus.

The ethmoid sinuses have been said to possess only a few lymphatic capillaries which apparently pass at the ostia onto the general nasal mucosa, where they join the lymphatics here.

The *innervation* of the anterior ethmoidal cells is through the ophthalmic division of the trigeminal nerve, by way of the anterior ethmoidal branch of the nasociliary (nasal) nerve, and in the case of frontal ethmoidal cells probably also by the twig which the supra-orbital branch of the ophthalmic gives off to the frontal sinus. The posterior ethmoidal cells receive their innervation from the maxillary branch of the fifth (and from the facial?) by way of the lateral posterior superior nasal branches of the spheno-palatine ganglion that supply the adjacent mucous membrane of the superior and middle nasal conchae; they are said to be innervated also by the orbital or ascending branches of the sphenopalatine ganglion (see p. 253). In addition, the posterior ethmoidal foramen may transmit a posterior ethmoidal branch of the nasociliary nerve, so that the posterior ethmoidal cells may be innervated by both ophthalmic and maxillary divisions of the fifth; as quoted by Whitnall, however, the posterior ethmoidal branch of the nasociliary is inconstant, and was found in only 2 of 6 cases.

SPHENOIDAL SINUS

The sphenoidal sinus regularly opens into the spheno-ethmoidal recess, that is, above and behind the superior nasal concha (see Fig. 135, p. 243, and Fig. 153, p. 268). The sphenoidal ostium is usually in the posterior wall of the recess, but sometimes in its lateral wall. While the anlage of the sphenoidal sinus, represented by a posterior recess of the nasal fossa, is recognizable as early as the fourth month of fetal life, it is only after the third year that the sinus begins to grow and actually excavate the body of the sphenoid bone.

The degree of growth of the sinus into the sphenoid bone varies enormously (Fig. 152); the capacity of this sinus has been said to vary from 0.5 to 30 cc., with an approximate average of about 7.5 cc. The sphenoid sinus may be entirely limited to the body of the sphenoid bone, or may extend into the great wing of the sphenoid, into the pterygoid process, and into the basilar portion of the occipital bone. The two sphenoid sinuses are rarely symmetrical in size and shape, and the sphenoidal septum between them is usually also asymmetrical in its position,

sinuses examined by Van Alyea varied from 4 to 44 mm. in length, from 2.5 to 34 mm. in width, and from 5 to 33 mm. in height. Dixon, noting that the sinus is larger in the Negro than in the white (which is generally true of all the sinuses and their ostia) found the average height of the sinus to be from 18 to 20 mm., the average width from 15 to 17 mm., and the average length from 19 to 22 mm., in 1600 skulls classified according to race and sex.

RELATIONSHIPS

The relationships of the sphenoidal sinus are of particular importance, and

Fig. 152. Medium and extremes of development of the sphenoid sinus.

especially posteriorly; sometimes the overlapping sinuses of the two sides lie above and below each other, rather than having the lateral relationship which would be expected. The two sinuses rarely communicate with each other, though Dixon found 5 cases (in 1600 skulls) in which the septum was deficient. Judging from a case described by Costen ('30), infection of a sphenoid sinus which extends markedly across the midline may cause pain referred to the side to which it has extended.

Congdon stated that the sphenoid sinus is the most variable in form of any bilateral cavity or organ in the human body, and Van Alyea ('41b) found it to be more variable in its anteroposterior dimension than in any other. The 100

have been detailed especially by Schaeffer ('20), by Van Alyea and by Dixon. Above, the sphenoid sinus is related to the middle cranial fossa and the pituitary gland in the sella turcica (Fig. 153); laterally, it is related to the cavernous sinus and the internal carotid artery (Figs. 154 and 155); posteriorly, it is in relation to that portion of the posterior cranial fossa in which the pons lies; and inferiorly, it lies above the roof of the nasopharynx. The thickness of the walls of the sphenoidal sinus obviously depends largely upon the extent of the development of the sinus; according to Dixon they average about 0.5 mm., the inferior wall, or floor, being usually the thickest. The posterior wall, between the sinus and the posterior cranial fossa, may be of ex-

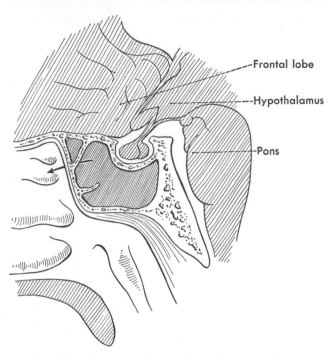

Fig. 153. Relations of the sphenoid sinus to the nose, brain, and hypophysis, in a nearly sagittal section. In this diagram an anterior overlapping of the two sinuses is indicated, as is also a septum partially subdividing the larger sinus.

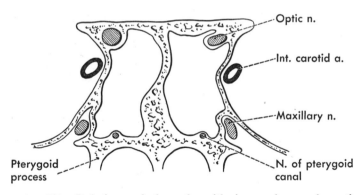

Fig. 154. Relations of the sphenoid sinuses in a schematic frontal section anterior to the hypophyseal fossa. The degree to which the structures related to the wall of the sinus project into this varies.

tremely heavy, compact bone, however, as much as a centimeter thick.

When a sphenoid sinus is well developed it is usual to see some of the structures adjacent to its walls modeling these, and thus appearing in more or less bas-

relief within the sinus. The sphenoid sinus may extend into the anterior and posterior clinoid processes, so that the hypophysis projects markedly into the sinus and the wall of the sella turcica is extremely thin (Dixon). The internal carotid artery

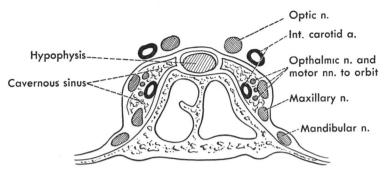

Fig. 155. Relations of the sphenoid sinuses in a schematic frontal section through the level of the hypophyseal fossa.

rather regularly indents the posterolateral wall (Fig. 156); Van Alyea found such a projection in 65 of 100 cases, and in 53 of these it was pronounced; Dixon has noted that actual gaps in the bony wall are not uncommon here.

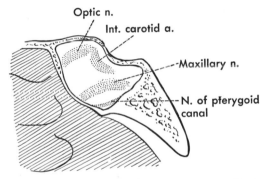

Fig. 156. Some markings that may be visible within the sphenoid sinus.

Dixon found a very deep projection of the optic canal into the sinus in 7 per cent of his cases, the wall of the optic canal being then very thin and sometimes presenting dehiscences in its floor; Van Alyea found a recognizable projection formed by the optic canal into the sphenoid in 40 per cent of his cases. The maxillary division of the fifth nerve may also indent the sinus; Dixon noted this in 32 (of 1600) while Van Alyea found it far more frequently, in 40 of his 100 cases. Dixon has noted that the ridge for

the Vidian nerve was often seen in the floor of the sinus; Van Alyea found such a ridge to be pronounced in 36 per cent and slight in 12 per cent. In 18 instances Van Alyea found that the sphenoid sinus extended far enough anteriorly to produce a bulge in the wall of the maxillary sinus. Diverticula of the sinus may extend through bony dehiscences to lie directly against the dura (Schaeffer). These various relationships to important structures indicate the care that should be exercised in exploring the sinus.

As noted on page 265, a posterior ethmoid cell may grow into the body of the sphenoid bone and lead to marked underdevelopment of the sphenoid sinus (Fig. 157); such posterior ethmoid cells may assume the relationship to the optic canal more frequently assumed by the sphenoid sinus. Vail has pointed out that

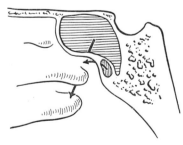

Fig. 157. A large posterior ethmoid cell largely surrounding and almost replacing a small sphenoid sinus. (Adapted from Riggle, P. P.: *Arch. Otolaryng. 16:*532, 1932.)

sometimes the wall between the sphenoid sinus or a posterior ethmoid cell and the optic nerve is dense and nonporous, sometimes it has large spongelike marrow spaces; he has visualized the sphenoid sinus by placing radiopaque oil within it, and then, by putting the patient's head so that the upper outer angle of the sinus is dependent, studied the relationship between the optic nerve and the sinus.

DRAINAGE

Van Alyea stated that the sphenoid sinus has been said to be involved in 15 per cent of all clinical cases of sinusitis, and to be responsible for approximately 35 per cent of all intracranial complications arising from the nose. He reported that examination of necropsy and cadaveric material has shown an incidence of low-grade chronic infection of these sinuses in approximately 13 to 14 per cent. Poor drainage of any sinus obviously favors its infection, and Van Alyea has emphasized the relation of anatomical variations to poor drainage of the sphenoid.

Normally, drainage from the sphenoid sinus in the erect posture is entirely through ciliary action, since the ostium is located typically well above (about 1.5 cm.) the floor of the sinus. Gravity drainage obtainable by turning the face down may be interfered with by septa or rows of spurs which project into it and partially subdivide it. Congdon found 122 bony septa or rows of spurs in 212 sinuses; Dixon found septa, partly bony and partly membranous, in 32 per cent of his 1600 cases; and Van Alyea found partial septa in 44 of his 100 cases. Obviously, whatever the actual incidence of such septa may be, it is quite high.

The ostium of the sinus in the fresh condition is rarely as large as the actual bony ostium seen on the dried skull, since it is normally blocked in part by a membranous septum, but among the variations interfering with drainage Van Alyea listed an ostium smaller than 2 mm. in diameter, one particularly near the roof, and one encroached upon by a posterior ethmoid cell. The frequent presence of recesses and septa within the sinus, already mentioned, and the occurrence of a shallow spheno-ethmoidal recess, through which heavy secretions pass only with difficulty, are also variations which may interfere with drainage. Pathological blockage may result, as he has noted, from thickening of inflammatory mucosa, hyperplasia, polyps and the like.

BLOOD SUPPLY AND INNERVATION

The innervation and vascular supply of the sphenoid sinus are similar to those of the posterior ethmoid cells, that is, branches of the sphenopalatine ganglion and artery, the posterior ethmoid artery, and sometimes a posterior ethmoid nerve (p. 266). Apparently, little is known concerning its possible lymphatics.

MAXILLARY SINUS

The maxillary sinus (antrum of Highmore), usually the largest of the paranasal sinuses, is located in the body of the maxilla. Its anterior wall is the facial surface of this bone, its posterior wall the infratemporal surface, and its medial wall the lateral wall of the nasal cavity. The roof of the sinus is also the floor of the orbit, and its floor is the alveolar process of the maxilla (Fig. 158). The average dimensions of the maxillary sinus in the adult are said to be a height of 33 mm., a width of 23 mm., and a length (in the anteroposterior direction) of 34 mm.; it varies considerably in capacity, however, as it may extend into the various bony processes from the body of the maxilla, or may have unusually thick walls, or there may be an inward bulging of the facial and nasal walls. The apex of the cavity usually extends into the zygomatic process of the maxilla, and may extend even into the zygomatic bone itself.

the first and second premolars are similarly related. The floor of the sinus in relation to these teeth may be relatively smooth, or it may be modeled over the root of one or more teeth so that these project upward into the sinus, separated from it only by a very thin lamina of bone (Fig. 161), or even by no bone at all (Fig. 162).

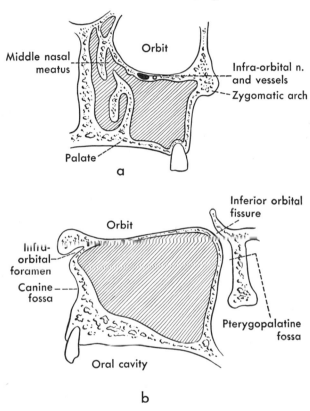

Fig. 158. Some relations of the maxillary sinus in frontal section, *a*, and sagittal section, *b*.

In the same way, the relation of the maxillary sinus to the teeth is inconstant, depending upon the extent to which the sinus invades the alveolar process (Figs. 159-162). According to Schaeffer ('10b) the three most constant teeth in relation to it are the three molars (Fig. 159), though there may be fewer (Fig. 160); he has found that only occasionally does the canine tooth have a direct relation to it and in a slightly larger percentage

Ridges and septa in the maxillary sinus are common; Schaeffer has pointed out that larger ones may turn upward so that they prevent adequate drainage of the sinus from below, serving as small basins which catch the fluid. Occasionally the ridges may form complete septa dividing the sinuses into two separate portions, in which case one portion may empty by a small foramen into the other, or by an accessory ostium into the nasal cavity;

lary sinusitis and the roots of the teeth at the same time in order to see what percentage might have been caused by bad teeth. In only 11 per cent of these

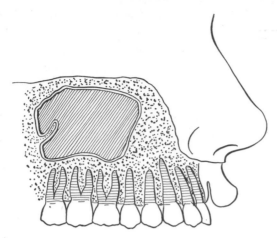

Fig. 159. Approximately average relations of the maxillary sinus and the roots of the teeth.

quite rarely two maxillary sinuses develop in one bone. The infra-orbital vessels and nerves, which run in the roof of the sinus, may be separated from the mucous mem-

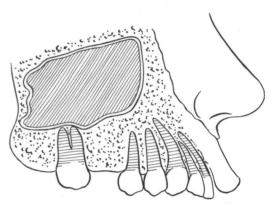

Fig. 161. Moderately thick alveolar process, with the roots of the second molar tooth very close to the mucous membrane of the antrum. (Adapted from Schaeffer, J. P.: *Am. J. Anat.* *10*:313, 1910.)

cases did all the teeth seem healthy; in 41 per cent there was a dead tooth in the floor of the antrum, and an origin of the infection from the tooth seemed possible; in 30 per cent there was an abscessed

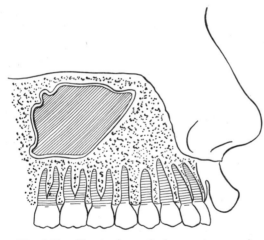

Fig. 160. Shortening of the ventrosuperior diagonal of the maxillary sinus, so that the only teeth in direct relation to it are the second and third molars. (Adapted from Schaeffer, J. P.: *Am. J. Anat. 10:*313, 1910.)

brane of the sinus by a bony wall of only papery thinness, and are occasionally even in direct contact with it, as may be also the superior alveolar nerves, both anterior and posterior.

Berry investigated 152 cases of maxil-

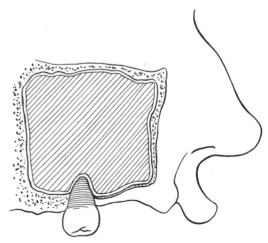

Fig. 162. Extreme development of the maxillary sinus, with marked thinning of the alveolar process: the root of the sole remaining tooth projects into the sinus, covered only by the mucous membrane of this. (Adapted from Schaeffer, J. P.: *Am. J. Anat. 10:*313, 1910.)

tooth present here, and the origin seemed probable; in 18 per cent the maxillary sinusitis was very definitely traced to an infection about the dental apex, and further sinus infection was obviated after the elimination of this primary infection. Stafne has described the occasional retention of dental roots which have been forced up into the maxillary sinus as another factor in chronic maxillary sinusitis.

The *innervation* and *blood supply* of the maxillary sinus is through small twigs derived from the posterior superior alveolar, infra-orbital and anterior superior alveolar nerves and arteries.

OSTIUM OF MAXILLARY SINUS

The ostium of the maxillary sinus is on the highest part of the medial wall of the sinus, and is therefore poorly placed from the point of view of free drainage; in addition, it opens not directly into the nasal fossa but into the narrow ethmoidal infundibulum, inflammation of which can further interfere with drainage. Van Alyea ('46b) has stated that the maxillary ostium in a healthy state is of ample size and provides adequate drainage for the sinus (with the aid of ciliary action) but that in any large group of specimens there may be found some with a complete absence of drainage because of adherence between the uncinate process and the ethmoidal bulla, with obliteration of the semilunar hiatus.

Simon ('33, '39) has insisted that the maxillary ostium is actually more frequently a canal, as he found the length from medial to lateral ends to be 4.44 mm. among 36 ostia, and in his later paper stated that in 82.7 per cent of 110 cases examined the canals were 3 mm. or more in length, the average length being 5.55 mm. This surely indicates the thick-

ness of the infundibular and sinus mucosa rather than the presence of a bony canal, since the ostium is usually located in that region of the lateral nasal wall which is partly very thin bone and partly membranous.

It is in this thin and partly membranous lateral nasal wall that accessory ostia may also be located; Myerson ('32a) found an incidence of accessory ostia of 30.7 per cent, and Schaeffer ('20) found an incidence of almost 41 per cent in 295 sinuses. Van Alyea found accessory ostia in 23 per cent of 163 specimens;

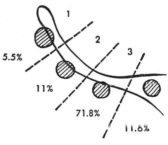

Fig. 163. Variation in positions of the ostium of the maxillary sinus in relation to the anterior, middle and posterior thirds (*1, 2, 3*) of the ethmoidal infundibulum. The percentages given are those of Van Alyea ('36).

Rosenberger observed them in only 4 per cent of Negroes and 17 per cent of whites, an incidence much lower than that reported by other workers.

The ostium of the maxillary sinus is commonly said to open into the posterior half of the infundibulum; Van Alyea ('36), analyzing his 163 specimens, found only 9 ostia in the anterior third of the uncinate groove, 18 in the middle third and 117 or 71.8 per cent in the posterior third; the remaining 19 ostia opened at the extreme posterior tip of the groove, and were visible, rather than hidden by the uncinate process (Fig. 163). Rosenberger also has stated that the ostium opens into the lower or posterior third in about 70 per cent of cases.

The accessibility of the ostium varies both with its position and the shape of the infundibulum (Fig. 164). In 25 per cent of Van Alyea's cases the uncinate wall was high and probing the ostium would apparently have been almost impossible in the living, while in 8 cases it was noticeably low; in 18 cases the hiatus was especially narrow and in 12 a low and overhanging bulla blocked the ostium.

subject to infection, as are the other sinuses, from general nasal infection, but may also be infected from the teeth, or from the frontal sinus or anterior ethmoid cells (Schaeffer, '16, found the ethmoidal infundibulum acting as a channel between these and the maxillary sinus in approximately 50 per cent of adults), the accessibility of the maxillary ostium for catheterization and lavage becomes of considerable clinical importance. This obviously varies not only with the skill of the worker, but with the anatomy of

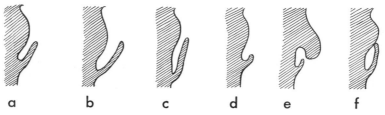

Fig. 164. Some variations in the semilunar hiatus and ethmoidal infundibulum which would affect the accessibility of a maxillary ostium opening into it. In *a* the uncinate process is moderately tall and the hiatus moderately wide; in *b* there is an extreme development of the process but the hiatus is also especially wide; in *c* the hiatus is narrow; in *d* the uncinate process and therefore the infundibulum are rudimentary; in *e* the bulla overhangs the uncinate process; and in *f* the two are in contact.

Myerson found that the uncinate process varied in length from 14 to 22 mm., and was usually about 5 mm. high —that is, the ethmoidal infundibulum was therefore about 5 mm. deep. In 114 lateral nasal walls which he investigated he found the uncinate process to be absent 3 times, rudimentary in 10 cases, moderately developed in 69 and pronounced, that is, more than 5 mm. high, in 32; he noted that the ethmoidal bulla may bulge so as actually to touch the uncinate process, and that the greatest width of the semilunar hiatus was 3 mm. The actual depth of the ethmoidal infundibulum was found in this study to vary from 0.5 to 10 mm.

Since the maxillary sinus is not only

the region—a high uncinate process and a deep and narrow ethmoidal infundibulum necessarily render access to the ostium difficult or impossible. Myerson ('32b) has stated that in about 81 per cent of clinical cases he was able to reach the normal ostium, but Rosenberger found that he could catheterize this in only about 46 per cent of white and 40 per cent of Negro skulls; Van Alyea ('36) similarly concluded from his anatomical study of the location of the maxillary ostium that in nearly one half of the 163 specimens he examined it was so located that catheterization of the antrum would have been impossible or at least very difficult.

APPROACHES TO MAXILLARY SINUS

Accessory, surgical, openings into the maxillary sinus may be either intranasal or facial. In making the former, it is necessary to penetrate the lateral nasal wall; this is commonly done through the inferior meatus, in which case the possibility of damage to the nasolacrimal ostium must be borne in mind (p. 241), but has also been done above the attached edge of the inferior concha. Myerson ('32b) has stated that there is no particular point in attempting to drain the maxillary sinus through a surgical opening in the inferior meatus, where one must traverse bone, when the sinus can be opened quite easily through the membranous portion of the lateral nasal wall; the former opening, however, has the advantage of better gravity drainage in the upright position, a factor which may be of considerable importance (see the last paragraph of this section).

In contrast, Goodyear ('49), stressing the importance of normal ciliary action about the natural ostium of the sinus, has strongly disapproved of interrupting this by antrostomies through the middle meatus, and stated that a very large and permanent opening under the inferior turbinate should be made. Simon ('33) apparently preferred the external approach to the maxillary sinus, finding that it usually gave a better chance of viewing the mucosa of the sinus, and the ostium, than did an opening through the wall of the inferior meatus. Simple punctures of the antral wall are of course most easily made through the thin wall of the middle meatus.

The extranasal approach to the maxillary sinus is usually through the canine fossa, the depression on the front of the maxilla extending from the infra-orbital foramen (or the lower margin of the orbit) above to the alveolar process below; the anterior superior alveolar nerves and vessels run in the bony wall between the canine fossa and the antrum, and Mellinger, pointing out that their exact arrangement is very variable, has found transmitted light to be often of value in locating these nerves and vessels as they cross the fossa.

Shapiro, Fabricant, and Stephan, noting that operations upon the maxillary sinuses through the canine fossa are sometimes accompanied by anesthesia or paresthesia of the cheek, upper lip or teeth, studied the results following vertical incisions into the mucosa, as compared to horizontal ones, in regard to sparing of the infra-orbital nerve. While they stated that vertical incisions gave better exposure and less bleeding, there was apparently no appreciable difference in so far as sensation was concerned between the two incisions. They concluded that the course of the alveolar nerves, particularly the anterior, is such that damage to one or more of these is practically unavoidable in performing the usual radical type of operation on the antra.

It should be realized that artificial openings into the sinus are probably effective only through gravity drainage, and that complete gravity drainage in the upright position frequently cannot be obtained by an intranasal approach, as the floor of the sinus may lie below the level of the nasal floor. Hilding ('41) concluded from experiments on rabbits that supplementary openings between the nasal cavity and the maxillary sinus may upset the normal physiology of the sinus, especially if they are made near the normal ostium, because of interference with the ciliary mechanism; McMurray expressed the belief that even large normal accessory ostia probably interfere with drainage from the maxillary sinus, by diminishing the normal negative pressure produced in the antra by inspiration. King placed radiopaque oil in the antrum of a patient with an artificial opening, and found that the oil usually did not flow out through the larger artificial opening but through the natural orifice, being drained therefore by ciliary action rather than by gravity. Hilding ('44) likewise has stated that the direction of flow in the maxillary sinus due to ciliary activity is not altered by making a window into the inferior meatus.

ANOMALIES

WHILE variations in the nasal cavities and sinuses are, as described under these structures, exceedingly common, major anomalies of the nose are relatively rare.

CONGENITAL ATRESIA OF NOSE

Probably the most common of these is congenital atresia or obstruction of the nose. Blair classified patients with this anomaly into five general groups: (1) atresia at the anterior nares, (2) atresia at the posterior nares, (3) obstruction by some malformation within the passages, (4) total absence of the nasal passages, and (5) pharyngeal narrowing due to backward displacement of the maxilla. He pointed out that congenital obstructions of the nose vary greatly in their origin, but expressed the belief that many are due to a partial reduplication of the nose.

Jervey has described a case of congenital *occlusion of both anterior nares*; in this case there was a complete occlusion of the nasal passage a quarter of an inch back from each anterior naris; the nose otherwise appeared normal. Jervey concluded that this condition must be the result of "faulty dislocations" of tissue before birth. He stated that this condition is apparently quite rare, even less common than occlusion of the choanae.

Blair described atresia at the anterior naris as characterized also by lack of the ala on that side, and a turning downward of the inner canthus; this obviously differs from the case described by Jervey, and rather seems to correspond to what Blair, Brown, and Byars described as total absence of one lateral half of the external nose and of the anterior naris. They reported several cases of such *hemi-absence*, accompanied by a marked downward inclination of the inner canthus, and a flattening of the cheek; 1 patient was shown to have no maxillary sinus, and 3 had complete blockage of normal tear drainage. In the 4 cases in which they operated there was also no evidence of a medial palpebral ligament.

Congenital *atresia of the posterior nares* is more common than that of the anterior nares, but is nevertheless apparently rare; Wright, Shambaugh, and Green found 230 cases reported in the literature up to 1945, and Kazanjian found 19 cases among the records of more than 6200 patients at the hospital at which he worked. The condition may be unilateral or bilateral, and the obstruction may be a bony one or due to a membranous septum. Kearney, in reporting a case of unilateral atresia, has stated that congenital choanal atresia is more frequently osseous than it is membranous, most commonly unilateral, and occurs more often in females and on the right side of the nose; Wright, Shambaugh, and Green gave a ratio of 90 per cent bony to 10 per cent membranous atresia. Colver noted both that unilateral atresia has been said to be more common, and that bilateral atresia has been said to predominate in the proportion of three to one. In 4 of Kazanjian's 19 cases the atresia was on the right side, in 3 it was on the left, and in 3 it was bilateral.

Colver has pointed out that unilateral atresia, because it is less serious than bilateral, may remain unsuspected for years, and has suggested that bilateral atresia has probably been the unsuspected cause of many deaths within the first several postnatal days. It appears obvious that the true incidence of this condition is not known. Wright, Shambaugh, and Green listed three theories as to the origin of choanal atresia: persistence of the upper part of the buccopharyngeal membrane, with fusion of the septum and the palatine processes to it; persistence of the naso-buccal membrane; growth of the palatine processes at the choanae so that they fuse not only with the septum but also with the sphenoid bone. They regarded none of these theories as proved. Stewart discussed several ways in which a persistent nasobuccal membrane might contribute to the deformity, and stated that when the buccopharyngeal membrane persists the atresia is bilateral.

Membranous occlusions of the choanae may be relatively easily corrected, of course, or even spontaneous rupture may occur in early infancy. Bony atresia, however, offers more difficulty, though it must be corrected at least on one side if it is bilateral. According to Wright and his co-workers, the occluding bone typically extends from the junction of hard and soft palates to the base of the sphenoid bone, and Colver stated that the bony obstruction has been reported as being as much as 12 mm. thick. Colver, and Wright, Shambaugh and Green, emphasized the removal of the posterior portion of the nasal septum as being of fundamental importance in ensuring a free and permanent choanal opening, and Kazanjian also followed this procedure.

One operative approach has been along the nasal septum, following this up to the site of occlusion, but Wright and his co-workers preferred an approach through the antrum, stating that this gave both a better exposure and more ready control of hemorrhage through ligation of the internal maxillary artery, if this should prove necessary. The transantral approach would, of course, not be feasible in the infant.

CEREBROSPINAL RHINORRHEA

Cerebrospinal rhinorrhea, although more commonly resulting from fractures of the skull, may also be due to congenital defects in the cribriform plate with the formation of a meningocele protruding into the nasal fossa; in this case it is known as spontaneous cerebrospinal rhinorrhea. Symptoms may not occur, or at least may be unnoticed, until adult life, and the condition must therefore be differentiated from allergic and vascular rhinorrhea.

Cerebrospinal rhinorrhea is discussed in more detail on page 45; it need only be pointed out here that intranasal medication with silver nitrate does not attack the rhinorrhea at the logical point—the defect in the cribriform plate—and, as meningitis is a common consequence of spontaneous cerebrospinal rhinorrhea, an intracranial operation is usually indicated. The cerebrospinal rhinorrhea resulting from fractures of the skull usually disappears in some six to eight weeks or less, as a result of spontaneous healing.

OTHER ANOMALIES

Anomalies of the external nose, besides hemi-absence (p. 276), include harelip and bifid nose. The former is discussed on pages 336 and 348. Bifid nose is characterized by separation at the columella; more commonly the tip only is cleft, but the separation between the medial crura of the two alar cartilages may be extreme, so that connective tissue and skin sink deeply between them.

REFERENCES

AVERBUKH, S. S., BREVDA, I. S., LUBOTSKY, D. N., and SEMENOVA, O. S. The palatine access to the ganglion sphenopalatinum and to the second branch of the trifacial nerve. *Ann. Surg. 101:*819, 1935.

AYMARD, J. L. Some new points in the anatomy of the nasal septum, and their surgical significance. *J. Anat. 51:*293, 1917.

BERRY, G. Further observations on dental caries as a contributing factor in maxillary sinusitis. *Arch. Otolaryng. 11:*55, 1930.

BLAIR, V. P. Congenital atresia or obstruction of the nasal air passages. *Ann. Otol., Rhin. & Laryng. 40:*1021, 1931.

BLAIR, V. P., BROWN, J. B., and BYARS, L. T. Observations on sinus abnormalities in congenital total and hemi-absence of the nose. *Ann. Otol., Rhin. & Laryng. 46:*592, 1937.

BROOKOVER, C. The nervus terminalis in adult man. *J. Comp. Neurol. 24:*131, 1914.

BROOKOVER, C. The peripheral distribution of the nervus terminalis in an infant. *J. Comp. Neurol. 28:*349, 1917.

BROWNELL, D. H. Postoperative regeneration of the mucous membrane of the paranasal sinuses: A summary of the published investigations. *Arch. Otolaryng. 24:*582, 1936.

BURNHAM, H. H. The anterior ethmoidal nerve syndrome: Referred pain and headache from the lateral nasal wall. *Arch. Otolaryng. 50:*640, 1949.

CHRISTENSEN, K. The innervation of the nasal mucosa, with special reference to its afferent supply. *Ann. Otol., Rhin. & Laryng. 43:*1066, 1934.

COHEN, S. Dislocation of the septal cartilage. *Arch. Otolaryng. 46:*601, 1947.

COLVER, B. N. Congenital choanal atresia: Two cases of complete bilateral obstruction. *Ann. Otol., Rhin. & Laryng. 46:*358, 1937.

CONGDON, E. D. The distribution and mode of origin of septa and walls of the sphenoid sinus. *Anat. Rec. 18:*97, 1920.

COSTEN, J. B. Relief of right-sided headache by resection of left sphenoid (anatomic variation of sphenoid sinuses): Report of a case. *Ann. Otol., Rhin. & Laryng. 39:*1074, 1930.

COSTEN, J. B. Anatomic phases involved in the surgery of the naso-antral wall and the floor of the mouth. *Ann. Otol., Rhin. & Laryng. 41:*820, 1932.

CUSHING, H. The sensory distribution of the fifth cranial nerve. *Bull. Johns Hopkins Hosp. 15:*213, 1904.

DALEY, J. Morphologic deformities of the lower lateral cartilages. *Arch. Otolaryng. 47:*49, 1948.

DIXON, F. W. A comparative study of the sphenoid sinus: A study of 1600 skulls. *Ann. Otol., Rhin. & Laryng. 46:*687, 1937.

FENTON, R. A. Pathways of referred pain from the nose. *Am. J. Surg. n.s.42:*194, 1938.

FITZ-HUGH, G. S., and RISHER, J. C. Epistaxis: Report of a case of ligation of the external carotid and anterior ethmoid arteries. *Arch. Otolaryng. 49:*564, 1949.

FOLEY, J. O., and DuBOIS, F. S. An experimental study of the facial nerve. *J. Comp. Neurol. 79:*79, 1943.

FOLEY, J. O., PEPPER, H. R., and KESSLER, W. H. The ratio of nerve fibers to nerve cells in the geniculate ganglion. *J. Comp. Neurol. 85:*141, 1946.

GOODYEAR, H. M. Ophthalmic conditions referable to diseases of the paranasal sinuses. *Arch. Otolaryng. 48:*202, 1948.

GOODYEAR, H. M. Intranasal surgery of the maxillary sinus. *Arch. Otolaryng. 50:*795, 1949.

GRAVES, G. O., and EDWARDS, L. F. The Eustachian tube: A review of its descriptive, microscopic, topographic and clinical anatomy. *Arch. Otolaryng. 39:*359, 1944.

HIGBEE, D. Functional and anatomic relation of sphenopalatine ganglion to the autonomic nervous system. *Arch. Otolaryng. 50:*45, 1949.

HILDING, A. The physiology of drainage of nasal mucus: I. The flow of the mucus currents through the drainage system of the nasal mucosa and its relation to ciliary activity. *Arch. Otolaryng. 15:*92, 1932.

HILDING, A. C. Experimental sinus surgery: Effects of operative windows on normal sinuses. *Ann. Otol., Rhin. & Laryng. 50:*379, 1941.

HILDING, A. C. The physiology of drainage of nasal mucus: IV. Drainage of the accessory sinuses in man; rationale of irrigation of the infected maxillary sinuses. *Ann. Otol., Rhin. & Laryng. 53:*35, 1944.

HILL, F. T. Local anesthesia for surgical treatment of the sinuses. *Arch. Otolaryng. 27:*197, 1938.

HIRSCH, C. Ligation of the internal maxillary artery in patients with nasal hemorrhage. *Arch. Otolaryng. 24:*589, 1936.

HUNT, J. R. Geniculate neuralgia (neuralgia of the nervus facialis): A further contribution to the sensory system of the facial nerve and its neuralgic conditions. *Arch. Neurol. & Psychiat. 37:*253, 1937.

JERVEY, J. W., JR. Congenital occlusion of both anterior nares. *Ann. Otol., Rhin. & Laryng. 53:*182, 1944.

JOHNSON, M. C., and FOSTER, M. E. Ligation of the external carotid artery for traumatic nasal hemorrhage. *Ann. Otol., Rhin. & Laryng. 42:*588, 1933.

KASPER, K. A. Nasofrontal connections: A study based on one hundred consecutive dissections. *Arch. Otolaryng. 23:*322, 1936.

KAZANJIAN, V. H. The treatment of congenital atresia of the choanae. *Ann. Otol., Rhin. & Laryng. 51:*704, 1942.

KEARNEY, H. L. Congenital bony atresia of the right posterior naris. *Ann. Otol., Rhin. & Laryng. 45:*583, 1936.

KING, E. A clinical study of the functioning of the maxillary sinus mucosa. *Ann. Otol., Rhin. & Laryng. 44:*480, 1935.

LARSELL, O., and BURNS, E. M. Some aspects of certain of the cranial nerves. *Ann. Otol., Rhin. & Laryng. 40:*661, 1931.

LARSELL, O., and FENTON, R. A. Sympathetic innervation of the nose: Research report. *Arch. Otolaryng. 24:*687, 1936.

LATTA, J. S., and SCHALL, R. F. The histology of the epithelium of the paranasal sinuses under various conditions. *Ann. Otol., Rhin. & Laryng. 43:*945, 1934.

LEDERER, F. L., and DINOLT, R. Influence of avulsion of the trigeminal nerve on the human nose. *Arch. Otolaryng. 37:*768, 1943.

LILLIE, H. I., and SIMONTON, K. M. Developmental extension of an anterior ethmoid cell within the frontal sinus: Report of a case. *Arch. Otolaryng. 32:*32, 1940.

LITTELL, J. J. Disturbances of the ethmoid branches of the ophthalmic nerve, with description of a syndrome associated with chronic suppuration of the olfactory fissure. *Arch. Otolaryng. 43:*481, 1946.

LUCAS, A. M. The nasal cavity and direction of fluid by ciliary movement in *Macacus rhesus* (Desm.). *Am. J. Anat. 50:*141, 1932.

McMURRAY, J. The intra-antral air pressure incident to the respiratory excursion and its effect on antral drainage. *Arch. Otolaryng. 14:*581, 1931.

MELLINGER, W. J. The canine fossa. *Arch. Otolaryng. 31:*930, 1940.

MOSHER, H. P. Symposium on the ethmoid: The surgical anatomy of the ethmoidal labyrinth. *Tr. Am. Acad. Ophth.* p. 376, 1929.

MOST, A. Ueber den Lymphgefässapparat von Nase und Rachen. *Arch. f. Anat. u. Physiol.* p. 75, 1901.

MYERSON, M. C. The natural orifice of the maxillary sinus: I. Anatomic studies. *Arch. Otolaryng. 15:*80, 1932a.

MYERSON, M. C. Natural orifice of the maxillary sinus: II. Clinical studies. *Arch. Otolaryng. 15:*716, 1932b.

PEARSON, A. A. The development of the nervus terminalis in man. *J. Comp. Neurol. 75:*39, 1941.

PROETZ, A. W. Effect of temperature on nasal cilia. *Arch. Otolaryng. 19:*607, 1934.

RIGGLE, P. P. Ethmosphenoidal cells with agenesis of the sphenoidal sinus. *Arch. Otolaryng. 16:*532, 1932.

ROSENBERGER, H. C. The clinical availability of the ostium maxillare: A clinical and cadaver study. *Ann. Otol., Rhin. & Laryng. 47:*176, 1938.

ROWBOTHAM, G. F. Observations on the effects of trigeminal denervation. *Brain 62:* 364, 1939.

ROY, D. Some clinical observations on nasal hemorrhage. *Ann. Otol., Rhin. & Laryng. 42:*1117, 1933.

SCHAEFFER, J. P.   On the genesis of air cells in the conchae nasales. *Anat. Rec. 4:*167, 1910a.

SCHAEFFER, J. P.   The sinus maxillaris and its relations in the embryo, child, and adult man. *Am. J. Anat. 10:*313, 1910b.

SCHAEFFER, J. P.   Types of ostia nasolacrimalia in man and their genetic significance. *Am. J. Anat. 13:*183, 1912.

SCHAEFFER, J. P.   The genesis, development, and adult anatomy of the nasofrontal region in man. *Am. J. Anat. 20:*125, 1916.

SCHAEFFER, J. P.   *The Nose, Paranasal Sinuses, Nasolacrimal Passageways, and Olfactory Organ in Man.*   Philadelphia, Blakiston, 1920.

SEWALL, E. C.   Surgical removal of the sphenopalatine ganglion: Report of three operations elaborating an original technic to expose the pterygopalatine fossa, command the internal maxillary artery and its terminals and the infraorbital nerve and its branches. *Ann. Otol., Rhin. & Laryng. 46:* 79, 1937.

SHAPIRO, S. L., FABRICANT, N. D., and STEPHAN, R. M.   Sensory disturbances following radical operations on the antrums: With an evaluation of the vertical incision. *Arch. Otolaryng. 19:*303, 1934.

SIMON, E.   Antroscopy and its relation to the anatomy of the maxillary sinus. *Ann. Otol., Rhin. & Laryng. 42:*198, 1933.

SIMON, E.   Anatomy of the opening of the maxillary sinus. *Arch. Otolaryng. 29:*640, 1939.

SLUDER, G.   The control of mandibular pain through nasal (sphenopalatine or Meckel's) ganglion. *South. M. J. 15:*856, 1922a.

SLUDER, G.   The control of earache through the nasal (sphenopalatine, Meckel's) ganglion. *J.A.M.A. 78:*1708, 1922b.

SLUDER, G.   A case of glossodynia with lingual tonsillitis as its etiology: Control through the nasal ganglion. *J.A.M.A. 81:* 115, 1923.

SMITH, C. G.   Incidence of atrophy of the olfactory nerves in man. *Arch. Otolaryng. 34:*533, 1941.

SMITH, C. G.   Age incidence of atrophy of olfactory nerves in man: A contribution to the study of the process of ageing. *J. Comp. Neurol. 77:*589, 1942.

SPAR, A. A., and HALLBERG, O. E.   Severe epistaxis and its management: Report of 11 cases in which the external carotid artery was ligated. *Ann. Otol., Rhin. & Laryng. 56:*141, 1947.

STAFNE, E. C.   Dental roots in the maxillary sinus. *Am. J. Orthodontics & Oral Surg. (Oral Surg.). 33:*582, 1947.

STEWART, J. P.   Congenital atresia of the posterior nares. *Arch. Otolaryng. 13:*570, 1931.

TRIBLE, G. B.   Epistaxis of antral origin: Report of cases. *Arch. Otolaryng. 10:*633, 1929.

VAIL, H. H.   Retrobulbar optic neuritis originating in the nasal sinuses: A new method of demonstrating the relation between the sphenoid sinus and the optic nerve. *Arch. Otolaryng. 13:*846, 1931.

VAN ALYEA, O. E.   The ostium maxillare: Anatomic study of its surgical accessibility. *Arch. Otolaryng. 24:*553, 1936.

VAN ALYEA, O. E.   Ethmoid labyrinth: Anatomic study, with consideration of the clinical significance of its structural characteristics. *Arch. Otolaryng. 29:*881, 1939.

VAN ALYEA, O. E.   Frontal cells: An anatomic study of these cells with consideration of their clinical significance. *Arch. Otolaryng. 34:*11, 1941a.

VAN ALYEA, O. E.   Sphenoid sinus: Anatomic study, with consideration of the clinical significance of the structural characteristics of the sphenoid sinus. *Arch. Otolaryng. 34:* 225, 1941b.

VAN ALYEA, O. E.   Sphenoid sinus drainage. *Ann. Otol., Rhin. & Laryng. 53:*493, 1944.

VAN ALYEA, O. E.   Frontal sinus drainage. *Ann. Otol., Rhin. & Laryng. 55:*267, 1946a.

VAN ALYEA, O. E.   Maxillary sinus drainage. *Ann. Otol., Rhin. & Laryng. 55:*754, 1946b.

WASSON, W. W.   Changes in the nasal accessory sinuses after birth. *Arch. Otolaryng. 17:*197, 1933.

WEDDELL, G., MACBETH, R. G., SHARP, H. S., and CALVERT, C. A.   The surgical treatment of severe epistaxis in relation to the ethmoidal arteries. *Brit. J. Surg. 33:*387, 1946.

WHITNALL, S. E.   *The Anatomy of the Human Orbit and Accessory Organs of Vision.*   London, Oxford, 1921.

WICKLIFFE, T. F. Abscess of the frontal lobe due to acute frontal sinusitis. *Arch. Otolaryng. 15:*290, 1932.

WILLIAMS, H. L., and HEILMAN, F. R. Spreading osteomyelitis of the frontal bone secondary to disease of the frontal sinus: With a preliminary report as to bacteriology and specific treatment. *Arch. Otolaryng. 25:* 196, 1937.

WRIGHT, W. K., SHAMBAUGH, G. E., JR., and GREEN, LOIS. Congenital choanal atresia: A new surgical approach. *Ann. Otol., Rhin. & Laryng. 56:*120, 1947.

ZIEGELMAN, E. F. The surgery of the great superficial petrosal nerve: Its possible relation to some of the pathology of the nasal and paranasal mucous membranes. *Ann. Otol., Rhin. & Laryng. 43:*1091, 1934.

CHAPTER 5

Fascia and Fascial Spaces of the Head and Neck

IT SEEMS probable that there are few subjects in gross anatomy that have suffered so many diverse descriptions as the fascia and fascial spaces of the neck. As quoted by Grodinsky and Holyoke "the cervical fasciae appear in a new form under the pen of each author who attempts to describe them" and, it may be added, the fascial spaces are apt also to appear under new names.

In spite of this, however, there is a good deal of agreement on the fundamentals of the relationships which have been thought to be of clinical importance; moreover, although they are difficult to describe clearly, the major fascial layers and spaces are actually relatively simple. If the reader will recall that there is no generally accepted definition as to how dense connective tissue must be before it can be regarded as forming a fascia, and that fascial spaces are simply areas of relatively loose connective tissue, the reasons for many of the discrepancies in the various descriptions will be obvious.

Connective tissue naturally forms a padding between and around the various structures in the neck, and, as occurs also elsewhere in the body, the connective tissue tends to be somewhat more dense where it is arranged immediately about organs. When the fascia and spaces of the head and neck of normal bodies are investigated by means of dissection or injection, as they must be, the looser connective tissue intervening between organs is torn and pressed against these organs, thereby exaggerating any fascial layer which was already present here. Thus Parsons was unable to identify in histological sections the carotid sheath or most of the other fascial layers usually described in the neck unless the material had been partly dissected beforehand; he therefore regarded the usually described layers as being formed entirely artificially by pressing together loose connective tissue which really serves simply as a padding around all structures. In so far as infections tend to spread through the looser connective tissue, however, these produce the same effects—that is, they exaggerate both the "spaces" and their fascial walls.

For practical purposes, it makes little difference to the surgeon operating in an uninfected neck whether, for instance, the connective tissue about the internal jugular vein, common carotid artery, and vagus nerve is described as forming a fascial sheath or not, if he realizes that these closely grouped structures are of course surrounded by connective tissue; at operation, he can easily dispose of this carotid sheath with one sweep of his scissors, or if he wishes to stay away from these structures, push them aside with their surrounding tissue. Of some practical importance, however, are the relations of the loose connective tissue areas, the fascial spaces, of the head and neck, both because of the structures which traverse or abut against them, and because they may become infected and harbor abscesses.

The relationships of these spaces to each other have been regarded as of especial importance in the spread of infection, and many surgeons have urged accurate knowledge of the anatomy of these spaces, and prompt drainage of them when they become infected. On the other hand, other workers (for instance, New and Erich) have doubted the importance of spread of infection through fascial spaces, and have advocated conservative treatment, with initiation of drainage only after an abscess has pointed. According to this latter view, the anatomy of the fascial spaces is of little moment.

It is not within the province of an anatomist to decide between these sharply divergent views as to pathological processes and clinical treatments, and the present account of the anatomy of these spaces and of the surgical approaches to them is presented without prejudice in this regard. It should be noted that with the widespread use of the newer antibiotics the anatomy of these spaces is necessarily becoming less important.

As a description of the fascial spaces is not understandable without some discussion of the fascial layers, these also are described briefly. For a fuller description of the spaces and fascial layers, the detailed works of Coller and Yglesias ('35, '37) and of Grodinsky and Holyoke should be consulted.

SUPERFICIAL FASCIA

The subcutaneous tissue of the head and neck, usually referred to as the superficial fascia, resembles this tissue elsewhere in that it contains a variable amount of fat; its distinguishing characteristic, as compared with subcutaneous tissue in general, lies primarily in the fact that it encloses voluntary muscles in its deep portion. Thus the platysma is embedded in this layer in the neck, while in the face the connective tissue is more dense and the muscles of expression lie within it. Except for the subcutaneous tissue of the eyelids, which is loose on both sides of the orbicularis oculi muscle and permits considerable accumulation of fluid, and a corresponding layer in the scalp deep to the epicranial aponeurosis (sometimes known as the danger space of the scalp), the subcutaneous tissue of the head and face is rather tightly attached about the muscles and to the underlying bone, and spaces can hardly be said to exist here. A space has been described in the neck between the superficial and deep fascial layers, but is of little practical importance.

DEEP FASCIA

In the neck the deep fascia upon dissection forms several more or less distinct layers. If, however, it is borne in mind that fasciae or connective tissue layers in general split to surround muscles and other soft tissues, and then unite again on the other side, blending with other layers where possible, it should be apparent that any description of the fascia of the neck is largely an arbitrary one. As a rule, some three layers of the deep fascia are described in the neck: these are frequently named the *superficial or anterior layer* of the deep fascia, the *middle layer* and the *posterior layer*; other terms have also been applied to some of these layers, and some of the descriptions seem needlessly complicated. The fascia is most easily described by considering separately its relations below and above the hyoid bone.

THE FASCIA AND SPACES BELOW THE HYOID BONE

FASCIA

SUPERFICIAL LAYER

The superficial investing, or anterior layer of the deep fascia may be thought of as arising from the vertebral spinous unite to form a single layer which crosses the posterior triangle of the neck to the posterior border of the sternocleidomastoid muscle; in so doing it splits to surround that portion of the omohyoid muscle which extends across the pos-

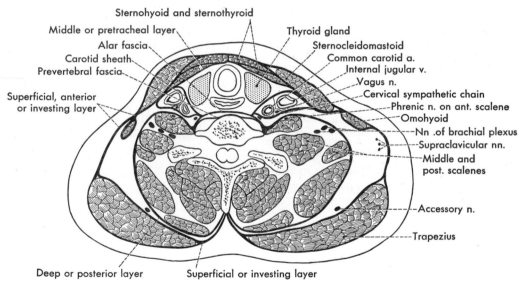

Fig. 165. Chief layers of the deep fascia of the neck below the hyoid bone. Note the relations of the various nerves. The fasciae and fascial spaces shown in this and the succeeding drawings on this subject are all, of course, both schematically shown and exaggerated.

processes and ligamentum nuchae and completely encircling the neck to attach again to these (Fig. 165). This fascia is usually described as enclosing the trapezius muscle, but it is the layer deep to the trapezius which is thicker. At the anterior border of the trapezius the two layers terior triangle, and, uniting below this muscle, acts as a ligament which holds the omohyoid in a relatively constant relation to the clavicle. At the posterior border of the sternocleidomastoid muscle the superficial layer of the deep fascia splits again to surround this muscle, and at the lateral borders of the strap muscles splits again to pass in front of, between, and behind these muscles. Thus it crosses the midline, unites again at the lateral borders of the strap muscles and proceeds around the other sternocleidomastoid and hence to the vertebral column in the manner already described.

layers to unite between the closely adjacent sternal heads of the sternocleidomastoid muscle, and therefore contains both of these heads; in addition, the lower ends of the anterior jugular veins and their transverse connecting branch lie within this space, and there may sometimes be a lymph node here.

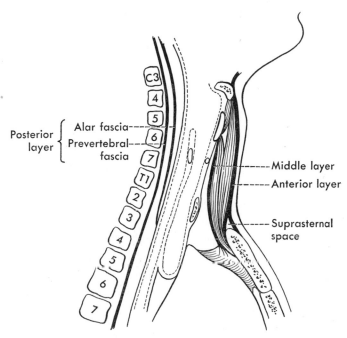

Fig. 166.   The chief deep fascial layers of the neck, below the hyoid bone, in longitudinal section. (Redrawn from Grodinsky, M., and Holyoke, E. A.: *Am. J. Anat. 63*:367, 1938.)

When the layer of the deep fascia anterior to the strap muscles is traced upward, it may be seen to attach to the hyoid bone (Fig. 166). When it is traced downward between the two sternocleidomastoid muscles it will be found to split into two layers just above the sternum; one attaches to the anterior and one to the posterior surface of the sternum, and the small space between these two layers is the *suprasternal space* (of Burns). It is due essentially to a failure of the fascial

MIDDLE LAYER

It is that part of the anterior layer of the deep fascia which passes behind the strap muscles, hence in front of the thyroid gland and trachea, which is most commonly described as the middle layer of the deep fascia (Fig. 167), usually known also as the pretracheal fascia (though the latter term has also been used as synonymous with the visceral fascia). In contrast to the layer in front of the strap muscles, the connective tissue behind them is apt to be filmy and therefore not very obvious, except in the lowest part of the neck where it is thicker and may contain some fat; it is probably not so much this layer of fascia as it is the

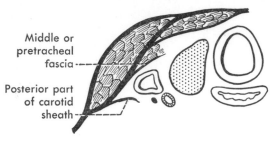

Fig. 167.   Disposition of the anterior part of the superficial (anterior, investing) layer of the deep fascia.

strap muscles and their fascia as a whole that should be regarded as forming a layer here.

The fascia behind the strap muscles (that is, the so-called middle layer) is of course continuous with the anterior layer at the lateral borders of these muscles (Fig. 168). Traced downward, it follows

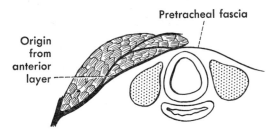

Fig. 168.   The so-called pretracheal, or middle layer of fascia.

these muscles behind the sternum to about their origin, where it fuses with the fibrous pericardium as this is prolonged out along the great vessels in the superior mediastinum. Above, this layer of fascia ends with the strap muscles, that is, it fuses to the thyroid cartilage and the hyoid bone. Theoretically, there are of course spaces about the strap muscles,

and these have been grouped together and named (by a number, 2A) by Grodinsky and Holyoke; actually, however, there seems no more point in naming these than in naming a sternocleidomastoid space, or a trapezius space—none are of clinical importance, and all consist merely of the potential planes of separation which lie between any muscle and its surrounding fascia.

POSTERIOR LAYER

The posterior layer of deep fascia may, like the anterior layer, be thought of as beginning from cervical spines and the ligamentum nuchae (Fig. 165, p. 284). It lies deep to the trapezius muscle, and upon the outer surface of the muscles of the back as they extend into the neck (sending, of course, septa among these muscles). For the most part, as this layer lies deep to the trapezius and as it extends across the posterior triangle, it is in contact with the anterior layer (for the "middle" layer exists only on the front of the neck), so that both layers appear as the fascial sheet between the trapezius and the underlying vertebral musculature, and both together form the fascial carpet of the posterior triangle, which is also the fascia on the lateral surface of the scalene muscles. They can, of course, be split apart so as to leave some fascia on the muscles of the back, and some on the deep surface of the trapezius, but this is a cleavage plane rather than an actual space except in very fat individuals. Above and behind the clavicle, however, and under the anterior edge of the trapezius as its more anterior fibers arise from the clavicle, the two layers are distinctly separated: the posterior layer follows the scalenes (and is reflected outward as a sleeve along the brachial plexus and axillary vessels as these structures run laterally from the scalenes), while the anterior layer remains against the trapezius and attaches below to the clavicle.

This area of separation (Space 4A of Grodinsky and Holyoke) is occupied by loose connective tissue and fat, in which lies the lower end of the external jugular vein and through which run the transverse scapular and transverse cervical (or superficial cervical) arteries, the supraclavicular nerves, and the posterior belly of the omohyoid muscle. Except for these structures, the space is of little clinical importance, since it communicates with no other space in the neck. Grodinsky and Holyoke regarded it as extending to the posterior midline through the cleavage plane deep to the trapezius.

The posterior layer of the deep fascia passes from the posterior triangle deep to the posterior border of the sternocleidomastoid, close to that portion of the anterior layer which also runs deep to this muscle. Lateral to the internal jugular vein, however, these layers separate: the anterior layer continues forward anterolateral to the vein and the common carotid artery toward the strap muscles, and in so doing forms the anterolateral wall of the carotid sheath; the posterior layer, however, turns medially behind these vessels and the vagus nerve, from which it is separated by loose connective tissue and the posterior wall of the carotid sheath. As it lies behind the carotid sheath on the scalene muscles, this part of the posterior layer is usually called the scalene fascia.

Between this fascia and the anterior scalene muscle is the phrenic nerve, and deep to the fascia, between the anterior and middle scalenes, the brachial plexus takes form; some of this fascia is carried outward about the plexus as it passes beyond the lateral edges of the scalenes,

to form a sheath about them and the subclavian artery, and blend with the axillary sheath.

Upon reaching the transverse processes, to which the scalenes are attached, the posterior layer of fascia attaches here also, and at about this position has embedded in its anterior surface the cervical sympathetic chain. From the transverse processes of one side the posterior fascia crosses the midline to attach to the transverse processes of the other side, passing behind the esophagus and in front of the vertebral column. This portion, passing

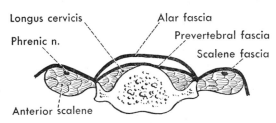

Fig. 169. Disposition of the anterior part of the posterior or deep layer of the deep fascia.

across the vertebral centra between the transverse processes, has usually been called the prevertebral or the retrovisceral fascia; Grodinsky and Holyoke have quite properly pointed out, however, that it actually consists of two layers here (Fig. 169), separated by extremely loose connective tissue; they have termed the anterior layer the alar fascia, the posterior the prevertebral fascia.

CAROTID SHEATH

The carotid sheath, surrounding the internal jugular vein, common carotid artery and vagus nerve, is interposed between the anterior and middle layers, on the one hand, and the posterior layer on the other. Its anterolateral wall is, in fact, the anterior layer of fascia deep to the sternocleidomastoid muscle, and to a lesser extent the middle layer of fascia where the strap muscles overlap the great vessels. Its posterior wall is formed by a lamina given off medially by the anterior layer as the latter reaches the level of the vessels (Fig. 170); this lamina passes behind the vessels and nerve to form the posterior wall of the sheath, and the medial wall of the sheath is then completed by fascia passing between the anterolateral and posterior walls, between the contents of the sheath and the trachea and esophagus. The sheath is attached medially to the posterior layer of fascia. The sympathetic trunk lies behind it; within it are separate compartments for the vein, artery and nerve.

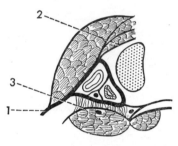

Fig. 170.   Formation of the carotid sheath. The anterior, middle, and posterior layers of the deep fascia are labeled 1, 2, and 3, respectively.

SPACES

Since a derivative of the anterior layer of the deep fascia (the middle layer, reinforced by the strap muscles) passes in front of the thyroid gland and the trachea, while the posterior layer of the deep fascia passes between the vertebral column and the esophagus, these layers form a compartment about the esophagus and trachea; laterally, the walls of this compartment are completed by the fascia on the deep surface of the sternocleidomastoid, where it is continuous with the middle layer of the deep fascia, and by the anteromedial wall of the carotid

sheath as it extends from the fascia on the deep surface of the sternocleidomastoid to the posterior layer of deep fascia.

VISCERAL COMPARTMENT

The area of loose connective tissue surrounding the thyroid gland, trachea and esophagus as a whole (Fig. 171)

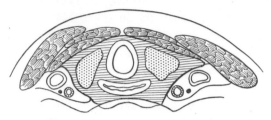

Fig. 171.   The visceral compartment of the neck.

was long known as the visceral compartment, and has been regarded as of particular importance in infections in the neck. Around the upper parts of the trachea, esophagus, and thyroid gland the visceral compartment is usually described as completely surrounding these, but below the level at which the inferior thy-

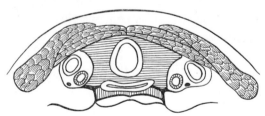

Fig. 172.   Subdivision of the visceral compartment into pretracheal (horizontally lined) and retrovisceral (vertically lined) portions by connective tissue attaching laterally to the esophagus, at a level below that shown in Figure 171.

roid artery enters the thyroid gland it is divided into two portions by denser connective tissue which attaches the esophageal wall laterally to the posterior layer of deep fascia (Fig. 172).

The anterior part of the compartment,

more or less surrounding the trachea and lying against the anterior wall of the esophagus, has been known by a number of different names, the more common ones being the previsceral space or the *pretracheal space*. The posterior part of the compartment, lying behind the hypopharynx and the esophagus, has been variously termed the *retrovisceral,* retropharyngeal, retro-esophageal, or postvisceral space. Grodinsky and Holyoke have emphasized the continuity of the pretracheal and retrovisceral spaces (the visceral compartment) by calling the two combined spaces part of their Space 3.

It is the visceral compartment which has usually been regarded as of particular importance in transmitting infections from the head and upper part of the neck to the mediastinum, for anatomically (as will be evidenced shortly) its posterior part is directly continuous above with the major spaces of the upper portion of the neck.

PRETRACHEAL SPACE

The pretracheal portion of the visceral compartment is limited above by the attachments of the strap muscles and their fascia to the thyroid cartilage and to the hyoid bone; below, it continues into the anterior portion of the superior mediastinum. It extends to about the upper border of the arch of the aorta according to Grodinsky and Holyoke (that is, to about the level of the fourth thoracic vertebra) where the posterior surface of the sternum and the fibrous pericardium along the aorta are united by heavy connective tissue.

The pretracheal portion of the visceral compartment could be infected by spread from the retrovisceral portion, around the sides of the esophagus and thyroid gland between the levels of the inferior thyroid

artery and the upper border of the thyroid cartilage, or directly by anterior perforations of the esophagus, which then open into this space. Both pretracheal and retrovisceral spaces descend into the superior portion of the mediastinum (Fig. 173). According to Pearse, however, infections descending from higher in the

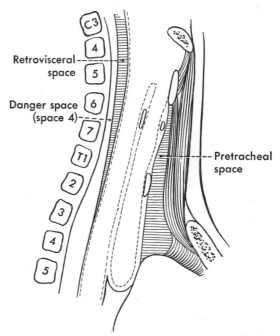

Fig. 173. The visceral compartment (horizontally lined) in a sagittal section of the neck. The danger space is also indicated. (Adapted from Grodinsky, M., and Holyoke, E. A.: *Am. J. Anat. 63:*367, 1938.)

neck reach the mediastinum through the pretracheal space rather rarely, only some 8 per cent of mediastinal suppurations of cranial or cervical origin having apparently traveled this route in the cases which he studied. This space has been opened by an incision anterior to the sternocleidomastoid muscle, carried medial to the carotid sheath (Hunt).

RETROVISCERAL SPACE

The posterior, retro-esophageal or retrovisceral portion of the visceral compartment in the lower part of the neck is not at all limited above, for it extends upward behind the pharynx to the base of the skull (Fig. 175, p. 293); while this upper part is usually known as the retropharyngeal space, this terminology should not be allowed to obscure the fact that the retropharyngeal and retro-esophageal spaces are just as continuous with each other as are their anterior walls, the pharynx, and esophagus, and actually form a single retrovisceral space.

Inferiorly, the retrovisceral space usually extends, like the pretracheal, into the mediastinum. The lower level of extent varies, according to Grodinsky and Holyoke, from the sixth cervical to the fourth thoracic vertebral level, where the space is obliterated through fusion of the fascia on the posterior surface of the esophagus to the posterior layer of the deep fascia of the neck. Coller and Yglesias ('37) gave the lower level of this space as being that of the bifurcation of the trachea, thus at about the fourth vertebral level. The latter workers also described a retro-esophageal space below this level; apparently they believed it represents a lower, but separate, portion of the retrovisceral space, but it is probably the same as that described by Grodinsky and Holyoke as "the danger space," or Space 4 (p. 292).

Since the retrovisceral portion of the visceral compartment extends upward behind the pharynx to the base of the skull, it has been described as an important pathway by which infections originating from various locations in the head and the upper portion of the neck reach the mediastinum; Pearse reported that this was the route followed in 71 per cent of the cases he studied in which infection had descended from the neck into the mediastinum. The retrovisceral space may also be infected directly from posterior perforations of the esophagus, or by infections of the deep cervical nodes which lie adjacent to it. The most convenient surgical approach to the retrovisceral space, according to Iglauer, is by an incision posterior to the sternocleidomastoid, carried medially behind the carotid sheath and its great vessels.

"VISCERAL SPACE"

The esophagus is of course enclosed in a connective tissue coat, continuous above with the more obvious fascia (buccopharyngeal fascia) on the posterior surface of the pharynx, and delicate connective tissue also is adjacent to the surface of the thyroid gland and that of the trachea. This connective tissue is frequently referred to as a fascia, though it more nearly corresponds to the subperitoneal connective tissue of the serous coat of most of the digestive tract, and can hardly be said to form a definite layer over the thyroid gland or the trachea.

If it must be designated as a fascia, it should probably be called the visceral fascia, as has been done by Grodinsky and Holyoke; that part on the thyroid gland is frequently referred to as the capsule of the thyroid gland (but see p. 518), and sometimes the entire layer in the neck, whether related to trachea, thyroid gland, or esophagus, is known as the pretracheal fascia.

Thus the term "pretracheal fascia" has been applied both to the connective tissue associated most closely with the posterior surface of the strap muscles (the so-called middle layer of the deep fascia) and to all the connective tissue surrounding and immediately adjacent to the viscera; correspondingly, the previsceral or pretracheal space has sometimes been described as lying behind the pretracheal fascia, and sometimes as lying anterior or external to it.

Confusingly, also, in view of the widespread use of the term "visceral compartment" for the pretracheal and retrovisceral spaces, the potential space which may be imagined to exist between this layer of fascia and the organs themselves is also referred to as the visceral space. Actually, such connective tissue as exists here to form a visceral fascia is firmly united to the structures which it covers, and the visceral space in the latter sense does not really exist; infections lying deep to the fascia on the esophagus, for instance, do not tend to spread within this fascia up and down the esophagus, but rather perforate it to reach the visceral compartment.

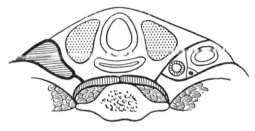

Fig. 174. The space of the carotid sheath (horizontally lined), and the "danger space" or space 4 of Grodinsky and Holyoke (vertically lined).

OTHER SPACES

In the lower part of the neck there are two other compartments which may be of clinical importance (Fig. 174). One of these is the potential *cavity within the carotid sheath*, into which, according to Coller and Yglesias ('35), infections from the visceral space readily spread; indeed, they have grouped the two under the name "visceral-vascular space." These authors have conceived of the space of the carotid sheath as being, like the retrovisceral space, a pathway for the spread

of infections from the upper to the lower part of the neck and into the mediastinum. Pearse has apparently also agreed with this, as he has attributed 21 per cent of mediastinal suppurations originating in the neck to spread along this pathway (as against 8 per cent along the pretracheal space, and 71 per cent through the retrovisceral).

In contrast to this concept, Grodinsky and Holyoke found that injections within the carotid sheath were usually closely limited to the area of injection, and never extended higher than the hyoid bone or lower than the root of the neck, since above and below these levels the sheath was too closely adherent to the vessels. They concluded that infections within it would tend to be localized within the cervical region, and that it has no important relations to either the head or the thorax. They stated that infection within the carotid sheath usually arises from thrombosis of the internal jugular vein, or from infection of the internal group of the deep cervical lymph nodes, which lie within the sheath.

The second important remaining space to be described in the lower part of the neck is that lying between the two laminae of the posterior layer of deep fascia as it passes from the transverse processes on one side to those of the other, between the viscera and the vertebral column. Its presence has apparently been ignored in many studies of the fascial spaces of the neck, yet it is easily demonstrated in most dissections.

It will be recalled (p. 287) that after the posterior layer of deep fascia attaches to the transverse processes, it divides into two layers, an anterior alar fascia which forms the posterior boundary of the retrovisceral space, and a posterior prevertebral fascia which consists of the connective tissue immediately against the anterior surfaces of the prevertebral muscles and the vertebral centra. Between these two layers lies an area of very delicate loose connective tissue, which Grodinsky and Holyoke have designated *Space 4* or the *danger space*.

It is possible that this has also been called the prevertebral space, but most descriptions of the latter space are not sufficiently clear to decide this; Grodinsky and Holyoke reserved the term "prevertebral space" for the potential cleavage plane existing between the prevertebral fascia and the vertebral centra. Whatever the space between the alar and prevertebral fasciae is called, it should be realized that it is not the same as that already designated as the retrovisceral space, and the confusion in terminology has been only more compounded by the implications of some authors that the retrovisceral and prevertebral spaces are synonymous.

As noted by Grodinsky and Holyoke,

the texture of the connective tissue within the danger space is such that it is almost an actual rather than a potential space. It has been thought to be of particular importance since it extends upward as far as the base of the skull, and is said to extend downward as far as the diaphragm. Since the space is closed above, below, and laterally, it could be infected only through its walls: Grodinsky and Holyoke concluded that infections of this should arise most commonly from infections of the retrovisceral space, for in their injections behind the prevertebral fascia they found that there was little tendency to break forward into Space 4. It is quite possibly the lower portion of this space, below the bifurcation of the trachea, which Coller and Yglesias ('37) described as a resumption of the retrovisceral space. Infections within this space (Space 4) are not limited to the superior mediastinum, according to Grodinsky and Holyoke, but may extend throughout the length of the posterior mediastinum.

THE FASCIA AND SPACES ABOVE THE HYOID BONE

ABOVE the level of the hyoid bone the fascial layers become perhaps slightly less complicated, since there is no middle layer of deep fascia here, but the fascial spaces themselves become more complicated.

FASCIA

ANTERIOR LAYER OF DEEP FASCIA

The superficial or anterior layer of the deep fascia extends from its attachment on the hyoid bone upward to the mandible (Fig. 175), and from the anterior border of the sternocleidomastoid upward to the mandible and zygomatic arch; in so doing, it passes across the superficial sur-

face of the muscles of the floor of the mouth (the mylohyoid and the anterior belly of the digastric), and thus forms the floor of a potential space lying above the fascia and below the muscles. As it attaches to the mandible it is usually described as splitting into two layers, one attaching on the inner and one on the outer surface of the mandible.

More posteriorly, at the level of the submaxillary gland, the anterior layer of the deep fascia also splits to form a capsule about this gland; still more posteriorly, about the insertions of the masseter and internal pterygoid muscles, it splits to enclose these muscles and the intervening angle and ramus of the mandible, one portion following the external surface of the masseter to the zygomatic arch and the other portion following the internal surface of the internal pterygoid to the pterygoid plate.

Finally, behind the angle of the jaw and anterior to the sternocleidomastoid this layer of fascia passes upward toward the zygomatic arch in relation to the parotid gland; Grodinsky and Holyoke have described it as splitting to form a

verse processes of the vertebrae, and across the front of the vertebrae splits into alar and prevertebral portions enclosing the danger space or Space 4.

BUCCOPHARYNGEAL FASCIA

The only other layer of fascia to be considered here is that on the pharynx itself, which is distinctly better developed than that upon the esophagus and is frequently referred to as the buccopharyn-

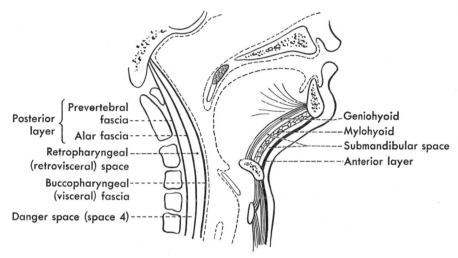

Fig. 175. Fascial layers and spaces above the hyoid bone, in a sagittal section. Note that the "danger space" and the retropharyngeal space show no interruption, but are continuous with the danger space and the retrovisceral space, respectively, below the level of the hyoid bone. (Redrawn from Grodinsky, M., and Holyoke, E. A.: *Am. J. Anat. 63*:367, 1938.)

capsule about this gland before attaching to the zygoma. The potential spaces formed by the splitting of the anterior layer of deep fascia are all closed spaces; those lying immediately deep to this fascia, however, communicate, or can be made to communicate, fairly freely with each other.

POSTERIOR LAYER OF DEEP FASCIA

The relations of the posterior layer of the deep fascia are identical to those lower in the neck—that is, it encloses the vertebral muscles, is attached to the trans-

geal fascia, since it is continuous with the fascia on the buccinator muscle; it is of course identical with the visceral fascia on the esophagus. The buccopharyngeal fascia separates the muscular wall of the pharynx from certain potential spaces which largely surround it.

SPACES

The fascial spaces above the level of the hyoid have been especially investigated by Coller and Yglesias ('35), and these relationships have been also generally agreed upon by Grodinsky and Holyoke, and by other workers who have had occasion to investigate some of them. Tschiassny ('45) has attempted to clarify the relationships of the spaces about the pharynx by pointing out that they can be regarded as consisting of posterior and lateral portions, and as arranged in three rows centering about the pharynx—an outer row, an intermediate row, and an inner row. Thought of in another way, the suprahyoid spaces consist of blind spaces formed by a splitting of the deep fascia, of intercommunicating spaces surrounding the pharynx and lying between the deep fascia and the pharyngeal wall, and of blind potential spaces within the pharyngeal wall itself, deep to the bucco-pharyngeal fascia.

Intrafascial Spaces

The "danger space" has already been described (p. 292) as being formed by a splitting of the posterior layer of deep fascia, and as extending from the base of the skull into the thorax; although its upper portion is suprahyoid, the relationships of this portion do not vary from those already described, and need not, therefore, be repeated here.

The other intrafascial spaces related to the upper part of the neck are all formed by a splitting of the anterior or superficial layer of deep fascia as it attaches to the skull: thus as this layer of fascia reaches the lower border of a limited portion of the mandible, it is said to attach to the outer and inner surfaces of this; as it reaches the insertions of the masseter and internal pterygoid muscles on the outer and inner surfaces of the mandible, respectively, it splits to follow the free surfaces of these muscles, and as it reaches the submaxillary and parotid glands it is usually described as surrounding these (p. 292).

Since the potential spaces thus formed do not communicate with each other or with other spaces, infections within them can spread only through rupture of their walls. The only one of these four spaces which contains any appreciable quantity of loose connective tissue is that associated with the muscles of mastication.

SPACE OF THE BODY OF THE MANDIBLE

The space of the body of the mandible, according to Coller and Yglesias, is formed by the attachment of the anterior layer of the deep fascia to both the outer and inner surfaces of the body of the mandible; the attachment to the outer surface is at the lower border of the mandible, but the deeper leaflet is said to be easily elevated from the mandible up to the origin of the mylohyoid muscle (Fig. 176).

As an actual space in the sense of an area of loose connective tissue, this space does not exist; rather it seems to be a potential cleavage plane between the fascia and the bone. This cleavage plane is apparently limited anteriorly by the attachment of the anterior belly of the digastric, and posteriorly by the attachment of the internal pterygoid, to the jaw; below, it is of course closed by the continuity of the fascial layers, and above it is closed by the attachment of these layers to the mandible. These attachments are said to prevent osteomyelitis from spreading either superficially or deeply; apparently an infection here may remain localized, may discharge into the mouth or may spread to the masticator space. This "space" has been drained by an incision through the buccal gingival mucous membrane, or by one externally along the inferior border of the mandible, the incision in either case being carried to the bone.

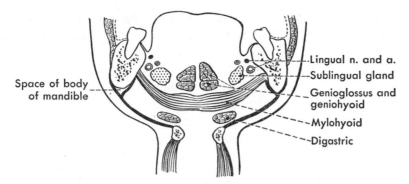

Fig. 176. Frontal section through the mandible and tongue, illustrating the attachment of the anterior layer of the deep fascia to the mandible, and some of the general anatomy here. Compare with Figures 175 and 184.

SPACE OF SUBMAXILLARY GLAND

The capsule of the submaxillary gland is usually described as enclosing a space, the submaxillary space (or, less confusingly, the space of the submaxillary gland) but again this description is apt to be misleading: the submaxillary gland does not lie loosely within its sheath, so that this latter can be opened and the gland easily shelled out; rather it and its associated lymph nodes are embedded in this fascia, and the septa of the gland are continuous with the capsule; essentially, therefore, the "submaxillary space" is the substance of the gland and nodes (Fig. 177).

The outer layer of the capsule, the continuation upward of the main portion

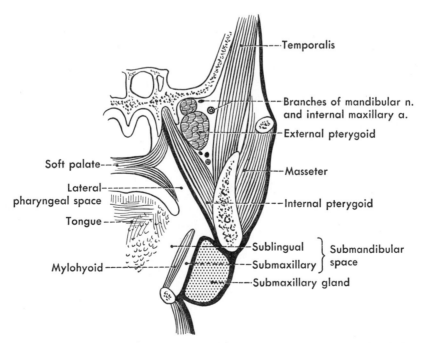

Fig. 177. Schema of half of a frontal section close to the angle of the jaw, to show the splitting of the superficial layer of the deep fascia about the submaxillary gland and the muscles of mastication.

of the anterior layer of the deep fascia, is strong, while the inner layer is thinner and is of course perforated by the duct of the gland; infections arising in the region of the gland generally break inward, therefore. The term "submaxillary space" has also been commonly used to describe the space between the superficial layer of deep fascia and the mylohyoid muscle (p. 300).

MASTICATOR SPACE

The masticator space is formed by the splitting of the anterior layer of the deep

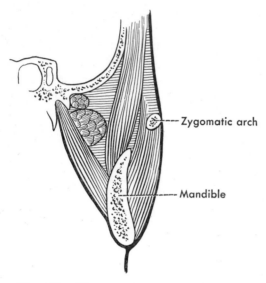

--- Zygomatic arch

--- Mandible

Fig. 178. The masticator space. Compare Figures 177 and 182.

fascia to enclose the ramus of the mandible, the masseter, the internal pterygoid and the lower portion of the temporal muscle (Fig. 178). As these structures lie between the fascial layers on the outer surface of the masseter and the inner surface of the internal pterygoid, the loose connective tissue about them forms the potential space. The internal maxillary artery, and most of the branches of the mandibular nerve, traverse it; the area of loose connective tissue lies medial

to the ramus of the mandible, between this and the internal pterygoid, and medial and anterior to the lower portion of the insertion of the temporal muscle.

The fascial walls of this space come together anterior and posterior to the borders of the ramus of the mandible, and the space is thus closed about this and its surrounding muscles except superiorly, where it extends upward both superficial and deep to the temporal muscle, and around its anterior border; its upward extent is limited deeply by the origin of the temporal muscle from the skull, but superficially it extends above the zygomatic arch, being limited here by the attachment of the thick temporal fascia.

This extension of the masticator space upward about the temporal muscle has been termed the temporal space, but can be more simply regarded as a part of the masticator space. Kostrubala similarly described several spaces about the muscles of the jaw below the level of the zygoma, but they seem to be largely, at least, also subdivisions of the masticator space.

Infections of the zygoma or of the temporal bone may pass to the masticator space, and so may also abscesses from the lower molar teeth (Coller and Yglesias); Hall and Morris reviewed 20 cases of infection of this space and found that they most commonly resulted from extraction of a lower molar tooth. Abscesses within this space may apparently point at the anterior aspect of the masseter muscle, either into the cheek or the mouth, or they may point posteriorly beneath the parotid gland.

SPACE OF PAROTID GLAND

The parotid space (Fig. 179) encloses the parotid gland and its associated lymph nodes, and the facial nerve and great

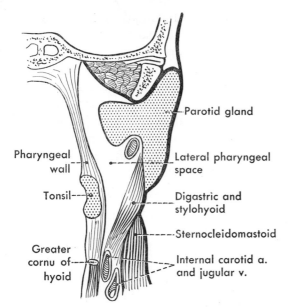

Fig. 179. Part of a diagrammatic semi-frontal section, slanted somewhat anteriorly from behind the ramus of the mandible, to show the relations of the anterior layer of the deep fascia to the parotid gland.

vessels which traverse it. Although Grodinsky and Holyoke found that injections into the parotid space broke out either superficially or deeply, and Coller and Yglesias regarded the tissue on the deep surface of the parotid gland as the stronger layer, both have pointed out that infections may readily pass deeply, and therefore into the important lateral pharyngeal space which lies deep to the parotid gland. As in the case of the submaxillary gland, the parotid gland is strongly attached to its surrounding fascia, and the parotid "space" is therefore not so much an anatomical as a clinical one; infections within it are infections of the gland or its nodes, not a cellulitis in loose connective tissue.

PERIPHARYNGEAL SPACES

These lie immediately posterior and lateral to the pharynx, and extend forward into the sublingual region, so that together they actually form a ring about the pharynx (Fig. 180). They lie entirely deep to the superficial or anterior layer of the deep fascia, and communicate more or less freely with each other around the muscles and vessels which traverse them.

Since they intervene between the interfascial spaces and the mandible, on the one hand, and the pharynx on the other, they are liable to infection from either of these sources by extension from them;

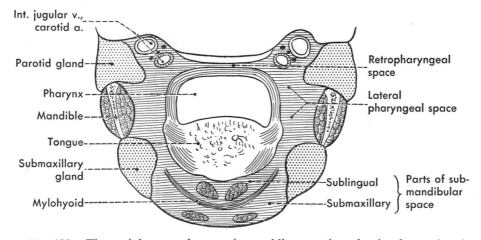

Fig. 180. The peripharyngeal spaces in an oblique section, slanting forward and downward. This illustrates the general relations of these spaces, and their continuity with each other. (Adapted from Grodinsky, M., and Holyoke, E. A.: *Am. J. Anat. 63*:367, 1938.)

moreover, it is these spaces which are most intimately related to the lymph nodes receiving the drainage from the nose, throat, and jaw, so that abscesses within them may form from breakdown of nodes secondarily infected from their regions of drainage. It is one or more of these spaces that is more commonly infected in the neck; while, as already noted, clinical opinions vary sharply as to the extent to which spread of pus or of a cellulitis occurs along fascial planes, it has been emphasized by many workers that injections of inert materials into certain of these spaces spread readily into others, and that infections may spread rapidly from one space to another.

RETROPHARYNGEAL SPACE

The central or posterior space of this group, and the key to an understanding of such downward spread of infections of the head and neck within fascial spaces as occurs, is the retropharyngeal space. This is simply the upper portion of the retrovisceral space, already described in connection with the infrahyoid spaces; it, also, is logically termed the retrovisceral space, though the term retropharyngeal is perhaps more commonly used. (Like the lower part of the retrovisceral space, this upper part has also been called the prevertebral space, a terminology which is to be deplored.)

The retropharyngeal space is the area of loose connective tissue lying behind the pharynx and in front of the posterior layer of the deep fascia, uniting the pharynx loosely to the vertebral column (Fig. 181). It extends upward between the pharynx and the vertebral column to the base of the skull; it extends downward behind the lower portion of the pharynx and the esophagus, as already described, to form the posterior portion of the

visceral compartment of the neck, communicate with the so-called pretracheal compartment, and end at about the level of the bifurcation of the trachea (p. 290). The connections of this space are therefore such that injections within it may spread into either the anterior or the posterior portions of the superior mediastinum without breaking through its walls; Grodinsky and Holyoke found that their injections sometimes broke through the

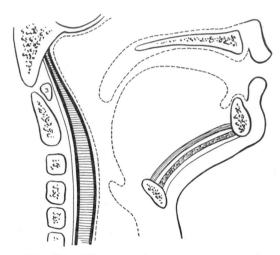

Fig. 181. The retropharyngeal or retrovisceral space in a sagittal section. Compare with Figure 175.

posterior wall of the retropharyngeal space, that is, through the alar fascia, and entered Space 4, the danger space, between the two lamellae of the posterior layer of the deep fascia; this space, as already noted, extends from the base of the skull to the level of the diaphragm.

Because of these relations, the retropharyngeal space has been commonly regarded as a route through which infections of the mouth and throat reach the mediastinum. New and Erich stated that they had not found a single case of mediastinitis secondary to cervical infection in the 267 cases that they studied. Pearse, however, although he concluded that suppurative mediastinitis is due to spread from the neck in not more than one fifth of the cases, reviewed 110 cases in which such spread was apparently the source of the mediastinitis, and stated that in by far the majority of these (71 per cent) the mediastinitis was due to spread in the retrovisceral space.

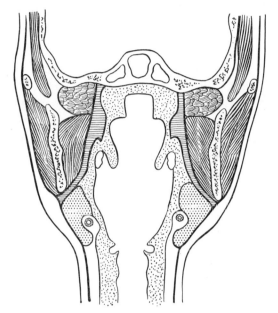

Fig. 182. The lateral pharyngeal space (horizontally lined) and its relations in frontal section. Lateral to it are the muscles of mastication and the masticator space, medially the pharyngeal wall including the tonsil, and below and medially the submaxillary gland. (Adapted by permission of *Surg. Gynec. & Obst.*, from Coller, F. A., and Yglesias, L., vol. 60, p. 277, 1935.)

LATERAL PHARYNGEAL SPACE

The retropharyngeal space extends also laterally about the pharynx, and these lateral portions, although continuous with the retropharyngeal space, are usually spoken of as the lateral pharyngeal spaces (Fig. 182). The lateral pharyngeal space has been variously termed the parapharyngeal, peripharyngeal, pharyngomaxillary, pterygopharyngeal, pterygomandibular, and

pharyngomasticatory space; it consists of the loose connective tissue on the lateral wall of the pharynx, and is bounded medially by the fascia of the pharynx itself, laterally by the pterygoid muscles and the sheath of the parotid gland.

Like the retropharyngeal portion of this visceral ring, the lateral pharyngeal space extends upward to the base of the skull, but it does not extend inferiorly below the level of the hyoid bone, as it is limited here by the sheath of the submaxillary gland and the attachments of this sheath to the sheaths of the stylohyoid muscle and the posterior belly of the digastric. This space is traversed by the styloglossus and stylopharyngeus muscles, and is by some authors (for instance, Hall) divided into a prestyloid and a poststyloid portion; both above and below these muscles it opens medially into the retropharyngeal space.

The posterior wall of the lateral pharyngeal space is formed by the carotid sheath, or at least by the connective tissue about the internal jugular and internal carotid vessels; some authors do not consider the carotid sheath to extend above the level of the hyoid bone. Anterosuperiorly the lateral pharyngeal space extends to the pterygomandibular raphe; anteriorly and inferiorly, above the submaxillary gland, it communicates with the spaces about the floor of the mouth.

Because of its relationships, the lateral pharyngeal space is more subject to infection than any of the other peripharyngeal spaces. Through its connection with the spaces about the tongue, it may receive and transmit to the retropharyngeal space infections originating here, as from the teeth; similarly, it is adjacent to the submaxillary gland and infections in this gland may spread into the space; in a like manner, both the masticator and the

Fig. 183. The submandibular space in a frontal section through the floor of the mouth. The continuity between the spaces above and below the mylohyoid muscle, and their connection with the lateral pharyngeal spaces, may be seen in Figures 177 and 180. For identification of other structures shown here, refer to Figure 176.

parotid spaces border the lateral pharyngeal space, and infections within either of these which perforate deeply instead of superficially will necessarily invade the lateral pharyngeal space. The tonsillar region of the pharynx is the medial wall of the lateral pharyngeal space, and infections originating about the tonsils may also involve this space.

The lateral pharyngeal space is thus subject to infection from several sources; among those workers who regard the fascial spaces as being of particular importance in the spread of infections, therefore, the lateral pharyngeal space is considered to be the route by which infections of diverse origins may be transmitted to the highway—the retropharyngeal space—which in turn leads to the mediastinum. Infections of the retropharyngeal, lateral pharyngeal, and sublingual spaces are most easily discussed together, therefore.

SUBMANDIBULAR SPACE

The anterior element of the peripharyngeal spaces is conveniently referred to as the submandibular space (Grodinsky and Holyoke). It actually consists of a group of spaces (Fig. 183) which, however, either communicate with each other or can be made to do so with relatively little pressure upon injection. The submandibular space as a whole is limited above by the mucous membrane of the tongue, while its floor is the anterior or superficial layer of deep fascia as it extends from the hyoid bone to the mandible. Its inferior extent is the attachment of the fascia to the hyoid.

Some of the subdivisions of the submandibular space are fairly obvious: the mylohyoid muscle, stretching across the floor of the mouth, divides the submandibular space into a portion above this muscle and a portion below; about the submaxillary gland, which lies partly above and partly below the posterior portion of the mylohyoid, these two subdivisions communicate with each other, however (Fig. 184).

The space beneath the mylohyoid muscle, often termed the *submaxillary space,* is sometimes said to be subdivided into subsidiary submental and submaxillary spaces by attachment of the deep fascia to the anterior belly of the digastric muscle; the submental space, corresponding to the triangle of the same

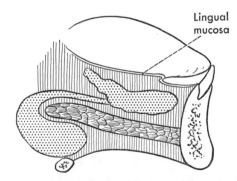

Lingual mucosa

Fig. 184. Continuity of the sublingual and submaxillary parts of the submandibular space around the posterior border of the mylohyoid muscle, and adjacent to the submaxillary gland, as it might be seen from the lateral aspect after removing the body of the mandible.

name, lies medial to the anterior belly of the digastric, the submaxillary space lateral and posterior to it, but Grodinsky and Holyoke found that injections spread readily beneath the anterior belly of the digastric from one space to the other. These spaces consist only of an easy line of cleavage between the fascia and the muscles, unless they are abnormally distended.

The spaces above the mylohyoid muscle can be collectively termed the *sublingual space,* and consist of the loose connective tissue lying between the muscles of the tongue and about the sublingual gland, the lingual and hypoglossal nerves and a portion of the submaxillary gland and its duct. The sublingual space is largely paired according to Williams but spaces of the two sides communicate anteriorly. The sublingual space has in turn been subdivided (for example, Coller and Yglesias, '35) into as many as three compartments, based upon their relationships to the genioglossus and geniohyoid muscles, but this subdivision seems needlessly complex.

INFECTIONS OF THE PERIPHARYNGEAL SPACES

Grodinsky ('39a) described infection of the peripharyngeal spaces as occurring more commonly in children less than 3 years of age, and it is frequently stated that such infections are relatively rare in adults. Beck ('42, '47) reported, however, that among 100 cases which he studied only 11 occurred in the age group 1 month to 2 years, 45 occurred in the age group 2 to 12 years inclusive, 12 in the age group 13 to 20 years inclusive, and 32 in the age group 21 to 81 years inclusive; in Boemer's series of 75 cases 26 were in adults; in Smith's series, there

were more cases of retropharyngeal abscesses in adults than in children.

Grodinsky regarded the majority of the acute abscesses of the retropharyngeal and lateral pharyngeal spaces as resulting from infections of the nose, throat, and middle ear, and stated that infection through lymphatic drainage (to the pharyngeal nodes in these spaces) is the most common method of involvement, where trauma is not involved. Faier also stressed the relation of infection of the retropharyngeal and deep cervical nodes to involvement of these spaces and Boemer reported such infection to be involved in all 49 of the children in his series. Beck found that about 50 per cent of the infections involving fascial spaces in the neck arose from infections of the pharynx and tonsils; Lake also has stressed the relationship of infections of those spaces to infections of the tonsils. About 20 per cent of the deep infections of the neck in Beck's series, and about one third of the adult cases in Boemer's series, arose from infections of dental origin. Faier expressed the belief that infections of the ear are not a common cause of retropharyngeal abscess, but that infections of this origin, which may reach the space not only along lymphatics but also by following canals in the bone which transmit vessels and nerves, are frequently severe; Beck has pointed out that infections within the petrous portion of the temporal bone may rupture directly into the lateral pharyngeal space, and infection at the tip of the mastoid process may follow the digastric groove and extend along the styloid and digastric muscles to this space; in 2 of the adult cases from Boemer's series infection of the peripharyngeal spaces resulted from mastoid infections.

Beck described the lateral pharyngeal

space as the one more frequently involved in deep infections of the neck, but not infrequently more than one space was involved simultaneously. In 12 cases of infection of the lateral pharyngeal space, for instance, the submaxillary region was also infected, and in 8 cases of lateral pharyngeal infection the carotid sheath was also infected.

Lifschutz has reported a case of fatal hemorrhage resulting from extension of a retropharyngeal abscess to the deep vessels of the neck; while this is comparatively rare, he found that it has been reported in the majority of cases as arising from the internal carotid artery rather than from the jugular vein; he concluded that the vein is more often occluded by the infectious process than it is eroded to the point of hemorrhage. Havens has emphasized that a sudden enlargement of a retropharyngeal mass may indicate erosion of a large vessel, and that in such a case aspiration of the mass before its incision is wise; if forewarned by the presence of blood, ligation of the carotid may prevent fatal hemorrhage. Barlow expressed the belief that thrombosis of the jugular vein from a deep infection of the neck is probably not due to direct infection of the carotid sheath, but rather to the fact that infectious material follows tributaries of the internal jugular vein to reach the sheath.

SURGICAL DRAINAGE

Opinions differ sharply as to the advisability and necessity of surgical drainage of fascial spaces (p. 283). However, the lateral pharyngeal space and the retropharyngeal one may be approached through the mouth and opened by appropriate incisions through the pharyngeal wall; Iglauer concluded that this approach to the retropharyngeal space is usually preferable except for large abscesses,

cellulitis, and infections due to caries of the spinal column. Boemer stated that external drainage of the lateral pharyngeal space should be carried out in practically all cases. External drainage of the lateral pharyngeal space can be obtained by making an incision immediately behind the submaxillary gland and passing upward along the medial or deep surface of the internal pterygoid muscle, into the lateral pharyngeal space; if desired, the stylohyoid and posterior belly of the digastric can be reflected to give entrance to this space. The retropharyngeal space may be drained externally by an incision behind the sternocleidomastoid muscle, carried medially behind the great vessels of the neck.

The sublingual space may be drained through the mucosa of the mouth, or, as described by Williams, the entire submandibular space may be opened by an incision extending parallel to the medial border of the mandible and carried through the suprahyoid fascia and the mylohyoid and digastric muscles. If this opening is to be carried posteriorly, the facial artery and vein must be ligated and the submaxillary gland may be removed. Tschiassny ('47) has suggested a different approach: he has used a transverse incision medial to the angle of the mandible to approach the submaxillary gland; after cutting the suprahyoid fascia he ligated the submental branch of the facial artery, freed the submaxillary gland and retracted it laterally; he then divided the mylohyoid muscle, sectioning its fibers at right angles, but did not extend the incision forward to involve the digastric or the geniohyoid muscles.

LUDWIG'S ANGINA

Ludwig's angina is the term given to the symptoms resulting from infection of the submandibular space, and is characterized especially, therefore, by extreme hardness of the floor of the mouth. The infection here may eventually extend to the lateral pharyngeal space also, and thence may enter the retropharyngeal space and even descend to the mediastinum. Beck estimated that in about 20 per cent of the cases in his series deep infection of the neck originated from the submandibular space, and Boemer expressed the belief that in about a third of the adult cases in his series the infection had this origin. Trout ('40a) has pointed out that the original criteria of Ludwig's angina are sufficiently indefinite to explain the various reports on the mortality, which has been said to be as high as 75 per cent or as low as 5 per cent; he found that the mortality rates reported at that time (before the use of the antibiotics) ranged usually from about 30 to 75 per cent.

As pointed out by Grodinsky ('39b) death from Ludwig's angina occurs as a result of suffocation due to edema of the mouth, tongue, and the glottis, or from mediastinitis due to spread, or from septicemia or pneumonia. Grodinsky noted that infections starting from the nose and throat may spread from the retropharyngeal and lateral pharyngeal spaces into the submandibular, and resemble Ludwig's angina in their later stages, but stated that such secondary extension is not characterized by the boardlike swelling of the neck centering about the floor of the mouth and by the ensuing elevation of the mucosa of the mouth and tongue, and should not be classified as true Ludwig's angina.

Trout ('40a) has stated that extraction of a lower molar tooth precedes Ludwig's angina in about 82 per cent of cases. He has also ('40b) agreed with most workers that the mylohyoid muscle tends to confine infections from these teeth to the deep tissues under the tongue, and has advocated cutting the deep fascia and the mylohyoid and digastric muscles to obtain adequate drainage; Taffel and Harvey have also emphasized that this is the only way in which pressure can be relieved, and have stated that the mylohyoid must be completely divided, as must the anterior belly of the digastric, regardless of whether pus or edema seems to be present or not; they then cut the geniohyoid if the infection seems to lie above this. Houser stated that Ludwig's angina always starts with involvement of the sublingual space, that is, always lies at first above the mylohyoid muscle, and suggested therefore that the logical method of evacuating pus is through an intra-oral incision; when this is done as a result of early diagnosis he concluded that involvement of the neck may be avoided.

The accepted fact that in the majority of cases Ludwig's angina originates from infections about the lower molar teeth is usually explained as a consequence of the eccentric setting of these teeth, so that their roots are closer to the inner than the outer side of the jaw. While the anterior teeth are also usually set eccentrically, they are nearer to the outer than the inner surface of the jaw and therefore infections about their roots, if they erode the thinner area of bone, would tend to break outward rather than inward.

Tschiassny ('43) stated, however, that it is not necessarily true that the medial border of the alveolar socket of the molar teeth is thinner than is the outer border, and found some jaws in which the reverse was true; he concluded that the decisive factor is rather the depth to which the roots penetrate, for he regarded Ludwig's angina as regularly starting below the mylohyoid muscle. According to his investigations, the roots of the second and third molar teeth almost always reach downward at least as far as the level of the attachment of the mylohyoid muscle, and usually below it, while most of those of the first molar teeth, and usually all of those anterior to this, are located above this ridge. He found it probable, therefore, that an infected second or third molar tooth might produce infection in the submaxillary space, which he would regard as true Ludwig's angina, while infections of the first molar or of a premolar would produce infections first in the sub-

exists within this fascia, between it and the muscular wall of the pharynx. Infections here, like those within the visceral fascia lower in the neck, tend either to remain localized or to break through into the lateral pharyngeal and retropharyngeal spaces.

PARATONSILLAR SPACE

Of more importance as a space is the peritonsillar or paratonsillar space, the area of loose connective tissue lying in the tonsillar bed, and uniting the capsule

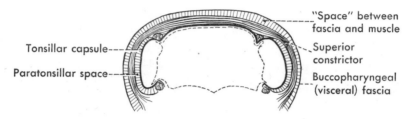

Fig. 185.   Potential intrapharyngeal spaces, in a section at the level of the tonsil.

INTRAPHARYNGEAL SPACES

As the pharynx is covered by a relatively dense pharyngeal or buccopharyngeal fascia, a potential space theoretically

lingual space, which he apparently would not classify as Ludwig's angina. Upon reviewing the literature he concluded that the back molars are almost exclusively responsible for the genesis of Ludwig's angina, as he has defined it. In a later ('47) article, however, he also has emphasized the importance of cutting the mylohyoid muscle for the relief of tension in Ludwig's angina; whether the infection starts above or below this muscle seems to be of little moment, therefore. Most workers have emphasized the involvement of the sublingual space.

of the tonsil loosely to the underlying pharyngeal muscles (Fig. 185). Infections here (quinsy) produce bulging of the tissue about the pillars of the tonsil, and can most easily be drained by incisions through the mucosa under which they point; often the opening is made through the supratonsillar fossa. According to Wood ('34) injections into the paratonsillar spaces tend to spread longitudinally but not transversely; in his study they extended as high as the hard palate or the pharyngeal orifice of the Eustachian tube, and some extended downward as far as the piriform sinus. Abscesses in the paratonsillar space may drain internally spontaneously; if they break laterally, they open into the lateral pharyngeal space.

REFERENCES

BARLOW, D. The surgical anatomy of the neck in relation to septic lesions: An investigation of the cervical connective tissue. *J. Anat. 70:*548, 1936.

BECK, A. L. Deep neck infection. *Ann. Otol., Rhin. & Laryng. 51:*592, 1942.

BECK, A. L. Deep neck infection. *Ann. Otol., Rhin. & Laryng. 56:*439, 1947.

BOEMER, L. C. The great vessels in deep infection of the neck. *Arch. Otolaryng. 25:* 465, 1937.

COLLER, F. A., and YGLESIAS, L. Infections of the lip and face. *Surg., Gynec. & Obst. 60:*277, 1935.

COLLER, F. A., and YGLESIAS, L. The relation of the spread of infection to fascial planes in the neck and thorax. *Surgery 1:*323, 1937.

FAIER, S. Z. Retropharyngeal abscess of otitic origin: Anatomy and pathogenesis with report of cases. *Ann. Otol., Rhin. & Laryng. 42:*408, 1933.

GRODINSKY, M. Retropharyngeal and lateral pharyngeal abscesses: An anatomic and clinical study. *Ann. Surg 110:*177, 1939a.

GRODINSKY, M. Ludwig's angina: An anatomical and clinical study with review of the literature. *Surgery 5:*678, 1939b.

GRODINSKY, M., and HOLYOKE, E. A. The fasciae and fascial spaces of the head, neck and adjacent regions. *Am. J. Anat. 63:*367, 1938.

HALL, C. The parapharyngeal space: An anatomical and clinical study. *Ann. Otol., Rhin. & Laryng. 43:*793, 1934.

HALL, C., and MORRIS, F. Infections of the masticator space. *Ann. Otol., Rhin. & Laryng. 50:*1123, 1941.

HAVENS, F. Z. Severe hemorrhage secondary to retropharyngeal abscess. *Am. J. Dis. Child. 58:*1256, 1939.

HOUSER, K. M. Ludwig's angina: Intra-oral incision in infections of the floor of the mouth. *Arch. Otolaryng. 16:*317, 1932.

HUNT, W. M. Periesophageal abscesses: The importance of early surgical interference. *Ann. Otol., Rhin. & Laryng. 48:*128, 1939.

IGLAUER, S. Surgical approaches to deep suppuration in the neck and posterior mediastinum. *Arch. Otolaryng. 21:*707, 1935.

KOSTRUBALA, J. G. Potential anatomical spaces in the face. *Am. J. Surg. n.s.68:*28, 1945.

LAKE, C. F. Infection of the neck after tonsillectomy. *Minnesota Med. 30:*851, 1947.

LIFSCHUTZ, J. Fatal hemorrhage resulting from the extension of a retropharyngeal abscess to the deep vessels of the neck. *Arch. Otolaryng. 14:*149, 1931.

NEW, G. B., and ERICH, J. B. Deep infections of the neck: Collective review. *Internat. Abstr. Surg. (Surg., Gynec. & Obst.). 68:*555, 1939.

PARSONS, F. G. On the carotid sheath and other fascial planes. *J. Anat. & Physiol. 44:*153, 1910.

PEARSE, H. E., JR. Mediastinitis following cervical suppuration. *Ann. Surg. 108:*588, 1938.

SMITH, J. E. Retropharyngeal abscess with reference to abnormally large percentage of adult cases. *Ann. Otol., Rhin. & Laryng. 49:*490, 1940.

TAFFEL, M., and HARVEY, S. C. Ludwig's angina: An analysis of forty-five cases. *Surgery 11:*841, 1942.

TROUT, H. H. Ludwig's angina. *Arch. Surg. 41:*532, 1940a.

TROUT, H. H. Von Ludwig's angina. *Surgery 8:*1024, 1940b.

TSCHIASSNY, K. Ludwig's angina: An anatomic study of the role of the lower molar teeth in its pathogenesis. *Arch. Otolaryng. 38:*485, 1943.

TSCHIASSNY, K. The "juxtapharyngeal" spaces as carriers and barriers of suppurations: A new anatomical classification. *Cincinnati J. Med. 26:*337, 1945.

TSCHIASSNY, K. Ludwig's angina: A surgical approach based on anatomical and pathological criteria. *Ann. Otol., Rhin. & Laryng. 56:*937, 1947.

WILLIAMS, A. C. Ludwig's angina. *Surg., Gynec. & Obst. 70:*140, 1940.

WOOD, G. B. The peritonsillar spaces: An anatomic study. *Arch. Otolaryng. 20:*837, 1934.

{CHAPTER 6}

The Face

THE subcutaneous connective tissue or "superficial fascia" of the face, as noted in the preceding chapter, closely invests the numerous facial muscles but is so bound down around them that, from the point of view of the spread of infections, fascial spaces in the face can generally be disregarded. The exception to this is in the lids, where loose connective tissue exists both superficial and deep to the palpebral portion of the orbicularis oculi muscle; the spaces here are discussed on page 100. Deep to and between the facial muscles, also enclosed in the connective tissue, are the nerves and blood vessels of the face. Except for the few deeper-lying facial muscles, the nerves to the muscles enter their deep surfaces, and typically do so close to the posterior border of the muscle.

FACIAL PARALYSIS

Facial paralysis is a particularly disfiguring condition, as it leads not only to inactivity of one side of the face or a portion of this during the active movements of smiling, frowning, and the like, but also to an obliteration of the facial furrows which even in repose are so im-

portant in facial expression. Ultimately there is also distortion of the face from the pull of unopposed muscles. In cases of injury to the facial nerve as a whole the most satisfactory procedure, when possible, is undoubtedly re-anastomosis of the facial stem, since this may restore both voluntary and emotional responses of the face. A procedure of secondary choice is a spinofacial or a hypoglossofacial anastomosis, which if successful restores voluntary movements of the face even though involuntary emotional responses are lacking. These procedures are discussed further in the section on the facial nerve (p. 327). In some cases, however, as discussed by Owens ('51), they are not possible and a plastic operation, using either fascial or muscle slips, must be used if the condition is to be improved. It may also be necessary to remove excess sag in the skin.

Lodge described a technic in which he used a single strip of fascia passing from the temporal region across beneath the eye to the bridge of the nose, downward to the corner of the mouth and upward again to the temporal region. Adams regarded muscle transplantation as much superior to the use of fascial strips or other nonactive means of suspension; he has transplanted anterior fibers of the masseter muscle into both lips, fibers of the temporal muscle into the eyelids, and used a part of the frontalis of one side to improve the forehead on the other. He stated that two to three months is required for the transplants to function properly, but that function improves as the patient re-educates the muscles. The improvement may continue for a period of a year or more.

Owens ('50) has used both muscle transplants and fascial implants inserted through the muscles. He agreed that muscle transplants give superior results, and presented clinical observations which suggest that the paralyzed facial muscles may become re-innervated by nerve fibers entering them from the innervated transplants.

THE FACIAL MUSCLES

THE facial or mimetic muscles may be conveniently divided into five chief groups, concerned especially with the mouth, the nose, the orbit, the ear, and the scalp, respectively; in addition, the platysma muscle in the neck belongs to the facial group. The muscles are characterized by the fact that their chief action is upon skin, into which for the most part they insert. All of them are innervated by the facial nerve, and are therefore facial in innervation as well as position; in addition to these muscles the facial nerve supplies only three more deeply lying ones: the stylohyoid, the posterior belly of the digastric (extending from the otic region to the hyoid bone), and the tiny stapedius muscle in the middle ear.

The muscles of the face vary considerably in their development and in the degree to which they interlace, and have been subdivided and named in several different ways. In the present account the B.N.A. terminology is used; the B.R. differs considerably from this.

PLATYSMA

The bulk of the platysma muscle lies in the superficial fascia of the neck, but its origin extends downward across the clavicle to the upper portion of the thorax, and its insertion similarly extends upward over the border of the jaw, superficial to the facial vessels, toward the lateral angle of the mouth; here it is more or less blended with some of the muscles connected with the lower lip, especially the triangularis. Over the two platysma muscles just beneath the chin there may be superficially placed transverse muscle bundles to form a transversus menti muscle. The platysma is innervated by the cervical branch of the facial nerve, the lowest and probably also the least important branch of the facial.

ORAL MUSCLES

The muscles most directly concerned with movements of the lips and cheek include a lower group, an upper group, the orbicularis oris encircling the mouth, and, laterally, the buccinator (Fig. 186).

Lower Group

The muscles of the lower group consist of the triangularis, the quadratus labii inferioris, and the mentalis.

TRIANGULARIS

The triangularis muscle, usually well developed, arises from the side of the body of the mandible below the canine, bicuspid, and first molar teeth; its fibers converge to the corner of the mouth, where they are partly inserted into the skin and partly become continuous with the upper part of the orbicularis oris.

The posterior border of this muscle may be somewhat blended with the upper fibers of the platysma, which also converge toward the corner of the mouth. The transversus menti is sometimes regarded as an aberrant portion of the triangularis.

muscle placed deep to the quadratus labii inferioris; the two muscles converge toward their insertions.

INNERVATION AND ACTION

These three muscles of the lower group are innervated by the marginal mandibular branch of the facial, and perhaps also from lower buccal branches. The triangularis depresses the corner of the mouth, the quadratus labii inferioris depresses the lower lip; the mentalis draws the skin of the lip upward, and thus aids

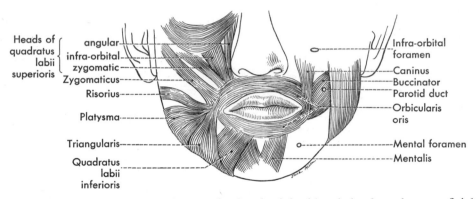

Fig. 186. Muscles about the mouth. On the left side of the face the superficial muscles are removed, and the lower part of the masseter is shown.

QUADRATUS LABII INFERIORIS

The quadratus labii inferioris arises from the front of the mandible, in part under cover of anterior fibers of the triangularis; it passes upward in front of the mental foramen, the fiber bundles running somewhat medially so as to converge with the muscle of the other side, to pass among the fiber bundles of the lower portion of the orbicularis oris and insert into skin and mucosa of the lower lip.

MENTALIS

The mentalis, the deeper-lying muscle of this group, arises from the mandible at the level of the root of the lower lateral incisor; in contrast to the preceding muscles it passes downward, to insert into the skin of the chin. It is a short, stout

in forcing the lower lip against the gum, and in protracting it. Damage to the branch of the facial nerve supplying these muscles can easily be inflicted during a block dissection of the neck for carcinomatous nodes, and, as is obvious from the actions of these muscles, such damage would upset the activity and symmetry of the mouth.

UPPER GROUP

The upper group of labial muscles consists of the risorius, the zygomaticus, the quadratus labii superioris, and the caninus.

RISORIUS

The risorius is a thin, usually poorly developed muscle which differs from most of the facial muscles in that it does not arise from bone, but in the subcutaneous tissue over the external surface of the parotid gland. It is a bandlike or slightly triangular muscle lying at about the upper border of the facial portion of the platysma, partly overlapping this superficially and often separable from it with difficulty. From its origin the risorius runs forward and slightly downward, across the masseter muscle to the lateral corner of the mouth where it inserts into skin and mucosa. Like the facial portion of the platysma, this muscle crosses superficial to the anterior facial vein and the external maxillary or facial artery.

ZYGOMATICUS

The zygomaticus arises from the posterior portion of the lateral surface of the zygomatic bone beneath the orbicularis oculi, and passes obliquely downward and forward to the corner of the mouth where it attaches to skin and mucosa. It is a superficially located, ribbon-like muscle, which passes superficial to the masseter and buccinator muscles, and to the anterior facial vein and facial artery.

QUADRATUS LABII SUPERIORIS

The quadratus labii superioris, better developed than the preceding muscles, arises by three heads, a zygomatic, an infra-orbital, and an angular one.

The *zygomatic head* arises from the zygomatic bone beneath the orbicularis oculi, anterior to the origin of the zygomaticus muscle, and runs toward the mouth parallel to this latter muscle, lying anterior to and above it. It inserts into the upper lip just medial to the corner of the mouth.

The *infra-orbital head*, broader than the zygomatic, arises from the infra-orbital margin of the maxilla, likewise under cover of the orbicularis oculi. It

extends downward and somewhat medially to mingle with the orbicularis oris and insert into much of the skin of the lateral half of the upper lip.

The *angular head* of the quadratus labii superioris arises alongside the margin of the nose; a small slip, sometimes known as the levator nasi, inserts into the skin and the alar cartilage of the nose, but the major portion passes obliquely downward to the skin and musculature of the upper lip, overlapping somewhat the infra-orbital head as it nears the lip. These three heads are sometimes described as separate muscles; they vary in their development, and the zygomatic head especially may be absent.

CANINUS

The fourth muscle of this group, the caninus, lies more deeply than do the others, and is covered by the quadratus labii superioris. It arises from the canine fossa of the maxilla and runs downward to the corner of the mouth to attach to the skin, sending also fasciculi around the corner of the mouth to blend with the lower part of the orbicularis oris. The facial artery runs across the lower part of the caninus, and the branches of the infra-orbital nerve and vessels spread out in the connective tissue between it and the overlying quadratus.

INNERVATION AND ACTION

The risorius is innervated through the buccal division of the facial nerve, the remaining, higher placed, muscles primarily through the zygomatic division. The risorius and the zygomaticus both draw the corner of the mouth laterally and upward, but the risorius contributes relatively little to the upward movement; the three heads of the quadratus act together in raising the upper lip, while a portion of the angular head widens the aperture of the external naris; the caninus raises the angle of the mouth.

ORBICULARIS ORIS

Under the term orbicularis oris are usually grouped a number of muscle bundles arranged in diverse directions; the major portion of the muscle, or the orbicularis oris proper, consists of fibers arranged in a sphincteric fashion about the mouth. To what extent true sphincteric fibers actually exist is not known; at least some of the fibers as they reach the corner of the mouth simply cross those of the other lip to insert into mucosa and skin, some are prolonged into the lips from the laterally placed buccinator muscles, and some of the fibers of the upper lip seem to be a direct continuation of the triangularis muscle, while some of those of the lower lip seem to be correspondingly a continuation of the caninus. Lee, for instance, investigated the orbicularis muscle in a case of double harelip, and found it well developed at the corner of the mouth; serial sections revealed, however, only a relatively few sphincteric muscle fibers here.

In addition to the sphincteric or pseudosphincteric fibers which encircle the mouth (some of them, in the midline of both upper and lower lips, inserting here also into the skin) the orbicularis oris contains the insertions of many of the muscles already described as reaching the upper and lower lips. For practical purposes, the latter muscles may be regarded as blending with the orbicularis, although most of them, as already noted, are usually described as inserting at least in part into skin and mucosa of the lip.

Finally, there are a few fibers in both upper and lower lips that are said to arise from the bony jaws at the levels of the canine teeth and pass laterally to insert into the corners of the mouth, and there are other, deep, fibers, said to be best developed in infants, which pass at right angles to most of the fibers, from the skin to the mucosa of the lip. Through the action of the whole and of the various parts, the orbicularis oris draws the lips together, draws inward the corners of the lips, and either protrudes them or draws them against the teeth. It is innervated by the buccal portion of the facial nerve.

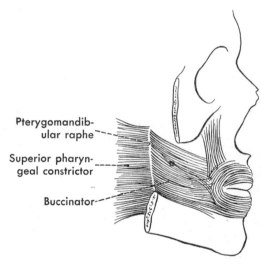

Fig. 187. The buccinator muscle. Note its continuity with fibers of the orbicularis oris, and its union posteriorly, at the pterygomandibular raphe, with the superior constrictor.

BUCCINATOR

The buccinator muscle (Fig. 187), forming the muscular substance of the cheek, arises from the posterior portion of the alveolar process of the maxilla; from the upper medial surface of the mandible at the junction of body and ramus, just posteromedial to the last molar tooth; and from the pterygomandibular raphe (pterygomandibular ligament) which stretches from the medial pterygoid process to the inner surface of the mandible, and which represents the line of junction between the buccinator muscle and the superior constrictor of the pharynx. The fibers pass forward to become apparently continuous with fibers of the orbicularis oris both of the upper and lower lips, and to pass through this to attach to the mucosa of the lips and to a lesser extent into the skin.

The muscle is crossed superficially by the facial artery and the anterior facial vein. The buccal (buccinator) artery and the similarly named branch of the mandibular nerve emerge through the buccal fat pad, between the buccinator and the insertion of the temporal muscle. The parotid duct passes forward upon the muscle and pierces it to enter the mouth, and the transverse facial artery roughly parallels the duct, lying usually above it. The buccinator muscle is innervated through the buccal branch of the facial nerve (not through the buccinator branch of the mandibular, which also lies on its outer surface and sends twigs through it to the buccal mucosa); it flattens the cheek against the teeth, thus keeping food from passing between teeth and cheek, and prevents the cheek from being distended unduly by air pressure, as when wind instruments are blown.

THE NASAL GROUP

The muscles connected with the external nares vary considerably in their developmnt, and have been variously described. Essentially, however, they consist of dilators and compressors of the nasal aperture (Fig. 188).

NASALIS

The best developed of these muscles is the nasalis, the chief part of which (compressor naris) is sometimes described as arising from the maxilla and inserting with the muscle from the opposite side on an aponeurosis across the dorsum of the nose, and is sometimes said to arise from the aponeurosis mentioned above and to insert into skin in the nasolabial sulcus. A few fibers are said also to insert into the great alar cartilage; these have been variously regarded as dilators or compressors of the nasal aperture, and have also been said to be a part of the depressor septi nasi.

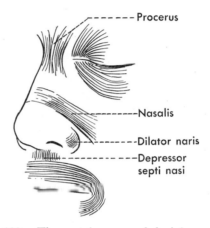

Fig. 188. The nasal group of facial muscles.

DEPRESSOR SEPTI NASI

The depressor septi nasi arises from the incisive fossa of the maxilla, and its fibers extend upward to be inserted both into the septum and the posterior part of the ala of the nose. At its origin it lies beneath the orbicularis oris.

DILATOR MUSCLES

Two small dilator muscles of the nose, an anterior and a posterior, are usually also described, although they are difficult to demonstrate as they consist of very delicate muscle bundles. The posterior dilator arises from the lesser alar cartilages, the anterior from the greater alar cartilage; both pass downward, the anterior in front of the posterior, close to the border of the nasal aperture to insert into skin near the margin.

In addition to the muscles just described, the *procerus* lies partly upon the dorsum of the nose; it is therefore sometimes described as a nasal muscle, but as its action is on the skin over the glabella it is here described as one of the muscles about the orbit.

INNERVATION AND ACTION

The muscles of the nose are supplied from the infra-orbital and buccal branches of the facial nerve. The nasalis and depressor septi narrow the external naris; the dilator muscles, aided by fibers of the angular head of the quadratus labii superioris, dilate it.

run superiorly and inferiorly about the orbit, so that they form a fairly broad ring extending beyond the orbital rim, which covers the origins of some of the other muscles in this neighborhood, and may contribute to them (Winckler). Apparently some of the fibers are truly circular ones.

The *palpebral portion* of the orbicularis oculi is described in detail in connection with the orbit (p. 95); it need only be stated here that it arises in part from the medial palpebral ligament and in part from the posterior lacrimal crest (therefore both in front of and behind the lacrimal sac) and that the fibers of the two lids interdigitate at the lateral palpebral raphe. The medial palpebral arteries,

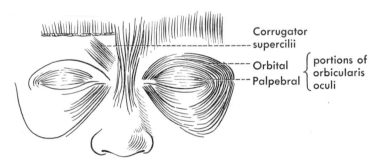

Fig. 189.   The facial muscles about the orbit.

THE ORBITAL GROUP

ORBICULARIS OCULI

The chief muscle about the orbit is the orbicularis oculi. This lies upon the bone surrounding the orbit, and extends also into the lids; it is therefore divided into two major portions, an orbital and a palpebral one (Fig. 189).

The *orbital portion* arises from the more medial part of the medial palpebral ligament, from the nasal portion of the frontal bone and from the medial portion of the inferior rim of the orbit; from this origin the fiber bundles spread out as they

the larger arteries of the lids, lie deep to this portion at the medial corner of the eye, and so also do the upper ends of the facial vessels.

The palpebral portion of the muscle is separated from the skin and from the deeper tissues by loose connective tissue, but the orbital portion is embedded in dense connective tissue; hence accumulations of fluid in the eyelids do not tend to spread much beyond the orbital rim.

PROCERUS

The procerus lies superficial to the nasal bone, and arises from this and the upper part of the lateral (upper lateral) cartilage of the nose; it attaches into the skin at the root of the nose.

CORRUGATOR SUPERCILII

The corrugator supercilii is a small, deeply situated muscle arising from the frontal bone above the rim of the orbit close to the nasofrontal suture, and extending laterally and upward to insert into the skin of the medial half of the eyebrow. It lies directly against the bone, and is covered by the orbicularis oculi, the procerus and the frontalis. The supraorbital vessels and nerves pass deep to it as they turn upward across the orbital rim into the forehead.

INNERVATION AND ACTION

These muscles are supplied by the infra-orbital and temporal branches of the facial nerve. The orbicularis closes the eyelids, the palpebral portion alone being able to do this, or in forced closure the entire muscle may contract. Contraction of the orbital portion draws the skin of the forehead and the eyelids downward, and the skin of the cheek upward, thus tending to shade the eyes. The procerus draws the skin of the forehead downward, producing transverse wrinkles at the root of the nose; the corrugator supercilii draws the eyebrows medially, producing vertical wrinkles in the forehead above the root of the nose.

According to Ehni and Woltman, it is in the orbicularis oculi that *hemifacial spasm* usually begins; it may slowly spread to adjacent muscles or to the entire side of the face. Women are said to be more often afflicted than men, in the proportion of about six to four, and children do not show it. Since the precipitating lesion is probably in the facial nucleus or the proximal portion of the nerve, they

advocated spinofacial anastomosis as probably the best remedy; more recently, Woltman, Williams and Lambert have described 2 cases in which decompression of the nerve within the facial canal relieved the spasm.

MUSCLES OF THE EAR AND SCALP

EXTRINSIC MUSCLES OF EAR

The extrinsic muscles of the ear, that is, the muscles arising from the head and inserting into the ear, are three in number, an anterior, a superior, and a posterior (Fig. 190).

The *anterior auricular muscle* is a small triangular one which arises from the galea aponeurotica to extend downward and slightly backward and insert into the helix. The *superior auricular muscle,* lying just behind the anterior, is also triangular; it arises from the galea aponeurotica and descends to insert upon the auricle. The *posterior auricular muscle* arises from the base of the mastoid process and extends over the insertion of the sternocleidomastoid muscle to reach and insert upon the convexity of the concha.

The anterior auricular muscle is supplied by the temporal branch of the facial, the posterior by the posterior auricular branch, while the superior is supplied by both branches. The anterior muscle draws the ear forward and upward, the superior elevates it, and the posterior retracts and elevates, but the muscles are usually not subject to voluntary control in man. The muscles vary considerably in development, the most constant being the superior.

MUSCLES OF SCALP

The two pairs of muscles connected with the scalp are the occipitalis and the frontalis muscles, sometimes grouped together as the epicranius. The *frontalis* is a thin muscle covering with its mate the larger portion of the forehead; it has no attachments to bone. Below, its fibers originate intermingled with the upper fibers of the procerus and with the fibers of the corrugator supercilii and orbicularis oculi; the muscle passes upward to end in the tendinous galea aponeurotica.

The *occipitalis* muscles, smaller than the frontales, arise from the mastoid portion of the temporal bone and from the

galea. Since the latter is firmly attached to the skin of the scalp by dense connective tissue, but is loosely attached to the periosteum of the bone, contraction of the occipitalis and frontalis muscles moves the scalp. Beneath the galea is the danger space of the scalp, an area of loose connective tissue in which fluid can accumulate and spread. Most of the nerves and vessels enter the scalp superficial to the galea; those leaving the orbit to run to the forehead lie at first, however, deep to

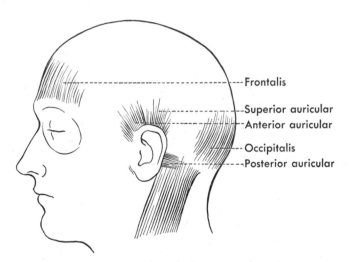

Fig. 190.   Muscles of the ear and scalp.

superior nuchal line on the occipital bone; unlike the frontales, these muscles are usually separated by a considerable space which is occupied by the galea aponeurotica. The fibers of the occipitales, like those of the frontales, end in the

the frontalis muscle, which they subsequently pierce to lie in the dense connective tissue between the skin and galea. The frontalis is supplied by the temporal branch of the facial nerve, the occipitalis by the posterior auricular.

VESSELS

ARTERIES

FACIAL ARTERY

The facial or external maxillary artery, after its origin from the external carotid, has at first a cervical course during which it is carried upward medial to the man-

dible and in fairly close contact with the pharynx; in this course it runs upward deep to the digastric (posterior belly) and stylohyoid muscles, then crosses above them to descend on the medial surface of the mandible, grooving or passing through the submaxillary (submandibular) gland as it rounds the lower border of the bone. From its appearance on the external surface of the mandible, at about the anterior border of the masseter muscle, the artery runs upward and medially to the side of the nose and the medial angle of the eye (Fig. 191). In this course it lies successively beneath the platysma, risorius, zygomaticus, quad-

LABIAL ARTERIES

The inferior and superior labial arteries run tortuously in the lips, in or behind the deeper fibers of the orbicularis oris and therefore fairly superficial in relation to the labial mucosa. Because of their tortuosity, they wind in and out in the deeper part of the muscle, sometimes lying in this and sometimes between the

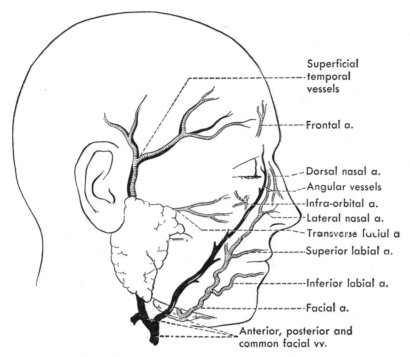

Superficial temporal vessels

Frontal a.

Dorsal nasal a.

Angular vessels

Infra-orbital a.

Lateral nasal a.

Transverse facial a.

Superior labial a.

Inferior labial a.

Facial a.

Anterior, posterior and common facial vv.

Fig. 191. Chief blood vessels of the face. These lie beneath the superficial facial muscles (see text) and only their general courses rather than their relations are indicated here.

ratus labii superioris, and orbicularis oculi muscles, but crosses superficial to the buccinator and caninus muscles. Above the mandibular margin it lies anterior to the anterior facial vein, which takes a corresponding course on the face (but reaches the face by crossing the submaxillary gland superficially, rather than emerging between the gland and the mandible). The chief branches of the artery on the face are labial, lateral nasal, and angular branches.

muscle and the mucosa. The tortuosity is more marked in the aged. In doing "lip shaves" for superficially located carcinoma of the lower lip the inferior labial artery is therefore frequently uncovered just under the mucosa.

There may be two inferior labial arteries, in which case the lower arises from the facial below the level of the alveolar border of the mandible and courses farther from the free margin of the lip, and less close to the mucosa, while the upper has the course already described. The superior labial gives off the artery of the nasal septum, which is a common source of bleeding from the nose.

LATERAL NASAL ARTERY

The lateral nasal artery usually ascends on the side of the nose, sends minute branches into the lateral portion of the nasal fossa, and anastomoses on the dorsum of the nose with the dorsal nasal artery from the ophthalmic.

ANGULAR ARTERY

The terminal portion of the facial artery is usually known as the angular artery, and proceeds alongside the margin of the nose toward the medial angle of the eye.

In its course the facial artery has anastomoses with the buccinator branch of the internal maxillary, with the transverse facial artery (usually a branch of the superficial temporal), and with the infra-orbital artery from the internal maxillary, while the angular portion usually terminates by anastomosing broadly with the dorsal nasal branch of the ophthalmic artery at the medial side of the orbit (p. 317). The anastomoses of the two facial arteries across the midline of the face, and probably especially the labial vessels, form an important part of the collateral circulation available after ligation of the external or common carotid artery on one side (p. 475).

ABNORMALITY OF FACIAL ARTERY

Rarely, the facial artery is deficient, and its place is taken in part by other branches. Grönroos has recorded a case in which it ended essentially as a submental branch, sending only a tiny branch upward along the anterior border of the masseter muscle; in this case the buccinator branch of the internal maxillary was very much enlarged, and after appearing on the cheek turned upward in the usual position of the facial to supply buccal, nasal, and angular branches. The present writer has recently seen a case in which the facial artery ended with the labial branches, its place above the mouth being taken by enlarged branches from the transverse facial artery and by the similarly enlarged dorsal nasal branch from the ophthalmic.

OTHER ARTERIES

The other arteries to the face are those already mentioned as anastomosing with the facial artery. The buccal or *buccinator branch of the internal maxillary artery* enters the cheek from a position deep to the ascending ramus of the mandible and the associated insertion of the temporal muscle, to supply the buccal fat pad and other tissue lying external to the buccinator muscle; this is usually a small vessel.

The *transverse facial artery* arises from the terminal portion of the external carotid or from the superficial temporal, and as its name implies runs almost transversely across the face, lying upon the outer surface of the masseter muscle, and below the zygomatic arch but above the parotid duct. This vessel gives off branches to the orbital region and anastomoses across the cheek with the facial.

The *infra-orbital artery* emerges with the nerve of the same name from the infra-orbital foramen, lying therefore at first deep to the quadratus labii superioris; it may or may not have a large branch of communication with the facial artery, but in any case its branches tend to spread out over the infra-orbital region, some of them also reaching the lower eyelid.

The *dorsal nasal artery,* one of the large terminal branches of the ophthalmic, penetrates the orbital septum in the upper eyelid, usually anastomoses broadly with the angular artery at the medial angle of the eye, and then proceeds downward on the dorsum of the nose, where it also anastomoses with the lateral nasal artery. If the anastomosis between the dorsal nasal and the angular artery directly is poorly developed, that between the lateral nasal and the dorsal nasal is usually better developed.

In addition to these vessels to the major portion of the face, the frontal and supra-orbital arteries, branches of the ophthalmic, turn upward around the superior orbital rim deep to the frontalis muscle, pierce it, and supply the skin on the forehead, while other branches of the ophthalmic deep to the orbicularis oculi form the palpebral arterial arches. Finally, the superficial temporal artery arises under or in the parotid gland and emerges between the condyle of the mandible and the external auditory meatus to pass upward, superficially, immediately in front of the ear. In this position it is accompanied by the corresponding vein, a tributary of the posterior facial, and by the auriculo-temporal branch of the mandibular nerve. This artery ascends in front of the ear over the root of the zygomatic process, and divides into parietal and frontal branches which are distributed to the scalp and to the skin of the forehead; twigs from the frontal branch also reinforce the circulation to the skin of the eyelids.

Smaller branches, in addition to the transverse facial, include twigs to the parotid gland, an anterior auricular branch to an anterior portion of the ear, a branch to the temporal muscle, and sometimes a twig which enters the orbit to anastomose with lateral branches of the ophthalmic artery. Although the artery is subcutaneous in front of the ear, it is crossed superficially by the upper (temporal and zygomatic) branches of the facial nerve, and by the anterior auricular muscle. The auriculotemporal nerve usually lies a little bit behind and deep to it; the superficial temporal vein frequently lies at first behind the artery, but the branches of the two vessels tend to intertwine on the forehead and temporal region.

VEINS

ANTERIOR FACIAL VEIN

The anterior facial vein is the chief vein of the face. This begins in the angle between the nose and the eye, where it communicates freely with the ophthalmic vein (see chapter on the orbit). It runs downward roughly parallel to the facial artery, but behind it, and usually ends by joining the posterior facial vein to form the common facial vein, which drains into both the internal and external jugular veins. Unlike the facial artery, to which the anterior facial vein corresponds, the anterior facial vein does not have a course medial to the mandible, but runs superficially downward across the outer surface of the submaxillary gland. In its facial course it, like the artery, runs beneath most of the facial muscles.

DANGER AREA OF FACE

Since the veins of the head and face are without valves, the communications of the anterior facial vein with the ophthalmic veins, and to a less extent, because they are smaller, with the infra-orbital and buccinator veins, have been of especial clinical importance. The ophthalmic veins drain directly into the cavernous sinus

(Fig. 192); the infra-orbital and buccinator veins drain into the pterygoid plexus, which has, however, also connections with the cavernous sinus through the foramen ovale and, by way of the inferior orbital fissure, to the inferior ophthalmic vein and hence to the cavernous sinus.

Infections of the face, especially about the upper lip and the nose, may therefore

usually result in spread of infected blood or other septic material, without evacuating any large amount of pus and with added danger of transmitting infection to branches of the vein.

Treatment of such infections should be conservative; Maes has stated that local surgical treatment should usually not be initiated, as the less that is done locally the better. Roeder suggested ligation of

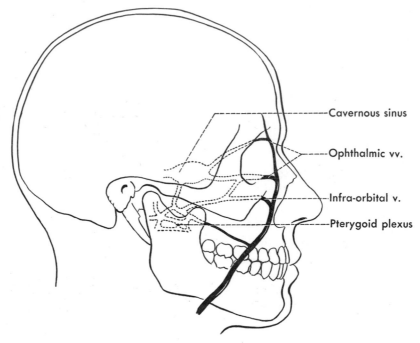

Fig. 192.   Chief connections of the anterior facial vein to the cavernous sinus.

carry considerable danger if unwisely handled. Areas of infection about the upper lip are almost impossible to immobilize; the actions of the muscles aid in rapid dissemination of septic material into adjacent venules with the production of facial vein thrombosis. Because of the connections of the anterior facial vein, it has often been emphasized that infections above the area of the mouth should not be touched from the point of view of attempting to evacuate them (for instance, Pratt; Maes). Such attempts

veins as a prophylactic measure, in order to prevent spread to the cavernous sinus, but Maes regarded this as of dubious value, even though he pointed out that once the thrombosis has reached the cavernous sinus, surgical treatment is of little avail because of the prompt development of meningitis. Writing in the days before the modern antibiotics, he found that it had been estimated that while only 7 per cent of patients afflicted with cavernous sinus thrombosis recovered without surgical intervention, less than 7 per cent recovered with such intervention. With the newer chemotherapeutic agents, the dangers of the venous connections recounted here can be largely obviated.

SMALLER VEINS

The branches of the smaller veins reaching the face are those corresponding to the arteries—that is, the transverse facial and the superficial temporal veins,

conspicuous nodes, arranged roughly along the pathway of the facial artery, and also by the preauricular and parotid nodes.

ANTERIOR FACIAL NODES

The anterior facial nodes are said to form two chief groups (Fig. 193), one group lying upon the lateral aspect of the mandible where the facial artery

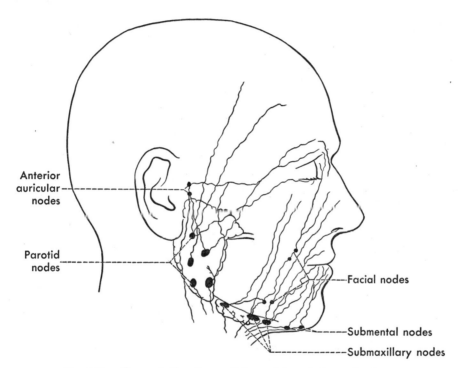

Fig. 193.   General directions of flow of lymph from the face.

emptying into the posterior facial vein which runs through the parotid gland; the buccinator vein, already mentioned as communicating with the pterygoid plexus of veins; and the branches of the ophthalmic vein which appear about the eye.

LYMPHATICS

The lymph nodes on the face are represented by a variable number of in-

crosses this, and another on the buccinator muscle; occasional nodes are said to occur also at the lateral border of the nose and in the infra-orbital region.

POSTERIOR FACIAL NODES

The posterior facial nodes include one or several anterior auricular (preauricular) nodes, situated immediately in front of the tragus, and the larger parotid group of nodes situated both on the surface of and buried in the parotid gland.

DRAINAGE FROM FACE

The lymphatic vessels from the forehead empty into the parotid nodes; those from the larger lateral part of both eyelids, and from a part of the external nose, empty into the anterior auricular and parotid nodes; the lymphatics from the medial corner of the eye, from the greater part of the external nose and from most of the lower part of the face pass largely downward through the anterior facial nodes to reach the submaxillary nodes; and the lymphatics from the medial portion of the lower lip drain into the submental nodes. Havens has stated that in his experience, however, metastatic involvement of the submental nodes secondary to carcinoma of the lower lip is relatively rare. The submental and submaxillary nodes (see p. 374) in turn drain into the superficial cervical and upper deep cervical nodes; the anterior auricular nodes drain either into the parotid nodes or directly into the upper deep cervical nodes, and the parotid nodes drain also into the upper deep cervical group.

McClure and Lam concluded, from a study of their own and others' cases, that in cases of small early carcinoma of the lip with no palpable evidence of involvement of the cervical nodes, dissection of the nodes of the neck is unnecessary, though they also stressed the importance of repeated examination of the neck in the two years following operation. Figi stated that removal of squamous cell epitheliomas of the lip of Grade 2 or 3 should be followed by removal and examination of the submental and submaxillary nodes, and if these are involved, by block dissection of the neck. This program was recommended regardless of the size of the primary lesion on the lip.

THE PAROTID GLAND

THE tough connective tissue about the parotid gland, united intimately to the surface of the gland, has been described as being formed by a splitting of the anterior layer of the deep fascia of the neck about the gland; as already noted, the deeper portion of the parotid gland lies in part adjacent to the lateral pharyngeal space, and this relationship presumably accounts for the sometimes severe consequences of parotitis. At its lower pole this gland is separated from the submaxillary (submandibular) gland by a thickening of fascia termed the stylomandibular ligament.

The parotid gland, located anterior to and below the lower part of the ear (Fig. 194), extends subcutaneously backward over the anterior portion of the sternocleidomastoid muscle and forward over the masseter muscle, and also deeply behind the ramus of the mandible to lie between this and the external auditory meatus and mastoid process. Superficial and deep parts of the gland have been described, and regarded both as broadly continuous with each other and as being united only by an isthmus about which run the branches of the facial nerve; the relationship of the gland to the facial nerve constitutes the chief hazard of surgery of this gland, and is discussed in detail, in connection with the facial nerve, on page 325.

SUPERFICIAL RELATIONS

The outer surface of the parotid gland is practically subcutaneous, and is related only to the skin and fascia and to a few inconstant superficial parotid nodes which

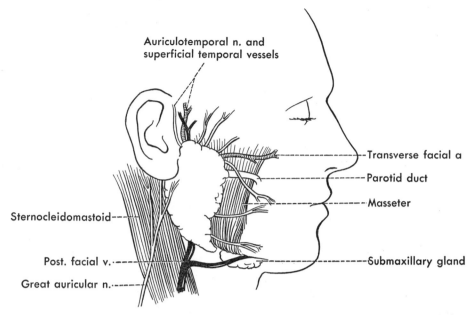

Fig. 194. Some relations of the parotid gland. Branches of the facial nerve (un-labeled) are seen radiating outward from the anterior border of the gland. The gland actually varies considerably in size and shape.

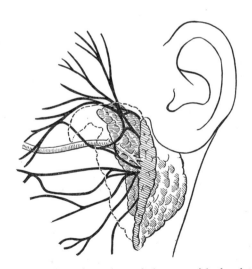

Fig. 195. Dissection of the parotid gland to show the duct and the facial nerve. This is supposed to show the separation of superficial and deep lobes of the gland by the facial nerve, but see also page 325 and Figure 201. A part of the superficial lobe, indicated by the broken line, has been cut away. (Redrawn from Mc-Whorter, G. L.: *Anat. Rec. 12*:149, 1917.)

may occur on its surface; from the anterior edge of this superficial part the *parotid* (Stensen's) *duct* (Figs. 194 and 195), often accompanied by accessory parotid tissue, passes forward across the masseter muscle, at a level about half-way between the zygoma and the angle of the lip. After passing beyond the anterior border of the masseter the duct turns medially to penetrate the buccinator muscle and open into the mouth at about the level of junction of the root and crown of the upper second molar tooth.

External fistulas of the parotid duct are troublesome, for they tend to heal slowly because of the constant secretion of saliva; surgical repair of an injured duct, or drainage of it, is necessary, since it will not heal spontaneously, and several ingenious methods of repair have been suggested (for example, Glascock and Glascock). A drain from the severed end of the duct into the mouth allows healing of it, or the formation of a fistulous

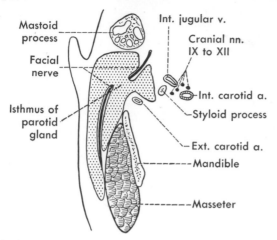

Fig. 196. Schema of the parotid gland in horizontal section, showing its supposed division into superficial and deep lobes and some of its relations. (Redrawn from McWhorter, G. L.: *Anat. Rec. 12:*149, 1917.)

channel to the mouth, as the case may be.

A short distance above the parotid duct the transverse facial artery and vein appear beneath the edge of the parotid gland, and run forward usually above and roughly parallel to the duct, but sometimes descending to cross superficial to it. The parotid duct may also be crossed superficially by anastomosing branches of the facial nerve connecting the zygomatic and buccal branches.

Also appearing at the anterior edge of the parotid gland are the major branches of the facial nerve which, having traversed the gland, radiate downward, forward, and upward across the masseter muscle and the zygomatic arch. The relations of the nerve within the gland are discussed in the following section. Obviously, vertical incisions over the anterior portion of the parotid gland carry with them great danger of injury to the parotid duct or some branch of the facial nerve, while horizontal incisions render either of these much more unlikely.

At the upper border of the parotid gland the temporal branch of the facial nerve, the superficial temporal artery and vein, and the auriculotemporal nerve, having traversed the parotid gland, cross the zygomatic arch subcutaneously. This branch of the facial nerve tends to lie anterior to the vessels and to cross them superficially; the superficial temporal vein lies slightly superficial to and behind the corresponding artery, while the auriculotemporal nerve lies deeper and usually slightly more posteriorly. All these structures, however, tend to be concentrated immediately in front of the ear.

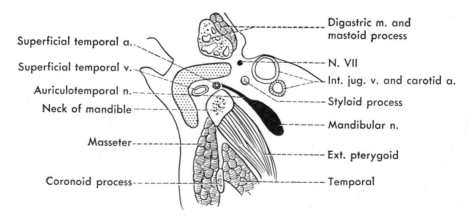

Fig. 197. Relations of the parotid gland as seen in horizontal section through the neck of the condyle of the mandible. (Redrawn from Symington, J.: *J. Anat. & Physiol. 46:*173, 1912.)

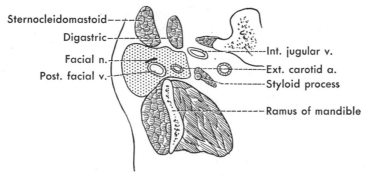

Sternocleidomastoid

Digastric

Facial n.

Post. facial v.

Int. jugular v.

Ext. carotid a.

Styloid process

Ramus of mandible

Fig. 198. Relations of the parotid gland as seen in a horizontal section about 16 mm. below the plane of section in Figure 197. The leader to the external carotid artery crosses the internal carotid. (Redrawn from Symington, J.: *J. Anat. & Physiol. 46:* 173, 1912.)

INTERNAL RELATIONS

The important relations of the deep portion of the parotid gland (Figs. 196–199) are vascular ones. Adjacent to the medial portion of the gland as a whole, and typically embedded in it for some distance, are the external carotid artery and the posterior facial vein; in this position the external carotid divides into the superficial temporal and internal maxillary arteries, and the posterior facial vein receives the corresponding venous branches. The deep auricular and transverse facial arteries also originate here, and the auriculotemporal nerve passes upward through or just deep to the upper portion of the gland.

Anteromedial to the deep portion of the gland are the internal jugular vein, the internal carotid artery, and the styloid process and its muscles; more anteriorly, the posterior belly of the digastric is against the anteromedial surface of the gland.

Above and anteriorly, the deep portion of the gland is related to the ramus of the mandible and the posterior border of the internal pterygoid muscle; posteriorly it is related to the mastoid process and the external auditory meatus. The pain produced by movements of the jaw in parotitis or mumps is due to a compression of the deep portion of the parotid gland by the ramus of the mandible, especially against the anterior wall of the external auditory meatus.

BLOOD SUPPLY AND INNERVATION

The parotid gland receives its blood supply from the vessels traversing it, and its sensory and secretory nerve fibers are received from the auriculotemporal nerve, which also traverses it. The sensory fibers are true trigeminal nerve fibers, with cells of origin in the semilunar ganglion, but

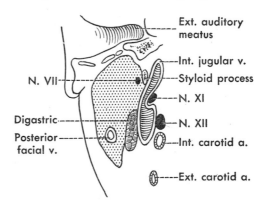

Ext. auditory meatus

Int. jugular v.

N. VII

Styloid process

N. XI

N. XII

Digastric

Posterior facial v.

Int. carotid a.

Ext. carotid a.

Fig. 199. Relations of the parotid gland as seen in a frontal section behind the mandible. (Redrawn from Symington, J.: *J. Anat. & Physiol. 46:*173, 1912.)

the secretory fibers are derived originally from the glossopharyngeal nerve. These take a devious course to reach the parotid gland: the preganglionic parasympathetic fibers leave the ninth nerve by way of its tympanic branch to join the tympanic plexus on the promontory of the middle ear cavity, subsequently leaving the plexus through the lesser superficial petrosal nerve; this nerve ends in the otic ganglion, otic ganglion, through connections between the greater and lesser superficial petrosal nerves as these run forward through the skull parallel to each other, or through a twig by which the chorda tympani is connected to the otic ganglion; the evidence for this, clinical rather than anatomical, is subject to other interpretations.

As is the case also with the other

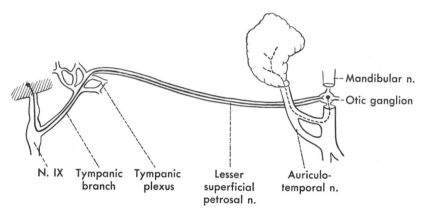

N. IX   Tympanic   Tympanic   Lesser   Auriculo-
         branch   plexus   superficial   temporal n.
                                      petrosal n.

—Mandibular n.

—Otic ganglion

Fig. 200. Schema of the parasympathetic innervation of the parotid gland. The preganglionic pathway is indicated by a solid line, the postganglionic one by a broken line.

where the preganglionic fibers make synapse (Fig. 200).

The otic ganglion lies just outside the foramen ovale on the medial surface of the mandibular nerve, and gives off filaments to the roots by which the auriculotemporal nerve arises from the mandibular; these fibers then leave the auriculotemporal with sensory fibers to form the parotid branches of this nerve. Some writers have stated that preganglionic fibers from the facial nerve also reach the salivary glands, relatively little is known concerning the sympathetic supply to the parotid gland; sympathetic fibers from the superior cervical ganglion presumably reach it by way of the external carotid plexus and its branches, thus traveling along the blood vessels, but the functional significance of the sympathetic supply is not clearly understood. This question is discussed further, in relation to the salivary glands as a whole, in the chapter on the jaw and tongue.

NERVES

FACIAL NERVE

In connection with the facial nerve after it leaves the skull there are two questions to be considered: the relation of the nerve to the parotid gland, and the anatomical and functional distribution of the nerve on the face.

RELATION TO PAROTID GLAND

As the facial nerve emerges through the stylomastoid foramen, typically situated slightly posterolateral to the styloid process and hence between this and the mastoid process (but very superficially located in the infant—page 195), it almost immediately comes into relation to the deeper and posterior aspect of the parotid gland. In the very occasional cases in which the nerve has an aberrant course and emerges rather from the anterior surface of the mastoid process, it still comes into immediate relation to this gland. In either case the nerve enters the substance of the parotid gland and divides into two chief divisions, an upper temporofacial and a lower cervicofacial one.

McWhorter described these two divisions of the facial nerve as passing between superficial and deep parts of the parotid gland, on either side of an isthmus which unites these two parts; according to his description the superficial and deep parts of the gland thus form lobes which are usually distinct and readily separable, and have separate duct systems, except where they are united through the isthmus. Essentially, therefore, according to this description, it is not so much a matter of the facial nerve traversing the substance of the parotid gland as a matter of the lobes of the gland being folded about the nerve. This description has been followed also by McCormack, Cauldwell and Anson and largely also by Hurford. Hurford stated that of 11 specimens which were especially dissected for this purpose there was evidence of a division into superficial and deep lobes in 10, and among the latter 7 showed a fairly clear isthmus and 3 showed a well-defined one. He added, however, that among these bilobed parotids there were only 4 in which the branches of the facial nerve remained strictly in the plane between the lobes, and that careful dissection was required to demonstrate the isthmus in every case.

The present writer has not seen a clear division along the plane of the branches of the facial nerve, although in the dissecting room it is certainly possible to produce such a plane about the main nerve branches by following the facial nerve through the gland. This has been done surgically also (for example, State), but does not of course prove that a natural subdivision of the gland exists. McKenzie has recently adduced rather compelling evidence that this concept of deep and superficial portions connected by an isthmus and otherwise separated by a plane in which lie the branches of the facial nerve is a simplification which does not actually exist (Fig. 201). He injected the ducts of the parotid system and upon subsequent dissection found that there was not only an isthmus passing between the upper and lower divisions of the facial nerve, but that there were multiple isthmi passing between and among the further branches of the facial nerve as it forms the parotid plexus within the gland; the isthmi which he described were not simply cases of contact between superficial and deep lobes, for he found that each isthmus had ducts connecting the deeper and the superficial parts. Rather than the parotid gland being simply folded about the branches of the facial nerve, therefore, his results indicate that parotid

the more superficial and the deeper portions of the parotid gland was found to vary from one individual to another, just as there is also variation in the pattern of branching of the facial nerve.

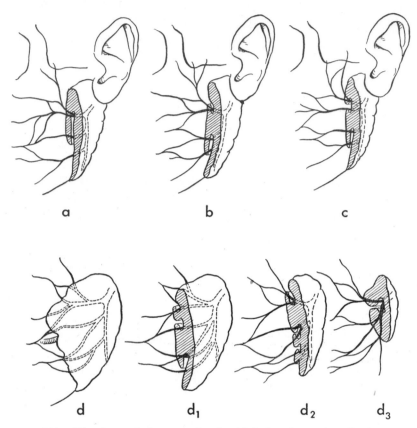

Fig. 201. Varying relations, each of which has been described as commonly prevailing, between the parotid gland and the facial nerve. In *a*, *b*, and *c* the nerve is shown passing between deep and superficial lobes of the gland, but the relationship of these lobes is variously depicted: *a* shows superficial and deep lobes united above, so that the gland is essentially folded over the nerve; *b* shows the two lobes united by an isthmus; *c* shows a combination of *a* and *b*. In *d* and its subnumbers is shown the relationship according to McKenzie: gland and nerve intertwined, with no superficial and deep lobes, and the relationship varying according to the plane of section. (Redrawn from McKenzie, J.: *J. Anat. 82:*183, 1948.)

tissue, ducts and facial nerve are intimately interwoven; he compared the parotid gland to a climbing vine which had interwoven itself in the meshes of a trellis-work fence (the facial nerve). The pattern of the connecting isthmi between

Regardless of the concept adopted, any operation for removal of a portion of the parotid gland, unless it involves only a very superficial part, necessarily carries with it the danger of damage to the facial nerve, and complete removal of the gland without damage to the nerve is a delicate procedure. Hurford found that in 5 of the 10 cases in which he recognized a deep lobe (that is, one deep to the facial nerve), this was larger than the superficial lobe, in contrast to what is ordinarily stated; he expressed the belief that in such cases removal of the deep lobe without damaging the facial nerve would be difficult, and perhaps impossible when a tumor was present also; he suggested that perhaps the superficial lobe, however, is more apt to be the site of tumors than is the deeper part of the gland.

Saltzstein carried out total removal of the parotid gland, without damage to the facial nerve, by locating the inframandibular (cervical) branch and following it up into the gland to the bifurcation of the facial into its two divisions; he traced these and the main stem of the facial, and first removed the part of the gland superficial to the nerve, then the deeper part. Furstenberg has preferred to identify the main stem of the facial nerve as it lies close to the styloid process, and trace it forward through the parotid gland by careful dissection; after this was done he removed the gland from about the nerve. McCune reported that in his hands the latter method, although faster, frequently led to more serious facial paralysis because of damage to the nerve before it was recognized.

SURGICAL REPAIR OF FACIAL NERVE

Sufficient damage to the main trunk of the facial nerve produces paralysis of the entire facial musculature on that side. Coleman ('44), in discussing this condition, has pointed out that the paralysis is less obvious in the upper facial area than in the lower, for it is not exaggerated by the activity of the muscles on the normal side as is paralysis in the lower facial area, especially about the mouth. In cases of injury to the facial stem as a whole, the nerve trunk is of sufficient size to allow end-to-end anastomosis, the use of a nerve graft or a hypoglossofacial or spinofacial anastomosis. Unfortunately, operations upon the parotid gland are of course more apt to injure smaller branches of the facial nerve, the surgical repair of which is difficult or impossible.

Duel and Tickle stated that surgical repair of the main stem of the facial nerve is worthwhile as long as the muscles will respond to galvanic current. They have suggested that following surgical injuries it is best to attempt immediate repair of the nerve, since the peripheral end retains its response to faradic stimulation for from forty-eight to seventy-two hours, and can therefore be more easily located by this means. It is generally recognized that an end-to-end anastomosis of the facial stem offers the best opportunity for successful repair; as pointed out by Furstenberg the anastomosis may sometimes be made possible by lifting the facial nerve from its bony canal in the mastoid, and freeing it in its course into the parotid gland.

Duel and Tickle have stated that one cannot expect perfect repair upon re-anastomosis of the ends of the facial, since some neurons may always be expected to reach the wrong destination. Howe, Tower, and Duel produced evidence that the *facial tic* sometimes occurring after injury to the nerve is due in part at least to bifurcation of some of the regenerated fibers in the nerve, so that one branch of a fiber goes to one muscle of the face, the other branch to another muscle; under these conditions, of course, there is no ability to relearn (because of the splitting of the axons) and the tic is therefore apparently permanent. Duel and Tickle have used previously degenerated femoral cutaneous or long thoracic nerves for nerve grafts.

In regard to anastomosis of the spinal accessory or hypoglossal nerves with the facial in cases of facial paralysis, Coleman ('40) has preferred the use of the hypoglossal. In his series he found that a hypoglossofacial anastomosis restored movement about the mouth in practically every case, even though function of the frontalis, far less important, was recovered in only one instance. In analyzing the results, he pointed out that function of muscle groups cannot be individualized after such an anastomosis, that emotional stimuli are registered only on the healthy side of the face, and that associated movements of the face may be produced by action of the tongue in individuals so treated. He stated that the ensuing hemiatrophy of the tongue caused no appreciable interference with either speech or swallowing.

Other workers prefer to use the proximal end of the spinal accessory nerve as a graft upon the distal end of the facial; this is subject to some of the same drawbacks found in hypoglossofacial union, but again the disability due to denervation of the sternocleidomastoid and trapezius muscles is apparently slight and usually not objected to by the patient, in comparison to the disfigurement of a facial paralysis. The course and distribution of the accessory nerve are discussed briefly beginning with page 514.

BRANCHES OF FACIAL NERVE

As the facial nerve emerges from the stylomastoid foramen its first branch is the posterior auricular, which runs upward between the parotid gland and the anterior border of the sternocleidomastoid muscle, and then in the notch between the external auditory meatus and the mastoid process; this branch supplies the more posterior muscles of the facial group: the occipitalis, the auricularis posterior and part of the auricularis superior, and the intrinsic muscles of the auricle.

Many of the sensory fibers emerging in the facial from the stylomastoid foramen also run in this branch, which has a cutaneous sensory distribution to the ear (p. 170).

The facial nerve then passes forward and downward lateral to the styloid process and its attached muscles, supplying branches to the posterior belly of the digastric and to the stylohyoid. After entering the parotid gland and separating into temporofacial and cervicofacial divisions it branches further; these branches then usually divide and anastomose to form a plexus within the parotid gland, and from the plexus a variable number of branches emerge, leave the parotid gland, and are distributed to the face (Fig. 202).

While it is customary and convenient to describe the branches of the facial nerve on the face as being divided into five sets—temporal, zygomatic or infraorbital, buccal, marginal mandibular (supramandibular), and cervical (inframandibular)—these terms actually do not so much indicate definite branches of the facial nerve as regions of distribution. The temporal and zygomatic branches of distribution arise from the temporofacial division, the marginal mandibular and cervical branches from the cervicofacial division; however, even the two major divisions of the facial nerve may anastomose with each other within the parotid gland, or may anastomose farther forward on the face so that both contribute to the buccal branches, which otherwise arise from the lower division. Between the branches of each division of the facial nerve anastomoses are even more numerous, commonly occurring both in the substance of the parotid gland and farther out upon the face. In the latter location there may be fairly definitive branches, or the facial may be represented by a plexiform arrangement. McCormack, Cauldwell, and Anson attempted to classify the facial nerves from 100 dissections according to the method

also supply the orbicularis oculi, the muscles about the nasal aperture, and most of the elevators of the upper lip; the buccal branches supply especially the musculature about both lips, the marginal mandibular the musculature beneath the lower lip, and the cervical branch supplies the platysma.

It is paralysis of the buccal and marginal mandibular branches which produces the most facial deformity, since they are concerned with the highly mobile lips;

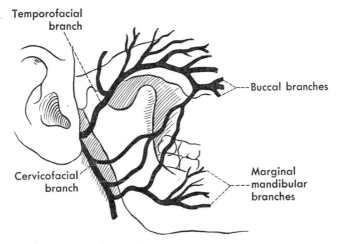

Fig. 202. Relationship of the facial nerve to the mandible. (Redrawn, by permission of *Surg., Gynec. & Obst.,* from McCormack, L. J., Cauldwell, E. W., and Anson, B. J., vol. 80, p. 620, 1945.)

of branching and the major anastomoses found, and divided them into eight types (Fig. 203); undoubtedly, the various patterns could also be allocated to double that number of types, if desired, or divided simply into those that show no major anastomoses upon the face, and those that do.

In general, the temporal branch or branches supply the anterior auricular and a portion of the superior auricular muscle, and the muscles upon the forehead including the major portion of the orbicularis oculi; the zygomatic branches

both the cervical and the marginal mandibular branches of the facial lie within the field of operation in radical dissections of the neck for metastatically involved lymph nodes, but it is the marginal mandibular branch which must be watched for and spared if the patient is not to suffer from a facial deformity following the operation.

The main portion of this branch runs, as its name implies, approximately along the lower margin of the mandible—sometimes actually overlying the bone, sometimes below the margin of the mandible.

The surgeon should take pains to identify and preserve this nerve if possible. It is frequently spared in accidental cuts upon the face in this region (Coleman, '44), since when it lies below the mandible it is protected by this bone.

from 27 to 40 per cent of the afferent fibers in the facial nerve of the cat leave it by way of the great superficial petrosal, from 45 to 62 per cent leave by way of the chorda tympani, while a minority (11 to 15 per cent) emerge with the facial

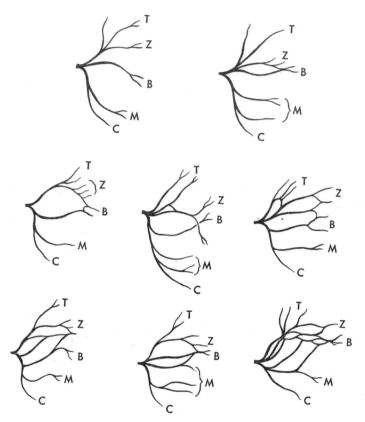

Fig. 203. Eight major types of branching and anastomosis of the facial nerve. *T, Z, B, M,* and *C* identify respectively the temporal, zygomatic, buccal, mandibular, and cervical branches of the nerve. (Redrawn, by permission of *Surg., Gynec. & Obst.,* from McCormack, L. J., Cauldwell, E. W., and Anson, B. J., vol. 80, p. 620, 1945.)

SENSORY FIBERS

Before emerging from the stylomastoid foramen, the facial nerve gives off its great superficial petrosal, stapedial, and chorda tympani branches. Presumably all of the parasympathetic fibers of the facial nerve leave through these branches, and so do the great majority of the sensory fibers—according to Foley and DuBois

through the stylomastoid foramen. Many of the latter are said to be distributed by way of the auricular branch of the facial, and undoubtedly account for the otalgia which apparently may be a symptom of geniculate ganglion neuralgia (Hunt); others, however, course toward the mimetic muscles, and have variously been regarded as proprioceptive to these muscles, and as subserving deep pain from the face.

Maloney and Kennedy concluded that the facial nerve transmits pressure pain from the skin, muscles, and bones of the face; Hunt described deep-seated pain from the face (prosopalgia) as being as characteristic of facial neuralgia as is pain in the ear. While prosopalgia may be due largely to conduction of pain over the great superficial petrosal nerve, there are observations to suggest that pain fibers run also in the superficial branches of the facial nerve. It is commonly recognized by surgeons that stimulation of the facial nerve in the region of the parotid gland may elicit pain, and Bruesch has described the myelinated afferent fibers coursing in the peripheral branches of the facial nerve of the cat (he did not study unmyelinated fibers) as being of the size usually considered to be concerned with pain and temperature rather than proprioception, and as ending primarily in connection with blood vessels. Pain conducted by the seventh nerve has undoubtedly been confused with trigeminal neuralgia (for example, Ruskin); Lyman, noting that the term "atypical trigeminal neuralgia" has been used to describe a number of different conditions, reported that some of them were apparently cases of "sphenopalatine ganglion neuralgia" (p. 254), hence from the deeper branches of the seventh.

Evidence that the afferent fibers in the superficial branches of the facial nerve are proprioceptive is entirely clinical. For instance, Carmichael and Woollard studied patients with presumably complete destruction of the semilunar ganglion, and stated that they were able to elicit no pressure pain upon the side of this destruction, but that movements and displacements of muscles upon the anesthetic side were recognized. They therefore concluded that pressure pain from the face is mediated entirely by the fifth nerve, but that proprioception is mediated by the seventh.

This latter statement, supported by the clinical observations of others, is in direct opposition to the much earlier report of Cushing, who concluded that the proprioceptive fibers are derived from the semilunar ganglion. Since proprioceptive endings have apparently not been found in the facial muscles, the question of proprioceptive fibers from them has not been investigated by direct anatomical experiments. Undoubtedly, however, cutaneous impulses over the fifth nerve contribute considerably to appreciation of movement in the face, and the numbness following destruction of the fifth nerve upsets this appreciation. This is witnessed by the common experience of the effects of local anesthesia administered by the dentist, and may sometimes explain also the occasional occurrence of a temporary facial paralysis following section of the fifth nerve—although the latter is usually blamed upon indirect damage to the facial nerve by way of its great superficial petrosal branch.

In summary, the anatomical evidence indicates that the facial nerve carries afferent fibers to the face, and that they are of the type usually associated with pain; the clinical evidence regarding the role of the facial nerve in pain and proprioception from the face is somewhat contradictory, but seems to be especially in favor of the afferent fibers in the superficial branches of the nerve being largely proprioceptive. The question cannot be regarded as settled, and bizarre observations on this subject are sometimes made. For instance, as recently as 1946 Jaeger stated that he had sectioned the roots of the fifth and ninth cranial nerves, and the upper five cervical sensory roots, and found not only persistence of pain from the ear but preservation of touch over the entire side of the face and forehead on the side of operation.

LOWER AND UPPER NEURON PARALYSIS

In attempting to localize the lesion in cases of facial paralysis, it is well to remember that paralysis of the facial muscles on the whole of one side of the face can result only from lesions of the facial nucleus or nerve; supranuclear (upper motor neuron) paralysis of the facial nerve spares the orbicularis oculi and the muscles of the forehead, as the portion of the facial nucleus supplying these muscles is controlled by fibers from both cerebral cortices, and only in the instance of a bilateral supranuclear lesion, therefore, is voluntary control of these muscles abolished. Monrad-Krohn also pointed out that central lesions may abolish voluntary control of the facial muscles, yet leave them active in emotional responses, such as smiling at a joke.

THE TRIGEMINAL NERVE AND THE SENSORY SUPPLY TO THE FACE

The sensory nerve supply to the face is largely through the trigeminal or fifth cranial nerve. Branches from the cervical plexus (transverse cervical or cutaneus colli and great auricular) supply a certain amount of skin along the lower border of the mandible and over its angle, and the seventh, ninth, and tenth nerves, with the cervical plexus, supply the greater portion of the skin of the external ear (p. 169); the scalp behind the ear is supplied by cervical nerves, but otherwise the skin of the entire face and of the scalp anterior to the level of the ear is supplied through the branches of the trigeminal nerve. Since the three primary branches of the fifth nerve separate before leaving the skull, and have widely different courses thereafter, sensation over the face must be tested in the distribution of each major branch; this is commonly done by testing sensation on the forehead, the prominence of the cheek, and the chin.

OPHTHALMIC BRANCHES

Each division of the trigeminal nerve sends several cutaneous branches to the face (Fig. 204). The largest branch of the ophthalmic nerve is the *supra-orbital*, which makes its exit from the orbit through the supra-orbital notch or supra-orbital foramen, situated on the upper margin of the orbit about a finger's breadth from the lateral side of the nose, and usually palpable. This nerve supplies most of the skin over the forehead, and the scalp back to about the level of a line connecting the two external auditory meatuses. A smaller branch of the ophthalmic, the *supratrochlear,* rounds the superior border of the orbit medial to the supraorbital nerve and supplies a limited medial region of skin over the forehead. Both of these at first lie deep to the frontalis muscle.

These branches, with the *infratrochlear* branch of the ophthalmic at the medial angle of the eye, and the small *lacrimal* branch of the ophthalmic at the lateral angle, supply also the skin of the upper lid, the medial and lateral angles of the lids, and the bridge and sides of the root of the nose.

Another branch of the ophthalmic, the *anterior ethmoidal* branch from the nasociliary, supplies skin on the lower half of the dorsum of the nose down to the tip through its external nasal branch (p. 246). The ophthalmic nerve thus sup-

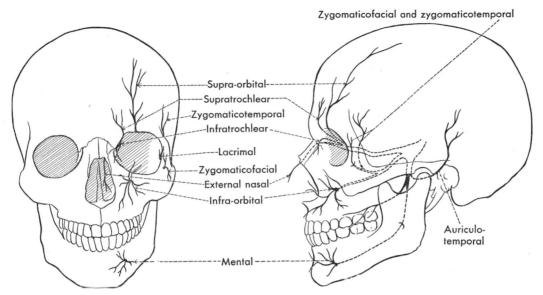

Fig. 204. Branches of the trigeminal nerve to the skin of the face. On the right is indicated the general courses of these nerves.

plies the forehead, the upper lid and most of the nose (Fig. 205), overlapping on the side of the nose with the distribution of the maxillary nerve.

MAXILLARY BRANCHES

The maxillary branch of the trigeminal nerve is represented on the face by three branches, the infra orbital, the zygomaticofacial, and the zygomaticotemporal. As

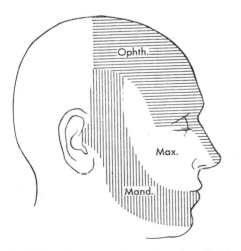

Fig. 205. Approximate cutaneous distribution of the three divisions of the fifth nerve.

a whole, this branch of the trigeminal supplies the lower eyelid, the prominence of the cheek and the side of the nose, the upper lip, and a relatively small area extending upward on the temple lateral to the lateral corner of the eye.

The *infra-orbital* nerve, by far the largest cutaneous branch of the maxillary, makes its exit through the infra-orbital foramen in the anterior wall of the maxilla, in company with the correspondingly named artery; this foramen may lie upon, but usually lies slightly lateral to a vertical line drawn downward from the supra-orbital foramen (see also p. 343). The nerve emerges under cover of the orbicularis oculi and the quadratus labii superioris, and ramifies in the connective tissue and fat lying between the latter muscle and the caninus, anastomosing here with zygomatic branches of the facial nerve. Its branches are distributed upward to the skin of the lower lid, medially to the side but not the dorsum of the lower part of the nose, laterally to most of the prominence of the cheek and downward to the upper lip.

The *zygomaticofacial* and *zygomaticotemporal* branches of the maxillary nerve leave the infra-orbital in the pterygopalatine fossa or as this nerve courses in the floor of the orbit, and then diverge from each other to appear separately upon the face. The zygomaticofacial nerve makes its exit through a small foramen on the lateral aspect of the zygoma, where it supplies a limited area of skin extending upward toward the lateral corner of the eyelids. The zygomaticotemporal nerve, after leaving the zygomaticofacial, passes more laterally to enter the anterior part of the temporal fossa, emerge around the anterior border of the temporal muscle, and supply skin over the anterior part of the temporal region.

MANDIBULAR BRANCHES

The cutaneous branches of the mandibular nerve are also three in number; through these branches the mandibular nerve supplies skin of the lower lip and of the chin, skin over the lateral aspect of the mandible and the fleshy part of the cheek, and an area extending upward in front of the ear and including much of the temporal region. According to Cushing the latter area of distribution includes only a small part of the ear, primarily the tragus and the crus of the helix, but extends also into the anterior and upper parts of the external auditory canal and to the external aspect of the tympanic membrane.

The *mental* branch of the mandibular nerve emerges through the mental foramen on the chin, where it lies at first beneath the quadratus labii inferioris; it immediately breaks up into a large number of twigs which are distributed to the skin and to the lower lip, extending later-

ally to about the level of the angle of the mouth. This nerve is a continuation of the inferior alveolar, which supplies the teeth of the lower jaw; the mental foramen lies approximately on the vertical line drawn downward from the supraorbital foramen, as discussed in more detail on page 368.

The *buccinator* (or buccal) branch of the mandibular nerve passes deep to or through the lower part of the temporal muscle and through the buccal fat pad to appear on the mobile part of the cheek between the upper and lower jaws and supply the skin here; this nerve also supplies the mucosa on the inner surface of the cheek.

The *auriculotemporal* nerve courses medial to and then behind the temporomandibular articulation, to which it gives a branch, traverses the upper part of the parotid gland and supplies branches to this, and emerges to cross the zygoma and supply the most anterior portion of the pinna and most of the temporal region. It is this branch of the mandibular that supplies portions of the external auditory meatus and tympanic membrane (Fig. 98, p. 172); in consequence of this distribution, pain about the mandible and tongue may be referred to the ear.

The distribution of the mandibular nerve is the most common area of involvement in trigeminal neuralgia (p. 62); the "trigger zone" is usually on the chin, the lip, or the tongue.

OTHER SUGGESTED PATHWAYS FROM FACE

Helson reported that following total or subtotal section of the sensory root of the trigeminal nerve there was, over a period of years, a gradual return of sensation to the denervated area; he stated that sensitivity to deep pressure increased one hundred fold, that there was pronounced improvement in the ability to localize a given point, and that extremely hot stimuli were usually reported as producing stinging or pricking sensations. He concluded that much of this functional return might be due to ingrowth of fibers from the cervical plexus, or to sensory fibers in the facial nerve; there seemed to be also the possibility that afferent fibers in the cervical sympathetic chain might be implicated.

The possible participation of the seventh nerve in sensation from the face has already been discussed in connection with this nerve (p. 330); similarly, it has been suggested that sensory fibers may accompany sympathetic fibers to the face and serve also, with the trigeminal, for conduction of sensations from the face. Thus Helson found that while the sensations of light touch, two-point discrimination, and pain were completely abolished over the area of distribution of the fifth nerve by section of its sensory root, sensitivity to extreme heat was regularly present except in those patients who had had both a section of the fifth root and a thoracic sympathectomy; in the latter patients, heat was not at all appreciated and the skin of the face could be seared without provoking a reaction from the patient.

Kuntz found experimental evidence of sensory fibers derived from the upper thoracic (but not upper cervical) nerves in the carotid plexuses, and suggested they might be concerned with certain atypical facial neuralgias which are not relieved by section of the trigeminal nerve, but Cleveland and Davis and Pollock could not confirm the presence of sensory fibers associated with the upper part of the sympathetic chain. Browder reported a case which he concluded indicated probable conduction of pain through fibers coursing with the sympathetic system to the head.

SYMPATHETIC DISTRIBUTION TO THE FACE

The sympathetic nerve supply to the face is usually assumed to be by way of the external carotid plexus, from the superior cervical ganglion. According to Hyndman and Wolkin all of the sweat fibers to the face arise within the first five thoracic segments of the cord, and many are apparently concentrated in the second thoracic nerve.

Gardner has pointed out that the external carotid plexus is not continuous with the common carotid plexus, and cannot therefore be interrupted by the more simple technic of stripping the adventitia from the common carotid artery. He described the external carotid plexus as originating in a fairly constant manner from at least two branches, one arising from the upper pole of the superior cervical ganglion and running directly to the external carotid artery, usually on its medial side; the other descending posterior and medial to the external carotid as far as the superior thyroid artery, around which it passes to turn upward along the anterior surface of the external carotid. In addition, fibers from the upper part of the ganglion also enter the intercarotid plexus, which can of course contribute to the external carotid plexus.

In addition to the sympathetic fibers reaching the face by means of the vessels, it is possible that sympathetic fibers may also reach the face by coursing with the several divisions of the fifth nerve, especially since these are so closely related in the cavernous sinus to the internal carotid artery and its nerve plexus. Simonton and Gay concluded that there is considerable evidence that only the portions of the face supplied by the maxillary and mandibular nerves receive their sympathetic fibers through the external carotid plexus, and that the portion supplied by the ophthalmic nerve receives its sympathetic fibers from the internal carotid plexus. As additional evidence for this view, they reported a case in which retraction of the internal carotid artery at operation was necessary, and following this retraction there was not only a temporary miosis but also a temporary anhidrosis of the frontal region on the side of operation; they interpreted this evidence as indicating that the ophthalmic division of the face receives its sweat fibers intracranially from the internal carotid plexus.

Lewy, Groff, and Grant ('38) produced in the cat movements of the eyelid, of the lip, and of the tongue (after sectioning the appropriate motor nerves) by stimulating the ophthalmic, maxillary, and mandibular branches of the fifth nerve.

Although they produced the same phenomena by stimulation of the cervical sympathetic, they concluded that this was through other fibers which acted similarly to those in the trigeminal nerve, and that autonomic fibers arising from the brain stem leave it with the branches of the fifth nerve. It is perhaps easier to believe that these workers were dealing with antidromic conduction, or with cervical sympathetic fibers which join the trigeminal nerve. These authors ('37) linked their findings with the associated movements of eyelid and jaw known as the Marcus Gunn phenomenon, and reported that in a case of the latter, relief was obtained by section of the motor root of the fifth nerve. This phenomenon and others similar to it are certainly not understood, however; they have been said to be due to abnormal innervation of the muscles concerned, and Wartenberg ('48a and b) regarded them as associated movements released by supranuclear (intracerebral) lesions.

ANOMALIES

CLEFT LIP

Davis listed thirty-one types of congenital deformities of the face in a series of 1000 studied; in this series, however, the chief defect in all except 63 cases was cleft lip or cleft palate. While cleft lips are commonly associated with clefts of the alveolar process and with cleft palates they may occur separately; Ritchie estimated that some 60 to 70 per cent of facial clefts involve also clefts of the alveolar process, and in Davis' series there were only 129 cases of cleft lip unassociated with cleavage of the alveolar process or palate, as opposed to 808 so associated.

By far the most common type of cleft lip is the unilateral one; bilateral cleft lip (harelip) is distinctly less common and median cleft lip is quite rare, and apparently always associated with absence of the anterior central ("premaxillary") portion of the alveolar process (Davis). The occurrence of these types is discussed further in the next chapter, in connection with cleft palate.

As pointed out by Ritchie, the problem in cleft lip is that of restoring muscle continuity and function, as well as cosmetic correction of the deformity. Peyton and Ritchie have stated that there is no tendency for the deformity of cleft lip to increase with age of the child, and that growth of the face of a child afflicted with cleft lip, seems to proceed at a nearly normal rate.

LABIAL PITS

A relatively rare deformity, constituting only 1.4 per cent of the cases in Davis' series, but nevertheless the most common other than facial clefts, is the occurrence of pits in the lower lip; as in a case described by Mason, Anson, and Beaton these may take the form of slits which produce a partial doubling of the lower lip. They are apparently due to improper development at the mucocutaneous junction.

OTHER ABNORMALITIES

Other abnormalities associated with the face include abnormalities of the external ear, ranging from complete absence to macrotia or, most common of all, simple protrusion; preauricular appendages, sinuses and fistulae (p. 174); palpebral coloboma (p. 100); and malformations of the nose (p. 276).

REFERENCES

ADAMS, W. M. Multiple muscle substitution for correction of facial paralysis. *Am. J. Surg. n.s.74:*654, 1947.

BROWDER, J. Do sympathetic nerves transmit painful impulses? Report of a case. *Am. J. Surg. n.s.18:*100, 1932.

BRUESCH, S. R. The distribution of myelinated afferent fibers in the branches of the cat's facial nerve. *J. Comp. Neurol. 81:*169, 1944.

CARMICHAEL, E. A., and WOOLLARD, H. H. Some observations on the fifth and seventh cranial nerves. *Brain 56:*109, 1933.

CLEVELAND, D. A. Afferent fibers in the cervical sympathetic trunk, superior cervical ganglion, and internal carotid nerve. *J. Comp. Neurol. 54:*35, 1932.

COLEMAN, C. C. Results of facio-hypoglossal anastomosis in the treatment of facial paralysis. *Ann. Surg. 111:*958, 1940.

COLEMAN, C. C. Surgical lesions of the facial nerve: With comments on its anatomy. *Ann. Surg. 119:*641, 1944.

CUSHING, H. The sensory distribution of the fifth cranial nerve. *Bull. Johns Hopkins Hosp. 15:*213, 1904.

DAVIS, L., and POLLOCK, L. J. The rôle of the sympathetic nervous system in the production of pain in the head. *Arch. Neurol. & Psychiat. 27:*282, 1932.

DAVIS, W. B. Congenital deformities of the face: Types found in a series of one thousand cases. *Surg., Gynec. & Obst. 61:*201, 1935.

DUEL, A. B., and TICKLE, T. G. The surgical repair of facial nerve paralysis: A clinical presentation. *Ann. Otol., Rhin. & Laryng. 45:*3, 1936.

EHNI, G., and WOLTMAN, H. W. Hemifacial spasm: Review of one hundred and six cases. *Arch. Neurol. & Psychiat. 53:*205, 1945.

FIGI, F. A. Malignant lesions of the face. *Collect. Papers Mayo Clin. & Mayo Found. 38:*410, 1946.

FOLEY, J. O., and DuBois, F. S. An experimental study of the facial nerve. *J. Comp. Neurol. 79:*19, 1943.

FURSTENBERG, A. C. Reconstruction of the facial nerve. *Arch. Otolaryng. 41:*42, 1945.

GARDNER, E. Surgical anatomy of the external carotid plexus. *Arch. Surg. 46:*238, 1943.

GLASCOCK, H., and GLASCOCK, H., JR. Repair of traumatic fistulas of Stenson's duct. *Surg., Gynec. & Obst. 65:*355, 1937.

GRÖNROOS, H. Eine seltene Anordnung der Arteria maxillaris externa bei einem Erwachsenen. *Anat. Anz. 20:*9, 1902.

HAVENS, F. Z. Personal communication, 1951.

HELSON, H. The part played by the sympathetic system as an afferent mechanism in the region of the trigeminus. *Brain 55:*114, 1932.

HOWE, H. A., TOWER, SARAH S., and DUEL, A. B. Facial tic in relation to injury of the facial nerve: An experimental study. *Arch. Neurol. & Psychiat. 38:*1190, 1937.

HUNT, J. R. Geniculate neuralgia (neuralgia of the nervus facialis): A further contribution to the sensory system of the facial nerve and its neuralgic conditions. *Arch. Neurol. & Psychiat. 37:*253, 1937.

HURFORD, F. R. The surgical anatomy of the parotid gland. *Brit. J. Surg. 34:*186, 1946.

HYNDMAN, O. R., and WOLKIN, J. Sweat mechanism in man: Study of distribution of sweat fibers from the sympathetic ganglia, spinal roots, spinal cord and common carotid artery. *Arch. Neurol. & Psychiat. 45:*446, 1941.

JAEGER, R. Neuralgic syndromes of the head: Anatomy and physiology of sensory nerves to the head. *Arch. Otolaryng. 44:*424, 1946.

KUNTZ, A. Nerve fibers of spinal and vagus origin associated with the cephalic sympathetic nerves. *Ann. Otol., Rhin. & Laryng. 43:*50, 1934.

LEE, F. C. Orbicularis oris muscle in double harelip. *Arch. Surg. 53:*407, 1946.

LEWY, F. H., GROFF, R. A., and GRANT, F. C. Autonomic innervation of the eyelids and the Marcus Gunn phenomenon: An experimental study. *Arch. Neurol. & Psychiat. 37:*1289, 1937.

LEWY, F. H., GROFF, R. A., and GRANT, F. C. Autonomic innervation of the face: II. An experimental study. *Arch. Neurol. & Psychiat. 39:*1238, 1938.

LODGE, W. O. A plastic operation for facial paralysis. *Brit. J. Surg. 17:*422, 1930.

LYMAN, H. W. The sphenoid sinus and the sphenopalatine ganglion as factors in so-called atypical trigeminal neuralgia. *Ann. Otol., Rhin. & Laryng. 44:*653, 1935.

MCCLURE, R. D., and LAM, C. R. Should the neck nodes be dissected in patients with carcinoma of the lip? *Ann. Surg. 125:*658, 1947.

MCCORMACK, L. J., CAULDWELL, E. W., and ANSON, B. J. The surgical anatomy of the facial nerve with special reference to the parotid gland. *Surg., Gynec. & Obst. 80:*620, 1945.

MCCUNE, W. S. Total parotidectomy in tumors of the parotid gland. *A.M.A. Arch. Surg. 62:*715, 1951.

MCKENZIE, J. The parotid gland in relation to the facial nerve. *J. Anat. 82:*183, 1948.

MCWHORTER, G. L. The relations of the superficial and deep lobes of the parotid gland to the ducts and to the facial nerve. *Anat. Rec. 12:*149, 1917.

MAES, U. Infections of the "dangerous area" of the face. *Surgery 2:*789, 1937.

MALONEY, W. J., and KENNEDY, R. F. The sense of pressure in the face, eye, and tongue. *Brain 34:*1, 1911.

MASON, M. L., ANSON, B. J., and BEATON, L. E. The surgical and anatomical aspects of a case of double lower lip. *Surg., Gynec. & Obst. 70:*12, 1940.

MONRAD-KROHN, G. H. On the dissociation of voluntary and emotional innervation in facial paresis of central origin. *Brain 47:*22, 1924.

OWENS, N. Preliminary report on the development of neuromuscular junctions in cases of facial paralysis followed by masseter muscle transplantations. *Plast. & Reconstruct. Surg. 6:*345, 1950.

OWENS, N. The surgical treatment of facial paralysis. *Plast. & Reconstruct. Surg. 7:*61, 1951.

PEYTON, W. T., and RITCHIE, H. P. Quantitative studies on congenital clefts of the lip. *Arch. Surg. 33:*1046, 1936.

PRATT, G. H. Furuncle of upper lip. *Am. J. Surg. n.s.36:*118, 1937.

RITCHIE, H. P. Congenital clefts of the face and jaws: A report of the operations used and a discussion of results. *Surg., Gynec. & Obst. 73:*654, 1941.

ROEDER, C. A. The treatment of infections of the face by prophylactic venous obstruction. *Ann. Surg. 104:*1112, 1936.

RUSKIN, S. L. Tic douloureux and trigeminal neuralgia relieved by treatment of the nasal (sphenopalatine) ganglion. *Arch. Otolaryng. 2:*584, 1925.

SALTZSTEIN, H. C. Total removal of parotid gland with preservation of facial nerve. *Ann. Surg. 103:*635, 1936.

SIMONTON, K. M., and GAY, J. R. Unilateral frontal anhidrosis and miosis occurring after petrous apicectomy (Ramadier technic): Report of a case. *Arch. Neurol. & Psychiat. 60:*86, 1948.

STATE, D. Superficial lobectomy and total parotidectomy with preservation of the facial nerve in the treatment of parotid tumors. *Surg., Gynec. & Obst. 89:*237, 1949.

SYMINGTON, J. The topographical anatomy of the salivary glands. *J. Anat. & Physiol. 46:*173, 1912.

WARTENBERG, R. Winking-jaw phenomenon. *Arch. Neurol. & Psychiat. 59:*734, 1948a.

WARTENBERG, R. "Inverted Marcus Gunn phenomenon" (so-called Marin Amat syndrome). *Arch. Neurol. & Psychiat. 60:* 584, 1948b.

WINCKLER, G. Contribution à l'étude et la région orbitaire externe chez l'homme. *Arch. d'anat., d'histol. et d'embryol. 24:*167, 1937.

WOLTMAN, H. W., WILLIAMS, H. L., and LAMBERT, E. H. An attempt to relieve hemifacial spasm by neurolysis of the facial nerves: A report of two cases of hemifacial spasm with reflections on the nature of the spasm, the contracture and mass movement. *Proc. Staff Meet., Mayo Clin. 26:*236, 1951.

CHAPTER 7

The Jaws, Palate, and Tongue

THE UPPER JAW

THE body of the maxilla forms the prominence of the cheek and encloses the maxillary sinus, and where it forms the roof of the latter it forms also much of the floor of the orbit. The frontal process of the maxilla extends upward to form the medial rim of the orbit and the lateral portion of the base of the nose; the zygomatic process extends laterally to articulate with the zygomatic bone and help form the prominence of the cheek at the zygomatic arch; the alveolar process projects downward to bear the teeth of the upper jaw, and the palatine process extends medially to form the larger part of the hard palate: thus maxillofacial injuries may involve not only the maxillary sinus, but also the orbit, nasal cavity, and mouth. Also, while there is relatively little soft tissue associated with the maxilla, the nerves and blood vessels to the upper teeth run upon or through it, as does also the large infra-orbital nerve, and fractures of the bone may therefore be associated with damage to these structures.

The maxillary sinus has already been described in more detail in the chapter on the nose (p. 270); in connection with its relations to the upper jaw it need only be pointed out here that it occupies a variable portion of the body of the maxilla and varies also in the extent to which it invades the zygomatic and alveolar processes; in the latter process, the sinus is more commonly in relationship to the apices of the three molars and of the second premolar, but this is variable both in regard to the number of teeth with which it is closely related and in regard to the thinness of the wall between the mucosa of the sinus and the roots of the teeth. It was this close relation between the teeth and the sinus that was responsible for the discovery of the antrum by Highmore, and infections about the apices of the more posterior teeth are a common cause of infection of the sinus (p. 272). As pointed out by Stafne broken roots of the molars are sometimes forced upward into the maxillary sinus in attempts to remove these teeth.

The alveolar process bears the upper teeth, consisting in the adult of medial (central) and lateral incisors, canine (cuspid), first and second premolars (bicuspids), and first, second and third molars, these being named from the anterior midline backward. The upper jaw is normally somewhat larger than the lower, and the premolars and molars typically slant slightly inward toward their occlusal surfaces. The third molar, the wisdom tooth, is quite commonly defective in its direction of growth, and may fail to emerge through the gum; it is also more apt to be congenitally absent than are the other teeth. Sometimes, also, there are supernumerary teeth posterior to the third molar. The external wall of the sockets of the teeth, especially those of the more anterior ones, is quite thin, as evidenced by the prominent ridges which the teeth make on the outer surface of the alveolar process, but the medial walls are strengthened by the attachment of the hard palate to the alveolar process. The third molar, closely related to the posterior surface of the maxilla, may have particularly thin walls, however, and efforts to remove it may result in fracture of the maxilla.

NERVES AND VESSELS

Except for some participation by the mandibular nerve in the innervation of the external gingival mucosa, the nerve supply of the upper jaw is entirely through the *maxillary nerve*, and, correspondingly, the chief blood supply is from the *internal maxillary artery*. Unlike the lower jaw, in which a single nerve branch (the inferior alveolar) supplies all the teeth, the branches to the upper teeth (superior alveolar nerves) are multiple and have divergent courses through the maxillary bone. Thus anesthesia of all the teeth on one side (except for the incisors, which may receive some innervation from the opposite side) can be ob-

tained only by injection about the maxillary nerve as a whole. This can be done, as for injection of the sphenopalatine ganglion, by delivering the anesthetic into the pterygopalatine (pterygomaxillary, sphenomaxillary, sphenopalatine) fossa by the external or lateral route into the fossa, by injection through the buccal mucosa deep to the mandible and the temporalis insertion, by the palatine route, or by injection backward through the infra-orbital foramen (pp. 251 and 343). A successful injection of this type produces also anesthesia of most of the nasal fossa and palate.

Production of anesthesia of specific groups of teeth depends upon delivering the anesthetic in the immediate neighborhood of the various nerves before they enter the small bony canals in which they run in the maxilla, and in injecting beneath the mucosa or periosteum of the alveolar process itself; this local infiltration not only produces anesthesia of the gingival mucosa, but also allows the anesthetic to reach the tooth sockets through the numerous small foramina for nerves and vessels that exist in the alveolar process. Submucous injections diffuse more widely, which is sometimes an advantage; subperiosteal injections should be made slowly, in order to minimize the pain produced by the elevation of the periosteum from the bone.

The nerve endings in and about the teeth have been described by Lewinsky and Stewart ('36a, '37), Van der Sprenkel, and Tiegs, among others; one of the questions apparently not completely settled is the extent to which nerve fibers penetrate into the dentine of the tooth. Of more physiological importance is the generally agreed upon fact that many of the nerve fibers to the teeth are not concerned with pain, but are large sensory fibers probably serving to control the strength of the bite.

INNERVATION OF UPPER TEETH

The innervation of the upper teeth is probably not accurately known, for the nerves are small and difficult to trace in their bony canals, show some gross variability, and, moreover, enter into a plexus through which it is impossible to trace fibers of a given branch to a specific tooth.

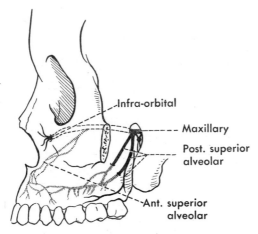

Fig. 206. Innervation of the upper teeth. The posterior superior alveolar nerves may be seen leaving the maxillary nerve in the pterygopalatine fossa, and coursing downward before entering the maxilla.

The superior alveolar (dental) nerves (Fig. 206) are usually described as consisting of three sets, a posterior, a middle and an anterior one, but according to Jones a middle alveolar nerve is probably quite rare.

Jones found the *posterior superior alveolar nerves* to number three as a rule. These are given off from the infra-orbital nerve just before it enters the infra-orbital canal, and therefore descend on the posterior wall of the maxilla, where this forms the anterior wall of the pterygopalatine fossa; one apparently usually does not enter the bone, but runs laterally to supply a posterior part of the gum and an adjacent part of the cheek, but the other two are true dental branches and enter canals on the posterior and lateral walls of the maxilla. They may be anesthetized before they enter their canals by passing a needle through the mucosa behind the last molar tooth and upward along the rounded tuberosity of the maxilla. As the jaw is opened widely the tendon of insertion of the temporal muscle is brought in close contact with the tuberosity, however, so that it may interfere with the passage of the needle here; this interference may be minimized by having the patient close his mouth somewhat, and even more successfully by combining this with deviation of the jaw toward the side to be injected. The posterior superior alveolar nerves which enter the maxilla course forward above the level of the roots of the teeth, the larger branch running, according to Jones, as far forward as the canine tooth. According to other descriptions, the posterior superior alveolar nerves supply only the molar teeth.

The *middle superior alveolar nerve* is usually described as arising from the infra-orbital nerve at the posterior part of the infra-orbital sulcus, and passing immediately into a canal in the bone which runs downward and forward at first behind and then inferior to the zygomatic process of the maxilla, where it is said to join the superior dental plexus and supply especially the bicuspid teeth; as already pointed out, Jones regarded this branch as rare.

Most texts describe the *anterior superior alveolar nerves* as numbering two or three, though Jones stated that there is typically a single stem of origin. The nerve leaves the infra-orbital canal in its middle or last portion and diverges laterally from the infra-orbital nerve in the floor of the orbit; it then turns medially and downward on the anterior wall of the antrum to run alongside and then beneath the external naris, reaching almost to the nasal spine. From this point descending branches spread downward in the anterior antral wall and form a superior alveolar plexus which is distributed to the roots of the canine and incisor teeth. According to Jones, the canine may be supplied either through this plexus or by the posterior nerves. The two plexuses apparently communicate across the midline, and the medial, and occasionally the lateral, incisors may receive a bilateral innervation.

As the anterior superior alveolar nerves run in the wall of the canine fossa, they (and the infra-orbital nerve) are subject to damage in external antrotomies (p. 275). Before they reach the teeth, the anterior superior alveolar nerves give off a nasal branch to a limited portion of the nasal fossa (inferior concha, inferior meatus) and twigs to the nasolacrimal duct, and all the superior alveolar nerves supply twigs to the mucosa of the maxillary sinus.

As the anterior superior alveolar nerves have no part of their course on the outer surface of the maxilla, they are difficult to inject; anesthesia of the incisors is therefore usually produced by infiltration rather than by nerve block. For a nerve block, the injection is typically into the infra-orbital foramen, which lies usually on a vertical line passed through the palpable supra-orbital notch (this line also passing usually through the mental foramen on the lower jaw), but may lie slightly lateral to this line. The injection can be delivered directly into the infra-orbital canal through the cheek, or may be made intra-orally into the region of the foramen.

In making the injection through the external surface of the cheek, it is well to remember that the canal does not usually approach the foramen in a straight postero-anterior line, but usually slants somewhat inward; thus the canal can be entered more readily if the syringe is directed slightly to the opposite side, so that the needle is directed posterolaterally. Also, care must be taken not to mistake the concavity on the front of the maxilla, the canine fossa, for the infra-orbital foramen itself; the infra-orbital foramen lies at the upper border of the fossa, and material delivered into the depths of the fossa, into or deep to the caninus muscle, may not affect the dental nerves appreciably. If injection is made intra-orally, the region of the infra-orbital foramen may be reached by passing the needle upward through the mucosa above the root of the first bicuspid, until it strikes the orbital rim overhanging the canine fossa; in this approach, however, the needle should not be introduced for any distance into the infra-orbital canal, since it would then necessarily impinge upon the roof of the canal, which may be exceedingly thin just behind the orbital rim and allow passage of the needle into the orbit.

BLOOD SUPPLY TO UPPER TEETH

The chief arteries to the teeth (Fig. 207) correspond approximately to the chief nerves already described. The *posterior superior alveolar (dental) artery* arises from the internal maxillary artery and descends on the posterior aspect of the maxilla, where its branches enter canals and run forward with the nerves above the upper teeth, supplying the molar and premolar teeth; like the nerves, these vessels give off branches to the gum, and to the cheek and the maxillary sinus. The *anterior superior alveolar or dental artery* is a branch of the infra-orbital artery (in turn a branch of the internal maxillary), and runs downward to supply the more anterior teeth and to anastomose with the posterior superior alveolar. A *middle superior alveolar artery* is also often described, leaving the infra-orbital artery to course in the lateral wall of the antrum to the region of the canine tooth, and anastomose with an-

nerve fibers which run toward the gum from the apical region of the teeth, that is, from the branches which enter the tooth pulp, but is also by nerve fibers from the gums which enter the periodontal membrane through minute foramina in the alveolar process; blood vessels from the gums also reach the periodontal membrane in this fashion.

BLOOD SUPPLY AND INNERVATION OF GUMS

The nerves and vessels to the gums and periodontal membrane are for the most

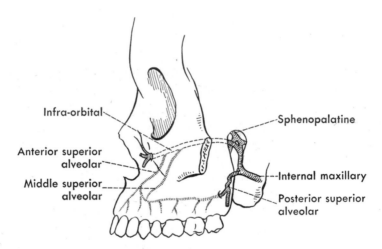

Fig. 207.   Arteries to the upper teeth.

teterior and posterior arteries. Bleeding into the nose following extraction of a tooth, apparently resulting from rupture of one of these vessels in the floor of the antrum, may be quite troublesome (Trible).

PERIODONTAL MEMBRANE

The pulp of the teeth is supplied entirely by branches of the nerves and vessels already described, which enter the foramen lying at the apex of the root; however, the periodontal membrane, or periosteum between the tooth and the alveolar process, has a double innervation (Fig. 208) according to Lewinsky and Stewart ('36b). This is in part from

part not connected with the alveolar nerves and vessels, hence the necessity for local injection if complete anesthesia of a tooth and its adnexa is desired. As indicated for the nerves in Figure 209, the labial (buccal) gingival mucosa about the more posterior teeth is supplied by branches from the posterior superior alveolar nerves and vessels, but also receives twigs from the buccinator or buccal nerve (from the mandibular) and buccinator artery (from the internal maxillary); they run together deep to the temporal muscle and emerge on the cheek over the buccinator muscle, but give off branches which supply both the outer

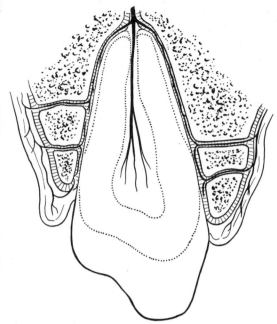

Fig. 208. The double innervation to a tooth. The nerve to the pulp gives off twigs to the periodontal membrane before entering the tooth, and minute branches from the nerves to the gum penetrate the bone of the alveolar process to reach the periodontal membrane. The periosteum (and its continuation as the periodontal membrane) is cross lined.

and inner surfaces of the cheek, and the adjacent gingival mucosa. The labial gingival mucosa of the more anterior teeth is supplied through the descending or labial branches of the infra-orbital nerve and vessels, which of course supply also the skin and mucous membrane of the upper lip.

The palatine (lingual) gingival mucosa of the upper teeth is supplied largely from the greater or anterior palatine nerve, which emerges from the great palatine foramen laterally at the junction of palatine and maxillary bones, and runs forward on the hard palate to supply the major portion of this and the adjacent gum (Fig. 210). A small anteromedial portion of the palate and gum, behind the medial incisors, is supplied by the nasopalatine nerves (p. 247) which emerge through the midline incisive foramen to anastomose with the greater palatine nerve.

The buccinator (buccal) nerve may be

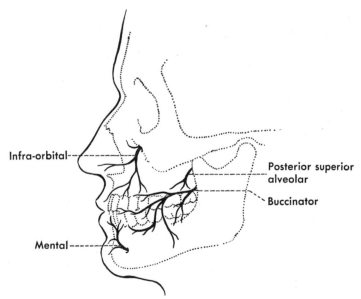

Fig. 209. Innervation of the buccal gingival mucosa and that of the adjacent cheek and lip. For the lower jaw it is entirely through the mandibular, but for the upper jaw only the posterior and anterior parts are innervated through the maxillary nerve.

blocked by anesthetic delivered through the mucosa on the inner surface of the temporal muscle, or into the buccal fat pad from the external surface; the twigs from the labial branches of the infraorbital nerve may be reached either through injection at the foramen or beneath the mucosa of the anterior teeth. The nasopalatine and greater or anterior palatine nerves can be most easily blocked at the foramina through which they emerge onto the palate: thus the naso-palatine nerves, both emerging through the incisive foramen (the left usually anterior to the right) may be blocked by injection immediately behind and between the central incisors, while the greater palatine nerve may be blocked by injection at the greater palatine foramen, which lies at the level of the third molar tooth. Insertion of a needle into this foramen may cause injury to the great palatine artery, and give rise to troublesome hemorrhage.

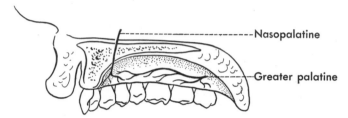

Fig. 210.   Nerves to the inner or lingual gingival mucosa of the upper jaw.

THE PALATE

THE palate intervenes between the nasal fossae and the cavity of the mouth; its functional efficiency, necessary to proper swallowing and to proper articulation of the sounds used in speech, depends upon the palate's ability to close off completely the nasal cavity from the mouth and oral pharynx. The musculature of the soft palate, acting in conjunction with that of the pharynx, normally brings about apposition between the soft palate and the posterior pharyngeal wall; Wardill ('28) has emphasized that this closure must be complete during certain stages of phonation, and stated that a gap between the soft palate and the posterior pharyngeal wall of even 1 mm., so small that it cannot be detected upon examination, may be responsible for defective speech. It should be remembered, however, that speech is a complex phenomenon involving the proper co-ordination of many parts; for instance, it is a matter of common knowledge that imperfect dentures may markedly interfere with clear enunciation.

HARD PALATE

Approximately the anterior three fourths of the palate is formed by the palatine processes of the maxillary and palatine bones, covered by a mucosa which is firmly adherent to the periosteum, but which contains in its submucosa numerous mucous palatine glands. The palatine processes of the maxillary bones form the larger part of the roof of the mouth, while the palatine bones articulate with these to form the posterior part of the hard palate, this articulation lying on a line drawn between the second molar teeth.

SOFT PALATE

The soft palate is a curved musculo-aponeurotic shelf covered by mucosa, projecting backward and downward from the posterior edge of the hard palate. From its free posterior edge, the velum, the nipple-like uvula projects downward in the midline, and laterally the palatine arches (p. 404) join it to the pharyngeal walls. On the oral (inferior and anterior) aspect of the soft palate are numerous palatine glands continuous with those on the hard palate, and the bulk of the uvula is largely made up of glands; because of this, and its especially abundant lymphatics, the uvula readily becomes edematous.

The central layer of the soft palate is the fibrous palatine aponeurosis, which attaches to the hard palate anteriorly, and laterally to the adjacent bone, and receives the attachments of the palatine muscles. Muscles attach upon both surfaces of the aponeurosis, but the more anterior portion of the soft palate is largely membranous, consisting of the aponeurosis and the tendon of the tensor veli palatini muscle; the bulk of the muscle of the palate occupies a middle segment, and Oldfield stated that the posterior segment is not sufficiently muscular to move actively, but moves passively as a result of movement of the middle segment.

The uvula is sometimes surgically shortened, especially in the course of tonsillectomy; Richardson and Pullen, however, expressed the belief that it should not be traumatized needlessly, for they regarded it as important in moistening and removing mucus from the posterior pharyngeal wall, and as a valuable aid in children in preventing middle ear disease. Froeschels pointed out normal variations in the shape of the uvula; he stated that the uvula shrinks after tonsillectomy, and this may obviate the clipping which sometimes seems indicated. The function of the uvula in helping to seal off the nasopharynx is perhaps best illustrated by Wodak's case, in which the uvula was turned forward and was adherent to the oral surface of the soft palate, with the result that the nasopharynx remained constantly open and the patient's speech was scarcely intelligible.

CLEFT PALATE

Developmentally, the palatine processes of the maxillae and of the palatine bones have arisen in shelves of tissue which have simply grown medially to meet the elements of the opposite side in the midline. The part of the alveolar process bearing the central incisor teeth, however, is formed by a median downgrowth (the medial nasal process) that also forms the mobile part of the nasal septum and the midpart of the upper lip; this normally fuses with the maxillary alveolar processes and the remainder of the hard palate (Fig. 211). The line of fusion between the medial and lateral processes apparently occurs at about the levels at which the tooth germs for the lateral incisors will appear later; although an unfused medial nasal process is often spoken of as the premaxilla (the part of the bone bearing the incisor teeth), the medial nasal process does not exactly correspond to this, and in failure of fusion the lateral incisor may be defective, or may lie on either side of the cleft.

Because of the method of development of the palate it occurs that cleft of the palate proper is always a defect in the midline, due to the failure of the palatine processes from the two sides to meet; on the other hand the alveolar process, like the upper lip, may show either a unilateral cleft or a bilateral cleft, due to improper fusion of the medial nasal process with the lateral nasal and palatine processes, or, rarely, a large midline defect due to failure of development of the medial nasal process.

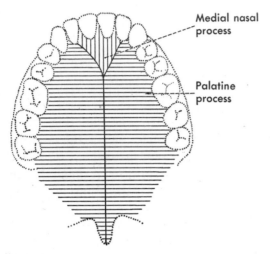

Fig. 211. Formation of the palate from two lateral and an anterior median process, thus determining the various types of cleft palate that may occur. Unless the medial nasal process fails to contribute to the upper jaw, clefts of the alveolar process must obviously be lateral ones, while clefts of the palate proper are necessarily midline.

INCIDENCE AND TYPES

Maxillofacial clefts (harelip and cleft palate) are by far the most common of facial anomalies; Smith and Johnson quoted other authors as having found that white children show cleft palate about once in 1000 births, Negro children once in 1800 births, and Slaughter and Brodie gave an occurrence of once in every 770 live births. Harelip and cleft palate are apparently also more common in the male

than in the female. Peyton found in a series of 2352 patients with congenital malformation of the upper lip and palate that 64.3 per cent were males.

Since harelip and cleft palate occur so frequently together, most of the figures do not break down these associated defects into their component parts. Actually, the lack of fusion may involve the entire hard and soft palates, the alveolar process and the upper lip, thus combining harelip with cleft palate; it may involve the entire palate alone; or it may be limited to either the anterior or posterior part of the palate. According to Ritchie ('41) the alveolar process is involved in about 60 to 70 per cent of all facial clefts. The alveolar process and the lip are apparently more commonly cleft on the left side than the right, and a midline defect of these is fortunately quite rare. In bilateral cleft of the alveolar process the superior alveolar nerves, from the maxillary, cannot of course grow across the gap to reach the central incisors, and the latter are in these cases, according to Goyder, innervated by the nasal (nasociliary) nerve.

Because of the sequence of closure of the palate, from before backward, the soft palate is usually cleft if the hard palate is; Goyder reported that tripartite palate (that is, bilateral alveolar clefts and complete cleft palate) occurred in 22.8 per cent of his cases, bipartite palate in 31.9 per cent, cleft of the soft and part of the hard palate in 28.7 per cent, of the soft palate alone in 15.7 per cent, and all other varieties, 0.9 per cent. Davis, in 804 cases of cleft palate, found unilateral clefts in the lip and alveolar process in 74, unilateral clefts of the entire palate in 342, bilateral cleft palate in 139, partial posterior clefts of the palate in 240, and submucous clefts of the hard palate in 9. It is apparent from his table that clefts of the lip and alveolar process do not always correspond, for he listed cases of unilateral cleft lip and bilateral cleft palate, and cases of bilateral cleft lip and unilateral cleft palate.

REPAIR

Repair of cleft lip is essentially a problem of restoring muscle continuity to the orbicularis oris, and the surgical problem is therefore different from that of the repair of cleft palate. Repair of the hard palate demands mobilization of the periosteum and mucosa on the palate, so that this can be moved to the midline and sutured to its fellow from the opposite side. In the Veau type of operation, the mucoperiosteum of either the nasal or buccal surface of the palate is sutured to that of the nasal septum; the raw surface may be left to heal spontaneously, or, if it is the lower surface, it may be covered by flaps from the buccal surface of the palate which are brought to the midline. Approximation of the two sides is necessary also in repair of the soft palate but, of equal importance, the soft palate must also be moved backward if it is abnormally short, in order to allow proper closure of the nasopharyngeal orifice.

As emphasized by most writers, the most difficult problem in obtaining a satisfactory functional repair of cleft palate is to obtain a really satisfactory improvement in the mechanism of speech. For instance, Lyons pointed out the role of the soft palate in proper speech, and the necessity of leaving it both soft and well back toward the normal position in repair of cleft palate, and Ritchie ('37) expressed the belief that mobility of the palate is probably more important than its length in regard to closure of the nasal cavity, both writers thus emphasizing the

care with which the soft tissues here should be handled.

Ritchie also described various types of defects in speech caused by openings in different portions of the palate; in an investigation of 100 cases of repair of cleft palate he found that apparently good anatomical results are not necessarily accompanied by good functional ones from the standpoint of speech, owing to insufficient closure of the nasal cavity. As evidence of the difficulty in obtaining a sufficiently long and mobile soft palate, he cited the fact that following repair the superior constrictor muscle of the pharynx, which aids in closing the nasal aperture, is usually hypertrophied; in order to facilitate proper closure, Wardill ('37) advocated suturing the pharynx along the line of the ridge of Passavant. Many writers have emphasized the importance of training in speech following correction of the palatine defect.

GROWTH FACTORS RELATED TO REPAIR

Wardill ('28) stated that he had been able to find no particular abnormalities of the musculature in cases of cleft palate, but that movement of the soft palate in such cases is either greatly deficient or almost entirely lacking. To what extent the deformity is due to an actual deficiency of tissue, and to what extent to malplacement, is a question which has been disputed for many years and yet cannot be regarded as settled. Among more recent workers Peyton reported that the general dimensions of cleft palate, usually arched upward higher than normal, are larger than those of the normal palate at an early postnatal date, except for the actual surface width of the palate; as has also been noted by others, he observed that subsequently there was sufficient growth of the palate to actually narrow the cleft. This can hardly be true of growth in length, for the cleft palate is usually described as being also short, hence the push-back operation—though, of course, the apparent shortness may depend in part upon insufficient movement.

Oldfield expressed the belief that there are probably two types of cleft palate, one with separation only and another with true deficiency as well. Dorrance emphasized that even in the absence of cleft palate the hard or soft palate may be abnormally short, and that in these cases also an operation for a push-back of the soft palate may be necessary.

Graber suggested that surgical correction of cleft palate in early childhood may limit the growth potential of the maxillary denture, as he found that in cases in which cleft palate had been repaired the maxilla was more deficient in its anteroposterior, lateral, and vertical dimensions than in unrepaired cleft palate; the latter apparently showed normal vertical and lateral growth in the absence of limiting bands of scar tissue. Five sixths of the growth in the lateral direction is said to be accomplished by the end of the fourth year of life, but most surgeons have preferred to perform the operation somewhat earlier. Recent trends are to repair cleft palate at a later age.

The importance of proper timing and of careful handling of the soft tissues so as to interfere with blood supply as little as possible has been stressed especially by Slaughter and Brodie, who have emphasized that surgical treatment may interfere with normal growth; Waldron has also stressed this point, and stated that the opinion of many surgeons and orthodontists experienced in this field is that surgical repair of the palate itself

should be postponed until the end of the fifth year.

MUSCULATURE

The skeletal core of the soft palate is the palatine aponeurosis, a layer of connective tissue firmly attached anteriorly to the posterior margin of the hard palate, and continuous laterally with the aponeurotic (submucous) layer of the pharynx, although fading out posteriorly toward the free palatal margin. This aponeurosis is also continuous laterally with the tendon of the tensor veli palatini muscle, while upon its upper surface are arranged most of the other muscles associated with the soft palate. In a push-back operation upon the soft palate, this aponeurosis must be detached from its attachment to the hard palate, in order that the musculofibrous mass of the soft palate may be actually moved backward. This is done by mobilizing the periosteum of the hard palate, with which the aponeurosis is continuous; Havens has found it useful also to extend the dissection onto the medial surface of the pterygoid plate, after fracturing the pterygoid process.

The most superficial muscle fibers on the upper surface of the soft palate are ones attributed to the *palatopharyngeus* (pharyngopalatinus, B.N.A.) muscle, (Fig. 212), but apparently consisting in part of special sphincteric fibers of the superior pharyngeal constrictor (p. 413); other and more numerous fibers of the palatopharyngeus arise from the inferior or anterior aspect of the palate. The anterior and posterior layers of this muscle enclose between them the musculus uvulae and the levator veli palatini, and come together laterally to form a muscle bundle which runs downward into the pharynx

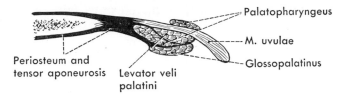

Fig. 212. Diagram of the aponeuroticomuscular structure of the soft palate, in longitudinal section.

to form the posterior pillar of the tonsil, also called the pharyngopalatine arch (Fig. 213). This muscle is considered further in connection with the pharyngeal wall, to which it more properly belongs.

The *musculus uvulae* is situated immediately deep to the posterior layer of the palatopharyngeus, and consists simply of longitudinally directed fibers that run downward into the uvula.

It is the fibers of the *levator veli palatini* (levator palati) that contribute the main muscular bulk of the soft palate; this muscle arises from the inferior surface of the petrous portion of the temporal bone, and in part also from the lower part of the cartilage of the Eusta-

chian tube, and runs downward and medially to curve into the soft palate, between the musculus uvulae and the anterior layer of the palatopharyngeus. Most of the fibers from the two muscles meet in the midline, the more anterior ones attaching to the palatine aponeurosis. It is primarily this muscle which forms what Oldfield described as the "middle segment" of the soft palate.

The *tensor veli palatini* (tensor palati) muscle, by its tendinous insertion into the anterior part of the palatal aponeurosis, contributes to the anterior, membranous, portion of the soft palate. This muscle originates from the base of the skull slightly anterior and lateral to the

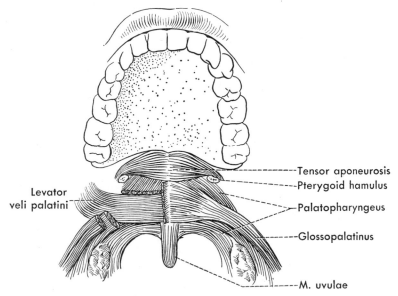

Fig. 213. Muscles of the soft palate from below. On the left side of the figure muscles are cut away to show the levator veli palatini.

origin of the levator veli palatini, and descends at first approximately parallel with this. Instead of simply passing into the soft palate when it reaches this level, however, the muscle passes farther downward (between the internal pterygoid muscle and the medial pterygoid plate) to pass lateral to the hamular process of

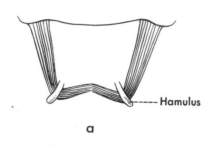

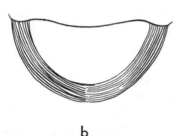

Fig. 214. The difference in the pull of the tensor veli palatini, *a*, and the levator, *b*. Note that by breaking the hamuli or removing the tendons from around them the tensors can be released so that they have a course similar to that of the levators.

the pterygoid plate; here it becomes tendinous, turns at almost a right angle below the hamulus, and as it runs medially and slightly upward expands into the soft palate and becomes continuous with the aponeurosis of this.

In an attempt to repair the soft palate, it is the tensor veli palatini which resists movement both toward the midline and backward; unlike the levators, which simply curve into the soft palate and can

therefore be fairly readily approximated, the tensors of the two sides are held apart by the two hamuli around which they run (Fig. 214). Wardill ('37), Dorrance and Bransfield, Havens, and others have emphasized that these muscles may make closure of the palate exceedingly difficult, or may subsequently by their contraction pull out the sutures; the tendons of the muscles may of course be cut, but these authors agree that a better method is to break the hamular processes. When this is done, the tensors of the palate then take a course into the palate essentially similar to that taken by the levators; they thus both lose part of their tensing powers on the palate and contribute to the elevation of this. The same result can be obtained by lifting the tendon off the hamular process, instead of breaking the latter.

The most superficial muscle fibers on the oral surface of the soft palate form the small *glossopalatine* (palatoglossus) muscle. This curves downward to the lateral margin of the tongue anterolateral to the tonsil, raising the mucous membrane to form the anterior pillar of the tonsil (glossopalatine arch).

ACTIONS

Acting upon the soft palate, the palatopharyngeus and the glossopalatinus muscles draw this downward, and hence narrow the pharyngeal and faucial isthmi. The musculus uvulae draws the uvula upward and forward. The levator has the action implied by its name, and in raising the velum of the soft palate helps to bring it in contact with the posterior wall of the pharynx, while the tensor veli palatini tenses the soft palate and also somewhat depresses it. The tensor is usually regarded as being instrumental in opening the auditory (Eustachian) tube, and the levator also is sometimes said to have this function (p. 185).

Because of the soft palate's action in closing the nasopharyngeal isthmus in swallowing, paralysis of it is particularly disabling; it allows food, and especially liquids, to pass upward into the nasal cavity rather than descend in the pharynx.

NERVES AND VESSELS

MOTOR NERVES

The tensor veli palatini muscle receives, on its lateral surface where it is adjacent to the mandibular nerve, a branch from this nerve by way of the otic ganglion; with the exception of this muscle, the remaining muscles of the soft palate are innervated by an ascending branch, not readily demonstrable, from the pharyngeal plexus (Sprague, and others). The motor fibers in the pharyngeal plexus are derived from the vagus nerve, probably reaching it in large part through the so-called bulbar rootlets of the spinal accessory.

It was once widely believed that the great superficial petrosal branch of the facial, ending at the sphenopalatine ganglion, supplied motor fibers to the muscles of the palate (for branches from the ganglion can be traced to the palate). This view has been largely discredited by observations such as those of Turner and of Rich, by most clinical observations of recent years, and by experimental analyses of the facial nerve, which have failed to reveal voluntary motor fibers in the great superficial petrosal. However, it is still apparently held by a few workers. For example, Tschiassny has stated that lesions of the facial nerve central to the origin of the greater superficial petrosal nerve sometimes produce deviation of the uvula and soft palate toward the opposite side, and expressed the belief that in such cases the palatine muscles are innervated through the great superficial petrosal, while in other cases the innervation of the muscles is different.

SENSORY NERVES

The sensory nerves of the palate are usually described as branches of the sphenopalatine ganglion, and therefore

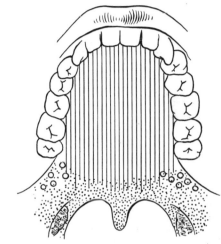

Fig. 215. Probable distribution of the fifth nerve (lines), seventh nerve (circles), and ninth nerve (stipple) on the palate.

might consist of (1) fibers from the facial nerve (through the great superficial petrosal) which traverse the ganglion; (2) fibers of the maxillary nerve; or (3) fibers of posterior cranial or upper spinal nerves which are said to reach the sphenopalatine ganglion via the Vidian nerve (p. 249). Actually, the details of the sensory innervation of the palate have apparently not been satisfactorily determined, and may indeed vary somewhat from one individual to another, but the major innervation is from the trigeminal nerve (Fig. 215), and the palate may be a "trigger zone" in trigeminal neuralgia.

Most texts describe the greater palatine

nerves as consisting of both maxillary and facial nerve fibers, and the other palatine nerves as largely, at least, composed of facial nerve fibers. However, Cushing

section of the ninth nerve only; and Hunt described eruptions on the soft palate, just in front of the anterior pillar of the fauces, associated with herpes of the

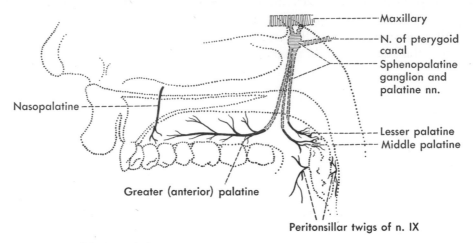

Fig. 216. Nerves of the palate from the medial aspect. Except for ascending twigs from the tonsillar plexus, all of them are so-called branches of the spheno-palatine ganglion.

('04) described anesthesia of the entire oral surface of the palate, including the uvula, and of at least the major part of the upper and posterior surface, as resulting

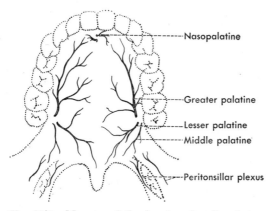

Fig. 217. Nerves of the hard and soft palates.

from destruction of the fifth nerve only; Dandy described anesthesia of the uvula, of a narrow strip on the anterior surface of the soft palate, and of most of the poste-rior surface of the soft palate following

geniculate ganglion. The sensory fibers are undoubtedly accompanied by secre-tory and vasomotor fibers from the sphenopalatine ganglion.

The sphenopalatine ganglion and its branches have been discussed in some detail in connection with the nose (p. 251). The palatine branches of the gan-glion are three in number (Fig. 216). Of these, the *great or anterior palatine nerve* is by far the largest; it passes downward through the pterygopalatine canal (greater palatine) in the lateral nasal wall, in company with the chief blood supply of the palate, the descending palatine artery. While it is in this canal the nerve supplies twigs to the lower posterior part of the nasal fossa. The nerve and its accompanying vessels emerge on the hard palate through the greater palatine foramen (posterior pala-tine foramen), situated at the level of the third upper molar tooth (Fig. 217).

The nerve then breaks up into branches which are distributed to the hard palate and to the gums on the inner surface of the alveolar process. A small area immediately behind the incisor teeth is supplied by terminal branches of the nasopalatine nerve (p. 247), also a branch from the sphenopalatine ganglion.

The *posterior, lesser or small palatine nerve* passes downward parallel to the greater and emerges through a lesser palatine foramen situated almost at the posterior edge of the hard palate, and therefore

tonsil. It and the posterior palatine together are frequently referred to as the lesser palatine nerves. The ninth nerve fibers which, according to Dandy, are distributed to the palate could reach this in several ways, but most easily through the tonsillar branch of the ninth nerve.

ARTERIES

The palate has an abundant arterial supply, its chief artery being the descending palatine, from the internal maxillary (Fig. 218). The main branch of the

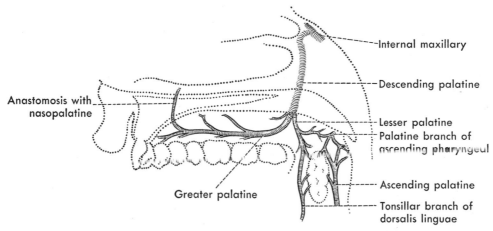

Internal maxillary

Descending palatine

Anastomosis with nasopalatine

Lesser palatine
Palatine branch of ascending pharyngeal

Ascending palatine

Greater palatine

Tonsillar branch of dorsalis linguae

Fig. 218.   Schema of the arteries of the palate.

slightly behind the greater palatine foramen; it turns backward and downward to be distributed to the soft palate. It is often stated to consist largely of facial nerve fibers, both for general sensation and for taste buds said to be present on the soft palate; it is this branch which has also been regarded as containing motor fibers from the facial which are distributed to the musculature of the soft palate.

The *middle or external palatine nerve,* a small twig, is usually said to contain sensory fibers from the facial nerve, and is distributed to the most lateral and posterior part of the palate, and to the adjacent area about the upper pole of the

descending palatine emerges on the hard palate with the greater palatine nerve at the level of the upper third molar tooth, and is the greater palatine artery; it runs forward on the lateral aspect of the hard palate at the junction of this and the alveolar process. The descending palatine artery also gives off lesser palatine arteries, which are distributed backward to the soft palate. The greater palatine artery may be a source of serious hemorrhage in repair of cleft palate, or may as it emerges onto the hard palate prevent proper mobilization of the soft tissues; probably the majority of surgeons purposely sacrifice it, if expedient, at the time of operation, but some have advocated its preliminary ligation with sufficient lapse of time to allow the development of the collateral circulation before repair is undertaken. This collateral circulation is provided both anteriorly and posteriorly, but especially from the latter position into the soft palate. Anteriorly, the greater palatine artery passes upward through the incisive or anterior palatine foramen to anastomose in the nasal fossa with the nasopalatine (septal) branch of the sphenopalatine artery; posteriorly, the minor palatine arteries anastomose on the soft palate with the palatine branch of the ascending pharyngeal artery (from the external carotid), the ascending palatine branch of the facial (external maxillary) and twigs from the tonsillar branch of the dorsalis linguae.

To recapitulate, the palate receives its blood supply from the descending palatine (a branch of the sphenopalatine) and from the ascending pharyngeal, facial, and lingual arteries. The branches of the descending palatine enter the palate from above, the remainder enter it from below and laterally. The anastomoses of these vessels in the nasal cavity and on the soft palate apparently suffice to supply the palate after ligature of the greater palatine artery.

VEINS AND LYMPHATICS

The veins of the palate drain both into the pterygoid plexus and, in the case of the soft palate, into the pharyngeal plexus; the latter in turn communicates with the pterygoid plexus and drains also into the internal jugular vein.

The lymphatics from the hard palate leave this at the level of the last molar tooth to pass downward and outward and end in the upper deep cervical nodes; those of the soft palate, which are especially numerous in the uvula, also pass largely into the upper nodes of the deep cervical chain, but those from the upper or posterior surface of the soft palate run also in part with pharyngeal lymphatics to end in the lateral pharyngeal (retropharyngeal) nodes.

THE MANDIBULAR REGION

MANY of the superficial relationships of the mandible have already been discussed in connection with the face; here are discussed primarily the mandible itself and its musculature and nerves, and the structures lying deeper to it, in the infratemporal fossa.

Although the mandible is apparently not developed from the cartilage of the mandibular arch (Meckel's cartilage), for it is believed to be a derm bone, it does develop from the mesenchyme around Meckel's cartilage, and therefore from the same source as the cartilage; the musculature of the mandible is likewise developed from this arch, hence the muscles most intimately connected with the lower jaw, including the mylohyoid and the anterior belly of the digastric in the suprahyoid region, are innervated by the mandibular branch of the trigeminal nerve. While Meckel's cartilage disappears from within the mandible, a fibrous remains of it stretches from the region of the mandibular foramen to that of the petrotympanic fissure as the sphenomandibular ligament, and it is the dorsal end of Meckel's cartilage which projects into the middle ear cavity to give rise to the malleus and incus (hence the innervation of the tensor tympani by the mandibular nerve).

MANDIBLE

The mandible consists of ramus and body, the region of junction being the angle. The ramus and angle are covered externally (Fig. 219) by the masseter muscle (which in turn is crossed by the facial nerve and parotid duct) and internally, between them and the internal pterygoid muscle, are the inferior alveolar and lingual nerves. Overlapping the posterior border of the ramus is the parotid gland, and within this, paralleling this border, is the upper portion of the

the nerves, vessels and muscles of the tongue.

While the mandible obviously varies considerably in form and proportions, anomalies of it are apparently rare. Congenital absence of the ramus has been reported (Kazanjian); Hrdlička has described a number of cases in which the condylar head was more or less doubled.

At the upper end of the ramus are, posteriorly, the condyloid process for articulation with the temporal bone, and, anteriorly, the more pointed coronoid

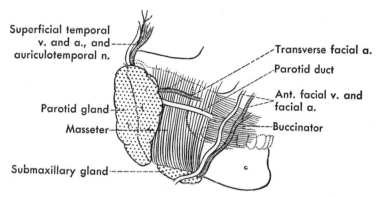

Fig. 219. Some superficial relations of the mandible, with the facial muscles and the branches of the facial nerve omitted. For these, see Figures 186, 194, and 202.

external carotid artery; the superficial temporal branch of this artery emerges from the parotid gland behind the temporomandibular joint, while its internal maxillary branch runs transversely deep to the ramus. Just in front of the insertion of the masseter muscle the facial artery and its accompanying vein cross the lower border of the body of the mandible, which, except for the thin facial muscles, is subcutaneous. Inferiorly and medially, the angle and posterior part of the body of the mandible are related to the submaxillary (submandibular) gland, and medially the anterior part of the mandible is adjacent to the sublingual gland and

process which receives much of the insertion of the temporal muscle; between the two is the mandibular notch. On the inner surface of the ramus is the mandibular foramen, for entrance of the inferior alveolar (dental) nerve (p. 368), and on the outer surface of the tooth-bearing body of the mandible is the mental foramen for the emergence of the mental branch of this nerve.

Fractures of the mandible are relatively common, and the most frequent of these lie between the bicuspid teeth and the angle of the jaw, while fractures of the ramus and the condyle occur less often (Moorehead). In these cases the long (anterior) fragment is always displaced downward (by the pull of the suprahyoid muscles), while the short or posterior fragment is displaced upward by the muscles that close the jaw.

Various aspects of the surgery of the mandible, including its plastic surgery, have been discussed by Byars. He has also pointed out that the periosteum of the mandible possesses a very considerable osteogenic capacity, so that relatively large defects may be healed if the periosteum can be left in place. Large defects may, however, require a bone graft in

downward in the alveolar process, and therefore approach closer to the labial surface as they are traced toward their tips.

TEMPOROMANDIBULAR JOINT

The parotid gland not only overlaps the mandible and the masseter muscle externally, but also extends deeply behind the mandible between its ramus and the external auditory meatus, the mastoid process, and the posterior belly of the digastric muscle; wide opening of the jaw as a strictly hinge movement is therefore

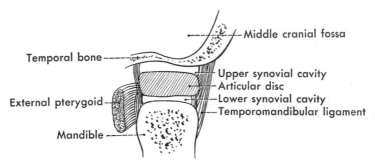

Fig. 220. Schema of the temporomandibular joint in a frontal section.

order to restore the necessary strength to the mandible.

The teeth of the lower jaw correspond in names and number to those of the upper jaw (p. 340). The more anterior teeth of the mandible, like all the teeth of the upper jaw, are set nearer the labial than the lingual surface of the alveolar process; the more posterior teeth, however, are in contrast usually set closer to the lingual surface of the alveolus. This has commonly been held to be responsible for the fact that Ludwig's angina occurs predominately as a result of infection of the lower molar teeth (p. 303). It has also been pointed out, however, that since these molars slant inward, their roots are necessarily directed outward as well as

impeded by the lack of space behind the ramus of the mandible, and the temporomandibular articulation is so formed that it allows for protraction of the jaw associated with opening of it. The temporomandibular ligament, passing from the zygoma to the head and neck of the condyloid process of the mandible, reinforces the articular capsule of the joint but is somewhat lax in order to allow for this protraction. Within the articular capsule an articular disc typically separates the temporomandibular joint into two separate synovial cavities (Fig. 220), the lower between the condyle of the mandible and the cartilage, the upper between the cartilage and the glenoid fossa of the temporal bone. These two joint cavities have separate functions: the cavity between the disc and the condyle acts as a hinge joint, while that between the disc and the temporal bone acts as a sliding joint, upon which both mandible and articular disc are carried forward together in protraction.

The *articular disc* is generally described as being fibrocartilaginous, but Lubosch, Wakeley ('39), and Robinson have all commented on the fact that much of it

dibular joint varies considerably in form, being apparently quite plastic in its development (Angel), and the disc also varies considerably (Fig. 221) in shape in different jaws (Lubosch); in general, however, it is from before backward concavoconvex on its upper surface, to fit the articular eminence and the articular fossa (mandibular fossa) of the temporal bone, and concave below to fit the mandibular condyle.

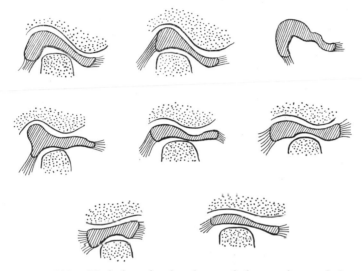

Fig. 221. Variations in the shape of the meniscus of the lower jaw. (Redrawn from Lubosch, W.: *Anat. Anz. 29:*417, 1906.)

may be plain dense fibrous connective tissue; Wakeley stated that sometimes he was unable to find any cartilage cells. The disc is usually also described as being thin in the center, or even sometimes perforated here, but Wakeley ('48) has particularly called attention to this as an erroneous description apparently copied from one text to another: he found the disc to be irregular in thickness, indeed, but thick in its center and thick anteriorly, with a thin part in between, while the posterior portion as it fuses with the capsule is very thin.

Aside from this, the temporoman-

Subluxation of the jaw is not rare, and occurs most frequently in young women (Doherty and Doherty). It may be due to a relaxed ligament or to a loose meniscus; constant clicking or snapping may occur upon movements of the jaw. Complete dislocation involves a forward slipping of the condyle and meniscus beyond the articular eminence. Morris has described plication of the joint capsule, or limiting forward movement of the condyle by a strip of temporal fascia, as being often satisfactory for the repair of snapping jaw. In some cases, however (Doherty and Doherty; Wakeley), the disc may be dislocated, being pulled away from its attachment to the posterior part of the capsule. According to Wakeley, the disc is never actually torn—for it is not firmly attached—but it may be crushed between the condyle and the glenoid fossa and give rise to acute pain; he has found that removal of the disc in such cases produces an excellently functioning joint.

In operations upon the joint, whether for a displaced disc or for an ankylosed joint, the relationships of the facial nerve and the superficial temporal vessels must be borne in mind. Trismus may obviously be due to pathology or even ankylosis of the temporomandibular joint, but may also be caused by spasticity of the closers of the jaw due to various causes, or by swelling induced especially by infections about or operations upon the wisdom teeth.

Upon reflection, it seems apparent that the temporomandibular joint is not designed to bear any very great stress; Robinson has emphasized this, pointing out that the thinness of the temporal bone here, and the fact that the disc may be largely dense connective tissue and even very vascular in places, both indicate that the muscles that close the jaw exert their force directly in bringing the teeth together, and do not act on the jaw as a lever which has the joint as its fulcrum. Apparently, however, in malocclusion of the teeth pressure is exerted on the joint, for proper function of the joint is dependent upon proper occlusion of the teeth (Greene). *Malocclusion* has been said to produce a variety of symptoms including pain in the tongue or the side of the head, disturbances of hearing, and so forth; these have been variously attributed to pressure upon the auriculotemporal and chorda tympani nerves, in-

creased tonus of the muscles supplied by the mandibular branch of the fifth nerve, possible obstruction of the outflow of lymph from the otic labyrinth, and other causes (Costen; Seaver; Young).

The *nerve supply* to the temporomandibular articulation is said to be from both the masseteric and the auriculotemporal nerves. According to Tanasesco the *lymphatics* from the joint empty into three groups of nodes, namely, the pre-auricular, the intraparotid, and the subdigastric (that is, deep cervical) but most of the lymph from the joint is said to reach the subdigastric group.

SPHENOMANDIBULAR AND STYLOMANDIBULAR LIGAMENTS

In addition to the temporomandibular ligament and the muscles which connect the mandible to the skull, the mandible also receives the attachments of the sphenomandibular and stylomandibular ligaments. The former, said to represent a fibrous remains of Meckel's cartilage, stretches from the region of the petrotympanic fissure to the lingula, a projection on the inner surface of the mandible just above the mandibular foramen. The internal maxillary artery passes transversely between this ligament and the ramus of the mandible, and farther up the auriculotemporal nerve also passes transversely between the ligament and the capsule of the temporomandibular joint. The middle meningeal artery runs upward between the ligament and the mandible, and the inferior alveolar nerve and its mylohyoid branch run downward between its lower part and the mandible as they approach the mandibular foramen.

The stylomandibular ligament stretches from the styloid process to the angle and posterior aspect of the ramus of the mandible, but is usually not too well defined; it lies between the masseter and internal pterygoid muscles and also separates the parotid gland from the submaxillary gland. It is usually regarded as representing merely a thickening of the deep cervical fascia associated with the parotid gland, but Lord has stated that it acts as a pivot through the action of which the external pterygoid muscle actively assists in opening the jaw.

MUSCULATURE

The musculature most intimately concerned with the mandible and its move-

pterygoids, and a portion of the temporalis are enclosed within a fascial compartment. The looser connective tissue deep to the ramus of the mandible, and between the various muscles in this location, constitutes the area referred to as the masticator space; through this run the branches of the mandibular nerve and of the internal maxillary artery, and in it lies also the pterygoid plexus of veins.

MASSETER

The masseter muscle rather completely covers the ramus of the mandible, arising from the zygomatic arch and usually also

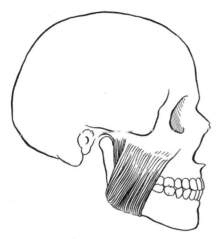 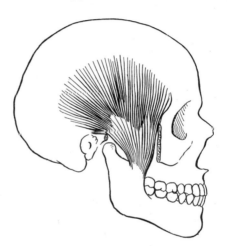

Fig. 222. The masseter and temporal muscles.

ments is a group of four muscles, namely, the masseter, the temporal, and the two pterygoids, external and internal. In addition, some of the suprahyoid muscles are attached to the mandible and assist in opening it, although not commonly classed as mandibular muscles.

As has already been described, the external layer of the deep fascia proceeding upward from the neck is said to split at the lower margin of the mandible to follow the external surface of the masseter and the internal surface of the internal pterygoid muscle, so that the masseter, the

by deep fibers from the fascia over the temporal muscle, and inserting along the ramus and down to the angle and lower margin of the jaw (Fig. 222). Its nerve supply, the masseteric nerve from the mandibular, enters the deep surface of the muscle by passing between the coronoid and condyloid processes of the jaw, being accompanied by the masseteric artery from the internal maxillary, and by a corresponding vein. In sectioning the ramus of the mandible, in order to reset it and overcome undue protraction or retraction of the mandible, the masseter muscle may be reflected upward from its insertion as far as the mandibular notch (the notch between coronoid and condyloid processes), but not above this point without injury to its nerve supply. In any operations in this area, it must be remembered that the masseter is crossed by both the parotid duct and by branches of the facial nerve.

The masseter is sometimes so enlarged, unilaterally or bilaterally, that the enlargement has been mistaken for a tumor; Hersh and Gurney have both reported cases of hypertrophy of the muscle, and concluded it was due to a nervous habit of grating the teeth or clenching the jaw in periods of emotional stress.

TEMPORAL

The temporal muscle has an extensive origin from the temporal fossa on the side of the skull, and inserts not only upon the coronoid process but also downward upon the medial surface of much of the more anterior part of the ramus of the mandible, being largely tendinous in its lower part (it is this part of the muscle which is forced against the maxillary tuberosity when the mouth is opened widely, and makes difficult the injection of the posterior superior alveolar nerves).

The nerves to the temporal muscle are typically two, an anterior and a posterior deep temporal, but there may be only one or there may be three. These nerves pass above the upper head of origin of the external pterygoid muscle, between this and the bone forming the margin of the infratemporal fossa; or the posterior nerve alone has this course, while the anterior one emerges between the two heads of the external pterygoid muscle. They turn upward on the deep surface of the temporal muscle and against the bone of the temporal fossa.

The temporal nerves are usually accompanied by corresponding arteries, but these again vary in number; the arteries, from the internal maxillary, have a more superficial origin than do the nerves and pass across the outer surface of the upper head of the external pterygoid to join the nerves on the deep surface of the temporal muscle; they supply both this and the adjacent bone.

EXTERNAL PTERYGOID

In contrast to the two preceding muscles, which run essentially vertically from above downward, the external pterygoid muscle lies primarily in the horizontal plane. It arises by two heads, a superior and an inferior (Fig. 223). The superior head, the smaller, arises from the lower portion of the temporal fossa and from the adjacent under surface of the great wing of the sphenoid bone; the inferior head arises from the lateral surface of the lateral pterygoid process. The two heads blend at their insertions, but the superior head inserts primarily into the anterior portion of the capsular ligament, the articular disc, and the upper portion of the neck of the condyle, while the inferior head inserts below this on the front of the neck of the condyle. According to Harpman and Woollard a portion of the tendon of the external pterygoid muscle in the human embryo passes through the temporomandibular joint to continue to the malleus, and it is this portion of the tendon which later gives rise to the disc; hence the insertion of the muscle into the disc is readily understandable.

RELATIONS OF NERVES AND VESSELS

The mandibular nerve emerges from the foramen ovale deep to the external pterygoid muscle, and its branches are therefore all intimately related to this muscle: the masseteric and deep temporal nerves pass above the superior head; the auriculotemporal nerve passes backward deep to the superior head and medial to the temporomandibular articulation; the buccinator nerve emerges from between the two heads of the muscle (so may the anterior deep temporal) to cross the

deep to the inferior head and emerge through the cleft between the two heads (p. 370), but in any case it then runs forward superficially in the groove between the heads to reach the posterolateral aspect of the maxilla and the pterygopalatine fossa. Both superficial and deep to the external pterygoid muscle is a plexus of veins, the two usually being

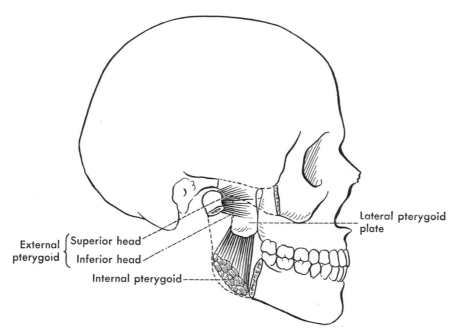

Fig. 223. External and internal pterygoid muscles after removal of a portion of the mandible.

lower head and run toward the cheek; the lingual and inferior alveolar nerves pass deep to both heads to emerge beneath the lower border of the inferior head and run across the external surface of the internal pterygoid muscle (Fig. 224).

The main stem of the internal maxillary artery, after it has passed forward medial to the mandible, also comes in intimate contact with the external pterygoid muscle; it may run superficial to both heads of this muscle, or may pass

grouped together and referred to as the pterygoid plexus.

INTERNAL PTERYGOID

The internal pterygoid muscle, the deepest of the four major paired muscles of the mandible, arises from the internal surface of the outer lamina of the pterygoid plate and inserts upon the body of the mandible where, uniting with the periosteum of the jaw, it forms a sling with the masseter on the outside of the jaw. This muscle receives its nerve supply from the mandibular nerve by a short branch lying deep to the inferior alveolar and lingual branches, and usually traversing or running against the otic ganglion.

The lateral surface of the internal pterygoid muscle forms the deep boundary of the looser tissue of the masticator space, and is crossed by the inferior alveolar and

INNERVATION

The nerves to these four muscles all arise close together, from the mandibular nerve soon after it has emerged from the foramen ovale; the masseteric and posterior deep temporal nerves may arise by a common stem, as may the anterior deep temporal and buccinator nerves; or the pattern may vary, the deep temporals arising by a common stem between the

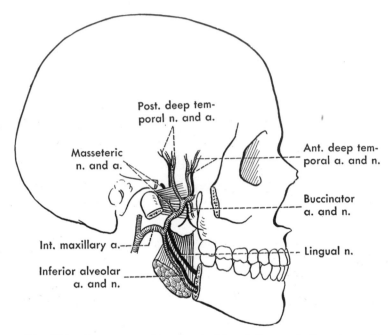

Fig. 224. Some neural and arterial relations of the pterygoid muscles.

lingual nerves and the inferior alveolar artery. The lingual nerve is joined at about the upper border of the muscle by the chorda tympani, and the lingual and inferior alveolar nerves then descend almost parallel with each other across the muscle, the lingual nerve being the more anterior. The medial surface of the internal pterygoid muscle with its covering fascia lies adjacent to the important lateral pharyngeal space, and commonly serves as a guide for the finger in opening this space (p. 302).

origin of the masseteric and the buccinator. The branches to the two heads of the external pterygoid usually arise in common with the buccinator nerve; the branch to the internal pterygoid usually proceeds, as noted, through the otic ganglion.

The masseter, temporal, and internal pterygoid muscles act to close the jaw; alternate action of the internal pterygoids of the two sides adds especially the grinding movements of the teeth involved in chewing. Because of its horizontal direction, the external pterygoid cannot aid in closing the jaw, but is rather a protractor of this; as it inserts upon both the mandible and the articular disc, it draws both of these forward and therefore produces a sliding movement between the disc and the temporal bone. Contraction of one internal pterygoid deviates the jaw to the opposite side. As protraction of the jaw is a necessary concomitant to wide opening of the mouth, the external pterygoids are usually regarded as aiding in opening of the mouth to this extent at least; Lord regarded them as playing an even more active part than this, and described the protraction of the condyle produced by the external pterygoid as producing also a rotation of the mandible about the stylomandibular ligament and perhaps also the sphenomandibular one, so that as the condyles move forward the body of the mandible necessarily moves downward.

OTHER MUSCLES OF MANDIBULAR REGION

The other muscles associated topographically with the ramus of the mandible include the posterior belly of the digastric and the muscles arising from the styloid process (Figs. 229-231, p. 375 ff.). These muscles belong to the suprahyoid, lingual, and pharyngeal groups, and will therefore not be discussed here other than to point out that the posterior belly of the digastric and the stylohyoid muscle pass down in close relationship to the posterior border of the ramus of the mandible, but inclining somewhat more forward than it so that they pass particularly close to its angle before attaching to the hyoid bone.

While the external jugular vein and its continuation upward, the posterior facial vein, pass superficially behind the mandible to enter the parotid gland, the external carotid artery lies more deeply, and is separated from the mandible by the posterior belly of the digastric and by the stylohyoid muscle. The other muscles originating from the styloid process run deep to the internal surface of the internal pterygoid muscle, thus through the connective tissue of the lateral pharyngeal space, which they partially subdivide.

NERVES

Most of the more posterior cranial nerves, and the great vessels extending upward from the neck into the head, are necessarily more or less related to the posterior and deeper aspects of the mandible; they are, however, more intimately concerned with the face, neck, tongue, and pharynx, and are therefore discussed in connection with these parts. It is the mandibular branch of the trigeminal nerve which is most closely related to the mandible, both topographically and because it is the motor supply to the muscles of the mandible and the sensory supply to the lower teeth. Similarly, it is the internal maxillary artery that must be regarded as the artery of the lower jaw, just as it is that of the upper jaw and of the nose.

Mandibular Nerve

The mandibular nerve, as it leaves the skull through the foramen ovale, consists of two rootlets, a large laterally lying sensory one which contains fibers derived from the semilunar ganglion, and a medial motor (and proprioceptive) root which is the direct continuation of the portio minor of the nerve, and is much smaller. As these two parts emerge through the foramen ovale in intimate contact they unite to form the mandibular nerve, a very short trunk which lies deep (medial) to the upper portion of the external pterygoid muscle, and lateral to the tensor veli palatini muscle. In this position the otic ganglion lies on the medial side of the nerve, between it and the tensor, and here also the nerve breaks up into a number of branches. Most of the muscular branches of the nerve leave it at its anterior border, while its larger sensory branches are from the posterior

their names. The anterior deep temporal nerve may also have this course, but often emerges with the buccinator nerve from between the two heads of the external pterygoid.

The *buccinator (buccal) branch* of the mandibular nerve also arises more or less in common with the preceding branches, and passes forward and laterally to emerge between the two heads of the external pterygoid, turn downward across the lat-

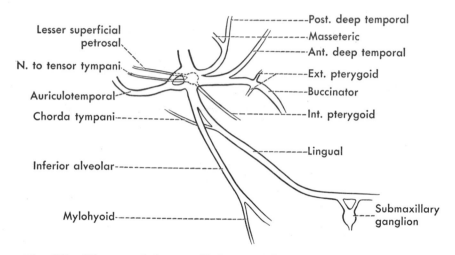

Lesser superficial petrosal.
N. to tensor tympani.
Auriculotemporal.
Chorda tympani
Inferior alveolar
Mylohyoid

Post. deep temporal
Masseteric
Ant. deep temporal
Ext. pterygoid
Buccinator
Int. pterygoid
Lingual
Submaxillary ganglion

Fig. 225. Diagram of the mandibular nerve in the region deep to the ramus of the mandible. In this lateral view the otic ganglion, situated on the medial side of the mandibular nerve, is indicated in outline. The branch of the mandibular to the tensor veli palatini, which passes medially through the otic ganglion, is not shown.

part of the nerve; it is frequently described, therefore, as forming two divisions, an anterior, mixed motor and sensory one, and a posterior, purely sensory one. This division is not, however, very obvious.

The first branches given off anteriorly are usually the *masseteric* and the *anterior* and *posterior deep temporal nerves* (Fig. 225); the first and last mentioned pass above the upper border of the superior head of the external pterygoid muscle, between this and the bone, to be distributed to the muscles indicated by

eral surface of the lower head, and come in contact with the medial surface of the insertion of the temporal muscle. Running forward and downward across this it penetrates the buccal fat pad and thus lies on the buccinator muscle in the cheek; some of its fibers are distributed to the skin here, while others penetrate the muscle to be distributed to the mucosa on the inner surface of the cheek and to the adjacent gingival mucosa.

As it passes between the two heads of the pterygoid muscle the buccinator nerve typically gives off a muscular branch to each, but thereafter is purely sensory. Thus, while it anastomoses with the buccal branch of the facial nerve on the cheek, it is the facial nerve fibers in the plexus that supply the buccinator muscle, and the buccinator nerve does not participate in this.

As already mentioned, the *otic ganglion*, a parasympathetic ganglion connected primarily with the parotid gland (see p. 324), is located on the medial side of the mandibular nerve just outside the foramen ovale. Three of the smaller muscular branches of the mandibular nerve typically pass through or in close association with the otic ganglion, so that they are sometimes described as branches of this; actually, they consist of voluntary motor (and proprioceptive) fibers which have joined the mandibular by way of the portio minor.

Of these three branches, the *nerves to the internal pterygoid, tensor tympani,* and *tensor veli palatini* muscles, respectively, the largest is the nerve to the internal pterygoid muscle, which runs forward and downward into the upper edge of this muscle. A tiny branch is given off posteriorly from the otic ganglion, and runs parallel to the lesser superficial petrosal nerve to supply the tensor tympani muscle. Finally, a twig proceeds medially from the otic ganglion to enter the tensor veli palatini muscle, the only muscle of the soft palate innervated by the fifth nerve.

Obviously, these branches have nothing to do functionally with the otic ganglion, but are simply associated with it; the function of the otic ganglion, as of all autonomic ganglia, is dependent upon preganglionic and postganglionic autonomic fibers. The otic ganglion does not receive any preganglionic fibers from the mandibular nerve, but rather receives these from the ninth nerve by way of the lesser superficial petrosal nerve; its postganglionic fibers are given off primarily to the auriculotemporal nerve, by which they reach the parotid gland; they may also, of course, be distributed to other branches of the mandibular nerve, but nothing definite seems to be known concerning this.

The three remaining branches of the mandibular nerve are sensory. From its posterior border the *auriculotemporal nerve* arises, typically by two stems between which runs the middle meningeal artery; these stems unite posterior to the middle meningeal artery, and the single auriculotemporal nerve thus formed then continues to pass posteriorly, medial to the temporomandibular joint, and behind the joint turns upward to pass between this and the external auditory meatus. Its further course has been described on page 334.

The two largest branches of the mandibular nerve are the *inferior alveolar* (dental) and the *lingual nerves*. These typically arise by a common stem which continues the downward direction of the mandibular nerve itself, but soon separate and cross the outer surface of the internal pterygoid muscle, lying at first between this and the external pterygoid and then between the internal pterygoid and the ramus of the mandible. On the surface of the internal pterygoid they diverge slightly, the lingual nerve passing somewhat more anteriorly while the inferior alveolar runs more directly downward. Because of their importance, these two nerves are described in some detail.

INNERVATION OF THE TEETH

Before it enters the mandibular foramen on the inner surface of the mandible the *inferior alveolar nerve* gives off its mylohyoid branch, which runs downward in a groove on the inner surface of the bone, and passes external to the mylohyoid muscle to supply this and the overlying anterior belly of the digastric. The inferior alveolar nerve enters the mandible through the mandibular foramen and is distributed to the teeth of the lower jaw.

Hensel has emphasized the fact that the inferior alveolar nerve lies in contact with the mandible before it enters the mandibular foramen. This foramen lies approximately 1.5 to 2 cm. below the mandibular notch, but according to Hensel the nerve is in immediate contact with the mandible for 3/16 inch (about 4.5 mm.) above the spine of the lingula and for a similar distance below this before it actually enters the mandible. He has stated that the distance from the bottom of the mandibular notch to the lingula varies from 7/16 to 10/16 inch (about 10.5 to 15 mm.), and pointed out that if the distance through which the nerve is in contact with the mandible above the lingula is subtracted from this, there is relatively little leeway in which a cut can be made across the ramus without involving either the mandibular notch or the inferior alveolar nerve. In cases in which the ramus of the mandible is to be sectioned in order to correct abnormal protraction or retraction, therefore, he advocated making the cut 5/16 inch (7.5 mm.) below the mandibular notch.

According to Starkie and Stewart the *distribution* of the inferior alveolar nerve *to the teeth* is as follows: soon after it enters the foramen, the nerve gives off an alveolar branch which runs parallel to the main stem, to supply the teeth posterior to the incisors; at the level of the canine tooth other fibers leave the nerve to form an intricate plexus external to the roots of the incisor teeth, while the remainder of the nerve leaves the mandible through the mental foramen. Starkie and Stewart found that the canines might be supplied either from the main alveolar branch or from the incisor plexus. In one third of the cases which they investigated they found no overlap between the incisor plexuses of the two sides, but in the others there was some; they felt that their anatomical observations agreed with clinical ones indicating that when such overlap between the nerves of the two sides is present, it usually does not extend beyond the central incisor and never beyond the lateral one on the opposite side.

The *mental nerve* is a large branch of the inferior alveolar that leaves the interior of the mandible to supply the skin of the chin and upper lip, and the mucosa of the lip and adjacent gum. In attempting to anesthetize the mental nerve or the more anterior lower teeth, the foramen may usually be found on the vertical line drawn downward from the palpable supra-orbital notch. In regard to its relation to the teeth, it lies in about 50 per cent of cases at the level of the apex of the second bicuspid tooth, between the apices of the two bicuspids in about 20 to 25 per cent, and posterior to the second bicuspid in about 24 per cent; in approximately 1 to 2 per cent it lies at the apex of the first bicuspid or of the first molar (Tebo and Telford—Fig. 226). Except for the distribution of the mental nerve, the inferior alveolar nerve does not supply the gingival mucosa; rather the outer gums behind the area of the mental nerve are supplied by twigs from the buccinator nerve, while the inner gums are supplied by branches of the lingual nerve.

Much of the bone about the alveoli of the more posterior teeth is dense, and good *anesthesia* here is best obtained by injection about the inferior alveolar nerve before it enters the mandible. This is usually done from the mouth by inserting the needle behind the oblique ridge which can usually be felt running upward from behind the last molar tooth on the inner border of the mandible; after the needle strikes the ramus of the mandible it can be guided upward along the bone to about the midpoint of the ramus, which corresponds approximately to the mandibu-

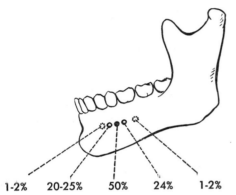

1-2%   20-25%   50%   24%   1-2%

Fig. 226. Variations in the relation of the mental foramen to the roots of the teeth. Percentages according to Tebo and Telford.

lar foramen. The gingival mucosa, with its different innervation, requires local infiltration.

LINGUAL NERVE

After leaving the inferior alveolar nerve, the lingual nerve receives the chorda tympani from the facial; this branch contains both sensory fibers from the geniculate ganglion and preganglionic parasympathetic fibers. Beyond this point it contains therefore fibers for general sensation which are true fifth nerve fibers, fibers for taste derived from the facial nerve, and autonomic fibers destined for the submaxillary (submandibular) ganglion and the innervation of the submaxillary (submandibular) and sublingual glands.

The nerve proceeds downward across the outer surface of the internal pterygoid muscle, anterior to the inferior alveolar, with which it may communicate; it then leaves the masseteric space to pass downward lateral to the styloglossus muscle, as this curves forward into the tongue, and then itself curves forward into the loose connective tissue spaces between the mylohyoid muscle and the musculature of the tongue. Its course and connections here are described in connection with the tongue (p. 384). In brief, most of the parasympathetic fibers leave the lingual nerve at the level of the submaxillary gland to end in the submaxillary ganglion, suspended from the nerve as it courses just above the gland; the fibers from the ganglion are distributed to the submaxillary and sublingual glands, while the sensory fibers of the lingual nerve are distributed to the anterior two thirds of the tongue.

VESSELS

INTERNAL MAXILLARY ARTERY

The main stem of the external carotid artery ascends approximately parallel to the posterior border of the ramus of the mandible, after having passed deep to the posterior belly of the digastric and the associated stylohyoid muscle; under cover of the angle of the mandible it gives off the external maxillary or facial artery which curves forward and downward over the submaxillary gland and around the lower margin of the mandible.

Above this level it gives off the posterior auricular artery (if this does not arise from the occipital), and at a point about two thirds of the distance between the angle of the mandible and the temporomandibular joint it divides deep to or within the parotid gland into its two terminal branches, the superficial temporal and the internal maxillary (Fig. 227). The further course of the superficial temporal through the parotid gland and to the scalp has been described on page 317.

The internal maxillary artery (or simply "maxillary artery" if the external is always referred to as the facial) leaves the external carotid at about a right angle, passing horizontally between the ramus apparently regarded the lateral course as an abnormal one, but in this country, at least, this course is seen more commonly than the deeper one. The deep course of the artery has been said to be most common in individuals with brachycephalic skulls, the superficial one in those with dolichocephalic skulls, but Lasker, Opdyke and Miller found no such correlation. They did report, however, a difference according to race, finding the artery deep to the muscle in 46 per cent

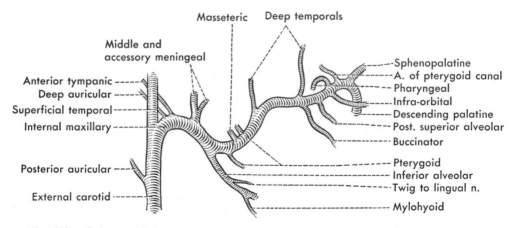

Fig. 227. Schema of the internal maxillary artery and its branches. The latter vary somewhat, especially in the order of their origins. Some of their relations are shown in Figure 224.

of the mandible and the sphenomandibular ligament at about the level of the lower border of the external pterygoid muscle, usually therefore slightly above the level of the midpoint between the mandibular condyle and the angle of the jaw. In front of the ramus of the mandible the artery passes upward across the lower part of the external pterygoid, but may cross either superficial or deep to the lower head of this muscle.

From an investigation of 200 arteries Lauber described only 16 as passing lateral to the lower head of the external pterygoid rather than medial to it, and of 147 sides in white persons, and in 31 per cent of 61 sides in Negroes (Fig. 228).

At any rate, if the artery passes medial to the lower head it then emerges with the buccinator nerve between the two heads, and its course is thereafter the same, lying upward and forward lateral to the groove between the two heads, or across the lateral surface of the upper head, of the external pterygoid.

FIRST PART

While it lies medial to the mandible (the so-called first part of the artery) the internal maxillary typically gives off four branches: small *deep auricular* and *anterior tympanic branches* which pass upward to aid in the supply of the external auditory meatus and the middle ear cavities (see pp. 169 and 183); the important *middle meningeal branch* which passes upward and slightly forward to pass between the two heads of origin of the auriculotemporal nerve and enter the skull by way of the foramen spinosum, situated just posterolateral to the foramen ovale; and the *inferior alveolar (inferior dental) artery* which passes downward

SECOND PART

While the artery is related to the external pterygoid muscle (the so-called second part of the artery) it gives off its muscular branches—the *masseteric*, the two *deep temporals* and the *buccinator*, or buccal, which accompany the nerves of the same names, and ʻalso *branches to the external and internal pterygoid muscles*. If the main stem of the artery lies deep to the inferior head of origin of the external pterygoid muscle, some of these branches necessarily pass between the two heads of the muscle to reach their

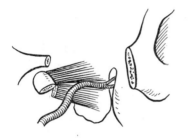

54% of white persons
69% of Negroes

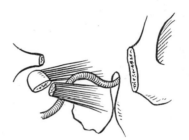

46% of white persons
31% of Negroes

Fig. 228. The two relations of the internal maxillary artery to the external pterygoid muscle. Percentages according to Lasker, Opdyke, and Miller.

and forward, gives off a mylohyoid branch that accompanies the nerve of the same name, and then enters the mandible with the inferior alveolar nerve to be distributed with it to the teeth and to send a small branch through the mental foramen to anastomose with other vessels on the face.

In this position also, the internal maxillary may give off an *accessory middle meningeal artery* which enters the foramen ovale on the deep surface of the mandibular nerve and supplies the semilunar ganglion and the meninges about this; more frequently, however, the accessory middle meningeal is a branch from the middle meningeal artery itself.

destinations; others leave the artery after it has bulged outward between the two heads. In either case, therefore, the main branches of this part of the artery run on the lateral surface of the external pterygoid muscle.

THIRD PART

The terminal (third or pterygopalatine) portion of the artery is that which lies against the posterolateral aspect of the maxilla and passes deeply between the two heads of the external pterygoid muscle to enter the lateral portion of the pterygopalatine fossa and lie lateral to the sphenopalatine ganglion.

This portion gives off the *posterior*

superior alveolar artery, described in connection with the upper jaw; the *infra-orbital artery*, accompanying the similarly named nerve through the infra-orbital groove and canal, and giving off orbital and anterior superior alveolar branches before it emerges on the face to anastomose with vessels there; the *descending palatine artery*, described in connection with the palate; the *artery of the pterygoid canal,* passing backward with the Vidian nerve (nerve of the pterygoid canal) to be distributed to a small upper portion of the pharynx and to a part of the auditory tube; a tiny *pharyngeal branch* to the upper part of the pharynx; and, finally, the important *sphenopalatine artery*, distributed to the nose and described in connection with this.

LIGATION

Because it lies deep to the parotid gland, the ramus of the mandible, and the zygoma, the internal maxillary artery is practically inaccessible from an external approach; therefore, if bleeding from it—for instance into the nose—cannot be controlled by local methods ligation of the external carotid is often resorted to; the third part of the artery may also be exposed through the transantral approach, as suggested by a number of writers, but carotid ligation is far simpler.

ANOMALIES

Aside from the variation in its position in relation to the inferior head of the external pterygoid muscle, variations or anomalies of the internal maxillary artery are apparently quite rare. The internal maxillary has been seen to arise by a common stem with the external (Delitzin, Bien), in which case it then ascended internal to and parallel with the long axis of the ramus of the mandible, instead of crossing this at right angles as usual. Usually the internal maxillary lies lateral to the major branches of the mandibular nerve in its course, but among 200 cases investigated by Lauber there were 42 in which he regarded this artery as following an abnormal course; in some of these cases the artery passed medial to all of the larger mandibular branches, in others it passed between the lingual and inferior alveolar nerves, and in a few it passed through a bifurcation of the inferior alveolar nerve.

THE SUPRAHYOID AND LINGUAL REGIONS

THE nerve-muscle relationships in the suprahyoid region are complicated but are largely understandable upon the basis of the probable embryology of this region. Representing as it does the junction of head and neck, it is a region of overlap between the voluntary muscles derived from various branchial arches and innervated by the cranial nerves concerned with these arches, and voluntary muscle developed from occipital and upper cervical myotomes.

Thus we have the mandibular arch represented not only by the muscles of mastication but also by the anterior belly of the digastric and by the mylohyoid muscle; these are innervated by the mandibular nerve, the nerve of the first branchial arch. The musculature derived from the second branchial arch is largely the mimetic muscles, but is represented in the suprahyoid region by the posterior belly of the digastric muscle and by the stylohyoid muscle, both innervated by the facial nerve. Musculature of the third branchial arch, innervated by the glossopharyngeal nerve, has almost disappeared, and is represented solely by the stylo-pharyngeus muscle; although it is in the suprahyoid region, it is described in this book with the muscles of the pharynx (p. 415). The musculature of the re-maining branchial arches, supplied by the tenth nerve (and by the eleventh, de-velopmentally a part of the tenth), is represented by the muscles of the palate, pharynx, and larynx (tensor veli palatini and stylopharyngeus excepted), and by the sternocleidomastoid and trapezius muscles.

Finally, both the extrinsic and intrinsic muscles of the tongue are believed to be developed largely from occipital myo-tomes in series with the cervical ones from which the strap muscles of the neck develop (for example, Bates); hence they are innervated largely by the hypoglossal nerve, not a branchiomeric nerve but a cranial one in direct series with the upper spinal nerves. The hypoglossal nerve rep-resents essentially several upper cervical nerves which have lost their sensory roots, fused together, and, through fusion of bony vertebral elements to the skull, at-tained a cranial exit.

The geniohyoid muscle represents the suprahyoid continuation of the strap muscles of the neck, is apparently derived from upper cervical myotomes, and is innervated by fibers from upper cervical nerves which travel with the hypoglossal; the genioglossus is sometimes classed with this and said to be innervated by the first cervical nerve, and sometimes stated to be innervated, like the other extrinsic muscles of the tongue, by the hypoglossal nerve. It is quite possible that the innervation of this muscle actually does vary, depending upon to what extent it is derived from occipital and to what extent from cervical myotomes; no exception to fundamental

principles is involved here, however, for such a variation in innervation is exactly comparable to the well-known variations in innervation, over a segment or so, of many of the other voluntary muscles of the body. Essentially, communications be-tween the hypoglossal nerve and the upper cervical ones represent the same tendency to plexus formation between spinal nerves as is seen in the cervical, brachial and lumbosacral plexuses.

The skin of the suprahyoid region is innervated by upper branches from the transverse cervical (cutaneus colli) nerve, derived from the second and third cervical nerves. Beneath the skin and the platysma muscle the cervical (inframandibular) branch of the facial nerve descends to anastomose with the sensory branches of the cutaneus colli, and supply the pla-tysma muscle; also under cover of the platysma muscle, and running approxi-mately along the lower margin of the mandible (but sometimes above this and sometimes definitely in the suprahyoid region) is the marginal mandibular branch of the facial, supplying muscula-ture connected with the lower lip. It is this branch which is especially endan-gered in the removal of the fascia and glands of the suprahyoid region during a radical dissection of the neck for carci-noma.

LYMPH NODES

Deep to the platysma, the structures of the suprahyoid region are also covered by the anterior or superficial layer of the deep fascia of the neck, which in the narrow region between the ramus of the mandible and the sternocleidomastoid muscle is continued upward to ensheath the parotid gland, and more anteriorly is reflected from the hyoid bone to the mandible, being attached to both; it is this part which encloses also the submaxillary gland. Embedded in the deep surface of this fascia are the lower superficial parotid lymph nodes, and the submaxillary and submental ones (Fig. 193, p. 319).

Since the fascia is not cleanly dissectible from the parotid and submaxillary glands, for there is no cleavage space between fascia and glands, it is impossible to be sure of removing all lymph nodes by dissection of the fascia from the glands. Therefore it is customary, in block dissections of the neck, to remove the lower tip of the parotid gland with its associated fascia, and to remove the submaxillary gland in its entirety with its associated fascia; in the latter procedure, the anterior facial vein and facial (external maxillary) artery, which penetrate the fascia and pass in close conjunction with the submaxillary gland to reach the face, must be sacrificed. Removal of the submental nodes is assured by making a clean anatomical dissection of the fascia from the surfaces of the suprahyoid muscles here.

SUBMENTAL LYMPH NODES

The submental lymph nodes are a few quite small ones which are, however, of considerable importance, for they receive the lymphatics from the medial part of the lower lip and from the chin, and from the more anterior part of the tongue. According to Stahr there are typically three submental nodes on each side, including both those which lie against the mylohyoid muscle between the two anterior bellies of the digastric, and those (usually described now as anterior nodes of the submaxillary group) which lie posterolateral to the anterior belly, upon the mylohyoid muscle as it forms the floor of the submaxillary or digastric triangle. It is in order to remove these nodes that the

external surface of the mylohyoid muscle must be cleanly dissected; this is obviously aided by removal of the anterior belly of the digastric muscle.

SUBMAXILLARY LYMPH NODES

The submaxillary or submandibular lymph nodes are larger and more numerous than the submental, and lie in general more superficially; they form a chain of from three to eight nodes situated largely along the upper border of the submaxillary gland, between this and the mandible, but also extending lateral or superficial to the gland, and often in front of and behind it against the floor of the submaxillary triangle.

According to Stahr, some of these nodes are constant and some are much less constant; the largest and most constant is the so-called middle submaxillary node, close to the point at which the facial artery crosses the mandible. These nodes receive the efferent vessels from the facial nodes (along the facial vein and artery) and therefore either directly or indirectly drain a large part of the face, receiving vessels from the nose, cheek, upper lip, lateral part of the lower lip, lateral parts of the anterior portion of the tongue, and much of the gingival mucosa. Their efferent connections are in part to the superficial cervical nodes (along the external jugular vein), but are largely into the upper deep cervical nodes along the internal jugular vein.

POSTERIOR PART OF SUPRAHYOID REGION

The narrow posterior part of the suprahyoid region is a direct continuation upward of the neck, and therefore contains the internal jugular vein, the internal and most of the external carotid artery, and the more posterior cranial nerves (that is, the seventh and the ninth to twelfth). The vascular and nerve relations here are described in connection with the neck, but this region also contains the posterior belly of the digastric muscle and the origins of the muscles arising from the styloid process. The sternocleidomastoid muscle and the ramus of the mandible largely overlap it, and much of the remaining interval is occupied superficially by the parotid gland; deep to this are the posterior belly of the digastric, and the stylohyoid muscle (Fig. 229).

reported 2 cases in the human being in which the stem of the external carotid artery giving rise to the internal maxillary and superficial temporal vessels passed superficial to the stylohyoid and the posterior belly of the digastric, but this is certainly exceedingly rare and should be readily appreciable before operation, since the artery in this case lies subcutaneously and should be easily palpable.

Much higher, under cover of the parotid gland and the posterior edge of the ramus of the mandible, these muscles are

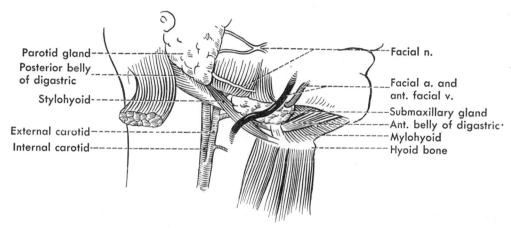

Fig. 229. Some relations in the suprahyoid region, with the sternocleidomastoid reflected backward.

The digastric and stylohyoid muscles originate a short distance apart, from a notch on the mastoid process and from the styloid process respectively, but as they run downward toward the angle of the mandible and the hyoid bone they converge; the important point here concerning them is that they cross lateral or superficial to the great ascending arteries and the internal jugular vein (Fig. 230, p. 376), and also the descending tenth, eleventh, and twelfth cranial nerves; at the level of the angle of the mandible, therefore, one can cut down to these muscles without fear of damaging vascular or neural structures. It is true that Pisk

crossed superficially by the posterior auricular artery; also, the facial nerve appears in front of the digastric to run lateral to the styloid process and its attached muscles, while the external carotid artery appears on the anterior surface of the stylohyoid muscle, between it and the styloglossus, and may lie somewhat lateral to the anterior fibers of this muscle.

HYOID BONE

The hyoid bone, to which are attached both infrahyoid and suprahyoid muscles and the superficial layer of the deep fascia in the front of the neck, effectively separates the anteriorly located suprahyoid and infrahyoid fascial compartments (Fig. 175, p. 293). As it is held in place primarily by the muscles which attach to it, it is freely movable and thus takes part in movements of swallowing and phonation. The thyrohyoid membrane stretches between it and the larynx. The sternohyoid, omohyoid, and thyrohyoid muscles attach to it below, the middle constrictor of the pharynx attaches laterally, and the stylohyoid muscle, the fascial sling of the digastric tendon, the mylohyoid, geniohyoid, and genioglossus muscles all attach to it above.

middle ear, lower portions by the lesser cornu and perhaps some of the body of the hyoid. Variations in the ossification of this intermediate segment lead to greater or less length of the styloid process (p. 410), and sometimes to complete ossification of the ligament. Chi-Min has described bilateral replacement of the ligament by an anomalous muscle.

SUPRAHYOID MUSCULATURE

The suprahyoid musculature as discussed here includes the digastric and

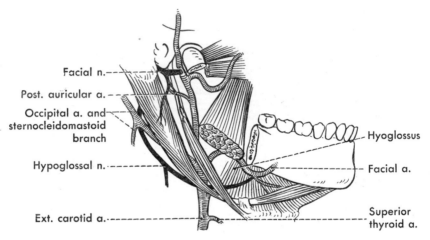

Fig. 230. Deeper relations in the suprahyoid region, after removal of the parotid and submaxillary glands and much of the mandible. The stylohyoid and the posterior belly of the digastric are shown more widely separated than they actually are.

The greater cornu may usually be palpated by lateral displacement of the bone toward the side to be palpated, but may lie under cover of the sternocleidomastoid muscle. The lesser cornu, at the level of junction of the greater cornu and the body, typically projects upward for only a few millimeters. The stylohyoid ligament attaches to the lesser cornu, and represents an unossified part of the skeleton of the second pharyngeal arch, upper portions of which are represented by the styloid process and the stapes of the

stylohyoid muscles, the mylohyoid, and the geniohyoid; the remaining muscles in this region are more easily discussed as muscles of the tongue.

DIGASTRIC MUSCLE

The digastric muscle (Figs. 229 and 230) consists of two bellies: the posterior belly arises from a notch on the inferior and medial surface of the mastoid process and passes downward and forward toward the hyoid bone, where the muscle fibers give place to a tendon; this tendon perforates the lower fibers of the stylohyoid muscle, is held downward against the hyoid by an aponeurotic attachment, and is continuous anteriorly with the anterior belly of the digastric. From its attachment to the hyoid bone the tendon between the two heads of the digastric curves forward and upward to be replaced by the fleshy fibers of the anterior belly, which are attached to the lower and inner surface of the mandible on either side of the midline. Sometimes there are aberrant fibers uniting the two anterior bellies of the digastric (du Bois-Reymond) or accessory muscles, derived either from them or the mylohyoid (Waern).

At its origin the posterior belly of the digastric lies beneath the sternocleidomastoid muscle; the facial nerve emerges from the stylomastoid foramen to lie slightly lateral to the anterior border of the muscle and supply this belly before curving forward lateral to the styloid process and the muscles attached to it. Deep to the origin of the posterior belly of the digastric are the upper fibers of origin of the levator scapulae, and the occipital artery which runs between these two muscles. The posterior border of the muscle is overlapped above by the insertions of the splenius capitis and semispinalis capitis muscles. Anterolaterally, the muscle is in relation to the deep portion of the parotid gland. The spinal accessory nerve, internal jugular vein, hypoglossal nerve and external carotid artery all lie deep to the posterior belly of the digastric behind the angle of the jaw; associated with the internal jugular vein in this position are the upper deep cervical lymph nodes. The internal carotid artery and the vagus nerve also lie here, but more deeply.

The intermediary tendon of the digastric is associated superficially with the submaxillary gland; the facial artery, after extending upward deep to the muscle, descends to emerge along the upper border of the submaxillary gland between this tendon and the lower margin of the mandible. The anterior belly of the digastric lies upon the lower surface of the mylohyoid muscle, and is covered by the external or anterior layer of deep fascia as this is reflected from the hyoid bone to the chin. It is innervated by a branch from the mylohyoid nerve, in turn a branch of the inferior alveolar nerve (from the mandibular division of the trigeminal).

The anterior belly of the digastric divides the region between the hyoid bone and the mandible into two triangles, the submaxillary (submandibular, digastric) triangle posteriorly and the submental or suprahyoid triangle anteriorly. The former lies between the posterior and anterior bellies of the digastric on the one hand, as they converge to attach to the hyoid bone, and the margin of the mandible on the other; the latter triangle lies between the anterior belly of the digastric, the hyoid bone and the midline of the submental region.

SUBMAXILLARY TRIANGLE

The submaxillary triangle is largely occupied by the major portion of the submaxillary gland, with its associated lymph nodes; the anterior facial vein crosses it on the superficial surface of the gland, and the facial (external maxillary) artery descends into it from a point internal to the mandible, to emerge by rounding the lower margin of the mandible. Anteriorly, the floor of the triangle is the mylohyoid muscle, while posteriorly the hyoglossus appears here; the deep process of the submaxillary gland leaves the triangle with the submaxillary duct by passing forward above the posterior border of the mylohyoid muscle, while in the posterior part of the triangle, against the hyoglossus muscle, the hypoglossal nerve with its accompanying vein runs forward to the tongue. Close to the angle formed by the two bellies of the digastric, the lingual artery is accessible before it disappears deep to the posterior border of the hyoglossus muscle (p. 386). The surfaces of these muscles in the triangle, and the hypoglossal nerve, must be carefully cleaned of their connective tissue if complete block dissections of the neck are to be done.

SUBMENTAL TRIANGLE

The submental triangle contains nothing other than the submental lymph nodes, already mentioned, and twigs of the submental branch of the facial artery and the corresponding submental vein (joining the anterior facial vein and also communicating with the anterior jugular vein). The floor of this triangle is the mylohyoid muscle; the relatively small amount of loose connective tissue lying between the covering deep fascia and the mylohyoid muscle, sometimes referred to as the submental space, is a part of the several anteriorly situated fascial spaces grouped together as the submandibular space (p. 300).

STYLOHYOID, MYLOHYOID, AND GENIOHYOID MUSCLES

The *stylohyoid muscle* arises from the posterolateral aspect of the styloid process and descends anterior to the posterior belly of the digastric to split into two parts, between which the tendon of the digastric runs, and then attach to the lateral portion of the body of the hyoid bone. Laterally, it is related to the parotid and submaxillary glands, medially to the great vessels of the neck. The muscle is innervated by a twig from the facial nerve as this nerve passes forward lateral to the origin of the muscle. Under cover of the submaxillary gland the facial artery passes above the insertion of the muscle to emerge between the gland and the lower margin of the mandible.

The *mylohyoid muscle* extends transversely from the inner surface of the mandible toward the midline. The most posterior fibers insert upon the body of the hyoid bone, the remainder insert with those of the muscle of the other side into a median raphe that extends from the hyoid bone almost to the mandible. The two muscles together form a diaphragm below the geniohyoid muscle and the muscles of the tongue. Superficially, or below, the mylohyoid is in contact with the anterior belly of the digastric, and with a major part of the submaxillary gland; the submental artery runs along its external surface, as does also the mylohyoid branch of the mandibular nerve (and its accompanying artery), which innervates both this muscle and the anterior belly of the digastric. Between the mylohyoid muscle and the overlying anterior layer of the deep fascia of the neck is the potential space sometimes involved in Ludwig's angina. Above, the muscle is in contact with the geniohyoid muscle and with the muscles of the tongue and the sublingual spaces about these; the submaxillary gland rounds the posterior border of the muscle to lie also in part in the connective tissue above it, where are also the submaxillary duct, the sublingual gland, the lingual and hypoglossal nerves, and the vessels of the tongue. The mylohyoid muscle occasionally has a gap between some of its fibers, through which a part of the sublingual gland may bulge into the submental region (for instance, Malpas).

The *geniohyoid muscle* (Fig. 231) lies upon the upper surface of the mylohyoid, arising from the inner surface of the mandible near the midline and inserting into the greater cornu of the hyoid bone; above it is the genioglossus muscle, and lateral to it the sublingual gland, the deep process and duct of the submaxillary gland, and the hypoglossal nerve. The lingual nerve and lingual artery also lie lateral to, but largely above the level of, the muscle. The geniohyoid is supplied by a twig from the hypoglossal nerve, which

the styloglossus; the glossopalatinus (palatoglossus) is sometimes described as a muscle of the tongue and sometimes as one of the soft palate, but receives its innervation from the vagus as do other muscles of the soft palate and in this book has been described as a palatine muscle. Of these muscles the two larger, the genioglossus and the hyoglossus, extend upward into the tongue from the sublingual region, while the styloglossus and glossopalatinus enter the tongue from above and laterally.

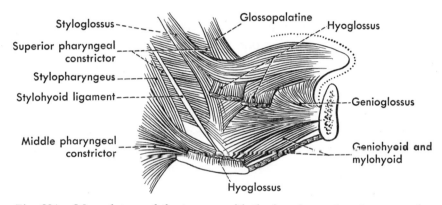

Fig. 231.   Musculature of the tongue, with the hyoglossus largely removed.

is usually stated to contain fibers derived from the first cervical nerve rather than true hypoglossal fibers.

ACTIONS

All four muscles of the suprahyoid group elevate the hyoid bone, and therefore the floor of the mouth and the base of the tongue, and thus take part especially in swallowing. The digastric, the mylohyoid and the geniohyoid also aid in opening the mouth.

LINGUAL MUSCULATURE

EXTRINSIC MUSCLES

The extrinsic muscles of the tongue are the genioglossus, the hyoglossus, and

The *genioglossus*, like the geniohyoid muscle, arises from the mental spine on the posterior surface of the mental portion of the mandible, and forms a broad fanlike sheet in the parasagittal plane, the fibers radiating from the origin so that the more anterior ones reach the anterior portion of the tongue, the middle ones reach the posterior portion, while the lower fibers curve backward and downward to insert into the hyoid bone (Fig. 231).

The *hyoglossus muscle* arises from a lateral part of the body of the hyoid bone and from its entire greater cornu, with sometimes a slip (chondroglossus) from the lesser cornu of the hyoid; its fibers pass upward and slightly forward, lateral

to the more posterior fibers of the genioglossus, to interlace with the styloglossus
muscle and the intrinsic muscles of the
tongue.

The hypoglossal nerve and the lingual
vein pass across the lateral (superficial)
surface of the hyoglossus muscle in their
course toward the tongue, but the lingual
artery passes deep to it, between it and the
genioglossus. Also lateral to the hyoglossus, between it and the inner surface
of the mandible, are, from below upward,
the submaxillary duct and the associated
deep part of the gland, the lingual nerve
and the sublingual gland; the latter, and
the nerves and vessels to the tongue, also
extend forward beyond the anterior border of the hyoglossus to lie on the lateral
surface of the genioglossus.

The *styloglossus muscle* arises from the
lower end of the styloid process, and
usually also from the upper part of the
stylohyoid ligament, and, broadening as
it runs downward and forward, passes
deep to the internal pterygoid muscle and
to the lingual nerve to reach the tongue;
here many of its fibers continue superficially on the lateral aspect of the tongue
as a longitudinal bundle, while others interdigitate with fibers on the hyoglossus
and pass more deeply into the tongue.
Like the hyoglossus, the lower part of this
muscle is related laterally to a portion of
the sublingual gland.

The small *glossopalatinus (palatoglossus) muscle,* not truly a muscle of the
tongue, lies deep to the superior constrictor muscle of the pharynx, and runs
upward from the posterolateral side of the
dorsum of the tongue to reach the soft
palate, lying adjacent to the mucosa of
the pharynx and forming the glossopalatine arch. It receives its innervation from
the pharyngeal plexus, and is in function
also a pharyngeal muscle.

INTRINSIC MUSCLES

The intrinsic muscles of the tongue are
complicated bundles of interlacing fibers,
among which are connective tissue septa;
the strongest of these is the median septum, which lies between the muscles,
nerves, and vessels of the two sides, rather
effectively separating the deeper structures of the tongue. Essentially, the intrinsic muscles consist of bundles which
are largely arranged in either a vertical
or a transverse direction, with a more
limited number running longitudinally.

ACTIONS AND INNERVATION

The intrinsic muscles are particularly
involved in producing changes in shape
of the tongue, such as the cupping of the
tongue which is used, when swallowing
liquids, to squirt the fluid through the
mouth (Whillis). The extrinsic muscles
also help to modify the shape of the
tongue, but especially assist in pulling
the tongue forward, backward, upward,
or downward, while both sets of muscles
may act with others of the suprahyoid
group, for instance the mylohyoid, in
such functions as swallowing.

Both intrinsic and extrinsic muscles of
the tongue are supplied by branches of
the hypoglossal nerve which are believed
to contain true hypoglossal fibers (with
perhaps some variation in this respect—
page 373—for the genioglossus). It is
well known that paralysis of the hypoglossal nerve causes a deviation of the
tongue to the paralyzed side when this
organ is protruded, and this is usually
accepted as being due to the actions of
both the intrinsic muscles and the genioglossus muscle of the sound side; Abd-El-
Malek denied that in the cat the genioglossus is at all concerned with contralateral movements of the tongue, but
Bennett and Hutchinson, in a reinvestiga-

tion of this in the dog, stated unequivocally that unilateral action of the genioglossus is an important factor in protrusion of the tongue to the opposite side. There seems no reason to doubt that this is also true in man.

The hyoglossus muscle flattens the dorsum of the tongue, while the styloglossus muscle pulls it upward and back, thus arching it; the glossopalatinus may both pull the soft palate downward and the tongue upward and is primarily therefore a narrower of the faucial isthmus. Except for the genioglossus muscle, therefore, the extrinsic muscles of the tongue are retractors.

NERVES AND VESSELS

The carotid and internal jugular vessels and the nerves associated topographically with them are discussed in connection with the neck; the present section deals with the more strictly suprahyoid nerves and vessels, primarily therefore those of the tongue.

MOTOR AND PROPRIOCEPTIVE INNERVATION OF THE TONGUE

The mylohyoid nerve and its associated artery (from the internal maxillary) and the submental branch of the facial artery have already been described as extending superficial to the mylohyoid muscle; the important nerves and vessels above the mylohyoid muscle are of course those connected with the tongue. As already stated in the discussion of the musculature of the tongue, the motor innervation to this is entirely by way of the hypoglossal nerve; this nerve also brings with it, however, sensory fibers which are derived from the first and second cervical nerves, and which are apparently proprioceptive

(Corbin and Harrison; Yee, Harrison, and Corbin).

Olmsted reported apparent paralysis of the tongue in the dog after section of the lingual nerve, and Barron concluded that the proprioceptive fibers run in the lingual nerve and not the hypoglossal, but Langworthy, also working on animals, found that bilateral section of both the lingual and ninth nerves caused no apparent ataxia of the tongue. It is probably true that in man movements of the tongue are guided both by proprioceptive impulses from the tongue musculature and its tendons, and by touch from the surface of the tongue (mediated especially by the lingual nerve). Weddell, Harpman, Lambley, and Young stated that after anesthetization of the lingual nerves in man there is no ataxia or tendency to bite the tongue, while Rowbotham stated that bilateral section of the fifth nerve markedly interferes with movements of the tongue at first, but there is much subsequent improvement. Carleton reported that anesthesia of the mucous membrane of the human tongue gave rise to complete loss of sense of position of the tongue in 4 of 8 cases in which this was tried, partial loss in 3, and no loss in 1.

TASTE AND GENERAL SENSATION ON THE TONGUE

The afferent supply to the mucous membrane of the tongue is almost entirely through the lingual and glossopharyngeal nerves, though the superior laryngeal branch of the vagus sends twigs upward to reach the epiglottis and a small area on the posterior basal aspect of the tongue. The fibers of the lingual nerve are distributed to approximately the anterior two thirds of the tongue, that is, the area in front of the circumvallate papillae, while those of the glossopharyngeal are distributed to the posterior third of the tongue, including the circumvallate papillae (Fig. 232).

Both nerves contain fibers both of general sensation (touch, pain, temperature) and of taste; the taste fibers in the lingual nerve are generally agreed to be derived from the geniculate ganglion of the facial,

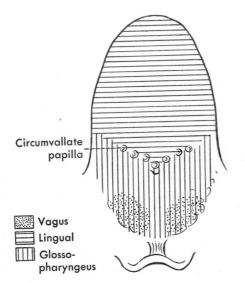

Fig. 232.   Sensory innervation of the tongue.

and to join the lingual by way of the chorda tympani, while the taste fibers of the glossopharyngeal are a component of this nerve as it leaves the brain stem, with their cells of origin situated in the petrosal ganglion of the ninth. The fibers of general sensation in the lingual nerve are derived from cells in the semilunar ganglion, and are therefore true trigeminal fibers, while the fibers of general sensation in the ninth enter the brain stem with the ninth nerve.

It is the distribution of the ninth nerve to the posterior part of the tongue and to the adjacent pharyngeal wall that accounts for the distribution of pain here in *glossopharyngeal neuralgia*; this pain is often initated by such actions as swallowing, eating, or talking, and usually arises from the tonsillar-pharyngeal-lingual region, with or without extension to the ear, but may occur first in the ear and extend to the tongue and throat.

Intracranial section of the ninth nerve for glossopharyngeal neuralgia produces both an anesthesia and a loss of taste on the posterior third of the tongue (Dandy; Reichert; Peet; and others). Perhaps there may sometimes be an overlap between the regions of distribution of the ninth and lingual nerves, for Peet reported that in 1 case of section of the ninth there was a slight diminution of taste on the anterior two thirds of the tongue, and stated that sometimes also the fifth nerve overlapped (for general sensation) onto the territory of the ninth, but this is apparently not very common, judging by the reports of other surgeons. Glossopharyngeal neuralgia has, however, apparently often been mistaken for trigeminal neuralgia.

The taste fibers in the ninth nerve, distributed especially to the numerous taste buds in the circumvallate papillae, are far more important than are those in the seventh, but nevertheless the loss of taste due to section of one glossopharyngeal nerve is apparently not noticed by the patient (Reichert); likewise, it is well known that injuries to the chorda tympani nerve in operations upon the mastoid or the middle ear cavity, although they must produce loss of taste on the anterior two thirds of the tongue, are often not complained of by the patient. However, patients may complain of a total loss of taste following tonsillectomy, even though it is certain that in these cases taste to the anterior two thirds of the tongue has not been disturbed, and that it is only the glossopharyngeal nerve whose function has been temporarily interrupted by edema about the nerve following the tonsillectomy. Arey, Tremaine, and Monzingo have stated that the taste buds of the circumvallate papillae undergo considerable degeneration during the later years of life, and may even almost entirely disappear after the seventieth year.

There is apparently little overlap between the nerves of the two sides: Whiteside, and Hayes and Elliott have described some slight overlap across the midline for the taste buds both of the ninth nerve and of the chorda tympani in animals, but according to Weddell and his coworkers the lingual nerve of man does not cross the midline in so far as taste fibers are concerned. They have reported some overlap in the neighborhood of the lower gum for pain and touch.

COURSE OF TASTE FIBERS

While much of the peripheral course and distribution of the taste fibers is generally agreed upon, the route by which they enter the brain stem was long a matter of dispute, and even today cannot be regarded as entirely accepted by clinicians. As long ago as 1903 Cushing took note of the fact that taste fibers from the tongue had been stated to enter the brain with the fifth nerve, and examined taste sensation in a number of patients in whom the semilunar ganglion had been removed. While he found that removal of the ganglion sometimes seemed to abolish or to lessen the acuity of taste over the anterior portion of the tongue temporarily, it never did so permanently or completely. Lewis and Dandy also reported that the fifth nerve carried no taste fibers into the brain stem, for no taste was lost in any of their cases, even in 1 in which the nerve had been sectioned bilaterally. Rowbotham also agreed that the fifth nerve

is not a part of the taste path into the brain stem, but stated that section of it may upset taste, apparently because of the removal of the normal accompanying sensation of touch.

Lewis and Dandy investigated patients in whom the fifth, seventh, or ninth nerves had been divided subtentorially, or in whom both fifth and seventh nerves had been divided at the same time. In all of their cases they found that section of the ninth nerve abolished taste on the posterior third of the tongue, while intracranial section of the seventh, similarly, immediately and permanently abolished taste over the anterior two thirds of the tongue on the operated side; they concluded therefore that the taste pathways are those described in modern texts, namely, that the fibers associated peripherally with the ninth nerve enter the brain stem with this, while taste fibers associated peripherally with the lingual and chorda tympani nerves enter the brain stem with the facial nerve. Tschiassny stated, however, that complete interruption of the facial nerve proximal to the geniculate ganglion spares taste, and has used this supposed fact in locating the site of a lesion on the facial nerve.

Schwartz and Weddell agreed that section of the root of the fifth nerve does not affect taste, but reported a case of loss of taste in 1 patient following excision of the greater superficial petrosal nerve, and 2 cases of preservation of taste over the anterior two thirds of the tongue following section of the chorda tympani. Since they also found, in the majority of individuals, loss of taste after injury to the chorda tympani or to the facial nerve in the canal, they concluded that the chorda is the usual pathway for taste from the anterior two thirds of the tongue, but that in some individuals the greater superficial petrosal nerve forms a part of this peripheral pathway (Fig. 233).

Carmichael and Woollard had previously reported that destruction of the semilunar ganglion by injection of alcohol was not infrequently accompanied by loss of taste, and attributed this to injury to the seventh nerve through the injection; since temporary paralysis of the facial sometimes follows section of the fifth nerve, possibly because of trauma

tongue from behind, and as they run forward curve up into it. The glossopharyngeal nerve also enters from behind, but lies deeper and is limited in its distribution to the posterior part of the tongue.

LINGUAL NERVE

The lingual nerve receives the chorda tympani of the facial at about the level of the posterior border of the internal pterygoid muscle; the chorda tympani emerges

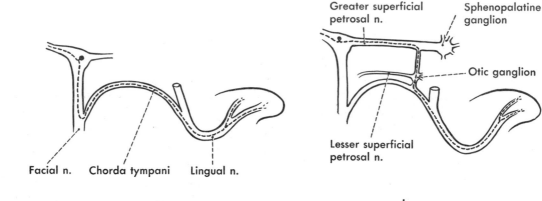

Fig. 233. *a*. The usually accepted pathway for taste from the anterior two thirds of the tongue. *b*. The pathway that apparently exists in some individuals, according to Schwartz and Weddell. Note that in both figures the taste fibers are shown entering the central nervous system by way of the facial nerve; in *b*, however, they are shown taking an unusual course to the geniculate ganglion of this nerve, through minute connections between the chorda tympani, the otic ganglion, and the greater superficial petrosal nerve.

transmitted through the canal of the greater superficial petrosal, it seems not impossible that the loss of taste attributed to section of the fifth nerve might be due to a similar cause; the apparent retention of taste following injury to the chorda tympani is not so easily explained, though it should be remembered that taste is at best somewhat difficult to test accurately in a patient.

COURSES AND RELATIONS OF THE
NERVES TO THE TONGUE

The lingual and hypoglossal nerves, and the lingual vessels, all enter the

from the petrotympanic fissure and passes downward and forward in a short course deep to the external pterygoid before joining the lingual. The lingual nerve then passes across the lateral surface of the internal pterygoid muscle, between this and the ramus of the mandible, to lie on the lateral surface of the styloglossus muscle as the latter curves forward into the tongue; in this position it bears the submaxillary (submandibular) ganglion, and then curves forward lateral to the hyoglossus and the other muscles of the tongue (Fig. 234). It then lies somewhat between the submaxillary duct below and the sublingual gland above, and also lateral to the sublingual gland. It sends off a number of small branches to this gland and across it to the gingival mucosa and the floor of the mouth, and then passes below the gland, turning around the submaxillary duct and the lower border of the sublingual gland to come in close connection with the hypoglossal nerve and the sublingual artery as these lie medial to the sublingual gland. The

ternal and external carotid vessels. In this course it usually passes downward until just lateral to the origin of the occipital artery, and then turns forward, being held at the turn by the sternocleidomastoid branch of the occipital artery so that it hooks around these vessels before it runs forward above the hyoid bone.

Accompanied by the main stem of the lingual vein (also called the vena comitans of the hypoglossal nerve) the nerve

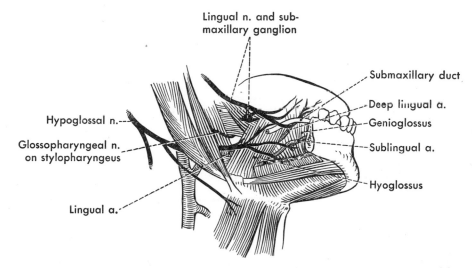

Fig. 234.   Chief neural and vascular relations of the sublingual region, with the mandible and the submaxillary and sublingual glands removed. Note that the hypoglossal nerve, submaxillary duct, and lingual nerve all lie on the lateral surface of the hyoglossus muscle, but that the lingual artery passes deep to this muscle.

lingual nerve then runs upward between the sublingual gland and the genioglossus muscle into the tongue.

HYPOGLOSSAL NERVE

The hypoglossal nerve typically emerges between the internal carotid artery and the internal jugular vein to descend in the lateral groove between them, to a point not far above the carotid bifurcation. It then gives off its descendens hypoglossi branch and curves forward across the lateral surfaces of both in-

then passes forward deep to the stylohyoid and posterior belly of the digastric muscles and enters the posterior part of the submaxillary or digastric triangle where it comes to lie upon the lateral surface of the hyoglossus muscle, under cover of the submaxillary gland. It passes forward upon the hyoglossus and then disappears above the posterior border of the mylohyoid muscle; here, beneath the tongue, it curves forward and upward upon the lateral surface of the genioglossus muscle, anastomoses with the lingual nerve, and enters the musculature of the tongue.

After giving off the descendens hypoglossi at about the level of its forward turn, the hypoglossal nerve gives twigs to the thyrohyoid and geniohyoid muscles, which are usually believed to contain only cervical nerve fibers, and branches to the extrinsic muscles of the tongue before ending in the intrinsic muscles.

GLOSSOPHARYNGEAL NERVE

The glossopharyngeal nerve, after giving off its carotid and pharyngeal anterior surface of the external carotid artery, but since it leaves this under cover of the posterior belly of the digastric and the angle of the jaw it is not very easily accessible here; from this origin the artery curves somewhat upward as a rule, gives off its tonsillar branch, and then curves downward to lie medial to, sometimes slightly above or below also, the hypoglossal nerve. In this position it lies above the attachment of the tendon of the two bellies of the digastric to the hyoid bone, and is here accessible, lateral to the middle pharyngeal constrictor, before it reaches

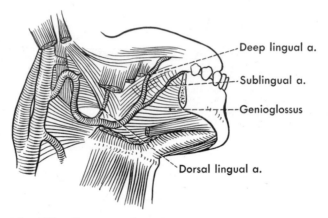

Deep lingual a.

Sublingual a.

Genioglossus

Dorsal lingual a.

Fig. 235. Course and main branches of the lingual artery. For other relations see Figure 234.

branches and its lone motor (stylopharyngeal) branch, passes lateral to the stylopharyngeus muscle, and under cover of the styloglossus and hyoglossus muscles gives off branches to the tonsil and to the posterior third of the tongue. In this position it lies close to the lower pole of the tonsil.

Finally, the superior laryngeal branch of the *vagus* is said to send a few ascending twigs to the base of the tongue, presumably from the branches which also supply the epiglottis.

LINGUAL ARTERY AND VEIN

The lingual artery (Fig. 235) is typically the second branch arising from the the posterior border of the hyoglossus muscle.

Since its stem of origin from the external carotid is accessible with difficulty, and is moreover sometimes difficult to identify (for instance, in about 20 per cent of cases the lingual and facial arteries were found to arise together by a common stem, according to Grant), the lingual artery is commonly ligatured above the hyoid bone if interruption of the entire vessel is desired. In seeking the lingual artery here, after pushing the submaxillary gland upward, the hypoglossal nerve is identified as it runs across the digastric triangle and if necessary is pushed somewhat upward so as **to form** a triangle between it and the angle of union of the two bellies of the digastric muscle. The triangle thus made is Lesser's triangle, and slightly more deeply within the posterior part of this is the lingual artery; it is visible for a short distance before it passes deep to the posterior border of the hyoglossus muscle.

At the posterior border of this muscle, the lingual artery gives off a twig to the strap muscles of the neck and then runs forward deep to the muscle, lying immediately above and parallel to the hyoid bone, and with the middle constrictor of the pharynx, the stylopharyngeus muscle and the stylohyoid ligament medial to it. In this position it is typically not accompanied by a vein, except posteriorly by the dorsal lingual vein, for the main lingual vein runs with the hypoglossal nerve lateral to the hyoglossus muscle.

Soon after it passes under cover of the hyoglossus muscle the lingual artery gives off its *dorsal lingual* branch, often doubled, to the posterior portion of the tongue and the tonsillar region, and at about the anterior edge of this muscle divides into its two terminal branches, the sublingual and the deep lingual or ranine.

The *sublingual artery* is the smaller branch; continuing the course of the chief vessel it passes along the side of the genioglossus muscle between this and the sublingual gland, and supplies both the gland and the muscles of the tongue. Beneath the mucous membrane of the anterior part of the floor of the mouth it anastomoses with its fellow of the opposite side, and this anastomotic branch gives off the artery to the frenulum; in cutting the frenulum for tongue-tie, this artery may have to be ligatured.

From its origin the *deep lingual artery* turns upward, and then once again forward, so that it runs not beneath the mucous membrane of the floor of the mouth but rather beneath that on the lateral part of the inferior surface of the tongue; its accompanying veins are here conspicuous when the mouth is open and the tongue lifted so that the under surface may be examined. Its branches pass upward into the tongue with the terminal branches of the lingual and hypoglossal nerves. In operations involving excision of only a portion of the tongue, the deep lingual artery may be identified through an incision of the mucous membrane in the lateral part of the floor of the mouth, and ligated as it emerges from beneath the cover of the hyoglossus muscle to lie on the lateral surface of the genioglossus. The anastomoses between the arteries of the two sides are largely submucous and are minute, so that unilateral operations upon the tongue may be carried out with practically no bleeding after ligation of the lingual artery on that side; bleeding is more free at the tip of the tongue, where the largest anastomoses between the two deep lingual arteries occur.

DEEP LINGUAL VEIN

The deep lingual or ranine vein, prominent on the lower surface of the tongue beneath the mucous membrane, accompanies the deep lingual artery to the anterior border of the hyoglossus muscle but thereafter separates from it. As it passes with the hypoglossal nerve lateral to the hyoglossus muscle, being therefore separated from its corresponding artery by this muscle, it is frequently termed the vena comitans of the hypoglossal nerve.

This vein receives the sublingual vein, and behind the posterior border of the hyoglossus it is joined also by the small dorsal lingual vein which emerges from deep to the hyoglossus. The main stem of the lingual vein thus formed crosses the common carotid artery and opens into the internal jugular vein, or may empty into the posterior or common facial veins, and typically communicates also with the pharyngeal plexus. On the other hand, veins which sometimes accompany the lingual artery may receive the dorsal lingual vein to form a lingual vein separate from the ranine; in this

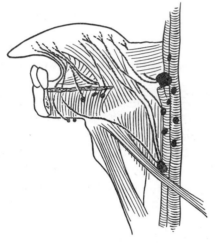

Fig. 236. Lymphatic drainage of the tongue. (Redrawn from Jamieson, J. K., and Dobson, J. F.: *Brit. J. Surg.* 8:80, 1920.)

case the lingual typically empties into the internal jugular, while the ranine usually empties into the common facial.

LYMPHATIC DRAINAGE OF THE TONGUE

The lymphatic drainage of the tongue is of particular importance from the point of view of metastasis in carcinoma of the tongue; while all of the lymphatics of the tongue eventually drain into the deep cervical nodes, they take divergent courses from different portions of the tongue, and may or may not end in regional nodes before reaching the deep cervical group (Fig. 236).

Lymphatic vessels from the base of the tongue, from behind the circumvallate papillae, run downward toward the hyoid bone and curve backward to penetrate the pharyngeal wall and enter nodes of the upper part of the deep cervical chain, especially a particularly large node situated on the lateral aspect of the internal jugular at about the point at which this vessel is crossed by the lower border of the posterior belly of the digastric muscle.

The lymphatics from the anterior two thirds of the tongue are divided into two sets (Jamieson and Dobson): marginal and central vessels. The *marginal vessels* drain the outer thirds of the upper surface of the tongue, the margin itself and the lower surface on the sides. The more anterior of these, originating behind the tip of the tongue, pass downward and penetrate the mylohyoid muscle to end in the submaxillary lymph nodes; the posterior ones course downward behind the margin of the mylohyoid muscle to reach the deep cervical lymph nodes directly, largely ending in the prominent node (jugulo-omohyoid node) situated at about the point at which the omohyoid muscle crosses the internal jugular vein.

Of the *central vessels,* those from the tip of the tongue pass downward through the mylohyoid muscle to end either in the submental nodes or course downward across the hyoid bone and end directly in nodes of the deep cervical chain, especially again in the jugulo-omohyoid node. The central vessels from the remainder of the upper surface of the tongue run down largely between the two genioglossus muscles; some of the more anterior ones drain, as do the marginal lymphatics, into the submaxillary nodes, while others by-pass these nodes and go directly to either the upper or the lower deep cervical nodes. The important fact stressed by Jamieson and Dobson is that the central vessels from one side of the tongue go to both deep cervical chains (Fig. 237), as do also some of the vessels from the base; thus while a carcinoma originating on the lateral margin of the tongue may be expected to metastasize first to nodes on the side of origin, carcinoma from the base, central portion of the dorsum or the tip of the tongue is apt to involve the nodes along both internal jugular veins.

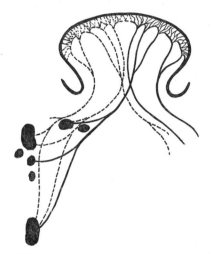

Fig. 237. Lymphatic drainage of the tongue, illustrated in a cross section. Note the bilateral drainage of the central vessels. (Redrawn from Jamieson, J. K., and Dobson, J. F.: *Brit. J. Surg. 8*:80, 1920.)

It should be apparent from the above description that metastatic carcinoma from the tongue may involve first the submental nodes, or (more frequently) the submaxillary nodes, or any of the nodes of either the upper or lower parts of the deep cervical chain; thus failure to find enlargement of the submental or submaxillary nodes upon palpation, or even failure to discover involvement of them at biopsy, does not indicate that carcinoma has not metastasized; it may rather have affected nodes of the deep cervical chain directly. It is because of the widespread locations of the nodes receiving the lymphatics of the tongue that block dissections of the neck are made in operations for lingual carcinoma. In these dissections the sternocleidomastoid muscle, the internal jugular vein, the digastric muscle and the submaxillary gland, and all of the connective tissue associated with these structures are removed, usually en bloc, while the surfaces of the deeper muscles are cleaned to the bare muscle, and the arteries and important motor nerves are carefully cleaned and spared—really a careful anatomical dissection of these parts (p. 490).

It is worth noting, incidentally, that none of the lymphatics of the tongue reach the superficial nodes associated with the facial artery or the parotid gland (Jamieson and Dobson). In carcinoma of the tongue, therefore, in contrast to that of some portions of the face, excision of the lower pole of the parotid gland offers no advantage except to render more accessible upper members of the deep cervical chain of nodes.

Jamieson and Dobson stated that unilateral block dissection of the neck should be efficacious for early carcinoma of the lateral border of the tongue, but because of the bilateral lymphatic drainage bilateral dissection should be performed if the tip of the tongue, the frenulum, or the dorsum is involved. Bilateral dissection of the nodes has traditionally been less thorough on the second side, since interruption and removal of both internal jugular veins, as required in a complete block dissection, has usually been regarded as necessarily fatal. Evans, however, recorded a number of cases in which individuals survived bilateral ligature of the internal jugulars, and bilateral block dissections of the neck have been shown to be practicable when certain precautions are taken (p. 491).

SUBMAXILLARY AND SUBLINGUAL GLANDS

SUBMAXILLARY GLAND

The submaxillary (submandibular) gland occupies most of the similarly named triangle, and expands beyond this over the superficial surfaces of the anterior and posterior bellies of the digastric. Its posterior border is close to the lower part of the parotid gland at the

and must also be sacrificed in removal of the gland; it is therefore ligatured both medial to the angle of the jaw and at the inferior border of the mandible as it emerges between this and the gland.

The anterior portion of the submaxillary gland lies directly against the mylohyoid muscle (Fig. 238), and the mylohyoid nerve is then the only structure of any importance related to the deep surface of this portion of the gland; more posteriorly, however, the hypoglossal nerve lies between the gland and the hyoglossus muscle, and this nerve should

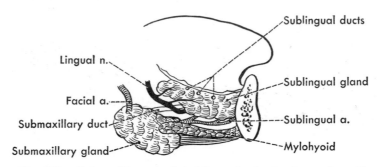

Fig. 238. Submaxillary and sublingual glands from the side, after removal of the mandible.

angle of the jaw, where it is separated from this gland by the sphenomandibular ligament. The submaxillary gland is crossed superficially by the anterior facial vein and sometimes by the marginal mandibular branch of the facial nerve. The larger submaxillary lymph nodes lie along the superficial upper border of the gland, between it and the mandible; other nodes may lie anterior and posterior to the gland if the lymph chain is particularly long.

In removing the gland the facial vein is sacrificed, but the marginal mandibular branch of the facial nerve is preserved if possible in order to avoid distortion of the mouth. The facial artery passes across the upper surface of the gland, usually grooving it deeply before rounding the lower border of the mandible,

therefore be sought and spared in removal of the gland. Higher up, medial to the mandible and above the level of the submaxillary gland (unless this extends upward unusually deeply), runs the lingual nerve in its course toward the tongue.

In removing the gland from its extension medial to the mandible, care should be taken that the lingual nerve is not pulled downward into the field of operation and injured here; this is possible because the submaxillary (submandibular) ganglion with its roots and branches forms a connection between the gland and the lingual nerve. Total removal of the gland involves also dissection about the posterior border of the mylohyoid muscle, as a deep portion of the gland rather regularly follows the submaxillary duct in this position, so that the gland is typically folded around the posterior edge of the muscle.

SUBMAXILLARY DUCT

The submaxillary duct (Wharton's duct) runs forward above the mylohyoid muscle between the inner surface of the mandible and the lateral surfaces of the hyoglossus and genioglossus muscles. The duct lies lateral to the hypoglossal nerve, and at first below the lingual nerve; as the lingual nerve descends it crosses lateral to the duct. Both the duct and the lingual nerve then pass around the lower border of the sublingual gland to lie medial to this, the lingual nerve at the same time passing below the duct and then crossing it medially (thus having looped almost completely around it) to turn upward on the genioglossus muscle, while the duct continues forward.

In the terminal portion of its course, therefore, the submaxillary duct is in immediate contact with the sublingual gland, lying at first below and then medial to it; at the anterior end of this gland it may receive a so-called major sublingual duct (Bartholin's duct) before it opens into the mouth. In the terminal part of its course the duct lies immediately beneath the mucosa of the floor of the mouth, which it raises slightly to form the sublingual fold, and then projects as the sublingual papilla or caruncle just lateral to the frenulum. The submaxillary duct is inelastic, and obstruction of it may cause intense pain.

SUBLINGUAL GLAND

The sublingual gland lies in the floor of the mouth beneath the mucosa and above the mylohyoid muscle; laterally it is related to the mandible itself, and medially it lies against the styloglossus and hyoglossus muscles posteriorly, and the genioglossus anteriorly; the glands of the two sides almost meet in the midline in front of the more anterior fibers of the genioglossus. The lingual nerve may descend lateral to the posterior end of the gland and at any rate runs along the lower border of this part, and sends small branches across its lateral surface toward the mucosa of the floor of the mouth; farther forward the lingual nerve and the submaxillary duct curve around the lower border of the gland to reach its medial surface. Between the anterior part of the gland and the genioglossus muscle the lingual and hypoglossal nerves both curve upward into the tongue, the sublingual artery runs forward to supply the gland and the adjacent genioglossus muscle, while the submaxillary duct continues along the upper medial border of the sublingual gland.

SUBLINGUAL DUCTS

Approximately a dozen or more small sublingual ducts (ducts of Rivinus) pass from the upper border of the gland to the sublingual fold to empty directly into the buccal cavity; sometimes some of the more anterior sublingual ducts unite together to form a larger duct, the "major" sublingual duct or duct of Bartholin, which joins the submaxillary duct to empty with this at the sublingual papilla. Bartholin's duct has been variously described as of usual occurrence, as occurring on only about 50 per cent of sides, or as being very rare in man; in any event, the variations in both its presence and size indicate that it is of too little importance to be designated the "major" sublingual duct.

CALCULI AND CYSTS

Calculi in the submaxillary and sublingual glands or their ducts are apparently not particularly common (Ziegelman) but according to Hamlin those of the submaxillary gland and its duct comprise about 75 per cent of all salivary calculi. He has stated that they occur about three times as commonly in males as in females; they can be demonstrated easily by roentgen ray. The operative approach to the submaxillary duct and the sublingual gland and its ducts is obviously through the mucosa of the floor of the mouth on the side of the tongue; since the duct and gland are in intimate contact with both the lingual and hypoglossal nerves, the anatomical relations here are of considerable importance, as emphasized by Ziegelman. Ranulas, which are cystic tumors of the floor of the mouth, are perhaps usually thought of as being due to obstruction of a duct of the sublingual gland, but New expressed the belief that this is not always the source of the cyst.

Smaller Glands

In addition to the three great pairs of salivary glands, there are of course numerous smaller glands opening into the mouth. These include the palatine glands, the so-called lesser sublingual (or alveololingual) glands in the lateral part of the floor of the mouth, glands (of Weber) between the submaxillary duct and the lateral surface of the tongue, and anterior lingual glands (of Blandin-Nuhn) on the inner surface of the tip of the tongue (Mullin). These latter are described as being ovoid glands of mixed (mucous and serous) cells, with one or two ducts apiece; it is said that they may become enlarged or cystic, or may contain calculi.

Innervation

The submaxillary and sublingual glands are both innervated by fibers from the submaxillary (submandibular) ganglion, which accompany sensory fibers of the lingual nerve. The preganglionic fibers for these glands are derived at least primarily from the facial nerve; like the fibers for taste to the anterior two thirds of the tongue they leave the facial nerve through the chorda tympani and join the lingual nerve to course thereafter with it: at the level of the submaxillary ganglion they leave the lingual nerve to end in this ganglion (Fig. 239).

According to Tschiassny, lesions of the facial nerve at, or proximal to, the geniculate ganglion typically cause a marked decrease in salivation; he expressed the belief that the facial nerve probably supplies fibers to all the salivary glands. Some authors (for example, Sewall; Reichert) have regarded these glands as receiving also an innervation through the ninth nerve; Reichert reported that intracranial section of the ninth nerve causes an immediate marked diminution in secretion of not only the parotid but also the submaxillary and sublingual glands, followed by a gradual return to almost normal by the end of the third postoperative month; he stated that section of the chorda tympani produces the same results, and concluded therefore that fibers from both seventh and ninth nerves reached all of the salivary glands.

The anatomical pathways by which this could occur are several, for connections may exist between the greater superficial petrosal of the seventh and the lesser superficial petrosal of the ninth, the auricular branches of the seventh and ninth usually join, and there is apparently typically a connection between the chorda tympani of the seventh and the otic ganglion (which receives the lesser superficial petrosal of the ninth). In contrast, many observers (for instance, Dandy; Peet) have been unable to detect any disturbance of salivary secretion after section of the ninth nerve.

Sympathetic fibers also reach these glands, either by way of other nerves or along the vessels; they are of course derived from the superior cervical ganglion. However, the exact function of this apparent double innervation, parasympathetic and sympathetic, is not clearly understood; stimulation of parasympathetic fibers is said to produce a watery secretion from these glands, while stimulation of sympathetic fibers is said to

clusively blood vessels. Rawlinson ('35) concluded that variations in blood flow are of considerable importance in the secretory activity of the glands, and it has been stated that the control of salivary secretion is almost entirely brought about by vasodilatation or vasoconstriction in the glands.

ANOMALIES

Major anomalies of the sublingual and lingual regions are rare. Although the

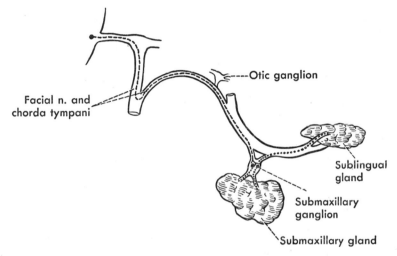

Fig. 239.   The usually accepted course for the secretory parasympathetic fibers to the submaxillary and sublingual glands. The preganglionic pathway is indicated by broken lines; the postganglionic one, originating in the submaxillary ganglion, by dotted lines.

produce a viscid one. Kuntz and Richins stated that in cats, dogs, and monkeys the parasympathetic fibers far exceed the sympathetic in number. In contrast to some workers (for example, Rawlinson, '33), who have stated that sympathetic fibers are distributed primarily to mucous cells and parasympathetic ones to serous cells, Kuntz and Richins concluded that both serous and mucous cells are innervated predominantly or exclusively by parasympathetic fibers, and that the sympathetic fibers supply mainly or ex-

sublingual artery varies in its origin, not uncommonly arising with the facial artery and sometimes arising with the superior thyroid, it usually shows no major variation in its course. According to Kren a few cases have been described in which there were marked anomalies of the lingual artery; he himself described a case in which one lingual artery was missing, and was replaced in the tongue by a branch from the other lingual artery that crossed above the two genioglossus muscles. Other rare variations which he found described in the literature include bilateral absence with replacement by branches from the facial artery, a lingual artery coursing on the inferior surface of the mylohyoid muscle and penetrating this muscle to reach the tongue, and a lingual artery passing across the outer surface of the hyoglossus muscle, in company with the hypoglossal nerve, instead of running deep to this muscle.

Either the submaxillary or the sublingual gland may very rarely be missing, and the sublingual gland varies considerably in size. Bilateral absence of the submaxillary gland has been reported, as well as a gland lying entirely above the mylohyoid muscle (Reid). When the mylohyoid muscle is deficient, as sometimes occurs (p. 378), the sublingual gland may bulge through this opening and appear therefore superficial to the muscle.

As evidenced by its ducts, the sublingual gland has developed by a number of outgrowths from the buccal mucosa, and apparently also sometimes from the region of the anterior end of the submaxillary duct; the variations in the latter connection have already been mentioned. The large, single, submaxillary duct is apparently quite constant (except, of course, in agenesis of the gland) but quite rarely a marked anomaly of this duct may occur. Thus Waller has described a case (in an embryo) in which a submaxillary duct opened into the pharynx near the isthmus of the fauces, and Rose described a case in which the chief duct seemed to bifurcate, one part emptying as usual at the sublingual papilla while the second limb, of equal size, appeared to empty in the floor of the mouth opposite the second molar tooth; the anterior limb in this case was blocked by a calculus, and Rose was not sure that the posterior limb might not have been a fistulous tract.

According to Bell and Millar *macroglossia* is usually defined as an enlargement of the tongue due to one of two conditions: either a lymphangiomatous enlargement or a true hypertrophy of the lingual muscles. They stated that lymphangioma is by far the most common cause of macroglossia; congenital hypertrophy of the musculature of the tongue is said to be usually associated with cretinism, mongolism, and idiocy. Janse described a case associated with cleft palate and micrognathia; in this case, the base of the tongue was especially enlarged and produced difficulty in breathing. Handley, and Bell and Millar, have discussed surgical technics for dealing with macroglossia.

In contrast to thyroglossal cysts and fistulas, *fistulas* of the body of the tongue are much rarer according to Montgomery. He has reported a case, and outlined the area in which such fistulas might be expected to be present if, as seems reasonable, they result from improper fusion of the swellings (paired, from the first branchial arches, and the unpaired tuberculum impar) normally forming the body of the tongue.

THYROGLOSSAL CYSTS AND LINGUAL THYROIDS

Since the thyroid gland develops as a median outgrowth from the floor of the pharynx in the region that gives rise also to the tongue, evidence of this origin is typically found in the posterior part of the midline of the body of the tongue in the form of a pit, the *foramen caecum*, that marks the cranial end of the usually evanescent thyroglossal duct. In a large series of children from a few weeks old up to the age of 10 years Marshall found that the foramen caecum was almost absent in 38 per cent of these, was a slight pit up to 1/8 inch long in 46 per cent, and was about 1/4 inch long in 15 per cent. Persistence of a more caudal portion of the thyroglossal duct may also occur, however, and such portions may give rise to sinus tracts, cysts or fistulas along the course of growth and migration of the thyroid gland to its definitive position in the neck. These are discussed in more detail in connection with the thyroid gland (p. 529), but since they may occur in the suprahyoid region they must also be discussed here.

If the thyroglossal duct has retained its connection at the foramen caecum, it obviously forms a *sinus tract* which extends among the muscles of the tongue; commonly it ends blindly somewhere in the neck, but it may through infection attain a fistulous opening, as in the cases which Kinsella described, in which a thyroglossal fistula extended from the foramen caecum to open externally on the surface of the neck.

As emphasized by a number of workers, treatment of thyroglossal sinuses and fistulas depends upon complete removal of the tract; as this tract may pass through or behind the hyoid bone, or sometimes even in front of it (Kinsella; Pemberton and Stalker), and the portion above the hyoid bone is often small and friable, it is customary to remove also the central segment of the body of the hyoid and the tissue above this in the midline between the muscles of the tongue. In their series of 293 cases, Pemberton and Stalker reported that 66.2 per cent of these sinuses occurred in males, 33.8 per cent in females. Both they and Marshall and Becker have reported a very low rate of recurrence (about 1 per cent) when the hyoid bone and the midline tissue up to the foramen caecum were removed.

Isolated segments of the thyroglossal duct, which have lost their connection to the foramen caecum, may persist along the path of growth of the thyroglossal duct and give rise to *cysts*. Most cysts derived from the thyroglossal duct lie below the level of the hyoid bone, but Hubert found 5 located above the hyoid among 43 cases, and Marshall and Becker reported that 61 of 310 occurred above the hyoid. Cysts of the thyroglossal duct

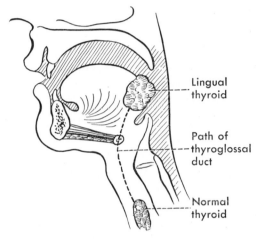

Fig. 240. The most common position of the rare lingual thyroid gland. Ectopic thyroid tissue and cysts of the thyroglossal duct lie approximately along the broken line, if they are not secondarily displaced, as this represents the pathway of "migration" of the thyroid gland into the neck.

above the hyoid bone may be situated in the base of the tongue (where, however, they are said to be even rarer than lingual thyroids), in the floor of the mouth, or immediately above the hyoid bone (Bailey).

LINGUAL THYROID

The most striking anomaly resulting from the development of the thyroid gland from the lingual portion of the pharynx is the retention of thyroid tissue here to form a lingual thyroid gland (Fig. 240). Of the various abnormalities in the position of the thyroid which may occur, a lingual thyroid is generally granted to be the rarest. Apparently some 250 cases of lingual thyroid have been reported in the literature. The lingual thyroid may consist of only a few small nodules or may be the size of a small orange (Smith); Rubin found that the incidence of myxedema after operations on lingual thyroid has been estimated to range from 15 to more than 50 per cent, and Smith, Ray, and Lemmon and Paschal have stated that in about 70 per cent of cases of lingual thyroid, thyroid tissue in the neck was said to be absent. Ray found that cretinism was reported as being present in about 10 per cent of the reported cases of lingual thyroid.

According to Goetsch the ectopic thyroid tissue was on the dorsum of the tongue in 142 of 144 cases of lingual thyroid reviewed from the literature, and buried in the body of the tongue in only 2; since the tissue is usually located beneath the mucosa at the back of the tongue, the usual symptoms are those of benign tumors of the tongue, that is, interference with swallowing, perhaps some dysphonia, and even respiratory symptoms. Lingual thyroid is apparently found more commonly in females than in males, about 75 per cent of the cases having been reported as occurring in females according to Ray (approximately the same sex ratio as seen in goiter), while Perlman found it had been estimated to occur perhaps eight times as frequently in females as in males; Rubin quoted the reverse of this, stating that it occurred eight times as frequently in males as females, but this was presumably a typographical error. Lingual thyroid glands have frequently not been noted until the physiological enlargement of the gland occurs at puberty, and sometimes have gone unnoticed until pregnancy; it may be, therefore, that the reported sex ratio is based not upon their actual occurrence, but rather upon the fact that they enlarge less frequently in the male, and are therefore often not recognized.

Rubin stated that carcinoma in a lingual thyroid is rare, as he found reports of only 2 such cases in the literature, but Smith regarded malignant growths and degenerative conditions as occurring in lingual thyroids in about the same proportion as when the thyroids are in the normal position. The removal of the gland is usually by way of the buccal route, with control of postoperative myxedema, if necessary, by thyroid extract. Rubin has warned that lingual thyroids usually have relatively large blood vessels traversing their surfaces, and sectioning the tissue for biopsy may mean severe hemorrhage.

REFERENCES

ABD-EL-MALEK, S. A contribution to the study of the movements of the tongue in animals, with special reference to the cat. *J. Anat. 73:*15, 1938.

ANGEL, J. L. Factors in temporomandibular joint form. *Am. J. Anat. 83:*223, 1948.

AREY, L. B., TREMAINE, M. J., and MONZINGO, F. L. The numerical and topographical relations of taste buds to human circumvallate papillae throughout the life span. *Anat. Rec. 64:*9, 1935.

BAILEY, H. Thyroglossal cysts and fistulae. *Brit. J. Surg. 12:*579, 1925.

BARRON, D. H. A note on the course of the proprioceptor fibres from the tongue. *Anat. Rec. 66:*11, 1936.

BATES, M. N. The early development of the hypoglossal musculature in the cat. *Am. J. Anat. 83:*329, 1948.

BELL, H. G., and MILLAR, R. G. Congenital macroglossia: Report of two cases. *Surgery 24:*125, 1948.

BENNETT, G. A., and HUTCHINSON, R. C. Experimental studies on the movements of the mammalian tongue: II. The protrusion mechanism of the tongue (dog). *Anat. Rec.* 94:57, 1946.

BIEN, GERTRUD Eine seltene Varietät der Arteria maxillaris interna. *Anat. Anz. 30:* 421, 1907.

DU BOIS-REYMOND, R. Beschreibung einer Anzahl Muskelvarietäten an einem Individuum. *Anat. Anz. 9:*451, 1894.

BYARS, L. T. Preservation and restoration of mandibular function and contour. *Ann. Surg. 127:*863, 1948.

CARLETON, ALICE Observations on the problem of the proprioceptive innervation of the tongue. *J. Anat. 72:*502, 1938.

CARMICHAEL, E. A., and WOOLLARD, H. H. Some observations on the fifth and seventh cranial nerves. *Brain 56:*109, 1933.

CHI-MIN, WANG An anomalous muscle in place of the stylohyoid ligament of a Chinese. *Anat. Rec. 107:* 375, 1950.

CORBIN, K. B., and HARRISON, F. The sensory innervation of the spinal accessory and tongue musculature in the Rhesus monkey. *Brain 62:*191, 1939.

COSTEN, J. B. Glossodynia: Reflex irritation from the mandibular joint as the principal etiologic factor; study of ten cases. *Arch. Otolaryng. 22:*554, 1935.

CUSHING, H. The taste fibres and their independence of the N. trigeminus: Deductions from thirteen cases of Gasserian ganglion extirpation. *Bull. Johns Hopkins Hosp. 14:*71, 1903.

CUSHING, H. The sensory distribution of the fifth cranial nerve. *Bull. Johns Hopkins Hosp. 15:*213, 1904.

DANDY, W. E. Glossopharyngeal neuralgia (tic douloureux): Its diagnosis and treatment. *Arch. Surg. 15:*198, 1927.

DAVIS, W. B. Congenital deformities of the face: Types found in a series of one thousand cases. *Surg., Gynec. & Obst. 61:*201, 1935.

DELITZIN, S. Arteria maxillaris communis. *Arch. f. Anat. u. Physiol.* p. 268, 1890.

DOHERTY, J. L., and DOHERTY, J. A. Dislocation of the mandible. *Am. J. Surg. 38:*480, 1937.

DORRANCE, G. M. Congenital insufficiency of the palate. *Arch. Surg. 21:*185, 1930.

DORRANCE, G. M., and BRANSFIELD, J. W. Studies in the anatomy and repair of cleft palate. *Surg., Gynec. & Obst. 84:*878, 1947.

EVANS, M. G. Bilateral jugular ligation following bilateral suppurative mastoiditis. *Ann. Otol., Rhin. & Laryng. 51:*615, 1942.

FROESCHELS, E. Uvula and tonsils. *Arch. Otolaryng. 50:*216, 1949.

GOETSCH, E. Lingual goiter: Report of three cases. *Ann. Surg. 127:*291, 1948.

GOYDER, F. W. The anatomy and treatment of cleft palate. *Brit. J. Surg. 1:*259, 1913.

GRABER, T. M. Craniofacial morphology in cleft palate and cleft lip deformities. *Surg., Gynec. & Obst. 88:*359, 1949.

GRANT, J. C. B. *An Atlas of Anatomy* (ed. 2). Baltimore, The Williams and Wilkins Company, 1947.

GREENE, E. Temporomandibular joint: Dental aspect. *Ann. Otol., Rhin. & Laryng. 46:* 150, 1937.

GURNEY, C. E. Chronic bilateral benign hypertrophy of the masseter muscles. *Am. J. Surg. n.s.73:*137, 1947.

HAMLIN, F. F. Calculus of the submaxillary gland and duct. *Arch. Otolaryng. 10:*177, 1929.

HANDLEY, S. The technique of Butlin's operation of marginal resection of the tongue. *Brit. J. Surg. 1:*42, 1913.

HARPMAN, J. A., and WOOLLARD, H. H. The tendon of the lateral pterygoid muscle. *J. Anat. 73:*112, 1938.

HAVENS, F. Z. Cleft lip and palate: Some technical procedures used in its treatment, with especial reference to closure of complete cleft of the anterior half of the palate. *Arch. Otolaryng. 48:*9, 1948.

HAYES, E. R., and ELLIOTT, R. Distribution of the taste buds on the tongue of the kitten, with particular reference to those innervated by the chorda tympani branch of the facial nerve. *J. Comp. Neurol. 76:*227, 1942.

HENSEL, G. C. The surgical correction of mandibular protraction, retraction, and fractures of the ascending rami. *Surgery 2:*92, 1937.

HERSH, J. H. Hypertrophy of the masseter muscle. *Arch. Otolaryng. 43:*593, 1946.

HRDLIČKA, A. Lower jaw: Double condyles. *Am. J. Phys. Anthropol. 28:*75, 1941.

HUBERT, L. Thyroglossal cysts and sinuses: Analysis of 43 cases. *Arch. Otolaryng. 45:* 105, 1947.

HUNT, J. R. The sensory field of the facial nerve: A further contribution to the symptomatology of the geniculate ganglion. *Brain* 38:418, 1915.

JAMIESON, J. K., and DOBSON, J. F. The lymphatics of the tongue: With particular reference to the removal of lymphatic glands in cancer of the tongue. *Brit. J. Surg. 8:*80, 1920.

JANSE, H. M. Macroglossia with an associated micrognathia causing respiratory dificulty. *Ann. Otol., Rhin. & Laryng. 39:*99, 1930.

JONES, F. W. The anterior superior alveolar nerve and vessels. *J. Anat. 73:*583, 1939.

KAZANJIAN, V. H. Congenital absence of the ramus of the mandible. *J. Bone & Joint Surg. n.s.21:*761, 1939.

KINSELLA, V. J. Complete thyroglossal fistulae. *Brit. J. Surg. 26:*714, 1939.

KREN, O. Über eine seltene Anomalie der Arteria lingualis nebst einer kurzen Zusammenfassung ihrer häufigsten topographischen Varietäten. *Anat. Anz. 73:*107, 1931.

KUNTZ, A., and RICHINS, C. A. Components and distribution of the nerves of the parotid and submandibular glands. *J. Comp. Neurol. 85:*21, 1946.

LANGWORTHY, O. R. A study of the innervation of the tongue musculature with particular reference to the proprioceptive mechanism. *J. Comp. Neurol. 36:*273, 1924.

LASKER, G. W., OPDYKE, D. L., and MILLER, H. The position of the internal maxillary artery and its questionable relation to the cephalic index. *Anat. Rec. 109:*119, 1951.

LAUBER, H. Ueber einige Varietäten im Verlaufe der Arteria maxillaris interna. *Anat. Anz. 19:*444, 1901.

LEMMON, W. T., and PASCHAL, G. W., JR. Lingual thyroid. *Am. J. Surg. n.s.52:*82, 1941.

LEWINSKY, W., and STEWART, D. The innervation of the dentine. *J. Anat. 70:*349, 1936a.

LEWINSKY, W., and STEWART, D. The innervation of the periodontal membrane. *J. Anat. 71:*98, 1936b.

LEWINSKY, W., and STEWART, D. The innervation of the periodontal membrane of the cat, with some observations on the function of the end-organs found in that structure. *J. Anat. 71:*232, 1937.

LEWIS, D., and DANDY, W. E. The course of the nerve fibers transmitting sensation of taste. *Arch. Surg. 21:*249, 1930.

LORD, F. P. Observations on the temporomandibular articulation. *Anat. Rec. 7:*355, 1913.

LUBOSCH, W. Ueber den Meniscus im Kiefergelenk des Menschen (Nebst ergänzenden literarischen Mitteilungen). *Anat. Anz. 29:* 417, 1906.

LYONS, D. C. Relationship of oral and pharyngeal abnormalities to speech. *Arch. Otolaryng. 15:*734, 1932.

MALPAS, P. Anomalies of the mylohyoid muscle. *J. Anat. 61:*64, 1926.

MARSHALL, C. F. Variations in the form of the thyroid gland in man. *J. Anat. & Physiol. 29:*234, 1895.

MARSHALL, S. F., and BECKER, W. F. Thyroglossal cysts and sinuses. *Ann. Surg. 129:* 642, 1949.

MONTGOMERY, M. L. Congenital fistulae of the body of the tongue. *Ann. Surg. 100:* 68, 1934.

MOOREHEAD, F. B. Fractures of the jaws and their management. *Am. J. Surg. n.s.38:* 474, 1937.

MORRIS, J. H. Chronic recurring temporomaxillary subluxation: Surgical consideration of "snapping jaw" with report of a successful operative result. *Surg., Gynec. & Obst. 50:* 483, 1930.

MULLIN, W. V. The anatomy, physiology and diseases of the salivary glands. *Tr. Am. Acad. Ophth.* p. 354, 1929.

NEW, G. B. Congenital cysts of the tongue, the floor of the mouth, the pharynx and the larynx. *Arch. Otolaryng. 45:*145, 1947.

OLDFIELD, M. C. Cleft palate and the mechanism of speech. (Arris and Gale Lecture.) *Brit. J. Surg. 29:*197, 1941.

OLMSTED, J. M. D. Taste fibers and the chorda tympani nerve. *J. Comp. Neurol. 34:* 337, 1922.

PEET, M. M. Glossopharyngeal neuralgia. *Ann. Surg. 101:*256, 1935.

PEMBERTON, J. DEJ., and STALKER, L. K. Cysts, sinuses and fistulae of the thyroglossal duct. *Ann. Surg. 111:*950, 1940.

PERLMAN, H. B. Lingual thyroid gland. *Arch. Otolaryng. 19:*594, 1934.

PEYTON, W. T. The dimensions and growth of the palate in the normal infant and in the infant with gross maldevelopment of the upper lip and palate: A quantitative study. *Arch. Surg. 22:*704, 1931.

PISK, E. Über eine seltene Varietät im Verlaufe der Arteria carotis externa beim Menschen und beim Hunde. *Anat. Anz. 45:*373, 1914.

RAWLINSON, H. E. Cytological changes after autonomic and adrenalin stimulation of the cat's submaxillary gland. *Anat. Rec. 57:* 289, 1933.

RAWLINSON, H. E. The changes in the cells of the striated ducts of the cat's submaxillary gland after autonomic stimulation and nerve section. *Anat. Rec. 63:*295, 1935.

RAY, B. S. Lingual thyroid. *Arch. Surg. 37:* 316, 1938.

REICHERT, F. L. Neuralgias of the glossopharyngeal nerve, with particular reference to the sensory, gustatory and secretory functions of the nerve. *Arch. Neurol. & Psychiat. 32:*1030, 1934.

REID, D. Notes on the salivary glands. *Anat. Rec. 32:*295, 1926.

RICH, A. R. The innervation of the tensor veli palatini and levator veli palatini muscles. *Bull. Johns Hopkins Hosp. 31:*305, 1920.

RICHARDSON, G. S., and PULLEN, E. M. The uvula: Its structure and function and its importance. *Arch. Otolaryng. 47:*379, 1948.

RITCHIE, H. P. Congenital clefts of the face and jaws: A report of the operations used and a discussion of results. *Surg., Gynec. & Obst. 73:*654, 1941.

RITCHIE, W. P. Cleft palate: A correlation of anatomic and functional results following operation. *Arch. Surg. 35:*548, 1937.

ROBINSON, M. The temporomandibular joint: Theory of reflex controlled nonlever action of the mandible. *J. Am. Dent. A. 33:*1260, 1946.

ROSE, B.-H. Bifurcation of the submaxillary duct. *Am. J. Surg. n.s.17:*257, 1932.

ROWBOTHAM, G. F. Observations on the effects of trigeminal denervation. *Brain 62:* 364, 1939.

RUBIN, H. Aberrant lingual thyroid: Report of a case. *Am. J. Surg. n.s.32:*150, 1936.

SCHWARTZ, H. G., and WEDDELL, G. Observations on the pathways transmitting the sensation of taste. *Brain 61:*99, 1938.

SEAVER, E. P., Jr. Temporomandibular joint malocclusion and the inner ear: A neuromuscular explanation. *Ann. Otol., Rhin. & Laryng. 46:*140, 1937.

SEWALL, E. C. Decompression of the facial nerve: Physiology of the seventh and ninth nerves and movements of the lid in facial paralysis. *Arch. Otolaryng. 18:*746, 1933.

SLAUGHTER, W. B., and BRODIE, A. G. Facial clefts and their surgical management in view of recent research. *Plast. & Reconstruct. Surg. 4:*311, 1949.

SMITH, A. E., and JOHNSON, J. B. Surgery of the cleft palate. *Am. J. Surg. n.s.45:*93, 1939.

SMITH, C. Lingual thyroid. *Arch. Otolaryng. 29:*78, 1939.

SPRAGUE, J. M. The innervation of the pharynx in the Rhesus monkey, and the formation of the pharyngeal plexus in primates. *Anat. Rec. 90:*197, 1944.

STAFNE, E. C. Dental roots in the maxillary sinus. *Am. J. Orthodontics. (Oral Surg. Sect.) 33:*582, 1947.

STAHR, H. Die Zahl und Lage der submaxillaren und submentalen Lymphdrüsen vom topographischen und allgemein-anatomischen Standpunkte. *Arch. f. Anat. u. Physiol.,* p. 444, 1898.

STARKIE, C., and STEWART, D. The intramandibular course of the inferior dental nerve. *J. Anat. 65:*319, 1931.

TANASESCO, J. G. Lymphatiques de l'articulation temporo-maxillaire. *Anat. Anz. 41:* 460, 1912.

TEBO, H. G., and TELFORD, I. R. An analysis of the relative positions of the mental foramina. (Abstr.) *Anat. Rec. 106:*254, 1950.

TIEGS, O. W. Further remarks on the terminations of nerves in human teeth. *J. Anat. 72:*234, 1938.

TRIBLE, G. B. Epistaxis of antral origin: Report of cases. *Arch. Otolaryng. 10:*633, 1929.

TSCHIASSNY, K. The site of the facial nerve lesion in cases of Ramsay Hunt's syndrome. *Ann. Otol., Rhin. & Laryng. 55:*152, 1946.

TURNER, W. A. On the innervation of the muscles of the soft palate. *J. Anat. & Physiol. 23:*523, 1889.

VAN DER SPRENKEL, H. B. Microscopical investigation of the innervation of the tooth and its surroundings. *J. Anat. 70:*233, 1936.

WAERN, A. Contribution à la connaissance des muscles interposés entre les ventres antérieurs des digastriques chez l'homme et présentation d'un projet de dénomination pour ceux-ci. *Arch. d'anat., d'histol. et d'embryol. 20:325*, 1935.

WAKELEY, C. P. G. The surgery of the temporomandibular joint. *Surgery 5:697*, 1939.

WAKELEY, C. P. G. The mandibular joint. *Ann. Roy. Col. Surgeons England. 2:111*, 1948.

WALDRON, C. W. Management of unilateral clefts of the palate. *Plast. & Reconstruct. Surg. 5:322*, 1950.

WALLER, W. H. Ectopic submaxillary ostium near the isthmus of the fauces. *Anat. Rec. 58:111*, 1934.

WARDILL, W. E. M. Cleft palate. *Brit. J. Surg. 16:127*, 1928.

WARDILL, W. E. M. The technique of operation for cleft palate. *Brit. J. Surg. 25:117*, 1937.

WEDDELL, G., HARPMAN, J. A., LAMBLEY, D. G., and YOUNG, L. The innervation of the musculature of the tongue. *J. Anat. 74:255*, 1940.

WHILLIS, J. Movements of the tongue in swallowing. *J. Anat. 80:115*, 1946.

WHITESIDE, BEATRICE Nerve overlap in the gustatory apparatus of the rat. *J. Comp. Neurol. 44:363*, 1927.

WODAK, E. Congenital anteflexion of the uvula accompanied by a swelling of the soft palate: Its correction by plastic methods. *Ann. Otol., Rhin. & Laryng. 53:581*, 1944.

YEE, J., HARRISON, F., and CORBIN, K. B. The sensory innervation of the spinal accessory and tongue musculature in the rabbit. *J. Comp. Neurol. 70:305*, 1939.

YOUNG, M. W. Anatomical and functional relationships between the jaw and the ear. (Abstr.) *Anat. Rec. 109:362*, 1951.

ZIEGELMAN, E. F. Calculi in the submaxillary and sublingual glands and their ducts. *Arch. Otolaryng. 19:318*, 1934.

CHAPTER 8

The Pharynx and Larynx

THE PHARYNX

THE wall of the pharynx consists of mucosa and voluntary muscle, with a more or less well defined connective tissue layer, the pharyngeal aponeurosis (pharyngobasilar fascia, pharyngobasilar lamina) interposed between the two, and of course a fascial layer (buccopharyngeal fascia) on the external surface of the muscles. The pharyngeal aponeurosis is well developed above, where it substitutes for a muscular wall in the sinus of Morgagni, and may also be distinguished at the level of the tonsil, for which it forms a fibrous bed; lower down, it becomes less and less distinguishable as a layer and finally disappears. It is said to be attached to the base of the skull, the pterygomandibular raphe (pterygomandibular ligament) and the posterior end of the mylohyoid line on the mandible, the hyoid bone, and the thyroid cartilage.

The mucosa of the pharynx varies in structure. That of the nasopharynx is for the most part ciliated and resembles the mucosa of the nose; in addition, it contains the lymphoid nodules which constitute the pharyngeal tonsil or adenoids. In the remainder of the pharynx the epithelium is stratified squamous (like that of the mouth with which it is continuous) and the mucosa tends to be tightly attached to the pharyngeal aponeurosis.

The muscular wall of the pharynx with its covering buccopharyngeal or visceral fascia is separated from the prevertebral fascia by an area of loose connective tissue which constitutes the retropharyngeal space; the lateral continuation of this connective tissue on both sides between the pharynx and the internal pterygoid muscles forms the lateral pharyngeal spaces. These spaces are discussed on pages 298–299. Posterolateral to the pharynx lie the ninth through the twelfth cranial nerves, the internal jugular and the carotid vessels and their branches, and the cervical sympathetic chain.

NASAL PHARYNX

The nasal pharynx (nasopharynx) is continuous anteriorly, through the choanae, with the nasal cavities; its floor is the upper surface of the soft palate, while its roof, the mucosa of which is at first attached closely to the base of the skull, slopes downward and backward to become continuous with its posterior wall (Fig. 241). At the level of the palate the nasal pharynx narrows to form the pharyngeal isthmus, through which the nasopharynx is continuous with the oral pharynx; the isthmus is bounded anteriorly by the velum and uvula of the soft palate, laterally by the pharyngopalatine

position of the sinus of Morgagni (p. 413).

In front of and below the pharyngeal recess, only slightly above the level of the floor of the nasal fossa, is the opening of the auditory (Eustachian or pharyngotympanic) tube. The anterior lip of the pharyngeal ostium of the tube is not well

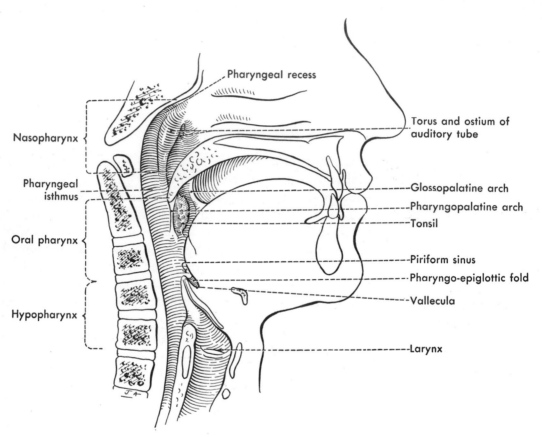

Fig. 241. General schema of the pharynx and larynx in sagittal section.

arches, and posteriorly by that part of the pharyngeal wall upon which is developed, during phonation, the ridge or fold of Passavant (p. 416). Above the isthmus the posterior part of the nasal pharynx is particularly wide, the lateral extension on each side constituting the pharyngeal recess or fossa of Rosenmüller; this recess corresponds to the

marked, but the posterior lip is elevated by the projecting cartilage of the tube to form the torus tubarius.

PHARYNGEAL TONSIL

The walls of the pharyngeal recess and the roof (fornix) of the nasal pharynx in contact with the basisphenoid and basioccipital bones contain in children and sometimes in adults a large amount of lymphoid tissue which constitutes the pharyngeal (nasopharyngeal) tonsil or adenoids. This tissue extends to a variable extent into the posterior wall and downward toward the orifice of the Eustachian tube; the wall of the tube itself is also sometimes described as containing lymphoid tissue (p. 185). Enlargements of the adenoids as a result of infection may interfere with nasal breathing and,

palate so as to occlude the nasopharynx. While rare, a majority of cases apparently have resulted from operations on the tonsils and adenoids (Kazanjian and Holmes).

PHARYNGEAL BURSA AND HYPOPHYSIS

In the posterior midline of the pharynx, surrounded by the pharyngeal tonsil, there may be a saclike depression, the pharyngeal bursa (Fig. 242); according

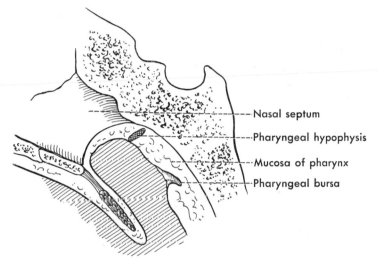

Nasal septum
Pharyngeal hypophysis
Mucosa of pharynx
Pharyngeal bursa

Fig. 242. Pharyngeal bursa and pharyngeal hypophysis as seen in a sagittal section of the head of an infant. (Redrawn from Dorrance, G. M.: *Arch. Otolaryng. 13:*187, 1931.)

through obstruction of the Eustachian tube, lead also to deafness because of the subsequent absorption of air from the middle ear cavity. Unlike the palatine and lingual tonsils, the pharyngeal tonsils have no epithelial crypts extending into them, although glands open through them (Arey).

Stenosis of the nasopharynx (not to be confused with congenital choanal atresia) may be produced by scarring and contracture of the posterior pharyngeal wall in the region of the adenoids or below, and may extend across toward the soft

to Dorrance it lies just above the uppermost fibers of the superior constrictor muscles and usually extends upward and backward toward the occipital bone; while it has apparently been mistaken for a persistent remnant of the craniopharyngeal canal (p. 54), it lies more posteriorly than this. Dorrance found the pharyngeal bursa to be more common in the embryo than in the adult. It is said to arise at the point of adhesion between the anterior end of the notochord and the pharyngeal endoderm (Snook). It may be the site of cyst formation, chronic infection of it being referred to as Torn-waldt's (Thornwald's, Tornwald's) disease.

Farther forward, deep to the mucosa or in the periosteum close to the vomerosphenoid articulation, and therefore corresponding in position to the diverticulum (Rathke's pouch, see p. 54) from which the anterior lobe of the hypophysis is developed, there apparently regularly occurs a pharyngeal hypophysis. Melchionna and Moore found this in 51 of 54 cases in which it was searched for, but unless it becomes cystic or gives rise to a tumor it is usually not grossly visible.

ORAL PHARYNX

The oral pharynx is continuous anteriorly, through the faucial or oropharyngeal isthmus, with the oral cavity; the boundary of this isthmus is the posterior edge of the soft palate above, the glossopalatine arches (anterior faucial or tonsillar pillars) laterally, and the dorsum of the tongue inferiorly. Below the faucial isthmus the anterior wall of the oral pharynx is formed by the base or root of the tongue, behind which projects the epiglottis. The base of the tongue and the epiglottis are connected by three low folds, the paired lateral ones being termed the pharyngo-epiglottic or lateral glosso-epiglottic folds, and the median one the (median) glosso-epiglottic fold. The shallow depressions between the median and the lateral folds are the valleculae; foreign bodies sometimes lodge here.

LINGUAL TONSIL

On the root of the tongue lie irregular nodules of lymphoid tissue into which dip small and shallow tubules or crypts of the surface epithelium. These nodules collectively form the lingual tonsil, and if enlarged may be partially removed at tonsillectomy; since, unlike the palatine tonsil, they have no well-defined deep surface or bed, it is impossible to remove them completely.

PALATINE ARCHES

The lateral wall of the oral pharynx is largely occupied by the palatine tonsil, the relationships of which are discussed in more detail in a following section. Anterior and posterior to the tonsil are the palatine arches, also called the tonsillar pillars or the pillars of the fauces. These are the rather inconspicuous (unless the tongue is pulled forward) anterior or glossopalatine (palatoglossal) arch passing between the tongue and soft palate, and the more prominent posterior or pharyngopalatine (palatopharyngeal) arch extending from the soft palate downward into the posterolateral wall of the pharynx. These arches are formed by the glossopalatine and pharyngopalatine (palatoglossus and palatopharyngeus) muscles, respectively.

WALDEYER'S TONSILLAR RING

The lingual tonsils anteriorly, the palatine tonsils laterally, and the pharyngeal tonsils or adenoids posterosuperiorly together form a ring of lymphoid or adenoid tissue about the upper end of the pharynx, known as Waldeyer's tonsillar ring (Fig. 243). Superficially located lymphoid nodules also extend upward along the posterior pillar of the tonsil and behind the soft palate to the pharyngeal recess to form a component of Waldeyer's ring; the tissue here is known as the lateral pharyngeal band or lateral band and has been the site of an hemangioma (Lillie and Heck).

POSTERIOR WALL

The posterior wall of the oral pharynx, related to the anterior surfaces of about the second and third vertebrae, is of course continuous above with the posterior wall of the nasopharynx and below with that of the laryngeal portion of the pharynx, and has no distinguishing markings.

posterior pharyngeal wall has apparently also sometimes been mistaken for a tumor.

LARYNGEAL PHARYNX

The laryngeal pharynx or hypopharynx extends from just above the level of the hyoid bone superiorly to the cricoid cartilage inferiorly, narrowing rapidly to be-

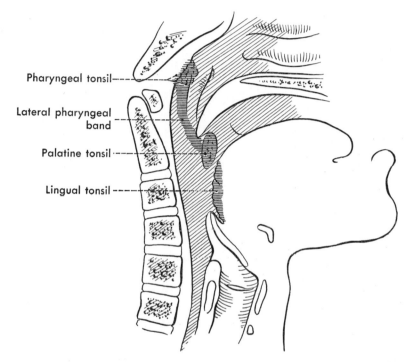

Pharyngeal tonsil
Lateral pharyngeal band
Palatine tonsil
Lingual tonsil

Fig. 243. Waldeyer's tonsillar ring.

The posterior wall of the nasal and oral pharynx is intimately related above and posteriorly to the antero-inferior surface of the base of the occipital bone, and posteriorly to the centra of the several upper cervical vertebrae. If the neck is hyperextended, the potential retropharyngeal space is obliterated and the wall of the pharynx forced directly against these bones—hence, in adenoidectomy, the neck should be in flexion in order to prevent injury to them. Protrusion of a portion of one of these bones against the

come continuous with the esophagus. Its posterior wall shows no markings, and neither do its lateral walls, which attach to the hyoid bone and the thyroid cartilage. The anterior wall of the hypopharynx is formed laterally by the medial surface of the thyroid cartilage, and centrally or in the medial line by the larynx and its appendages (Fig. 244): above is the epiglottis, and below this the aditus of the larynx. Below the aditus the anterior wall of the pharynx is also the posterior wall of the larynx, the pha-

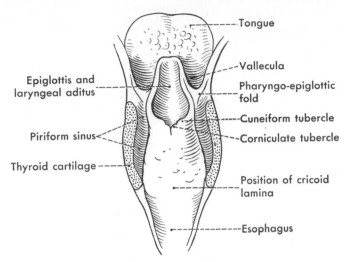

Fig. 244. Hypopharynx from behind, with its posterior wall removed.

ryngeal wall here being the posterior surfaces of the arytenoid cartilages and their connecting fold, and the lamina of the cricoid cartilage and its attached muscles. These are covered posteriorly only by the mucosa of the pharynx; it is this mucosa at the junction of the pharynx and esophagus which is reflected backward in the approach to the arytenoid cartilage in operations of the King type (p. 450).

PIRIFORM SINUSES

Lateral to the epiglottis are the pharyngo-epiglottic or lateral glosso-epiglottic folds, which are regarded as forming the upper boundary of the hypopharynx, and beneath the level of these folds the hypopharynx expands anterolaterally between the inner surface of the thyroid cartilage and the posterolateral surfaces of the arytenoid and cricoid cartilages; these bilateral expansions are the piriform sinuses, recesses, or fossae (Fig. 245).

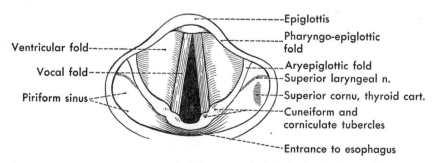

Fig. 245. Piriform sinuses and hypopharynx from above. Within the right sinus is indicated the positions in which the internal branch of the superior laryngeal nerve and the superior cornu of the thyroid cartilage may form folds protruding into it; the position of the nerve alone is indicated in the left sinus. Below and between the piriform sinuses the hypopharynx narrows toward its junction with the esophagus. (Adapted from Schugt, H. P.: *Arch. Otolaryng. 31*:626, 1940.)

Foreign bodies not infrequently lodge here, and both the piriform sinuses and the valleculae should therefore be investigated before such bodies are sought in the larynx, trachea, or esophagus.

According to Schugt markings within the piriform sinus or recess are not constant, but anomalies are relatively rare. The internal laryngeal nerve usually produces a slight fold in the anterior part of the floor of the sinus, as it runs beneath this after penetrating the thyrohyoid membrane; whether visible or not, it may be blocked by applying local anesthetic to the mucosa of the sinus. The upper border of the thyroid cartilage may be visible as a white line in the floor of the sinus, and Schugt found that one of the most common anomalies of the sinus was the projection into it of the superior cornu of the thyroid cartilage. Also running in the wall and across the floor of the piriform sinus are the superior laryngeal artery and vein, and many of the lymphatics from the larynx. Abscesses of the larynx may point in the piriform sinus, and edema of the hypopharynx and larynx may so elevate the mucosa as to obliterate it.

PALATINE TONSIL

The palatine tonsil represents the largest accumulation of lymphoid tissue in Waldeyer's ring, and in contrast to the lingual and pharyngeal tonsils constitutes a compact body having on its deep surface a definite though thin capsule. Tonsillar crypts, blind tubules from the epithelium on the surface of the tonsil, extend deeply into this tissue. According to Minear, Arey, and Milton the tonsillar crypts vary considerably in shape, but the majority are roughly platelike; since they originate as solid epithelial growths and the lumen usually develops first at the growing end, cystic crypts may be formed or the mouths of the crypts may be so narrowed that it is difficult for them to empty. Minear and his co-workers stated that degeneration of the tonsil with increasing age usually begins in the lower half. Kelemen investigated the involution of the tonsil during the sixth decade of life, and found that it is essentially a simple atrophy with gradual disappearance of the cells and tissues.

CAPSULE

The so-called capsule of the tonsil is usually regarded as a specialized portion of the pharyngeal aponeurosis, which covers the deep surface of the tonsil and extends into it to form septa that conduct the nerves and vessels. The tonsil is not, therefore, easily separable from its capsule, but the capsule in turn is united by loose connective tissue to the muscles of the pharynx; thus the tonsil can be partly displaced from its normal position, and its removal is most easily accomplished by separating the capsule from the muscle through this loose connective tissue which forms the peritonsillar space (Wood). After repeated attacks of quinsy or peritonsillar infection the tissue becomes dense and unites the tonsillar capsule firmly to the muscle. Painter apparently regarded the tonsillar capsule and the pharyngeal aponeurosis as separate layers of connective tissue, for he has described separating them in the course of a tonsillectomy; he has emphasized that the capsule must be removed if a clean dissection of tonsillar tissue is to be obtained.

TONSILLAR RELATIONS

The free surface of the tonsil is covered with mucosa from which are derived the tonsillar crypts, and in connection with this surface there are somewhat variable *folds* and *fossae* (Fig. 246): The triangular fold is a layer of mucosa and connective tissue, the latter said to be continuous with the capsule of the tonsil, that lies just behind the anterior palatine arch; this fold may be adherent to the medial surface of the tonsil, or may be separated from it by an anterior tonsillar fossa. Rarely there may be a similar fold posteriorly, and in about 40 per cent of

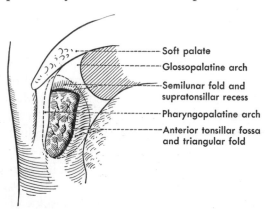

Fig. 246.   Folds and fossae about the tonsil. The size of the tonsil is indicated by the broken lines; its free surface is shown here partly covered by well-developed semilunar and triangular folds.

cases there is a semilunar fold and a supratonsillar fossa at the upper pole of the tonsil.

Since the tonsil lies in the depression (tonsillar fossa) between the glossopalatinus and the pharyngopalatinus muscles, the unenlarged tonsil is largely covered by the former muscle when viewed from the oral aspect; the enlarged tonsil varies much in its relations in different individuals, sometimes much of it being exposed whereas in other cases much of it is buried, depending upon the direction in which it has expanded. More of the buried tonsil can of course be displayed by pushing on the anterior pillar of the tonsil, and in children, especially, a buried

tonsil may virtually "pop out" when the mucosa behind which it has expanded is cut. The upper portion of the tonsil was said by Hett and Butterfield to be especially well developed during the early years of life, so that approximately the upper third of the tonsil extends up under cover of the soft palate; they stated that by middle age much of this higher tissue has undergone atrophy.

On its deep surface the tonsil is held in place, somewhat below its middle, by fibers of the palatopharyngeus muscle which attach into it (Todd and Fowler), and which have apparently been termed the triangular ligament or the retrotonsillar or transverse plica; according to Todd and Fowler, it is the presence of these fibers which has especially given trouble in snare enucleation of the tonsil, and been responsible for leaving tonsillar tags. Browne ('28) described two attachments of the lower part of the tonsil, an insertion of the palatopharyngeus and palatoglossus muscles into its capsule, and a fibrous suspensory ligament attaching the anterior portion of the lower part to the base of the tongue.

The *muscular relations* of the tonsillar bed (Fig. 247) are variously described and illustrated, and probably vary somewhat from one individual to another. The superior constrictor of the pharynx is frequently described and illustrated as forming the larger part of the tonsillar bed, with perhaps a variable posterior portion of this bed formed by more anterior fibers of the palatopharyngeus (pharyngopalatinus) muscle; Todd and Fowler have stated, however, that the tonsillar bed is formed entirely by the palatopharyngeus muscle, and that while the superior constrictor is related to the upper part of the tonsil it ends well above its lower part. This seems actually of no particular importance; in the region of the tonsil it is difficult to distinguish between the fibers of the superior constrictor and those of the palatopharyngeus, and both muscles probably vary considerably in their development.

In any case, the muscular wall is quite thin, and immediately against it on the the stylohyoid ligament and sometimes the styloid process, the ascending pharyngeal artery, and the ascending palatine branch of the facial artery. Usually there is a considerable space (the lateral pharyngeal space) between the posterolateral wall of the pharynx at the tonsillar level and the external and internal carotid

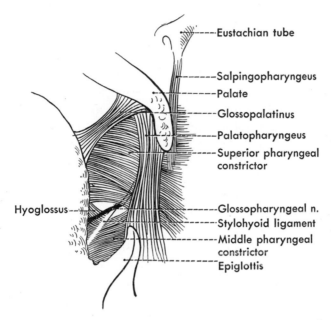

Eustachian tube

Salpingopharyngeus
Palate
Glossopalatinus
Palatopharyngeus
Superior pharyngeal constrictor

Hyoglossus

Glossopharyngeal n.
Stylohyoid ligament
Middle pharyngeal constrictor
Epiglottis

Fig. 247. Bed of the tonsil. It is here shown as being formed in great part by the superior constrictor. The course of the glossopharyngeal nerve lateral to the tonsillar bed, and the appearance of this nerve and the stylohyoid ligament beneath the lower border of the superior constrictor are indicated; since the stylohyoid ligament is a continuation of the styloid process, a long bony process is necessarily closely related to the tonsil.

outer wall of the pharynx is the glossopharyngeal nerve. Thus this nerve can be directly injured if the tonsillar bed is pierced, and not uncommonly it is temporarily affected by edema following tonsillectomy, producing a transitory loss of taste over the important posterior third of the tongue.

Also related to the lateral wall of the pharynx in the tonsillar region are the stylopharyngeus and styloglossus muscles, vessels and their main branches; sometimes, however, the facial artery or even the lingual may extend higher than usual and, in making the turn downward, bulge into close relation to the lower pole of the tonsil. The facial artery is apparently the more common important *vascular relation*. Probably even more rarely, a tortuous internal carotid artery may have its loop situated directly lateral to the tonsil (Cairney).

According to MacCready a visible pulsation of a large artery on the posterolateral wall of the pharynx is not uncommon, but as a rule the vessel itself is not identified—it has been thought to be an ascending pharyngeal, an ascending palatine, an aberrant vertebral, or a tortuous internal carotid. The pulsation has been mistaken for that of an aneurysm, as it may increase with age. MacCready reported a case in which he excised a portion of the vessel through an incision in the posterior pharyngeal wall and found that there was no true aneurysm here, but rather simply a tortuosity of the involved vessel; he did not identify the vessel other than to find that it was definitely not the internal carotid.

Cairney found tortuous internal carotids in 12 out of 36 adults examined, and pointed out that usually such arteries lie nearer the pharynx than normal and sometimes in actual contact with it; he expressed the belief that pulsation of the dorsal or lateral pharyngeal wall was probably due to such vessels. Since he found similar tortuosities in 5 of 20 fetuses, they obviously are not due entirely to changes in old age.

STYLOID PROCESS

Of the other relations of the pharyngeal wall at the tonsillar level, the only one of any importance seems to be the possible relation to the styloid process. Eagle ('48, '49) has pointed out that the normal styloid process does not reach the tonsillar fossa, but in about 4 per cent of individuals the process is elongated. In such cases, he has reported, the tip may be so deviated as to impinge upon either the internal or external carotid vessels, but more frequently it impinges upon the tonsillar region to produce pharyngeal pain, perhaps with extension to the ear.

Eagle found these symptoms primarily in persons who had had tonsillectomies, but Fritz reported that only 11 out of 43 patients with pain due to an elongated styloid process had had tonsillar operations. These workers and Loeser and Cardwell all agree that most elongated styloid processes do not cause symptoms, and that diagnosis can easily be made by palpation over the tonsillar fossa. Williams has stated his belief that fibrositis of the stylohyoid ligament is a far more frequent cause of throat pain, and pain referred to the ear.

Fritz and Eagle have preferred to remove the tip of a styloid process impinging upon the pharynx through a pharyngeal incision, while Loeser and Cardwell preferred the external approach, similar to that to the internal carotid artery. Babbitt has reported a rare case of spontaneous fracture of the styloid process, the symptomatology of which closely resembled that of simple protrusion of an elongated process against the tonsillar area. He has stated that the normal styloid process is about 30 mm. long, and that among 2000 skulls examined by another worker only 11 measured more than 1½ inches (38 mm.) and 1 more than 3 inches (76 mm.).

ARTERIES AND VEINS OF TONSIL

The arteries of the tonsil (Fig. 248) enter it especially toward its lower pole, with branches also at its upper pole, according to most descriptions. There are typically three arteries at the lower pole: the tonsillar branch of the dorsal lingual artery anteriorly, the tonsillar branch of the ascending palatine artery posteriorly, and the tonsillar branch of the facial artery between these (entering the tonsillar bed lower down). Toward the upper pole of the tonsil the tonsillar branch of the ascending pharyngeal artery enters the posterior aspect of the tonsil, and the tonsillar branch of the lesser palatine artery descends to enter the upper pole. Contrary to most descriptions such as this one, Browne ('28) stated that the real blood supply to the tonsil is from the tonsillar branch of the facial artery only, and that the other so-called tonsillar arterial branches end in adjacent muscles or in mucous membrane and do not actually

chief bleeding from tonsillectomy is due to this somewhat variable vein.

NERVE SUPPLY

The nerve supply of the tonsillar region is through the tonsillar branches of the glossopharyngeal nerve about the lower pole of the tonsil, and through descending branches from the middle and posterior (lesser) palatine nerves (usually assumed to be seventh nerve fibers cours-

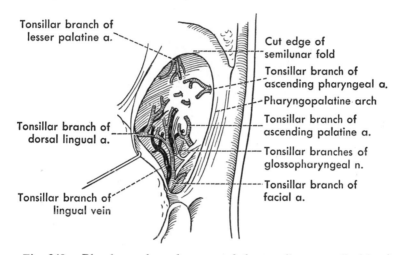

Fig. 248. Blood vessels and nerves of the tonsil, as usually identified. It has also been stated (see text) that the branch of the facial artery is the real blood supply of the tonsil, and that the other branches merely supply the neighborhood of the tonsillar bed. (Redrawn from Truex, R. C., and Kellner, C. E.: *Detailed Atlas of the Head and Neck.* New York, Oxford, 1948.)

pierce the capsule of the tonsil to be distributed to it.

The veins of the tonsil are usually described as forming a plexus about the capsule, though Browne regarded this as imaginary; the chief venous drainage is probably downward by way of the tonsillar branch of the lingual vein into this latter vein, with other vessels connecting to the pharyngeal plexus. A vein from the soft palate (the paratonsillar vein) runs downward to the pharyngeal plexus across the upper portion of the tonsillar bed; Browne expressed the belief that the

ing through the sphenopalatine ganglion, but Dandy described anesthesia over the entire tonsillar region as following section of the ninth nerve). In any event, the nerves thus form a circle about the tonsil, and adequate local anesthesia of this region necessitates infiltration beneath the mucosa all about the tonsil. The possibility of damage to the main trunk of the ninth nerve, which lies immediately outside the tonsillar fossa (p. 409) should be borne in mind; the nerve is sometimes seen crossing the fossa after removal of the tonsil.

LYMPHATICS

The lymphatic vessels leaving the tonsil are said to communicate with the submaxillary and superficial cervical lymph nodes, but the majority apparently pass to the upper deep cervical nodes, and especially to one located just behind the angle of the mandible; it is this node that has been called the tonsillar lymph node,

opposite side in the pharyngeal raphe of the posterior midline, while the longitudinal muscles, the palatopharyngeus and the stylopharyngeus, fan out and are lost in the pharyngeal wall. With the exception of the stylopharyngeus, which is innervated by the ninth cranial nerve, the muscles of the pharynx, like most of those of the palate, are innervated by the

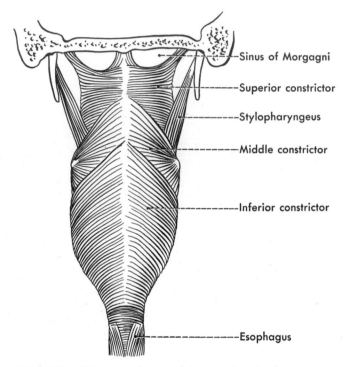

Fig. 249. Pharyngeal constrictors and stylopharyngeus from behind. The sinus of Morgagni is simply the postero-lateral, fascial, wall of the pharyngeal recess. For more details of the pharyngeal muscles see Figures 247 and 250.

because it is so frequently enlarged in tonsillar infections.

tenth nerve through the pharyngeal plexus.

MUSCULATURE OF THE PHARYNX

The musculature of the pharynx (Figs. 247, 249, 250) consists of three overlapping constrictors, superior, middle, and inferior, and two more longitudinally directed muscles. Each constrictor inserts with the corresponding muscle of the

SUPERIOR CONSTRICTOR

The superior constrictor of the pharynx, quadrilateral in shape, arises from the hamulus of the medial pterygoid process, from the pterygomandibular raphe or ligament (where it meets the buccinator muscle) and a posterior part of the mylohyoid line on the mandible, and from the side of the root of the tongue. It is sometimes described as arising from the medial lamina of the pterygoid process itself, but Oldfield and others have denied this attachment. Of more importance is the fact that some inner fibers at the upper border of the superior constrictor attach to the palatine apo-

into each other at the medial raphe of the pharynx; the upper fibers arch somewhat upward, however, to attach also to the pharyngeal tubercle on the occipital bone; the lower fibers arch somewhat downward and are overlapped by the middle constrictor. As the upper fibers run from the level of the hamulus of the

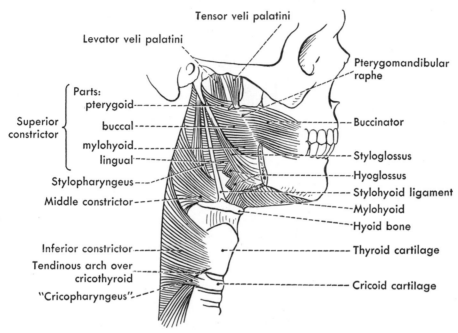

Fig. 250. Pharyngeal constrictors and related muscles from the side. In order to show the origin of the middle constrictor, that part of the hyoglossus arising from the greater cornu of the hyoid bone is here depicted as if cleanly cut away from this. Several parts of the constrictors are indicated. Note that the sinus of Morgagni is here largely obliterated by the levator and the tensor of the palate; the former and the Eustachian tube (hidden by the tensor) here penetrate the pharyngeal wall above the superior constrictor.

neurosis (Fig. 251); since they lie in the same plane as the palatopharyngeus muscle, they have apparently often been described as a part of this muscle. Whillis pointed out that these fibers are important in the formation of the ridge of Passavant (p. 416), and suggested that they be called the palatopharyngeal sphincter.

The muscle fibers of the superior constrictors of the two sides insert largely

pterygoid plate to the pharyngeal tubercle, there is left above their concave upper border an area deficient in muscle; this is the sinus of Morgagni, the wall of which is formed only by the mucosa of the pharynx and a thicker portion of the pharyngeal aponeurosis. The sinus lies against the basisphenoid bone, and represents essentially a gap in the upper border of the muscular wall of the pharynx which the Eustachian tube and the levator veli palatini muscle traverse; the enlargement of the nasopharynx at the sinus of Morgagni produces the pharyngeal recess (of Rosenmüller).

MIDDLE CONSTRICTOR

The middle constrictor of the pharynx is a fan-shaped muscle which arises from the greater and lesser cornua of the hyoid bone and the lower end of the stylohyoid ligament; between this muscle at its origin and the lower border of the superior con-

at about the lower pole of the tonsil, whatever space may exist between the lower fibers of the superior constrictor and the upper fibers of the middle one. The diverging muscle fibers of the middle constrictor insert with those of the other side into the median raphe of the pharynx, though a few of the upper fibers are said to reach the occipital bone.

Along or slightly above the level of the upper border of the middle constrictor the glossopharyngeal nerve curves for-

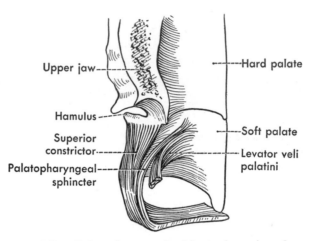

Fig. 251. Palatopharyngeal sphincter in a view, from above, of a horizontal section just above the floor of the nasal fossa. (Redrawn from Whillis, J.: *J. Anat. 65:*92, 1930.)

strictor there is laterally a potential gap, but as the upper fibers curve markedly upward and the lower ones curve similarly downward, the middle constrictor comes to overlap posteriorly the lower portion of the superior constrictor, and is in turn overlapped by the inferior constrictor.

At the posterior border of the lateral gap the stylopharyngeus muscle insinuates itself between the superior and middle constrictors to lie between the latter muscle and the mucous membrane of the pharynx; farther forward, fibers of the palatopharyngeus muscle lie internal to the upper two constrictors, and bridge,

ward into the tongue, and lateral to the muscle at its origin lie the lingual artery and the hyoglossus muscle.

INFERIOR CONSTRICTOR

The inferior constrictor of the pharynx arises on the lateral surface of the thyroid cartilage from an oblique line which also gives attachment to the thyrohyoid and sternothyroid muscles, from the cricoid cartilage, and from a tendinous line extending from the thyroid cartilage to the cricoid cartilage and arching across the cricothyroideus muscle. The upper fibers arch markedly upward, to overlap a large part of the middle constrictor, while the middle fibers ascend less obliquely and the lower fibers are approximately horizontal or even arched slightly downward. Some of the latter apparently blend with the circular fibers of the esophagus.

Because of the several origins of each of the constrictors, each muscle has been described as composed of a number of muscles which are then named according to their origins. Of the several parts of the superior constrictor, the only one of particular importance, the palatopharyngeal sphincter, has already been noted; the named parts of the middle constrictor are of no practical importance; in the inferior constrictor, those fibers arising from the cricoid cartilage are frequently designated as the *cricopharyngeus muscle,* and are commonly believed to be of some importance because of their supposed relation to hypopharyngeal pulsion diverticula (p. 418). The cricopharyngeus forms the musculature at the opening into the esophagus; spasm of it has been reported under the designation of globus hystericus. When the region of the "cardiac sphincter," that is, the gastroesophageal junction, has been abolished by resection, it is apparently the cricopharyngeus that prevents regurgitation from the stomach (Puppel). This muscle is discussed further in the section on hypopharyngeal diverticula.

PALATOPHARYNGEUS

The palatopharyngeus (pharyngopalatinus) muscle (Fig. 247, and Fig. 213, p. 351), arises chiefly from the anterior and inferior surface of the palate, passing between the tensor and levator palati; as the fibers run downward, they are joined by others arising from the upper surface of the posterior part of the palate, and many of them become aggregated into a conspicuous band which forms the posterior palatine or pharyngopalatine arch (posterior pillar of the fauces); the fibers gradually fan out to form a thin and scattered layer attaching to the pharyngeal aponeurosis, some few attaching also to the posterior border of the thyroid cartilage. As indicated by the alternative name, the origin and insertion of the muscle are frequently regarded as the reverse of those given here.

SALPINGOPHARYNGEUS

The salpingopharyngeus (Fig. 247) is a poorly developed muscle which arises from the lower part of the cartilage of the auditory or Eustachian tube and inserts into the wall of the pharynx; it lies immediately adjacent to the mucous membrane and may form a slight fold in the mucosa, the salpingopharyngeal fold, extending downward from the orifice of the Eustachian tube. It is frequently spoken of as being of considerable importance in swallowing movements, but its morphology does not support this; it is ordinarily quite poorly developed, and de Paula Assis has stated that it was absent in 30 per cent of 50 subjects dissected. In only 6 was it a strong muscle, and in the remainder it was extremely thin. Since it lies adjacent to the posterior fibers of the palatopharyngeus muscle, de Paula Assis has considered it actually part of this muscle.

STYLOPHARYNGEUS

The final muscle to be considered with the pharynx is the stylopharyngeus. This arises from the medial side of the base of the styloid process and passes downward and medially between the external and internal carotids to lie against the posterolateral surface of the superior constrictor of the pharynx and enter the pharynx between this muscle and the middle constrictor; here it spreads out beneath the mucous membrane.

MOVEMENTS OF THE PHARYNX AND THE SOFT PALATE

DURING SPEECH

Coordinated movements of the palate and pharynx normally occur during both speech and swallowing, and are therefore most easily discussed together. As pointed out in the discussion of the soft palate, apposition of the soft palate to the posterior wall of the pharynx is necessary for

palate upward and backward almost into contact with the posterior wall of the pharynx; the remaining gap is apparently sealed by the formation of a transverse fold (the fold or ridge of Passavant— Fig. 252) of the posterior pharyngeal wall, which develops simultaneously with the movement of the palate. According to some investigators, the ridge of Passavant is maintained during the period of phonation, while according to others it appears and disappears rapidly with the movements of the palate.

The ridge of Passavant can conceivably

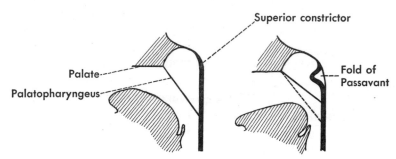

Fig. 252.   Formation of the fold of Passavant. The second figure indicates the upward movement of the pharyngeal wall with contraction of the palatopharyngeus, the relaxed position of the muscle being indicated by the broken line, its contracted one by the solid line. (Redrawn from Browne, D.: *Brit. J. Surg. 20:*7, 1932.)

proper speech; this involves both movements of the palate and a movement of the pharynx.

According to Wardill and Whillis the closure during speech is extraordinarily rapid, and involves first a contraction of the salpingopharyngeus muscle, then of the palatine levators and of the superior constrictor together. In spite of their emphasis upon the salpingopharyngeus, however, it must be primarily the palatopharyngeus that is involved here; see the account of the salpingopharyngeus. In the closure of the nasopharyngeal orifice, the levator veli palatini pulls the soft

be formed by either of two mechanisms: by an elevation of the pharynx produced probably especially by the palatopharyngeus (with the salpingopharyngeus assisting?) so as to produce passively a fold in the mucosa of the pharynx; and by the active constriction of the upper and inner horizontally disposed fibers (palatopharyngeal sphincter) of the superior constrictor muscle. There seems no reason to believe that both of these mechanisms are not working at the same time. De Paula Assis, from his study of the salpingopharyngeus muscle, expressed the belief that it could not help to close the pharynx but could assist in the opening of the pharyngeal orifice of the Eustachian tube.

IN SWALLOWING

In swallowing, the tongue, palate, and pharynx all work together. In rapid sequence contraction of the lips and cheek and elevation of the tongue force the food backward into the oral pharynx. Contraction of the glossopalatinus muscles narrows the faucial isthmus to deter return of the food to the mouth. The levator and tensor veli palatini muscles and the palatopharyngeus then tighten the soft palate and tend to close the passage into the nasal pharynx (according to Wardill and Whillis the tensor acts only in swallowing, and not in phonation). The stylopharyngeus and presumably also the palatopharyngeus draw the pharynx upward at the same time that the sphincters contract in a peristaltic fashion from above downward, thus passing the food through the pharynx into the esophagus.

The passage of food into the larynx instead of into the esophagus is undoubtedly prevented largely by the contraction of the musculature about the laryngeal aditus, and the closure of the larynx by the apposition of both the true and the false vocal cords; it has been both affirmed and denied that the epiglottis, during swallowing, is folded so as to cover the glottis. For instance, Stuart and M'Cormick observed the action of the epiglottis through a fistula, and stated that when solid food was swallowed the epiglottis did not fold down over the larynx as was commonly believed, but remained approximately erect and firmly applied to the back of the tongue. Negus ('27) accepted this view and stated that the epiglottis does not help to cover the glottis, but is rather a degenerate organ in man

and probably has no function. Subsequently, however, this view was combatted by Johnstone, who made a radiological study of swallowing; he stated that during swallowing the entire larynx is drawn up, as is also the hyoid bone, and that as the base of the tongue is pushed back it pushes upon the upper part of the epiglottis; he found that this push by the tongue, with the contraction of the epiglottic musculature, makes the tip of the epiglottis cover the glottis like a lid. Be that as it may, however, the epiglottis is not essential to normal swallowing; patients who have had the epiglottis removed because of carcinoma have no difficulty in swallowing.

Naffziger, Davis, and Bell have pointed out that paralysis of the last four cranial nerves produces a great difficulty in swallowing. Two important causes of this, in their opinion, are a lateral bulging of the paralyzed side of the pharynx, and the inability of the pharynx to move upward because of the paralyzed stylopharyngeus muscle. However, most surgeons reporting upon the effect of glossopharyngeal nerve section for neuralgia have reported that paralysis of the stylopharyngeus muscle alone produces no defective movement of the pharynx; the palatopharyngeus thus apparently suffices when it is not affected also. Naffziger and his co-workers have devised a reparative operation which they have tried upon both the monkey and man, as follows: to strengthen the weakened pharyngeal wall, they cut the carotid sheath laterally but left it attached to the prevertebral fascia and brought it forward around the pharynx to fasten to the anterior midline of the larynx and the cricoid cartilage; as a substitute for the paralyzed levators of the pharynx they attached the posterior belly of the digastric to the thyroid cartilage. The patient so treated is said to have swallowed very well after a little training.

PHARYNGEAL DIVERTICULA

Sinuses and fistulae of the pharynx connected with the development of the branchial pouches are discussed in connection with the neck in Chapter 9; these

often described as forming the cricopharyngeus muscle (Figs. 253 and 254). It is generally agreed that hypopharyngeal diverticula arise most commonly in the region of the cricopharyngeus muscle, although there is considerable diversity of opinion as to the exact site of origin of these diverticula. The several views advanced are that the diverticula arise in the midline below the cricopharyngeus,

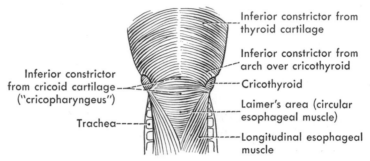

Fig. 253. Posterior wall of the hypopharynx. The "cricopharyngeus" is somewhat variably described, and is obviously difficult to delineate exactly, since its upper fibers blend with the lower fibers of the rest of the inferior constrictor, while its lower ones blend with the circular fibers of the esophagus.

most commonly open into the region of the supratonsillar fossa. The pharyngeal diverticulum referred to here is that encountered in the lower portion of the pharynx, close to its junction with the esophagus, and variously termed in the literature pharyngeal diverticulum, hypopharyngeal diverticulum, esophageal diverticulum, and pharyngo-esophageal diverticulum. Like the majority of diverticula found elsewhere in the digestive tract, these are commonly believed to be pulsion diverticula through an area of congenital weakness in the muscular coat, although causes other than congenital anatomical weakness have been suggested (p. 421).

The lowermost fibers of the inferior pharyngeal constrictor muscle arise from the cricoid cartilage, and these fibers are

or between two sets of fibers composing it, or above it; that they arise laterally below the cricopharyngeus, or above it; and that they arise also in higher locations. It seems not impossible that all the various accounts of this are correct, and

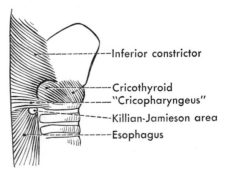

Fig. 254. The Killian-Jamieson area, the gap beneath the inferior constrictor for the entrance of the inferior laryngeal nerve and vessels into the larynx.

that there are several potential sites of herniation, though some of these are so close together that it hardly seems worth arguing as to which might be the site of a diverticulum.

McGillicuddy reported on a very large diverticulum of which one wall was composed of voluntary muscle (said to be derived from the hypopharynx) and the other wall of smooth muscle (said to be derived from the esophagus), and concluded that this hernia therefore arose at the junction of the hypopharynx and esophagus (although usually the upper part of the esophagus contains striated, not smooth, muscle). Just below the inferior border of the cricopharyngeus there is a triangular area, known as Laimer's triangular area, or the Laimer-Haeckermann area, in which the posterior esophageal wall is somewhat deficient because the longitudinal fibers of the esophagus are here swinging laterally and forward around the esophagus to reach an attachment on the cricoid cartilage. This area is therefore bounded laterally by the diverging bundles of longitudinal fibers, and above by the inferior border of the cricopharyngeus muscle; only the circular musculature of the esophagus forms the wall here, and it is conceivably a potentially weak area. However, Moynihan and Shallow, among others, denied that this area is the site of pharyngeal hernia; they stated that there were no recorded cases from this region.

Killian described the cricopharyngeus muscle as being composed of two parts, a superficial and upper oblique portion— frequently referred to as the constrictor portion—and a lower and deeper transverse or sphincteric portion. He expressed the belief that hypopharyngeal diverticula always occur between these two components of the cricopharyngeus muscle.

Wilkie and Hartley, and Bortone, agreed with this concept, and expressed the belief that the pouches are therefore of midline origin. Raven also agreed and stated (without citing evidence) that the upper or constrictor fibers of the cricopharyngeus are innervated by the tenth nerve through the pharyngeal plexus, the lower or sphincteric ones by the recurrent branch of the tenth, implying that asynergia between these two parts might be a precipitating cause for herniation.

Other workers (for instance, Moersch and Judd; Moynihan; and King, '47) have regarded the site of herniation as being above the upper fibers of the cricopharyngeus, between these and the remainder of the inferior constrictor of the pharynx. It is not clear, however, that this apparent difference in the location in which the diverticula are said to develop is not primarily one of definition of the cricopharyngeus muscle; after all, it is at best simply a poorly differentiated lower portion of the inferior constrictor, and its upper oblique fibers can easily be regarded as forming the lower part of the inferior constrictor proper, so that the cricopharyngeus could be defined as consisting only of the more transversely placed sphincteric fibers.

If this view is adopted, then there is actually no difference in opinion between those who state that the diverticulum occurs through the cricopharyngeus muscle and those who claim that it occurs between this muscle and the inferior constrictor. Babcock and Jackson stated that herniation might occur either through or above the cricopharyngeus muscle. In any event, however, it is difficult to believe that this is a matter of any real clinical importance, in spite of the emphasis which has been placed upon it.

While the midline diverticulum is generally granted to be most common, several writers have described also other areas of herniation in this region. Moynihan described a lateral diverticulum, occurring between the lowest fibers of the cricopharyngeus as they attached to the cricoid cartilage and the upper circular fibers of the esophagus; in this location there is a gap (Fig. 254) which transmits the inferior laryngeal nerve, a branch (inferior laryngeal) of the inferior thyroid artery and some lymphatics, and

agus, as they are said to do commonly, the relation between the nerve and the neck of the sac must necessarily be rather close.

Most of the diverticula arising in the hypopharynx, regardless of the exact site of their development, protrude to the left; in so doing, they come to lie in the visceral space, between the prevertebral or alar fascia and the pretracheal fascia about the strap muscles. The surgical approach to them is therefore usually from

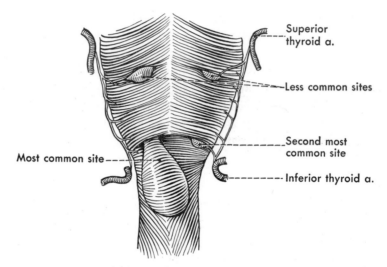

Fig. 255. Most common sites of hypopharyngeal diverticula according to Shallow. (Redrawn, by permission of *Surg., Gynec. & Obst.,* from Shallow, T. A.: vol. 62, p. 624, 1936.)

which is otherwise occupied by a small pad of fat. This area is sometimes known as the Killian-Jamieson area. Moersch and Judd have recognized the presence of diverticula from this area, and Shallow described it as a common (35 per cent) site of origin of pharyngeal diverticula. The distinction between diverticula here and in the midline may be of some importance because of the close relation between the neck of the sac and the inferior laryngeal nerve, although by the time diverticula about the cricopharyngeus muscle attain the diameter of the esoph-

the left side, either along the anterior or the posterior border of the sternocleidomastoid muscle.

Shallow apparently believed that not even the so-called midline diverticula are strictly this, for although he recognized the majority as arising between the cricopharyngeus (apparently the transverse portion) and the rest of the inferior constrictor (Fig. 255), he regarded the diverticulum as actually originating along a branch of the inferior thyroid artery which enters in this location, and therefore the weak places here as being bilateral rather than midline. He stated that of 79 cases of pharyngeal diverticula in various positions, the majority were in this location on the left side, and 4 were in a similar position on the right. Among these cases, the next most common area involved was said to be the slit between the cricopharyngeus and the upper circular fibers of the esophagus (Killian-Jamieson area), the diverticula arising here in slightly more than 35 per cent of the cases; in these, hoarseness preceding or following the operation was not unusual. He stated also, however, that occasional hernias arise higher, through the inferior constrictor muscle itself, where another branch of the inferior thyroid artery penetrates the pharyngeal wall; he regarded this as the least common locus.

Morley has pointed out that pharyngeal diverticula occur as a rule in late middle age, and King ('47) has stated that he has never heard of one occurring before the age of 15 years. They are apparently more common in men than women, according to King about three times so, and King has doubted that they are actually due to areas of congenital weakness. He has pointed out that the most common locus, at about the junction of the cricopharyngeus and the rest of the inferior constrictor, actually represents a point where the lower border of the cricoid cartilage rests against the cervical vertebral column, and expressed the belief that pressure from the mature male larynx produces the weakness here.

Furstenberg ('47) has also doubted that all cases of these diverticula are actually due to congenital weakness; he has regarded esophageal obstruction as a possible cause of these, and has described a case in which he observed the development of such a diverticulum following obstruction of the upper part of the esophagus. This would agree with the theory advanced by Killian, that spasm of the sphincteric fibers of the cricopharyngeus may be a cause of diverticula. It might be noted here, however, that the cricopharyngeus muscle, being a voluntary one, is not innervated by the sympathetic system, and there seems to be no ready explanation as to why a cervical sympathectomy should relieve spasm of this muscle, as it was reported to do by Rogers.

In many patients symptoms of pharyngeal diverticula have been present for from 5 to 10 years before they present themselves for operation: these symptoms may include some degree of dysphagia associated with regurgitation, and there may be complaints of disagreeable noises on swallowing; regurgitation may be accompanied by violent coughing and choking (Morley). Enlargement of the pouch gradually produces obstruction to the passage of food through the esophagus, so that while in early cases the weight may be well maintained, in late or neglected cases there may be considerable emaciation.

The surgical treatment is, of course, removal of the sac. Hershey has stated that the usual approach is an anterior one, that is, along the anterior edge of the sternocleidomastoid muscle, but he preferred a lateral approach, along the posterior edge of the muscle. The operation was once routinely done in two stages, the first stage including merely the mobilization of the diverticulum and its implantation in the superior portion of the wound, while the second included the actual incision of the sac and the closure of its opening. In recent years the one-stage operation, in which the sac is mobilized and removed at one operation, has been more favored. The technic has been described by many of the workers already cited and by Eliason, Tucker, and Thigpen; Lahey ('33, '46); and Sweet. Practically all of these workers have praised the one-stage operation as opposed to the two-stage one, though Lahey as recently as 1946 still preferred the latter.

NERVES

PHARYNGEAL PLEXUS

The motor nerve supply to the pharynx, and the sensory supply to all except a

forward medial to, then behind, then lateral to, the stylopharyngeus muscle. The pharyngeal branch of the glossopharyngeal, sometimes multiple instead of single, arises from the upper part of the nerve between the jugular foramen and the point at which the nerve passes across the posterior surface of the stylopharyngeus muscle.

This branch of the nerve extends downward, medially, and forward to join the pharyngeal branch of the vagus on the

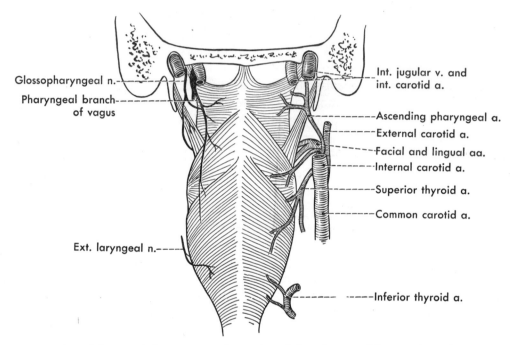

Fig. 256. Schema of the nerves and arteries of the pharynx. The arterial twigs from tonsillar and palatine vessels are not shown.

very small portion of it, is through the pharyngeal plexus, which is formed by the pharyngeal branches of the ninth and tenth cranial nerves (Fig. 256). The glossopharyngeal nerve at first descends between the internal carotid artery and the internal jugular vein, and then passes forward lateral to the artery to lie behind the styloid process and the muscles attached to this, and run downward and

lateral surface of the superior constrictor muscle and with it to form the pharyngeal plexus. The pharyngeal branch or branches of the vagus similarly leave this nerve high, and run forward lateral to the internal carotid artery, usually slightly below the level of the pharyngeal branch of the ninth nerve, to pass between internal and external carotids to the posterior or posterolateral surface of the pharynx. The pharyngeal branches of the ninth and tenth nerves may join as they cross the internal carotid, or may join more peripherally upon the pharynx.

The glossopharyngeal nerve contributes only sensory fibers to the pharyngeal plexus, while the vagus apparently contributes only voluntary motor fibers. The plexus is likewise joined by fibers from the superior cervical ganglion. The *motor fibers* in the pharyngeal plexus are distributed to all of the muscles of the pharynx and of the soft palate, with the exception of the tensor veli palatini (supplied by the mandibular branch of the fifth), the stylopharyngeus (supplied by the ninth nerve as it passes this muscle), and perhaps the lower part of the inferior constrictor, which may receive a branch from the external branch of the superior laryngeal nerve (vagus). The transverse fibers of the cricopharyngeus have been said to be supplied by the recurrent branch of the vagus, but upon what evidence is not clear. The motor fibers to the pharynx and larynx in the pharyngeal plexus leave the brain stem in the lower vagal roots and in the so-called bulbar rootlets of the accessory nerve, which join the vagus; this is true, however, of most of the voluntary motor fibers of the vagus, for the superior rootlets of the vagus are largely sensory ones (p. 77).

The *sensory fibers* of the glossopharyngeal nerve joining the pharyngeal plexus are distributed to a large portion of the pharynx, and most of the remainder of the pharynx is then supplied by the tonsillar branches of the ninth nerve, given off as this nerve passes medial to the hyoglossus muscle. The glossopharyngeal is thus the sensory nerve to practically the entire pharynx (Fig. 257). The only portion of the pharynx (palate

excepted—see p. 353) known definitely not to be supplied by the ninth nerve is a limited superior portion of the nasopharynx, which receives its sensory innervation from the pharyngeal branch of the sphenopalatine ganglion, the fibers apparently being supplied by the trigeminal nerve.

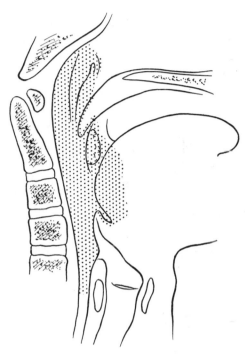

Fig. 257. Sensory distribution of the ninth nerve to the pharynx. The exact limits of this distribution vary somewhat—the orifice of the Eustachian tube may be supplied by the fifth nerve, and the anterior wall of the hypopharynx below the laryngeal aditus by the vagus.

GLOSSOPHARYNGEAL NEURALGIA

The distinction in the functional distribution of the ninth and tenth nerves to the pharynx is of no particular importance from the point of view of injury to these nerves, since they are usually involved together in tumors, vascular accidents, or other trauma; it is, however, of importance in surgery. Pain from the throat, tongue, or ear, corresponding in distribution to that of the glossopharyngeal nerve, may be initiated by swallowing or chewing movements; this pain is of the same character as major trigeminal neuralgia, and the condition is designated as glossopharyngeal neuralgia (p. 79). Since glossopharyngeal neuralgia involves the sensory distribution of this nerve, and the nerve contains no voluntary motor fibers except to the small stylopharyngeus muscle, the neuralgia may be abolished by intracranial section of the ninth nerve without appreciable damage to the voluntary muscles of the palate and pharynx. Indeed, many of the surgeons who have carried out this operation have emphasized that following it there was no difficulty in swallowing, and no abnormality of pharyngeal movements could be detected; this is, of course, in spite of the fact that the stylopharyngeus muscle must be paralyzed. Following section of the ninth nerve, however, the gag reflex on the side of operation is abolished, for the sensory side of its arc is cut.

VESSELS

ARTERIES

The blood supply of the pharynx (Fig. 256) is largely from the ascending pharyngeal and superior thyroid arteries. The ascending pharyngeal, the smallest branch of the external carotid, passes upward between the external and internal carotids and inclines medially to run along the posterolateral aspect of the upper portion of the pharynx, which it supplies before proceeding toward the jugular foramen. The superior thyroid artery as it descends gives off at about the level of the superior horn of the thyroid cartilage a branch which supplies the lower portion of the pharynx. The lowermost part of the pharynx is also supplied by branches from the inferior thyroid artery. Finally, the upper portion of the nasopharynx is supplied also by twigs from the artery of the pterygoid canal (Vidian artery, from the internal maxillary), and by similar twigs from the sphenopalatine branch of the internal maxillary artery; in addition, the pharyngeal wall in the neighborhood of the tonsil is presumably supplied also by the tonsillar arteries already described (p. 410).

VEINS

The veins of the pharynx form a plexus on the posterior wall of this organ, this plexus communicating above with the pterygoid plexus of veins and below with the superior thyroid and lingual veins. Batson has described a second pharyngeal plexus which lies internally, just beneath the mucous membrane of the pharynx; this is said to be particularly dense, composed of veins which are themselves some 1 to 3 mm. in diameter, and arranged in two parts, one on the anterior, the other on the posterior wall of the pharynx. The anterior plexus is said to communicate with the posterior one around the sides of the pharynx, to communicate with the superficial veins of the tongue, and to drain both into the superior laryngeal veins and the esophageal veins; Batson stated that the plexus on the posterior wall has a well-marked upper border but connects below with the veins of the esophagus, and also with the plexus on the outside of the constrictors. The plexus was described as particularly dense and ringlike around the entrance to the larynx, and Batson suggested that it might be concerned with pressure adjustments accompanying swallowing, as it seemed to be much greater in size than is necessary to supply the tissue here.

LYMPHATICS

The pharyngeal mucosa is rich in lymphatics, especially about the pharyngeal tonsil. According to Most the efferent lymphatics of the pharynx leave this in three areas: those from the roof and most of the posterior wall of the pharynx pass through the pharyngeal wall to the lateral pharyngeal node (a constant lymph node lying just medial to the internal carotid artery close to where this enters the skull, and against the lateral wall of the pharynx); the lymphatics from the tonsillar region drain laterally directly into the deep cervical nodes; the lymphatics from the hypopharynx group together in the piriform sinus, pierce the thyrohyoid membrane, and unite with other lymphatics from the region of the head to go to the deep cervical nodes.

The lymphatic plexus on the posterior pharyngeal wall receives most of the lymphatics from the nasal fossa, but near the ostium of the pharyngeal tube some of these lymphatics diverge to flow downward to the tonsillar region. Although it is customary to refer to the drainage of the pharynx as being into retropharyngeal nodes, the paired lateral pharyngeal nodes are usually the only ones seen in routine dissections, and Most has stated that, while these lateral pharyngeal nodes are constant, true retropharyngeal nodes are small and inconstant.

THE LARYNX

SKELETAL STRUCTURE

THYROID CARTILAGE

Since the larynx, as a portion of the air passageway, must remain open except when it is voluntarily closed, it is surrounded by cartilages which prevent its collapse and also give attachment to its muscles. The large and prominent thyroid cartilage forms most of the anterior and lateral walls of the larynx (Fig. 258). The upper border of this cartilage is attached above to the hyoid bone by the thyrohyoid membrane, while its inferior horns articulate with the sides of the cricoid cartilage. As its name implies, the thyroid cartilage is a shield-shaped one, open behind. Since it forms a major portion of the wall of the larynx, approaches to the larynx are often made through it. Jackson and Jackson ('35a) stated that laryngofissure, or cutting through the cartilage, and removing the inner perichondrium and everything inward of that in an area of carcinoma, is effective in a high percentage of carefully chosen cases; this approach, of course, avoids the necessity of removing the entire larynx.

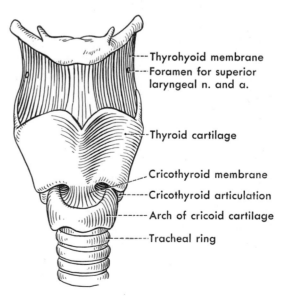

Fig. 258.   Cartilages of the larynx from the front.

Labels on figure:
- Thyrohyoid membrane
- Foramen for superior laryngeal n. and a.
- Thyroid cartilage
- Cricothyroid membrane
- Cricothyroid articulation
- Arch of cricoid cartilage
- Tracheal ring

CRICOID CARTILAGE

The lower portion of the laryngeal wall, and the entrance to the trachea, is supported by the cricoid cartilage which, unlike the thyroid cartilage, forms a complete ring; as it is the only supporting element of the larynx and trachea which extends completely around the air passage, the cricoid cartilage should never be cut in tracheotomies. The cricoid cartilage is shaped essentially like a signet ring, its anterior and lateral portions being a relatively narrow band while posteriorly it expands to form a lamina some 2 to 3 cm. in vertical length. Laterally and inferiorly, at the junction of arch and lamina, is the cricothyroid articulation; here the cricoid presents a small rounded depression which receives the inferior horn of the thyroid cartilage.

The cricoid and thyroid cartilages are also united to each other, anterior to this articulation, by the conus elasticus (cricothyroid or cricovocal membrane), and in the anterior midline by additional ligamentous tissue partly fused deeply with the conus elasticus and sometimes described as a part of this, sometimes as the (middle) cricothyroid ligament.

The posterior portion of the cricothyroid membrane is overlapped externally by the cricothyroid muscle, which also connects these two cartilages, but anterolaterally it is subcutaneous, and emergency tracheotomies have been made through it (but see p. 443). Because of the cricothyroid articulation the cricoid and thyroid cartilages cannot be actually moved away from each other, in spite of the elasticity of the cricothyroid membrane; however, the rotatory action possible at the cricothyroid articulation allows the cricoid and thyroid cartilages to be tilted upon each other in such a fashion as to increase or decrease

the distance between the thyroid cartilage and the upper border of the cricoid cartilage; Mitchinson and Yoffey ('48) expressed the belief that there may be also some slight sliding at this joint, though, judging from its shape, this must be extremely limited at best.

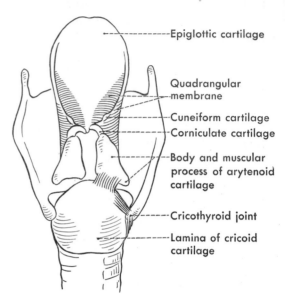

Fig. 259. Cartilages of the larynx from behind.

ARYTENOID CARTILAGES

On the upper surface of the lamina of the cricoid cartilage, and therefore located posteriorly, are the paired arytenoid cartilages (Fig. 259), particularly important because it is to these that the posterior ends of the vocal cords are attached. The base of the arytenoid cartilage is roughly triangular, and the cartilage as a whole is a somewhat misshapened triangular pyramid. In addition to its base, therefore, it presents three surfaces, a posterior, an anterolateral, and a medial. Similarly, its base has an anterior, a lateral, and a medial angle; the medial angle is not remarkable, but both lateral and anterior angles are prolonged. The lateral angle, short and broad, projects as the muscular process of the arytenoid cartilage, and to it are attached the posterior and lateral cricoarytenoideus muscles. The anterior angle of the base of the arytenoid cartilage forms a longer and more slender projection, the vocal process of the cartilage, and to the anterior apex of this is attached the vocal fold.

On the base of the arytenoid cartilage between the angles is the surface for articulation with the lamina of the cricoid cartilage. The ligaments of this joint allow some sliding movement of the arytenoid cartilages, so that the two bases can be brought closer together in the posterior wall of the larynx to close the interarytenoid gap, and also allow some tilting of the arytenoid on the cricoid. More important still, however, is the fact that rotation through the cricoarytenoid joint also goes on; thus a forward pull upon the muscular process at the lateral angle of the base produces a medial movement of the vocal process at the anterior angle of the base, the tip of the vocal process thus moving toward the midline and the vocal cord being adducted. Similarly, when the muscular process is pulled posteromedially, rotation through the cricoarytenoid joint swings the tip of the vocal process laterally, so that the vocal cord is abducted.

CORNICULATE CARTILAGES

The apices of the arytenoid cartilages are bent somewhat posteriorly and medially, and are in turn surmounted by the small corniculate cartilages (of Santorini), generally regarded as rudimentary and nonfunctional in man. According to Negus ('29) these cartilages, which necessarily move forward with the arytenoid cartilages during closure of the larynx, aid in opening of the esophagus in lower animals; Fishman has reported a case in man in which esophageal fibers attached to them.

CUNEIFORM AND EPIGLOTTIC CARTILAGES

In the aryepiglottic folds (p. 430) are usually, but variably, a pair of small isolated cartilages, the cuneiform cartilages (of Wrisberg). The curved, very thin epiglottic cartilage, forming the anterior wall of the laryngeal aditus, is anchored anteriorly to the posterior surface of the body of the hyoid bone by a hyo-epiglottic ligament, and its pointed inferior stalk (petiolus) is attached to the inner surface of the thyroid cartilage by a thyro-epiglottic ligament. The freely projecting upper portion of the epiglottic cartilage is simply covered with mucous membrane, but the lateral edges of the lower portion (below the aryepiglottic folds) have attached to them the quadrangular membrane. The potential space between the anterior surface of the epiglottis and the inner surfaces of the thyrohyoid membrane and thyroid cartilage has been described as the pre-epiglottic space; carcinoma of the larynx may invade this space, which is therefore sometimes regularly removed by resection of a portion or all of the hyoid bone and total removal of the epiglottis, where there is a carcinoma of the larynx.

Elastic Tissue

QUADRANGULAR MEMBRANE

The elastic tissue of the larynx deserves special description, since it forms what may be called the intrinsic ligaments of the larynx, and especially the vocal ligament. Lewis has described this tissue in considerable detail. Essentially, it consists of two fundamental parts. The upper part of this elastic skeleton of the larynx, termed the quadrangular membrane (Fig. 259), extends from the sides of the epiglottic cartilage to the corniculate and arytenoid cartilages; with the mucous membrane covering it, the upper border of the quadrangular membrane forms the aryepiglottic fold, while the remainder of the membrane forms the wall between the piriform sinus and the larynx.

The quadrangular membrane is usually not well pronounced except in its upper part, but is rather a thin sheet interposed between two layers of mucosa, with which are associated delicate bundles of muscle. Inferiorly, at or above the level of the false vocal fold, it becomes too attenuated to be identified grossly; Lewis has described,

part attaches to the arytenoid cartilage and its vocal process, while most of the remainder attaches into the vocal ligament or vocal cord, which can therefore be regarded as a thickened, specially developed free edge of the conus elasticus. The more anterior fibers of the conus are somewhat blended with the middle cricothyroid ligament, which is frequently regarded as a part of the conus; these fibers attach to the inner wall of the thyroid cartilage at the midline, and here the anterior ends of the two vocal ligaments come together.

The vocal ligaments consist therefore

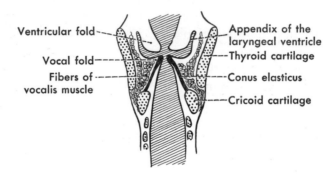

Fig. 260. Schema of the larynx and the conus elasticus in a frontal section.

from microscopic studies, a thin elastic membrane continuous above with the quadrangular membrane and below with the conus elasticus, and thus forming a third or intermediate segment of elastic tissue which is situated about the laryngeal ventricle.

CONUS ELASTICUS AND VOCAL LIGAMENTS

The conus elasticus (cricovocal or cricothyroid membrane) is a much more strongly developed layer of elastic tissue than the quadrangular membrane. It arises from the upper border of the cricoid cartilage, and sweeps medially and upward (Fig. 260); the more posterior

of thickened bands of elastic tissue attached anteriorly to the inner aspect of the thyroid cartilage at the midline, and posteriorly to the apices of the vocal processes of the arytenoid cartilages (Fig. 261); the anterior ends of the vocal ligaments are thus fixed, but the posterior ends move laterally or medially with the vocal processes of the arytenoid cartilages. The cords are parallel with each other only when they are completely adducted, and in any other position form two sides of a variable triangle, with the apex at the anterior midline of the larynx and the base an imaginary line drawn between the tips of the vocal processes.

GENERAL FORM AND RELATIONS

EXTERNAL RELATIONS

Anterolaterally, the thyroid and cricoid cartilages are in relation externally to the upper poles of the thyroid gland, and the isthmus of this gland lies across or just below the cricoid; the thyroid gland is attached, through its so-called adherent zone, either to the lateral surface of the cricoid cartilage or to the tracheal rings immediately below this. The cricoid cartilage is covered also by the strap muscles of the neck, which largely cover the thyroid cartilage; otherwise the thyroid cartilage is practically subcutaneous. Pos-

called the lateral thyrohyoid ligament) of the thyrohyoid membrane and lies against the lateral surface of the membrane, with the accompanying superior laryngeal artery and vein (from the superior thyroid vessels).

The external laryngeal branch of the superior laryngeal nerve descends upon the lateral surface of the inferior constrictor, as this muscle sweeps forward to attach to the oblique line on the thyroid cartilage, and here frequently gives off a twig to the lower portion of the constrictor; in the upper part of its course it is immediately medial to the superior

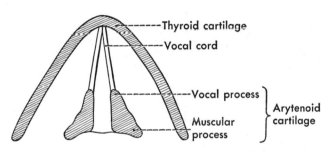

Fig. 261.   Attachments of the vocal cords, seen from above.

terolaterally, the larynx is related to the carotid sheath and its contents.

The recurrent laryngeal nerve, ascending approximately in the groove between the trachea and esophagus, passes just behind the cricothyroid articulation to enter the larynx, accompanied by a branch of the inferior thyroid artery. The palpable tip of the inferior horn of the thyroid cartilage thus serves as a guide to the point of entrance of this important nerve into the larynx. Descending medial to both the external and internal carotid arteries, the superior laryngeal nerve divides into two branches, internal and external; the internal branch curves forward across the lateral surface of the thickened posterior border (sometimes

thyroid artery, and can easily be injured here in clamping the artery. The external laryngeal branch then swings forward across the outer surface of the lower part of the inferior constrictor, between this and the upper pole of the thyroid gland, to supply the cricothyroid muscle.

INTERNAL ANATOMY

The laryngeal aditus (Fig. 262), or entrance into the larynx, is formed anteriorly by the epiglottis, laterally by the aryepiglottic folds, and posteriorly by the tips of the corniculate cartilages and the upper border of the arytenoideus muscle —these, of course, covered by mucosa. Between the anterior surface of the freely projecting portion of the epiglottis and the base of the tongue are the medial and lateral glosso-epiglottic folds, enclosing the shallow valleculae. The aryepiglottic folds are formed by the upper free edges of the quadrangular ligament and its covering mucosa, and extend from the lower part of the sides of the epiglottic cartilage to the arytenoid and corniculate cartilages; lateral to them, and thus between them and the inner surface of the thyroid cartilage, are the piriform sinuses of the hypopharynx (p. 406). As the aryepiglottic folds swing posteriorly and medially toward the corniculate cartilages they typically present small swellings, the cuneiform or cuneate tubercles, caused

receives on its sides the attachment of the circular muscle at this level and inserts upon the midline crest of the lamina; the larger part of the lateral portions of the posterior surface of the lamina are occupied by the cricoarytenoideus posterior muscles.

The larynx is considered to extend from the level of the aditus to the lower border of the cricoid cartilage, where it is continuous with the trachea (Fig. 263); it is divided into two parts, an upper and a lower, by the vocal folds which with their intervening aperture constitute the glottis. The upper portion of the larynx is the vestibule. It is bounded by the epiglottis,

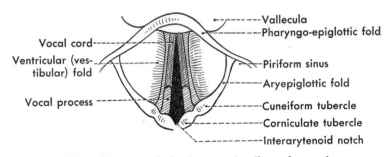

Fig. 262. Schema of the laryngeal aditus, from above.

by the presence of the cuneiform cartilages. Posteriorly, on either side of the midline, the corniculate tubercles formed by the projecting corniculate cartilages may be recognized. The depression between these is the interarytenoid notch.

The posterior surfaces of the corniculate and arytenoid cartilages and the lamina of the cricoid cartilage, covered by mucosa, form the anterior wall of the laryngeal pharynx. The potential gap between the arytenoid cartilages is largely occupied by the arytenoideus muscle; between the mucosa of the pharynx and the lamina of the cricoid cartilage the longitudinal musculature of the esophagus, swinging forward in two bands, one on either side, forms a single tendon which

the quadrangular ligaments, the arytenoid cartilages above the level of the vocal processes, and by the interarytenoideus muscle.

VENTRICULAR FOLDS

Low on the lateral walls of the vestibule are the ventricular folds (bands, vestibular folds, superior vocal cords, false vocal cords—Fig. 264), two thick folds of mucous membrane with a thin center of connective tissue; they are attached at their anterior ends to the thyroid cartilage just below the attachment of the epiglottis, and at their posterior ends to the bodies of the arytenoid cartilages. The false vocal cords thus move with the arytenoid cartilages, and are brought together in

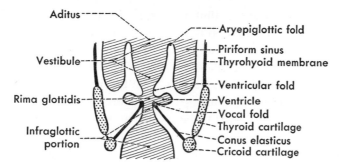

Fig. 263. Cavity of the larynx and its subdivisions in a frontal section. See also Figure 260.

forced closure of the glottis to help seal the air passage.

From above, the false vocal cords are simply inward bulges of the mucosa, which hide much of the true vocal folds; their lower free edges are however undermined by a recess, the ventricle of the larynx (ventricle of Morgagni, laryngeal sinus) which expands between the ventricular fold and the true vocal cord, separating these folds from each other. At the anterior end of the ventricle, under cover of the ventricular fold, there is normally a diverticulum known as the appendix of the laryngeal ventricle, or the laryngeal saccule (Fig. 260); this extends upward between the ventricular fold and the inner surface of the thyroid cartilage, and contains a number of mucous glands whose secretion is believed to lubricate the vocal folds. In addition to the mucous membrane, the wall of the ventricle and of the appendix consists of the thin thyro-arytenoideus muscle, the contraction of which probably aids in expressing the secretion from the appendix, and a delicate elastic lamina.

The size of the appendix of the laryn-

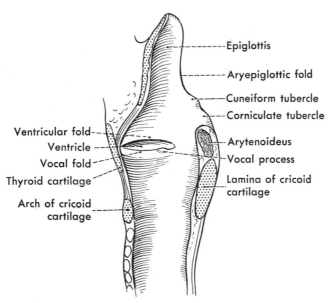

Fig. 264. Interior of the larynx.

geal ventricle varies so markedly that it is difficult to establish a normal, but it usually does not extend above the upper border of the thyroid cartilage; when it is markedly elongated it does so extend, and penetrates the thyrohyoid ligament to lie beneath the strap muscles of the neck.

LARYNGOCELE

An enlargement of the laryngeal saccule (a normal development in some animals, for instance, the howling monkey) is usually referred to as diverticulum of the larynx or as laryngocele. The incidence of laryngocele is unknown, and is indeed impossible to determine unless only true cystic formations of this are counted, or an arbitrary limit is placed upon the size of a so-called normal appendix; Campbell has noted, for instance, that one worker has reported 85 cases of laryngocele, while another of wide experience has seen only 2.

Most workers have regarded laryngeal diverticula as being of congenital origin, and representing an atavism; many of these diverticula apparently present no symptoms and are discovered only in the dissecting laboratory. Really large diverticula, extending markedly beyond the thyrohyoid membrane, are sufficiently unusual in the dissecting room to attract attention; the present author has seen only 1 such case, in which the diverticula were bilateral.

According to Schall only about 80 cases of laryngocele had been reported by 1943. The clinical symptoms described by Taylor in a case of unilateral diverticulum included recurring hoarseness, and swelling on the side of the neck, to some extent therefore resembling those of carcinoma of the larynx. The swelling associated with an enlarged ventricular saccule may be entirely internal, and present itself within the larynx above the false vocal cord, bulging the aryepiglottic fold (internal laryngocele); it may be outside the thyrohyoid membrane and therefore present itself in the neck (external laryngocele); or there may be both an internal and an external laryngocele.

Lindsay was not certain that laryngoceles are necessarily congenital, but expressed the belief that an elevation of air pressure within the larynx, thus exposing the ventricle to pressure, might be a major cause in such developments; he pointed out that an abnormally long appendix extending beyond the border of the thyroarytenoid muscle might predispose toward such development. Havens has stated that he believes that the necks of some laryngeal saccules are quite small, and that the opening may be further narrowed by an inflammatory reaction. He has suggested that this may be an important factor in the development of a laryngocele from an otherwise normal laryngeal saccule: the narrowed opening may allow air under pressure, as when holding the breath and straining, to enter and dilate the saccule, but prevent the ready emergence of the air once it has entered. Schall, on the other hand, noted that laryngoceles have been reported in children whose ages ranged from 1 to 13 years, and regarded this as lending support to the usual belief that they are congenital.

TRUE VOCAL FOLDS

Below the ventricle of the larynx are the true vocal folds. Strictly speaking, the vocal folds and the slit (rima) between them constitute the glottis, but the term is not infrequently used to mean the lower portion of the larynx in general. The edges of approximately the anterior three fifths of the vocal folds are formed by the vocal cords (the vocal ligaments and their covering epithelium), and the space between them is the rima glottidis vocalis, or intermembranous portion of the rima; those of about the posterior two fifths of the vocal folds, on the other hand, are formed by the vocal processes of the arytenoid cartilages, and the space between them is therefore the intercartilaginous or the respiratory part of the rima.

The glottis is normally, of course, the narrowest portion of the larynx, but its shape and size vary greatly with movements of the arytenoid cartilages and the membranous and intercartilaginous portions. In extreme abduction of the vocal cords in forced inspiration the vocal processes may turn outward so as to convert the rima into a somewhat diamond-shaped opening, the widest parts being the ends of the vocal processes to which the ligaments are attached. Finally, in forcible closure of the air pathway, as in fixing the thorax by holding one's breath, the arytenoid cartilages are both adducted and drawn forward, so that the cartilage and the ventricular fold of one side meet those of the other in the midline, thus obliterating the lower part of the vestibule.

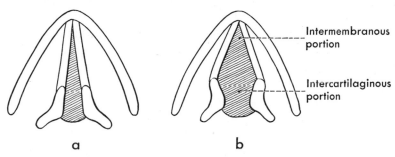

Fig. 265. Rima glottidis; *a*, quiet respiration and, *b*, forced respiration. Note that in the latter the arytenoid cartilages as a whole are abducted, and their vocal processes are externally rotated.

vocal folds. In quiet respiration the intermembranous part of the rima glottidis is triangular (Fig. 265), the two vocal folds extending from the separated ends of the vocal processes to their midline attachment on the inner surface of the thyroid cartilage; under these conditions, the vocal processes are parallel with each other and therefore the intercartilaginous portion of the rima is approximately rectangular.

The intermembranous portion of the rima may be closed by rotation of the arytenoid cartilages so as to bring the tips of the vocal processes together, but more commonly the arytenoid cartilages are adducted so as to close both inter-

This action apparently occurs also in swallowing, so that the ventricular folds tend to protect the larynx against any material which may pass the constrictors of the aditus.

MUCOSA OF LARYNX

The epithelium of the mucosa of the larynx is largely of the respiratory type (columnar ciliated) such as is found in the trachea, but a portion of it is stratified squamous epithelium like the lining of the pharynx. The squamous epithelium is largely limited to the upper half of the posterior surface of the epiglottis, the upper part of the aryepiglottic folds, and the vocal folds themselves, though scattered patches of such epithelium may be found elsewhere in the mucous membrane above the glottis; below the glottis, the epithelium is entirely of the respiratory type. Mucous secreting glands are numerous, especially in front of the arytenoid cartilages and in the ventricular appendages, but are absent from the free edges of the vocal folds.

The mucous membrane seems for the most part closely adherent to the adjacent structures of the laryngeal wall, but in certain locations can be raised from them by a submucosal collection of fluid, as in edema of the larynx. Miller has investigated the attachment of the mucosa by injecting fluid into the submucosa of the pharynx; he found that fluid so injected spread through the pharyngeal wall to the lateral glosso-epiglottic folds (pharyngo-epiglottic folds) but was here temporarily halted, and accumulated beneath the mucosa of the piriform sinus so as to almost obliterate this sinus. In so doing it of course invaded the aryepiglottic fold and also extended posteriorly over the esophageal aspect of the cricoid cartilage, but was halted abruptly here at the midline, and extended only a short distance downward below the lower margin of the cricoid. Passing forward from the piriform sinus the injected fluid eventually spread into the vallecula, and over the entire anterior surface of the epiglottis, crossing to the opposite side. It extended forward also to the base of the tongue. Spreading medially over the edge of the aryepiglottic fold the fluid passed downward beneath the mucosa of the vestibule of the larynx, and obliterated the ventricle, but was halted abruptly at the vocal cords; the tightness of the attachment of the mucosa to these was such that no real edema of them was produced, and in none of the specimens could edema be

demonstrated below the true cords. Clinically, this tight attachment at the vocal cords is evidenced by the independent occurrence of supraglottic and infraglottic edema; in acute laryngotracheo-bronchitis, for instance, the laryngeal edema is sharply limited above by the cords.

MUSCULATURE

EXTRINSIC MUSCLES

The muscles acting upon the larynx fall into two groups: the extrinsic muscles which tend to move the larynx as a whole, and the intrinsic muscles which are confined to the larynx and modify the size of the aditus and of the rima glottidis, and the length and position of the vocal cords. The extrinsic muscles include a number of diverse groups, such as the strap muscles (omohyoid, sternohyoid, sternothyroid, and thyrohyoid), which, with the exception of the thyrohyoid, are depressors of the larynx; the stylohyoid, digastric, and mylohyoid, which with the thyrohyoid elevate the larynx; the stylopharyngeus and palatopharyngeus muscles, which tend to elevate the pharynx and therefore the larynx, and are otherwise important in modifying the air passage above the larynx; and the middle and inferior constrictors of the pharynx, which arise from the hyoid bone and the larynx.

The exact parts which these various extrinsic muscles play in the physiology of the larynx, that is, in respiration and phonation, are certainly not clearly understood, but certain points appear fairly clear. In the first place, the larynx as a whole may participate in respiratory movements (Mitchinson and Yoffey, '47). The movements here are, however, not constant and probably not particularly important: in 23 individuals investigated by Mitchinson and Yoffey the larynx rose in 5 during inspiration, but descended in 4, and there was no appreciable vertical displacement in the remaining 14 as determined by x-ray; the maximal movement was about ¼ inch (6 mm.), the hyoid bone and larynx moving together. In 18 out of the 23 individuals there was an appreciable forward movement of the hyoid bone, the tongue, and the epiglottis in deep inspiration, this movement obviously tending to enlarge the aditus.

PRODUCTION OF TONES AND CHANGES IN PITCH

The extrinsic muscles may participate in this in several ways: they raise or lower the larynx as a whole, perhaps alter the direction of slope of the thyroid cartilage and therefore the length and tension on the vocal cords, and by their attachments afford relative fixation for the thyroid cartilage, upon which base the intrinsic muscles may further modify the cords. Sokolowsky has reviewed the literature concerning the action of extrinsic muscles on the larynx. Critchley and Kubik stated that paralysis of the strap muscles of the neck causes difficulty in singing high and low notes, and inability to whisper. Apparently one of the factors in producing the higher pitched, grating voice in psychophonasthenia is spasmodic contraction of the extralaryngeal muscles, with consequent elevation of the larynx.

According to Mitchinson and Yoffey ('48) the larynx moves upward for an average distance of about one vertebra in producing high tones (they studied the larynx while the patient was humming, by taking lateral roentgenograms), so that the supraglottic space is shortened or lengthened for high and low notes, respectively (Fig. 266), in a fashion reminiscent of the use of organ pipes; Griesman also agreed with this concept, which is likewise a matter of common observation.

A theory once supported by many students of the larynx, though perhaps not widely held today, is that the larynx functions essentially like a reed instrument, pitch depending essentially therefore upon the size of the aperture through which the air escapes. According to this concept, movements of the vocal cords affect changes in pitch in only a passive fashion, through increasing or decreasing the width of the rima glottidis, and the cords themselves are not a vibratory mechanism. Their changes in length, therefore, would according to this theory be purely adventitious, and of no importance in the production of various tones.

It has also been commonly assumed, however (for instance, Josephson and Willens), that the vocal cords act essentially like piano strings, vibrating as a whole, with the pitch of the voice determined by the length of the cord and its degree of tension; thus the usual explanation of the difference in pitch between the voices of men and women is that the larynx of the former is larger and the vocal cords longer. This is probably true, but the same principle does not seem to be involved in a given larynx—if it were, the vocal cords would elongate for low notes, shorten for high ones, while the observations of Griesman and of Mitchinson and Yoffey indicate that just the reverse occurs. According to Griesman, elevation of the larynx in producing high tones is accompanied by a forward movement of the thyroid cartilage which elongates the vocal cords (Fig. 267), while depression of the larynx similarly results in a shortening of the cords. To

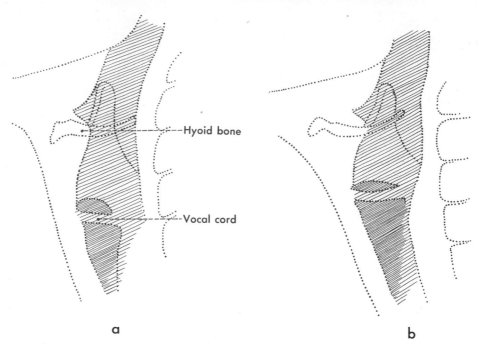

Hyoid bone

Vocal cord

a   b

Fig. 266. Semischematic line drawings indicating the changes in position of the larynx between, *a,* humming a low tone and, *b,* humming a high tone. Note the upward and forward movement of the pharynx and larynx and the lengthening of the vocal cords, in *b.* (Redrawn from the reproductions of the roentgenograms of Mitchinson and Yoffey, *J. Anat. 82*:88, 1948.)

what extent lengthening and shortening of the vocal cords is brought about by the extrinsic muscles is of course not known, for normally both sets of muscles must participate in these movements; that the lengthening for high tones is very definite, however, is indicated by the measurements of Mitchinson and Yoffey. These workers found an average increase of 5 mm. in length of the vocal cords in going from low to high tones, but practiced singers showed greater lengthening than others, the maximal increase being 9 mm. (in 1 case more than 100 per cent of the original length of the cord).

Actually, the functional implications

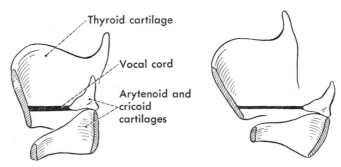

Thyroid cartilage

Vocal cord

Arytenoid and cricoid cartilages

Fig. 267. Schema indicating the production of a longer and thinner vocal cord upon tilting the thyroid and cricoid cartilages on each other.

of a lengthening of the vocal cords in forming high tones are not too clear. As already noted, the longer of two cords subject to the same tension should upon vibrating produce a lower tone, yet the cords are lengthened in taking high tones; furthermore, although it is usually assumed that this lengthening process produces an increase in the tension of the vocal cords, so that the pitch produced by their vibration is raised, this is not known to be true either.

Strong stated that the elasticity of the vocal ligament is somewhat like that of a rubber band, rather than that of a vibratory metal string, and therefore increased tension upon the vocal cord does not produce a rise in pitch such as is produced by increased tension upon a banjo or violin string. Further, he stated that during phonation the edges of the vocal cord are separated into tensed and nontensed segments of definite lengths, and that it is the nontensed segment which is vibrated by means of the air pressure from the lungs. According to his conclusions, in so far as pitch is determined by the vocal cords it is not through variations in the length or tension of the cords as a whole, but rather through the length of their nontensed, freely vibratile segments; through the action of intrinsic muscles of the larynx the nontensed portion of the cord can be made infinitely variable, to produce all the finer modulations of tones.

Pressman ('42), in an excellent discussion of the vocal mechanism, did not consider the effects of changes in the length of the cords as a whole, except as a matter of increased tension; he did, however, report (from his studies of slow-motion moving pictures of the larynx during phonation) exactly the same phenomenon described by Strong, although slightly differently interpreted. Pressman stated that during the formation of the higher notes a posterior part of each vocal cord is held in tight adduction, while an anterior part is abducted and then thrown into vibration by the escaping air. With progressively higher tones, there is an increase in the extent to which the posterior parts of the cords are held in adduction or muted, while the vibratile anterior segments become ever smaller.

The most reasonable explanation of the effect of the lengthening or shortening of the vocal cords in producing high or low tones, respectively, seems to be that lengthening causes the cord to become thinner, and shortening causes it to become thicker—the thinner cord producing the higher tones, the thicker the lower ones. In this respect, then, the cords might be compared to the strings of a violin or guitar in that their rate of vibration probably depends in part purely upon the mass of the vibrating segments. This concept is strengthened by the clinically observed lowering in pitch produced by polypoid thickening of the cords, and the lower pitch associated with use of the thicker ventricular bands for phonation. According to this concept, although elongation or shortening of the true vocal cord does not of course change the total mass, that of a segment of any given length is altered (Fig. 268); thus the changes in length of the cord lay the base for the action of the vocalis muscle in changing the mass of the vibrating (nontensed or abducted, anterior) segment.

This is not to say that the mechanisms of voice production are understood and agreed upon. There are obviously a number of factors operating at the same time —tension and length of the cords, size of the rima glottidis, length of the air column above the cords, and perhaps others, all of which may perhaps have an effect upon pitch. Pressman, for instance, has stated that the laryngeal picture may vary considerably even for the same note sung by individuals with similar voices.

VICARIOUS VOICE

In spite of the fact that the vocal cords are normally the chief vibrating mechanism for the production of voice, it should be noted that other mechanisms

vocal cord phonation with the ventricular folds is usually not so good, because of scars or injury to them. Morrison ('31) and Kallen also emphasized the fact that laryngectomized persons may produce a voice by allowing air to escape past a narrowed portion of the digestive tract—the cardiac end of the stomach, the upper end of the esophagus, or a portion of the pharynx. They discussed the methods of training for the production of such a vicarious voice, and seemed to believe

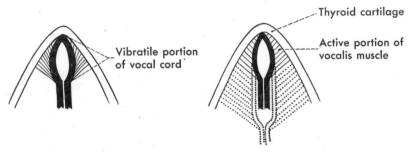

Fig. 268.   Illustrating how lengthening, and therefore thinning, of the vocal cords can result in a smaller mass for the vibratory portion of the vocal cords. Although the lengths of the vibratile segments are shown here as being equal, that of the second figure obviously has a lesser mass because of its thinness, and therefore should vibrate at a higher rate. As indicated by the dotted lines in the second figure, the vibratile portion of a cord of the same length and thickness can be varied by the action of the vocalis muscle, thus changing the mass of the vibratile portion (in the illustration, producing a lower tone).

can be used to produce vibrations and can therefore substitute for the normal one. Jackson and Jackson ('35b) stated that phonation by the ventricular bands may occur if the voice is forced during acute laryngitis, and that the same thing occurs after one or both true vocal cords have been destroyed by disease. They described the voice resulting from ventricular band phonation as being usually somewhat deeper in pitch and rougher in quality than the normal voice, but stated that it can be especially trained until phonation is smooth and not far from normal in pitch. They also noted, however, that after surgical removal of the

that it was more satisfactory than an artificial larynx.

INTRINSIC MUSCLES

The intrinsic muscles of the larynx are the cricothyroid, posterior and lateral cricoarytenoids, arytenoid or interarytenoid, and the thyroarytenoid muscles, plus various portions of these which have received special names (Fig. 269). Of these, the cricothyroid appears on the lateral and outer aspect of the larynx, while the others are covered either by the thyroid cartilage or by mucous membrane; corresponding to this difference in position is one of innervation, for the cricothyroid is innervated by the external branch of the superior laryngeal nerve, while the other muscles are innervated by the inferior laryngeal nerve, the continuation into the larynx of the recurrent branch of the vagus. All of the muscles are paired except the arytenoid.

CRICOTHYROID

The cricothyroid muscle (Fig. 254, p. 418) arises from the external surface of the arch of the cricoid cartilage, and cartilage backward through the cricothyroid joint, thus lengthening the vocal cords.

POSTERIOR CRICOARYTENOID

The posterior cricoarytenoid muscle arises from the the posterior surface of the lamina of the cricoid cartilage, largely covering a lateral half of this and being in turn covered by the mucosa of the anterior wall of the hypopharynx; between this muscle and its mate of the other side

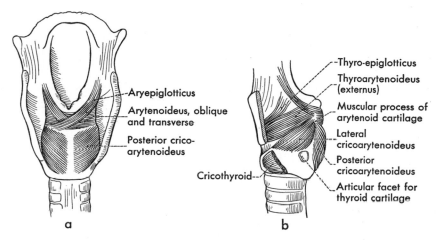

Fig. 269. Internal muscles of the larynx: *a*, from behind after removal of the pharynx and esophagus; *b*, from the side, after partial removal of the thyroid cartilage.

is partially divisible into two portions, an anterior and superior portion (so-called straight portion) which runs upward and laterally toward the inferior border of the thyroid cartilage, and a posterior and inferior, oblique portion which runs in the same direction but somewhat more obliquely backward. The more anterior portion inserts on the lower border of the thyroid cartilage, and some of the more posterior fibers are similarly inserted, but others extend backward to attach to the inferior horn and the inner surface of the thyroid cartilage. The muscle tilts the thyroid cartilage forward and the cricoid is the tendinous attachment (cricopharyngeal tendon) of the esophagus to the midline crest. From its origin on the lamina the fibers of the posterior cricoarytenoid pass obliquely laterad and upward to insert into the muscular process of the arytenoid cartilage; contraction of the muscle therefore pulls the muscular process posteriorly, medially, and downward, and abducts the vocal cords.

Sometimes associated with the lower border of this muscle is an aberrant muscular slip, the keratocricoid (ceratocricoid) muscle, stretching between the lamina of the cricoid cartilage and the inferior cornu of the thyroid cartilage; Hetherington found this present in 7.6 per cent of sides in the Negro and 12.9 per cent of sides in whites. Presumably this is an antagonist of the cricothyroid muscle.

LATERAL CRICOARYTENOID

The lateral cricoarytenoid muscle arises from the upper border and outer surface of the cricoid arch and extends upward and backward to insert upon the anterior surface of the muscular process of the arytenoid cartilage; by its contraction, therefore, it pulls the muscular process forward and downward, and thus is the antagonist of the posterior cricoarytenoid muscle, adducting the vocal cords.

ARYTENOIDEUS

The arytenoideus (interarytenoideus) muscle consists largely of transversely placed fibers stretching between the medial surfaces of the two arytenoid cartilages, and is therefore essentially unpaired. This major portion of the muscle is sometimes referred to as the transverse arytenoid muscle. It obviously approximates the two arytenoid cartilages and thus assists in closing the posterior (intercartilaginous) portion of the glottis. On the posterior surface of the relatively heavy transverse fibers of the arytenoideus there can usually be demonstrated two thin bands (oblique arytenoidei) which cross the transverse fibers obliquely, passing from the muscular process of the arytenoid upward and posteriorly to cross each other in the midline, and run toward the tip of the opposite arytenoid cartilage. Some of the fibers insert here, while others fan out upon the quadrangular membrane, those running in the aryepiglottic folds being termed the aryepiglottic

muscle, while other parts, of no practical significance and hardly demonstrable, have been given such names as thyroarytenoideus obliquus and arymembranosus. The arytenoid muscle as a whole is covered posteriorly by the mucosa of the hypopharynx; its anterior surface is covered laterally by the arytenoid cartilages, but in the space between these is directly in contact with the mucosa of the larynx.

THYROARYTENOIDEUS EXTERNUS

Above the lateral cricoarytenoid muscle, but sometimes inseparable from this, is a thin, frequently poorly developed and variable muscle which lies between the thyroid lamina and the elastic layer of the larynx largely above the cone. It arises on the inner surface of the thyroid cartilage where the laminae come together, and extends backward to insert upon the lateral surface of the arytenoid cartilage; it draws the arytenoid cartilage forward and rotates it medially, thus shortening the vocal cord; it is therefore somewhat an antagonist of the cricothyroid.

This muscle, the thyroarytenoideus externus, is frequently grouped with the constant and better developed fibers of similar attachment, lying deeper and in close contact with the conus elasticus (the vocalis muscle, or the thyroarytenoideus internus), the two together being referred to as *the* thyroarytenoideus muscle. Some few fibers of the external thyroarytenoideus muscle may usually be traced upward upon the quadrangular membrane to or toward the lateral border of the epiglottis, and constitute the thyro-epiglottic muscle.

VOCALIS

The vocalis muscle (thyroarytenoideus internus) is actually simply a deeper, thicker and better developed portion of the thyroarytenoideus muscle as a whole; in contrast to the thyroarytenoideus externus, from which, however, it is scarcely separable in a dissection, it lies against and intimately adherent to the conus elasticus. Like the thyroarytenoideus externus, its fibers arise from the inner surface of the thyroid cartilage at the angle formed by the junction of the laminae; some of these fibers insert upon the vocal process of the arytenoid cartilage, but, in addition, some insert directly onto the vocal ligament itself. From the upper edge of this muscle a few fibers extend around the ventricle and the saccule, these being sometimes known as the ventricular muscle.

By its action the vocalis muscle can draw forward the arytenoid cartilage, thus rendering lax the vocal cords as a whole, or through the insertion of its fibers along the length of the vocal cord it may draw a variable portion of the cord forward, rendering tense that part of the cord behind the insertion of the muscle fibers concerned, and relaxing or abducting, for phonation, the part of the cord in front of the attachment of the contracting fibers.

MOVEMENTS OF THE VOCAL CORDS

It has already been indicated in the discussion of the action of the extrinsic muscles upon the larynx that the mechanism of voice production is not too well understood; it follows, therefore, that the precise role of the intrinsic laryngeal muscles in the production of various tones is not understood, though it is generally believed that these muscles, or at least the cricothyroid and vocalis, are responsible for the finer modulations in tones. It is certainly these muscles primarily, however, that are responsible for the variations in the size of the rima glottidis,

and therefore for the opening or closing of the entrance into the trachea. In the following account the actions of the muscles are given as they relate to movements of the vocal cords, and to lengthening or tensing of the vocal cords, in regard to opening of the air passage but without prejudice as to the specific role in phonation played by variations in length and tenseness of the cords.

The *cricothyroid muscle* tilts the thyroid cartilage forward and the lamina of the cricoid cartilage backward; in so doing, it lengthens the distance between the angle of the thyroid cartilage, to which one end of each of the vocal cords is attached, and the arytenoid cartilage, to which the other end of each vocal cord is attached and which necessarily moves largely with the cricoid cartilage. This muscle by its contraction therefore lengthens the vocal cords (Fig. 267, p. 436), and in the process of so doing undoubtedly tenses them. Of greater clinical importance, however, even though it is frequently neglected in discussions of the actions of the muscles of the larynx, is the fact that in lengthening the vocal cords the vocal processes and the cords themselves are necessarily brought together toward the midline (adducted), in accordance with the principle that a straight line is the shortest distance between two points. With all muscles of the larynx intact this does not necessarily happen, for it may be opposed by other muscles, but if the cricothyroid alone is acting adduction must occur—this fact is of extreme importance in the development of respiratory symptoms following bilateral paralysis of the inferior laryngeal nerve (p. 448).

The *posterior cricoarytenoid muscle* is the most important one of the larynx, for it is the only abductor of the vocal cords as a whole. It rotates the arytenoid cartilage through the cricoarytenoid articulation: by rotating the arytenoid so that the muscular process swings medially and posteriorly it swings the vocal process laterally (Fig. 270a); the vocal processes necessarily carry with them the posterior ends of the vocal cords and therefore both the intercartilaginous and the intermembranous portions of the rima are widened.

The *lateral cricoarytenoid muscle* likewise rotates the arytenoid cartilage, but since it pulls the muscular process of this

would seem to tend to draw forward the arytenoid cartilage, thus relaxing the vocal ligament, and at the same time narrowing the cavity of the larynx; however, as noted on pages 437 and 441, the vocalis is said to be so inserted into the vocal ligament that it can make tense a variable posterior portion of this ligament, therefore relaxing the more anterior portion so that it may vibrate freely (or, according to Pressman, it is so inserted that it can abduct a limited segment of the cord). It is therefore commonly be-

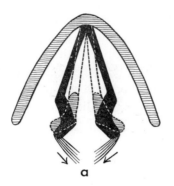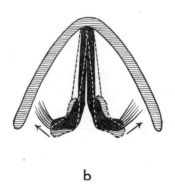

a   b

Fig. 270. Schema of the actions of the cricoarytenoid muscles in opening and closing the rima glottidis. In *a* the contraction of the posterior cricoarytenoid is shown to rotate the vocal process lateralward, therefore to abduct the vocal cords; in *b* the lateral cricoarytenoid is shown to have an opposing action, adduction of the vocal cords.

cartilage forward, it swings the tips of the vocal processes together, thus bringing the vocal cords together in the midline or adducting them (Fig. 270b). While it is obviously the most direct antagonist of the cricoarytenoideus posterior, it is only one of several muscles which may adduct the cords.

The *arytenoideus muscle*, and especially the heavy transverse portion, obviously brings the two arytenoid cartilages closer together in the midline, and in so doing therefore closes the posterior or intercartilaginous portion of the rima.

Acting as a whole, the *vocalis muscle*

lieved to be the muscle especially responsible for the finer modulations in tones during phonation and especially singing.

The *thyroarytenoideus externus muscle* has actions similar to those of the whole of the vocalis, relaxing the vocal cords by drawing forward the arytenoid cartilages and narrowing the laryngeal cavity; the various smaller slips of muscle, such as the thyro-epiglotticus and aryepiglotticus, presumably assist in narrowing the aditus of the larynx. Pressman ('41) discussed the three levels of sphincteric action (aditus, false vocal folds, and true vocal folds) which protect the trachea and lungs, and quite properly pointed out that while muscular action at the aditus is relatively weak, the two sets of cords themselves have valvelike forms which add greatly to the effectiveness of the larynx in resisting pressure. Thus the false cords, because of their downwardly directed concavity, are especially adapted to resist pressure outward, as in holding the

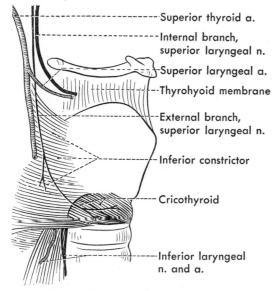

Superior thyroid a.

Internal branch, superior laryngeal n.

Superior laryngeal a.

Thyrohyoid membrane

External branch, superior laryngeal n.

Inferior constrictor

Cricothyroid

Inferior laryngeal n. and a.

Fig. 271. Nerves and arteries of the larynx, lateral view.

breath, while the true vocal cords when adducted resist especially downward pressure.

VESSELS AND NERVES

ARTERIES AND VEINS

The arteries of the larynx consist of two pairs, the superior and inferior laryngeal arteries (Fig. 271). The superior laryngeal artery arises from the superior thyroid artery as this runs downward toward the upper pole of the thyroid gland; it runs approximately horizontally across the posterior portion of the thyro-

hyoid membrane in company with the internal branch of the superior laryngeal nerve, and with the nerve penetrates the membrane to run downward beneath the mucosa of the lateral wall and floor of the piriform sinus, and supply mucosa and musculature of the larynx. The inferior laryngeal artery, a branch of the inferior thyroid (from the subclavian artery via the thyrocervical trunk), passes with the inferior laryngeal nerve to the back of the cricothyroid articulation and enters the larynx through a gap here (the Killian-Jamieson area) beneath the lower border of the inferior constrictor muscle (Fig. 254, p. 418); within the larynx it branches and supplies mucosa and musculature, and anastomoses with the superior laryngeal artery.

At the level of the cricothyroid membrane the superior thyroid artery also gives off a cricoid branch, which runs transversely across the membrane, somewhat closer to the thyroid than to the cricoid cartilage; sometimes, though apparently rarely, this may send a small branch through the cricothyroid membrane to anastomose with the laryngeal arteries. Emergency tracheotomies done through a transverse incision close to the upper border of the cricoid cartilage avoid the cricoid artery; this approach has largely been abandoned, however, since the incision must of course be carried through the conus elasticus and is so close to the vocal cords that it predisposes to laryngeal stenosis.

Superior and inferior laryngeal veins parallel the arteries; they join the superior and inferior thyroid veins respectively.

LYMPHATICS

The lymphatics of the larynx are numerous except over the vocal folds, where the mucosa is thin and tightly attached to the vocal ligament; by the vocal folds, the lymphatics are largely divided into a superior and an inferior group. The efferent channels from the superior group pass through the floor of the piriform sinus with the superior laryngeal artery and then upward with it, and join the nodes of the upper portion of the deep cervical chain; the efferents from the inferior group pass downward with the inferior artery and join the lower deep cervical nodes, some of them going as far as the supraclavicular nodes.

NERVES

The innervation of the larynx is likewise by two sets of nerves, superior and inferior laryngeal, but these two nerves are of different functional importance— the superior laryngeal nerve is largely sensory and secretory, and supplies only one muscle of the larynx, the cricothyroid; the inferior laryngeal nerve, the continuation upward of the recurrent branch of the vagus, probably also contains afferent and secretory fibers, but is largely voluntary motor and supplies all of the intrinsic muscles of the larynx except the cricothyroid.

The *superior laryngeal nerve* leaves the vagus trunk at the lower end of the nodose ganglion and passes downward medial to both the internal and external carotid arteries. As it curves downward and forward toward the larynx it divides into a small external and a large internal branch. The external branch of the superior laryngeal nerve (external laryngeal nerve) continues downward and forward on the lateral surface of the inferior constrictor, to which it may give a branch, and ends in the cricothyroid muscle. It is this branch which lies usually very close to the superior thyroid artery (p. 429). The internal branch (internal laryngeal

nerve) curves forward upon the thyrohyoid membrane, in company with the superior laryngeal artery, penetrates this membrane, and breaks up into a number of branches which are distributed to a small portion of the posterior aspect of the base of the tongue, the posterior or laryngeal but not the anterior surface of the epiglottis, the mucosa of the larynx itself, and possibly the pharyngeal mucosa on the posterior surface of the larynx (but not, apparently, to the piriform sinus which is, according to Dandy, innervated by the ninth cranial nerve).

One branch of the internal laryngeal nerve normally runs downward on the posterior surface of the larynx to anastomose with an ascending branch from the inferior laryngeal nerve; branches from this or from other descending branches of the superior laryngeal nerve penetrate the arytenoideus muscle to reach the mucosa of the posterior laryngeal wall, and several authors (for instance Dilworth; Berlin and Lahey; Nordland) have maintained upon the basis of dissections that the superior laryngeal nerve sometimes or always supplies the arytenoid muscle. Obviously, the fact that branches from the nerve may penetrate the muscle does not necessarily indicate that these are motor branches, and the problem in a dissection is further complicated by the fact that branches from the inferior laryngeal nerve usually anastomose with the superior (Fig. 272), and that the branch of the inferior laryngeal to the arytenoid muscle may run through or deep to the posterior cricoarytenoid muscle; in view of these facts, and the difficulty of accurate dissection of the smaller branches of the nerves in the larynx, gross anatomical observations upon this question are of relatively little value. Further, an innervation of the arytenoid by the superior laryngeal nerve has never been confirmed and is indeed contradicted by all experimental work, which indicates that there are no voluntary motor fibers in the internal branch of the superior laryngeal nerve. Finally, the clinical and physiological fact (the adduction of the vocal cords that may follow bilateral paralysis of the inferior laryngeal nerves) which these observations purport to explain can be explained completely by other uncontroverted facts.

The vagus nerve, and usually the superior laryngeal directly, receive communications from the superior cervical ganglion, and both the superior and inferior laryngeal nerves probably contain both sympathetic and parasympathetic fibers. Johnson showed on the cat that stimulation of either of these nerves causes secretion of tracheal mucus, and expressed the belief that such stimulation is responsible for the annoying accumulations of mucus sometimes occurring in the course of human thyroidectomies. He stated that mucous secretion was much reduced simply by taking care to prevent injury to the superior laryngeal nerve. In the dog (Lemere, '32b) there are ganglion cells, presumably parasympathetic, along the course of the internal laryngeal nerve.

The recurrent branch of the vagus (recurrent nerve, *recurrent laryngeal nerve*) runs upward more or less in the groove between the trachea and esophagus, giving off branches to these structures, and is in relation to the inferior thyroid artery and the posterior aspect of the thyroid gland; these relationships are considered in connection with the thyroid gland, and it only need be mentioned here that injury to both recurrent nerves is a serious consequence of thyroid surgery.

The inferior laryngeal nerve, the upper end of the recurrent, enters the larynx with the corresponding artery just behind the cricothyroid articulation, dividing into two branches, an anterior and a posterior one (Fig. 273), either before or after it enters the larynx (p. 527); sometimes the branches are multiple. The anterior branch, frequently referred to as

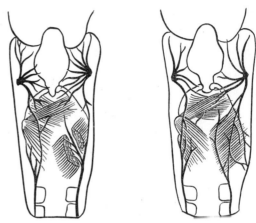

Fig. 272. Simple and complicated anastomoses between the superior and inferior laryngeal nerves. (Redrawn from Lemere, F.: *Anat. Rec. 54*:389, 1932.)

the adductor branch, passes upward and somewhat forward on the lateral surfaces of the lateral cricoarytenoideus and thyroarytenoideus muscles; it supplies these muscles and their subdivisions, including therefore the vocalis, aryepiglotticus, and so forth. The posterior branch, the so-called abductor branch, supplies the cricoarytenoideus posterior (the abductor of the vocal cord) but normally supplies also the arytenoideus muscle, transverse and oblique, which is of course an adductor. It is this branch which usually anastomoses with the descending branch of the superior laryngeal nerve.

It has already been stated that, in spite of the occasional description of the superior laryngeal nerve as innervating the arytenoid muscle, no experimental work indicating this has ever been brought forward; instead, work such as that of Lemere ('32a, '33) on dogs, DuBois and Foley on cats, and the observations of Clerf and Suehs on the human being all indicate the accuracy of the description just given: that all the voluntary motor fibers of the superior laryngeal nerve go into the external branch; that the cricothyroid is therefore the only laryngeal muscle supplied by the superior laryngeal nerve, which is otherwise sensory (and

adjustments for tones, are controlled on the sensory side not so much by muscle sense as by hearing: hence, for instance, the monotonous tone employed by the extremely deaf, and the lamentable efforts of the "tone deaf" to follow a tune.

PARALYSIS OF THE LARYNGEAL MUSCLES

INJURIES TO SUPERIOR LARYNGEAL NERVES

The external branch of the superior laryngeal nerve, lying as it usually does under cover of the superior thyroid artery,

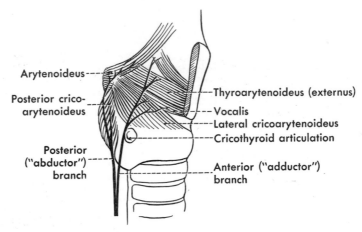

Fig. 273.　Schema of the distribution of the inferior laryngeal nerve.

secretory) to the larynx; and that the inferior laryngeal nerve is almost entirely motor, and supplies all of the intrinsic muscles of the larynx except the cricothyroid.

It is interesting that while Brocklehurst and Edgeworth found in the monkey that the external branch of the superior laryngeal nerve contains about 30 per cent of sensory (proprioceptive) fibers, the inferior laryngeal nerve was found to contain only about 3 per cent; this emphasizes the fact, already obvious upon reflection, that the internal muscles of the larynx, which are responsible for all the finer

is easily subject to damage in putting a clamp upon this vessel during the course of a thyroidectomy; it has undoubtedly often been so injured, but because injury to it, even bilateral, does not have dramatic or even dangerous aftereffects comparable to those of damage to the inferior laryngeal nerve, damage to it has probably frequently been overlooked. Paralysis of the superior laryngeal nerve or its external branch causes of course a paralysis of the cricothyroid muscle; as this muscle is primarily responsible for gross changes in the length of the vocal cords, bilateral damage to the nerves, although seldom seen, can be expected to make it difficult or impossible to sing high tones, and, since all the load of tensing the cords is then thrown on the less strong internal muscles, should cause easy tiring of the voice with some hoarseness and weakness. The quality of the voice is sometimes described as "flabby."

Lemere ('33), on the dog, and Clerf and Suehs on man, found that section of both superior laryngeal nerves or their external branches produced little or no effect on the appearance of the resting glottis; Lemere stated, however, that since the tension of the vocal cords was lost these wrinkled on attempted phonation and caused hoarseness; Clerf and Suehs reported that the immediate result of section of the superior laryngeal nerves was usually a loss of voice, even though the cords met in the midline on phonation. Obviously, however, injury to one or both superior laryngeal nerves should cause no difficulty in respiration or swallowing.

INJURIES INVOLVING RECURRENT NERVES

Injuries to the recurrent nerve, or injuries to both recurrent and superior laryngeal nerves, produce several different and understandably confusing clinical pictures, which have probably often been misinterpreted. Lemere's ('33) very careful experimental work on the dog, in which he cut various nerves and combinations of nerves, has served to clear up much of the confusion surrounding this subject; Clerf and Suehs, in analyzing 250 cases of injury to the nerves of the larynx, were apparently able to transfer Lemere's findings directly to man. This is not surprising in view of the close similarity which apparently exists between the larynx of the dog and of man.

One of the obvious difficulties in assessing damage to the movements of the vocal cords is that the cords are frequently assumed, in the absence of phonation, to be necessarily in one of three positions— extreme abduction, extreme adduction, and the midway position between these two, the cadaveric position. The cadaveric position implies, however, that no muscles whatever are acting upon the vocal cord, and should therefore be expected to be found only in paralysis of both the inferior and superior laryngeal nerves. Obviously, the difference between a true cadaveric position and a more medial one may not be very marked and may pass unnoticed unless the examiner is experienced. Since in any event it is difficult during laryngoscopy to estimate or record the exact relation of a cord to the midline, many experienced workers have preferred to classify "fixed" (paralyzed) cords into only two main groups, paralyzed straight cords and paralyzed bowed cords. The true cadaveric position of the cord is the extreme example of this latter.

As pointed out by Lemere, the musculature of the larynx serves three main functions: protection in swallowing, the maintenance of a patent airway, and vocalization. The first function depends on all of the intrinsic muscles of the larynx except the cricothyroid and the posterior cricoarytenoid; respiration, involving as it does the opening of the air passage, depends entirely upon the activity of the posterior cricothyroid; vocalization normally involves all of the laryngeal muscles except the posterior cricoarytenoid.

While Lemere emphasized that identical nerve lesions do not always give exactly the same picture in the glottis, his various combinations of lesions apparently explain most of the various clinical pictures that have been reported. In brief, paralysis of one recurrent nerve may cause some dyspnea upon exertion, since the cord may remain more adducted than in the cadaveric position; there is, however, little hoarseness, because on phonation the healthy cord crosses the midline to meet the paralyzed one. Swallowing is not interfered with, probably mainly because of the bilateral innervation of the arytenoid, from both inferior laryngeal nerves, so that the posterior portion of the glottis is properly closed.

In bilateral paralysis of the recurrent nerves in dogs, according to Lemere, both cords are adducted to about midway between the cadaveric position and the completely adducted position, and there is therefore both dyspnea and hoarseness. In man, however, dyspnea is not a significant finding while the voice is poor. Improvement in the voice, however, is regularly accompanied by increasing dyspnea, for both are due to gradual adduction of the vocal cords. Also, the least protection in swallowing would be expected to occur in bilateral paralysis, since all of the muscles which normally close the larynx are inactive; while difficulty in swallowing is typical of recent paralyses, patients somehow accommodate to this lack of sphincteric action and after a time have little or no trouble in swallowing. The dyspnea of bilateral recurrent nerve paralysis can, according to Lemere, be somewhat alleviated by anesthetization or section of the superior laryngeal nerves, since the cords then recede to a position of complete rest in the wider cadaveric position; however, he has noted that under the latter circumstances dyspnea becomes marked upon exertion, and that the incoming air during deep inspiration tends to appose the cords, for they act as valves owing to the ventricular sac above them. The results

of Lemere's experiments are shown diagrammatically in Figure 274.

The clinical application of these observations is obvious. They agree with the well-known fact that paralysis of one recurrent nerve is largely symptomless, since the normal vocal cord may be abducted to widen the airway, and adducted across the midline for phonation. They explain especially, without recourse to an anomalous innervation of the arytenoid muscle, the gradual adduction of the vocal cords which may follow injury to the recurrent nerves—as the cricothyroid muscles contract unopposed, the cords gradually become straightened and adducted. If this occurs the voice improves, thus signifying a gradual occlusion of the airway.

The variability of the state of the vocal cords following paralysis is well known, and depends in part upon the time lapse between the onset of the paralysis and the examination; this is only one factor, however, for paralyzed cords may be either straight or bowed, may or may not gradually become adducted, or may be adducted immediately after the onset of paralysis. These differences are undoubtedly dependent upon variations in the extent of the paralysis, but are difficult to analyze. They will vary with the degree of injury to the nerve, with whether the entire inferior laryngeal or only its anterior or posterior or a further subsidiary branch is involved, and with the state of the unparalyzed muscles. Certainly not all of the factors are understood. There is, for example, no ready explanation for the fact that paralysis of the left recurrent nerve caused by a lesion in the mediastinum is typically not followed by adduction of the vocal cord, while paralysis caused by injury to the nerve near the larynx always carries with

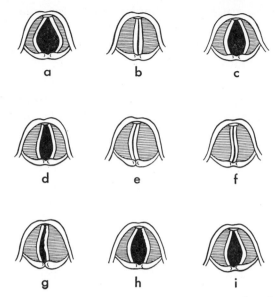

Fig. 274. Effects upon the vocal cords of the dog of sectioning various laryngeal nerves. (Redrawn from Lemere, F.: *Arch. Otolaryng.* *18*:413, 1933.) *a* and *b* indicate complete abduction and complete adduction respectively, of normal vocal cords; *c*, the cadaveric position, also characteristic of complete interruption of all four laryngeal nerves; *d*, slight adduction from the cadaveric position, which may become more marked, the result of bilateral paralysis of the recurrent nerves; *e*, attempted phonation with a unilateral paralysis of the recurrent nerve, the intact vocal cord crossing the midline to contact the paralyzed one; *f*, attempted phonation with bilateral paralysis of the external branch of the superior laryngeal nerve, with both cords therefore improperly tensed; *g*, attempted phonation with paralysis of the left recurrent nerve and the external branch of the right superior laryngeal nerve; the right vocal cord is shown crossing the midline toward the left one, but is lax; *h*, paralysis of the left recurrent nerve and of the external rami of both superior laryngeal nerves, in quiet respiration; the left cord is fixed in the cadaveric position but the right cord, although relaxed, can move across the midline; and *i*, bilateral paralysis of the recurrent nerves and paralysis of the external ramus of the right superior laryngeal nerve; neither cord can be moved, but the left one is partially adducted through the unopposed action of the cricothyroideus, while the right one is fixed in the cadaveric position.

it the danger of gradual adduction (Havens).

Havens has also stated that a vocal cord which moves normally immediately following a thyroidectomy may within a few days to a week become completely paralyzed. This late postoperative paralysis is presumably due to edema affecting the nerves, and rarely is permanent; if bilateral, however, it may be accompanied by such severe dyspnea that a tracheotomy is necessary.

Clerf and Suehs stated that about 90 per cent of paralyses of the vocal cord are due to injury to the peripheral nerves, and that central lesions account for only 10 per cent. Furstenberg ('37) pointed out that the laryngeal muscles, like other muscles commonly acting bilaterally, receive their innervation from nuclei (nucleus ambiguus) which are in turn bilaterally innervated from both cerebral cortices; thus a supranuclear (corticobulbar) lesion will not produce paralysis of the laryngeal muscles unless such a lesion is bilateral. Laszlo and Fiertz have discussed methods for assessing, by electrical stimulation, the extent of damage to the recurrent nerve.

It has long been known that partial damage to the inferior laryngeal nerve results in much more profound damage to the abductor muscle (the posterior cricoarytenoid) than it does to the other muscles, and this fact, that the abductor fibers of the recurrent laryngeal nerve are affected sooner and more profoundly than are the adductor fibers, has been termed Semon's law. In experiments on dogs, Lemere ('34) showed that after 4 months of age the adductors are stronger than the abductors; he found also that the nerve fibers to the abductor muscles are larger and have a lower threshold of stimulation, and that they are less resistant than are the adductor nerve fibers of the recurrent nerve. The latter is in line with the usually observed fact that larger fibers are more easily injured than smaller ones. When it is also recalled, as pointed out by Imperatori, that the abductor is a single muscle while the adductors are many, the increased susceptibility of the abductor muscle, as stated in Semon's law, seems readily explainable. Murtagh and Campbell concluded from physiological studies, however, that the fibers to the abductors (in goats and cats) are smaller than those to the adductors, and probably also very few in number.

Bach, Lederer and Dinolt reported degenerative changes in the laryngeal muscles in senile individuals, and concluded that these were sufficient to explain the peculiarities of the senile voice; they regarded the degeneration as due largely to poor vascular nutrition. In the 5 cases which they investigated, they found the abductor muscles to be more affected than the adductors. Whether the two facts are related is not apparent, but Lemere ('34) found in the dog that the abductor contained a considerably larger percentage of red muscle than did the other laryngeal muscles, which contained more admixture of red and white muscle fibers, or white fibers alone.

SURGICAL IMPROVEMENT OF THE AIRWAY

The dyspnea resulting from bilateral injury to the recurrent nerves may be so severe as to interfere seriously with the activity of the individual or indeed threaten death, and for these cases several operations have been devised. While, as noted by Lemere ('34), some improvement in the airway can be produced by interruption of the superior laryngeal nerves, this would result in complete denervation of the larynx and abolition of the cough reflex and of protection to the larynx during swallowing, and probably should not be attempted surgically.

The surgical methods which have been used to relieve the dyspnea resulting from bilateral paralysis of the vocal cords include a permanent tracheotomy, cordectomy or cordotomy by an intralaryngeal punch operation (portions of the arytenoid cartilage also being sometimes thus removed), laryngofissure with removal of one cord (for example, Lore) and lateral displacements of the vocal cords. Permanent tracheotomy is of course to be avoided if possible, and laryngofissure with cordotomy or cordectomy is apt to be followed by the production of scar tissue which not only interferes with phonation but also produces again a stenosis of the larynx. Bilateral submucous resections are more successful in producing a permanent widening of the air passage.

The method of choice, certainly in younger people, is undoubtedly one which produces a permanent lateral displacement of the posterior end of one of the vocal cords; while such operations are difficult technically they will, if properly done, relieve the dyspnea permanently and yet allow good phonation (through apposition of the anterior ends of the cords?).

The older operation and probably the most difficult, although offering at the same time good results without particular danger of scar tissue formation, is the King ('39a and b) operation or a modification thereof; this consists in incising the inferior constrictor of the pharynx along the posterior border of the thyroid cartilage and behind the cricothyroid ligament, working upward and medially between the mucosa of the anterior surface of the pharynx and the lamina of the cricoid cartilage until the arytenoid cartilage comes into view, and detaching the arytenoid cartilage from its muscular and ligamentous attachments so that it can be moved laterally. In the original King operation the arytenoid cartilage was sutured to the omohyoid muscle, on the theory that contraction of this muscle during respiration would lead to rhythmic separation of the vocal cords to produce the desired abduction, while in between the respiratory movements the vocal cords would be adducted and therefore the voice would be better preserved. It is now generally believed that the use of the omohyoid muscle has no advantages, and therefore the operation is usually somewhat modified, the arytenoid cartilage being attached not to the omohyoid muscle but rather sutured to the thyroid cartilage. This procedure has been described by Seed, Morrison ('43), and Shirer, among others. Seed has emphasized that the suture attaching the arytenoid cartilage to the thyroid should be through the vocal process, so as to produce good abduction of the cord, rather than through the stronger and more obvious muscular process. He has also pointed out that before the suture is finally tied the vocal cord should be visualized by laryngoscopy to be sure of optimal placement of the cord. When this operation is successfully carried out, good and permanent opening of the air passage is secured and the voice is said not to be appreciably affected.

Another extralaryngeal approach to the arytenoid cartilage is by way of a window made in the thyroid cartilage (Kelly, '43, '44; Wright). Kelly has apparently preferred this to the approach through the inferior constrictor, pointing out that scar tissue left after thyroidec-

tomy may complicate the latter approach. He has removed the arytenoid cartilage and fixed the cord by a suture attaching it to the cartilage about the window in the thyroid cartilage. He noted that the suture must not be placed too far forward on the cord if a satisfactory voice is to be obtained. Kelly and Wright both stated that this operation is simpler and more easily performed than is the King operation. Woodman has elevated the perichondrium from both outer and inner surfaces of the posterior border of the thyroid cartilage, thus avoiding cutting both the superior constrictor and the thyroid cartilage, separated the cricothyroid joint, and removed the major part of the arytenoid subperichondrially by dissecting beneath the perichondrium of the cricoid cartilage; he then sutured the remainder of the arytenoid, with the vocal process, to the thyroid cartilage.

While the King operation and its variants have usually given excellent results, their technical difficulties are considerable. For those surgeons who are trained in suspension laryngoscopy, the intralaryngeal approach of Thornell has apparently already completely replaced the King operation, because of its relative simplicity and high percentage of excellent results. The Thornell operation involves direct visualization of the larynx through the mouth, the approach being made through this route. An incision is made over the arytenoid cartilage and into the upper border of the aryepiglottic fold, the arytenoid is removed by a submucous resection, and the posterior part of the vocal cord is displaced laterally into the area from which the cartilage was removed; after it has been held in this position by an obturator for three to seven days, it becomes permanently fixed here by scar tissue. The obturator has been omitted, as unnecessary, by some surgeons. The operation can be performed only while using a suspension apparatus, and Thornell has warned that surgeons without this equipment and training in its use should continue to use the King operation or one of its modifications.

ANOMALIES

Congenital anomalies of the larynx are apparently rare; in addition to the presence of an enlarged laryngeal saccule, already discussed on page 432, congenital stenosis of the larynx has been reported occasionally, as has also the presence of congenital cysts. Rare cases of doubling of the vocal cords have been reported (for instance, Frank and Malev). Congenital stenosis of the larynx, usually referred to as a congenital web of the larynx, has been reported by, among others, Clerf; Iglauer; Tucker ('35); and Poe and Seager. Apparently a congenital web typically unites the anterior portions of the vocal cords, especially just behind the anterior commissure where the cords come together to attach to the thyroid cartilage. In accordance with this, the web is apt to be thickest anteriorly, and to thin out markedly posteriorly. It has been stated to be due to fusions occurring in the embryo, during stages in which the primitive vocal cords are normally adherent to each other. Diaphragms or webs of the larynx may of course also be acquired, due to adhesions following injury.

Cysts of the larynx are relatively rare according to Myerson and the large majority are located on either the epiglottis or the vocal cords, though they may occur also in the ventricle, on the arytenoid cartilage, the aryepiglottic fold, or the ventricular band. The usual symptoms are said to be hoarseness or dyspnea; Myerson found that at least some of them are congenital, and noted that their management in young infants is difficult. According to Kleinfeld congenital laryngeal cysts are quite rare, and he found only about 15 cases reported in the literature up to that time. He described them as usually thin walled and containing a milky fluid, and commonly arising from a broad base in the region of the laryngeal aperture, often from the aryepiglottic fold.

Tucker ('37) described a case of laryngoptosis due to a congenital anomaly of the sternohyoid and sternothyroid muscles, with displacement downward of both the larynx and the hyoid bone. He stated that other cases of laryngoptosis had been described, but none of them had apparently been due to downward displacement of the hyoid. In the case which he reported, the hyoid bone lay just above the suprasternal notch and the larynx lay approximately level with it, with the cricoid being situated behind the sternum. The larynx failed to rise normally in swallowing. At operation a tendinous mass replacing the sternohyoid and sternothyroid muscles on one side was found and sectioned, and the hyoid bone and larynx immediately ascended to almost normal position.

REFERENCES

AREY, L. B. On the development, morphology and interpretation of a system of crypt-analogues in the pharyngeal tonsil. *Am. J. Anat. 80:*203, 1947.

BABBITT, J. A. Fracture of the styloid process and its tonsil fossa complications, with report of a case. *Ann. Otol., Rhin. & Laryng. 42:*789, 1933.

BABCOCK, W. W., and JACKSON, C. The single stage operation for pulsion diverticulum of the oesophagus. *Surg., Gynec. & Obst. 53:* 667, 1931.

BACH, A. C., LEDERER, F. L., and DINOLT, R. Senile changes in the laryngeal musculature. *Arch. Otolaryng. 34:*47, 1941.

BATSON, O. V. Veins of the pharynx. *Arch. Otolaryng. 36:*212, 1942.

BERLIN, D. D., and LAHEY, F. H. Dissections of the recurrent and superior laryngeal nerves: The relation of the recurrent to the inferior thyroid artery and the relation of the superior to abductor paralysis. *Surg., Gynec. & Obst. 49:*102, 1929.

BORTONE, F. Esophageal diverticulum. *Am. J. Surg. n.s.70:*64, 1945.

BROCKLEHURST, R. J., and EDGEWORTH, F. H. The fibre components of the laryngeal nerves of Macaca mulatta. *J. Anat. 74:*386, 1940.

BROWNE, D. The surgical anatomy of the tonsil. *J. Anat. 63:*82, 1928.

BROWNE, D. The operation for cleft palate. *Brit. J. Surg. 20:*7, 1932.

CAIRNEY, J. Tortuosity of the cervical segment of the internal carotid artery. *J. Anat. 59:*87, 1924.

CAMPBELL, M. D. Laryngocele. *Arch. Otolaryng. 44:*219, 1946.

CLERF, L. H. Congenital stenosis of the larynx: Report of three cases. *Ann. Otol., Rhin. & Laryng. 40:*770, 1931.

CLERF, L. H., and SUEHS, O. W. Paralysis of the larynx. *Ann. Otol., Rhin. & Laryng. 50:* 762, 1941.

CRITCHLEY, M., and KUBIK, C. S. The mechanisms of speech and deglutition in progressive bulbar palsy. *Brain 48:*492, 1925.

DANDY, W. E. Glossopharyngeal neuralgia (tic douloureux): Its diagnosis and treatment. *Arch. Surg. 15:*198, 1927.

DILWORTH, T. F. M. The nerves of the human larynx. *J. Anat. 56:*48, 1921.

DORRANCE, G. M. The so-called bursa pharyngea in man: Its origin, relationship with the adjoining nasopharyngeal structures and pathology. *Arch. Otolaryng. 13:*187, 1931.

DuBois, F. S., and FOLEY, J. O. Experimental studies on the vagus and spinal accessory nerves in the cat. *Anat. Rec. 64:*285, 1936.

EAGLE, W. W. Elongated styloid process: Further observations and a new syndrome. *Arch. Otolaryng. 47:*630, 1948.

EAGLE, W. W. Symptomatic elongated styloid process: Report of two cases of styloid process-carotid artery syndrome with operation. *Arch. Otolaryng. 49:*490, 1949.

ELIASON, E. L., TUCKER, G., and THIGPEN, F. M. Esophageal diverticula: With a report of ten cases of the pulsion type originating in the pharynx. *Surgery 2:*188, 1937.

FISHMAN, L. Z. Laryngeal and esophageal atavism in man as indicated by the probable phylogenesis of the hypopharyngeal receptacle, concerned in the act of deglutition. *Ann. Otol., Rhin. & Laryng. 44:*139, 1935.

FRANK, D. I., and MALEV, M. Double vocal cord. *Arch. Otolaryng. 29:*713, 1939.

FRITZ, M. Elongated styloid process: A cause of obscure throat symptoms. *Arch. Otolaryng. 31:*911, 1940.

FURSTENBERG, A. C. An anatomical and clinical study of central lesions producing paralysis of the larynx. *Ann. Otol., Rhin. & Laryng. 46:*39, 1937.

FURSTENBERG, A. C. Diverticulum of the esophagus. *Ann. Otol., Rhin. & Laryng. 56:* 305, 1947.

GRIESMAN, B. L. Mechanism of phonation demonstrated by planigraphy of the larynx. *Arch. Otolaryng. 38:*17, 1943.

HAVENS, F. Z. Personal communication to the author, 1951.

HERSHEY, J. H. The lateral approach to a diverticulum of the esophagus. *Surg., Gynec. & Obst. 73:*355, 1941.

HETHERINGTON, J. The kerato-cricoid muscle in the American white and Negro. *Am. J. Phys. Anthropol. 19:*203, 1934.

HETT, G. S., and BUTTERFIELD, H. G. The anatomy of the palatine tonsils. *J. Anat. & Physiol. 44:*35, 1909.

IGLAUER, S. A new procedure for the treatment of web in the larynx: Report of a case. *Arch. Otolaryng. 22:*597, 1935.

IMPERATORI, C. J. Paralysis of the larynx: A suggested explanation of the so-called continued median position of the vocal cords in bilateral paralysis—a consideration of Semon's law. *Ann. Otol., Rhin. & Laryng. 44:*730, 1935.

JACKSON, C., and JACKSON, C. L. Malignant disease of the larynx: Its treatment by laryngofissure and laryngectomy. *Am. J. Surg. n.s.30:*3, 1935a.

JACKSON, C., and JACKSON, C. L. Dysphonia plicae ventricularis: Phonation with the ventricular bands. *Arch. Otolaryng. 21:* 157, 1935b.

JOHNSON, J. Effect of superior laryngeal nerves on tracheal mucus: An experimental study on the relationship. *Ann. Surg. 101:* 494, 1935.

JOHNSTONE, A. S. A radiological study of deglutition. *J. Anat. 77:*97, 1942.

JOSEPHSON, E. M., and WILLENS, MINNIE K. Physiology of the singing voice: With special reference to the relation of respiration and muscular physiology. *Arch. Otolaryng. 11:* 696, 1930.

KALLEN, L. A. Vicarious vocal mechanisms: The anatomy, physiology and development of speech in laryngectomized persons. *Arch. Otolaryng. 20:*460, 1934.

KAZANJIAN, V. H., and HOLMES, E. M. Stenosis of the nasopharynx and its correction. *Arch. Otolaryng. 44:*261, 1946.

KELEMEN, G. The palatine tonsil in the sixth decade. *Ann. Otol., Rhin. & Laryng. 52:* 419, 1943.

KELLY, J. D. A supplementary report on extralaryngeal arytenoidectomy as a relief for bilateral abductor muscular paralysis of the larynx. *Ann. Otol., Rhin. & Laryng. 52:*628, 1943.

KELLY, J. D. Some problems in the surgical treatment of bilateral abductor paralysis of the larynx. *Ann. Otol., Rhin. & Laryng. 53:*461, 1944.

KILLIAN, G. Ueber den Mund der Speiseröhre. *Zeitschr. f. Ohrenh. 55:*1, 1908.

KING, B. T. New and function-restoring operation for bilateral abductor cord paralysis: Preliminary report. *J.A.M.A. 112:*814, 1939a.

KING, B. T. A new and function-restoring operation for bilateral abductor cord paralysis: Preliminary report. *Tr. Am. Laryng. A. 61:*264, 1939b.

KING, B. T. New concepts of the etiology and treatment of diverticula of the esophagus. *Surg., Gynec. & Obst. 85:*93, 1947.

KLEINFELD, L. Laryngeal cysts in the newborn. *Arch. Otolaryng. 19:*590, 1934.

LAHEY, F. H. The surgical management of very small and early pulsion oesophageal diverticula. *Surg., Gynec. & Obst. 56:*187, 1933.

LAHEY, F. H. Pharyngo-esophageal diverticulum: Its management and complications. *Ann. Surg. 124:*617, 1946.

LASZLO, A. F., and FIERTZ, C. O. Prognosis of the recurrent nerve paralysis following thyroidectomy. *Arch. Otolaryng. 42:*372, 1945.

LEMERE, F. Innervation of the larynx: I. Innervation of laryngeal muscles. *Am. J. Anat. 51:*417, 1932a.

LEMERE, F. Innervation of the larynx: II. Ramus anastomoticus and ganglion cells of the superior laryngeal nerve. *Anat. Rec. 54:*389, 1932b.

LEMERE, F. Innervation of the larynx: III. Experimental paralysis of the laryngeal nerve. *Arch. Otolaryng. 18:*413, 1933.

LEMERE, F. Innervation of the larynx: IV. An analysis of Semon's law. *Ann. Otol., Rhin. & Laryng. 43:*525, 1934.

LEWIS, D. D. The elastic tissue of the human larynx. *Am. J. Anat. 4:*175, 1905.

LILLIE, H. I., and HECK, W. E. Hemangioma of the lateral pharyngeal band: Report of a case. *Ann. Otol., Rhin. & Laryng. 57:*519, 1948.

LINDSAY, J. R. Laryngocele ventricularis. *Ann. Otol., Rhin. & Laryng. 49:*661, 1940.

LOESER, L. H., and CARDWELL, E. P. Elongated styloid process: A cause of glossopharyngeal neuralgia. *Arch. Otolaryng. 36:* 198, 1942.

LORE, J. M. A suggested operative procedure for the relief of stenosis in double abductor paralysis: An anatomic study. *Ann. Otol., Rhin. & Laryng. 45:*679, 1936.

MACCREADY, P. B. So-called aneurysm of the ascending pharyngeal artery: Report of one case which developed under observation. *Ann. Otol., Rhin. & Laryng. 44:*513, 1935.

McGILLICUDDY, O. B. Hypopharyngeal diverticulum. *Arch. Otolaryng. 19:*247, 1934.

MELCHIONNA, R. H., and MOORE, R. A. The pharyngeal pituitary gland. *Am. J. Path. 14:*763, 1938.

MILLER, M. V. Edema of the larynx: A study of the loose areolar tissues of the larynx. *Arch. Otolaryng. 31:*256, 1940.

MINEAR, W. L., AREY, L. B., and MILTON, J. T. Prenatal and postnatal development and form of crypts of human palatine tonsil. *Arch. Otolaryng. 25:*487, 1937.

MITCHINSON, A. G., and YOFFEY, J. M. Respiratory displacement of larynx, hyoid bone and tongue. *J. Anat. 81:*118, 1947.

MITCHINSON, A. G. H., and YOFFEY, J. M. Changes in the vocal folds in humming low and high notes: A radiographic study. *J. Anat. 82:*88, 1948.

MOERSCH, H. J., and JUDD, E. S. Diagnosis and treatment of pharyngo-oesophageal diverticulum. *Surg., Gynec. & Obst. 58:*781, 1934.

MORLEY, J. Pharyngeal diverticula. *Brit. J. Surg. 33:*101, 1945.

MORRISON, L. F. Bilateral paralysis of abductor muscles of the larynx: Report on seven patients treated by the method outlined by Dr. Brien T. King. *Arch. Otolaryng. 37:*54, 1943.

MORRISON, W. W. The production of voice and speech following total laryngectomy: Exercise and practice for the production of the pseudovoice. *Arch. Otolaryng. 14:*413, 1931.

MOST, A. Ueber den Lymphgefässapparat von Nase und Rachen. *Arch. f. Anat. u. Physiol.* p. 75, 1901.

MOYNIHAN, B. Diverticula of the alimentary canal. *Lancet. 1:*1061, 1927.

MURTAGH, J. A., and CAMPBELL, C. J. The respiratory function of the larynx: II. The elementary physiology of the recurrent laryngeal nerve. *Ann. Otol., Rhin. & Laryng. 57:*465, 1948.

MYERSON, M. C. Cysts of the larynx. *Arch. Otolaryng. 18:*281, 1933.

NAFFZIGER, H. C., DAVIS, C., and BELL, H. G. Paralysis of deglutition—surgical correction. *Ann. Surg. 128:*732, 1948.

NEGUS, V. E. The function of the epiglottis. *J. Anat. 62:*1, 1927.

NEGUS, V. E. Function of the cartilages of Santorini. *J. Anat. 63:*430, 1929.

NORDLAND, M. The larynx as related to surgery of the thyroid based on an anatomical study. *Surg., Gynec. & Obst. 51:*449, 1930.

OLDFIELD, M. C. Cleft palate and the mechanism of speech. *Brit. J. Surg. 29:*197, 1941.

PAINTER, A. M. Important points in tonsillectomy. *Ann. Otol., Rhin. & Laryng. 39:*815, 1930.

DE PAULA ASSIS, J. E. Observações anatômicas sôbre o musculus salpingopharyngeus. *Rev. brasil. de oto-rino-laring. 15:*169, 1947.

POE, D. L., and SEAGER, P. S. Congenital laryngeal web: Its eradication. *Arch. Otolaryng. 47:*46, 1948.

PRESSMAN, J. J. Sphincter action of the larynx. *Arch. Otolaryng. 33:*351, 1941.

PRESSMAN, J. J. Physiology of the vocal cords in phonation and respiration. *Arch. Otolaryng. 35:*355, 1942.

PUPPEL, I. D. The role of esophageal motility in the surgical treatment of mega-esophagus. *J. Thoracic Surg. 19:*371, 1950.

RAVEN, R. W. Pouches of the pharynx and oesophagus: With special reference to the embryological and morphological aspects. *Brit. J. Surg. 21:*235, 1933.

ROGERS, L. The treatment of spasmodic dysphagia by sympathetic denervation. *Brit. J. Surg. 22:*829, 1935.

SCHALL, L. A. Laryngocele—associated with cancer of the larynx: Case report. *Ann. Otol., Rhin. & Laryng. 53:*168, 1944.

SCHUGT, H. P. The piriform sinus: Anatomic and clinical observations, with a review of the literature. *Arch. Otolaryng. 31:*626, 1940.

SEED, L. The King operation for bilateral abductor paralysis of the vocal cords. *Ann. Otol., Rhin. & Laryng. 51:*66, 1942.

SHALLOW, T. A. Combined one stage closed method for the treatment of pharyngeal diverticula. *Surg., Gynec. & Obst. 62:*624, 1936.

SHIRER, J. W. Modification of the King operation for bilateral vocal cord paralysis. *Ann. Surg. 120:*617, 1944.

SNOOK, T. The later development of the bursa pharyngea: Homo. *Anat. Rec. 58:*303, 1934.

SOKOLOWSKY, R. R. Effect of the extrinsic laryngeal muscles on voice production. *Arch. Otolaryng. 38:*355, 1943.

STRONG, L. H. The mechanism of laryngeal pitch. *Anat. Rec. 63:*13, 1935.

STUART, T. P. A., and M'CORMICK, A. The position of the epiglottis in swallowing. *J. Anat. & Physiol. 26:*231, 1892.

SWEET, R. H. Pulsion diverticulum of the pharyngo-esophageal junction: Technic of the one-stage operation; a preliminary report. *Ann. Surg. 125:*41, 1947.

TAYLOR, H. M. Ventricular laryngocele. *Ann. Otol., Rhin. & Laryng. 53:*536, 1944.

THORNELL, W. C. A new intralaryngeal approach for arytenoidectomy in the treatment of bilateral abductor vocal cord paralysis. *J. Clin. Endocrinol. 10:*1118, 1950.

TODD, T. W., and FOWLER, R. H. The muscular relations of the tonsil. *Am. J. Anat. 40:* 355, 1927.

TRUEX, R. C., and KELLNER, C. E. *Detailed Atlas of the Head and Neck.* New York, Oxford University Press, 1948.

TUCKER, G. Congenital web of the larynx. *Arch. Otolaryng. 21:*172, 1935.

TUCKER, G. Laryngoptosis: Ptosis of the larynx due to downward displacement of the hyoid bone resulting from fibrosis and shortening (congenital anomaly) of the left sternohyoid and sternothyroid muscles. *Arch. Otolaryng. 25:*389, 1937.

WARDILL, W. E. M., and WHILLIS, J. Movements of the soft palate: With special reference to the function of the tensor palati muscle. *Surg., Gynec. & Obst. 62:*836, 1936.

WHILLIS, J. A note on the muscles of the palate and the superior constrictor. *J. Anat. 65:*92, 1930.

WILKIE, D. P. D., and HARTLEY, J. N. J. Pharyngeal diverticulum and its surgical treatment, with a record of two cases. *Brit. J. Surg. 10:*81, 1922.

WILLIAMS, H. L. Personal communication to the author, 1951.

WOOD, G. B. The peritonsillar spaces: An anatomic study. *Arch. Otolaryng. 20:*837, 1934.

WOODMAN, DE G. A modification of the extralaryngeal approach to arytenoidectomy for bilateral abductor paralysis. *Arch. Otolaryng. 43:*63, 1946.

WRIGHT, E. S. The Kelly operation for restoration of laryngeal function following bilateral paralysis of the vocal cords: Report of three cases. *Ann. Otol., Rhin. & Laryng. 52:* 346, 1943.

CHAPTER 9

The Neck

GENERAL CONSIDERATIONS

THE fascia and fascial spaces of the neck, and the anatomy of the pharynx and larynx, have already been described in separate chapters on these subjects; they will be alluded to here, therefore, only in so far as is necessary in describing other anatomy of the neck. Some of the general anatomy of the neck is shown in Figure 275.

The skin and superficial connective tissue of the neck are thin and flexible. Within the subcutaneous tissue lies the platysma muscle, extending from the upper thoracic region over the clavicle and the anterolateral surface of the neck, and over the mandible toward the mouth. It is extremely thin, as its name implies, and varies considerably in development; it is generally and properly disregarded in planning incisions in the neck. Concerning the latter, transverse incisions are to be preferred when possible, since they produce more satisfactory cosmetic results than do longitudinal ones. This is based upon good anatomical and surgical principles. For one thing, it is generally recognized that incisions across flexion

creases in any part of the body are apt to produce undue scarring and interference with flexion. In the second place, Langer's lines (tension lines of the skin, cleavage lines) are arranged transversely in the neck, and it is well known that incisions parallel to these lines heal without the formation of the additional scar tissue produced by incisions across them; when the tension lines are cut across, undue retraction of the lips of the wound necessarily results.

The cutaneous innervation of the neck is largely through the transverse cervical (cutaneus colli) branch of the cervical plexus, containing fibers derived from the second and third cervical nerves. This nerve passes close around the posterior border of the sternocleidomastoid muscle and then forward on its lateral surface, dividing into two main branches which run upward toward the jaw and downward toward the base of the neck. The skin of the base of the neck, like that over the upper part of the thorax, is supplied by the supraclavicular nerves (C-3 and C-4) which descend behind the sternocleidomastoid in the posterior triangle and fan out as they descend.

TRIANGLES OF THE NECK

The prominent landmarks in the neck are the hyoid bone, the thyroid cartilage and trachea, and the sternocleidomastoid muscles. The sternocleidomastoid muscles divide each side of the neck into two

of the neck, and it is not until this fascia has been removed that the subsidiary triangles of each of these major triangles can be clearly seen.

The subsidiary triangles usually described in the anterior triangle of the neck (Fig. 276) are the *inferior carotid or muscular triangle,* below the hyoid bone and antero-inferior to the superior belly of the omohyoid muscle; the *carotid*

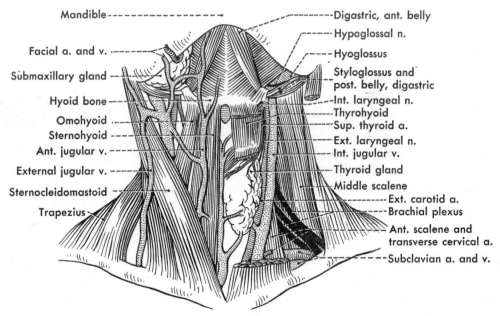

Mandible
Facial a. and v.
Submaxillary gland
Hyoid bone
Omohyoid
Sternohyoid
Ant. jugular v.
External jugular v.
Sternocleidomastoid
Trapezius

Digastric, ant. belly
Hypoglossal n.
Hyoglossus
Styloglossus and post. belly, digastric
Int. laryngeal n.
Thyrohyoid
Sup. thyroid a.
Ext. laryngeal n.
Int. jugular v.
Thyroid gland
Middle scalene
Ext. carotid a.
Brachial plexus
Ant. scalene and transverse cervical a.
Subclavian a. and v.

Fig. 275.   A general view of the neck. On the left side of the neck the sternocleidomastoid and strap muscles, the submaxillary gland, and other superficially located structures have been removed.

major triangles, the anterior and posterior triangles of the neck. The anterior triangle is thus delimited by the anterior border of the sternocleidomastoid muscle laterally, the midline medially, and the lower border of the mandible above; the posterior triangle is delimited by the posterior border of the sternocleidomastoid anteromedially, the anterior border of the trapezius muscle posterolaterally, and the clavicle below. These triangles are of course covered by the deep fascia

or superior carotid triangle, bounded below and anteriorly by the superior belly of the omohyoid, above by the stylohyoid and the posterior belly of the digastric, and posteriorly by the sternocleidomastoid; the *submaxillary (submandibular) triangle,* between the anterior and posterior bellies of the digastric and the lower border of the mandible, and the *suprahyoid or submental triangle,* bounded by the midline, the anterior belly of the digastric and the hyoid bone.

The subdivision of the posterior triangle of the neck (Fig. 276) into two parts is of little practical importance; the larger upper portion of this triangle is called the *occipital triangle,* while a small portion above the clavicle is termed the *subclavian (omoclavicular) triangle,* and corresponds to the supraclavicular fossa. The two are described as separated by the posterior belly of the omohyoid as this crosses the posterior triangle. This muscle runs close to and almost parallel with the clavicle, so that the subclavian approached through the subclavian triangle.

The floor of the occipital triangle is formed, from above downward, largely by the splenius capitis, the levator scapulae, and the posterior and middle scalene muscles; at the uppermost part of the triangle the occipital artery emerges from under cover of the splenius capitis to cross the semispinalis capitis and penetrate the trapezius muscle. The lesser occipital nerve, from the cervical plexus, runs upward in the triangle,

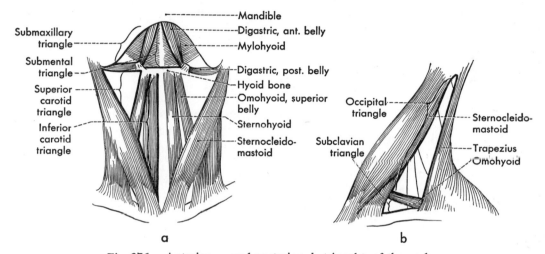

Fig. 276. Anterior, *a,* and posterior, *b,* triangles of the neck.

triangle is usually small; typically, the omohyoid muscle must be displaced upward if a surgical approach is to be through this triangle.

The brachial plexus and the subclavian artery pass through the subclavian triangle, and therefore are usually approached through this; the transverse cervical and transverse scapular arteries run across it, and the internal jugular vein, the termination of the external jugular vein, the termination of the thoracic duct, and the phrenic nerve, although actually lying under cover of the sternocleidomastoid muscle, may be most easily

emerging from under cover of the posterior border of the sternocleidomastoid, and the great auricular and cutaneus colli nerves turn sharply around the border of the sternocleidomastoid; the accessory nerve and the more lateral supraclavicular nerves run obliquely downward across the triangle, from the posterior border of the sternocleidomastoid toward the anterior border of the trapezius and the upper border of the clavicle.

It is important to note that the spinal accessory nerve crosses the posterior triangle not in contact with the muscles forming its floor, but separated from the muscle on which it lies (levator scapulae) by a distinct and heavy layer of fascia. The fascia crossing the posterior triangle of the neck represents a blending of two layers, the anterior or superficial layer of the deep fascia and the posterior (prevertebral) layer of the deep fascia; the accessory nerve runs between these two layers, and therefore is embedded in dense fascia or in connective tissue and fat between dense fascial planes. The same is true also in part of the supraclavicular nerves, and of the lower portion of the external jugular vein and the proximal portion of the transverse cervical artery.

Deep to the prevertebral fascia, and therefore immediately adjacent to the muscles, are the nerves of the brachial plexus and, more anteriorly, the phrenic nerve.

With the exception of the spinal accessory nerve, which emerges from behind or through the posterior border of the sternocleidomastoid in the middle third of the muscle and descends almost vertically to disappear beneath the anterior border of the trapezius muscle, the nerves appearing relatively superficially within the confines of the posterior triangle of the neck are all cutaneous branches of the cervical plexus.

MUSCULATURE

STERNOCLEIDOMASTOID

The sternocleidomastoid or sternomastoid muscle (Fig. 275) arises by a tendinous head from the sternum (the depression between these heads of the two muscles being known as the suprasternal notch) and by a wider muscular head from the proximal portion of the clavicle. It passes transversely upward and laterally in the neck, to insert upon the mastoid process, and is enclosed by the superficial or anterior layer of the deep fascia of the neck, which splits to pass around it. In addition to the platysma, which overlies it, the sternocleidomastoid is crossed superficially by twigs from the anterior supraclavicular nerve, by the cutaneus colli and great auricular nerves, and by the external jugular vein. In its lower part it covers the lateral borders of the strap muscles and the great vessels of the neck; farther up it crosses these and forms the posterior boundary of the carotid triangle.

In the lower part of the carotid triangle the sternocleidomastoid receives a branch from the superior thyroid artery, and at about the level of the hyoid bone it receives one from the occipital artery, or directly from the external carotid. The muscle is supplied by the spinal accessory nerve, which runs downward and a little posteriorly through or deep to it; this nerve typically emerges between the internal jugular and internal carotid vessels and crosses the lateral surface of the internal jugular to reach the deep surface of the sternocleidomastoid and supply it some 1½ to 2½ inches (about 4 to 6 cm.) below the tip of the mastoid process. Sensory fibers to the muscle are from the cervical plexus (p. 496).

STRAP MUSCLES

The strap muscles of the neck are surrounded by deep fascia, that running anterior to them usually being termed the anterior or superficial layer of the deep fascia, that running posterior to them being usually termed the pretracheal fascia. They form the floor of the inferior carotid or muscular triangle, but in their lower portions are largely covered by the sternocleidomastoid muscle. They lie in turn upon the trachea, the thyroid gland, and the larynx. There are four muscles in the infrahyoid group: the sternohyoid, the sternothyroid, the thyrohyoid, and the omohyoid (Fig. 277).

sling of deep fascia, and normally join by a tendon. Langsam reported that in 90 per cent of the cases he examined the two bellies of the omohyoid presented an intermediate tendon of some sort, although this was sometimes incomplete, sometimes constricted and sometimes not; in 10 per cent there was no tendinous intersection to be noted.

Deep to the sternohyoid and the su-

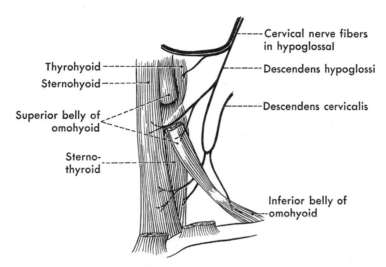

Fig. 277. The infrahyoid muscles and their nerve supply. A part of the superior belly of the omohyoid is shown cut away, and the hypoglossal nerve is shown diagrammatically as separated into its two components, cervical fibers and true hypoglossal fibers.

The *sternohyoid* is a relatively broad, flat, and thin muscle, which extends from an origin on the posterior surface of the sternum to an insertion upon the hyoid bone. Posterolateral to it, and descending at first parallel with it, is the superior belly of the *omohyoid muscle*; as this runs downward from the hyoid bone it gradually diverges, however, from the lateral border of the sternohyoid to become continuous with its lower belly. The inferior belly of the omohyoid is attached to the upper border of the scapula just medial to the suprascapular notch; the two bellies are typically attached to the clavicle by a

perior belly of the omohyoid are the *sternothyroid* and *thyrohyoid muscles*, also thin but extending posterolaterally farther than the border of the sternohyoid. The sternothyroid arises from the posterior surface of the sternum below the origin of the sternohyoid, and inserts upon the thyroid cartilage in an oblique line; the thyrohyoid arises from the thyroid cartilage at the line of insertion of the sternothyroid muscle, and continues upward to an insertion upon the hyoid bone.

The strap muscles of the neck are innervated by cervical nerve fibers which accompany the hypoglossal nerve in part:

the nerve to the thyrohyoid descends from the hypoglossal as this nerve curves forward under cover of the submaxillary (submandibular) gland to pass above the hyoid bone; the nerves to the remainder of the strap muscles of the neck are derived either from the descendens hypoglossi or the ansa hypoglossi. As a rule, a branch directly from the descendens hypoglossi supplies the upper belly of the omohyoid muscle and the upper portions of the sternothyroid, while branches from the ansa hypoglossi supply the inferior belly of the omohyoid, and the lower portion of the sternohyoid and sternothyroid. The latter muscles are frequently cut in exposing the thyroid gland, and efforts are sometimes made to avoid injuring their nerve supply. Unfortunately, the levels at which the nerves enter the muscles are not constant. Thus Langsam found the branch to the superior belly of the omohyoid muscle to pass beneath the posterior edge of this muscle anywhere from 2.5 cm. above the level of the superior thyroid notch to 5 cm. below the level of this notch; in 91 per cent of the cases that he studied, however, the level of crossing lay between the level of the notch and a horizontal plane 2 cm. inferior to this. Similarly, it is usual to find the upper branch to the sternohyoid and sternothyroid entering these muscles at the level of the thyroid cartilage, so that sectioning them below this level would not usually involve this nerve. The other branch or branches to the strap muscles are apt to enter the sternohyoid and sternothyroid only a little above the level of the suprasternal notch, so that, generally speaking, it would seem that the innervation of these muscles could best be avoided by sectioning them approximately halfway between the lower border of the thyroid cartilage and the suprasternal notch.

SCALENES

The muscles of the suprahyoid region have already been discussed in a preceding chapter (p. 376). Much of the muscle mass of the posterior and posterolateral portions of the neck is of course associated with the vertebral column, and is in this book described therewith; the deep musculature of the anterior and anterolateral aspects of the neck consists primarily of two muscle groups, the longus and the scalene muscles. The longus muscles are actually anterior vertebral musculature, and are therefore described with the other vertebral muscles. It is only necessary to note here that the two pairs of muscles, longus cervicis (colli) and longus capitis, cover much of the anterior surface of the cervical vertebral column; that the vertebral fascia covering them, and separating them from the pharynx and esophagus, is divisible into two layers—prevertebral fascia proper, on the surfaces of the muscles, and the alar fascia (p. 287)—between which lies very loose connective tissue forming the "danger space" of the neck; and that in front of the danger space and the alar fascia is the retrovisceral compartment, bounded anteriorly by the viscera.

POSTERIOR

The scalene muscles (Fig. 278) extend from the transverse processes of the cervical vertebrae to the ribs, and are therefore flexors and rotators of the vertebral column and elevators of the thoracic cage; their prime importance to the surgeon, however, is their relation to the brachial plexus, subclavian vessels, and phrenic nerve. Of the three scalene muscles, anterior, middle, and posterior, the posterior has no particularly important relations. It forms a part of the floor of the posterior triangle of the neck, lying between the levator scapulae (above and posteriorly) and the scalenus medius (anteriorly), and is crossed superficially by the nerve to the rhomboids and by the long thoracic nerve as this descends to the upper border of the serratus anterior. The scalenus posterior (scalenus posticus) is a rather short muscle, usually arising

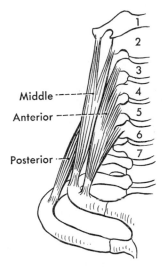

Fig. 278. The scalene muscles, the minimus not being shown. For some of the relations to the brachial plexus, see Figures 300 and 303.

from the transverse processes of about the fifth and sixth cervical vertebrae, and attaching onto the lateral surface of the second rib or occasionally even the third. Nat has regarded it as being a posterior part of the scalenus medius which passes beyond the first rib; in fact, except at their insertions, these two muscles are often difficult to separate from each other.

MIDDLE

The middle scalene (scalenus medius), typically the largest of the scalene group, arises from the transverse processes of most of the cervical vertebrae; according to Cave it arose from all of the cervical vertebrae in about 61 per cent of 60 subjects, from the second to the seventh

vertebrae in 15 per cent, from the third to the seventh in 10 per cent, and from the third to the sixth in 10 per cent (in the percentage not accounted for, the origin was not determined). The muscle inserts into the first rib behind, or postero-lateral to, the subclavian groove. In its lower portion the scalenus medius is separated from the scalenus anterior by the brachial plexus and the subclavian artery; the subclavian vein, however, runs in front of the anterior scalene. Higher up, the muscle is usually pierced by the nerve to the rhomboids (dorsal scapular nerve), and by the major portion (fifth and sixth cervical portions) of the long thoracic nerve. If the insertion of the medius is farther forward than usual, it may be very close to or even blend with that of the anterior, thus lessening the room between the lower ends of the two muscles, and forcing the subclavian artery and the lower part of the brachial plexus into a higher position than usual.

ANTERIOR

The scalenus anterior (scalenus anticus) muscle, clinically the most important of the scalenes, is usually described as arising from the anterior tubercles of the transverse processes of the third or fourth to the sixth cervical vertebrae; Reed ('48) has stated that many fibers arise also from the posterior tubercles of the fourth to sixth vertebrae, and that the fourth to sixth cervical nerves normally emerge therefore through the fibers of the anterior scalene rather than between this and the middle scalene as usually described. As they extend downward, however, all elements of the brachial plexus come to lie between these two scalenes. From its origin the fibers of the anterior scalene run downward and slightly laterally to insert on the upper edge of the first rib, in front of the subclavian groove.

Although in the lower part of the neck the sternocleidomastoid is running inferiorly and medially, while the anterior scalene is running inferiorly and slightly laterally, the lateral boundaries of the two muscles for a short distance above the clavicle correspond approximately, and the lateroposterior edge of the sternocleidomastoid may therefore be used to locate the anterior scalene muscle.

Because of its intimate relations to the brachial plexus the anterior scalene has been thought to be responsible for certain clinical manifestations of pressure upon the plexus (scalenus anticus syndrome): spasm of the muscle has been thought to exert pressure upon the brachial plexus either directly or by elevation of the first rib against the plexus. This question is discussed later in more detail (p. 505), but it may be noted here that Reed deduced from his dissections that the nerves of the plexus could be compressed by spasm of only those fibers passing posterior to them. He found an especially large group of fibers posterior to the sixth nerve.

The brachial plexus and the subclavian artery emerge from behind the lateral border of the scalenus anterior muscle, and are therefore the important posterior relations of this muscle; anteriorly, the most important relation is the phrenic nerve. Toward the upper end of the muscle the phrenic nerve crosses its lateral border and then descends with a slightly medial inclination, lying directly against the muscle fibers and therefore behind the posterior layer of the deep fascia of the neck, here of course termed "scalene fascia." Since the fibers of the scalenus anterior are inclined slightly laterally, the phrenic nerve and the muscle bundles do not run exactly parallel with each other. As the muscle reaches its insertion the phrenic nerve passes across its medial border to proceed behind the first rib and enter the thorax.

Close to its insertion, and therefore behind the clavicle, the anterior scalene is crossed anteriorly by the subclavian vein; above this, and typically only slightly above the level of the clavicle, the transverse scapular (suprascapular) artery crosses the muscle transversely, and still higher is the transverse or superficial cervical artery, when these arteries arise, as usual, medial to the scalene. The short thyrocervical trunk, which typically gives rise to these vessels, runs upward along the medial border of the muscle, and so does its main branch, the inferior thyroid artery; above these the ascending cervical branch of the inferior thyroid artery ascends along the muscle close to its origin. The cervical sympathetic chain parallels the phrenic nerve, and has been mistaken for the phrenic, although it lies medial to this, at about the level of the tips of the transverse processes. The vagus nerve also descends in front of the anterior scalene, but lies within the carotid sheath with the common carotid artery and the internal jugular vein. Finally, in operations upon either the phrenic nerve or the anterior scalene muscle, the thoracic duct is liable to injury; this attains a more superficial position in the neck by passing medial to the anterior scalene and then crossing the lower part of this muscle, between the muscle and the internal jugular vein, to enter approximately the angle of juncture between the internal jugular and subclavian vessels. In this terminal portion of its course the thoracic duct may be entirely hidden by the veins until it actually reaches the angle between them, or it may loop upward and outward so as to have a short course in which it is particularly exposed.

MINIMUS

In addition to the three scalenes already described, an additional one, the scalenus minimus (scalenus pleuralis, scalenus anticus minor), is frequently present (Fig. 279); it is usually stated to be present, bilaterally or unilaterally, in about two thirds of bodies; Sunderland and Bedbrook found it more often, in 80 per cent on the right side and 69 per cent on the left of 100 specimens.

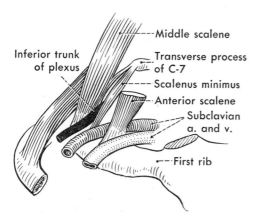

Fig. 279. A scalenus minimus muscle. In this case it separates the inferior trunk of the brachial plexus from the remainder of that plexus (not shown) and the subclavian artery. If it inserted farther forward, it might raise the subclavian artery well above the first rib. (Redrawn from Shore, L. R.: *J. Anat. 60:*418, 1926.)

It consists typically of a small bundle of muscle fibers which arises from the anterior tubercle of the sixth, sometimes the seventh, cervical vertebra, and usually attaches both into the first rib and into the fascia of the pleural cupula (Sibson's fascia). Fawcett regarded it as a detached portion of the anterior scalene. The insertion into the first rib may be quite close to or some distance removed from the insertion of the anterior scalene, but the two muscles are apparently always separated by the subclavian artery—that is, the scalenus minimus inserts between the subclavian artery and at least a portion of the brachial plexus (Shore, Stott); it may also separate elements of the plexus. When the insertion of the minimus is close to that of the anticus, the subclavian artery may be held well above the upper surface of the first rib.

INNERVATION

The scalene muscles are all innervated by short branches from the anterior rami of the nerves forming the brachial plexus, given off before these enter into the plexus: the anterior scalene usually receives branches from the fifth through the seventh cervical nerves; the middle, branches from the fourth through the eighth; the posterior, fibers from the seventh or seventh and eighth; and the minimus, fibers from the eighth.

ANOMALIES AND PATHOLOGY

Anomalies of the infrahyoid muscles are occasionally encountered, but are usually anatomical curiosities rather than of clinical importance; since the strap muscles come from a common mass it is easy to see how faulty cleavages of this mass may produce these anomalies. Doubling of a belly of the omohyoid, attachment of the superior belly to the mandible, or to the clavicle instead of to the posterior belly, or additional anomalous muscles are the ones most frequently reported (for instance, Jung; Frazer, '01; Rutherford; Taylor; and Jackson). The levator glandulae thyroideae (p. 519) apparently sometimes represents a development from the strap muscles, and is in any case closely associated topographically with them; it is of surgical interest merely because of its attachment to the thyroid gland. Tucker has reported a case of congenital shortening of the sternohyoid muscles which resulted in downward displacement of the larynx to about the level of the suprasternal notch.

The scalenus anticus syndrome is discussed in connection with the brachial plexus (p. 502).

TORTICOLLIS

Torticollis, or wryneck, is usually classified as being either congenital or spasmodic. According to Hough the incidence has been variously reported as 0.3 per cent, 0.5 per cent, or 1 in 150,000 births, and appears to be about one tenth as common as clubfoot. He found that involvement of the right side was only slightly more common than the left, and that no sexual or racial predisposition had been shown.

CONGENITAL TORTICOLLIS

Congenital torticollis is apparently usually limited to involvement of the sternocleidomastoid muscle, but may involve the platysma, the scalenes, or even the splenius muscles. As reviewed by Hough, this condition has been variously thought to be due to heredity, a constitutional defect, arrested development, birth injury, infective myositis, or ischemic fibrosis. Middleton stated that "congenital torticollis" is not hereditary (but it has been reported in twins) nor as a rule congenital, and that it usually appears months or years after birth. More recent investigators (for instance, Chandler and Altenberg; Larson and Rosenow) have agreed that a tumor-like ovoid swelling develops in the muscle some ten to fourteen days after birth; although it may regress and even disappear in ensuing months, the muscle fibers are gradually replaced by fibrous tissue.

Middleton regarded a temporary acute venous obstruction, occurring during labor, as being the precipitating cause of the disease, and Eddy, noting that the several vascular supplies to the muscle have been said to lack anastomosing channels between them, expressed the belief that extreme rotation of the head might cause ischemia in the lower part of the muscle by compression of the artery supplying this portion. Chandler and Altenberg have shown, however, that this concept of the circulation to the muscle is incorrect, for they were able to demonstrate anastomoses both between the arteries and the veins of the muscle.

The latter authors have regarded congenital torticollis as resulting from any of a number of factors, acting separately or together; while many cases of torticollis are associated with difficult labor, the attractive theory that a birth injury of some type is necessarily responsible is ruled out by their report of a case of torticollis in which the diagnosis was made in utero and delivery was by Caesarian section—in spite of the nontraumatic delivery, the torticollis was present at birth and the "tumor" appeared in the muscle at fourteen days. As they suggest, it seems possible that the torticollis may be responsible for the difficult delivery, rather than vice versa.

Copland stated that the anterior scalene may apparently be involved secondarily in torticollis, and suggested that this may sometimes be responsible for failure of relief following section of the sternocleidomastoid muscle. Stewart ('35) reported a case due to abnormal attachment of the left sternocleidomastoid to the right clavicle, and Grieve has warned that care should be taken to distinguish between ocular and sternocleidomastoid torticollis.

SPASMODIC TORTICOLLIS

Herz and Hoefer felt that in so-called spasmodic torticollis the electrical activity in the muscles affected hardly justified the term "spasmodic," although the activity of the muscle was sustained—the defect is not in the muscle, but in the nervous system. Putnam, Herz, and Glaser have pointed out that spasmodic torticollis usually involves three groups of muscles: the short muscles between the atlas, axis, and skull; the larger muscles of the neck including the sternocleidomastoid, trapezius, vertebral musculature, and the scalenes; and the hyoid musculature. They concluded that favorable results can be obtained by reducing the strength of the participating muscles, and have had varying degrees of success in so doing by sectioning motor branches of the cervical nerves. The spinal root of the accessory nerve has also been sectioned intracranially in attempting to relieve this condition (p. 77).

Rugh expressed the belief that there are actually two types of spasmodic torticollis, one being due to a basic functional weakness of the nerve cells and the other to lesions in the basal ganglia or perhaps to disturbed labyrinthine function. He has suggested that the best treatment is the use of a cast for as long as two years.

ARTERIES

SUBCLAVIAN ARTERY AND BRANCHES

AT THE base of the neck on the right side the right subclavian artery arises from the innominate behind the sternoclavicular articulation; it arches upward and laterally, rising usually above the level of the upper border of the clavicle and above the subclavian vein, to pass behind the anterior scalene muscle and leave the neck by crossing the first rib, where it changes its name to axillary. The left subclavian artery arises, of course, lower than the right, as it comes typically from the arch of the aorta; it therefore ascends through the superior mediastinum to the base of the neck where it arches laterally behind the anterior scalene and like the right artery crosses the first rib to become the axillary (Fig. 280). The anterior scalene muscle is the landmark by which the subclavian artery is divided for descriptive purposes into three portions; the first part of each vessel is medial to the scalene, the second behind it, the third lateral to it. Except for their first parts, the relations of the two subclavian arteries are essentially similar.

FIRST PART

The first part of the right subclavian artery is fairly short; it is covered superficially by the sternal head of the sternocleidomastoid muscle, and as it arches laterally is crossed anteriorly by the internal jugular and vertebral veins, the vagus nerve and usually cardiac branches of both vagal and sympathetic trunks. As the vagus passes across the subclavian it gives off the right recurrent nerve, which turns below and then behind the artery to ascend in the neck. Medial to this sympathetic fibers, forming the ansa subclavia, pass across, below and then behind the artery to unite the middle and inferior cervical ganglia. The artery is partly overlapped by the sternohyoid and sternothyroid muscles, and in front of these, between them and the sternocleidomastoid, the anterior jugular vein runs laterally.

Postero-inferiorly the subclavian artery rests upon the pleura of the cupula of the lung. Behind it the sympathetic trunk extends from the thorax into the neck, there may be additional descending cardiac branches, and the recurrent nerve and ansa subclavia turn upward. The inferior cervical ganglion lies either behind it or deep to its upper border, and the middle cervical ganglion, when in its low position, lies on its anterosuperior aspect.

The first part of the left subclavian

left lung; as the artery reaches the neck the thoracic duct passes forward between it and the carotid and then arches laterally in a plane anterior to the subclavian artery to enter the angle between internal jugular and subclavian veins.

The most striking anomaly of the subclavian artery is the rather rare (about 1 per cent) so-called anomalous right subclavian artery (retro-esophageal subclavian artery), due to a maldevelopment of the aortic arch system; far less frequently, a retro-esophageal left sub-

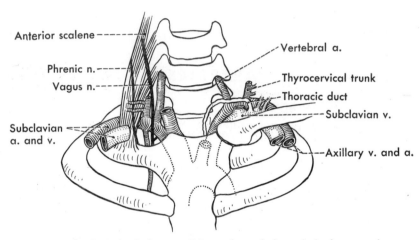

Anterior scalene

Phrenic n.

Vagus n.

Subclavian a. and v.

Vertebral a.

Thyrocervical trunk

Thoracic duct

Subclavian v.

Axillary v. and a.

Fig. 280.   Some relations and branches of the subclavian arteries.

artery as it passes into the neck is also related anteriorly to the sternocleidomastoid and the strap muscles of the neck. Behind these the vagus and phrenic nerves, and cardiac branches of the vagus and sympathetic, pass downward parallel to the vessel along its front; as on the right side, cardiac branches often also pass behind it. At the base of the neck the left internal jugular and vertebral veins lie between the nerves and the strap muscles, and the left common carotid artery lies anteromedial to the subclavian. Posteromedial to it are the esophagus, trachea, thoracic duct, and left recurrent nerve, and lateral to it the cupula of the

clavian artery is found. These conditions are discussed in a chapter on the thorax (Volume 2) in connection with other anomalies of the aortic arch system.

SECOND PART

The second part of both subclavian arteries is typically the highest part of the arch of each, and lies between the anterior and middle scalene muscles. It is here separated from the pleura by the middle scalene. The lower part of the brachial plexus usually lies immediately above this part of the artery. As already noted, the subclavian artery may be raised higher than usual by the presence of a scalenus minimus muscle or a more anterior insertion of the scalenus medius.

THIRD PART

The third part of the artery is related also posteriorly to the scalenus medius, with the lowest trunk of the brachial plexus lying between the vessel and the muscle; above and lateral to it are the upper trunks of the brachial plexus, or their derivative cords. This part of the vessel is crossed superficially by the supraclavicular nerves and the nerve to the subclavius as these descend, and in front of it lies also the external jugular vein which here usually receives the transverse scapular, transverse cervical, and anterior jugular veins.

The third part of the artery lies within the subclavian triangle, and, being free of the lateral border of the sternocleidomastoid, is the most readily accessible portion of the vessel. It has been, therefore, the favored portion for ligation of the subclavian; the chief anastomotic channels available after this is done are the anastomoses between the transverse scapular and transverse cervical arteries on the one hand and the subscapular artery on the other, and those between branches of the internal mammary and intercostals, and the lateral thoracic and subscapular arteries.

Vertebral Artery

The important branches of the subclavian artery at the base of the neck are the vertebral artery, the thyrocervical trunk, the internal mammary artery, and the costocervical trunk. These branches tend to come off close together, from the first part of the subclavian artery and close to the medial border of the scalenus anticus muscle. The vertebral artery, a large and rather constant branch, is typically the first to arise; it takes its origin from the upper and posterior part of the first portion of the subclavian artery and running upward enters the foramen of a transverse process—usually that of the sixth, but sometimes as high as the fourth or as low as the seventh.

This part between the origin of the artery and its entrance into the foramen of the transverse process is called the first part of the artery, and therefore varies in length (Fig. 281); the second portion of the artery consists of that portion which courses through the vertebral foramina, and varies in length inversely with the first part. The branches of the second portion of the artery are segmental twigs given off to supply the vertebrae and to accompany the roots of the spinal nerves to supply the meninges and the spinal cord itself. The third and fourth parts of the artery are the part in the suboccipital region, above the atlas, and that between the point at which the artery pierces the atlanto-occipital membrane and its ending to form the basilar artery. These parts are described in connection with the suboccipital region and the cranium, respectively.

At its origin the vertebral artery lies usually directly in front of the inferior cervical ganglion, while the middle cervical ganglion, when it has a low position, lies in front of the artery; thus not infrequently inferior and middle cervical ganglia, lying at the same horizontal level, are separated only by the vertebral artery itself. The vertebral vein runs in front of the artery, and sympathetic fibers derived from the inferior cervical ganglion run upward upon the artery; some of these are actually rami communicantes between the inferior cervical ganglion and some of the nerves of the brachial plexus, and therefore leave the artery to join the nerves as they emerge from the intervertebral foramina. Other fibers are, strictly speaking, the vertebral sympathetic plexus, and accompany the artery into the cranium.

Occasionally, perhaps in from 3 to 4 per cent (McDonald and Anson), the left vertebral arises directly from the aortic

toid muscle, and of most of the second part by approaching along the anterior border of this muscle; for the upper portion of the second part of the artery, or for the third, they have reflected the sternocleidomastoid from its insertion in order to reach the transverse process of the atlas.

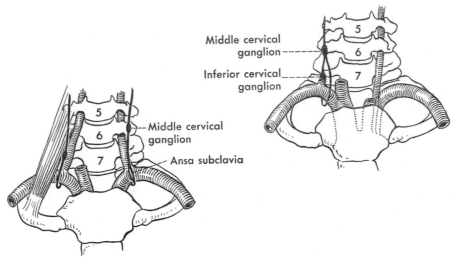

Fig. 281. Some relations and varations of the vertebral artery. In the figure on the left the vertebral artery is shown entering the canal in the transverse process of the fifth cervical vertebra on one side, that of the sixth on the other, and different relations of the middle cervical sympathetic ganglion are shown. In the figure on the right the right vertebral artery is shown cut away to reveal the inferior cervical ganglion (or upper part of the stellate, as the case may be), while the left vertebral is shown arising, as it does occasionally, directly from the arch of the aorta.

arch and, rarely, a vertebral may arise by two stems, one from the innominate and one from the subclavian, as reported by Neuberger.

Aneurysms and arteriovenous fistulas of the vertebral vessels are apparently rare; Elkin and Harris have stated that arteriovenous fistulas of the vertebral vessels are among the rarest of arterial injuries, presumably because of the location of the vessels, and that only about 100 cases have been reported. They suggested that adequate exposure of the first part of the artery is best obtained by an incision through the sternocleidomas-

THYROCERVICAL TRUNK

The thyrocervical trunk (thyroid axis) arises from the upper and front part of the subclavian artery, quite close to the medial margin of the scalenus anterior, and divides almost immediately into several branches (Fig. 282). These are typically the transverse scapular (suprascapular), the transverse cervical, and the inferior thyroid artery. The so-called typical pattern of branching of this vessel, which, however, was found to hold in only 29 per cent of 544 bodies in a British series (Thomson), is for the transverse scapular to be given off first, and for the transverse cervical to be given off above this; the inferior thyroid artery is the most constant branch in its origin from the thyrocervical trunk, yet it has been reported missing in about 6 per cent of cases. The variations in the branches, and the exact manner of branching, of the thyrocervical trunk are numerous; they have been classified, for instance, by Thomson, and by Bean, although the figures as to the occurrence of the different types are not in agree-

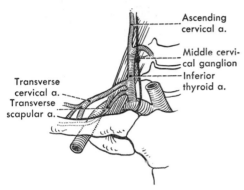

Ascending cervical a.

Middle cervical ganglion

Inferior thyroid a.

Transverse cervical a.

Transverse scapular a.

Fig. 282. The thyrocervical trunk.

ment. In general, either the transverse scapular or transverse cervical artery, or both, may arise directly from the subclavian artery instead of from the thyrocervical trunk. Also, these two arteries may arise by a common stem, from either the thyrocervical trunk or the subclavian; or a fourth branch of the trunk, a superficial cervical artery, may also occur.

TRANSVERSE SCAPULAR ARTERY

The transverse scapular (*suprascapular*) artery, usually a branch of the thyrocervical trunk, passes transversely across the neck in front of the anterior scalene muscle, the brachial plexus, and the third part of the subclavian artery; from its origin it usually runs at first slightly downward, so as to lie behind the upper border of the clavicle. It reaches the scapula at the level of the scapular (lesser scapular) notch, and its further course is described in connection with the shoulder. In a goodly number of cases the transverse scapular artery arises from the third part of the subclavian, and therefore has an origin independent of the thyrocervical trunk. The stated occurrence of this in the British series already cited is undoubtedly far too low; Bean described this origin in 22 per cent of his cases, and Read and Trotter found it in 28 per cent of their series. It may also arise from the internal mammary; although Bean's figure of 10 per cent for this origin seems somewhat high, Read and Trotter reported this origin in 5.1 per cent; occasionally, it may arise from the axillary artery rather than the subclavian. Instead of passing in front of the brachial plexus, this artery may pass through it or behind it; it is more apt to have one of the latter courses when it arises from the third part of the subclavian.

TRANSVERSE CERVICAL ARTERY

Even more variable in its origin is the vessel known as the transverse cervical artery (Fig. 283). More commonly, this artery arises from the thyrocervical trunk and runs almost transversely across the neck anterior to the anterior scalene muscle and the brachial plexus; it roughly parallels the transverse scapular artery but lies somewhat higher, and above the level of the upper border of the clavicle. According to some terminologies, when it has this origin and course it is called the superficial cervical. It passes across the posterior triangle of the neck to reach the deep surface of the trapezius, where it divides into superficial and deep branches (usually described in American texts as ascending and descending, respectively).

The superficial branch divides to ascend and descend upon the deep surface of the trapezius, and the deep (descending, posterior scapular) branch descends on the deep surface of the rhomboids. It not infrequently happens, however, that the ascending and descending branches

the third part of the subclavian, as has been done, for as already noted the transverse scapular artery frequently has this origin. Doubling of the ascending branch may occur, with one branch arising from the thyrocervical trunk and the other from a transverse cervical that arises from the third part of the subclavian; altogether, the origin of one or both

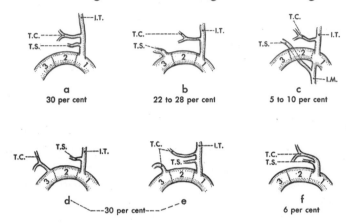

Fig. 283. Some of the numerous variations in the origins of the vessels which are normally branches of the thyrocervical trunk, and the approximate percentages in which these particular patterns have been reported to occur. *a.* The so-called normal arrangement. *b.* and *c.* Other origins of the transverse scapular. *d.* and *e.* Other origins of the transverse cervical. *f.* Absence of the inferior thyroid. The numerals upon the subclavian artery identify its parts. Abbreviations used are: *I.M.*, internal mammary; *I.T.*, inferior thyroid; *T.C.*, transverse cervical; and *T.S.*, transverse scapular. The superficial cervical is not identified in these sketches because of the various ways in which it has been defined.

have separate origins; for instance, in 22 per cent of the 544 cases in the British series the superficial branch arose from the thyrocervical trunk while the deep branch arose from the third part of the subclavian artery. In these cases the superficial branch is often referred to as the superficial cervical artery, although various distinctions have been made between the two terms "transverse cervical" and "superficial cervical." Certainly it is not correct to define the transverse cervical artery as the only vessel arising from

branches of the transverse cervical artery from the third part of the subclavian has been reported as occurring in as high as 30 per cent of cases.

SUPERFICIAL CERVICAL ARTERY

As already indicated, the superficial cervical artery has been variously defined, and this term has been applied to what is in this text described as the transverse cervical artery. Otherwise the term is usually applied to an independently arising superficial branch of the transverse cervical or to an accessory vessel which has a similar course. In the latter sense it arises from the thyrocervical trunk and somewhat parallels the transverse cervical, but is distributed to the trapezius only. Bean identified a superficial cervical artery in 30 per cent of cases, as a branch of the thyrocervical trunk; Read and Trotter felt that it has been so variably defined that its incidence cannot be established.

INFERIOR THYROID ARTERY

The inferior thyroid artery normally runs upward in front of the vertebral artery, continuing the direction of the thyrocervical trunk. At about the level of the sixth cervical vertebra the inferior thyroid artery gives off its ascending cervical branch and then passes medially and usually somewhat downward to make an arch behind the carotid sheath, penetrate the prevertebral fascia, and reach the posterior aspect of the thyroid gland. As it makes its medial turn, the artery lies on the longus colli muscle and crosses the cervical sympathetic trunk; the relation to this varies, as the trunk may be behind or in front of the artery, may be split by the artery, or cardiac branches may cross anterior to the artery while the trunk itself passes behind. When the middle cervical ganglion has its high location, it usually rests upon the artery or in the concavity of its curve. As the inferior thyroid artery reaches the thyroid gland it typically divides, and also necessarily comes in close relation to the recurrent nerve. The terminal portion of this artery and its relation to the recurrent nerve are discussed in detail in connection with the thyroid gland (pp. 521 and 525).

The inferior thyroid artery goes primarily to the thyroid gland, and its other branches are small. In its course it gives off muscular twigs to the scalenus anterior, the longus colli, the infrahyoid strap muscles, and the inferior constrictor of the pharynx; esophageal and tracheal branches; and the inferior laryngeal artery. The latter passes along the trachea with the inferior laryngeal nerve to enter the larynx with it. The largest of the branches of the inferior thyroid artery other than to the thyroid gland is the small ascending cervical artery. This leaves the inferior thyroid as that artery turns to pass behind the carotid sheath, and runs up along the anterior tubercles of the transverse processes of the cervical vertebrae; it gives twigs to the muscles of the neck, and spinal branches which, like those of the vertebral, are distributed to the bodies of the vertebrae and to the spinal cord and its membranes, and forms anastomoses with the ascending pharyngeal and occipital arteries.

When the inferior thyroid artery is not a branch of the thyrocervical trunk (rather rare in the present writer's experience, but reported in as high as 6 per cent of sides in one series), its place may be taken by an artery which arises from the subclavian or the common carotid; such an aberrant vessel is usually called the thyroid ima artery.

INTERNAL MAMMARY ARTERY

The internal mammary artery arises from the lower surface of the arch of the subclavian artery close to the medial edge of the anterior scalene muscle, and therefore at about the same level as the thyrocervical trunk. It passes downward with a slight inclination medialward to enter the thorax behind the first rib; its further course is described in connection with the thoracic wall (see Volume 2).

COSTOCERVICAL TRUNK

The costocervical trunk is a short vessel arising from the posterior surface of the subclavian artery, usually just medial to the edge of the anterior scalene on the left, and behind the anterior scalene on the right. It runs upward and backward above the dome of the pleura and as it turns downward behind the pleura divides into two branches, the supreme or superior intercostal, and the deep cervical.

The supreme intercostal crosses the neck of the first rib and gives rise to the first intercostal artery, with which it may terminate, but usually helps also to form the second intercostal, anastomosing with the uppermost intercostal branch from the aorta.

The deep cervical artery passes directly backward between the seventh and eighth cervical nerves, and below the transverse process of the seventh cervical vertebra, and then runs upward between the semispinalis capitis and semispinalis cervicis on the posterolateral aspect of the neck. Occasionally the two branches of the costocervical trunk arise separately from the subclavian.

COMMON CAROTID ARTERY

The two common carotid arteries differ in length, for the right usually arises from the innominate artery behind the sternoclavicular joint (Fig. 284), while the left arises from the arch of the aorta and has therefore a thoracic as well as a cervical course. Both arteries normally end by bifurcating into external and internal carotids at approximately the level of the hyoid bone. At the base of the neck, as they emerge from behind the sternoclavicular articulations, the two common carotid arteries lie deeply, being covered not only by the various layers of fascia but also by the sternocleidomastoid muscle and the strap muscles of the neck; in the carotid triangle, however, they are more readily accessible, being covered anteromedially only by skin, the platysma,

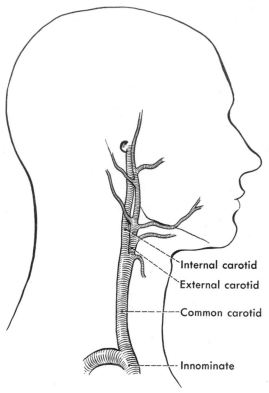

Fig. 284. The right common carotid artery and its branches.

and fascia, although overlapped somewhat, laterally, by the medial margin of the sternocleidomastoid.

Each common carotid artery is enclosed in a carotid sheath, a layer of connective tissue which contains also, in separate compartments, the internal jugular vein and the vagus nerve; within this sheath the internal jugular vein lies laterally and the common carotid medially, while the vagus lies behind and somewhat between the two. Anteromedially, the common carotid artery is related to the trachea, the thyroid gland, and the larynx; posterior to the artery are the longus colli and longus capitis muscles over the transverse processes of the cervical vertebrae, and in the connective tissue between these muscles and the carotid sheath is the cervical sympathetic trunk, which therefore lies behind the artery. The inferior thyroid arteries also course behind the carotid arteries to reach the thyroid gland.

In the lower part of the neck the right recurrent nerve crosses obliquely behind the right common carotid to attain a more medial position, while the left recurrent nerve lies behind the left common carotid as both pass from the thorax into the neck. On the left side also the thoracic duct lies behind the common carotid as they enter the neck, but some 3 to 4 cm. above the clavicle it passes lateral to it to cross the anterior surfaces of the vertebral, thyrocervical and subclavian arteries.

Above the level at which it is crossed by the omohyoid muscle the carotid is crossed by few structures of importance, and this is therefore the usual site of election for ligature of the vessel. The superior thyroid vein, the sternocleidomastoid branch of the superior thyroid artery, and sometimes a communication between the facial and the anterior jugular veins cross superficial to the artery in the carotid triangle, and may be wounded in the operation for ligature; the descendens hypoglossi nerve usually can be found here also on the front of the carotid sheath or within the sheath, and may join the descendens cervicalis on the front of the sheath to form the ansa hypoglossi, but these are more closely associated with the jugular vein than with the artery.

In the operation for ligature, a skin incision at the level of the hyoid bone, therefore at about the level of the carotid bifurcation, allows access to the common carotid or its branches. The internal jugular vein is best avoided in opening the carotid sheath by doing this well to the medial side; some care in passing the ligature about the artery may be necessary to avoid inclusion of the vein or of the vagus nerve. Ligature of the external carotid is most easily carried out through the same approach, identifying the bifurcation of the common carotid and placing the ligature about the first part of the external carotid, usually between the superior thyroid and lingual branches.

LIGATION OF CAROTID ARTERIES

The collateral circulation available after ligature of the common carotid artery on one side is relatively abundant (Fig. 285); it includes the anastomoses between the branches of the external carotids of the two sides, especially across the face and scalp; also the anastomoses between branches of the external carotid and subclavian arteries, especially between the superior and inferior thyroid arteries of both the same and the opposite sides, and between the occipital artery and the deep and superficial cervical arteries.

In ligation of the external carotid artery above the superior thyroid a majority of these channels are still available, and may be supplemented also by the anastomosis between the ophthalmic artery and the facial. More collateral circulation would be available to the external carotid artery if the ligature were placed below the superior thyroid artery, but this is not necessary, and the superior thyroid frequently arises so low that there is not room for a ligature on the external carotid below its point of origin.

It might be noted here that while the

external and internal carotid arteries lie parallel to each other at their origins, they are not situated in that relation to each other which would seem to be implied by their names; rather the external carotid artery lies anteromedial while the internal carotid lies posterolateral; the vessels are named not from their relations

Ligation of the common carotid has been said, according to Pemberton and Livermore, to reduce the blood flow through the internal carotid by about 50 per cent; in a series of 44 collected cases in which this operation was done they found only 2 deaths (a mortality rate of 4.5 per cent) reported. Ligation of the internal carotid

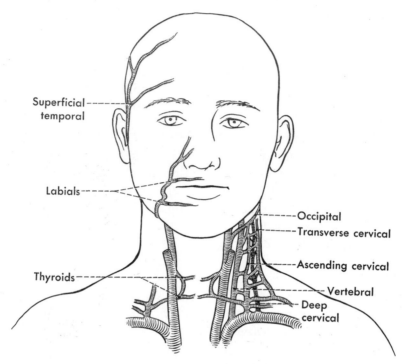

Fig. 285. Some of the collateral channels available after ligation of the common carotid artery. On the right side of the body are shown the chief communications between the two sides, on the left the chief longitudinal anastomoses.

to each other but from their distributions. Any doubt as to which vessel is which can be resolved by identifying branches as arising from one of them: the internal carotid has no branches in its cervical course, as contrasted with the external carotid which gives off several branches close to its origin.

Ligation of the external carotid artery has no serious sequelae unless the internal carotid is injured during the operation.

is, however, an exceedingly serious procedure. Pemberton and Livermore noted that valid statistics are not available; however, they stated that while Dandy had had a death rate of less than 4 per cent in ligations of this artery for intracranial aneurysm, the death rate was 15.7 per cent in a collected series of 51 cases of internal carotid ligation (for other than aneurysm) which they reviewed, and in half again as many additional patients there were cerebral complications. They found that about 30 per cent of patients operated upon for tumors of the carotid body have in the past died as a direct result of the ligation.

CAROTID BIFURCATION

Beyond the rare origin of a thyroid ima artery from the common carotid at the level of the thyroid gland, and the

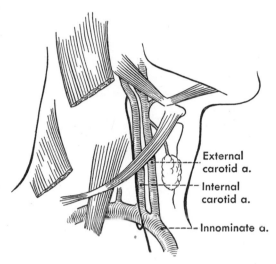

External
carotid a.

Internal
carotid a.

Innominate a.

Fig. 286. Absence of the common carotid (independent origins of the external and internal carotids). (Redrawn from Boyd, J. D., J. Anat. 68:551, 1934.)

occasional origin of the superior thyroid artery from the uppermost portion of the common carotid, the common carotid artery gives off no branches except for its terminal ones, the external and internal carotids. Extremely rarely, as in a case described by J. D. Boyd, external and internal carotids may arise independently from the subclavian and there may be therefore no common carotid (Fig. 286); Kantor has recorded 2 similar cases in which the common carotid bifurcated immediately after its origin. The bifurcation of the common carotid ordinarily occurs, however, at about the level of the hyoid

bone; Kantor quoted Quain as having found 31 cases of abnormally low bifurcation among 295 individuals. In 26 of these 31 cases, the bifurcations lay at about the levels of the upper or middle portions of the thyroid cartilage, while in the other 5 they were at the level of the cricoid. On the posteromedial surface of the common carotid artery immediately below its bifurcation is the carotid body (p. 481).

INTERNAL CAROTID ARTERY

From its origin the internal carotid artery ascends directly toward the jugular foramen, being crossed laterally, in ascending order, by the hypoglossal nerve, the occipital artery, the posterior belly of the digastric and the associated stylohyoid muscle, and the posterior auricular artery (Figs. 287 and 288). Still higher, and close to the base of the skull, it has the external carotid artery situated anterolateral to it; the stylopharyngeus muscle and the associated glossopharyngeal nerve, the pharyngeal branch of the vagus, and the stylohyoid ligament all pass lateral to the internal carotid, between it and the external carotid. Eagle has regarded deviation of the tip of an elongated styloid process, with impingement upon either the internal or external carotid artery, as a cause of some facial pains and headaches. In the upper part of its course the internal carotid lies deep to the parotid gland, and the internal jugular vein, which at first lay lateral to the artery, runs behind it. Medially, the internal carotid is related to the pharynx, and especially therefore to the superior constrictor muscle and the tonsillar region; except when it is unusually tortuous it does not come into direct contact with the pharyngeal wall in the tonsillar region (although it does higher), but is rather separated from the pharynx by the retropharyngeal space. The artery lies upon the longus capitis muscle, and between it and the muscle are the superior cervical ganglion and the vagus nerve; higher up, where the internal jugular vein lies behind the artery, the ninth, tenth, eleventh, and twelfth cranial nerves all

of its course. Close to its origin the superior laryngeal nerve lies behind it at first, and then crosses it medially to descend toward the larynx; at approximately the same level the hypoglossal nerve crosses the artery laterally, and within the substance of the parotid gland the facial nerve also crosses superficial to it. In addition to these nerves, the artery

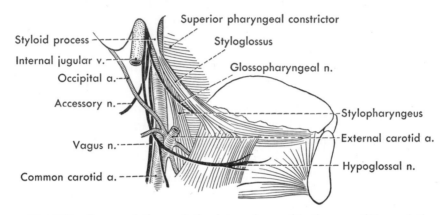

Fig. 287. Some relations of the internal carotid, the mandible and the digastric and stylohyoid muscles having been removed.

normally pass behind the artery, between it and the internal jugular vein.

EXTERNAL CAROTID ARTERY AND BRANCHES

After its origin in the carotid triangle anteromedial to the internal carotid, the external carotid artery (Fig. 288) passes upward deep to the posterior belly of the digastric and the stylohyoid muscle (although a superficial course has been reported in at least 2 cases—p. 375), crosses the styloglossus and the stylopharyngeus muscles on their lateral side (these muscles separating it from the internal carotid) and, approximately paralleling the ramus of the mandible, passes into the deeper portion of the parotid gland. Joessel reported 3 cases in which the external carotid was double for a part

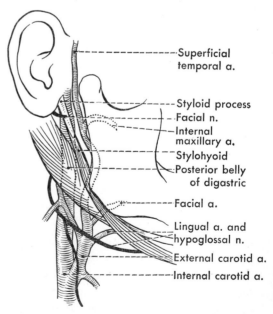

Fig. 288. The deep course of the external and internal carotid arteries, diagrammed as if the parotid gland had been removed.

is crossed laterally by the superior thyroid, common facial, lingual and ranine veins, and within the substance of the parotid gland it lies deep to the temporal (or posterior facial) and internal maxillary veins as these join. In the upper part of its course the external carotid lies anterolateral to the internal carotid, being separated from this not only by a portion of the parotid gland and the stylopharyngeus and styloglossus muscles, but also by the glossopharyngeal nerve and the pharyngeal branch of the vagus.

SUPERIOR THYROID

The superior thyroid artery is typically the first branch from the external carotid, arising usually from the anterior surface of the latter quite close to its origin; in approximately 16 per cent of cases, the superior thyroid arises from the common carotid. This artery runs downward and forward to supply the adjacent muscles, the larynx, and the thyroid gland; its course is further described with the thyroid gland (p. 520).

ASCENDING PHARYNGEAL

The ascending pharyngeal artery, the smallest branch of the external carotid, arises from the posterior surface of the latter close to its origin, and ascends vertically anteromedial to the internal carotid and upon the side of the pharynx; it supplies several branches to the pharynx, a branch to the palate and tonsil, the inferior tympanic branch to the tympanum, and several meningeal branches; of these, the larger terminal branch is usually a posterior meningeal which enters the cranium through the jugular foramen. It also supplies twigs to adjacent muscles, nerves, and lymph nodes, and anastomoses with branches of the ascending cervical artery. In approximately 14 per cent of cases the ascending pharyngeal arises not from the external carotid but from the occipital artery.

LINGUAL

The lingual artery arises from the anterior surface of the external carotid above the superior thyroid artery, usually at or above the level of the hyoid bone; depending upon the level of its origin it may run almost straight forward at the level of the upper border of the greater cornu of the hyoid, may run upward above this level and then curve downward and forward again, or simply curve downward and forward toward the tongue. In any case, it passes deep to the digastric and the stylohyoid to lie against the lateral wall of the pharynx, and runs forward to disappear medial to the hyoglossus muscle. The variations in its origin, its relationships in Lesser's triangle (the usual site of ligation of the vessel) and its further course and branches are described in connection with the tongue (p. 386).

FACIAL OR EXTERNAL MAXILLARY

The facial (external maxillary) artery also arises from the anterior surface of the external carotid artery, at about the lower border of the digastric muscle, and somewhat under cover of the angle of the mandible; it passes forward and upward beneath the digastric and stylohyoid, arching above the latter to come in contact with the submaxillary (submandibular) gland. As already stated, this artery may arise in common with the lingual (Fig. 289), or more rarely in common with the internal maxillary; its further course and its branches are described in connection with the face (p. 314). The cervical branches of the artery are the ascending palatine, the tonsillar branch, branches to the sub-maxillary salivary gland, the submental artery running forward upon the mylo-hyoid, and muscular branches to some of the masticator muscles.

OCCIPITAL

The occipital artery arises from the posterior surface of the external carotid, at about the same level as the facial artery, and therefore close to the lower margin of the posterior belly of the di-

sternocleidomastoid. In the latter part of its course it is joined by the greater occipital nerve.

In addition to muscular branches to adjacent muscles, it gives off a named muscular branch, the sternocleidomastoid artery, to this muscle; this branch passes downward and backward over the hypo-glossal nerve as the nerve loops around the occipital artery. The artery's auricular branch supplies the back of the concha, and its mastoid branch, which is usually

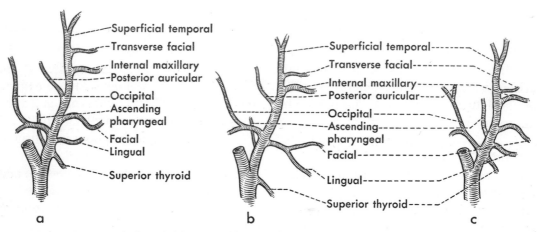

Fig. 289.   Some variations in the branching of the external carotid artery. In *a* is shown what is usually described as the more common arrangement; in *b* the superior thyroid is shown arising from the common carotid, and the lingual and facial arteries as having a common stem; and in *c* the posterior auricular artery is a branch of the occipital, while the ascending pharyngeal arises higher than usual.

gastric. It runs backward to cross the internal carotid artery and internal jugular vein superficially. Close to its origin the hypoglossal nerve emerges between the internal jugular and the internal carotid, therefore deep to the occipital artery, and turns forward lateral to the artery toward the tongue; thus the nerve and artery hook around each other. The occipital artery runs obliquely upward and backward among the vertebral muscles, then turns upward onto the scalp in the interval between the cranial attachment of the trapezius and that of the

from the auricular but sometimes directly from the occipital, enters the skull through the mastoid foramen to supply diploë, mastoid cells and dura; a meningeal branch usually ascends with the internal jugular vein to enter the skull through the jugular foramen and the condyloid (pos-terior condylar) canal, and, at the base of the skull, the occipital gives off de-scending branches which anastomose with the ascending branch of the trans-verse cervical artery, and the vertebral and deep cervical arteries. These branches help to maintain the collateral circulation following ligature of either the common carotid or the subclavian artery.

POSTERIOR AURICULAR

The posterior auricular artery also arises from the posterior surface of the external carotid, but above the level at which this artery is crossed by the digastric and stylohyoid muscles; it is largely covered by the parotid gland and ascends along the styloid process to the groove between the external ear and the mastoid process. It may arise as a branch of the occipital rather than as an independent branch from the external carotid. It gives off twigs to adjacent muscles and to the parotid gland, the stylomastoid artery to mastoid cells and the

tympanum, an auricular branch to the back of the auricle, and an occipital branch to the scalp above and behind the ear.

SUPERFICIAL TEMPORAL AND INTERNAL MAXILLARY

The terminal branches of the external carotid artery, the superficial temporal and the internal maxillary, arise within the substance of the parotid gland; the superficial temporal continues the upward direction of the parent stem, while the internal maxillary passes forward medial to the ramus of the mandible. These vessels have been described especially in connection with the face (p. 317) and with the jaws (p. 369).

CAROTID BODY AND CAROTID SINUS

THE region of the carotid bifurcation contains two sensory structures, sometimes confused, but actually quite different anatomically and physiologically, and of different surgical importance. One of these is the carotid body ("glomus" caroticum, carotid "gland"), the other the carotid sinus.

CAROTID BODY

The carotid body is a small (from about 2.5 by 5 mm. to about 4 by 7 mm.) flattened structure lying at about the level of the carotid bifurcation. Although sometimes described as lying in the bifurcation, it is typically rather on the posteromedial side of the common carotid artery, and held firmly against this by connective tissue; its upper pole may, however, extend above the carotid bifurcation (Fig. 290).

The parenchyma of the carotid body

consists of epithelioid cells, and among these are numerous capillaries or sinusoids which seem to come in contact with every cell; structurally, therefore, the carotid body resembles an endocrine organ, and was indeed thought to be one for

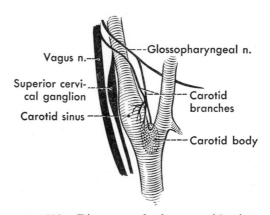

Fig. 290. Diagram of the carotid sinus, carotid body, and their innervation. What part the carotid branch of the vagus plays in this innervation is not known (see text). Note that the carotid body lies not so much in, as medial to the carotid bifurcation.

many years. In contrast to the carotid body of some animals, which forms a rounded and compact unit, the carotid body of the human being is divided into many lobules by the dense connective tissue which binds it together and also binds it to the adventitia of the common carotid artery. It is probably the varying development and position of these lobules which have led to the report that the carotid body tends to degenerate in the adult years of life; actually, there is no good evidence that it does so, and no apparent reason why it should. The carotid body contains numerous nerves and nerve endings, and was once regarded as a part of the chromaffin system of the body—portions of which do undergo degeneration after birth.

Although the carotid body does resemble chromaffin tissue in certain aspects of its morphology, its cells do not give a "chromaffin reaction," and neither do they secrete epinephrine. The nerve supply of the carotid body is not a sympathetic one, as is true of chromaffin tissue, but is sensory; the carotid body represents a specialized sensory organ, or vascular chemoreceptor, which responds to chemical changes in the blood and through its afferent connections to the nervous system reflexly produces changes in the cardiovascular output and in respiration.

The most important stimulus to the carotid body is anoxia; such stimulation leads to a pronounced increase in blood pressure and cardiac rate, and a correspondingly pronounced increase in the depth and rapidity of respiratory movements—that is, with the onset of anoxia, the carotid body initiates reflexes which have the effect of tending to overcome this anoxia. The fundamental anatomical work upon the carotid body was done by de Castro ('26, '28), and the physiological work by Heymans and Bouckaert ('33, '39); reviews of its anatomy and physiology have been published by Hollinshead ('40a) and by Schmidt and Comroe; more recent studies include those of von Euler and Zotterman, and Hollinshead ('43, '45).

The surgical importance of the carotid body is that it sometimes gives rise to a tumor. This tumor may be largely vascular or largely epithelial; it has sometimes been referred to as a glomus tumor, but this is an unfortunate term since it is not of the same origin as true glomus tumors (tumors of arteriovenous anastomoses), and is not characterized by the excruciating pain produced by pressure upon true glomus tumors. Actually, tumors of the carotid body present no pathognomonic symptoms; the symptoms are those which might be produced by any tumor in this general location, and many carotid body tumors are not diagnosed preoperatively. Recognition of the fact by pathologists that the carotid body is not composed of chromaffin tissue should lead to the abandonment of attempts to demonstrate the chromaffin reaction in carotid body tumors. LeCompte has reviewed the subject of carotid body tumors from the standpoint of the pathologist. Apparently about 300 cases of such tumors have been reported in the literature. They may embarrass the circulation, and at operation are frequently found to so surround the common or internal carotid arteries that they cannot be completely removed without ligation and section of these vessels. Complete removal of carotid body tumors therefore has carried a rather high death rate (p. 477), because of inadequacy of collateral circulation to the brain, or of an ascending thrombosis of the internal carotid artery. The majority of carotid body tumors are said to occur after the age of 30.

The carotid bodies do not represent the only chemoreceptor tissue present in the neck, although the exact distribution of this tissue, especially in man, is certainly not known. It is known, however, that tissue of similar structure, and presumably similar function, is located at the superior bulb of the internal jugular vein, therefore adjacent to the floor of the middle ear cavity; in recent years some tumors in this region have been recognized as being similar to carotid body tumors, and are believed to derive therefore from the so-called glomus jugularis (p. 486). Similar tissue also occurs in the mediastinum, and in animals, at least, in the base of the neck at the point where the right vagus nerve crosses the subclavian artery.

CAROTID SINUS

The carotid sinus is completely different in structure and function from the carotid body. It is that portion of the base of the internal carotid artery the wall of which is characterized by much elastic tissue and little muscle, and by numerous and complicated sensory nerve endings. Grossly, the carotid sinus is usually identified as a dilatation at the proximal end of the internal carotid artery, but the physiological carotid sinus does not necessarily correspond to this, as nerve endings may be situated above the gross sinus. In contrast to the carotid body, a chemoreceptor, the carotid sinus is a pressoreceptor: its nerve endings are stimulated by pressure—normally, of course, the pressure of the blood itself. Stimulation of the carotid sinus causes reflex slowing of the heart rate and reduc-

tion of general blood pressure, so that the carotid sinus represents the sensory organ of a reflex mechanism by which the blood pressure can be reduced if it begins to get too high.

Although the carotid sinuses are probably the best known of the pressoreceptor areas, they are certainly not the only ones in the body; exactly similar areas occur on the right subclavian artery and the arch of the aorta, and possibly also on blood vessels elsewhere. Denervation of both carotid sinuses and of the pressoreceptor areas at the base of the neck and in the thorax produces a prolonged and apparently permanent rise in blood pressure (for instance, Heymans); however, denervation of one or both carotid sinuses has no such effect, for the fibers of pressoreceptor function in the cervical portions of the vagus nerves (the depressor branch of the vagus) prevent a rise in blood pressure when the carotid sinuses alone are denervated.

The clinical, as distinguished from the physiological, importance of the carotid sinus is that it may become unduly sensitive to pressure, whereupon relatively slight pressure upon the sinus from without, as in turning the head, may produce an abnormal flow of impulses from it, with consequent slowing of the heart, reduction of blood pressure, and loss of consciousness.

The carotid sinus syndrome—that is, the syndrome of a hypersensitive carotid sinus—can be abolished by denervation of the sinus. The nerve to both the carotid body and the carotid sinus is the sinus nerve (or intercarotid nerve) of Hering or de Castro; it arises largely or entirely from the glossopharyngeal nerve after this has left the skull. The carotid sinus nerve descends in the connective tissue between the internal and external carotids, or upon the internal carotid. In dissections in man connections to this nerve from the vagus, from the superior cervical ganglion, and even from the hypoglossal nerve are sometimes seen; certainly neither the hypoglossal nerve nor the sympathetic system have anything in particular to do with the function of the carotid body, and it is doubtful that the tenth nerve does. Experiments upon animals have indicated that the ninth nerve is the sole nerve supply to the carotid body and the chief one to the sinus, and Ray and Stewart have apparently shown that in man the ninth nerve is at least the primary nerve, since they have found that the carotid sinus reflex is abolished by intracranial division of the ninth.

Mulholland and Rovenstine, and Cattell and Welch have denervated the carotid sinus by stripping the adventitia from about the common and internal carotid vessels, and the latter have also sectioned the intercarotid tissue above the bifurcation; as the carotid sinus nerve usually seems to enter the internal carotid close to the bifurcation, stripping the adventitia should presumably be effective in most cases, but might depend upon the levels at which fibers entered the carotid. Sheehan, Mulholland and Shafiroff have suggested that it might be more feasible to divide the carotid sinus nerve (that is, the intercarotid tissue below the ninth nerve), in preference to extensive stripping of the carotid artery. Pick and Wertheim have described a technic for local anesthetic block of the carotid sinus nerves.

Although carotid body tumors, because of their situation, might be thought to be a not unusual cause of the carotid sinus syndrome, this is not the case; McSwain and Spencer, in reporting 2 cases in which there was such an association, found only a few similar cases in the literature. Apparently the carotid sinus syndrome is due to definite but unknown physiological changes in this sinus.

VEINS

THE veins of the neck vary considerably in their connections with each other, and in their relative sizes; those conducting blood downward from the head and face include the external jugular, the anterior jugular, the internal jugular, and the vertebral; at the base of the neck are the transverse scapular and transverse cervical veins, and the subclavian which unites with the internal jugular to form the innominate vein. The subcutaneous veins, the external and anterior jugulars, are especially variable in size and course; the connections between the various veins, both superficial and deep, are also extremely variable.

SUPERFICIAL VEINS

EXTERNAL JUGULAR

The external jugular vein, quite variable in size, begins in the substance of the parotid gland where it is most often (about 35 per cent, according to Brown, '41) formed by the union of the posterior facial and the posterior auricular veins, or, quite variably, by a single one or some combination of these and the common facial, internal maxillary or other veins in the parotid region; close to the parotid gland it usually receives a communication from the internal jugular vein. It runs vertically downward across the superficial surface of the sternocleidomastoid muscle (very rarely deep to it) to pierce the deep fascia of the posterior triangle of the neck at the posterior border of this muscle just above the clavicle (Fig. 291).

At about the middle of the neck the external jugular receives the posterior external jugular vein, from the back part of the neck, and in the posterior triangle it usually receives the transverse cervical, transverse scapular and, frequently, the

laterally, from the posterior or common facial veins, or parotid veins. It has variable communications with the internal jugular or the common facial vein, and descends on the strap muscles of the neck; the paired veins typically parallel each other, but when they arise in the parotid region they tend to descend along the anterior borders of the two sternocleidomastoid muscles, and hence to con-

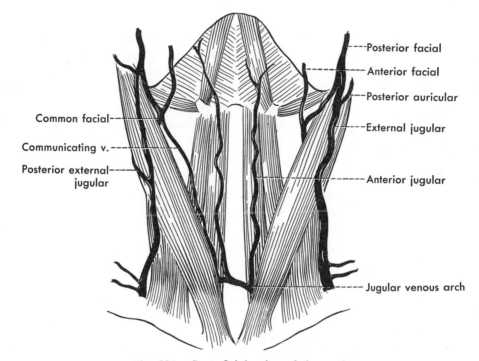

Fig. 291. Superficial veins of the neck.

anterior jugular veins, although these may end directly in the subclavian. It more commonly terminates in the subclavian vein, but in about a third of cases ends in the internal jugular. It may be double, or have a bifid termination.

ANTERIOR JUGULAR

The anterior jugular vein usually begins in the suprahyoid region through the confluence of various and variable superficial veins here; or it may arise more

verge. In the lower portion of the neck, above the sternum, the two veins are commonly united by a transversely disposed jugular venous arch, which is then one of the vessels encountered in a low tracheotomy. Below the jugular venous arch each anterior jugular curves laterally to empty into the terminal portion of the external jugular vein, or into the subclavian vein between the external and internal jugulars. Sometimes, usually when one anterior jugular is missing from its more lateral location, an unpaired vein (median cervical vein) descends from the submental region in the midline of the neck. A number of the variations in the superficial veins of the neck have been described by Pikkieff. She found a median cervical vein in 6.2 per cent of 96 subjects, absence of one anterior jugular in 13.5 per cent, and an arcus venosus juguli in only about 58 per cent.

DEEP VEINS

INTERNAL JUGULAR

The internal jugular vein, the right being usually the larger, begins at the jugular foramen as the continuation of the sigmoid sinus; its first part is somewhat enlarged to form the superior bulb, and projects into the floor of the tympanum. Close against the jugular bulb, and connected with the glossopharyngeal nerve, is a minute bit of tissue, demonstrable only microscopically, which is probably chemoreceptor tissue, therefore similar to the carotid body (p. 481). This is the jugular glomus (Guild). Tumors in this location, believed to arise from this tissue, may invade the adjacent temporal bone (for instance, Rosenwasser); exactly similar tissue is said to occur also on both the tympanic branch of the ninth cranial nerve and the auricular branch of the tenth within the temporal bone, and may give rise to tumors here (Winship and Louzan).

In the uppermost part of its course the internal jugular lies posterior to the internal carotid artery, from which it is separated by the ninth, tenth, and eleventh cranial nerves as they emerge from the anterior portion of the jugular foramen; lower down it lies lateral to the internal carotid and also to the common carotid artery. The glossopharyngeal and hypoglossal nerves usually pass forward between the internal carotid and internal jugular, and the accessory nerve passes backward and downward across the internal jugular, sometimes lying superficial to this and sometimes deep to it (p. 515). As the vein assumes a lateral position in relation to the artery, the vagus nerve lies behind and somewhat between the two vessels, just as it does lower down in relation to this vein and the common carotid artery. During much of its course in the neck the internal jugular vein is intimately related to deep cervical lymph nodes, many of which are embedded in that portion of the carotid sheath surrounding the vein.

At its upper end the internal jugular vein receives the inferior petrosal sinus, which typically passes through the internal jugular foramen anterior to the sigmoid sinus, separated from it by the vagus and spinal accessory nerves. At about the level of the hyoid bone it receives the common facial vein, formed by the union of the anterior facial and the anterior branch of the posterior facial veins, and at about this same level receives also the pharyngeal veins, veins from the tongue (which may, however, join the common facial), and the superior thyroid vein (Fig. 292). The middle thyroid vein, which is not uncommonly absent, typically joins the internal jugular at about the level of junction of the middle and lower thirds of the thyroid gland, passing in front of the common carotid artery to do so.

At the root of the neck the right internal jugular vein lies slightly lateral to the common carotid artery, and crosses in front of the right subclavian artery to join the subclavian vein, while on the left the internal jugular usually somewhat overlaps the common carotid anteriorly. Just above its termination the internal jugular vein may show a second dilation, the inferior bulb; below the level of the subclavian artery on the right, and in front of the subclavian artery on the left, the internal jugular veins join the subclavians to form the two innominate veins. Just above this level the vertebral vein enters the internal jugular on its posteromedial surface, or enters the first portion of the innominate vein, and the external

through the atlanto-occipital membrane from the internal vertebral venous plexuses, and from small veins from the deeper muscles of the upper part of the neck; it descends as a plexus about the vertebral artery, in the canal formed by the transverse foramina of the cervical vertebrae; at the lower end of the canal the plexus unites into a single vein which

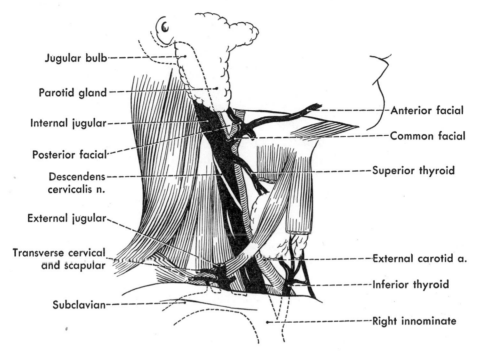

Fig. 292. Some of the deeper veins of the neck. These, like the superficial veins, are quite variable in both size and connections. The descendens cervicalis, shown here lying superficial to the internal jugular, may lie deep to it; thus the ansa hypoglossi may or may not surround the vein.

jugular vein may also open into the lower portion of the internal jugular. The thoracic duct on the left, and the right lymphatic duct or its constituent vessels on the right, open approximately into the angle of union between the internal jugular and subclavian vessels (p. 492).

VEINS AT THE BASE OF THE NECK

The vertebral vein begins in the suboccipital triangle, being formed here by numerous small vessels which pass

lies in front of the vertebral artery and opens into the posterior surface of the first part of the innominate vein or the lower end of the internal jugular.

The deep cervical vein drains the posterior vertebral venous plexus and the deep muscles of the neck. Like the artery of the same name, it passes beneath the transverse process of the seventh cervical vertebra; it opens into the innominate close to the vertebral, or into the vertebral.

The thyroid veins are discussed in connection with the thyroid gland (p. 523).

The subclavian vein, the continuation of the axillary, begins at the outer border of the first rib. Close to its origin it may receive one or more branches corresponding to the thoraco-acromial artery, and sometimes the cephalic vein or a branch of it crosses superficial to the clavicle to enter the subclavian instead of the axillary. The subclavian usually receives the external jugular, may receive the transverse scapular, transverse cervical and other deep veins, and terminates by uniting with the internal jugular to form the innominate close to the sternoclavicular joint. Each subclavian vein lies anterior to the corresponding artery, and at a slightly lower level. Anteriorly it is related to the clavicle; at the level of the anterior scalene muscle it passes across the front of this muscle, by which it is then separated from the artery. Normally the phrenic nerve passes behind it, but sometimes the nerve, or especially an accessory nerve, crosses the vein anteriorly. The right lymphatic duct and the thoracic duct, or tributaries to these, may empty into the terminal portions of the subclavian veins.

The transverse scapular and transverse cervical veins, and sometimes also a superficial cervical vein, accompany the arteries of the same name; like these, they tend to pass in front of or through the brachial plexus. They end variably, in the subclavian vein, the external jugular, or both.

LYMPH NODES AND LYMPHATICS

THE lymphatic system of the neck consists of numerous lymph nodes intimately connected with each other by lymphatic channels, and of the terminations of the thoracic and right lymphatic ducts.

The lymph nodes of the neck are usually divided for convenience of description into some four or five groups, although these groups are continuous with each other (Fig. 293). A convenient

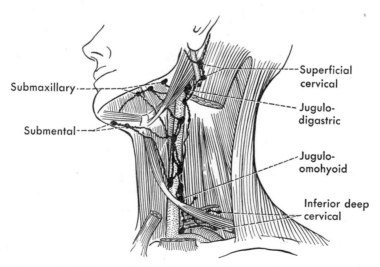

Submaxillary

Submental

Superficial cervical

Jugulo-digastric

Jugulo-omohyoid

Inferior deep cervical

Fig. 293. Schema of the lymph nodes of the neck. The anterior cervical nodes are not shown here, but pretracheal ones of this group appear in Figure 314.

classification is that which describes the lymph nodes as being divided into submaxillary (submandibular), submental, superficial cervical (or external deep cervical) and deep cervical (or internal deep cervical) groups; in addition, an anterior cervical or pretracheal group is usually also described.

The submaxillary and the submental (or suprahyoid) nodes have already been described in a preceding chapter (p. 374) and it need only be pointed out here that they are intimately connected with the fascia over the anterior belly of the digastric and the mylohyoid muscles, and with the submaxillary gland itself. The submental nodes receive their afferent lymphatics from the skin of the chin, the middle portion of the lower lip and the tip of the tongue, and from mucous membrane of the mouth; their efferents pass in part to the submaxillary nodes and in part into the deep cervical chain directly. The submaxillary nodes receive afferents not only from the submental nodes but from the lower portion of the nasal fossae, from the buccal cavity and the upper lip, the gums, much of the anterior part of the tongue, and the lateral parts of the lower lip; their efferent vessels pass into the upper deep cervical nodes.

The superficial cervical nodes, also classified as the external group of the deep cervical nodes, lie about the external jugular vein as it emerges from under cover of the parotid gland, and therefore upon the external surface of the sternocleidomastoid muscle. Their afferents are said variously to consist of cutaneous lymphatics from the face, especially the auricular and parotid regions; of the efferents of posterior auricular (mastoid) and parotid nodes; and sometimes also of occipital nodes; their efferents drain around the anterior border of the sternocleidomastoid

muscle into the deep cervical nodes at about the level of the hyoid bone.

The anterior cervical nodes are an irregular and inconstant group placed in front of the larynx and trachea; some of them are along the anterior jugular vein while others lie deeper on the cricothyroid ligament and the front of the trachea (Fig. 314, p. 524). The latter drain the lower part of the larynx and the upper part of the trachea, and a medial part of the thyroid gland (p. 524). Their efferents pass to the lower deep cervical nodes.

DEEP CERVICAL NODES

The deep cervical lymph nodes are numerous and prominent, and many of them are large. They form a chain embedded in the connective tissue of the carotid sheath; the majority are in that portion of the sheath about the internal jugular vein, rather than concentrated about the artery as lymphatics frequently are. They extend from the base of the skull to the base of the neck.

The nodes of the deep cervical chain are usually described as constituting two groups, although actually there is no subdivision; the upper or superior deep cervical nodes are those lying above the level at which the omohyoid muscle crosses the carotid artery and jugular vein, and the inferior or supraclavicular deep cervical nodes are those lying below this level.

The *superior deep cervical nodes* are especially closely related to the internal jugular vein; they receive their afferents from both superficial and deep structures of the head and upper portion of the neck, some of these afferents reaching these nodes primarily, others being derived from facial, parotid, auricular, occipital, submental, submaxillary and pharyngeal nodes. The superior deep cervical nodes are largely under cover of the sterno-cleidomastoid muscle; the especially large nodes of this group are the jugulodigas-tric (subdigastric) node, situated on the internal jugular and internal carotid vessels where the posterior belly of the digastric crosses these, and the jugulo-omohyoid node, forming the lower end of the superior cervical group, at the point at which the omohyoid crosses the vessels.

The *inferior deep cervical lymph nodes* lie largely posterior and lateral to the internal jugular vein, and extend into the subclavian triangle. The more anterior ones are adjacent to the internal jugular vein, and therefore under cover of the posterior margin of the sternocleido-mastoid, but the more posterolateral ones are more closely associated with the sub-clavian vessels and the brachial plexus.

The inferior deep cervical nodes receive afferents from the back of the scalp and of the neck, from many of the superior deep cervical nodes, from some of the axillary nodes, and even from vessels directly from the skin of the arm and from the pectoral region. Altogether, there-fore, the inferior cervical nodes receive a great deal of the lymphatic drainage from the entire head and neck, plus some drainage from the arm and superficial aspects of the thorax. The efferent vessels of the inferior cervical nodes unite to form the jugular lymphatic trunk, which may be reinforced by efferents from the superior deep cervical nodes, and on the left side typically joins the thoracic duct, while on the right it joins the right lymphatic duct or empties independently at the junction of internal jugular and subclavian veins. The lymphatic drainage of the head and neck has been sum-marized by Trotter and by Looney, among others.

Because of their wide connections, the deep cervical nodes may be involved in carcinoma originating anywhere in the head or neck; in addition, the supra-clavicular or lower deep cervical nodes (also known as the nodes of Virchow or of Trosier, or as the signal nodes) may be involved by carcinoma originating within the abdominal or thoracic cavities. In a study by Viacava and Pack the lower deep cervical nodes were found to be involved (presumably by retrograde ex-tension) in 2.8 per cent of patients with tumors in the abdomen and thorax. The nodes on the left were more frequently involved, probably because of their re-lationship to the thoracic duct, while the nodes on the right were usually involved only when there were tumors in the thorax. In 41 patients, however, the supraclavicular metastatic growths were the first clinical signs of a malignant tumor and led to a search for the primary site of this tumor.

BLOCK RESECTIONS

Since it is impossible to dissect out in-dividually all of the cervical lymph nodes, the technic of block resection of lymph nodes, or radical dissections of the neck, has been developed. This operation ap-parently offers the best hope of "five-year cures" of metastatic carcinoma, and the operation itself is associated with a low mortality rate.

Essentially, the technic of block dissec-tion includes removal of the sternocleido-mastoid muscle and the internal jugular vein, with all the connective tissue about them and all that overlying the muscles of the floor of both the posterior and the anterior triangles of the neck. In the technic described and illustrated by Brown and McDowell the dissection is started from below by sectioning the muscle and ligaturing and sectioning the vein; as the block of tissue is lifted the omohyoid muscle is included, the brachial plexus is cleaned of connective tissue, and so also are the common carotid artery and vagus and phrenic nerves; these structures are of course left intact. The scalene and levator scapulae muscles are carefully cleaned, and the cutaneous branches of the cervical plexus are sacrificed and lifted with the block, leaving only the stumps of this plexus, and its muscular branches. The portion of the accessory nerve passing through the posterior triangle to the trapezius is saved if possible, but may have to be sacrificed owing to the fact that it may pass through the sternocleidomastoid muscle; some workers prefer to sacrifice it to avoid interrupting the dissection at this level.

Above the level of the hyoid bone the posterior belly of the digastric is removed, and so is the stylohyoid (this is omitted by some surgeons), in order to afford access to the upper nodes of the superior cervical group; in the submental region the deep cervical fascia over the mylohyoid muscle is removed with the anterior belly of the digastric, leaving the bare muscle of the mylohyoid, thus assuring removal of the nodes here; the submaxillary gland and its associated nodes are removed after ligature of the facial artery and vein. Two nerves are especially watched for here, the hypoglossal nerve passing deeply across the submaxillary triangle, and the marginal mandibular branch of the facial running approximately along the lower margin of the mandible (p. 329). The lingual nerve also appears, for although normally well under cover of the mandible it is dragged downward by traction on the submaxillary gland.

The dissection is completed by removing the lower tip of the parotid gland with its associated lymph nodes, ligating the upper end of the internal jugular, and sectioning the posterior belly of the digastric, the stylohyoid, and the sternocleidomastoid muscles close to their origins.

Obviously, this type of careful anatomical dissection down to the surfaces of the deeper muscles, removing all overlying muscles and connective tissue and sparing only the important vessels and motor nerves, offers the nearest obtainable approach to a complete removal of the lymph nodes of the neck. When the nodes on both sides have been involved dissections of the second side simultaneously with the first have usually not been complete, for it is impossible to do a thorough dissection and yet spare the internal jugular vein. Bilateral occlusion of this vein is not necessarily fatal (Evans), but bilateral dissections of the neck remove not only this pathway but also many veins which would, with simple ligation of the internal jugular, be available as collateral channels. Dissections of the second side have usually therefore been limited to the removal of such nodes as possible without sacrifice of the internal jugular. If the internal jugular must be sacrificed, the operation is apparently fairly safe after an interval of time, perhaps three months. Simultaneous bilateral block dissections, sacrificing both internal jugular veins, produce extreme edema of the soft tissues of the nose and throat, and a severe rise in intracranial pressure; this radical procedure can however be successfully carried out, in selected cases, if a tracheotomy is done to prevent suffocation as a result of the edema, and if the pressure of the cerebrospinal fluid is kept within reasonable limits by withdrawing fluid as the pressure rises (Morfit).

The collateral circulation after bilateral neck dissections is obviously scanty. Drainage from within the cranial cavity is dependent upon the emissary veins, and the internal vertebral venous plexus; the further pathway for blood both of intracranial and extracranial origin is necessarily the vertebral venous plexuses, the vertebral veins, and veins, such as the deep cervical and the transverse cervical, in the posterior part of the neck.

THORACIC AND RIGHT LYMPHATIC DUCTS

The large lymphatic channels which terminate at the base of the neck are the thoracic duct on the left and the right lymphatic duct on the right. In the upper part of the thorax the thoracic duct lies at first behind the first part of the left subclavian artery, but as it enters the base of the neck it lies somewhat to the right of this and behind the left common carotid artery. From this deep position, between the esophagus and the left pleura and behind the left common carotid and left vagus, it arches upward, forward and laterally; in so doing it emerges between the left common carotid and left subclavian arteries; as it turns laterally it runs in front of the vertebral artery and the thyrocervical trunk, and arching above the level of the subclavian artery passes between the internal jugular vein and the anterior scalene muscle to the (lateral) angle of junction between the left internal jugular and subclavian veins, crossing the subclavian artery superficially (Fig. 294). The duct may loop high into the neck and then downward, or may not rise above its level of termina-

tion; Lissitzyn stated that the high-looping duct is typical of individuals with narrow thoracic apertures, the lower duct of individuals with broad thoracic apertures.

At its termination it is typically joined by the left jugular and left subclavian trunks, and may also receive the left bronchomediastinal (mediastinal) trunk; the bronchomediastinal trunk, and less often a jugular or subclavian trunk, may empty into the veins independently of the thoracic duct. Typically, however, the

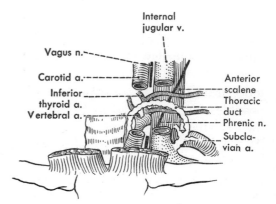

Fig. 294. Relations of the upper end of the thoracic duct. A segment of the contents of the carotid sheath has been cut away.

thoracic duct obviously drains both lower limbs, most of the abdomen and its contents, and the left side of the thorax, head, and neck.

The exact point of ending of the thoracic duct varies, as it may open into the internal jugular, the subclavian, or the angle of junction between these; at its mouth it is provided with a pair of valves which apparently prevent the passage of venous blood into the duct during life, but in the cadaver the terminal portion of the duct may be filled with blood. Davis described the duct as opening into the subclavian vein in 59 per cent of his cases, into the jugulo-subclavian angle (angulus venosus) in 22.7

per cent, into the left innominate, left internal jugular, and right internal jugular in 4.5 per cent each, and, bifid, into the left internal jugular and left angle, or into the left internal jugular and left vertebral, in 4.5 per cent each. The upper end of the duct may be doubled, tripled, or quadrupled; Davis found a single termination of the thoracic duct in only 77 per cent of cases.

At least sometimes the thoracic duct has communications with the right lymphatic duct; Simpson and Graham apparently believed that a potential anastomosis regularly exists, although often so small that it functions in only 1 out of 5 patients. They stated, however, that an anastomosis here becomes functional if the thoracic duct itself is closed in the neck.

The terminal portion of the thoracic duct may be injured in accidents, or in operations at the base of the neck; since it is separated from the phrenic nerve only by the posterior or prevertebral layer of deep cervical fascia as it passes in front of this nerve and the anterior scalene muscle, it is especially liable to injury in operations upon the phrenic nerve or the anterior scalene muscle. Various procedures which have been suggested as treatment for injured thoracic ducts are discussed in connection with the description of this duct in the thorax (Volume 2); injuries to it in the neck are frequently treated by temporary pressure, or when necessary by ligation. Simpson and Graham, and Snedecor have reported satisfactory results from simple ligation here. In animals, Lee was not very successful in producing complete occlusion of the thoracic duct by ligations of it in the neck or high in the thorax, because of the several entrances of the duct into the venous sys-

tem, and its branches of communication with the right lymphatic duct.

RIGHT LYMPHATIC DUCT

The right lymphatic duct is usually defined as being formed by the union of the right jugular and right subclavian trunks, which may be joined by the right bronchomediastinal trunk; therefore, in its fullest development, it receives lymph from the right side of the head and neck, from the right upper extremity, and from the right side of the thorax including the right lung (and part of the left lung), the right side of the heart, and a portion of the convex surface of the liver. The three channels which go to make up the right lymphatic duct usually empty separately or in various combinations into the angle of union between the subclavian and internal jugular veins, or into one of these veins (Fig. 295); a true right lymphatic duct, as a single vessel draining the right side, is apparently rare. Like the thoracic duct, the right lymphatic duct is provided with two semilunar valves at its opening into the venous system.

RIGHT THORACIC DUCT

It has already been mentioned that there may be a communicating channel between the thoracic duct and the right lymphatic duct; in the thorax, where the thoracic duct was once bilateral, parts of both ducts may remain and parallel each other. In cases of anomalous (retroesophageal) right subclavian artery, or of a persistent right aortic arch with a left descending aorta, the development of the upper end of the (left) thoracic duct is apparently frequently interfered with, for in these cases the thoracic duct commonly deviates to the right instead of the left in the posterior mediastinum, and empties into the right side of the venous system instead of into the left as it does normally. This has been true in the few cases seen by the present writer, and was thought by Szawlowski to be always true; it is apparently not invariable, however, for Hammer and Meis reported 3 cases of anomalous right subclavian artery, in 2 of which the thoracic duct emptied into the veins of the left side.

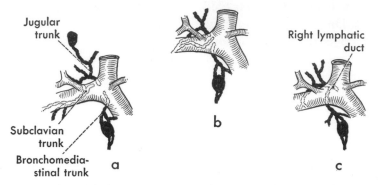

Fig. 295. Various manners of ending of the lymphatic ducts on the right side of the neck. In *a* all three trunks are shown ending separately; in *b* a right lymphatic duct is formed by the union of jugular and subclavian trunks, but the latter trunk branches and ends also independently; in *c* all three major ducts unite to form a right lymphatic duct. (Redrawn from Poirier, P., and Charpy, A.: *Traité d'Anatomie humaine.* Paris, Masson, 1909, Tome 2, Fasc. 4.)

NERVES

CERVICAL PLEXUS

THE cervical plexus is formed by the union of the anterior rami of the second, third, and fourth cervical nerves, with sometimes also a contribution from the first. (Of the posterior rami of these nerves, to skin and musculature of the dorsum, the one from the second cervical has an especially large cutaneous component which chiefly forms the greater occipital nerve.) Close to their origins the anterior rami of these nerves receive communications (rami communicantes) from the cervical sympathetic chain, and give off muscular branches to the adjacent muscles—the longus capitis and cervicis, the levator scapulae, and the scalenus medius.

The first, or more frequently the second, cervical nerve also gives off fibers which join the hypoglossal and run for some distance with this, part of them leaving it as the so-called descendens hypoglossi and the remainder running farther forward to supply the thyrohyoid and the geniohyoid muscles (Fig. 296). Similarly, fibers from the second or second and third cervical nerves form the descendens cervicalis, which in turn unites with the descendens hypoglossi to supply the infrahyoid strap muscles of the neck. These branches, with the contribution to the phrenic (from the third and fourth cervical) and fibers sent either directly or by way of the spinal accessory nerve to the sternocleidomastoid and trapezius muscles (second, third, and fourth cervical) constitute the so-called deep branches (except for the latter, largely motor) of the plexus.

The superficial or cutaneous branches of the plexus are derived from a series of simple loops between the second, third, and fourth cervicals; they are the lesser occipital, great auricular, cutaneus colli, and supraclavicular nerves. The *lesser occipital nerve* is derived from the second

directly upward toward the ear, where it supplies skin over the parotid gland and, with the lesser occipital, skin over the back of the auricle and over the mastoid process.

The *cutaneus colli*, also called the transverse or superficial cervical nerve and the anterior cutaneous nerve of the neck, typically arises by a common stem

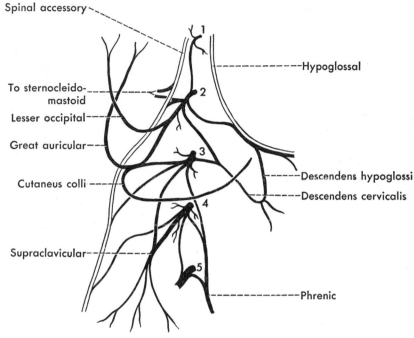

Fig. 296. Schema of the cervical plexus. The short, unlabeled, branches arising from the nerves close to their origins are muscular branches to the longus muscles, the scalenes, and the levator scapulae.

or the second and third cervicals, passes upward around the posterior border of the sternocleidomastoid muscle, and follows approximately this border of the muscle upward to the skin over the side of the head behind the ear.

The *great auricular nerve* is typically derived with the superficial cervical (cutaneus colli) nerve from the loop between the second and third cervical nerves; it also rounds the posterior border of the sternocleidomastoid and passes almost

with the great auricular, from C-2 and C-3, and turns sharply around the posterior border of the sternocleidomastoid near its middle, running at first almost transversely but subsequently dividing into branches which ascend and descend to supply most of the skin of the anterior portion of the neck. The upper branches of this nerve anastomose with the cervical branch of the facial.

The *supraclavicular nerves* arise from a loop between the third and fourth cervicals, and divide typically into three sets, anterior, middle, and posterior; the anterior supraclavicular nerve supplies skin over the anterior portion of the clavicle and the adjacent portions of the neck and thorax, and also filaments to the sternoclavicular joint; the middle supraclavicular nerve supplies especially skin over the anterior portion of the deltoid and the clavicular head of the pectoralis major; while the posterior supraclavicular crosses the outer surface of the trapezius and the acromion, and supplies skin on the upper and posterior parts of the shoulder. It is the superficial branches of the plexus which are routinely sacrificed in block dissections of the neck.

The branches which the cervical plexus sends to the sternocleidomastoid and trapezius muscles have been a source of much confusion, both as to their component fibers and their distribution in the muscles as compared with the spinal accessory. It used to be maintained that the innervation of the sternocleidomastoid and trapezius muscles by both spinal accessory and cervical nerve fibers indicated an origin of these muscles from both branchial arches and myotomes. Corbin and Harrison have, however, shown that in the monkey these connections from the upper cervical nerves to the spinal accessory or directly to the sternocleidomastoid and trapezius muscles contain sensory fibers only, and it seems entirely probable that this is true also of man.

PHRENIC NERVE

The phrenic nerve usually arises from the third, fourth, and fifth cervical nerves, so that it is derived from both cervical and brachial plexuses (Fig. 297); it passes downward with a slight medial

inclination on the front of the anterior scalene muscle, between this muscle and the prevertebral fascia, and is commonly attacked surgically as it lies in this position. The vagus nerve lies within the carotid sheath anterior to the phrenic nerve, and the cervical sympathetic chain lies somewhat more medially, posterior to the carotid sheath but not upon the anterior scalene muscle; both of these nerves have at operation been mistaken

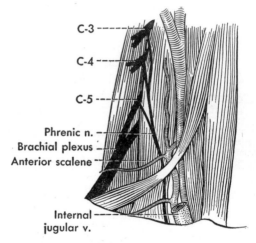

Fig. 297. The phrenic nerve and some of its relations. On the left side these include the thoracic duct (Fig. 294).

for the phrenic nerve. The important point in the identification of the phrenic nerve is that it lies behind the fascia and directly on the anterior surface of the muscle fibers of the anterior scalene muscle.

ACCESSORY PHRENIC NERVES

Simple crushing or section of the phrenic as it lies on the scalene has often failed to produce the desired paralysis of the diaphragm, for these procedures do not necessarily interrupt the entire nerve; accessory phrenic nerves, not closely paralleling the main nerve, frequently exist and because of their aberrant courses may be overlooked.

The most common accessory phrenic nerves arise from the fifth or sixth cervical nerve and run usually lateral to the normal phrenic to join it at about the level of the first rib, but may join the phrenic nerve in the neck, or may not unite with it until the level of the root of the lung, or even until close to the diaphragm. Decker found accessory phrenic nerves in 30 per cent of 72 sides, the majority arising from the fifth cervical nerve, but a smaller

additional or accessory phrenic; in the laboratory such a branch, if it joined the phrenic after only a short course, would probably not be termed an accessory phrenic nerve. Perhaps these figures of Kelley's simply emphasize the importance of seeking the phrenic nerve well below the level of emergence of the fifth cervical, if the nerve as a whole is to be crushed.

Although the accessory phrenic may loop in front of the subclavian vein to join the main phrenic, Decker did not regard this as a deterrent to avulsion of

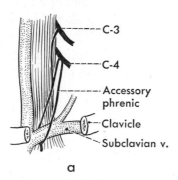

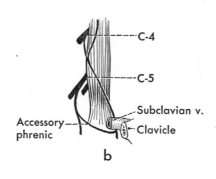

Fig. 298.   Two types of accessory phrenic nerve. In *a* a long accessory from C-4 loops in front of the subclavian vein to join the phrenic proper; in *b* the accessory phrenic arises from the fifth cervical nerve in common with the nerve to the subclavius, and after leaving this runs almost horizontally to join the phrenic. (Adapted from Decker, H. R.: *J. Thoracic Surg. 2:*538, 1933.)

group from the third and fourth (Fig. 298). Kelley, reviewing 309 operations upon the phrenic nerve, stated that there was a second phrenic nerve in addition to the main phrenic in 99.2 per cent, and conclusive proof of the existence of an "accessory phrenic" (defined as one smaller than the main phrenic) in 75.7 per cent. This is far larger than is found in the dissecting room; from Kelley's discussion, it seems probable that any root from the fifth cervical nerve which did not join the remainder of the phrenic before this passed onto the anterior surface of the scalene was regarded as an

the nerve, stating that the nerve usually breaks before it can damage the vein. The nerve to the subclavius, of no clinical significance otherwise, is fairly frequently the source of an accessory phrenic derived from the fifth cervical nerve. If the phrenic is avulsed from well within the thorax, it is probable that in almost all cases all accessory phrenic nerves will also be torn out; if, however, the nerve is simply crushed as it lies on the anterior scalene muscle it might be prudent to locate and crush the nerve to the subclavius, if possible, and to seek other branches descending from the brachial plexus along the lateral border of the anterior scalene. Turner has described a case in which an accessory phrenic nerve was derived from the ansa hypoglossi, this apparently representing the usual contribution from the third cervical nerve to the phrenic; this branch, on the left side, passed in front of the left innominate vein and the arch of the aorta and joined the phrenic at the level of the root of the left lung.

Apparently complete interruption of the phrenic nerve does not always produce the expected effect on the diaphragm (Volume 2).

BRACHIAL PLEXUS

The brachial plexus is formed primarily by the union of anterior rami of the lower four cervical and the first thoracic nerves. At its origin the plexus is related anteriorly to the anterior scalene muscle, and posteriorly to the middle scalene; Reed has stated that the fourth to sixth cervical nerves typically emerge first between the fibers of the anterior scalene muscle, but the plexus as a whole makes its appearance between the anterior and middle scalenes. The ascending cervical branch of the inferior thyroid artery ascends across the anterior surface of the plexus, and the transverse scapular and transverse cervical arteries cross it, either anteriorly or among its branches, as they run laterally and posteriorly. The distal portion of the plexus is of course in close relation to the subclavian and axillary arteries.

The anterior rami of the nerves forming the brachial plexus lie almost completely behind the anterior scalene muscle, and the union of these anterior rami to form trunks occurs close to the lateral edge of this muscle. Passing in front of the brachial plexus and onto the anterior

surface of the anterior scalene muscle is the phrenic nerve, typically receiving a branch from the fifth cervical. The variations in this have already been discussed (p. 496).

TRUNKS, DIVISIONS, AND CORDS

In the formation of the brachial plexus, the anterior rami of the fifth and sixth cervical nerves unite at about the lateral edge of the anterior scalene to form an upper trunk, the seventh nerve emerges by itself as a middle trunk, and the eighth cervical and first thoracic nerves, usually uniting behind the anterior scalene muscle, form a lower trunk (Fig. 299). Each of these trunks in turn forms two divisions, an anterior and a posterior one; the splitting of the superior and middle trunks into anterior and posterior divisions usually occurs soon after they have emerged from between the two scalenes, while that of the lower trunk occurs farther distally, as a rule behind the subclavian artery and either behind the clavicle or in the axilla. Also, it should be noted that whereas the superior and middle trunks usually split into divisions of approximately equal size, the divisions of the lower trunk are markedly unequal; the anterior division of the inferior trunk is always much the larger, while the posterior division of the trunk, contributed to the radial nerve, is usually quite small. It therefore follows that the radial nerve contains relatively few fibers of eighth cervical and first thoracic origin, and apparently few of these usually belong to the first thoracic nerve.

The divisions of upper, middle, and lower trunks typically unite in a standard pattern to form the cords of the brachial plexus. The anterior divisions of upper and middle trunks unite to form the lateral cord, formed at about the level of the clavicle; as this passes between the clavicle and first rib it becomes associated with the anterolateral aspect of the axillary artery (Fig. 300). The anterior division of the lower trunk continues alone to form the medial cord of the plexus, lying at first somewhat behind the subclavian artery as they cross the first rib

of the posterior cord typically take place in the lower part of the neck, or the union of their posterior divisions may occur in the upper part of the axilla. The inferior trunk usually divides relatively late, as or after it crosses the first rib (lying here typically behind the subclavian artery, between it and the first rib); at this point

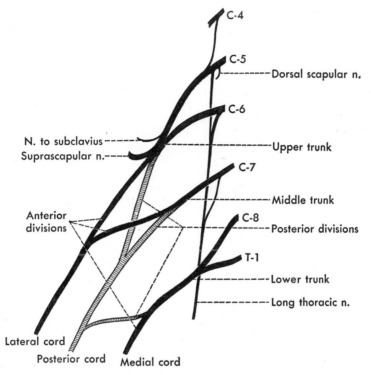

Fig. 299. Schema of the formation of the brachial plexus, and its branches in the neck. The twigs to the longus and scalene muscles are not shown.

together, but subsequently passing slightly forward to lie medial to the axillary artery. The posterior divisions of all three trunks unite to form the posterior cord of the brachial plexus, which then lies behind the axillary artery.

The level at which the cords are formed varies somewhat; the divisions of the upper and middle trunks, and the unions of their component divisions to form the lateral cord and the greater part

of division, of course, the medial cord is formed, while the definitive posterior cord is not completely formed until the posterior division of the lower trunk joins the already united posterior divisions of the middle and upper trunks. The posterior cord is usually formed therefore in the apex of the axilla.

The nerves given off from the three cords typically arise in the axilla, and are described in connection with the upper limb (Volume 3). Not infrequently, however, the lateral pectoral (or lateral anterior thoracic) nerve (to the pectoralis major), which is described as the first branch from the lateral cord, arises in the lower part of the neck, sometimes even from the anterior divisions of the upper and middle trunks before these have united.

cle. It is of importance only because it may contribute to the origin of the phrenic nerve (p. 497).

SUPRASCAPULAR NERVE

In addition, the upper trunk before its division gives off the larger and important suprascapular nerve (to the supraspinatus and infraspinatus muscles) which at first

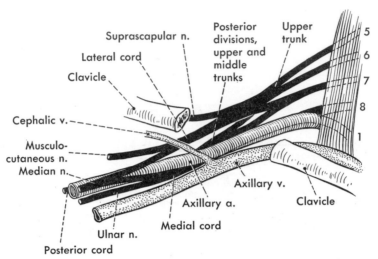

Fig. 300. The relation of the brachial plexus to the subclavian and axillary arteries, a section of the clavicle having been removed and the arm being abducted and externally rotated. The transverse scapular, transverse cervical, and superficial cervical arteries are also closely related to the plexus at the base of the neck, one or more of these usually passing anterior to or through the plexus. The posterior cord is exaggeratedly prolonged in order to show its position.

BRANCHES IN THE NECK

NERVE TO THE SUBCLAVIUS

While most of the branches of the brachial plexus arise, as noted, in the axilla, several have higher origins, and leave the brachial plexus in the neck. Thus, in addition to its contribution to the phrenic nerve, the fifth nerve or the upper trunk gives rise to the small nerve to the subclavius which passes downward in front of the lower portion of the brachial plexus and in front of the subclavian artery and vein to reach this mus-

parallels the upper trunk of the brachial plexus, running lateral to it, but subsequently swings laterally at about the level of the clavicle to parallel the transverse scapular vessels, and pass backward toward the lesser scapular notch.

DORSAL SCAPULAR NERVE

Of the other supraclavicular branches of the brachial plexus, several are twigs to the longus colli and to the scalenes, and arise from the lower four cervical nerves as these leave the intervertebral foramina. They are thus completely hidden by the scalene muscles. The dorsal scapular nerve (to the rhomboidei) also has an origin close to the interverte-bral foramen, arising from the fifth cervi-cal nerve under cover of the anterior scalene, turning backward through the scalenus medius, and running downward and backward in the neck on the deep surface of or through the levator scapulae muscle.

LONG THORACIC NERVE

The long thoracic nerve (to the ser-ratus anterior muscle) is the only one of the deeper branches of the brachial plexus to be obvious in dissections in the anterior region of the neck. It is usually said to arise from the fifth, sixth, and seventh cervical nerves, close to the exits of these nerves from the intervertebral foramina. The root of this nerve from the sixth cervi-cal vertebra seems to be constant and relatively large; those from the fifth and the seventh are more variable, the root from the seventh being least frequently found. The roots from the fifth and sixth cervicals pass through, that from the seventh nerve usually behind, the middle scalene muscle, to emerge upon the an-terolateral surface of the muscle (where they unite if they have not done so pre-viously) and descend on this surface behind the brachial plexus and onto the superficial surface of the serratus anterior muscle.

It has been stated that the long thoracic nerve has sometimes been crushed mis-takenly for the phrenic, since its relation to the middle scalene is somewhat like that of the phrenic to the anterior sca-lene; however, the phrenic nerve lies far medial to the long thoracic, and more-over the long thoracic nerve passes down-ward behind the brachial plexus, while the phrenic is of course in front of the plexus, separated from this by the anterior scalene muscle. There would seem to be relatively little excuse for confusing these two nerves.

VARIATIONS

The brachial plexus is rather constant in the gross anatomy of its formation, although varying somewhat in the size of the contribution which it receives from the fourth cervical and the first thoracic nerves, and also in the fact that it may sometimes receive fibers from the second thoracic nerve. Occasionally, real anom-alies such as the formation of a single anterior cord (instead of a lateral and medial cord), or the union of all elements of the plexus into a single cord such as described by Singer, may occur.

The more common variations in the brachial plexus have been described by Harris and Kerr. Kerr, in a study of 175 plexuses, divided them into three groups: (1) those receiving fibers from C-4; (2) those receiving no fibers from C-4 but all of the anterior ramus of C-5; and (3) those receiving only a part of the anterior ramus of C-5. In his series, more than 62 per cent of the brachial plexuses belonged to Group 1, 30 per cent to Group 2, and 7 per cent to Group 3.

Normally, therefore, there is little shift in origin of the brachial plexus, although plexuses are sometimes classified, accord-ing to the segments which contribute to them, as prefixed, normal, or postfixed. While these variations affect somewhat the segmental innervation of the muscles to which the nerves of the brachial plexus are distributed, the range is, as will be noted, no more than a segment. There may be a small communication from the second thoracic nerve to the brachial plexus; Todd ('12) described this communication as consisting largely of small myelinated and unmyelinated fibers, and expressed the belief that these were sympathetic in nature, although some cutaneous sensory or voluntary motor fibers probably run through this connection also, on occasion.

OTHER RELATIONS

Kolodny has pointed out that while birth injuries of the brachial plexus are usually either of the upper (Erb-Duchenne) or lower (Déjerine or Klumpke) type, owing to the nerves entering into the plexus being angulated sharply over the upwardly directed transverse processes, this is not usually true in the adult; here the transverse processes run downward, and traction usually traumatizes the tissue and blood vessels about the nerve trunks, so that the plexus as a whole becomes embedded in scar tissue.

Since the brachial plexus passes in the relatively narrow space between the clavicle and the first rib, and in the upper part of the axilla is related to the coracoid process, the tendon of insertion of the pectoralis minor on this process, and the head of the humerus, it is apparent that extreme postures of the upper limb might bring the brachial plexus into contact with some of these structures, pressing it against them or stretching it across them. Clausen has pointed out that the danger of injury through such positions is increased when the patient is under general anesthesia, where the muscular protection is largely absent, and has discussed some of the positions to be avoided if such damage is not to occur.

Brachial plexus anesthesia is apparently most commonly carried out by injection through the supraclavicular fossa, the first rib serving as a landmark and the plexus being injected as it crosses this rib. At the level at which the plexus crosses the first rib, most of it is lateral to and above the subclavian artery, and the site of the injection can be therefore somewhat guided by placing a finger upon the artery, or starting laterally on the first rib and proceeding medially. The lateral and posterior cords or the divisions entering into them tend to lie respectively somewhat anterior and posterior to the artery, but on its lateral aspect, while the medial cord (or more commonly the lower trunk, which consists largely of fibers which form the medial cord) lies somewhat behind it, between the artery and the middle scalene muscle, or between the artery and the rib.

The subclavian artery, the subclavian vein and the dome of the pleura are all liable to injury in performing a brachial plexus block; according to some authors, neither puncture of the pleura nor of the subclavian artery carries any particular danger, but Patrick, and de Pablo and Diez-Mallo, have warned that injection into the vein may be fatal, and thus must be avoided. One of the difficulties in attaining successful brachial plexus blocks is undoubtedly the connective tissue surrounding the brachial plexus, carried downward around it from the prevertebral fascia, which presumably somewhat protects the nerves from the action of the anesthetic unless the latter is delivered within this heavy sheath. The position of the lower trunk behind the subclavian artery also makes it difficult to obtain good anesthesia in the area of distribution of the ulnar nerve.

CERVICAL RIB, RUDIMENTARY FIRST THORACIC RIB, AND SCALENUS ANTICUS SYNDROME

These three conditions, with similar clinical symptoms, are characterized by evidences of pressure upon the brachial plexus, and frequently also by evidence of disturbed circulation to the limb. In all three conditions the precipitating causes are similar or identical, and consist in the fact that the brachial plexus is stretched or angulated over a bony projection or a fibrous band, or compressed through narrowing of the space behind the anterior scalene muscle.

CERVICAL RIB

The incidence of cervical rib is said to be between 0.5 and 1 per cent of individuals (Hill), or 6 patients per 1,000 (Adson, '47), but symptoms are said to occur in only about 10 per cent of such

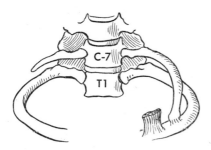

Fig. 301. Two types of cervical ribs—a short one ending freely, and a longer one articulating with the first thoracic rib. Observe in the latter case the very limited space that may exist between the rib and the anterior scalene muscle for the passage of the subclavian artery and brachial plexus into the axilla.

individuals (Hill). The condition has been said to be bilateral in from about 50 to 80 per cent of cases, and when unilateral to be more common on the left (Hill; Kasman and Bernstein); Adson ('51) quoted the occurrence of cervical ribs as being twice as frequent in females as males, bilateral in 50 per cent, and if unilateral as common on one side as the other.

Cervical ribs vary considerably in their development, sometimes being quite short and sometimes long (Fig. 301). They may end freely or articulate with

the first rib through a cartilage, but are apparently more frequently united to the normal first thoracic rib by a fibrous band. This band may in turn act in the same manner as a rib, by affording a rather dense structure against which the brachial plexus can be compressed.

Cervical ribs and their fibrous bands may interfere with the brachial plexus in one of two ways: they may narrow the space available behind the insertion of the anterior scalene muscle, through which the brachial plexus and subclavian artery must pass over the first rib; or they may so project that a portion of the brachial plexus must pass across them. If the rib is short, the seventh nerve alone may lie in contact with the rib; if it is long, the entire brachial plexus may pass over it. In the latter case the lower trunk of the plexus rests against the cervical rib, and in order to reach its point of exit between the normal first thoracic rib and the clavicle has to run upward to pass over this extra obstruction. In such a case, obviously, the angulation of the plexus produced by a cervical rib would be increased by any lowering of the shoulder.

RUDIMENTARY FIRST THORACIC RIB

Rudimentary first thoracic ribs are not so well known, and their incidence has apparently not been established, but their occurrence may be associated with exactly the same symptoms as those commonly attributed to a cervical rib (Dow; White, Poppel and Adams). A rudimentary first thoracic rib is one which fails to reach the sternum, its anterior end being usually fixed to the second rib by ligaments. Apparently there is always associated with a rudimentary first thoracic rib a downward shift in the segmental origin of the brachial plexus, so that the second thoracic nerve contributes largely to this plexus (Dow; Hertslet and Keith). Since it is obvious that the vertebral relations between the second thoracic nerve and the first rib are the same as those between the first thoracic nerve and a cervical rib —that is, in each case the lowest nerve must ascend in order to cross above the rib—the angulation produced by a first

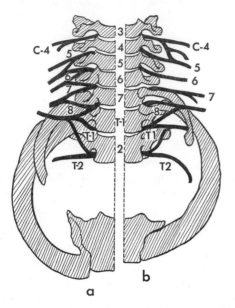

Fig. 302. Comparison of the composition and relations of the brachial plexus in *a*, a case of rudimentary first thoracic rib and, *b*, a case of cervical rib. Note that in both cases the lowest element contributing to the plexus tends to hold the lower trunk down against the highest rib. (Redrawn from Hertslet, L. E., and Keith, A.: *J. Anat. & Physiol. 30:*562, 1896.)

thoracic rib with a postfixed plexus is somewhat similar to that produced by a cervical rib with a normal plexus (Fig. 302).

NEUROCIRCULATORY COMPRESSION

Either of the two anatomical abnormalities just described may therefore apparently produce signs of compression of the brachial plexus through angulation of the plexus across them, and this would be increased by any abnormal lowering of the shoulder. In a similar fashion, ab-

normal lowering of the shoulder or abnormal elevation of the first rib may conceivably bring about compression of the plexus and of the subclavian artery against a normal first thoracic rib. There are, indeed, a variety of anatomical and physiological factors which may, individually or collectively, produce evidences of pressure upon the brachial plexus; Walshe, Jackson, and Wyburn-Mason; and Telford and Mottershead have especially emphasized this fact.

It is obvious that the presence of a cervical rib is not necessarily, in itself, responsible for signs of neurocirculatory compression, for the great majority of cervical ribs present no symptoms and are found incidentally upon x-ray examination, while similar symptoms occur when the bony conformation is entirely normal. It has been recognized by a number of workers that the symptoms attributed to the presence of a cervical rib occur predominantly on the right side, and that they are apt to occur in later life; Spurling and Bradford regarded this as being due to a gradual dropping of the shoulder girdle and to the fact that the dominant, usually the right, side drops lower than does the other. One possible factor in the production of symptoms, therefore, is an abnormally lowered shoulder or, the converse of this, an abnormally raised thoracic cage.

The possibility of alleviating neurocirculatory compression (whether or not there is a cervical or rudimentary first thoracic rib) by improving the muscular tone of the elevators of the scapula should be considered in all cases in which diminished tone may appear to be a contributing factor. Naffziger and Grant as early as 1938 reported that exercise of the upper part of the trapezius and other elevators of the shoulder sometimes relieved the conditions of compression, and Spurling and Grantham reported that conservative treatment (infrared and postural therapy) gave relief in 300 out of 400 cases of such compressions.

Since identical symptoms may or may not be associated with the presence of a cervical rib, many authors have expressed the belief that it is actually spasm or hypertrophy of the anterior scalene muscle which is usually responsible for the disturbances to the brachial plexus, even when a cervical rib is present. Such changes in the muscle produce elevation of the first rib and a limitation of the space behind the anterior scalene, either or both of which may contribute to compression of the plexus. An additional factor having to do with the width of this space would be the presence of a scalenus minimus (scalenus anticus minor) which is found unilaterally or bilaterally in a majority of bodies (p. 465).

Naffziger and Grant apparently felt that scaleniotomy was especially of value because it allowed the first rib and the remainder of the thoracic cage to drop somewhat, and thus reduce the pressure upon the brachial plexus. Adson ('51) stressed a combination of factors as contributing to the signs of neurocirculatory compression in the presence of a cervical rib: according to his view, the anatomical basis is that the patients so afflicted have long necks, and the posterior cervical triangle is narrow (and so far as the brachial plexus is concerned, may be still further narrowed by the presence of a cervical rib), so that there is less width than usual behind the anterior scalene; to this is added the descent of the shoulder, and an hypertrophy of the anterior scalene muscle, with extra width at its insertion. Gage and Parnell, and Kirgis and Reed have also emphasized that some of the nerve

roots of the plexus pass through the anterior scalene muscle, and regarded them as subject to compression by contraction of the muscle, especially of its more posterior fibers.

Resection of a cervical rib is more difficult technically than is section of the anterior scalene muscle (for the anatomy of which see page 463), and scaleniotomy alone is therefore often carried out even in the presence of a cervical rib; the rationale of scaleniotomy, whether or not a cervical rib is present, is to allow the thoracic cage to drop if possible and to increase the available space behind the anterior scalene muscle (Fig. 303). Patterson, and Kirgis and Reed, have suggested that for either purpose it would seem logical to section not only the anterior scalene but also the middle one (which both helps to raise the first rib and, because it is directly posterior to the brachial plexus, may presumably contribute to irritation of the plexus through its spasticity). Adson ('51) has described the subclavian artery and the lower part of the plexus as dropping downward and forward after section of the anterior scalene, and has found that such section frequently so increases the space available that removal of a cervical rib, when that is present, is unnecessary. Of course, if some of the brachial plexus actually overrides a cervical rib, a portion of the rib should be resected. Adson has also reported that compression of the plexus may be caused by a taut omohyoid muscle instead of by the anterior scalene.

Kaplan has suggested procaine infiltration of the muscle as a diagnostic test, and stated that repeated injections may obviate the need for scaleniotomy. Adson's test for compression of the plexus by the anterior scalene, which he regarded as pathognomonic whether or not a cervical rib is present, is obliteration of the pulse in the affected limb when the contracted muscle is forced backward: the muscle is contracted by having the patient take a deep breath, and forced backward by having him extend his neck and turn his head toward the affected side. This must be carried out while the patient is sitting erect with the hands resting upon the knees. According to Adson, scaleniotomy for cervical rib or scalenus anticus syndrome accomplishes little unless the result of this vascular test is positive.

tests have ruled out the presence of a protruded disc.

The symptoms directly referable to pressure upon the brachial plexus are most commonly pain, frequently paresthesia and anesthesia, and, less often, paralysis. Since it is more commonly the lower portion of the plexus that is affected, the sensory disturbances usually occur on the ulnar side of the hand, and the muscles supplied by the ulnar nerve are the ones which are most apt to show paralysis or atrophy. Vascular symptoms

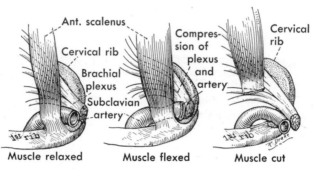

Fig. 303. Illustrating the manner in which contraction of the anterior scalene muscle in the presence of a cervical rib can produce compression of the subclavian artery and brachial plexus, and how scaleniotomy alone may relieve this compression by allowing the vessel and nerves to drop forward. (From Adson, A. W.: *J. Internat. Coll. Surgeons 16:*546, 1951.)

Even when neurocirculatory compression seems definitely due to scalene spasm, the possibility that the spasm is secondary to irritation of the nerve roots should be considered. Reflex spasm of the muscle, a protective device to prevent further compression of a nerve root, may be a prominent feature of protruded cervical intervertebral discs, and the neurocirculatory signs thus evoked may even overshadow the clinical features due to the disc (Spurling and Scoville). Kristoff and Odom have on this account warned that section of the scalene should not be undertaken until after myelography or other

also frequently accompany these other ones, but to what extent they are due to pressure upon the plexus and to what degree to more direct disturbances of the circulation is not agreed upon. The vascular symptoms are those of poor circulation to the affected limb, and may somewhat simulate Raynaud's disease.

ORIGIN OF VASCULAR SYMPTOMS

Eden, McGowan, and Shumacker, among others, have all expressed the belief that the vascular symptoms might be due, directly or indirectly, to compression of the subclavian artery between the clavicle and a normal or cervical rib, accentuated by downward movements of the shoulder or upward movements of the thorax. On the other hand, Telford and Mottershead have argued that since depression of the shoulder is usually accompanied by a forward movement of the clavicle, this cannot result in a pinching of the vessel. Moreover, according to these writers, depression of the shoulder with obliteration of the radial pulse does not abolish the axillary pulse, and therefore cannot be due to pressure of the subclavian artery upon the rib or clavicle. They interpreted their evidence as indicating rather that such obliteration of the radial pulse (produced by a downward movement of the arm in some individuals) results from constriction of the axillary artery by the two heads of the median nerve.

While the subclavian artery has been reported as being narrowed as it passed between the scalenus anterior and a scalenus minimus (G. I. Boyd), Telford and Stopford have pointed out that even sudden occlusion of the subclavian artery does not usually produce marked vascular symptoms in the limb, and found it difficult to believe that chronic compression of the vessel, as by a cervical rib, could have any real effect upon the peripheral circulation. Mechanical constriction of the subclavian artery has been felt by many to be an unsatisfactory explanation, although Adson ('51) has attributed some of the vascular symptoms to this cause.

Obvious anatomical changes in the vessels may also occur, and Eden regarded the peripheral vascular changes as probably the sequelae of intimal damage with the formation of multiple emboli. Aneurysmal dilatations of the subclavian artery have not been reported very fre-quently, but were found in 27 of 100 cases of cervical rib reviewed by Lindskog and Howes; Smith reported a case in which a thickened band of cervical fascia pressing upon the subclavian artery had produced a thrombosis of it; Adson ('51) has pointed out that atheromatous plaques may occur in the subclavian artery behind the anterior scalene, and has had 2 cases of rupture here following scaleniotomy.

Why most dilatations of the arterial stem are distal to the anterior scalene muscle, and therefore to the point of possible mechanical interference with the vessel, is not quite clear; MacFee considered this as evidence that they are probably not caused by a simple constriction or compression with local damage. It has been suggested that the aneurysmal dilatations may be due to pinching of the vessel between the clavicle and the first rib, or to interference with sympathetic fibers normally distributed to the dilated portion of the vessel (Todd, '13). That the first suggestion is true has been denied on the ground that such pinching cannot occur; as for the second, modern knowledge of the sympathetic system would seem to indicate that aneurysmal dilatations of vessels are not produced by local denervation.

There have been, therefore, proponents of the concept that the vascular symptoms are due primarily to mechanical constriction of the vessel, or that the mechanical constrictions are accompanied by pathological changes in the vessels of the limb. Finally, it has also been suggested that the symptoms are a result of stimulation of the sympathetic fibers passing into the limb with the plexus. Adson ('51) has accepted each of these as being probably responsible for some of the vascular symptoms.

Telford and Stopford described a case in which the sympathetic fibers in the first thoracic nerve were found to be concentrated especially in the lower border of this nerve where they would be easily subject to pressure from a cervical rib, and suggested that the sympathetic fibers to the limb were therefore directly stimulated through such pressure. Blair, Davies, and McKissock, and Sunderland, have failed to confirm a concentration of sympathetic fibers in the lower part of the first thoracic nerve, however, but rather described them as distributed throughout the nerve. The former workers regarded chronic inflammation of the nerve, extending throughout it, as stimulating the sympathetic fibers. In opposition to the concept of sympathetic stimulation, Eden has pointed out that chronic irritation of a nerve is usually succeeded by paralysis, and stated that this has not usually been reported to occur in cases of cervical rib. Adson, however, has stated that Horner's syndrome has often been observed in association with evidence of brachial plexus compression.

CERVICAL SYMPATHETIC CHAIN

The cervical sympathetic chain consists of three ganglia, inferior, middle, and superior, and the trunk connecting these (Fig. 304). While a few postganglionic fibers may descend in the cervical chain (Foley) its fibers consist largely of ascending preganglionic ones which have emerged through the anterior roots of the upper several thoracic nerves, and are passing upward to make synapse in either the middle or superior cervical ganglia, though some may pass beyond the latter to end in ganglia of the carotid plexus itself. It is generally believed that few or no sensory fibers of spinal nerve origin

run in the trunk, but it is not uncommon, at least in the cat, for vagal fibers (probably sensory ones) to be incorporated in relatively large numbers in the sympathetic chain (for instance, Hinsey, Hare, and Wolf; Foley).

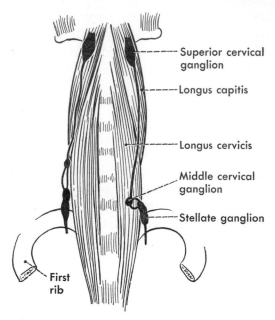

Fig. 304. Cervical sympathetic chain. Both the high and the low positions of the middle cervical ganglion are illustrated.

THE GANGLIA

SUPERIOR CERVICAL GANGLION

The large superior cervical ganglion lies on the longus capitis muscle at about the levels of the centra of the second and third cervical vertebrae; it is therefore above the carotid bifurcation, and lies somewhat posteromedial to the first portion of the internal carotid artery, being related also anteriorly to the nodose ganglion of the vagus. It typically gives off rami communicantes to approximately the upper three cervical nerves, and also has communications with the vagus, the hypoglossal, and other nerves in this neighborhood; it also gives off the external carotid plexus (p. 335) which accompanies the branches of this vessel, and the large and important internal carotid plexus which leaves the upper end of the ganglion as a broad sheet of fibers that subsequently form a plexus about the internal carotid artery. The very slender superior sympathetic cardiac nerve likewise arises from the superior cervical ganglion, and descends behind the great vessels.

The internal carotid plexus, the chief continuation from the superior cervical ganglion, consists primarily of postganglionic fibers derived from the cells of this ganglion. Within the cavernous sinus many of the fibers of the plexus leave the artery to be distributed to the orbit (p. 156), and others leave it, as the deep petrosal nerve, to join the great superficial petrosal, course to the sphenopalatine ganglion, and be distributed through the branches of this ganglion. Perhaps some fibers (p. 336) also reach the skin of the upper part of the face, which is otherwise, however, supplied through the external carotid plexus. Still others are distributed along the intracranial branches of the internal carotid. It has already been mentioned that the internal carotid plexus may contain ganglia, although whether they are all simply misplaced portions of the superior cervical ganglion, as usually supposed, or some are parasympathetic ganglia (p. 41) is not known. It has likewise been pointed out (p. 252) that there is evidence that the internal carotid plexus may contain some afferent fibers from upper thoracic spinal nerves.

The preganglionic fibers reaching the superior cervical ganglion are derived largely from the upper three thoracic nerves by means of their so-called white rami communicantes, which enter the upper thoracic chain and then run upward through this and the cervical chain

to end in the superior cervical ganglion. Interruption of the cervical chain anywhere along its course will therefore interrupt all impulses to the superior cervical ganglion, and be followed by the temporary flushing, the absence of sweating, the myosis, and the ptosis of the upper lid which characterize Horner's syndrome. According to the evidence of Ascroft obtained on the monkey, and that of Ray, Hinsey and Geohegan from experiments in man (p. 155), however, the majority of preganglionic fibers destined for the innervation of the orbit are derived from the first thoracic nerve, so that section of the sympathetic chain below the first thoracic ganglion, sparing the fibers from the first thoracic nerve, apparently leaves the eye unaffected (p. 511).

MIDDLE CERVICAL GANGLION

The middle cervical ganglion is variable both in size and position; sometimes it is impossible to recognize it macroscopically, though there are probably in these cases cells scattered along the nerve trunk, corresponding to this ganglion; in other cases the ganglion may be small or large, or may be doubled. When it can be recognized, it is commonly found in one of two positions: it may lie at about the level of the transverse process of the sixth cervical vertebra (the carotid tubercle), where it is usually associated with the inferior thyroid artery as this vessel loops medially toward the thyroid gland, or it may lie close to the vertebral and subclavian arteries at about the level of the seventh cervical vertebra. The latter seems to be the more common location (for instance, Axford), and a ganglion here is often called the "intermediate" ganglion. The middle cervical ganglion usually sends rami communicantes to about the third and fourth cervical nerves, and from it or the chain close to it arises the middle cardiac nerve.

INFERIOR CERVICAL GANGLION

The inferior cervical ganglion (termed the stellate when it is fused with the first thoracic ganglion and in the English literature sometimes referred to as the stellate ganglion even when it is not so fused) lies typically at about the level of the disc between the seventh cervical and first thoracic vertebrae; the first thoracic ganglion lies upon the transverse process of the first thoracic vertebra and the head of the first rib, behind the pleura. Perlow and Vehe found the two ganglia fused in 40 of 48 sides.

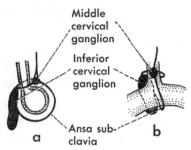

Fig. 305. Relations of the middle and inferior cervical (or stellate) ganglia to each other and to the subclavian and vertebral arteries when the middle ganglion is in a low position. *a.* In a parasagittal section. *b.* From the front.

Depending upon the height to which the subclavian artery ascends, the inferior cervical ganglion or the upper end of the stellate lies either behind or immediately above the upper border of the first part of the artery, and in the latter case usually behind or posteromedial to the vertebral artery (Fig. 305). Perlow and Vehe, however, reported considerable variation in this relation: they described the ganglion as anterior to the vertebral in 2 cases, anteromedial in 16, medial in 23, medial

and posterior in 5, and posterior in only 2. When the middle cervical ganglion is in its low position, it and the upper end of the stellate ganglion lie at about the same vertical level, but are usually separated from each other by the vertebral artery. They are connected both by direct fibers which constitute the lower end of the cervical chain, and by other fibers which loop around the subclavian artery to connect the two ganglia, these fibers constituting the ansa subclavia (ansa Vieussens). The inferior cervical ganglion typically supplies fibers to the sixth, seventh, and eighth spinal nerves, so that with the first thoracic ganglion it would seem to supply most of the postganglionic fibers to the upper limb.

FUNCTIONAL CONNECTIONS

All of the ganglia of the cervical sympathetic chain show considerable variation in their connections to the spinal nerves. The rami communicantes of these nerves have been investigated in considerable detail by Axford and by Siwe; it should be sufficient to point out here that the ganglia vary both in regard to the number of spinal nerves with which they are connected, and in regard to the course which their rami communicantes take. These rami may have small ganglia upon them (Skoog); otherwise, they are composed of postganglionic fibers which are leaving the ganglia to be distributed through the cervical nerves. They may run directly to the nerves, may run along the longus muscles upon which the sympathetic chain lies, or may pierce muscles. Generally speaking, the superior cervical ganglion is connected with about the upper three cervical nerves, the middle cervical with the third and fourth cervical nerves, and the inferior cervical with the lower four cervical nerves. The fibers along the vertebral artery, forming the so-called vertebral nerve, are derived from the inferior cervical ganglion and, except for some which follow the vertebral artery into the cranium as the vertebral plexus, constitute rami communicantes to the sixth or seventh cervical nerves, or both.

The general distribution of postganglionic fibers from the cervical chain, as demonstrated by the anhydrosis produced by injuries to the chain, has been reported for man by List and Peet and by Guttmann; the present writer would emphasize, however, the variations in the chain and its connections, so numerous that any blanket statements about it are apt to be misleading.

Since the postganglionic fibers to the upper limb are derived from the inferior cervical ganglion and upper ganglia of the thoracic sympathetic chain, sympathetic impulses to the limb may be largely blocked by injection of the ganglion or surgical interference with it. In stellate ganglion blocks, the position of the ganglion in relation to the subclavian and vertebral arteries must be clearly borne in mind; the bony landmark for this injection is the transverse process of the seventh cervical vertebra. Murphrey has described a technic which he has found successful in 95.7 per cent of the cases in which it was tried. In the anterior approach for removal of the stellate ganglion, now seldom used, the anterior scalene muscle must be cut and the subclavian artery retracted downward in order to allow an approach to the ganglion.

As discussed in more detail in connection with the thoracic sympathetic chain (Volume 2), removal of the stellate ganglion was for many years the operation of choice in attempts to alleviate the symptoms of Raynaud's disease in the upper limb. Stellectomy and removal of the upper several segments of the thoracic chain result in a postganglionic or anatomical denervation of the blood vessels of the upper limb, and in view of the ensuing sensitivity to epinephrine which has been said to occur after postganglionic denervation was for a time abandoned by many surgeons. In recent years, however, a number of workers have reverted to the postganglionic denervation as the one giving the most favorable and lasting results.

Since the preganglionic fibers to the upper limb are derived largely from below the first thoracic nerve (for instance, Hyndman and Wolkin), an approximate preganglionic denervation such as that described by Smithwick can be carried out through an upper thoracic approach. This usually includes sectioning the thoracic chain below at least the third thoracic ganglion, then reflecting the chain cranially and severing the rami communicantes uniting the more cranial ganglia with the spinal nerves, up to but not including the connection to the first thoracic nerve. Apparently the first thoracic nerve distributes most of its preganglionic fibers to the orbit, and few or none to the limb; thus if its rami communicantes are left intact the limb is at least almost completely denervated, and yet the disagreeable sequelae of Horner's syndrome are avoided.

CRANIAL NERVES IN THE NECK

In addition to the cervical branch of the facial nerve, which descends into the neck to supply the platysma muscle, the ninth through the twelfth cranial nerves are all related to the upper portions of the great vessels of the neck, and the tenth and eleventh run through the neck for a considerable distance.

NINTH NERVE

Within the jugular foramen the glossopharyngeal nerve bears its two ganglia (superior and petrous or inferior) and gives off its tympanic branch to the middle ear cavity (p. 181) and its auricular one to the external ear (p. 170); since section of the nerve outside the foramen is useless in abolishing the pain of glossopharyngeal neuralgia when it involves the ear, and since the approach to the nerve as it leaves the foramen is quite difficult, this nerve is typically sectioned intracranially for glossopharyngeal neuralgia (p. 79). The auricular branch of the ninth nerve typically joins that of the tenth, and apparently varies inversely in size with the latter. Just outside the jugular foramen the ninth nerve sometimes has also a branch of communication with the facial nerve; the functional importance of this branch is not known.

As it emerges from the jugular foramen the glossopharyngeal nerve lies anterolateral to the vagus and spinal accessory nerves, medial to the internal carotid artery and anteromedial to the jugular bulb. Almost immediately upon its exit it passes laterally between the jugular vein and the internal carotid artery (Fig. 306), and then forward between the internal and external carotids, to lie deep to the styloid process and the muscles attached to it. It is most easily located here by looking along the medial surface of the lower border of the stylopharyngeus muscle. It supplies this muscle and curves around its lateral border to lie on the lateral surface of this and subsequently on the middle constrictor of the pharynx as it runs forward toward the tongue

(pp. 382 and 386); as it passes deep to the hyoglossus muscle it gives off its tonsillar and lingual branches.

While the glossopharyngeal is related to the internal carotid artery it gives off its carotid branch or branches (nerve of Hering, carotid sinus nerve, intercarotid nerve) which descends between internal and external carotids to unite with the carotid branch of the vagus and supply the carotid body and carotid sinus (p.

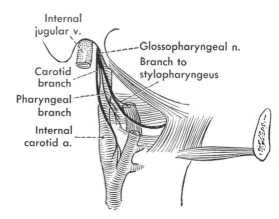

Fig. 306. Course of the glossopharyngeal nerve.

483). Also in this location it gives off its pharyngeal branch or branches which pass forward between internal and external carotid vessels, below the main trunk of the ninth nerve, to unite with the pharyngeal branches of the vagus on the middle constrictor muscle. The pharyngeal branches of the ninth are entirely sensory to the pharynx (p. 423). The motor distribution of the nerve is to the stylopharyngeus muscle only, and is given off while the nerve lies deep to the muscle.

TENTH NERVE

The vagus nerve also makes its exit through the jugular foramen, lying between the glossopharyngeal and the spinal accessory nerves. Within the foramen the vagus bears its jugular or superior ganglion, and at or just distal to this ganglion it receives the internal ramus (accessory branch to vagus) of the accessory nerve, a branch consisting of the so-called bulbar or cranial rootlets of the accessory, the fibers of which are thereafter distributed entirely with the vagus. The bulbar rootlets and internal ramus of the accessory contribute to the vagus the majority of

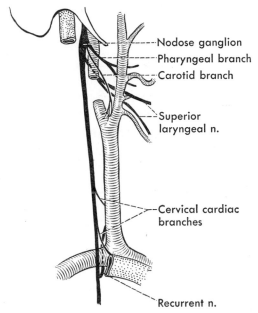

Fig. 307. Course of the right vagus nerve in the neck.

Labels in figure: Nodose ganglion / Pharyngeal branch / Carotid branch / Superior laryngeal n. / Cervical cardiac branches / Recurrent n.

its voluntary motor fibers (p. 76). Just outside the foramen the vagus expands again to form the large nodose or inferior vagal ganglion (Fig. 307). The vagus at first lies medial to both the jugular vein and the carotid artery, but as it descends, and as the vessels shift slightly so that the jugular vein comes to lie lateral to the artery, the vagus lies behind and somewhat between the two. Below the bifurcation of the common carotid it is related in a similar fashion to this vessel and to the

internal jugular vein. As the vagus is enclosed within the carotid sheath, and therefore anterior to the prevertebral fascia, there is no necessity of exposing it in searching for the phrenic nerve; however, it has been mistaken for the phrenic when the carotid sheath was unintentionally opened.

Anomalous positions of the cervical vagus are quite rare; Gibson has described one of the few cases in which the nerve has been found in front of the common carotid instead of behind it. Partial doubling of the trunk in the neck has been reported, according to Taguchi (1888), who himself described a case in which an abnormal branch of the vagus helped to form an ansa "hypoglossi." Von Lippmann described a similar case, in which the origin of the abnormal branch was seen to be from cervical fibers which first joined the vagus and then separated from it.

MENINGEAL, AURICULAR, AND PHARYNGEAL BRANCHES

The meningeal and auricular branches of the vagus (pp. 71 and 170) arise from this nerve within the jugular fossa; the pharyngeal branch arises from the upper part of the nodose ganglion and passes across the lateral side of the internal carotid artery, between this and the external carotid, to join the pharyngeal branch of the glossopharyngeal in forming the pharyngeal plexus (p. 422). The pharyngeal branch of the tenth nerve is the chief motor supply to the pharynx. The vagus also can be shown to contribute fibers to the carotid nerve of Hering, although this is primarily a glossopharyngeal branch. The nodose ganglion usually has communications with the spinal accessory and hypoglossal nerves, the superior cervical ganglion and the upper two spinal nerves, but the nature of these is not understood.

SUPERIOR LARYNGEAL NERVE

From the lower end of the ganglion nodosum arises the superior laryngeal nerve, which usually receives a branch from the superior cervical ganglion of the sympathetic, descends behind the internal carotid artery and divides into its two terminal branches, external and internal. The smaller external branch (external laryngeal nerve) descends and runs forward on the larynx, being closely associated with the superior thyroid artery (p. 521); it usually gives a branch to the inferior pharyngeal constrictor and ends by supplying the cricothyroid muscle. The larger internal branch (internal laryngeal nerve) curves forward on the thyrohyoid membrane and enters the larynx with the superior laryngeal artery, to supply the mucous membrane of the larynx. The superior laryngeal nerve is discussed more fully in the chapter on the larynx (p. 444).

DEPRESSOR NERVES AND CERVICAL CARDIAC BRANCHES

The vagus also contains fibers destined for chemoreceptor tissue and vasodepressor areas in the lower part of the neck and the upper part of the thorax; these constitute the depressor nerves, which usually run with the cervical vagus, but, at least in the cat, may be partly incorporated in the cervical sympathetic chain (Hollinshead, '40b). After their connections and branches high in the neck, the vagus nerves have no other branches until they approach the middle of the neck; here each nerve gives off two or more small cervical cardiac branches (usually termed superior and inferior); the superior cardiac branch arises at about the level of the thyroid cartilage, communicates with cardiac branches of the sympathetic, and runs to the deep cardiac plexus; the inferior cardiac branch typically arises just above the level of the first rib, that on the right passing usually in front of the subclavian artery and across the front of the innominate artery to enter the deep cardiac plexus, while that on the left passes across the arch of the aorta to the superficial cardiac plexus (Volume 2).

RECURRENT NERVES

The recurrent nerves (recurrent laryngeal nerves) are especially important branches of the vagi in the neck, although only the right recurrent arises in the neck; this leaves the right vagus in front of the subclavian artery, and loops below and behind the artery to ascend obliquely to the posterolateral aspect of the trachea and pass upward toward the larynx. The left recurrent nerve arises from the left vagus as this passes across the arch of the aorta, and therefore has a mediastinal origin; it likewise runs upward alongside the trachea to reach the larynx. The somewhat variable relations of the recurrent nerves are described in connection with the thyroid gland (p. 524); their distribution within the larynx is described in connection with this structure (p. 444).

ELEVENTH NERVE

The spinal accessory nerve divides within the jugular foramen into its internal and external rami, and the internal ramus, also called the accessory branch to the vagus, joins the vagus nerve just outside the foramen. The accessory nerve of gross anatomy is therefore purely the spinal portion, derived from the external ramus and taking origin from upper seg-

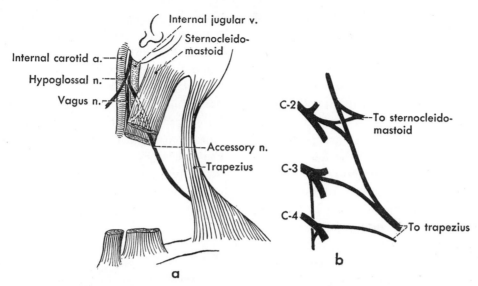

Fig. 308. Usual course and relations, *a*, of the spinal accessory nerve, and its connections, *b*, with the cervical plexus.

ments of the spinal cord (p. 76); it consists entirely of voluntary motor fibers which are distributed to the sternocleidomastoid and trapezius muscles. It is the most posterior of the three nerves leaving the jugular foramen; it at first lies medial to and somewhat between the internal jugular and the internal carotid vessels, and typically passes between the vein and the artery to cross the lateral surface of the vein (Fig. 308). This is not a fixed relation, however, for the nerve sometimes passes behind the vein rather than in front of it. Tandler found the accessory nerve passing anterior to the vein in two thirds of 150 cases, and passing behind it in the other third; similarly, Parsons and Keith summarized it as anterior in 70 per cent, posterior in 26.8 per cent, and passing through the vein in 3.2 per cent of 415 sides (Fig. 309). This apparently depends upon the fact that in the embryo a venous ring is about the nerve, and the relation of the latter to the vein varies according to which segment of the ring persists.

After crossing the internal jugular vein, the accessory nerve descends obliquely downward and backward to the upper part of the sternocleidomastoid; it gives

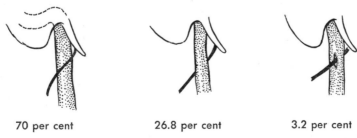

70 per cent   26.8 per cent   3.2 per cent

Fig. 309. Variations in the relations of the spinal accessory nerve to the internal jugular vein. The percentages given are those of Parsons and Keith.

off its branch into the deep surface of this muscle some 1½ or more inches (4 cm. or more) below the tip of the mastoid process, and may pass downward and backward either deep to the sternocleidomastoid or through it (about 18 and 82 per cent, respectively, according to Parsons and Keith) to course across the posterior triangle and enter the deep surface of the trapezius. In the posterior triangle it lies between two layers of fascia, the anterior (or superficial) layer of the deep fascia and the prevertebral layer of this fascia. The accessory nerve is typically joined before it enters the sternocleidomastoid by a branch from the second cervical nerve, and is also joined as it enters the trapezius by branches from the third and fourth cervical nerves. These are believed to be entirely sensory (p. 496).

Coleman and Walker have indicated their belief that the spinal accessory nerve is highly variable, and have described it as dividing into sternocleidomastoid and trapezius branches so high that one branch passes behind, the other in front of, the internal jugular vein. They have also stated that the nerve may fail to reach the trapezius, which in these cases is then supplied by cervical nerves. As they have given no detail of their anatomical researches—for instance, the number of cadavers investigated, and whether the observations were on students' dissections or on dissections carried out personally—it is impossible to assess these statements. The present writer would however call attention to the fact that sensory fibers only have been demonstrated in the cervical nerve supply to the trapezius in carefully controlled experiments, and that the sole evidence of a motor supply from this source rests upon

debatable clinical evidence. The variation in the obvious crippling of the shoulder following section of the accessory nerve, which these observations purport to explain, can undoubtedly usually be explained upon the basis of variation in the degree to which other muscles compensate for paralysis of the trapezius. The accessory nerve is sometimes purposefully sectioned so that it can be used in a spinofacial anastomosis for alleviation of facial paralysis (p. 328).

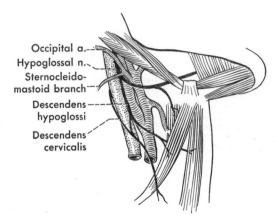

Occipital a.
Hypoglossal n.
Sternocleido-
mastoid branch
Descendens
hypoglossi
Descendens
cervicalis

Fig. 310. Hypoglossal nerve in the neck. The branches shown (descendens hypoglossi and nerve to the thyrohyoid) are not actually composed of hypoglossal fibers (Fig. 277).

TWELFTH NERVE

The hypoglossal nerve emerges through the hypoglossal foramen (anterior condylar canal), and therefore medial to the internal jugular vein and internal carotid artery. It passes laterally and downward to lie against the posterior aspect of the vagus nerve, where it exchanges branches of communication with this nerve and with the sympathetic, and then runs downward and outward between the jugular vein and the internal carotid artery (Fig. 310). Close to its exit from the skull it receives branches of communication from upper cervical nerves, usually the second; it is these fibers which leave it as the descendens hypoglossi, the nerve to the thyrohyoid, and the nerve to the geniohyoid. The hypoglossal nerve itself probably supplies only muscles of the tongue.

As the nerve emerges between the jugular and internal carotid vessels or, rarely, posterior to the internal jugular—Löwy found this in only 8 of 100 cases—it lies under cover of the posterior belly of the digastric muscle. It passes forward across the lateral surfaces of both the internal and the external carotid arteries, giving off the descendens hypoglossi as it does so, and passing lateral to the origin of the occipital artery from the external carotid, so that it loops forward about this vessel and its sternocleidomastoid branch. Below the angle of the jaw it is accessible as it lies deep to the posterior end of the submaxillary gland, before it passes forward to the tongue. Its further course has been described in connection with the tongue (p. 385). Like the accessory nerve, the hypoglossal is sometimes sectioned and united to the distal stem of the facial nerve in paralysis of the facial muscles (p. 328).

The two branches of the hypoglossal nerve in the neck are the descendens hypoglossi and the nerve to the thyrohyoid muscle. The descendens hypoglossi leaves the hypoglossal stem as this turns forward around the origin of the occipital artery, and descends on the internal carotid and then the common carotid arteries, either in front of or within the carotid sheath, gives off a branch to the superior belly of the omohyoid and then joins the descendens cervicalis to form the ansa hypoglossi. As both the descendens hypoglossi and the descendens cervicalis are composed of cervical nerve fibers, the strap muscles of the neck are innervated entirely through cervical nerves and not by the hypoglossal nerve itself. The ansa hypoglossi may be either a short or a long loop, that is, the union between the descendens cervicalis and the descendens hypoglossi may be situated high or low in the neck; also, the descendens cervicalis may pass either medial to the internal jugular vein to join the descendens hypoglossi between the internal jugular and carotid, or may pass posterior and then lateral to the vein to join the descendens hypoglossi and form an ansa hypoglossi across the front of the internal jugular vein. Both these relationships occur frequently; Grant reported that the descendens cervicalis passed medial to the internal jugular vein in 43 per cent of 118 cases, and lateral to it in 57 per cent.

VISCERAL STRUCTURES OF THE NECK

THE visceral structures of the neck include the thyroid and parathyroid glands, a portion of the pharynx, the larynx, trachea, and esophagus, and sometimes portions of the thymus. The pharynx and larynx have already been described in Chapter 8. Only the other structures in the neck will therefore be described here.

THYROID GLAND

The thyroid gland lies below and on the sides of the thyroid cartilage, covered (Fig. 275, p. 458) by the infrahyoid strap muscles of the neck with the exception of the thyrohyoid muscle. In seeking access to the thyroid gland, the sternohyoid and sternothyroid muscles must be separated from the gland, or cut and reflected; if they are sectioned transversely at about the level of the isthmus of the gland their innervation is probably least apt to be injured, although the levels at which the nerves enter these muscles vary considerably (p. 462). If the gland is much enlarged, the strap muscles may be so thinned as to be barely identifiable.

The thyroid gland consists of two lateral lobes situated anterolateral to the larynx and trachea and united across the front, just below the cricoid cartilage, by an isthmus. It therefore partially surrounds the trachea, and enlargements of it may early produce dyspnea. Sometimes the gland expands also somewhat behind the trachea; this is important clinically, since it brings the gland into close contact with the recurrent nerve even when this is situated deeply in the tracheo-esophageal groove; Else regarded this relationship as often responsible for the recurrence of goiter, owing to incomplete removal of this part of the gland. From the isthmus, but not always in the midline, a process of thyroid tissue may project upward; this is the pyramidal process, and may be a short stump or rise high enough to be attached to the hyoid bone (Fig. 311).

THYROID FASCIA AND CAPSULE

The thyroid gland lies in the visceral compartment of the neck, and is of course invested by connective tissue. The thin layer of connective tissue between the posterior surfaces of the strap muscles and the thyroid gland is usually referred to as the pretracheal fascia; connective tissue in relation to the thyroid has been called the perithyroid sheath, thyroid fascia, and false thyroid capsule. The terminology here as used in the clinical

literature is confusing, however, for this delicate connective tissue layer, united loosely to the thyroid gland, has also been called simply *the* capsule of the thyroid gland. Thus, for instance, Fowler and Hanson identified the capsule of the thyroid gland as the tissue usually described

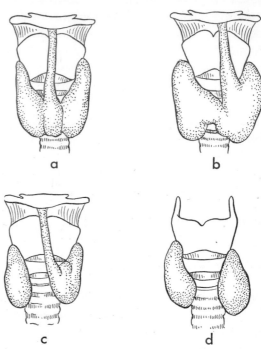

Fig. 311. Some unusual forms of the thyroid gland. *a*, *b*, and *c* all have large pyramidal processes extending to the hyoid bone; in *b* and *c* the process is asymmetrically attached to the thyroid gland; in *c* and *d* the isthmus is lacking. (Redrawn from Marshall, C. F.: *J. Anat. & Physiol. 29*:234, 1895.)

as pretracheal fascia, and failed to find it as definitely developed as it is often described. They also found that it did not envelop the thyroid gland posteriorly, but rather ran behind the esophagus; they stated that the recurrent nerves lie inside this so-called capsule when it is well developed. Ziegelman described the false capsule as failing to envelop the gland posteriorly, while others have described or diagrammed it as completely surrounding the gland. There thus appears to be no clear agreement as to what constitutes the thyroid fascia.

It is presumably also the varying development of the connective tissue adjacent to the thyroid gland that accounts for the various statements concerning the relations of the parathyroid glands to this layer. For instance, Walton has stated that the normal superior parathyroid glands always lie between the thyroid fascia and the gland itself, while the inferior parathyroids may lie either within or without this fascia, or be embedded in it. Most anatomy texts describe the parathyroid glands as lying between the fascia and the thyroid gland itself, except of course for aberrant ones which are not so closely connected with the thyroid gland.

While it seems reasonable, therefore, to regard the perithyroid sheath or thyroid fascia as being the more or less well developed condensation of connective tissue about the thyroid gland after the visceral compartment has been entered, this "fascia" should not be confused with the true capsule of the thyroid gland. The latter term should be reserved for the connective tissue forming the surface of the gland, binding it together and sending septa between the lobules; the true capsule is thus an integral part of the gland, not separable from the parenchyma except by sharp dissection; in it run the larger branches of the vessels as they enter the gland, and subcapsular dissections are made by incising it.

VARIATIONS IN SHAPE

Although the two lobes of the thyroid are usually approximately symmetrical, Marshall recorded a number of variations in the form of the gland in children; while he reported upon 60 cases, a great majority of which he apparently regarded as in some degree abnormal, it is not evident that these were not largely selected cases. The percentages which he quoted are certainly not encountered routinely in the dissecting laboratory. In 7 per cent of his cases one lateral lobe was markedly larger than the other, and in 1 case the right lobe was absent entirely, while in 6 cases (10 per cent of the 60 he investigated) the isthmus was entirely absent (Fig. 311). In these children, also, a pyramidal process was present in 43 per cent, but in not all of these was it symmetrically placed. The pyramidal process was sometimes found connected to the isthmus and sometimes to one of the lateral lobes; similarly, the isthmus was sometimes found to be symmetrically placed while in other cases it was quite broadly confluent with one of the two lateral lobes.

LEVATOR GLANDULAE THYROIDEAE MUSCLE

An occasional anomaly encountered in connection with the thyroid gland is the occurrence of a muscular slip, or sometimes of paired slips, which attach to it, descending from the region of the pharynx or the hyoid bone. Such a slip, known as the levator glandulae thyroideae muscle, is more frequent on the left side, but may be more or less bilaterally symmetrical or occur only on the right (Fig. 312). It is usually assumed to be a derivative from the strap muscles of the neck, but its innervation is not always in accord with this. In the case recorded by Keyes, for instance, a left levator of the thyroid gland was supplied by a branch from the external laryngeal ramus of the right superior laryngeal nerve, while no branch was found to the right levator.

Eisler, in an extensive study of these

muscles and their innervations, has pointed out that they probably represent any one of several discrete muscle bundles. He stated that the levator of the thyroid gland may be innervated either through the ansa hypoglossi or through the vagus, usually in the latter case by the superior laryngeal branch. He regarded levators of the thyroid as divisible into three groups—anterior levators, derived from the cricothyroid and innervated by the external branch of the

superior laryngeal branch of the vagus, and he expressed the belief that it represented a derivative of the cricothyroid muscle.

BLOOD SUPPLY

The thyroid gland and the adrenal gland have each been stated to have the most abundant blood supply of any organ in the body for their size. Whichever really deserves this honor, the thyroid is

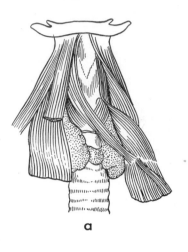
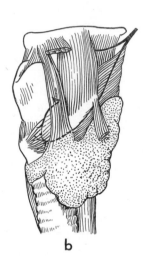

Fig. 312. Two forms of the levator glandulae thyroideae. In *a* it is pretracheal and runs obliquely from one side to the other; its nerve supply was not identified. In *b* it is confined to one side and seems to be associated with the strap muscles, but is innervated by the external branch of the superior laryngeal nerve. (Redrawn from Eisler, P.: *Anat. Anz. 17:*183, 1900.)

vated by the external branch of the superior laryngeal nerve; lateral levators, derived from the thyrohyoid muscle or from the infrahyoid muscle group as a whole, attaching to the hyoid bone, and innervated from the ansa hypoglossi; and posterior levators, innervated like the anterior ones by the superior laryngeal branch of the vagus, and apparently derived from the inferior constrictor of the pharynx. In a case which he described, the muscle, although attached to the hyoid bone, was innervated through the

a very vascular structure, being supplied by four main arteries—two superior thyroid and two inferior thyroid (Fig. 313 and Fig. 320, p. 533).

SUPERIOR THYROID ARTERY

Of these arteries the superior thyroid, although the smaller, is the more constant. It arises usually as the first branch of the external carotid in the superior carotid triangle, but may (about 16 per cent) be a branch from the common carotid. In its descent toward the apex of the lateral lobe of the thyroid gland this artery lies close against (usually just superficial to, but sometimes slightly below) the external branch of the superior laryngeal nerve; the nerve is therefore liable to damage in placing a clamp upon the artery, and, if the upper pole of the gland is particularly high, the internal branch

membrane to enter the larynx; a crico-thyroid artery which runs upon the crico-thyroid membrane close to the lower border of the thyroid cartilage; and numerous branches to the thyroid gland.

Delitzen described one of the rare cases of an abnormal superior thyroid artery—in this case, it continued in-

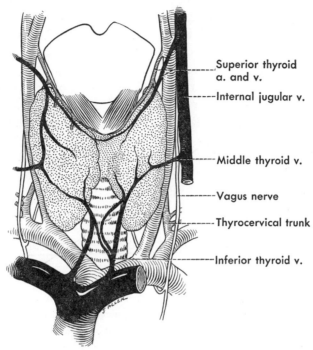

Superior thyroid a. and v.
Internal jugular v.

Middle thyroid v.

Vagus nerve

Thyrocervical trunk

Inferior thyroid v.

Fig. 313. Arteries and veins of the thyroid gland, from the front. (From Hollinshead, W. H.: *S. Clin. North America 32*:1115, 1952.)

of the superior laryngeal may also be liable to damage in this manner (Roeder). These nerves are discussed in connection with the larynx (p. 444). The superior thyroid arteries descend on the anterior surface of the medial side of the lateral lobes of the thyroid and usually anastomose above the isthmus with each other.

In its course each vessel gives off a superior laryngeal artery, which accompanies the internal branch of the superior laryngeal nerve across the thyrohyoid

feriorly after supplying the thyroid gland, and ended in the upper part of the pectoralis major.

INFERIOR THYROID ARTERY

The usual origin of the inferior thyroid artery from the thyrocervical trunk has already been described (p. 470). While the superior thyroid artery is variable primarily only in regard to its exact origin, the inferior thyroid is much more variable in both its origin and relations. Typically it ascends along the medial side of the anterior scalene muscle and behind the prevertebral fascia, loops downward and medially on the anterior surface of the longus cervicis, here being variously related (p. 473) to the cervical sympathetic chain and frequently also to the middle cervical ganglion, penetrates the prevertebral fascia and, at about the point of its branching, crosses the more vertically directed inferior laryngeal nerve. The artery typically divides into two major branches, an upper and a lower, but may be subdivided into a larger number; the lower artery runs toward the lower pole, the upper lies on the posterior surface of the gland at about the junction of its upper two thirds and lower third and is, according to Bachhuber, frequently the major branch of the vessel. He found it absent in only 3 of 200 sides.

One inferior thyroid artery is sometimes absent; Faller and Schärer found this to be true in 6 per cent of 100 sides which they investigated, and reported that the incidence of absence has been given in the literature as from 0.2 to 5.9 per cent. In the absence of an inferior thyroid artery, its place is usually taken by a branch from the superior thyroid artery of the same side, or from the inferior thyroid artery of the other side; less frequently, its place is taken by a thyroid ima artery (see the following section). Rarely, doubling of an inferior thyroid artery may occur, as in the case reported by Jenny.

Normally, anastomoses of considerable size exist between the superior and inferior thyroid arteries, of the same and the opposite sides. Stewart ('32) has stated that it has been shown that the superior and inferior thyroid arteries on the same side always communicate; that the two superior, or one superior and a contralateral inferior, anastomose in 80 per cent of cases; that direct communications between all four vessels occur in 20 per cent of cases. Presumably he was describing large superficially placed anastomoses; although the superior thyroid artery has been regarded as being distributed primarily to the septa, while the inferior really supplies the parenchyma (for instance, Rogers), this view is scarcely tenable; whether large anastomoses exist or not, the smaller branches of the various vessels anastomose abundantly with each other; moreover, there are also numerous fine anastomoses between the thyroid vessels and those of the trachea and esophagus, and one or all of the thyroid arteries may be ligated without fear of producing necrosis of the gland.

The relationship of the inferior thyroid artery to the recurrent nerve is of considerable importance; this is recounted in more detail in a following section (p. 525), but it may be stated here that the nerve more commonly passes behind the inferior thyroid artery or its main branches on the left than on the right, but may pass in front of these, or between the major branches, on either side.

THYROID IMA ARTERY

Occasionally there is present, as either accessory to or replacing the inferior thyroid artery, a vessel known as the thyroid ima artery. This has been variously defined, so much so that Pratt concluded that it would never have received a special name were it not for its importance in tracheotomy, but would have been regarded simply as an aberrant inferior thyroid. As usually described, the thyroid ima artery arises from the innominate (probably the most common origin), from the right common carotid (reported as occurring in as much as 2 per cent of bodies), from the aortic arch directly (reported to have an incidence of 0.36 per cent or more), or, even more rarely, from the internal mammary, an anterior mediastinal vessel (Kimmel), or either subclavian.

With the exception of the latter origin, in which case the vessel may be regarded as a thyroid ima but is more commonly regarded as an inferior thyroid of aberrant origin, any vessel to the thyroid with such origin is usually designated as a thyroid ima, regardless of whether an inferior thyroid proper is present or not. The vessel more commonly arises on the right, and tends to ascend in front of the trachea—hence its importance in tracheotomy. The reported incidence of occurrence of the thyroid ima artery varies widely, presumably because of the variations in the way the vessel is defined. Faller and Schärer found a reported incidence in the literature of from 1.5 to 12.2 per cent, and 2 cases (4 per cent) in the 50 bodies they themselves investigated. The thyroid ima may be a large trunk fully capable of replacing an inferior thyroid, or merely an accessory twig.

VENOUS DRAINAGE OF THYROID

The venous drainage of the thyroid gland is by two or three pairs of veins, which anastomose freely on the gland. The superior thyroid vein emerges from the upper part of the thyroid gland and accompanies the superior thyroid artery, emptying into the internal jugular vein or the common facial vein at about the level of the carotid bifurcation. The middle thyroid vein, variable both as to its presence and its size, arises from the lateral surface of the thyroid at about the level of junction of the upper two thirds

and lower third, and drains laterally into the internal jugular vein, crossing in front of the common carotid artery; it may be torn in separating the gland from the carotid sheath. Bachhuber found a middle thyroid vein in only slightly more than half of the 100 bodies he investigated. When it is not present, its place is taken by a vein which drains into either the superior or inferior thyroid vein.

The two inferior thyroid veins descend from the lower part of the thyroid gland; the right passes typically anterior to the innominate artery to empty into the right innominate vein, or in front of the trachea to join the left innominate, while the left passes obliquely over the trachea to join the left innominate vein. When, as sometimes happens, the right inferior thyroid vein joins the left, so that both veins drain by a common stem into the left innominate vein, the common stem is referred to as the thyroid ima vein. Even when this junction does not occur, the two inferior thyroids may anastomose freely with each other, or may form a plexus in front of the trachea. They are always, therefore, a definite potential source of bleeding in a tracheotomy. The thyroid veins receive also branches from the strap muscles, and from the larynx and trachea.

NERVES

Nerve fibers have been described as reaching the thyroid gland from both the superior cervical ganglion and the superior laryngeal branch of the vagus (Nonidez, '31), but degeneration experiments have apparently shown that the great majority of the fibers are sympathetic ones (Holmgren and Naumann). The vagal fibers are said to form sensory arborizations upon the blood vessels (Nonidez, '35).

Within the gland the nerves form

perivascular and interfollicular (or peri-
follicular) plexuses; a few observers (for
instance, Rhinehart) have reported nerve
endings about the bases of the follicular
cells, but the majority of workers have
failed to find such endings. Most observations have indicated that the interfollicular plexus is really a portion of
the perivascular one, and is actually
not in contact with the follicular cells.
Similarly, a variety of experiments (Smith
and Moloy; Holmgren and Naumann)
have indicated that the nerves are entirely related functionally to the blood
vessels and that, as is usual in the case of
endocrine glands, their stimulation or
ablation does not materially affect the
function of the glandular tissue itself.

LYMPHATICS

The lymphatic drainage of the thyroid
gland is chiefly by vessels which accompany the arterial blood supply (Fig. 314).
The superior lymphatic channels drain
the cranial border of the isthmus, much
of the medial surface of the lateral lobes,
and the ventral and dorsal surfaces of the
upper part of the lateral lobes. The inferior channels drain the major portion
of the isthmus and the lower portions of
the lateral lobes. The upper channels
empty into the upper deep cervical nodes,
the lower ones into the lower deep cervical nodes including the supraclaviculars,
and into the pretracheal and prelaryngeal
nodes. Mahorner, Caylor, Schlotthauer,
and Pemberton described an additional
drainage, from the middle of each lateral
lobe, which passes directly laterally to
enter the deep cervical nodes. While they
found the majority of the efferents from
the thyroid to end in regional nodes as
expected, in 3 of 23 cases they traced a
lymph channel from the right lobe di-

rectly into the right subclavian vein, without passing through a node.

RELATIONS OF THE RECURRENT NERVE

Among the most important relations
of the thyroid gland are those to the recurrent (recurrent laryngeal) nerves and

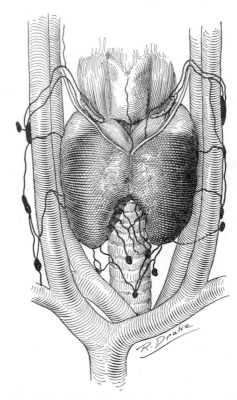

Fig. 314. Usual lymphatic drainage of the
thyroid gland. Deep cervical and anterior
cervical nodes are shown. (From Mahorner,
H. R., Caylor, H. D., Schlotthauer, C. F., and
Pemberton, J. de J.: *Anat. Rec. 36*:341, 1927.)

the parathyroid glands. The right recurrent nerve arises from the vagus as this
trunk passes in front of the subclavian
artery, curves below and behind the subclavian, and then passes upward, angling
somewhat medially, to run within the so-
called pretracheal or visceral compartment of the neck. The left recurrent nerve
arises from the left vagus as this passes

in front of the arch of the aorta, the nerve passing below and upward behind the aorta at the point of attachment of the ligamentum arteriosum. Its course in the neck is essentially similar to that on the right side, as it ascends more or less in the angle between the esophagus and trachea, within the visceral compartment.

Close to their origins the two recurrent nerves usually give rise to cardiac branches, and as they ascend on either side of the trachea they give off branches to the trachea and the esophagus. The terminal portion of each recurrent nerve, before it enters the larynx, is usually termed the inferior laryngeal nerve; the distribution of this to the laryngeal musculature has already been discussed in connection with the larynx (p. 445).

As the recurrent nerves ascend in the neck they necessarily cross the inferior thyroid arteries (which arise lateral to them) and turn medially to reach the thyroid gland; situated as they are somewhat close to the trachea, the nerves also come in more or less direct contact with the posterior or posteromedial surface of the thyroid gland. The relationship between the nerve on the one hand and the artery and gland on the other is of considerable importance to surgeons, and especially so if a total thyroidectomy or removal of tumors from the posterior surface of the gland is to be attempted. Unfortunately, these relations are not constant.

RELATIONSHIP TO TRACHEA

In the first place, the two recurrent nerves are not necessarily tucked into the groove between the trachea and esophagus, as so often stated; they may run considerably farther laterally than this, and the right is especially apt to do so (Fig. 320, p. 533). Berlin, for instance,

noted that the right recurrent nerve may be as much as a centimeter lateral to the trachea; in dissections upon 70 cadavers he found the right recurrent nerve to be in the tracheo-esophageal sulcus in only 42 of these, the left to be similarly situated in 49; in a similar series of 70 operations, in only some of which the nerve was exposed, he concluded that the nerve was in the sulcus in 41 cases on the right, and 45 on the left.

RELATIONSHIP TO INFERIOR THYROID ARTERY

The relationship of the recurrent nerve to the inferior thyroid artery is also variable (Fig. 315). Depending upon the distance from the tracheo-esophageal groove at which the recurrent nerve lies, and upon the point at which the artery divides, the nerve may cross either the main artery or its branches. Further, it may pass behind the artery, in front of it, between its two major branches or among minor branches of these; or the recurrent itself may divide before reaching the level of the artery and a part pass in front of and another part behind the main inferior thyroid or some of its branches. These variations have been the subject of a number of investigations which have sought to establish the relative frequency of the different patterns so constantly observed in the dissecting room, but the tabulations of various workers do not agree very closely.

From the combined series of Taguchi (1889) and Fowler and Hanson, totalling 522 sides, it would appear that the nerve is more commonly posterior to the artery than anterior to it (in 299 instances it was posterior, in 114 anterior); Taguchi described it as passing between the branches of the artery in 75 of his 122 cases, however, while Fowler and Hanson, disregarding the smaller branches of the artery, reported the nerve as between branches of the artery in only 34 of their series of 400.

Neither of these papers indicated a possible difference between the right and left sides, for sides were not recorded. Nordland, in a short series of 62 sides, found the nerve anterior to the artery more often than posterior, but no marked difference in sides, while Berlin and Lahey, and Berlin, the latter in a series

Bachhuber found the nerve posterior in 55 per cent, anterior in 11 per cent and between in 33 per cent, while Reed found it posterior in 51.4 per cent, anterior in 11.5 per cent, and between in 33.1 per cent. Bachhuber found the nerve dividing into branches while related to the artery in only 2 cases (1 per cent), while Reed found it thus dividing in 5.4 per cent.

From the various figures quoted above, it is obviously impossible to establish

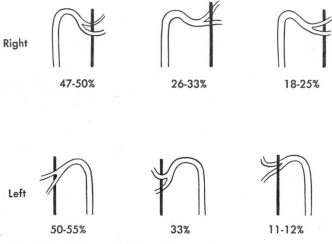

Right 47-50% 26-33% 18-25%

Left 50-55% 33% 11-12%

Fig. 315. Three chief relations between the recurrent nerve (black) and the inferior thyroid artery, and the approximate percentages in which these have been described as occurring on each side. (From Hollinshead, W. H.: *S. Clin. North America* 32:1115, 1952.)

of 70 dissections, found that the left nerve was more commonly posterior to the artery than was the right. Bachhuber's series of 200 sides, and Reed's ('43) series of 506 sides support this conclusion, and are also in fair agreement with each other. On the right side, Bachhuber found the nerve posterior to the artery in 33 per cent, anterior to it in 18 per cent, and passing between branches of the vessel in 48 per cent, while Reed found it posterior in 26.9 per cent, anterior in 25.7 per cent, and between branches in 47.6 per cent; on the left side,

any statistically valid conclusions; the situation appears even more complicated by the fact that in 253 bodies Reed found a total of twenty-eight different types, and that in only 17 per cent of bodies were the relations of the nerve to the artery alike on both sides. However, it appears obvious that the nerve rather frequently passes between either the main or minor branches of the artery, and that this is somewhat more common (about 50 per cent) on the right; that on the left the most common position of the nerve (approximately 50 per cent) is behind the artery, and only relatively rarely (about 10 to 12 per cent) does it pass in front, while on the right side it is in front and behind in more nearly equal proportion (roughly 25 per cent).

It is the varying but close relation between the inferior thyroid artery and the recurrent nerve that makes it dangerous to attempt to control bleeding at this level by the use of hemostats, and that has led to the practice of ligating the artery well laterally. Also, the fact that the nerve may pass in front of the artery or some of its branches means that it is held relatively close to the gland, and is necessarily dragged forward as the lateral lobe is rotated at operation.

RELATIONSHIP TO THYROID GLAND

Obviously, the closeness of the relationship between the recurrent nerve and the thyroid gland during operation varies in part according to whether the nerve lies deeply in the tracheo-esophageal groove or more laterally, where it is necessarily more closely applied to the posterior surface of the lateral lobe, and in part according to whether the nerve passes in front of the inferior thyroid artery or some of its branches. There is also an additional factor affecting this relationship: At the level of the upper two or three tracheal rings, the thyroid gland is attached to the larynx by a considerable quantity of connective tissue; the recurrent nerve at this level—that is, at about the middle third of the thyroid gland—is here in closest contact with the thyroid gland and may lie against its posterior surface, pass through the adherent zone, or even penetrate the gland itself (Fig. 316).

Of 140 nerves dissected in cadavers, Berlin found 10 per cent actually penetrating the gland for a short distance,

and 25 per cent passing through the adherent zone; in a similar number of operations he identified the recurrent nerves in 52 per cent, and found the recurrent penetrating the thyroid gland in 7 per cent, and passing through the adherent zone in 31 per cent. Thus in a total thyroidectomy or removal of a tumor from the posterior surface of the thyroid

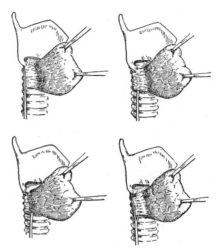

Fig. 316. Varying relations of the recurrent nerve to the adherent zone of the thyroid gland. (From Berlin, D. D.: by permission of *Surg., Gynec. & Obst. 60:19, 1935.*)

it is entirely possible to elevate the recurrent nerve with the lateral lobe of the thyroid, and therefore to section it inadvertently in removing thyroid tissue.

EXTRALARYNGEAL DIVISION OF NERVE

The recurrent or inferior laryngeal nerve is usually described as dividing into anterior and posterior ("adductor" and "abductor") branches as it enters the larynx, but may do so outside the larynx. It has already been noted that Bachhuber found this to be true in at least 1 per cent, and Reed found it in at least 5.4 per cent of cases (they apparently listed only the extralaryngeal divisions which occurred while the nerve was in contact with the inferior thyroid artery), but Weeks and Hinton found such a division to be quite common in the small number of cases which they investigated—in only 1 of 20 sides did the nerve fail to divide before entering the larynx, and the level of division varied from 1 to 4 cm. below this point.

This extraordinarily high percentage has not been found in more extensive series, but investigations on this particular point indicate that extralaryngeal division of the nerve is certainly common rather than rare. King and Gregg described the nerve as dividing while in relation to the thyroid gland in 8 of 32 sides (25 per cent); they stated that in some of these cases the two branches of the nerve were a full quarter of an inch (0.6 cm.) apart, and called attention to the significance of this fact, which may allow differential injury to the abductor and adductor portions of the nerve, in the interpretation of the behavior of paralyzed vocal cords. Armstrong and Hinton have reported extralaryngeal division of the recurrent nerve in 73 per cent of 100 sides; Morrison found the nerve divided 0.5 cm. or more below the level of the cricothyroid joint on at least one side in 43 per cent of 100 cadavers, and stated that in the majority of these the divided nerve lay in the region involved in operations upon the thyroid gland. There is apparently no significant difference in the incidence of extralaryngeal division of left and right nerves. The distribution of the recurrent nerve within the larynx, and the consequences of its injury during operations on the thyroid, are discussed in connection with the larynx (pp. 445 and 447).

ANOMALOUS RECURRENT NERVE

Finally, it should be mentioned that the recurrent laryngeal nerve may be anomalous, in that it may arise from the cervical portion of the vagus at about the level of the larynx or thyroid gland, and run rather directly to the larynx without looping about the subclavian artery, and thus without ascending through the major part of its usual course. An anomalous inferior laryngeal (which is not, strictly speaking, a recurrent nerve, though it

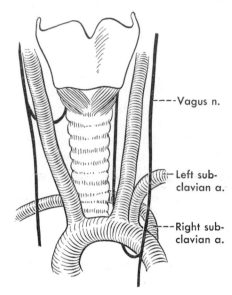

Fig. 317. Anomalous right "recurrent" nerve. Note the anomalous (retroesophageal) right subclavian artery, the occurrence of which is responsible for the anomaly of the nerve.

may loop around the inferior thyroid artery) is found far more frequently on the right side, since it is always associated with an anomalous (retro-esophageal) subclavian artery (Fig. 317). Only in the rare cases in which there has been a persistent right instead of a left aortic arch, and at the same time an anomalous or retro-esophageal left subclavian artery, can a similar disposition of the inferior laryngeal nerve occur on the left side. Retro-esophageal right subclavian arteries are believed to occur in about 1 per cent of individuals. They are discussed in connection with the thorax, and the embryology which is responsible for the associated anomaly of the inferior laryngeal nerve is there explained (Volume 2).

THYROGLOSSAL CYSTS AND FISTULAE

Since the thyroid gland, or at least the major portion of it, develops as a diverticulum from the floor of the pharynx at the level of the first pharyngeal pouches, ectopic thyroid glands and remains of the one-time connection of the thyroid to the pharynx (thyroglossal duct) may be located anywhere along the original pathway of this duct between the foramen caecum on the tongue and the thyroid gland itself. A common occurrence of thyroid tissue outside the major body of the gland is the pyramidal lobe, usually in the midline and sometimes extending as high as the hyoid bone; although this is generally not regarded as ectopic thyroid tissue, because of its common occurrence, failure to remove it may sometimes be the cause of a recurrence of goiter. The most striking type of ectopic thyroid, which may represent the entire thyroid anlage or may be coexistent with thyroid tissue in the neck, is the lingual thyroid, discussed on page 395.

Persistence of portions of the thyroglossal duct itself, which normally begins to atrophy about the fifth to sixth week of development, may give rise to fistulous tracts connected to the tongue, or to cysts along the original course of the duct. External fistulous openings on the neck, if developed from the thyroglossal duct, are necessarily secondary openings, for the duct does not, of course, open to the outside.

Thyroglossal cysts and fistulae have been discussed in connection with the tongue (p. 394), for the cysts may have a suprahyoid position; the large majority, however, are infrahyoid (for instance, Bailey, '25; Hubert; Marshall and Becker). They occur most commonly immediately below the hyoid bone, and according to Marshall and Becker cysts at this level are often displaced to the left side. Some retrosternal cysts have also been thought to be thyroglossal ones, but if so must represent an abnormal migration of the remains of the duct. Finally, it should be emphasized again that thyroglossal cysts and fistulae require complete surgical removal; if the tract extends both above and below the hyoid bone a midsection of the bone itself should be removed, and the tissue about the fistulous tract should be dissected with care. While His expressed the belief that the thyroglossal duct always lies deep to the hyoid bone, it has since been shown that the relationship varies—the duct may pass behind the hyoid bone, in front of it, or even through it.

LATERAL ABERRANT THYROID GLANDS

Weller described the thyroid gland as arising from three primordia, namely, the large unpaired primordium from the floor of the pharynx, which contributes by far the greater amount of tissue to the thyroid gland, and small lateral paired diverticula from the junction of the fourth pharyngeal (branchial) pouch and the pharynx; these diverticula are sometimes regarded as rudimentary fifth branchial pouches, but are usually known as the ultimobranchial or postbranchial bodies (Fig. 318). The ultimobranchial bodies and the parathyroid glands derived from the fourth branchial pouches are closely associated in their development, and in an early stage of development become associated with the lateral lobes of the thyroid gland.

SUPPOSED EMBRYOLOGY

Weller has maintained that the ultimo-branchial body constitutes actually a lateral thyroid primordium, which undergoes the same change that occurs in the thyroglossal portion of the thyroid gland, becoming transformed into true thyroid tissue which is normally added to the lateral lobes of the gland. This view has been supported also by the investigations of Norris ('37), but does not agree with extensive researches carried out by Kings-

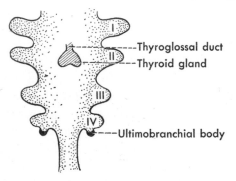

Fig. 318. Diagram of a ventral view of the pharynx to show the origin of the thyroid gland and the position of the ultimobranchial body (which has been regarded as contributing to the thyroid—see text). The Roman numerals identify the pharyngeal pouches.

bury on the fate of the ultimobranchial bodies in animals.

There are therefore two views as to the fate of the ultimobranchial bodies: one that they become transformed into true thyroid tissue and the other that they join the thyroid but lose their identity by degenerating. An attempt to answer the question as to which of these views is correct has been reported by Ramsay; he transplanted in the embryo of the mouse a portion of the pharyngeal pouch which gives rise to thymic and parathyroid tissue, and to the ultimobranchial body; in the successful transplants he was able to recognize both thymic and parathyroid tissue, but no thyroid tissue; on the other

hand, when he transplanted the thyroid anlage either before or after it was visible as a diverticulum in the floor of the pharynx, he was able to identify thyroid material in the transplant in 88 per cent of the experiments. On the basis of these experiments, it seems reasonable to conclude that if the ultimobranchial body (of the mouse) does produce thyroid tissue, it must be through an induction brought about by its relation to the thyroid gland, and not through its own inherent thyroid-forming potentialities. It seems quite probable that the contribution of the ultimobranchial body to the thyroid in the human being has been much exaggerated.

TUMORS

The concept of a separate lateral contribution to the thyroid gland has undoubtedly influenced views concerning the identity of so-called lateral aberrant thyroid tumors, and has in turn been thought to be supported by the occurrence of such tumors. Warren and Feldman have stated that lateral aberrant thyroid tumors have been found in slightly more than 0.3 per cent of 20,000 patients with surgically removed thyroid glands.

Obviously, occurrence of even normal aberrant thyroid tissue does not necessarily indicate an origin of the thyroid gland from several anlagen, for aberrant tissue can undoubtedly develop by fissure from the main part of the gland; that lateral aberrant thyroid tumors actually develop from misplaced but otherwise normal tissue has long been doubted by a number of workers. The suspicious fact that these "aberrant tumors" are in the position of the deep cervical lymph nodes, and increasing acknowledgement that they are always associated with a tumor within the gland itself, as Pemberton and his colleagues have long claimed (for instance, King and Pemberton), have finally brought general recognition of the fact that "lateral aberrant thyroid tumors" are actually metastatic tumors from the thyroid gland to the deep cervical lymph nodes. They have no relation, therefore, to the embryological development of the thyroid gland.

INTRATHORACIC GOITER

In addition to the undoubted occasional occurrence of thyroid tissue along the path of the thyroglossal duct, the thyroid gland may also be displaced downward so as to become "substernal" (really retrosternal) in position, or actually intrathoracic. This is apparently not due, however, to an actual caudal migration of the thyroid gland, but simply represents a goitrous expansion of the gland behind the sternum. Lahey and Swinton found that the sex incidence of intrathoracic goiter corresponds to the occurrence of goiter of any type—that is, that most of the individuals showing this are females. An intrathoracic goiter normally exerts pressure upon the trachea, thus interfering with breathing; Lahey and Swinton stressed the fact that any patient with mechanical interference with breathing, or with dilation of superficial thoracic veins (from pressure upon the innominate veins or superior vena cava) should be regarded as possibly goitrous.

Sharer reviewed 212 cases in which the lower border of the thyroid gland upon swallowing remained definitely below the suprasternal notch; in 4 per cent of these the thyroid or a part of it reached below the aortic arch. He stated that most aberrant retrosternal goiters probably have some connection with the parent gland, though this may be merely a fibrous cord. As pointed out by Lahey and Swinton, a goitrous expansion of the thyroid in a retrosternal position must be farther into the thorax if its diameter is to be increased, and therefore it tends to spread downward still more. Sweet has pointed out that while the majority of intrathoracic goiters are in the anterior portion of the mediastinum, occasional ones are in its posterior portion; he suggested that this is due to a difference in their development, "substernal" and anterior mediastinal tumors having arisen from the isthmus or the lower pole of a lateral lobe, while posterior mediastinal tumors have arisen from more lateral or posterior parts of the lateral lobe.

OTHER ABERRANT THYROID TISSUE

Thyroid tissue has also been reported as being found in the larynx, trachea, pons, pleura, pericardium, and ovaries; in some of these cases it is obviously impossible to conceive of the thyroid gland of pharyngeal origin as having participated in the formation of these misplaced bits of thyroid tissue; for instance, the thyroid tissue occasionally reported as present in the ovaries (for example, Masson and Mueller) must be due to a teratoma or metaplasia of the tissues there.

Krafka expressed the belief that intratracheal thyroid was due to an abnormal early fixation of the tip of the lateral lobe to the trachea, so that the cartilages grow around and enclose it—he did not regard the trachea as actually being invaded by the thyroid. At the time of his writing, he was able to find only 39 cases which had been reported in the literature.

PARATHYROID GLANDS

DEVELOPMENT

The parathyroid glands, typically four in number, develop from the dorsal extremities of the third and fourth pharyngeal (branchial) pouches (Fig. 319), and are sometimes therefore designated as parathyroid glands III and parathyroid glands IV. In the course of their development the parathyroids derived from the third pouches soon become associated with the thymus, which also develops from these pouches, while those developing from the fourth pouches become associated with the thyroid gland itself. It is the association between the parathyroids

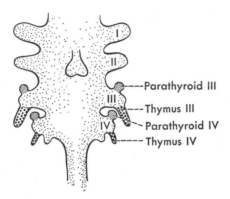

Fig. 319. Diagram of a ventral view of the pharynx showing the origin of the parathyroid glands from the pharyngeal pouches (identified by the Roman numerals). The thymus, arising chiefly from the third pouch, and the thyroid gland (unlabeled) are also shown.

III and the thymus which has induced Weller to refer to these glands as the "parathymus"—justifiable embryologically perhaps, but a needless addition to the already formidable group of anatomical synonyms.

As the thyroid and thymus, with their associated parathyroid glands, move caudally from the region in which they originate the thymus normally, of course, descends beyond the level at which the thyroid halts. The parathyroids derived from the third branchial pouches are therefore typically carried farther caudally than are those derived from the fourth

branchial pouches. Thus the parathyroids from the fourth pouches are typically located more cranially on the thyroid gland, and are called the superior parathyroid glands, while those derived from the third pouches are typically freed from the thymus and become associated with the thyroid gland toward its lower pole, and therefore constitute the inferior parathyroid glands.

NUMBER

From this method of development, one would expect exactly four parathyroids in each individual, but both more and less have been reported. Thus Heinbach, for instance, found an average of only 3.2 parathyroids in 25 individuals and expressed the belief that exactly four parathyroids occur in no more than 50 per cent of persons. On the other hand Norris ('37), working on embryos and fetuses, found no case in which there were less than 4 parathyroids, and suggested that reports of fewer are due to the difficulty of finding them in gross dissection. It might be remarked that the parathyroid glands are usually difficult to recognize in the cadaver with any certainty, and may easily be overlooked, or even improperly identified unless they are checked histologically; some of the data upon these glands are probably inaccurate because of failure to do this. It is said that they are somewhat more easily recognized in the living individual, as their pinkish or yellowish color contrasts somewhat with the darker red of the thyroid gland itself.

Gilmour and Martin, in a very detailed anatomical study, found four parathyroids in about 80 per cent of 527 persons, more than four in 6 per cent, and less than four in only 14 per cent; they attributed the finding of less than four to failure to find all that were present, and stated that the combined weight of the glands in these cases suggested that one had been overlooked. Supernumerary parathyroids apparently arise by division of a single parathyroid; Godwin has described this as a regular occurrence in the dog, and Norris found evidence of its occasional occurrence in the human fetus.

found the "typical" arrangement in only 20 of 64 carefully studied necropsy specimens.

It must be recognized that while parathyroid tissue usually lies in the thyroid region, it may occur anywhere between the level of the bifurcation of the common carotid and the mediastinum; in the

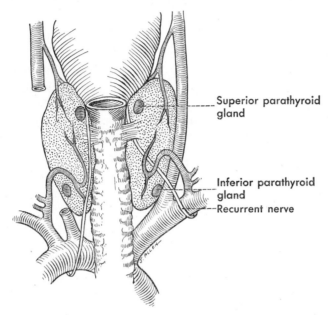

Fig. 320. Common positions of the parathyroid glands on the posterior aspect of the thyroid gland. (From Hollinshead, W. H.: *S. Clin. North America* *32*:1115, 1952.)

LOCATION

Both sets of parathyroid glands are often described as being typically located upon the posterior aspect of the lateral lobes of the thyroid gland (Fig. 320), but this is only a very general rule with many exceptions; because of the manner in which they arise and migrate into the neck the glands are often displaced, and may be located in other positions on the thyroid gland or may lie above or below it (Figs. 321 and 322). MacCallum, for instance, in one of the early experimental and anatomical studies of these glands,

one case, the parathyroid tissue has essentially remained in the location in which it first developed, while in the second case it has probably failed to free itself from the thymus, and has therefore traveled with this tissue into the mediastinum. A search for a parathyroid tumor may therefore be a task of considerable difficulty; however, parathyroid glands are not found scattered indiscriminately through the tissues of the neck, but are confined to the visceral compartment or the tissue connected with the thymus.

According to Lahey and Haggart the

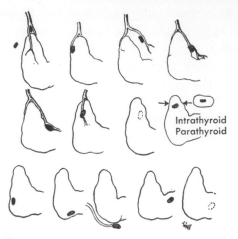

Fig. 321. Some of the various positions in which histologically identified parathyroid tissue has been found. While most of these show parathyroids related to the anterior surface of the gland, the most common position was behind the gland (indicated by the broken lines). (From Lahey, F. H., and Haggart, G. E.: by permission of *Surg., Gynec. & Obst. 60:* 1033, 1935.)

most constant position for the superior parathyroid gland (parathyroid IV) is on the posterolateral aspect of the upper pole of the thyroid gland, where it rests against the "laryngeal cartilage"; that for the inferior is close to the entrance of the inferior thyroid artery, and below the lateral exits of the middle and superior thyroid veins. Black, more specifically, has described the upper parathyroid gland as normally situated well posteriorly, lying upon the pharynx or esophagus rather than directly on the thyroid gland; it then lies dorsal to the recurrent nerve and the inferior thyroid artery, and is usually not so near the upper pole as about the level of junction of middle and upper thirds of the lateral lobe. It is, in his experience, more easily found than is the inferior parathyroid gland. He has stated that the inferior parathyroid gland usually lies near the inferior pole of the thyroid, in a more ventral plane than the

superior, and usually anterior to the recurrent laryngeal nerve and the inferior thyroid artery. He found it most commonly associated with the posterolateral surface and inferior pole of the thyroid gland, usually near, but anterior to, branches of the inferior thyroid artery and somewhat medial to branches of the inferior thyroid vein. In contrast, Heinbach, among the glands which he identified, found 7 per cent opposite the cranial third of the thyroid, 57 per cent opposite the middle third, 25.6 per cent opposite the caudal third, and 10.4 per cent entirely caudal to the thyroid gland (Fig. 322); he found only one gland lying partly on the anterior surface, and none inside the thyroid gland. Because of the varying positions he questioned the advisability

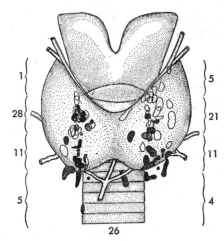

Fig. 322. Composite diagram indicating the positions of all the parathyroid glands found in 25 bodies, represented as if the thyroid gland were transparent. The brackets along the sides indicate, from above downward, the upper, middle, and lower thirds of the thyroid gland, and a region below the gland; the figures indicate the numbers of parathyroid glands found in each of these regions. Those glands which appeared to be superior ones are shown in outline, those which appeared to be inferior ones are shown solid, while those which could not be assigned to either group are shaded. (From Heinbach, W. F., Jr.: *Anat. Rec. 57:* 251, 1933.)

of trying to designate the glands as superior and inferior.

Because of these more usual positions posterior to the thyroid gland, it has long been an axiom among surgeons particularly concerned with the thyroid gland that the posterior part of the capsule of the gland should be left intact if possible, in order to preserve sufficient parathyroid tissue to support life. This is undoubtedly a good general rule, but its fulfillment does not guarantee that the parathyroids will be left intact, nor does the sometimes necessary infraction of it always predicate a total removal of parathyroid tissue. It has already been stated that "normal" or accessory parathyroid glands are sometimes found in various locations in the neck, where they would be spared even if all the thyroid capsule were removed; conversely, one or more of the glands intimately associated with the thyroid may be so located (fortunately, this would seldom or never be true of all) that they are removed even when the posterior part of the capsule is spared.

Thus Millzner found parathyroid glands on the anterior or lateral part of the capsule of the thyroid in approximately 30 per cent of all cases, and actually on the anterior capsule in approximately 10 per cent; in these observations, made upon 740 surgical specimens and 56 cadavers, he found that the inferior parathyroids assume such positions approximately twice as often as do the superior. Norris, in fetuses, found parathyroid III (the lower parathyroid) lying in the tissue lateral to the trachea and back of the posterior edge of the lateral thyroid lobe in 75 per cent of cases, embedded in the posterior edge of the lateral thyroid lobe in 15 per cent, embedded in the lateral surface of the thyroid in 5 per cent and anterior to or below the lower thyroid

pole in 5 per cent. He found parathyroid IV between the posterior edge of the lateral lobe and the lateral aspect of the esophagus (in the loose areolar tissue here) in 60 per cent, in much the same position except against the posterior edge of the thyroid lobe in 25 per cent, in close relationship to the anterolateral wall of the esophagus in 10 per cent and lateral to the thyroid lobe in 5 per cent. Lahey and Haggart have illustrated the many positions (posterior, lateral, anterior) in which they have identified parathyroid tissue, including the rare intrathyroid position of the parathyroid.

In view of these varying positions of the parathyroid gland, it is obviously useless to describe them as having a fixed relation to fascial layers associated with the thyroid gland—that is, as being either routinely embedded in the true capsule of the gland, or between the true and the false capsule. Walton stated that in his experience the superior parathyroids always lie between the thyroid fascia and the gland, but actually superior parathyroids may be located some distance upward, along the superior artery, for instance. He described the inferior parathyroids as having two normal positions: upon the thyroid gland below the inferior thyroid artery as it lies on the posterior surface of the gland, in which case, he stated, they lie anterior to the thyroid fascia; and above the inferior thyroid artery, in which case they lie outside of the thyroid fascia. Rarely, he noted, they are actually embedded in the gland. He regarded the relationship of the parathyroid to the fascia as important, from the standpoint of the directions in which tumors of it may be displaced, but to what degree this is so is not clear.

Black stated that an abnormally placed parathyroid tumor in the mediastinum may be in either the anterior or posterior portions of the superior mediastinum if derived from the inferior gland, while mediastinal tumors of the superior gland usually lie in the posterior portion of the mediastinum. He subscribed to the belief that this displacement may be due either to abnormal migration depending upon their embryology, or a consequence of their enlargement, in which the same forces that cause intrathoracic thyroid tumors play a part. Rienhoff has stated that approximately 20 per cent of parathyroid tissue is displaced as a result of these two factors; Norris ('47), in an extensive review of parathyroid adenomas, found that 10.7 per cent of 322 of them were reported to be definitely aberrant in position—the majority being located in the mediastinum.

BLOOD SUPPLY

However close their relation to the thyroid gland and the thyroid arteries, there need be no hesitation about ligating the blood supply to the thyroid gland for fear this will interfere with the function of the parathyroids. These glands, when located upon the thyroid gland, share with it the abundant anastomoses which exist between the thyroid arteries and the arteries of the larynx, pharynx, trachea and esophagus; Curtis has stated that each gland normally receives a single artery which is usually derived from the inferior thyroid (for both the inferior and superior parathyroids), but may be derived from anastomotic vessels, and in the present writer's experience must often, for the superior parathyroids, be derived from the superior thyroid artery; Curtis has shown that injection masses reach the parathyroid glands after ligation of both inferior thyroid arteries, after this is supplemented by ligation of the anterior branches of both superior thyroids, and when all four arterial trunks are ligated.

CERVICAL THYMUS

Because of the origin of the thymus from the branchial region (the third pharyngeal pouches) it sometimes occurs that during its migration into the mediastinum accessory bits of thymic tissue may be disconnected from the body of the thymus and remain in the neck, or processes from the lobes of the thymus, marking the path of migration, may extend upward through the superior thoracic aperture to reach the border of the thyroid cartilage or even extend higher. Harman has, for instance, described a case in which two processes, continuous with the main portion of the thymus, passed up into the neck, the longer one continuing above the level of the thyroid cartilage to lie under cover of the angle of the mandible; in this case also there was an accessory thymus, detached from the main body, at about the lower border of the thyroid gland. Similarly, Bien described 2 cases in which in newborn infants a portion of the thymus extended upward into the neck to come into close relation to the hyoid bone.

TRACHEA AND ESOPHAGUS

TRACHEA

The pharynx and larynx have already been discussed in the preceding chapter. The trachea begins at the lower border of the cricoid cartilage, extending downward therefore from about the level of the sixth cervical vertebra. Its walls are kept from collapse, and largely formed, by a series of cartilages having a somewhat C-shaped form, with the open ends directed posteriorly; these rings are united to each other by an elastic membrane, and the posteriorly lying space between the ends of the cartilage is occupied by a thin muscular coat, the trachealis muscle.

The important anterior relationships of the trachea in the neck include the thyroid gland, the isthmus of which crosses the anterior surface of the trachea at about the level of the second, third, and fourth cartilages; below this are the in-

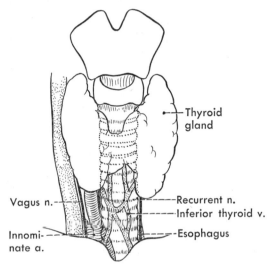

Fig. 323. Some relations of the trachea. The strap muscles and the great vessels of the left side, are not shown.

ferior thyroid veins (p. 523), tracheal lymph nodes and sometimes a thyroid ima artery (p. 522), and anterior to all these are the strap muscles of the neck (Figs. 275, p. 458, and 323). Laterally are the lobes of the thyroid gland, which may extend somewhat behind, and the great vessels of the neck; posterolaterally are the recurrent nerves lying more or less in the tracheo-esophageal groove (p. 525). Posteriorly, the trachea is related throughout its length to the esophagus. The innominate artery usually crosses the trachea obliquely in a retrosternal position, but sometimes it appears anterior to the trachea in the lower por-

tion of the neck. Close to the suprasternal notch, the jugular venous arch (between the two anterior jugular veins) frequently passes transversely superficial to the strap muscles.

The relations of the structures in front of the trachea must be borne in mind in doing a tracheotomy; because of the attendant dangers of subsequent stenosis of the larynx (p. 443) high tracheotomies, that is, above the level of the thyroid gland, are not considered safe; tracheotomies are done below the level of the thyroid isthmus, at about the level of the fourth, fifth, and sixth tracheal rings, or through or behind the isthmus, at about the levels of the second, third, and fourth rings. Many surgeons much prefer this higher approach, finding that the lower ones are more difficult in their subsequent management, and in general less satisfactory. In incisions at the lower level, moreover, the inferior thyroid veins are necessarily encountered, and even if an uncosmetic incision in the anterior midline is made large midline vessels may be observed. Further, longitudinal incisions carried too close down to the suprasternal notch may easily damage the anterior jugular venous arch or even the left innominate vein. The short transverse incision at the proper level, with due regard for the positions of the external and internal jugular vessels, would seem to be a better anatomical approach, with ligation of vessels as necessary on the front of the trachea.

The most important anomaly connected with the trachea is tracheo-esophageal fistula; this is discussed in connection with the thorax (Volume 2).

ESOPHAGUS

The esophagus begins at the lower border of the cricoid cartilage, where it is continuous with the pharynx. This is said to be its narrowest point, and spasm of the transverse fibers of the cricopharyngeus muscle, further narrowing the esophageal orifice, has been held responsible for the occurrence of hypopharyngeal diverticula (p. 418). Unlike the trachea, which runs straight downward in the midline, the cervical portion of the esophagus is somewhat curved, with its convex side to the left; it therefore projects somewhat to the left of the trachea, and incisions for approach to the esophagus are commonly made on this side. On its anterior surface the esophagus is largely related to the trachea; anterolaterally are the lateral lobes of the thyroid gland, especially the left lobe, the inferior thyroid arteries, and the carotid sheath with its contents. Because of the lateral curvature of the esophagus, the left recurrent nerve tends to lie on the anterior surface of the esophagus, the right recurrent along the right border of the esophagus, when these nerves are in the tracheo-esophageal sulcus. Posteriorly, the esophagus lies upon the vertebral column, being separated from it however by the two layers of fascia usually termed prevertebral fascia, and the longus colli muscles.

The muscular coat of the cervical portion of the esophagus is largely voluntary muscle, arranged in an inner circular and an outer longitudinal layer; the fibers of the inner layer are continuous with the inferior constrictor of the pharynx. The longitudinal fibers of the esophagus, which over most of this organ form an even layer, diverge at the upper end of the esophagus so as to form two bands between which, posteriorly, are exposed the inner circular fibers (Fig. 249, p. 412); these bands swing laterally and then anteriorly around the esophagus to attach to a common tendon on the midline of

the back of the cricoid cartilage (for example, Birmingham; Abel). The circular fibers on the posterior aspect of the esophagus are apparently continuous with those of the inferior constrictor, while, as described by Birmingham, the highest fibers laterally attach in part to the edge of the common tendon of the longitudinal fibers, and thus into the cricoid cartilage, and above this point cease (Fig. 324). The tendon of attachment of the esophagus to the cricoid cartilage has been called the cricopharyngeus tendon, but crico-esophageal would be more fitting.

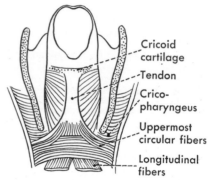

Fig. 324. Attachment of the esophagus to the cricoid cartilage, the hypopharynx and esophagus having been opened from behind.

In addition to its esophageal glands proper, the cervical portion of the esophagus fairly frequently (in perhaps 70 per cent of cases) contains also superficially located glands similar to those found in the cardia or even the fundus of the stomach, and therefore referred to as cardiac, fundic or peptic glands; the secretion of these glands may give rise to erosion of the wall of the esophagus, just as that of similar glands in the stomach apparently influences the formation of gastric ulcers.

NERVE AND BLOOD SUPPLY

The cervical portions of both the trachea and esophagus have similar nerve and blood supplies; the nerve supply is derived from the recurrent nerves, which give off branches to both structures as they ascend to the larynx, while the blood supply is primarily through the inferior thyroid arteries. The arteries are multiple and small; Swigart, Siekert, Hambley, and Anson, for instance, found esophageal arteries derived from the terminal branches of the inferior thyroids, and from the ascending or the descending segments of these vessels; they also found, more rarely (12.8 per cent), branches to the esophagus from the superficial cervical, the subclavian, the ascending pharyngeal, vertebral and common carotid arteries, and the costocervical trunk. In addition, of course, the thoracic portions of the trachea and esophagus, and the pharynx and larynx, have their own blood supply which through anastomoses may aid in supplying the cervical portions.

Shapiro and Robillard found a somewhat similar origin of the arteries to the esophagus in the 50 cases in which they carried out dissection; they described major arteries to the cervical portion of the esophagus as originating from the inferior thyroid in 34 cases, from the subclavian in 12, from a thyroid ima in 3, and from the common carotid in 1, with accessory arteries derived variously from the subclavian, aorta, carotid, and vertebral. They described also the gross anastomoses which they observed in the vessels of this region, and commented upon the fact that separation of the esophagus from the trachea here may jeopardize the blood supply, since the main vessels tend to run in the tracheo-esophageal groove and supply both structures. According to Demel the left wall of the cervical segment of the esophagus receives fewer blood vessels than does the right side,

and Shapiro and Robillard found the main branches on the right to be more voluminous in about two thirds of cases.

ANOMALIES AND PATHOLOGY

Congenital anomalies of the esophagus are fortunately relatively rare, but their incidence is not really known; they may account for a number of deaths in infants, and never be reported. Phelps, in reviewing the various types of congenital anomalies, listed nine varieties: (1) absence; (2) a solid cord throughout; (3) doubling of the esophagus, complete or partial; (4) spasmodic contraction; (5) diverticula, either traction or pulsion; (6) tracheo-esophageal fistula; (7) cysts of the esophagus; (8) atresia, varying from a solid cord between segments to a fold, valve, web or diaphragm; and (9) stenosis, either from a developmental narrowing of the lumen or from pressure from without. None of these anomalies are limited to the cervical portion of the esophagus, and the majority are associated especially with the longer thoracic segment, and are therefore discussed in connection with the thorax (Volume 2).

Since both the trachea and the esophagus are located in the visceral compartment of the neck, perforations of either of these lead to swelling within the fascial layers of the neck. Lichtenstein has stated that tracheotomy may be necessary in such cases, but that usually incision into the fascial spaces of the neck is sufficient to relieve the signs of obstruction. It may be noted again here that anterior perforations of the esophagus tend to lead to spread into the anterior portion of the superior mediastinum, while posterior perforations tend to spread into the posterior mediastinum.

BRANCHIOGENIC CYSTS AND FISTULAE

Cysts and fistulae in the neck may be similar in origin to cysts and fistulae found elsewhere in the body—for instance, dermoid cysts—or may be connected especially with the development of the pharyngeal region and its derivatives. Thyroglossal cysts and fistulae have already been discussed (pp. 394 and 529); so also have laryngoceles (p. 432), and pharyngo-esophageal diverticula (p. 418), which, although not strictly congenital may be associated with congenital weaknesses. The other type of cysts and fistulae found most frequently in the neck are those referred to as branchiogenic cysts and fistulae, although there is some dispute concerning their exact origin.

ORIGIN

There appear to be at least three theories as to the origin of the so-called branchiogenic cysts and fistulae: The first is that they represent remains of the branchial pouches which extend laterally as diverticula from the pharynx, or of the branchial clefts which indent the ectoderm to come in contact with the branchial pouches, or represent a fusion of these two elements (Fig. 325). The second, closely related, is that they represent remains of the precervical or cervical sinus, formed in the embryo by the growth of an operculum from the second branchial arch; this covers the third and fourth arches and the last three clefts and, fusing with the ectoderm below the fourth arch, encloses a blind ectodermally lined cavity. The third is that they represent remains of the thymic or thymopharyngeal duct, that is, the original connection between

the thymus and the third branchial pouches from which it takes origin.

Because of the complicated developmental history of the cervical region, and the shifting relationships which occur here during development, it may fairly be stated that none of these theories have been, or probably can be, entirely substantiated through embryological investigation. Rather what has been done is to

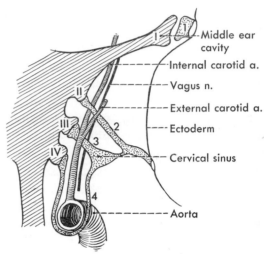

Fig. 325. Schema of the branchial pouches and clefts and their important vascular relations, in a ventral view. The branchial pouches are identified by Roman numerals, the clefts by Arabic ones. The second to fourth clefts are here shown drawn out into tubes communicating with the cervical sinus, which in turn opens to the exterior. (Redrawn from Frazer, J. E.: *Brit. J. Surg. 11*:131, 1923.)

consider the presumably known facts of embryology, and attempt to correlate these with the relationships of cysts and fistulae identified and investigated anatomically and clinically. Some writers have said that somewhat similar cysts and fistulae may actually be of different origin: for instance, it has been stated that fistulae of the neck opening above the hyoid bone are necessarily of branchiogenic origin, while those opening below the level of the hyoid are never of branchiogenic origin, but rather of "thymic duct" origin (see p. 542).

It is difficult to believe that this statement can be true, since complete fistulae opening internally into the supratonsillar region (the region of the second branchial pouch) and externally low in the neck have been described a number of times; the present writer would doubt that the position of the external opening of a fistulous tract has anything to do with the origin of that tract. It seems to this writer that only those fistulae which have an internal opening or extend into close relation to the carotid bifurcation can be at all positively identified as to their origin, and this because of their relationship to the portions of the pharynx and the vessels associated developmentally with the several branchial pouches and arches; the position of branchial cysts may or may not be a clue to their identification, and, unless external fistulae run deeply toward the pharynx, their relationships would usually give no clue as to their origin. Apparently, however, the cervical sinus could not normally contribute to branchial cysts and internal fistulae, as it is closed, according to Frazer ('26), and Garrett, by a fusion of its ectodermal lining from within toward the surface.

TYPES OF FISTULAE

According to Bailey's ('33) excellent review of branchial fistulae, the most common variety is that which is blind internally, having no connection with the pharynx; the next most common, although rare, is the complete fistula, while the least common is an incomplete internal fistula. Branchial fistulae occur about three times as often in females as in males; in 80 per cent of the cases, according to Bailey, the external opening is in the lower third of the neck, at about the anterior border of the sternocleidomastoid muscle—although cysts are more typically present in the upper third of the neck. Bailey has pointed out also that the rare "branchial cartilages" and cervical auricles are found typically likewise in the lower third of the neck. The internal opening, when present, is usually into the pharynx close to the tonsil, thus indicating the origin of these fistulae from the second branchial pouch.

RELATIONS

Practically all complete branchial fistulae, as reported for instance by Bolman, Kleinert, Berry, Brown ('35), and others, open into the tonsillar fossa. This is understandable since, as pointed out by Frazer ('26) and emphasized by Raven, complete connections from the third and fourth branchial pouches to the skin would necessarily have to pass across the hypoglossal nerve, and would most likely be severed by the upward movement of that nerve during development; further, a fourth pouch which retained its connection to the ectoderm would have to pass below the subclavian artery on the right, the aortic arch on the left. Fistulae and sinuses arising from the second pouch necessarily pass between the external and internal carotid vessels if they are long enough to reach this level, and the majority of fistulae do so. Raven has discussed branchiogenic pouches and fistulae in considerable detail; in addition to tracts which were apparently derived from the second pharyngeal pouch, he has identified also pharyngeal diverticula which he considered to be derivatives of the third and fourth pharyngeal pouches (Fig. 326). Apparently, a derivative from the third pouch should open into the piriform sinus, while one of the fourth should open into the hypopharynx below this level. Branchiogenic fistulae derived from the third pouch necessarily run posterior and lateral to the internal and external or common carotids.

CYSTS

Branchiogenic cysts are said to be lined by stratified squamous epithelium, or by columnar ciliated or nonciliated epithelium resembling that of the respiratory tract; some authors have described them

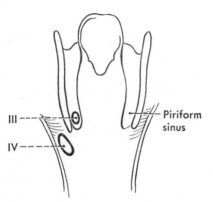

Fig. 326. Positions of the openings of two pouches of the pharynx, one presumably derived from the third pouch, one from the fourth, according to Raven.

as being apparently primarily endodermal in nature, although how one identifies "endodermal epithelium" is not clear to this writer. They may contain lymphoid tissue, and this has been interpreted to mean that they are not truly branchiogenic cysts but are rather derived from thymic tissue; Ladd and Gross have pointed out that the presence of lymphoid tissue may be due to chronic infection.

According to Ladd and Gross, branchiogenic cysts tend to lie higher in the neck than the cutaneous opening of a branchial fistula, and are apt to be located opposite the middle third of the sternocleidomastoid muscle. Bailey has pointed

out the various relationships of branchiogenic cysts—they may lie close against the sternocleidomastoid, close against the internal jugular, lie within the bifurcation of the carotid, or be small and situated against the pharyngeal wall. It is important to realize that any branchiogenic cyst or fistula is apt to be closely associated with the great vessels of the neck, and also with the lower cranial nerves, especially the vagus, accessory and hypoglossal.

THYMIC DUCT THEORY

The theory that branchiogenic cysts and fistulae arise from the thymic duct has been supported by a number of clinicians, upon what grounds it is not plain; it is apparently largely a matter of the histological findings, of prejudice, and an understandable confusion regarding the embryological details and their relations to the surgical and anatomical findings. The thymic duct theory was propounded by Wenglowski, and based upon a detailed study which led him to conclude that no remnants of the branchial apparatus proper can occur below the level of the hyoid bone and hence, by elimination, cysts or fistulae below this level must arise from some other source. Wenglowski's fundamental thesis, that the hyoid bone constitutes the lowest level of branchial derivatives, is obviously not correct, and his entire argument thereby collapses.

Presumably no one can state positively that thymic duct remnants never form cysts, but so far as the present writer is aware no modern student of embryology has supported this theory. Weller, in his discussion of the development of the thymus, has stated that persistent thymic ducts occur, but has not himself described their development; 1 of the cases he cited as evidence of their occurrence was a complete fistulous tract opening internally into the tonsillar region—that is, into the region of the second pouch, and not that of the third from which the thymus develops.

The facts seem to be that the very great majority of lateral cysts and fistulae which can, from their anatomical relations, be reasonably accurately assigned to a definite origin, arise from the second branchial pouch, and cannot conceivably be related to the development of the thymus; other cysts, and external fistulae, cannot so definitely be assigned to a certain origin, but there is no evidence that they ever develop from a "thymic duct." Surely, if this were so, occasional examples of tracts between the pharynx and the thymus would be found.

REFERENCES

ABEL, WILLIAMINA The arrangement of the longitudinal and circular musculature at the upper end of the oesophagus. *J. Anat. & Physiol. 47:*381, 1913.

ADSON, A. W. Surgical treatment for symptoms produced by cervical ribs and the scalenus anticus muscle. *Surg., Gynec. & Obst. 85:*687, 1947.

ADSON, A. W. Cervical ribs: Symptoms, differential diagnosis and indications for section of the insertion of the scalenus anticus muscle. *J. Internat. Coll. Surgeons. 16:*546, 1951.

ARMSTRONG, W. G., and HINTON, J. W. Multiple divisions of the recurrent laryngeal nerve: An anatomic study. *A.M.A. Arch. Surg. 62:*532, 1951.

ASCROFT, P. B. The basis of treatment of vasospastic states of the extremities: An experimental analysis in monkeys. *Brit. J. Surg. 24:*787, 1937.

AXFORD, M. Some observations on the cervical sympathetic in man. *J. Anat. 62:*301, 1928.

BACHHUBER, C. A. Complications of thyroid surgery: Anatomy of the recurrent laryngeal nerve, middle thyroid vein and inferior thyroid artery. *Am. J. Surg. n.s.60:*96, 1943.

BAILEY, H. Thyroglossal cysts and fistulae. *Brit. J. Surg. 12:*579, 1925.

BAILEY, H. The clinical aspects of branchial fistulae. *Brit. J. Surg. 21:*173, 1933.

BEAN, R. B. A composite study of the subclavian artery in man. *Am. J. Anat. 4:*303, 1905.

BERLIN, D. D. The recurrent laryngeal nerves in total ablation of the normal thyroid gland: An anatomical and surgical study. *Surg., Gynec. & Obst. 60:*19, 1935.

BERLIN, D. D., and LAHEY, F. H. Dissections of the recurrent and superior laryngeal nerves: The relation of the recurrent to the inferior thyroid artery and the relation of the superior to abductor paralysis. *Surg., Gynec. & Obst. 49:*102, 1929.

BERRY, G. Branchial cyst: Two instructive cases. *Ann. Otol., Rhin. & Laryng. 43:*287, 1934.

BIEN, GERTRUD Ueber accessorische Thymuslappen im Trigonum caroticum. *Anat. Anz. 29:*325, 1906.

BIRMINGHAM, A. A study of the arrangement of the muscular fibres at the upper end of the oesophagus. *J. Anat. & Physiol. 33:*10, 1898.

BLACK, B. M. Surgical aspects of hyperparathyroidism: Review of sixty-three cases. *Surg., Gynec. & Obst. 87:*172, 1948.

BLAIR, D. M., DAVIES, F., and McKISSOCK, W. The etiology of the vascular symptoms of cervical rib. *Brit. J. Surg. 22:*406, 1935.

BOLMAN, R. M. Bilateral branchial cleft cyst. *Am. J. Surg. n.s.71:*96, 1946.

BOYD, G. I. Abnormality of subclavian artery associated with presence of the scalenus minimus. *J. Anat. 68:*280, 1934.

BOYD, J. D. Absence of the right common carotid artery. *J. Anat. 68:*551, 1934.

BROWN, J. B., and McDOWELL, F. Neck dissections for metastatic carcinoma. *Surg., Gynec. & Obst. 79:*115, 1944.

BROWN, J. M. Branchial and thyroglossal duct cysts and fistulas. *Ann. Otol., Rhin. & Laryng. 44:*644, 1935.

BROWN, S. The external jugular vein in American whites and Negroes. *Am. J. Phys. Anthropol. 28:*213, 1941.

DE CASTRO, F. Sur la structure et l'innervation de la glande intercarotidienne (glomus caroticum) de l'homme et des mammiferès, et sur un nouveau système d'innervation autonome du nerf glossopharyngien. *Trav. du lab. d. recherches biol. de l'Univ. de Madrid 24:* 365, 1926.

DE CASTRO, F. Sur la structure et l'innervation du sinus carotidien de l'homme et des mammiferès: Nouveaux faits sur l'innervation et la fonction du glomus caroticum. *Trav. du lab d. recherches biol. de l'Univ. de Madrid 26:*331, 1928.

CATTELL, R. B., and WELCH, M. L. The carotid sinus syndrome: Its surgical treatment. *Surgery 22:*59, 1947.

CAVE, A. J. E. A note on the origin of the M. scalenus medius. *J. Anat. 67:*480, 1933.

CHANDLER, F. A., and ALTENBERG, A. "Congenital" muscular torticollis. *J.A.M.A. 125:* 476, 1944.

CLAUSEN, E. G. Postoperative ("anesthetic") paralysis of the brachial plexus: A review of the literature and report of nine cases. *Surgery 12:*933, 1942.

COLEMAN, C. C., and WALKER, J. C. Technic of anastomosis of the branches of the facial nerve with the spinal accessory for facial paralysis. *Ann. Surg. 131:*960, 1950.

COPLAND, S. M. The scalenus anticus factor in congenital torticollis. *Surgery 11:*624, 1942.

CORBIN, K. B., and HARRISON, F. The sensory innervation of the spinal accessory and tongue musculature in the Rhesus monkey. *Brain 62:*191, 1939.

CURTIS, G. M. The blood supply of the human parathyroids. *Surg., Gynec. & Obst. 51:*805, 1930.

DAVIS, H. K. A statistical study of the thoracic duct in man. *Am. J. Anat. 17:*211, 1915.

DECKER, H. R. The results of phrenic nerve operations in 222 cases with a discussion of the technic of the operations. *J. Thoracic Surg. 2:*538, 1933.

DELITZIN, S. Ueber eine Varietät des Verlaufes der Arteria thyroidea superior. *Arch. f. Anat. u. Physiol.,* p. 105, 1892.

DEMEL, R. Die Gefässversorgung der Speiseröhre: Ein Beitrag zur Oesophaguschirurgie. *Arch. f. klin. Chir. 128:*453, 1924.

Dow, D. R. The anatomy of rudimentary first thoracic ribs, with special reference to the arrangement of the brachial plexus. *J. Anat. 59:*166, 1925.

EAGLE, W. W. Symptomatic elongated styloid process: Report of two cases of styloid process-carotid artery syndrome with operation. *Arch. Otolaryng. 49:*490, 1949.

EDDY, H. C. Vascular origin of congenital torticollis: Case report. *Am. J. Surg. n.s.17:* 100, 1932.

EDEN, K. C. The vascular complications of cervical ribs and first thoracic rib abnormalities. *Brit. J. Surg. 27:*111, 1939.

EISLER, P. Der M. levator glandulae thyreoideae und verwandte praelaryngeale Muskelbildungen. *Anat. Anz. 17:*183, 1900.

ELKIN, D. C., and HARRIS, M. H. Arteriovenous aneurysm of the vertebral vessels: Report of ten cases. *Ann. Surg. 124:*934, 1946.

ELSE, J. E. Anatomical variations in the thyroid as a cause of recurrent goiter. *Am. J. Surg. n.s.8:*92, 1930.

v. EULER, U. S., and ZOTTERMAN, Y. Action potentials from the baroceptive and chemoceptive fibres in the carotid sinus nerve of the dog. *Acta physiol. Scandinav. 4:*13, 1942.

EVANS, M. G. Bilateral jugular ligation following bilateral suppurative mastoiditis. *Ann. Otol., Rhin. & Laryng. 51:*615, 1942.

FALLER, A., and SCHÄRER, O. Über die Variabilität der Arteriae thyreoideae. *Acta anat.* (Suppl.) *4:*119, 1947.

FAWCETT, E. What is Sibson's muscle (scalenus pleuralis)? *J. Anat. & Physiol. 30:* 433, 1896.

FOLEY, J. O. The components of the cervical sympathetic trunk with special reference to its accessory cells and ganglia. *J. Comp. Neurol. 82:*77, 1945.

FOWLER, C. H., and HANSON, W. A. Surgical anatomy of the thyroid gland with special reference to the relations of the recurrent laryngeal nerve. *Surg., Gynec. & Obst. 49:* 59, 1929.

FRAZER, J. E. Anomaly of omo-hyoid. *J. Anat. & Physiol. 35:*494, 1901.

FRAZER, J. E. The nomenclature of diseased states caused by certain vestigial structures in the neck. *Brit. J. Surg. 11:*131, 1923.

FRAZER, J. E. The disappearance of the precervical sinus. *J. Anat. 61:*132, 1926.

GAGE, M., and PARNELL, H. Scalenus anticus syndrome. *Am. J. Surg. n.s.73:*252, 1947.

GARRETT, F. D. Development of the cervical vesicles in man. *Anat. Rec. 100:*101, 1948.

GIBSON, A. Bilateral abnormal relationship of the vagus nerve in its cervical portion. *J. Anat. & Physiol. 49:*389, 1915.

GILMOUR, J. R., and MARTIN, W. J. The weight of the parathyroid glands. *J. Path. & Bact. 44:*431, 1937.

GODWIN, M. C. The development of the parathyroids in the dog with emphasis upon the origin of accessory glands. *Anat. Rec. 68:* 305, 1937.

GRANT, J. C. B. *An Atlas of Anatomy* (ed. 2). Baltimore, Md., Williams and Wilkins, 1947.

GRIEVE, J. The relative incidence of sternomastoid and ocular torticollis in aircrew recruits. *Brit. J. Surg. 33:*285, 1946.

GUILD, S. R. A hitherto unrecognized structure, the glomus jugularis, in man (Abstr.). *Anat. Rec. 79* (Suppl.2):28, 1941.

GUTTMANN, L. The distribution of disturbances of sweat secretion after extirpation of certain sympathetic cervical ganglia in man. *J. Anat. 74:*537, 1940.

HAMMER, DONNA L., and MEIS, A. M. Thyroid arteries and anomalous subclavian in the white and the Negro. *Am. J. Phys. Anthropol. 28:*227, 1941.

HARMAN, N. B. "Socia thymi cervicalis," and thymus accessorius. *J. Anat. & Physiol. 36:* 47, 1901.

HARRIS, W. The true form of the brachial plexus, and its motor distribution. *J. Anat. & Physiol. 38:*399, 1904.

HEINBACH, W. F., JR. A study of the number and location of the parathyroid glands in man. *Anat. Rec. 57:*251, 1933.

HERTSLET, L. E., and KEITH, A. A comparison of the anomalous parts of two subjects, the one with a cervical rib, the other with a rudimentary first rib. *J. Anat. & Physiol. 30:*562, 1896.

HERZ, E., and HOEFER, P. F. A. Spasmodic torticollis: I. Physiologic analysis of involuntary motor activity. *Arch. Neurol. & Psychiat. 61:*129, 1949.

HEYMANS, C. Some aspects of blood pressure regulation and experimental arterial hypertension. *Surgery 4:*487, 1938.

HEYMANS, C., and BOUCKAERT, J. J. Dissociation des deux sensibilités réflexogènes de la bifurcation carotidienne: Sensibilité chimique et sensibilité a la pression. *Compt. rend. Soc. de biol. 112:*1240, 1933.

HEYMANS, C., and BOUCKAERT, J. J. Les chémo-récepteurs du sinus carotidien. *Ergebn. der Physiol. 41:*28, 1939.

HILL, R. M. Vascular anomalies of the upper limbs associated with cervical ribs: Report of a case and review of the literature. *Brit. J. Surg. 27:*100, 1939.

HINSEY, J. C., HARE, K., and WOLF, G. A., JR. Structure of the cervical sympathetic chain in the cat. *Anat. Rec. 82:*175, 1942.

HIS, W. Der Tractus thyreoglossus und seine Beziehungen zum Zungenbein. *Arch. f. Anat. u. Physiol.*, p. 26, 1891.

HOLLINSHEAD, W. H. Chromaffin tissue and paraganglia. *Quart. Rev. Biol. 15:*156, 1940a.

HOLLINSHEAD, W. H. The innervation of the supracardial bodies in the cat. *J. Comp. Neurol. 73:*37, 1940b.

HOLLINSHEAD, W. H. A cytological study of the carotid body of the cat. *Am. J. Anat. 73:*185, 1943.

HOLLINSHEAD, W. H. Effects of anoxia upon carotid body morphology. *Anat. Rec. 92:* 255, 1945.

HOLLINSHEAD, W. H. Anatomy of the endocrine glands. *Surg. Clin. North America 32:* 1115, 1952.

HOLMGREN, H., and NAUMANN, B. A study of the nerves of the thyroid gland and their relationship to glandular function. *Acta endocrinol. 3:*215, 1949.

HOUGH, G. DEN., JR. Congenital torticollis: A review and result study. *Surg., Gynec. & Obst. 58:*972, 1934.

HUBERT, L. Thyroglossal cysts and sinuses: Analysis of forty-three cases. *Arch. Otolaryng. 45:*105, 1947.

HYNDMAN, O. R., and WOLKIN, J. Sympathectomy of the upper extremity: Evidence that only the second dorsal ganglion need be removed for complete sympathectomy. *Arch. Surg. 45:*145, 1942.

JACKSON, J. L. An infra-hyoid muscular anomaly in man. *Anat. Rec. 59:*41, 1934.

JENNY, H. Abnorme einseitige Verdoppelung der Arteria thyreoidea inferior. *Anat. Anz. 40:*623, 1912.

JOESSEL. Neue Anomalien der Carotis externa und der Maxillaris interna. *Arch. f. Anat. u. Physiol.*, p. 433, 1878.

JUNG, A. Eine noch nicht beschriebene Anomalie des Musculus omo-hyoideus. *Anat. Anz.* 7:582, 1892.

KANTOR, H. Tiefe Teilung der Arteria carotis communis. *Anat. Anz. 26:*492, 1905.

KAPLAN, L. Relation of the scalenus anticus muscle to pain in the shoulder: Diagnostic and therapeutic value of procaine infiltration. *Arch. Surg. 42:*739, 1941.

KASMAN, L. P., and BERNSTEIN, W. Cervical ribs. *Am. J. Surg. n.s.30:*372, 1935.

KELLEY, W. O. Phrenic nerve paralysis: Special consideration of the accessory phrenic nerve. *J. Thoracic Surg. 19:*923, 1950.

KERR, A. T. The brachial plexus of nerves in man, the variations in its formation and branches. *Am. J. Anat. 23:*285, 1918.

KEYES, E. L. Demonstration of the nerve to the levator glandulae thyreoideae muscle. *Anat. Rec. 77:*293, 1940.

KIMMEL, D. L. Anterior mediastinal origin of the thyroidea ima artery (Abstr.). *Anat. Rec. 103:*544, 1949.

KING, B. T., and GREGG, R. L. An anatomical reason for the various behaviors of paralyzed vocal cords. *Ann. Otol., Rhin. & Laryng. 57:*925, 1948.

KING, W. L. M., and PEMBERTON, J. deJ. So called lateral aberrant thyroid tumors. *Surg., Gynec. & Obst. 74:*991, 1942.

KINGSBURY, B. F. The question of a lateral thyroid in mammals with special reference to man. *Am. J. Anat. 65:*333, 1939.

KIRGIS, H. D., and REED, A. F. Significant anatomic relations in the syndrome of the scalene muscles. *Ann. Surg. 127:*1182, 1948.

KLEINERT, MARGARET N. Branchial fistula. *Arch. Otolaryng. 18:*510, 1933.

KOLODNY, A. Traction paralysis of the brachial plexus. *Am. J. Surg. n.s.51:*620, 1941.

KRAFKA, J., JR. Intratracheal thyroid occurring in a seven months human fetus. *Ann. Surg. 106:*457, 1937.

KRISTOFF, F. V., and ODOM, G. L. Ruptured intervertebral disk in the cervical region: A report of twenty cases. *Arch. Surg. 54:*287, 1947.

LADD, W. E., and GROSS, R. E. Congenital branchiogenic anomalies: A report of 82 cases. *Am. J. Surg. n.s.39:*234, 1938.

LAHEY, F. H., and HAGGART, G. E. Hyperparathyroidism: Clinical diagnosis and the operative technique of parathyroidectomy. *Surg., Gynec. & Obst. 60:*1033, 1935.

LAHEY, F. H., and SWINTON, N. W. Intrathoracic goiter. *Surg., Gynec. & Obst. 59:* 627, 1934.

LANGSAM, C. L. M. omohyoideus in American whites and Negroes. *Am. J. Phys. Anthropol. 28:*249, 1941.

LARSON, L. M., and ROSENOW, J. H. Fibrous sternomastoid "tumors" of infancy: Their role in the etiology of muscular torticollis. *Minnesota Med. 31:*1243, 1948.

LeCOMPTE, P. M. Tumors of the carotid body. *Am. J. Path. 24:*305, 1948.

LEE, F. C. The establishment of collateral circulation following ligation of the thoracic duct. *Bull. Johns Hopkins Hosp. 33:*21, 1922.

LICHTENSTEIN, M. E. Acute injuries to the neck involving the food and air passages. *Surg., Gynec. & Obst. 85:*734, 1947.

LINDSKOG, G. E., and HOWES, E. L. Cervical rib associated with aneurysm of the subclavian artery: Report of a case and review of the recent literature. *Arch. Surg. 34:*310, 1937.

VON LIPPMANN, R. Abnormer Ursprung des Ramus descendens n. hypoglossi aus dem N. vagus. *Anat. Anz. 37:*1, 1910.

LISSITZYN, M. S. Ductus thoracicus. *Arch. f. klin. Chir. 128:*215, 1924.

LIST, C. F., and PEET, M. M. Sweat secretion in man: II. Anatomic distribution of disturbances in sweating associated with lesions of the sympathetic nervous system. *Arch. Neurol. & Psychiat. 40:*27, 1938.

LOONEY, W. W. Lymphatic drainage of head and neck—emphasizing special structures. *Ann. Otol., Rhin. & Laryng. 44:*33, 1935.

LÖWY, R. Ueber das topographische Verhalten des Nervus hypoglossus zur Vena jugularis interna. *Anat. Anz. 37:*10, 1910.

MacCALLUM, W. G. The surgical relations of the parathyroid glands. *Brit. M. J. 2:*1282, 1906.

MacFEE, W. F. Cervical rib causing partial occlusion and aneurysm of the subclavian artery. *Ann. Surg. 111:*549, 1940.

McDONALD, J. J., and ANSON, B. J. Variations in the origin of arteries derived from the aortic arch, in American whites and Negroes. *Am. J. Phys. Anthropol. 27:*91, 1940.

McGowan, J. M.   Cervical rib: The rôle of the clavicle in occlusion of the subclavian artery. *Ann. Surg. 124:*71, 1946.

McSwain, B., and Spencer, F. C.   Carotid body tumor in association with carotid sinus syndrome: Report of two cases. *Surgery 22:*222, 1947.

Mahorner, H. R., Caylor, H. D., Schlotthauer, C. F., and Pemberton, J. deJ.   Observations on the lymphatic connections of the thyroid gland in man. *Anat. Rec. 36:* 341, 1927.

Marshall, C. F.   Variations in the form of the thyroid gland in man. *J. Anat. & Physiol. 29:*234, 1895.

Marshall, S. F., and Becker, W. F.   Thyroglossal cysts and sinuses. *Ann. Surg. 129:* 642, 1949.

Masson, J. C., and Mueller, Selma C.   Ovarian tumors of thyroid tissue. *Surg., Gynec. & Obst. 56:*931, 1933.

Middleton, D. S.   The pathology of congenital torticollis. *Brit. J. Surg. 18:*188, 1930.

Millzner, R. J.   The normal variations in the position of the human parathyroid glands. *Anat. Rec. 48:*399, 1931.

Morfit, H. M.   Simultaneous bilateral radical neck dissection: Total ablation of both internal and external jugular venous systems at one sitting. *Surgery 31:*216, 1952.

Morrison, L. F.   Recurrent laryngeal nerve paralysis: A revised conception based on the dissection of one hundred cadavers. *Ann. Otol., Rhin. & Laryng. 61:*567, 1952.

Mulholland, J. H., and Rovenstine, E. A.   Surgery in the carotid sinus syndrome. *Surgery 9:*751, 1941.

Murphrey, D. R., Jr.   Stellate ganglion block: A new anterior approach. *Ann. Surg. 120:* 759, 1944.

Naffziger, H. C., and Grant, W. T.   Neuritis of the brachial plexus mechanical in origin: The scalenus syndrome. *Surg., Gynec. & Obst. 67:*722, 1938.

Nat, B. S.   The scalenus medius. *J. Anat. 58:* 268, 1924.

Neuberger, H.   Über einige Arterienvarietäten am Hals. *Anat. Anz. 41:*618, 1912.

Nonidez, J. F.   Innervation of the thyroid gland: II. Origin and course of the thyroid nerves in the dog. *Am. J. Anat. 48:*299, 1931.

Nonidez, J. F.   Innervation of the thyroid gland: III. Distribution and termination of the nerve fibers in the dog. *Am. J. Anat. 57:* 135, 1935.

Nordland, M.   The larynx as related to surgery of the thyroid based on an anatomical study. *Surg., Gynec. & Obst. 51:*449, 1930.

Norris, E. H.   The parathyroid glands and the lateral thyroid in man: Their morphogenesis, histogenesis, topographic anatomy and prenatal growth. *Contrib. Embryol. 26:*247, 1937.

Norris, E. H.   The parathyroid adenoma: A study of 322 cases. *Internat. Abstr. Surg. 84:*1, 1947.

de Pablo, J. S., and Diez-Mallo, J.   Experience with three thousand cases of brachial plexus block; its dangers: Report of a fatal case. *Ann. Surg. 128:*956, 1948.

Parsons, F. G., and Keith, A.   Seventh report of the Committee of Collective Investigation of the Anatomical Society of Great Britain and Ireland, for the year 1896-97: Question III. The position of the spinal accessory nerve. Whether it passes outward between the jugular vein and internal carotid artery, or between the jugular vein and the atlas? Whether it perforates the sterno-mastoid or not: If so, does the whole nerve perforate, or only a part? Which division of the sternomastoid does it perforate? *J. Anat. & Physiol. 32:*177, 1897.

Patrick, J.   The technique of brachial plexus block anaesthesia. *Brit. J. Surg. 27:*734, 1940.

Patterson, R. H.   Cervical ribs and the scalenus muscle syndrome. *Ann. Surg. 111:* 531, 1940.

Pemberton, J. deJ., and Livermore, G. R., Jr.   Surgical treatment of carotid body tumors: Value of anticoagulants in carotid ligation. *Ann. Surg. 133:*837, 1951.

Perlow, S., and Vehe, K. L.   Variations in the gross anatomy of the stellate and lumbar sympathetic ganglia. *Am. J. Surg. n.s.30:* 454, 1935.

Phelps, K. A.   Congenital anomalies of the esophagus with a report of nine cases. *Ann. Otol., Rhin. & Laryng. 39:*364, 1930.

Pick, J., and Wertheim, H.   A technic for blocking the carotid sinus nerves. *Ann. Surg. 127:*144, 1948.

PIKKIEFF, ELLEN. On subcutaneous veins of the neck. *J. Anat.* 72:119, 1937.

POIRIER, P., and CHARPY, A. *Traité d'Anatomie Humaine.* Paris, Masson et Cie, Tome 2, Fasc. 4, p. 1306, 1909.

PRATT, G. W. The thyroidea ima artery. *J. Anat.* 50:239, 1916.

PUTNAM, T. J., HERZ, E., and GLASER, G. H. Spasmodic torticollis: III. Surgical treatment. *Arch. Neurol. & Psychiat.* 61:240, 1949.

RAMSAY, A. J. Experimental studies on the developmental potentialities of the third pharyngeal pouch in the mammalian embryo (mouse) (Abstr.). *Anat. Rec.* 106:234, 1950.

RAVEN, R. W. Pouches of the pharynx and oesophagus with special reference to the embryological and morphological aspects. *Brit. J. Surg.* 21:235, 1933.

RAY, B. S., and STEWART, H. J. Role of the glossopharyngeal nerve in the carotid sinus reflex in man: Relief of carotid sinus syndrome by intracranial section of the glossopharyngeal nerve. *Surgery* 23:411, 1948.

RAY, B. S., HINSEY, J. C., and GEOHEGAN, W. A. Observations on the distribution of the sympathetic nerves to the pupil and upper extremity as determined by stimulation of the anterior roots in man. *Ann. Surg.* 118:647, 1943.

READ, W. T., and TROTTER, MILDRED The origins of transverse cervical and of transverse scapular arteries in American whites and Negroes. *Am. J. Phys. Anthropol.* 28:239, 1941.

REED, A. F. The relations of the inferior laryngeal nerve to the inferior thyroid artery. *Anat. Rec.* 85:17, 1943.

REED, A. F. Anatomic relations of the anterior scalene muscle (Abstr.). *Anat. Rec.* 100:706, 1948.

RHINEHART, D. A. The nerves of the thyroid and parathyroid bodies. *Am. J. Anat.* 13:91, 1912.

RIENHOFF, W. F., JR. The surgical treatment of hyperparathyroidism: With a report of 27 cases. *Ann. Surg.* 131:917, 1950.

ROEDER, C. A. Operations on the superior pole of the thyroid. *Arch. Surg.* 24:426, 1932.

ROGERS, L. The thyroid arteries considered in relation to their surgical importance. *J. Anat.* 64:50, 1929.

ROSENWASSER, H. Carotid body tumor of the middle ear and mastoid. *Arch. Otolaryng.* 41:64, 1945.

RUGH, J. T. Spasmodic torticollis: Its cause and treatment. *Am. J. Surg.* n.s.49:490, 1940.

RUTHERFORD, N. C. A curious arrangement of the retro-clavicular musculature. *Anat. Anz.* 37:148, 1910.

SCHMIDT, C. F., and COMROE, J. H., JR. Functions of the carotid and aortic bodies. *Physiol. Rev.* 20:115, 1940.

SHAPIRO, A. L., and ROBILLARD, G. L. The esophageal arteries: Their configurational anatomy and variations in relation to surgery. *Ann. Surg.* 131:171, 1950.

SHARER, R. F. Substernal thyroid. *Am. J. Surg.* n.s.32:56, 1936.

SHEEHAN, D., MULHOLLAND, J. H., and SHAFIROFF, B. Surgical anatomy of the carotid sinus nerve. *Anat. Rec.* 80:431, 1941.

SHORE, L. R. An example of the muscle scalenus minimus. *J. Anat.* 60:418, 1926.

SHUMACKER, H. B., JR. A case of costoclavicular compression of the subclavian artery simulating arterial aneurysm. *Surgery* 20:478, 1946.

SIMPSON, W. L., and GRAHAM, D. G. Injuries of the cervical thoracic duct. *Ann. Otol., Rhin. & Laryng.* 52:834, 1943.

SINGER, E. Human brachial plexus united into a single cord: Description and interpretation. *Anat. Rec.* 55:411, 1933.

SIWE, S. A. The cervical part of the gangliated cord, with special reference to its connections with the spinal nerves and certain cerebral nerves. *Am. J. Anat.* 48:479, 1931.

SKOOG, T. Ganglia in the communicating rami of the cervical sympathetic trunk. *Lancet* 2:457, 1947.

SMITH, B. C. Thrombosis of third portion of subclavian artery associated with scalenus anticus syndrome. *Ann. Surg.* 111:546, 1940.

SMITH, I. H., and MOLOY, H. C. The effect of nerve stimulation and nerve degeneration on the mitochondria and histology of the thyroid gland. *Anat. Rec.* 45:393, 1930.

SMITHWICK, R. H. The problem of producing complete and lasting sympathetic denervation of the upper extremity by preganglionic section. *Ann. Surg.* 112:1085, 1940.

SNEDECOR, S. T. Injuries to thoracic duct. *Am. J. Surg. n.s.26*:64, 1943.

SPURLING, R. G., and BRADFORD, F. K. Scalenus neurocirculatory compression. *Ann. Surg. 107*:708, 1938.

SPURLING, R. G., and GRANTHAM, E. G. The painful arm and shoulder with especial reference to the problem of scalenus neurocirculatory compression. *J. Missouri M. A. 38*:340, 1941.

SPURLING, R. G., and SCOVILLE, W. B. Lateral rupture of the cervical intervertebral discs: A common cause of shoulder and arm pain. *Surg., Gynec. & Obst. 78*:350, 1944.

STEWART, J. D. Circulation of the human thyroid. *Arch. Surg. 25*:1157, 1932.

STEWART, W. J. Torticollis due to the aberrant sternal portion of the sternocleidomastoid muscle. *J. Bone & Joint Surg. n.s.17*:493, 1935.

STOTT, C. F. A note on the scalenus minimus muscle. *J. Anat. 62*:359, 1928.

SUNDERLAND, S. The distribution of sympathetic fibres in the brachial plexus in man. *Brain 71*:88, 1948.

SUNDERLAND, S., and BEDBROOK, G. M. Narrowing of the second part of the subclavian artery. *Anat. Rec. 104*:299, 1949.

SWEET, R. H. Intrathoracic goiter located in the posterior mediastinum. *Surg., Gynec. & Obst. 89*:57, 1949.

SWIGART, L. L., SIEKERT, R. G., HAMBLEY, W. C., and ANSON, B. J. The esophageal arteries: An anatomic study of 150 specimens. *Surg., Gynec. & Obst. 90*:234, 1950.

SZAWLOWSKI, J. Über das Verhalten des Ductus thoracicus bei Persistenz der rechten absteigenden Aortenwurzel. *Anat. Anz. 3*:839, 1888.

TAGUCHI, K. Ueber eine seltene Anomalie des Verlaufes des Vagusstammes und eines seiner Aeste. *Arch. f. Anat. u. Physiol.*, p. 365, 1888.

TAGUCHI, K. Die Lage des Nervus recurrens nervi vagi zur Arteria thyreoidea inferior. *Arch. f. Anat. u. Physiol.*, p. 309, 1889.

TANDLER, J. Die Entwickelung der Lagebeziehung zwischen N. accessorius und V. jugularis interna beim Menschen. *Anat. Anz. 31*:473, 1907.

TAYLOR, J. An unusual variation of the omohyoid muscle. *J. Anat. 59*:331, 1925.

TELFORD, E. D., and MOTTERSHEAD, S. Pressure at cervico-brachial junction: An operative and anatomical study. *J. Bone & Joint Surg. s.B.30*:249, 1948.

TELFORD, E. D., and STOPFORD, J. S. B. The vascular complications of cervical rib. *Brit. J. Surg., 18*:557, 1931.

THOMSON, A. Second annual report of the Committee of Collective Investigation of the Anatomical Society of Great Britain and Ireland for the year 1890-91. *J. Anat. & Physiol. 26*:76, 1891.

TODD, T. W. The hinder end of the brachial plexus in man and mammals. *Anat. Anz. 42*:129, 1912.

TODD, T. W. The arterial lesion in cases of "cervical" rib. *J. Anat. & Physiol. 47*:250, 1913.

TROTTER, H. A. The surgical anatomy of the lymphatics of the head and neck. *Ann. Otol., Rhin. & Laryng. 39*:384, 1930.

TUCKER, G. Laryngoptosis: Ptosis of the larynx due to downward displacement of the hyoid bone resulting from fibrosis and shortening (congenital anomaly) of the left sternohyoid and sternothyroid muscles. *Arch. Otolaryng. 25*:389, 1937.

TURNER, W. A phrenic nerve receiving a root of origin from the descendens hypoglossi. *J. Anat. & Physiol. 27*:427, 1893.

VIACAVA, E. P., and PACK, G. T. Significance of supraclavicular signal node in patients with abdominal and thoracic cancer: A study of one hundred and twenty-two cases. *Arch. Surg. 48*:109, 1944.

WALSHE, F. M. R., JACKSON, H., and WYBURN-MASON, R. On some pressure effects associated with cervical and with rudimentary and "normal" first ribs, and the factors entering into their causation. *Brain 67*:141, 1944.

WALTON, A. J. The surgical treatment of parathyroid tumours. *Brit. J. Surg. 19*:285, 1931.

WARREN, S., and FELDMAN, J. D. The nature of lateral "aberrant" thyroid tumors. *Surg., Gynec. & Obst. 88*:31, 1949.

WEEKS, C., and HINTON, J. W. Extralaryngeal division of the recurrent laryngeal nerve: Its significance in vocal cord paralysis. *Ann. Surg. 116*:251, 1942.

WELLER, G. L., JR. Development of the thyroid, parathyroid and thymus glands in man. *Contrib. Embryol. 24:*93, 1933.

WENGLOWSKI, R. Ueber die Halsfisteln und Cysten: Zweiter Theil. Die seitlichen Halsfisteln und Cysten. *Arch. f. klin. Chir. 100:* 789, 1913.

WHITE, J. C., POPPEL, M. H., and ADAMS, R. Congenital malformations of the first thoracic rib: A cause of brachial neuralgia which simulates the cervical rib syndrome. *Surg., Gynec. & Obst. 81:*643, 1945.

WINSHIP, T., and LOUZAN, J. Tumors of the glomus jugulare not associated with the jugular vein. *A.M.A. Arch. Otolaryng. 54:* 378, 1951.

ZIEGELMAN, E. F. Laryngeal nerves: Surgical importance in relation to the thyroid arteries, thyroid gland and larynx. *Arch. Otolaryng. 18:*793, 1933.

INDEX

With few exceptions, the individual structures and parts listed in this index are arranged according to the noun which identifies them, rather than according to descriptive adjectives. Thus, for instance, the various muscles are listed alphabetically under the heading *Muscle or muscles,* but are not listed under the qualifying adjective—the sternocleidomastoid muscle, for example, occurs in the index under *M*, but not under *S*.

The index is also a regional one, listing under the specific part of the body concerned the page numbers on which discussions of the nerves, blood vessels, muscles, and so forth, of that part will be found. The page references in italics identify a more complete description or discussion.

Accommodation, of lens of eye, 122
Actions, of muscles in general, *see under* Muscle or muscles *or* discussions of specific muscles or muscle groups
Adenoids, 402
Agger nasi, 241
Angina, Ludwig's, 302
Angles, of eye, *94, 100*
Annulus, of Zinn, 114, *131*
Anomalies, *see* listings under specific parts of body
Ansa hypoglossi, 462, 517
Ansa subclavia, 510
Antrum, of Highmore, *see* Sinus, maxillary
tympanic, 189
Aponeurosis, epicranial, 1, 314
of levator palpebrae, *99,* 101, 105, 129
palatine, 347
pharyngeal, 401
Appendages, preauricular, 174
Appendix, of laryngeal ventricle, 431
Approaches, surgical, *see* discussions of specific regions and parts
Aqueduct, cochlear, 204, 205
Fallopian, 179, *194*
vestibular, 204
Arachnoid, cranial, 25
Arcades, arterial palpebral, 101, *103*

Arches, palatine, 404
Area, of Kiesselbach, 257
of Killian-Jamieson, 420
of Laimer or Laimer-Haecker-mann, 419
of Little, 257
Arnold, nerve of, 57, 170
Arteries or artery, *see also* arteries, *or* vessels, under various regions and organs
alveolar, 343, 371, 372
angular, 102, *316*
auditory, internal, 81, 87, 219
origin of, 33
of auditory meatus, external, 169
auricular, deep, *169,* 172, 371
posterior, 183, *481*
basilar, *33,* 87
variations of, 37
of brain, general distribution, 34
innervation of, 40
physiological control of, 41
variations of, 37
buccinator, 316, 371
caroticotympanic, 183
carotid, common, 474
bifurcation of, 477
external, 478
internal, 477
in chiasmal region, 48, 51
in cranium, 34
tortuous, 409, 410
ligation of, 475

Arteries—*Continued*
central, of retina, 126, 142, *157*
cerebellar, anterior inferior, 33, 81, 87
relations to cranial nerves, 81
posterior inferior, 33, 87
relations to cranial nerves, 75
superior, 33, 87
cerebral, 32
anterior, *36,* 48, 51
middle, *36,* 51
posterior, *34,* 87
cervical, deep, 474
superficial, 472
transverse, 471
of chiasmal region, 48
choroidal, 49, 51
ciliary, 120, *126,* 157
of circle of Willis, 36
cochlear, 219
communicating, anterior, 36, 39, 48
posterior, 36, 38, 49, 51, 87
of conjunctiva, 104
costocervical, 474
of cranial fossa, anterior, 46
posterior, 86
cricoid or cricothyroid, 443, 521
dental, 343, 371, 372
dorsal lingual, 387
dorsonasal, 103, 159, 233, *317*

Arteries—*Continued*
　of ear, external, 169
　　internal, 219
　　middle, 183
　of esophagus, 538
　ethmoidal, 159
　　anterior, external nasal branch of, 233
　　in nose, 256
　of eyeball, 126
　of eyelids, 103
　of face, 314
　facial, 102, *314,* 479
　　transverse, 103, *316*
　frontal, 103, 159
　hyaloid, 126
　infra-orbital, 160, 316, 372
　intercostal, supreme, 474
　of iris, 124
　of jaw, lower, 371
　　upper, 343
　labial, 315
　lacrimal, 158
　of larynx, 443
　lingual, *386,* 479
　　deep, 387
　mammary, internal, 473
　maxillary, external, 102, *314,* 479
　　internal, 254, 316, 363, *369,* 481
　of meatus, external auditory, 169
　of membrane, tympanic, 172
　meningeal, 21
　　anterior, 46
　　middle, *21,* 56, 371
　　　accessory, 56, 371
　　　course and variations, 21
　　posterior, 71
　mental, 371
　mylohyoid, 371
　nasal, dorsal, 103, 159, 233, *317*
　　lateral, 316
　of nasal cavity, 254
　of neck, 467
　of nose, external, 233
　　internal, 254
　occipital, in neck, 480
　　in occipital region, 69
　ophthalmic, 35, 141, *156*
　　anastomoses of, 160
　　connection with middle meningeal, 133, *158*
　　about orbital margin, 103
　　terminal branches of, 103, 159
　　variations of, 158, 160
　about orbit, 103
　of orbit, 156
　of palate, 355
　palatine, 255, *355,* 372
　palpebral, 101, *103,* 159
　petrosal, superficial, 183

Arteries—*Continued*
　pharyngeal, ascending, 479
　of pharynx, 424
　of pterygoid canal, 372
　pulsation of, against pharyngeal wall, 410
　retinal, 126
　of scalp, 1
　　aneurysms of, 4
　scapular, transverse, 471
　sphenopalatine, *255, 257,* 372
　stylomastoid, 183
　subclavian, 467
　　retro-esophageal, 468
　sublingual, 387
　supra-orbital, 3, 103
　suprascapular, 471
　supratrochlear, 103, 159
　of teeth, 343, 371
　temporal, superficial, 3, 103, 317, 481
　　deep, 44, 371
　thyrocervical, 470
　thyroid ima, 522
　thyroid, inferior, 470, *473,* 521, 525
　　relations to recurrent nerve, 525
　　superior, 520
　　origin of, 479
　of tonsil, 410
　of tube, auditory, 185
　tympanic, *183,* 371
　of tympanic cavity, 183
　of tympanic membrane, 172
　vertebral, in cranial cavity, *32,* 86
　　in neck, 469
　　in occipital region, 70
　　variations of, 37
　vestibular, 219
Articulation, temporomandibular, 358
Atresia, of external auditory meatus, 174, 197
　of nose, congenital, 276
Auricle, cervical, 541
　of ear, *see* Ear, external
Axis, thyroid, 470

Band, *see also* Fold or folds
　pharyngeal, lateral, 404
Bartholin, duct of, 391
Bodies or body, carotid, 481
　ciliary, 122
　foreign, in pharynx, 404, 407
Bone or bones, of ear, middle, 180
　　conduction of sound by, 186
　hyoid, 375
　nasal, 229
Brain, arteries of, 32
　relations to skull, 28
　veins of, 12, *41*
Bulb, olfactory, 47

Bulbus, oculi, *see* Eyeball
Bulla, ethmoidal, 243
　frontal, 261
Bursa, pharyngeal, 403

Calculi, in salivary ducts, 391
Calvaria, 5
　approaches through, 44, *55,* 68, 73
　thickness of, 5
　trephining of, 5, 12
Canal or canals, *see also* Duct or ducts
　auditory, 167
　carotid, 34, 193
　of Cloquet, 126
　craniopharyngeal, 54
　of Dorello, 146
　facial, 179, *194*
　Fallopian, 179, *194*
　hyaloid, 126
　infra-orbital, 152
　optic, 109, *112*
　of Petit, 123
　of Schlemm, 120
　semicircular, 179, *202, 206*
　　function of, 210, 214
Canaliculi or canaliculus, cochlear, 204, 205
　lacrimal, 106
　vestibular, 204
Canthi, *94,* 100
Capsule, of crystalline lens, 123
　of Tenon, *115,* 119
　of thyroid gland, 518
　of tonsil, 407
Cartilage or cartilages, alar, greater, 232
　　minor or lesser, 232
　arytenoid, 426
　branchial, 541
　corniculate, 427
　cricoid, 426
　cuneiform, 427
　of ear, external, 166
　　in ear, middle, 198
　epiglottic, 427
　of larynx, 425
　of meatus, external auditory, 167
　nasal, lateral, 231
　　septal, 231, *238*
　of nose, 231, 238
　　quadrangular, of nose, 238
　of Santorini, 427
　thyroid, 425
　of trachea, 536
　triangular, 231
　vomeronasal, 239
　of Wrisberg, 427
Caruncle, lacrimal, 94
Cave, trigeminal or Meckel's, 61
Cavity, endolymphatic, 200, *206*
　nasal, 234
　　see also Nose, internal

Cavity—*Continued*
  perilymphatic, 200, *201*
    connections of, 204
  tympanic, *see* Ear, middle
Cells, ethmoid, *see* Sinus or
      sinuses, ethmoid
  mastoid, 190
    false bottom of, 191
  of petrous apex, 192
Chain, sympathetic, 508
Chambers, of eye, 124
Chemoreceptors, 481
Chiasma, optic, 140
  composition of, 50
  general relations of, 47
  position and variations, 49
  vascular relations of, 50
Chorda, tympani, *196, 369*
  and taste, 383
Choroid, 121
Cilia, of nasal cavity, 235
  of paranasal sinuses, 258, 275
Circle, arterial, of iris, 124, 126
  of Willis, 36
    aneurysms of, 40
    variations, 38
Circulation, collateral, for carotid
      arteries, 475
Circulus arteriosus, *see* Circle, of
      Willis
Cisterns, subarachnoid, 25
Clefts, branchial, 540
Cloquet, canal of, 126
Cochlea, bony, 202
  function of, 216
  membranous, 208
Compartment, visceral, of neck,
      288
  see also Space or spaces
Compression, neurocirculatory,
      of arm, 504
Conchae, nasal, 241
Cone, of light, 172
Confluence of sinuses, 16, 20
Conjunctiva, 99
  blood supply, 104
Conus elasticus, 428
Cords, vocal, 428, 432
    action in producing tones,
        435
    false, 430
    movements of, 441
  of brachial plexus, 498
Cornea, 120
Corti, organ of, 208, 211
Craniopharyngioma, 54
Craniotomy, 44, 55, 73
Cranium, bony, *see* Calvaria
  contents of, 8
  epidural space of, 8
Crest, lacrimal, 98, 107
Cristae, of semicircular canals,
      210
Cryptophthalmia, 100
Cup, optic, 125

Cysts, branchiogenic, 540
  of hypophysis, 54
  of larynx, 452
  preauricular, 174
  sublingual, 392
  thyroglossal, 394, 529

Deafness, *see also* Hearing, mech-
      anisms of
  nerve, 189
Defects, in floor of skull, 45
Diaphragma sellae, 52
Diploë, 7
Disc, optic, 125
  choked, 162
  of temporomandibular joint,
      359
Disease, Ménière's, 213
  Raynaud's, operations for, 511
Diverticula, of larynx, 432
  pharyngeal (hypopharyngeal
      or pharyngo-esophag-
      eal), 418
Divisions, of brachial plexus,
      498
Dorello, canal of, 146
Drum, of ear, *see* Ear, middle,
      and Membrane, tym-
      panic
Duct or ducts, *see also* Canal
      or canals
  of Bartholin, 391
  cochlear, 203, *208,* 216
  endolymphatic, 204, 207
  lacrimal, 106
  of lacrimal gland, 106
  lymphatic, right, 493
  nasolacrimal, 108, 241
  parotid, 321
  periotic, 204, 205
  of Rivinus, 391
  salivary, 321, 391
    calculi of, 391
  sublingual, 391
  submaxillary, 391
  thoracic, in neck, 492
    right, 493
  thymic, 542
  thyroglossal, 394
  utriculosaccular, 207
  Wharton's, 391
Dura mater, cranial, 8
  innervation and sensitivity of,
      general, 24
  nerve and blood supply of, in
      anterior cranial fossa,
      46
    in middle cranial fossa, 56
    in posterior cranial fossa, 71

Ear, 166
  external, 166
    anomalies of, 173
    cartilage of, 166
    muscles of, 313

Ear—*Continued*
  external—*Continued*
    nerves of, 169
    supernumerary, 174
    vessels of, 169
  internal, 200
    anomalies of, 219
    bony, 201
    embryology of, 200
    fenestration of, 199
    hydrops of, 213
    lymphatics of, 206, 221
    membranous, 206
    nerves of, 221
    physiology of, 210, 212, 214
    vessels of, 219
  middle, 175
    anomalies of, 197
    arteries of, 183
    bones in, 180
    conduction of sound through,
        186, 188
    markings of medial wall of,
        179
    muscles of, 180
    nerves of, 181
    pouches of, 176
    veins and lympathics of, 184
Ectropion, 96
Eminence, pyramidal, 178
Endolymph, 206, *212*
Epiglottis, 417, 427
Epistaxis, 257
Esophagus, in neck, 537
Exophthalmos, *114,* 156
Eyeball, 118
  chambers of, 124
  humors of, 124, *125*
  layers of, 119
  muscles of, extrinsic, *see* Mus-
      cle or muscles, ocular
    intrinsic, 122, 124
  nerves of, *see* Nerve or nerves,
      optic *and* ciliary
  vessels of, 126
Eyelashes, 94
Eyelids, 94
  anomalies of, 100
  fascial spaces of, 100
  lymphatics of, 104
  nerves and vessels of, 101
  ptosis of, 99, 100, *102,* 129,
      130

Face, 306
  anomalies of, 336
  arteries of, 314
  danger area of, 317
  lymphatics of, 319
  muscles of, 307
  nerves of, 325, 332, 335
  sensation from, 330, 332, 334
  veins of, 317
Fallopius, aqueduct or canal of,
      179, *194*

Falx cerebelli, 71
  cerebri, 10
Fascia or fasciae, alar, 287
  buccopharyngeal, 293
  bulbi, *115,* 119
  cervical, above hyoid bone, 292, 294
    below hyoid bone, 284
    deep, 283
      anterior layer of, 284, 292
      middle layer of, 285, 290
      posterior layer of, 286, 293
  of head and neck, 282
  lacrimal, *107,* 114
  orbital, 114
  of orbital muscles, 114, *116*
  palpebral, *97,* 113
  of pharynx, 401
  pretracheal, 285, 290
  prevertebral, 287
  retrovisceral, 287, 298
  scalene, 287
  superficial, of face, 306
    of head and neck, 283
  thyroid, 518
  visceral, 290
Fenestra cochleae (rotunda), 179, 204
Fenestra vestibuli (ovalis), 179, *187,* 204, 216
Fenestration, 199
Fissula ante fenestram, 204
Fissure or fissures, cerebral, relations to skull, 29
  ethmoidal, 151
  orbital, inferior (sphenomaxillary), 110, 111, 114
    superior (sphenoidal), 111
  palpebral, 94
Fistula, arteriovenous, of vertebral vessels, 470
  of body of tongue, 394
  branchiogenic, 540
  of ear, 174, 197
  thyroglossal, 529
Fold or folds, *see also* Plica
  aryepiglottic, 430
  glosso-epiglottic, 404, 430
  of Passavant, 416
  pharyngo-epiglottic, 404
  tonsillar, 408
  ventricular or vestibular, 430
  vocal, *see* Cords, vocal
Foramen, caecum, 394
  ethmoidal, 110
  infra-orbital, 152, 343
  mandibular, 368
  mental, position of, 368
  oculomotor, 131, 132, *133*
  optic, 109, *112*
  ovale, 61, 365
  rotundum, 60, 247
  spinosum, 22
  supra-orbital, 111, 150, 332

Fornix, conjunctival, 99, 100
Fossa or fossae, *see also* Recess *and* Sinus or sinuses
  canine, 309, 343
  cranial, anterior, 43
    vessels and nerves of, 46
    middle, 55
      cranial nerves in, 59
      meningeal vessels and nerves of, 56
    posterior, 67
      approach to, 67
      cranial nerves in, 74
      dura and floor of, 70
      venous sinuses related to, 72
  lacrimal, 105, 111
  of lacrimal sac, 107, 110
    relations of, 109
  nasal, *see* Nose, internal
  preauricular or juxta-auricular, 174
  of Rosenmüller, 402
  tonsillar, 408
Fossula, cochlear, 179
Fossula post fenestram, 204
Fovea centralis of retina, 125
Fractures, of floor of skull, 45, 55, 70
  of mandible, 357

Galea aponeurotica, 1, 314
Galen, great vein of, 43
Ganglion, cervical, inferior, 510
  middle, 509
  superior, 508
  ciliary, 133, *152*
  cochlear (spiral), 222
  Gasserian, 60
  Meckel's, *see* Ganglion, sphenopalatine
  nasal, *see* Ganglion, sphenopalatine
  otic, 324, *367*
  Scarpa's, 221
  semilunar, 60
  sphenopalatine, 149, 247, *251*
    block of, 251
    branches of, 253
    neuralgia of, 254
    roots of, 252
    surgical approaches to, 251
  stellate, 510
    block of, 511
  submaxillary, 369
  trigeminal, 60
  vestibular, 221
Gland or glands, of Krause, 106
  lacrimal, 99, *105*
    accessory, 106
    innervation of, 106, *149*
  lymph, *see* Nodes, lymph
  of Meibom, 95, 97
  of Moll, 94
  of oral cavity, 392

Gland—*Continued*
  parathyroid, 519, *531*
    blood supply, 536
  parotid, 320
    nerve and blood supply, 323
  pituitary, *see* Hypophysis
  sublingual, 391
    innervation of, 392
  submaxillary, 390
    innervation of, 392
  tarsal, *95,* 97
  thyroid, 517
    aberrant, 529, 531
    abnormalities and variations of, 394, 519, 529
    adherent zone of, 527
    arteries of, 520
    development of, 529
    innervation of, 523
    lingual, 395
    lymphatics of, 524
    relation to recurrent nerve, 527
    retrosternal or substernal, 531
    veins of, 523
  of Zeis, 94
Glaucoma, 100, 121, 126
Glomus caroticum, 481
Glomus jugulare or juglaris, 182, 486
Glottis, 432
Goiter, intrathoracic, 531
Gruber, ligament of, 146
Gums, nerves and vessels of, 344

Harelip, 336, 348
Hasner, valve of, 108
Headache, 40
Hearing, mechanisms of, 186, 188, 211, 216
Hemispheres, cerebral, general relations, 28
Hemorrhage, extradural, 21
  nasal, 257
  into retropharyngeal space, 302
Hering, nerve of, 483
Hiatus, semilunar, 244
Highmore, antrum of, *see* Sinus, maxillary
Hilton, water bed of, 26
Horner, muscle of, *96,* 107
Humor, aqueous, 124, *125*
  vitreous, 126
Hypopharynx, 405
  diverticula of, 418
Hypophysis, 52
  general relations of, 47, 52
  pharyngeal, 54, 404
  tumors of, 54
  vessels and nerves of, 53
Hypothalamus, 48, *52*
Hyrtl, ophthalmopetrous sinus of, 20

Incisions, *see* discussions of various regions
Incus, 180
Infundibulum, ethmoidal, 244
Innervation, *see* Nerve or nerves, *and* listings and discussions under organs and parts of the body
Iris, 123
innervation of, 154, 155
vessels of, *124,* 126
Isthmus, faucial, 404
pharyngeal, 402

Jacobson, nerve of, 181
Jaw, lower, 356
muscles of, 361
nerves of, 365
"snapping," 359
upper, 340
nerves and vessels of, 341
Joint, crico-arytenoid, 427
cricothyroid, 426
temporomandibular, 358
Junction, sclerocorneal, *100,* 119, 121

Kelch, accessory venous sinus of, 20
Kiesselbach, area of, 257
Killian-Jamieson, area of, 420
Korner, septum of, 191
Krause, glands of, 106

Labbé, anastomotic vein of, 43
Labyrinth, bony, 201
function of, 210, 214, 216
membranous, 206
finer structure of, 210
Lacrimal apparatus, 105
Laimer or Laimer-Haeckermann, area of, 419
Lake, lacrimal, 94, 106
Lamina cribrosa, 120
Lamina papyracea, 110
Laryngocele, 432
Larynx, 425
anomalies of, 452
cartilages of, 425
edema of, 434
in high trachectomy, 443
innervation of, 444
interior of, 429
mucosa of, 433
muscles of, extrinsic, 434
intrinsic, 438
innervation, 438, 444, 527
operations for paralysis of, 450
paralysis of, 446
in phonation, *435,* 441
ptosis of, 452
relations of, 429
stenosis of (webbed), 452
vessels and nerves of, 443
Lens, crystalline, 122

Leptomeninges, cranial, 25
about cranial nerves, 27
Lesser, triangle of, 387
Lids, *see* Eyelids
Ligament or ligaments, atlanto-occipital, 70
check, of orbital muscles, 117
denticulate, 75
of Gruber, 146
of Lockwood, 116
palpebral, 96, 97, *98,* 107
petroclinoid, 146
petrosphenoidal, 146
pterygomandibular, *310,* 412
sphenomandibular, 181, 360
spiral, of cochlea, 209
stylohyoid, 376, 410
stylomandibular, 360
suspensory, of eyeball, 116
of lens, 122
tarsal, *see* Ligament or ligaments, palpebral
vocal, *see* Cords, vocal
Ligation, arterial, for nasal hemorrhage, 257
of carotid arteries, 475
of lingual artery, 386, 387
Limbus, of eyeball, *100,* 119, *121*
Lines (Langer's or cleavage), in neck, 457
Lingula, of mandible, 368
Lip, cleft and pitted, 336
Little, area of, 257
Lockwood, ligament of, 116
Lymphatics, *see also* Nodes, lymph
at base of neck, 492
of ear, external, 169
internal, 206, 221
middle, 184
of eyelids, 104
of face, 319
of larynx, 443
of nasal cavity, 258
of palate, 356
of pharynx, 425
of scalp, 4
of thyroid gland, 524
of tongue, 388
of tonsil, 412

Macroglossia, 394
Macula lutea, 125
Maculae, of utricle and saccule, 210, 215
Maier, sinus of, 107
Malleus, 180
Mandible, 357
Marcus Gunn phenomenon, 336
Mastication, muscles of, 361
Mastoid process, 190
false bottom of, 191
Maxilla, 340

Meatus, external auditory, 167, 169
atresia of, 174
internal auditory, 81, 194
nasal, 240
Meckel, cave of, 61
ganglion of, *see* Ganglion, sphenopalatine
Meibom, glands of, 95, 97
Membrane, *see also* Ligament or ligaments
basilar, 209, 212, 216
cricovocal, 428
mucous, *see* Mucosa
periodontal, 344
quadrangular, 427
tectorial, 209, *212,* 216
tympanic, *171,* 173
incision of, 173
movements of, 186
vessels and nerves of, 172
vestibular (Reissner's), 206, *209*
Ménière's disease, 213
Meninges, *see* Dura mater, Arachnoid, *or* Pia mater
Meningocele, 45
Moll, glands of, 94
Morgagni, sinus of, 413
ventricle of, 431
Mouth, *see also* Teeth, Gums, Palate, *and* Tongue
glands of, 392
Mucosa, of larynx, 433
of nasal cavity, *235,* 244
olfactory, 244
of paranasal sinuses, 258
of pharynx, 401
Müller, muscles of, *see* Muscle or muscles, ciliary, orbitalis, *and* tarsal
Muscle or muscles, aryepiglotticus, 440
arytenoid, *440,* 442
auricular, 313
buccinator, 310
bulbar, *see* Muscle or muscles, ocular
caninus, 309
ceratocricoid, 439
chondroglossus, 379
ciliary, 122, 123
of Riolan, 96
constrictors, pharyngeal, 412
corrugator supercilii, 313
crico-arytenoid, *439,* 441
cricopharyngeus, 415, 419
cricothyroid, *439,* 441
depressor septi nasi, 311
digastric, 376
dilator naris, 311
dilator pupillae, 124
of ear, external, 313
epicranius, 314

Muscle—*Continued*
  of eyeball, *see* Muscle or mus-
    cles, ocular, ciliary,
    and pupillary
  of eyelids, innervation of, 101
  of face, 307
    innervation of, 307, 329
  frontalis, 313
  genioglossus, 379
  geniohyoid, 379
  glossopalatine, 352, 380
  of Horner, *96, 107*
  hyoglossus, 379
  infrahyoid, 460
  of jaw, 361
  keratocricoid, 439
  of larynx, actions of, 441, 447
    extrinsic, 434
    intrinsic, 438
      innervation of, 438, 444,
        445
      paralysis of, 446, 448
  laxator tympani, 197
  levator glandulae thyroideae,
    519
  levator of palate, 351
  levator palpebrae, 128
    aponeurosis of, *99,* 101, 105,
      129
  levator scapulae, 460, 463
  longissimus capitis, 68
  longus, 462
  of mandible, 361
    innervation of, 364
  masseter, 361
  mentalis, 308
  about mouth, 307
    innervation and actions of,
      308, 309
  of Müller, *see* Muscle or mus-
    cles, ciliary, orbitalis,
    and tarsal
  mylohyoid, 378
  nasalis, 311
  of neck, 460
    anomalies of, 465
  about nose, 311
  oblique, of orbit, 130, 135, 137
  obliquus capitis, 69
  of occipital region, 68
  occipitalis, 313
  ocular, 128
    actions of, 136
    innervation of, *128,* 155
      see also the discussions of
        the various muscles and
        nerves concerned
    sensory fibers to, 146
    testing of, 137
    variations of, 139
  omohyoid, 461
  orbicularis oculi, *95, 98,* 312
    paralysis of, 96, 102
  orbicularis oris, 310
  about orbit, 312

Muscle—*Continued*
  of orbit, *see* Muscle or muscles,
    ocular
  orbitalis (inferior orbital), 114
  of palate, 350
    actions of, 352
    innervation of, 353
  palatoglossus, 352, *380*
  palatopharyngeus, 350, 415
  palpebral, *see* Muscle or mus-
    cles, tarsal
  pars lacrimalis of orbicularis
    oculi, 96
  pharyngopalatinus, 350, 415
  of pharynx, 412
    innervation of, 412, 422
  platysma, 307
  procerus, 312
  pterygoid, external, 362
    internal, 363
  pupillary, 124
  quadratus labii, inferioris, 308
    superioris, 309
  recti, of orbit, *131,* 138
  rectus capitis posterior, 70
  of Riolan, 96
  risorius, 308
  salpingopharyngeus, 415
  scalene, 462
    innervation of, 465
    syndrome, 504
  of scalp, 313
  semispinalis capitis, 69
  sphincter, palatopharyngeal,
    413
  sphincter pupillae, 124
  splenius capitis, 68
  stapedius, 178, 180, 187
  sternocleidomastoid, 460
  sternohyoid, 461
  sternothyroid, 461
  strap, of neck, 460
  styloglossus, 380
  stylohyoid, 378
  stylopharyngeus, 415
  suboccipital, 68
  of suprahyoid region, 376
  tarsal, inferior, 99
    superior, 99
      innervation of, 129, 156
  temporal, 362
  tensor of palate, 351
  tensor tarsi (Horner's), *96,* 107
  tensor trochleae, 139
  tensor tympani, 179, *181,* 187
  thyroarytenoideus, *440,* 442
  thyro-epiglotticus, 440
  thyrohyoid, 461
  of tongue, 379
    actions and innervation of,
      380
    intrinsic, 380
  trapezius, innervation of, 516
  triangularis, 307
  of uvula, 351

Muscle—*Continued*
  vocalis, 440, 442
  zygomaticus, 309

Nares, 229, 234
Nasopharynx, 401
Neck, 457
  arteries of, 467
  fascia of, 282
  lymph nodes and lymphatics,
    of, 443
    dissections of, 374, 389, *490*
  muscles of, 460
  nerves in, 457, *494*
  triangles of, 458
  veins of, 484
  viscera of, 401, 507
  wry, 466
Nerve or nerves, *see also* discus-
    sions of muscles and
    muscle groups
  abducens, 59
    in cranial cavity, 85
    in orbit, 146
    paralysis of, 86, 146
  accessory, *see* Nerve or nerves,
    spinal accessory
  acoustic, in cranial cavity, 80
    in ear, 221
  alveolar, inferior, 367
    superior, 342
  of Arnold, 57, 170
  auditory, 80, 221
  of auditory tube, 185
  auricular, of glossopharyngeal,
    171
    great, 3, 495
    of vagus, 170
  auriculotemporal, 3, 334, 367
    distribution to ear, 169
    origin of, 367
  autonomic, to ear, 222
    to face, 335
    to nose, 250
    to orbit, 152
    to salivary glands, 323, *392*
  block, *see* specific nerves or
    parts of body
  of brachial plexus, 498, 501
  buccal of facial, 328
    or buccinator, of mandibular,
      334, 366
  cardiac, 509, 510, 514
  caroticotympanic, 181
  carotid (intercarotid, of Her-
    ing), 483
  of cervical plexus, 494
  chorda tympani, *196,* 369, 383
  ciliary, long, 120, 121, *151*
    short, 120, 121, *155*
  cochlear, in cranial cavity, 80
    in ear, 222
  cranial, *see also* listing of
    nerves by name

Nerve—*Continued*
cranial—*Continued*
composition of, *see* under individual nerves, in cranial cavity
meningeal relations of, 27
in middle cranial fossa, 59
neuroglia in, 27
in posterior cranial fossa, 74
cutaneous, *see* Nerve or nerves, of face, in neck, etc.
dental, 342, 367
depressor, 514
descendens cervicalis, *494, 517*
descendens hypoglossi, 462, 494, *517*
of dura, *see* Dura mater
of ear, external, 169
internal, 221
endings, sensory, in eye muscles, 146
ethmoidal, 46, 151
anterior, 46, 151, 234, *246*
of eyelids, 102
facial, 325
afferent fibers in, 330
anastomosis of, 196, 327
branches of, 328
course through temporal bone, 194
in cranial cavity, 80
cutaneous distribution to ear, 170
to eyelids, 101
paralysis of, 66, 195, 332
relation to parotid gland, 325
frontal, 150
glossopharyngeal, 382, 386, *512*
in cranial cavity, 78
to pharynx, 422
of gums, 344
of Hering, 483
hypoglossal, 385, *516*
in cranial cavity, 84
infra-orbital, 102, 110, *152,* 333
infratrochlear, 102, *151,* 234, 332
intercarotid, 483
of Jacobson, 181
of jaw, lower, 365
upper, 341
lacrimal, 102, *149,* 332
of larynx, 444
inferior, *445,* 447, 514, *524*
paralysis of, 446
superior, *444,* 446, 514
block of, 407
lingual, 367, 369, *385*
mandibular, in cranial cavity, 61
on face, 334
in jaw, 362, *365*

to mandibular muscles, 364
maxillary, 151
in cranial cavity, 61
on face, 333
to nasal cavity, 247
of membrane, tympanic, 172
meningeal, *see* Dura mater
mental, 334, 368
mylohyoid, 368
nasal, 150
anterior, 234, *246*
external, 332
from sphenopalatine ganglion, 247
see also Nerve or nerves, nasociliary
of nasal cavity, 244
block of, 249, 251
nasociliary, 150
in nasal cavity, 245
in neck, 457, *494*
of nose, external, 234
internal, 244
occipital, greater, 4, 68
lesser, 495
oculomotor, in cranial cavity, 59, *86*
in orbit, 143
paralysis of, 144
olfactory, 244
ophthalmic, in cranial cavity, 61
on face, 332
in orbit, 148
optic, 139
"head," 125, 162
localization of fibers in, 50
relation to paranasal sinuses, 265, 269
vascular relations of, 50
see also Chiasma, optic
of orbit, 59, *139*
of palate, 353
palatine, 253, *354*
parasympathetic, *see* Nerve or nerves, autonomic
to parotid gland, 323
petrosal, deep, 252
great superficial, 66, *248, 252*
surgical approaches to, 252
lesser superficial, *182, 324*
pharyngeal, of maxillary, 253
of pharynx, 422
phrenic, 496
accessory, 496
plexuses, *see* Plexus
of pterygoid canal, 252
recurrent, 445
anomalous, 528
division of, 527
relations of, 524
to salivary glands, 392

of scalp, 2
block of, 2
scapular, dorsal, 500
sinocarotid, 483
spinal accessory, 514
in cranial cavity, 76
in posterior triangle, 459
spinosus, 57
to subclavius, 500
supraclavicular, 495
supra-orbital, 3, 102, *150*
suprascapular, 500
supratrochlear, 3, 102, *150,* 234
sympathetic, *see also* Nerve or nerves, autonomic
cervical chain, 508
of teeth, 342, 367
tentorial, 57
terminal (nervus teminalis), 47, *248*
thoracic, long, 501
of thyroid gland, 523
of Tiedemann, 155
of tongue, 381
trigeminal, 60
arrangement of fibers in sensory root of, 63
branches of, *see* Nerve or nerves, mandibular, maxillary, *or* ophthalmic
decompression of, 66
on face, 332
in posterior cranial fossa, 82
relationships in middle cranial fossa, 61
roots of, 60
section of sensory root of, 62, 82
temporal approach to, 65
trochlear, 59, *145*
in cranial cavity, 59, 84
paralysis of, 145
tympanic, of glossopharyngeal, 181
of tympanic membrane, 172
vagus, 386, 422, 444, *512*
in cranial cavity, 77
vestibular, in cranial cavity, 80
in ear, 221
Vidian, 252
zygomatic, of facial, 101, 328, 329
of maxillary, 152
zygomaticofacial, 102, 152, 334
zygomaticotemporal, 102, 152, 334
Neuralgia, glossopharyngeal, 79, 382, 423
of sphenopalatine ganglion, 254
trigeminal, 62
Neuritis, retrobulbar, 134, *142*
Neuroglia, of cranial nerves, 27

Niche, round window, 179
Nodes, lymph, *see also* Lymphatics
  cervical, deep, 489
    dissections of, 374, 389, *490*
  of face, 319
  of neck, 488
  parotid, 374
  submaxillary, 374, 489
  submental, 374, 489
Nodules, preauricular, 174
Nose, 229
  anomalies of, 276
  bifid, 278
  external, 229
    skeleton of, 229
    vessels and nerves of, 233
  hemi-absence of, 100, 276
  internal, 234
    nerves of, 244
    vessels of, 254
  muscles of, 311
  "saddle," 239

Operations, *see* indexing *and* discussions of specific regions or parts
Ora serrata, 122, 125
Orbit, 94
  bony, 109
  decompression of, 112
  fascia of, 113
  muscles of, 128
  nerves of, 59, *139*
  relations, general, 109
  vessels of, 156
Organ, of Corti, 208, 211
  vomeronasal or Jacobson's, 240
Ossicles, auditory, 180, 186
Otoliths, 211
Otosclerosis, 198

Palate, 346
  blood supply, 355
  cleft, 347
    repair of, 349
  development of, 347
  innervation, sensory, 353
  lymphatics of, 356
  muscles of, 350
    innervation, 353
  in phonation, 346, 349, 416
  soft, 347, 350
    movements of, 416
Palpebrae, *see* Eyelids
Papilla, lacrimal, 95
  optic, *see* Disc, optic
  sublingual, 391
Papilledema, 162
Paralysis, *see also* discussions of individual muscles, muscle groups, and nerves
  facial, 306, 327, 332

Paralysis—*Continued*
  of hypoglossal nerve, 380
  of laryngeal muscles, 446
    operations for, 450
  of levators of eyelid, 102
  of orbicularis oculi, 96
  of palate, 353
  of pharyngeal muscles, 417
Passavant, ridge of, 416
Perilymph, 205, 206, 216
Periorbita, 113
Petit, canal of, 123
Pharynx, 401
  diverticula of, 418
  laryngeal, 405
  lymphatics of, 425
  movements of, 416
  muscles of, 412
  nasal, 401
  nerves of, 422
  oral, 404
  paralysis of, 417
  relations of posterolateral wall of, 409
  vessels of, 424
Phenomenon, Marcus Gunn, 336
Phonation, action of palate and pharynx in, 347, 349, 416
  mechanism of tone production, 435
Pia mater, cranial, 25
Pillars, of fauces, 404
Pits, of lip, 337
Plates, tarsal, 96, *97*
Plexus, basilar (venous), 15
  brachial, in neck, 498
    block of, 502
    injuries to, 502
  carotid, external, 335
    internal, 35, 41, 156, 335, *509*
  cervical, 494
  pharyngeal (nerve), 353, 422
  tympanic, 181
Plica, *see also* Fold or folds
  lacrimal, 108
  semilunaris, 94
Pneumatization, of temporal bone, 189
Pouch or pouches, of larynx, 432
  of middle ear, 176
  of pharynx, 418
  Rathke's, 54
Pressoreceptors, 483
Process or processes, ciliary, 122
  cochleariform, 179
  mastoid, cell groups of, 190
    false bottom of, 191
  styloid, 410
    syndrome of, 410
  uncinate, nasal, 244, 274
Prominence, of facial canal, 179
  of lateral semicircular canal, 179

Promontory, of middle ear, 179
Proptosis, of eyeball, *114,* 156
Prosopalgia, 331
Prussak, pouch of, 177
Pterion, 29, 32
Ptosis, of eyelid, 99, 100, *102,* 129, 130
Puncta, lacrimal, *95,* 106
Pupil, of eye, 124
  segmental innervation of, 155
Pyramid, nasal, 229
  orbital, 109
  petrous, infection of, 193
    pneumatization of, 192

Quinsy, 304

Ranula, 392
Raphe, lateral palpebral, 96, 98
Rathke's pouch, 54
Recess, *see also* Fossa or fossae *and* Sinus or sinuses
  epitympanic, 177
  pharyngeal, 402
  piriform, 406
  spheno-ethmoidal, 241
Reissner's membrane, 206, *209*
Resections, block, of neck, 374, 389, *490*
Retina, 124
  detachment of, 125, 127
  development of, 124
  nerve head of, 125, 162
Rhinorrhea, cerebrospinal, 45, 277
Rib, cervical, 503
  thoracic, rudimentary first, 503
Ridge, arcuate, 202
  of Passavant, 416
  petrous, 55
  sphenoid, 44, 55
Rima glottidis, 432
Ring, tonsillar (Waldeyer's), 404
  tympanic, 171, 175
Riolan, muscle of, 96
Rivinus, duct of, 391
Rolando, fissure of, 29

Sac, endolymphatic, 207
  lacrimal, 107
    blood and nerve supply of, 109
    operations on, 98, 103, 107, 108
    relations to ethmoidal cells, 109
Saccule, of ear, *207,* 215
  laryngeal, 431
Santorini, cartilage of, 427
Scala media, 203, *208,* 216
  tympani, 203
  vestibuli, 203
Scaleniotomy, 505
Scalp, 1
  aneurysms of, 4

Scalp—*Continued*
  danger space of, 1, 101, 314
  incisions of, 3, 44, 55, 68
  lymphatic vessels of, 4
  muscles of, 313
  nerves and vessels of, 1
  sensitivity of, 4
  veins of, 4
Scarpa, ganglion of, 221
Schlemm, canal of, 120
Sclera, 120
Septum, Korner's, 191
  nasal, 237
    deviation of, 239
    mobile, 233, *239*
    nerves and vessels of, 240,
      247, 255
    resection of, 239
  orbital, *97*, 113
Sheath or sheaths, carotid, 287
  space of, 291
  of eyeball, *115*, 119
  of optic nerve, 140
  of orbital muscles, 114, 116
Sinus or sinuses, *see also* Fossa
      or fossae *and* Recess
  accessory (venous), of Kelch,
      20
    of Verga, 20
  basilar (venous), 15
  carotid, 483
  cavernous, *15*, 47, 58
    thrombosis of, 318
  cervical, 540
  cranial, venous, 11
    accessory or anomalous, 20
    blood flow in, 19
    related to anterior cranial
      fossa, 47
    related to middle cranial
      fossa, 58
    related to posterior cranial
      fossa, 72
    sizes of, 16
    variations of, *16*, 73
    see also listings by name
  ethmoid, 109, 110, 112, 113,
      263
    important relations of, 265
    vessels and nerves of, 266
  frontal, 111, *259*
    vessels and nerves of, 262
  intercavernous (venous), 15
  laryngeal, 431
  lateral (venous), 14, 72
    relation to skull, 29, 73
    variations of, 17
  of Maier, 107
  marginal (venous), 14, 73
  maxillary, 111, 270
    antrostomy, 275
    ostium of, 273
    relation of teeth to, 340
    vessels and nerves of, 273
  of Morgagni, 413

Sinus—*Continued*
  occipital (venous), 13, 73
  ophthalmopetrous (venous) of
      Hyrtl, 20
  paranasal, 258
  petrosal, inferior (venous), 14,
      73
    superior (venous), 14, 55,
      58, 72
  petrosquamous (venous), *16,*
      20, 58
  piriform, 406
  sagittal, inferior (venous), 13
    superior (venous), 12
      lacunae of, 12
      resection of, 12
  sclerovenous, 120
  sigmoid (venous), *see* Sinus or
      sinuses, lateral
  sphenoid, 112, 146, *266*
    drainage of, 270
    important relations of, 267
    vessels and nerves of, 270
  sphenoparietal (venous), 15,
      47, 58
  straight (venous), 13
  transverse (venous), *see* Sinus
      or sinuses, lateral
  tympani, 179
  venous, *see* Sinus or sinuses,
      cranial
Skeleton, of ear, 166
  of larynx, 425
  of nose, external, 229
Skull, *see* Calvaria
Sound, bone conduction of, 188
  conduction through middle ear,
      186
  localization in cochlea, 218
Space or spaces, of body of
      mandible, 294
  of carotid sheath, 291
  danger, or Space 4, of neck,
      292
  danger, of scalp, 1, 101, 314
  endolymphatic, 206
  epidural, cranial, 8
  of eyelids, 100
  fascial, of head and neck, 282,
      288, 292, 293
    infections of, 283, 289, 291,
      294, 296, 298, 299, 301,
      302, 304
  intrafascial, of head and neck,
      294
  intrapharyngeal, 304
  masticator, 296
  parapharyngeal or peripharyn-
      geal, 297, 299
  paratonsillar or peritonsillar,
      304
  of parotid gland, 296
  perichoroidal, 121
  perilymphatic, 201, 204
  perivascular, 27

Space—*Continued*
  pharyngeal, lateral, 299
  pharyngomaxillary or pharyn-
      gomasticatory, 299
  postvisceral, 289
  pre-epiglottic, 427
  preseptal, 101
  pretarsal, 101
  pretracheal or previsceral, 289,
      290
  pterygopharyngeal or pterygo-
      mandibular, 299
  retro-esophageal, retropharyn-
      geal, or retrovisceral,
      289, 298
  subaponeurotic (danger space
      of scalp), 1, 101, 314
  subarachnoid, 25
    about cranial nerves, 27
  subdural, 9
  sublingual, 301
  submandibular, 300
  submaxillary, 300
    of submaxillary gland, 295
  submucosal, of larynx, 434
  temporal, 296
  visceral, 288, 290
  zonular, 123
Speech, *see* Phonation
Spot, blind, 125
Stapes, 179, *180*
Stellectomy, 511
Stria vascularis, of cochlea, 209
Suture, petromastoid, 191
Swallowing, mechanism of, 416
Sylvius, fissure of, 29
  vein of, 43
Sympathectomy, of upper limb,
      511
Sympathetic system, cervical, 508
Syndrome, carotid sinus, 483
  cervical rib, 502
  Costen's, 360
  Horner's, 102, 156
  Ménière's, 213
  Raynaud's, 511
  scalenus anticus, 502

Tarsi, 96, *97*
Taste, 381, 383
Teeth, lower, 358
  innervation of, 367
  upper, 340
    nerves and vessels of, 341
    relation to maxillary sinus,
      271
Tendon or tendons, in general,
      see discussions of vari-
      ous muscles
  of muscles of eyeball, 136
  of Zinn, 114, *131*
Tenon, capsule of, *115,* 119
Tentorium cerebelli, 11
Thymus, cervical, 536

Thyroidectomy, anatomical relations in, 517, 524
Tic douloureux, 62
Tiedemann, nerve of, 155
Tones, formation of, 435
 perception of, 218
Tongue, anomalies of, 393
 arteries of, 386
 innervation of, 381
 lymphatics of, 388
 muscles of, 379
 veins of, 387
Tonsil, lingual, 404
 palatine, 407
  folds and spaces about, 408
  lymphatics of, 412
  relations of, 408
  vessels and nerves of, 410, 411
 pharyngeal, 402
 tubal, 185
Torcular, 16, 20
Torticollis, 77, 466
Trachea, in neck, 536
 relation of recurrent nerves to, 525
Tracheotomy, 443, 537
Tract, olfactory, 47, 48
 spinal, of fifth nerve, section of, 67
 uveal, 121
Triangle or triangles, carotid, 458
 Lesser's, 387
 muscular, 458
 of neck, 458
 occipital, 459
 subclavian, 459
 submaxillary, 377, 458
 submental, 378, 458
 suboccipital, 70
 suprahyoid, 458
Trochlea, of orbit, 130
Trolard, anastomotic vein of, 43
Trunk or trunks, of brachial plexus, 498
 costocervical, 474
 sympathetic, 508
 thyrocervical, 470
Tube, auditory, Eustachian, or pharyngotympanic, 184

Tube—Continued
 blood supply and innervation of, 185
Tubercle, orbital or zygomatic, 98, 110
Turbinates, nasal, 240
Tympanum, see Ear, middle

Utricle, 207, 215
Uvea, 121
Uvula, 347

Vallecula, 404
Valve, of Hasner, 108
 utriculo-endolymphatic, 213
Vein or veins, angular, 107, 160, 317
 of brain stem, 43
 central, of retina, 128, 142, 161
 cerebellar, 43
 cerebral, 12, 42
  anastomotic, 43
  great (of Galen), 43
  internal, 43
 cervical, deep, 487
  transverse, 488
 ciliary, 128
 cortical, 42
 in cranial cavity, see Sinus or sinuses, venous and Vein or veins, cerebral
 diploic, 7
 of ear, external, 169
  internal, 220
  middle, 184
 emissary, 12, 14, 15, 16, 20, 492
 of eyelids, 104
 of face, 317
 facial, anterior, 102, 317
  connections to cavernous sinus, 317
 frontal, 160
 infra-orbital, 162
 jugular, anterior, 485
  external, 484
  internal, 486
 of Labbé, 43
 of larynx, 443

Vein—Continued
 lingual, 387
 meningeal, 15
 of nasal cavity, 258
 of neck, 484
 ophthalmic, 160
  anastomoses of, 160, 162
  inferior, 133, 162
  superior, 133, 161
 about orbit, 102
 of orbit, 160
 of palate, 356
 of pharynx, 424
 ranine, 387
 scapular, transverse, 488
 subclavian, 488
 supra-orbital, 104, 160
 Sylvian, 43
 thyroid, 523
 of tongue, 387
 of Trolard, 43
 vertebral, 487
 vorticose, 128, 161, 162
Ventricle, cerebral, lateral, relations to skull, 31
 laryngeal (Morgagni's), 431
Verga, accessory venous sinus of, 20
Vestibule, of ear, inner, 201, 214
 of larynx, 430
 of nose, 234
Viscera, of neck, 517
Voice, see also Phonation
 production of, 435
 vicarious, 438

Waldeyer, tonsillar ring of, 404
Web, of larynx, 452
Wharton, duct of, 391
Window, oval, of ear, 179, 204
 round, of ear, 179, 187, 204, 216
Wrisberg, cartilage of, 427
Wry neck, 466

Zeis, glands of, 94
Zinn, annulus of, 114, 131
 zonule of, 122
Zonule, ciliary, 122

Set in Linotype Times Roman
Format by Katharine Sitterly
Manufactured by The Haddon Craftsmen, Inc.
Published by HARPER & BROTHERS, *New York*